CW01024518

MOTOCOURSE

THE WORLD'S LEADING GRAND PRIX ANNUAL

HAZLETON PUBLISHING

WAYNE GARDNER – WORLD 500cc CHAMPIONSHIP

WORLD CHAMPION 1987.

ANTON MANG – WORLD 250cc CHAMPIONSHIP

WORLD CHAMPION 1987.

GEORGES JOBE – WORLD 500cc MOTOCROSS CHAMPIONSHIP

WORLD CHAMPION 1987.

ERIC GEBOERS – WORLD 250cc MOTOCROSS CHAMPIONSHIP

WORLD CHAMPION 1987.

There we go, repeating ourselves again.

1987 has been rather a success story for Honda. An outstanding number of wins, topped off by four of the most prestigious World Championship titles (including the 250cc road race, where we took the first four places). Not that it was entirely unexpected, though. After all, nothing comes near a Honda, as we've always said. Over and over again.

HONDA

CONTENTS

Motocourse is published by Hazleton Publishing, 3 Richmond Hill, Richmond, Surrey TW10 6RE. Typeset by G.W. Young (Photosetters) Ltd, Thames Ditton, Surrey. Colour Reproduction by Adroit Photo Litho Ltd, Birmingham. Printed in The Netherlands by drukkerij de lange/van Leer bv, Deventer.

ISBN: 0-905138-48-1

DISTRIBUTORS

UK & OTHER MARKETS
Osprey Publishing Limited
12-14 Long Acre
London WC2E 9LP

USA
Motorbooks International
PO Box 2
729 Prospect Ave
Osceola
Wisconsin 54020

AUSTRALIA
Technical Book & Magazine Co. Pty
289-299 Swanston Street
Melbourne
Victoria 3000

NEW ZEALAND
David Bateman Ltd
PO Box 65062
Mairangi Bay
Auckland 10

All photography in *Motocourse 1987-88,* unless otherwise credited, is by Malcolm Bryan.
Other photographs have been contributed by: Doug Baird, Peter Clifford, Colorsport, Kel Edge, Bernd Fischer, Flyin' Fast Photos, Tomáš Gescheidt, David Goldman, Henk Keulemans, Phil Masters, John McKenzie, Stan Perec, Tom Riles, Alexander Savel and John Ulrich.

ACKNOWLEDGEMENTS
The Editor would like to thank the following for their help throughout the year:
E.J., Anne-Marie Gerber (FIM), Charlie Henneken, Henk Keulemans, Hans van Loozenoord, Ian MacKay, Toni Merendino, Paolo Scalera, Gary Taylor, Mike Trimby and Gunther Wiesinger.

PUBLISHER
Richard Poulter

EDITOR
Peter Clifford

EXECUTIVE PUBLISHER
Elizabeth Le Breton

ART EDITOR
Steve Small

HOUSE EDITOR
S.G. Spark

PRODUCTION CONTROLLER
Jane Doyle

PRODUCTION ASSISTANT
Peter Lovering

PUBLICITY & PROMOTION
Jane Payton

SECRETARY
Liz Renton

RESULTS AND STATISTICS
Kay Edge and John Taylor

CHIEF PHOTOGRAPHER
Malcolm Bryan

Dust-jacket illustration by Malcolm Bryan depicts 1987 World Champion Wayne Gardner on his 500 cc Rothmans Honda during the Portuguese Grand Prix meeting at Járama.

Title page photograph features 1987 Sidecar World Champions Steve Webster and Tony Hewitt at the Swedish Grand Prix.

The Grand Prix title page photograph shows Tadahiko Taira and Eddie Lawson in action on their Marlboro Yamahas at Monza 1987.

WAYNE SUPREME!

NGK-equipped riders again swept up all the top places in the World 500 series, led by Wayne Gardner and his Honda.

NGK are also proud to have fired the ultra-competitive 250 winner and the victorious Krauser sidecar of British pair Steve Webster/Tony Hewitt.

World Moto Cross saw NGK top again, so, whatever you ride, with a pedigree like this can you really consider fitting any other spark plug in your engine?

In tune with today's engines

FOREWORD

by Wayne Gardner

Colorsport

Winning the 1987 500 cc World Championship has been a childhood dream come true and being the first Australian to have done so makes it, for me, all the more rewarding.

One of the many duties of being World Champion is to write the Foreword to the 1987 *Motocourse,* and to appear on the front cover itself is an honour.

I attribute my success to my team, who morally and mechanically gave me the support needed to win the title. Their hard work and dedication will always be appreciated.

I would like to take this opportunity to thank all those people who have encouraged and supported me throughout my career.

Together we have reached this ultimate goal and we have this 1987 *Motocourse* to reflect upon.

Without a doubt, 1987 will be the year I will always remember.

A triumphant homecoming for Australia's first 500 cc World Champion.

Colorsport

YAMAHA FZR 1000. PROVIN

The Yamaha FZR1000. Four-stroke motorcycling in a new dimension.

Proving the genius of Yamaha's "Genesis technology." by totally-integrated development of engine and chassis.

The most powerful, most compact engine in its class in the most-advanced chassis on

G THE GENIUS OF GENESIS.

today's roads... the alloy 'delta box' chassis from our World Championship and Endurance racers. Four-stroke engineering that leads the world!

Forward-inclined, parallel four-cylinder engine − Downdraft carburation − 20-valve cylinder head − Twin overhead-camshafts − Digital electronic ignition control − Lightweight alloy 'delta box' frame − Twin 320mm front disc brakes − Hollow-spoke cast-alloy wheels − Monocross suspension.

YAMAHA
A TRADITION OF PERFECTION.

THE TURNING POINT?

There is a strong feeling in the sport that we have arrived at the brink. Not Armageddon but a possible breakthrough that could ensure the prosperity of Grand Prix racing for the next decade. Either that or there could be hard times ahead as the costs continue to escalate and some of the major sponsors withdraw as they become disenchanted by the lack of progress.

This feeling is based on the fact that, at long last, the problems surrounding the sale and distribution of television rights for the World Championship are about to be resolved. One company will have control of all TV rights instead of these being sold individually by the promoters. Previously, a television company in, say, Australia wanting to take pictures from each race would have been obliged to make agreements with all fifteen promoters.

Not only had the difficulties discouraged the television companies themselves, but it also limited the amount of trackside advertising, because this is often dependent on the sale of TV rights.

The FIM decided to bring motor cycle racing into line with Formula 1 car racing, where one company has the TV rights. It is no coincidence that F1 car races reach television audiences in twice as many countries. Typically, the FIM made a major mistake when they first decided to contract-out the rights by selling them while they were still owned by the promoters; the FIM promptly found themselves facing the threat of legal action. Second time around, they changed the FIM rules, so the promoters have now to accept the rights organised by the FIM through a nominated third party.

The choice of this third party has been the subject of much argument and negotiation behind the scenes all year and it has been obvious to all that whoever obtains the rights will wield considerable power in the sport. Bernie Ecclestone has used this TV power as part of his influence which dictates the direction F1 car racing is taking.

Ecclestone has been one of those trying to gain the motor cycle TV rights. The other two main players are IRTA, the teams' organisation, and ROPA, the organisers' and promoters' organisation which is aligned with the pairing of Brian Kriesky and Sean Roberts. Roberts led Rothmans into motor cycle racing and has since resigned from that company to join Kriesky in this new venture while still working as a consultant to Rothmans.

IRTA contracted Alex Whittaker (who had worked with Ecclestone), reasoning that he knew the ins and outs of international television rights selling from his experience in F1. With the backing of all the teams – and apparently all the sponsors – IRTA held a strong hand. The sponsors proved to be the weak link, however, as they carried on struggling for power amongst themselves.

Sean Roberts was representing Rothmans in IRTA, so he had a good idea of their intentions. It seems that Kriesky and Roberts, along with Ecclestone, thought that IRTA's chance of getting the rights was too high. Kriesky declared: 'Between us, we agreed to get some of IRTA's support taken away.' Kriesky does not say what he and Roberts managed to do, but states that Ecclestone used his F1 involvement to get some of the sponsors' support withdrawn. Kriesky's stated reason for trying to force IRTA out of the picture was that Whittaker was not well respected within the TV industry and his involvement would be bad for the sport.

Meanwhile, ROPA started to gain strength by offering the FIM an attractive deal that included a lump sum for the European Championship out of the proceeds of the television rights. The FIM were left to decide to whom they should give the rights at the October Congress. Not wishing to rush into anything the FIM dithered so much at the October congress that they could make no decision and put it off presumably until the tea leaves are more favourable.

The natural hope is that the decision would be made purely on the grounds of who would do the best job for the sport . . . but, knowing the FIM, that is likely to have been furthest from their minds. Too many committee members at the FIM are solely interested in power and realise that owning the TV rights means power and money, both being interchangeable.

The choice provided the FIM with something of a dilemma. If they gave the rights to the promoters, then ROPA would have had control of the circuits, the organisation and the rights. Why would they still need the FIM? If the rights went to IRTA, then that group would be in effective control of the riders' machines and the television rights; they would need only to find some non-ROPA tracks and they could set up their own championship. Remember World Series?

Choosing either of the other two possibilities might be even worse, depending on your point of view. Ecclestone has done nothing for the sport in the past and may just wish to control the rights to make sure that our sport can never grow to challenge his own. On the other hand, if he pushes motor cycling hard and makes a huge success of it, he could run it as he has done F1. There, he has already demonstrated that he has no time for the blazer wearers of the FIM.

Plenty of colour and money is evident at the start of the Swedish Grand Prix. But this is one of the backwater events that has not kept pace with the higher profile of the World Championship, and television coverage is rudimentary. Even the national station did not wish to cover it.

SILVERSTONE 4.710km

SUZUKA 6.004km

ISLE OF MAN 60.720km

It's a rare production bike that can genuinely lay claim to having been developed on some of the world's most gruelling race circuits.

But then the RC30 is a very rare kind of machine.

Based, like the VFR750F, on Joey Dunlop's winning RVF750, it's streets ahead of a mere race replica.

With its slim V4 engine, aluminium twin tube frame and single sided Pro-Arm, it's a full production version of the RVF. Street legal, but with the capacity to be a serious competition machine.

Not that you'll be seeing a lot of them on the open road. We're only making 1000 available worldwide. Though, of course, you should be able to track one down at a Honda Dealer near you. If you're quick, that is.

After all, a bike that's as far advanced as the RC30 is bound to go like lightning.

VFR

ME A LONG WAY.

WAYNE GARDNER
500cc World Motorcycle Champion

ERIC GEBOERS
250cc World Motocross Champion

JACK VALENTINE
European Pro-stock Champion

JIMMY McRAE
British Open Rally Champion

JOHNNY HERBERT
British Formula 3 Champion

CHRIS HODGETTS
British Touring Car Champion

SEPPO NIITTYMAKI
European Rallycross Champion

DAVE THORPE
500cc British Motocross Champion

WITH GEMINI BEHIND THEM, NO WONDER THEY ENDED UP IN FRONT.

In 1987, Shell Gemini technology lubricated more riders and drivers to championship winning positions in the UK, than any other motor oil.

Which just goes to show that drivers who make the grade, use the oil that stays in grade.

You won't find a motor oil that comes close to Gemini. But you'll find Gemini at your nearest Shell filling station.

ROGER MARSHALL
ACU Super Bike 1 Champion

SIMON STUBBINGS
British National Rally Group N Champion

MARK RENNISON
British Rallycross Champion

KEEP ON RUNNING. USE THE OIL THAT STAYS IN GRADE.

GEMINI

OFF TRACK

In this week's episode Freddie Spencer loses a contact lens and Rob McElnea slips off on it, crashing up the road on the Marlboro Yamaha. Watching all this, Randy Mamola runs off the track, letting Wayne Gardner past. That allows the Australian to catch Eddie Lawson, who promptly stops at the pits and hands the bike back to the Yamaha technician saying he doesn't want to ride it any more. Yamaha give the bike to Cagiva so that they can repaint it as

their '88 model. Suzuki, realising that their Yamaha copy is going to be a waste of time, send all the bikes back to Japan and sack the entire team. Their rider, Kevin Schwantz, then goes to Ago and declares that if Lawson doesn't like the bikes, he will ride. Suzuki see themselves losing Schwantz as they had Mackenzie, Roche, Baldwin and de Radiguès the year before. They agree to hire Schwantz at his vastly over-inflated fee and begin work copying the plans leaked from Yamaha's racing department for the single-crank '88 machine, which is a copy of Honda's '87 design, which Honda are about to

Michael Jackson before plastic surgery, looking very much like ex-Sheene fan George Harrison.

15 parts of a never ending soap, or It's better than a day job

Little and Lars, stars of the before and after ads for that well known dietitian O'Lean, are full of the joys of spring and proof positive that Sweden can produce more than ugly cars and drunks.

abandon because Freddie Spencer says it is no good. Spencer agrees to another three-year contract with HRC, providing he alone can ride the 200 bhp turbo in the 500 class which Honda have got legalised by the FIM through promising to run ten HRC riders in 125, 250 and 500 classes at all the 1988 Grands Prix boycotted by IRTA. IRTA have decided that they need neither ROPA nor the FIM to run a World Championship and are going to run a seven-round series, with four races in Macau and two at Michelin's La Doux test track and the final round at Goiania in Brazil because no-one else will take an event. IRTA have dispensed with their year-long pass

Max cannot cope with the high-tech autofocus and loses all the pics for his new mini-volume 'Fred – The Truth', while Honda's happy heroes rumble Volker who's still looking for the eight-cylinder NR. Charlie Heineken and Mac are 'just good friends'; Chuck most admires the old Scot for his break-dancing. Judith Sillytummy is working hard as Trim decides immediately to pen his resignation, having finally found that IRTA Pres. Metro does not know Goldwyn or Mayer and therefore cannot cast him in the lead of their forthcoming blockbuster 'If I ruled the World'.

system for 1988, realising that all members are recognisable from the radioactive glow given off since they attended the Brazilian Grand Prix at Goiania. The yearly trip to Brazil is to be maintained because the radioactivity is said to counteract any other unfortunate infections that may have been picked up on the first trip. Marlboro decide that McElnea must go because their cowboys are worn out from rounding up all the red cows and herding them off to Dianese. As a replacement they try to sign Kevin Magee, but Kenny Roberts has other ideas, trying to hook up a deal with Fosters Lager. He convinces them to compete with Swann, who got Gardner to put their sticker on the top of his helmet instead of the Rothmans one by convincing him that 400 crates of beer are worth more than a Porsche. In fact, most of the beer had to be given to customs officials to get the Porsche back after it had been seized because it was still being driven on German temporary export plates. The loss of the beer did not greatly upset Digger as Donna told everyone the 105-foot motorhome is chock full of

Moët et Chandon bottles. Donna is friends with everyone except motorhome driver Mick Roberts, who has no idea how to keep the thing tidy and is more interested in chatting up the girl from the Parisienne team. Despite the fact that the front window leaks when it rains, Gardner's new Foretravel home has the desired effect of looking more impressive than Spencer's Newell, which has been dubbed the 'Zanussi' because of the way it beams in and out of the paddock like the TV advert and is never seen to arrive or depart – unlike Mamola, who is always seen and heard. Mamola is the most popular man in the paddock with everyone . . . except Kenny Roberts, who has the peculiar idea that winning World Championships is important and tries to sign Lawson but does not have enough cash because of money spent hiring John Mockett to build bigger seat fairings so that Paul Butler can fill his long day applying bigger Dunlop stickers. Roberts also tried to sign Gardner, but then realises he has to stick to Rothmans because Toni Mang said that painting the bike the right colour is the most important factor in winning the championship (having tried all other available liveries). Gardner hangs on Mang's every word and follows his example by training for his next job – beer testing. Gardner, in turn, has his follower: Shunji Yatsushiro, who he wakes up at four in the morning telling him that drinking beer and racing in Rothmans colours is all that is required to be World Champion. Deprived of this advice because he is sponsored by the wrong cigarette company, Niall Mackenzie decides that the curse put on him by Suzuki's Martin Ogborne for pulling out of their team must be working. Mike Baldwin and Raymond Roche have been injured in mysterious circumstances, so Mackenzie decides that a life on the boards is safer and tries to hone his two acts to perfection. His imitation of a fish swimming up Niagara Falls is an unparalleled success, but his impersonation of the lunar landscape needs polishing. He takes advice from the more

15

Birmingham's best make tea and balance the odd bowler while Pingley looks tyred and emotional about the notion that he might have finally found a tyre round enough for Randy to win on.

Determined to find out how it is possible to crash three times in three races, the team send Rob out with a home movie camera taped to his helmet so they can capture the next occasion on film. Then Ago can sell the footage to Spielberg which might compensate for the cost of frame replacements.

experienced pairing of Randy and fiancée Alex, who learnt too little during her time as a Rothmans girl to help Mamola win the championship once he left to join Lucky Strike. They have the marketing of their cigarettes taped by demanding that all riders in the team are American because that is important for the US. When they race in the US the bikes are painted in Kool colours as a fiendishly clever ruse to keep the opposition guessing. Lucky Strike scored another first over the opposition by hiring a new writer for their press releases. They looked for someone unimpeachable. They find a man who had stated in print that he was more believable because he was the only journalist who did not take money from sponsors. Finding such an honest person – someone so much less biased than Clifford, Harris, Fowler, Brown, Wiesinger, Carter *et al.*, who had sold their souls to the devil – they promptly hire him. Mike Scott's successful job application has nothing to do with the fact that, for the first year, he can go to Grands Prix in countries like Yugoslavia and Czechoslovakia, having just swapped his South African passport for a British one after spending enough time in Britain to gain British nationality and enough money to consider buying a home in South Africa or Spain because he so hates the British

weather. The 'journos' (or 'scum', as Mike Trimby calls them) go from strength to strength, finding their organisation, IRRPA, as strong as the League of Nations. Volker Rauch, a legend since he revealed to the world the 8-cylinder NR500, falls for a Carter ruse when he overhears Carter discussing with Brown how delightful it is that the Argentine organisers have provided all the top journalists with free tickets to South America, two freeloaders having fun at the expense of the greatest exponent. Everyone loves the press, at least while they are within hearing. Helmut Diehl has even started a Paolo Scalera fan club. President of the fan club is Serge Rosset, who suggests that all other IRTA team managers should sign a petition to have him sent on an expenses-paid trip to Coventry. Rosset is one of the busiest characters in the saga because, in between playing with the most expensive kids' engineering kit ever raced and getting Honda to reimburse Elf for a decade of children's parties, he is also IRTA's militant tendency and sees quite clearly that a collection comprising an ex-banker, ex-riders, ex-travel agent, ex-cigarette executive, ex-tyre salesman and ex-computer salesman are more capable of running the sport than the FIM, who are merely ex. Megolomania rules, and in their usual self-congratulatory manner an awards evening is organised. Mike Trimby walks off with the Tact,

Good Grace and Forgiveness Award. Ago is the winner of the Honest Look Trophy and Serge Rosset is given an Oscar for Best Imitation of a French Accent, but it is a close-run thing with Christian Sarron, who instead takes home the Bump on the 'ed Cup for most damage to ROPA property. Marlboro get the Most Conspicuous Expenditure Award for their new bus, and, for the fourth year running, Eddie Lawson is Personality of the Year. To show their appreciation of the press corps, a whole heap of awards go their way. Nick Harris wins the Award for Broadcasting for bringing the flavour of a quiet Sunday soccer match on an Oxfordshire village green to his BBC broadcast from the German Grand Prix at Hockenheim. Fred MacNaulty gets the Gold Cup, donated by Gerald Davison, for covering all the Grands Prix for the *Mirror* and *Today* without straying from the hotel swimming pool. Alan Cathcart wins the Insomniacs' Trophy for writing most about least and is edged out of the Book of the Year Award by Peter Clifford's masterpiece, *The Frustration of Never Having Made It as a Road Racer. Motocourse* receives the Sprocket Trophy for most esoteric publication.

Confused? You won't be after the next episode, in which all the cigarette companies compete to see who can spend the most money before international anti-tobacco legislation limits their sponsorship to 'existing levels'. To get around legislation in an increasing number of European countries that prevents riders from having their names linked to cigarette brands, the sponsorship contracts insist that the riders change their names to that of the cigarette, and the FIM change all their records so that Eddie Marlboro and Wayne Rothmans are the most recent winners. HRC make their FIM World Championship look prettier by getting even more sponsors to back the otherwise identical machines, so they take the money from HB, Elf, Ducados, Campsa, Parisienne, Marlboro, Camel, Shell and ICI. The World Bank decide that this one-way flow of currency in favour of the Yen can no longer be tolerated, bringing pressure to bear on the European nations with their collapsing economies, so the teams are forced to send all the racing bikes back to Japan. With no bikes, all the sponsors withdraw: there are no hospitality tents, so all the journalists stay home; and the overpaid riders all retire to their tax havens. Things look pretty grim until Roberto Gallina reminds his fellow team managers that he has just finished refurbishing all the old MVs, which are then wheeled out to be raced. Gallina dusts off his leathers, as do Agostini and Carruthers, and after ringing round a few old friends they have a continental circus to put back on the road. So they return to the circuits like Imatra, Opatija, Brno and the Isle of Man. Then they get the FIM to run the series so that they can have more fun whingeing about a common enemy.

Max Revs
Room 20
George Hotel

A BLIND DATE

In 1987, Michelin took an unprecedented risk to prove the superiority of their new A59X/M59X road radials by pitting them against their rivals' high-performance tyres. The venue was Donington Park. The plan was simple: a straight competition, out there on the track, in rain or shine, come what may.

Ten riders were selected to ride and performance-rate all tyres. Half the riders were notable Grand Prix racers. The other half, bike-wise members of the press.

Each rating would be publicly scored and, to avoid biased assessment, the identity of all tyres was hidden from the riders until the final result was announced.

The race-bred A59X/M59X tyres were the road-going counterparts of the company's world championship winning racing radials and as in racing, Michelin yet again came out on top.

Understandably it was the racers, used to depending on the right rubber for their success, who were more acutely aware of why the Michelin radial was so convincingly better in every performance aspect.

Reflecting the day and the overall result, they were unstinting in their praise of a new road tyre that's turning out to be a very hard act to follow:

The bikes are lined up ready to be test fitted with a variety of tyres which are covered, hiding their identity *(above right)*.

Wayne Gardner *(right)*, **prepared to go tyre testing on the Honda VFR750.**

The hard figures at the end of the day *(centre right)* **leave no doubt about the winner: MICHELIN.**

ADVERTISEMENT FEATURE

WITH SUCCESS

Wayne Gardner

I immediately found an unbelievably close relationship between the road Michelins and the Michelins I race on. As soon as I got on the road Michelins I knew which ones they were because the feel was the same as the racing tyres and they provided the same sort of predictable grip.

On the Honda VFR they impressed me so much. It was not only the grip, but the good feeling they gave. I could put the bike where I wanted because the Michelins didn't have that soft feeling of some road tyres. They give you confidence in your riding. I am going to fit some on my road bike as soon as I get home. I don't want to ride on anything else.

Rob McElnea

I think Michelin were pretty confident that we would come out with the right answer. It was near the end of the day that I got the Michelins and there was no doubt what tyre it was without seeing the name. It totally transformed the bike.

I was riding a 750 Genesis and every lap down Craner Curves on the normal road tyres it wobbled like a heavy tourer. The Michelins transformed it completely.

It handled like a racer and gave me so much more confidence. It was stable in a straight line, and under heavy braking I could still change direction, and I could flick it into the corners right over onto my knee like I was on a racing bike with slicks.

Michelin must have known we were going to find their radials the best, they were so different to the other tyres it was ridiculous.

Ron Haslam

They're really good – I mean lap after lap. They just don't go off. They're better than the others and very responsive on braking too.

Martin Wimmer

Overall I scored them well in every department, but if you want an all-round impression – the best!

Kenny Irons

The best. They feel good – you can do anything with them.

MICHELIN *radial day*	A	B	C	D	E
Ride Number	20	20	20	20	20
Stability	115	113	145	114	126
Braking	109	115	151	114	122
Handling	120	110	146	103	120
Grip Factor	124	119	155	110	127
Comfort	115	112	131	111	122
Confidence	118	108	160	106	130
Points Total	701	677	888	658	747

TT SENSATION

Following their success at Donington Park, Michelin's new road radials performed sensationally under Dave Leach at this year's Isle of Man TT. With his Formula 1 bike out of action, Dave, refusing to scratch, borrowed a standard, ex-showroom Suzuki GSX 750R fitted with A59X/M59X Michelins and rode in the opening Formula 1 race.

Competing against factory-entered machines on slicks he finished a remarkable eighth – beaten only by the TT's best riders.

Dave was the first privateer home and was credited with the fastest lap (112·98 mph) for a standard production 750 cc machine on standard road tyres. Standard road tyres indeed! Michelin radials have proved that they are the best tyre equipment that money can buy, which means there's no better reason for making sure it's a Michelin.

MAKE SURE IT'S A MICHELIN *radial*

Congratulations Keith.

(One of the very few winners who didn't make sure it was a Michelin)

This year, seven World and five British Championships were won on Michelin tyres. The competition really didn't get a look in. So why then are we showing Keith Huewen (MCN/EBC) Superstock Champion?

Simply because when you get as many winners as we did, it's easier to picture someone who didn't ride on our rubber than all those who did.

On the other hand we must give credit where credit's due. So let's hear it for the winning Michelin Men.

And Congratulations to all the winning Michelin Men!

Wayne Gardner
500 cc World Champion

Anton Mang
250 cc World Champion

Fausto Gresini
125 cc World Champion

Jorge Martinez
80 cc World Champion

Virginio Ferrari
Formula 1 World Champion

Herve Moineau
Endurance World Champion

Jordi Tarres
Trials World Champion

Steve Saunders
British Trials Champion

Robin Milton
125 cc British Champion

Roger Marshall
1300 cc British and
Shell Oils Superbike Champion

Phil Mellor
Metzeler Production Series
Champion

MAKE SURE IT'S A MICHELIN · THE CHAMPIONS DO
Michelin's range of road bike tyres are race-bred and available from your local dealer.

The Italian crowd went absolutely wild at Misano as Loris Reggiani won the San Marino Grand Prix on the Aprilia.

In his first full Grand Prix season Honda's Japanese 'hopeful', Shunji Yatsushiro, put in some good performances, especially late in the season, but he did not progress as much as HRC had hoped.

THE HONDA CBR 600. RACE-TRACK TESTED FOR OUTSTANDING ROAD PERFORMANCE

The Honda CBR 600 The machine that proved itself time and again this year in some of the closest, most competitive one-make series racing in the UK. Don't miss next year's action. The new colours: red and white for '88.

TOP TEN RIDERS OF 1987

Toni Mang

1	**TONI MANG**
2	**WAYNE GARDNER**
3	**EDDIE LAWSON**
4	**RANDY MAMOLA**
5	**REINHOLD ROTH**
6	**LORIS REGGIANI**
7	**SITO PONS**
8	**JORGE MARTíNEZ**
9	**RON HASLAM**
10	**LUCA CADALORA**

1. Toni Mang

A fifth World Championship is a remarkable achievement by any standards and he won against very strong opposition. There is no more competitive class and, with five other factory Hondas and five factory Yamahas, the machinery was as strong as the riders. He beat a different man each weekend and no-one could match him.

His approach to racing through the season was virtually beyond criticism; he practised only with the intention of winning races. He sat on pole position just once this year yet the bike was always set up to run race distance and to make the tyres last.

He often had to fight his way through a group to take victory and his performances in the British, Czechoslovakian and the Portuguese Grands Prix provided perfect examples of his ability to get in front. To see him dictate the pace of a race only five bike lengths in front of the opposition, as he did in Austria, was a privilege for the spectator.

His season did not all run smoothly and after the crash early in the second round at Jerez many would have suffered a loss of form. He won the next race, as he did after being knocked off in the wet at Le Mans. The only point of criticism that could be raised about his riding is the aggressive manner in which he occasionally dealt with the opposition. His clash with Dominique Sarron was particularly hard and riding of that kind was not necessary in order to win the championship.

Eddie Lawson

Wayne Gardner

Randy Mamola

2. Wayne Gardner

He rides harder than anyone else in the class and frequently forces the bike well out of shape. In 1986 that was not enough to win him the championship, but this season Honda built him a better machine and with that he was able to beat the Yamahas.

Had he won only one or two races it would be understandable to call his style wild and risky; having watched him finish fifteen Grands Prix without even running off the track it has to be said that he is clearly able to ride like that and get away with it – it is simply his style.

Off the track, the pressure seemed to be getting to him a little towards the end of the season, but on the motor cycle he was just as devastating as he had been at the beginning of the year. The way in which he clinched the championship in Brazil demonstrated that he had no doubts about his own ability.

His dealings with the public and media are very professional and he will be a better ambassador for the sport worldwide than the recent American champions because he fully realises that his duties do not stop when he climbs off the machine.

3. Eddie Lawson

It would be simple to say that he lost the World Championship because the Honda was just too fast. The Yamaha's lack of speed also affected his approach and he began to get dispirited. That could hardly be wondered at, for the opposition's machinery was fast, but his loss of spirit may well have taken the edge off his riding at a couple of races.

In the end, he did not lose the championship by a mere couple of points, as the tyre problem in Japan and the mechanical failure in Austria broadened the points gap. Lawson's one clear mistake was the second-lap crash at Le Mans, and Lawson allows himself no errors. From that point on, he was fighting back and ended the season with some great rides.

4. Randy Mamola

More than ever he was Mr Entertainment throughout 1987, and he is fast becoming the best-known rider in the world. He could teach everyone else about publicity and has little to learn as a rider.

There were times when no-one was doing the job better. He was trying hard enough in practice to get the bike and tyres sorted out and he rode the races with enough determination to win.

Perhaps his only limitation is that he is a natural sceptic. Despite his apparent brashness and incredible confidence, he doubts that he can ever be World Champion. If he won one title he could surely win several, but he still has that hurdle to cross. There is no doubt that he will be one of the great riders of '88, for his form seems to vary little. The only question is whether he has that little extra that will make him champion.

The Marlboro Yamaha team once more won races throughout 1987, spearheaded by Eddie Lawson's determined attempt to hang on to the 500 cc World Championship. It was a team effort and everyone pulled their weight, making it one of the most cohesive teams in the paddock.

Reinhold Roth

Loris Reggiani

Sito Pons

5. Reinhold Roth

Those who suggest that nice guys finish last should listen to Reinhold Roth and watch him ride. The West German is a perfect gentleman yet determined enough to finish a great second in the championship – one which he might have won but for his bad shoulder injury.

His ride to the rostrum after breaking his collarbone during practice at Hockenheim was truly heroic and he battled for the second half of the year against a recurring problem caused by two further falls. Those falls showed a possible weakness in Roth's riding attitude and in his resistance to pressure.

He was quite unaccustomed to the success he attained throughout the year and he had never prepared himself for a long struggle to wrest the championship from a man as cool as Mang. In '88 he will be in fine fettle to fight for the championship and, with a cooler approach himself when things are tight, he could well succeed.

6. Loris Reggiani

Aggression is the name of his game. Though by no means a dangerous rider, he looks to ride a 250 harder than anyone else.

He was never likely to win the championship because of the unreliability of the Rotax engine and pushing so far on to the ragged edge was always risky, although he made few mistakes apart from the fall in Argentina.

His cheerful and friendly personality makes him a celebrity, particularly in Italy, and the rest of the Aprilia team matched his enthusiasm. He has great strength of character, which has helped him bounce back from some very nasty injuries in the past and it enabled him to keep his spirits up when things went wrong this season.

Typically, when a rider fell in front of him at Assen and Reggiani injured his foot by clipping the fallen bike, he refused to accept that his bad luck had struck once more, saying that far from being unlucky he was fortunate that the foot had not been seriously damaged.

7. Sito Pons

The Spaniard rarely makes mistakes but he started the year with a couple of falls that resulted in injury and these affected his performance. He also suffered from more mechanical problems than other riders on the factory 250 Honda.

Pons' riding remained consistent when he was fit and he was often fighting for the lead. The fact that he only won a single Grand Prix, and that the last of the season, had more to do with his injured hand than lack of ability.

One problem he does have during practice is finding the enthusiasm to ride at anything like race speed. When getting faster during the race he often uncovers handling problems, and for that reason Pons found it difficult to match Mang and Roth.

Ron Haslam

Jorge Martínez

Luca Cadalora

David Goldman

8. Jorge Martínez

In winning his second World Championship in a row he has started to show something of the style of Angel Nieto, the all-time hero of Spanish road racing. That is not to suggest that he could exercise a Nieto-like domination for a decade, but there are few who seem able to race with him.

There is no doubt that riding an 80 requires a special skill, yet it cannot be so different from riding a single-cylinder 125 and therefore it will be very interesting to see what Martínez does as the new class gains importance. His matchless judgement of high corner speed should be equally valuable on the 125 and he could well turn his talent to that championship in the near future.

9. Ron Haslam

On the NSR he was often fighting for a place in the top three during the first half of the year and clearly established himself in fourth place in the World Championship.

Once the Elf 4 arrived on the scene the performances tailed off, because although continuing to race the NSR for several races, he practised on the Elf and found the NSR less than perfectly set up when it came to the race.

He finds it difficult to ride at 100 per cent on a machine that is not working perfectly, but on the other hand he is probably a better test rider than anyone. There is a fine balance between a rider sensitive enough to recognise what needs changing on a motor cycle and one who cannot push the bike to the limit because of that awareness.

10. Luca Cadalora

In his first season on a 250 he was a revelation. There was no guarantee that being 125 World Champion would make him a great 250 rider but he soon proved that he could make the switch.

A number of factors prevented Cadalora from finishing higher in the championship and the most important was the superiority of the Hondas. The young Italian refused to give up early in the year, but a nasty fall in Austria, where he was trying to make up for a woefully slow machine, taught him that there were limits to what cornering ability could achieve.

It took time for him to recover from the effects of the concussion he suffered in Austria and some poor results followed. The end of the season was much better and Cadalora had learnt to ride at 105 per cent only when his Yamaha was within 6 per cent of the opposition, and he impressed everyone. He was still capable of making mistakes (like the start at Misano), but his riding left little to be desired. Another year of experience will see him win races and challenge for the championship.

Rob McElnea – where now?

Raymond Roche – nearly, but not quite.

Christian Sarron – a bump too many.

Freddie Spencer – lost contact and out of touch.

AUTOCOURSE 1987-88

For the first time in its 37-year history, AUTOCOURSE presents the entire Grand Prix season in sensational colour.

Detailed race reports and lively features by the sport's top journalists spotlight the leading personalities and technical innovations.

And, of course, there's also full coverage of US racing, Sports-Prototype, Formulas 3 and 3000, plus comprehensive results sections.

160 colour and 40 BW photographs
ISBN: 0-905138-47-3
● **Price: £19.95**

MOTOCOURSE 1987-88

Now in its 12th year, MOTOCOURSE is bigger and better than ever, with more pages, more colour and more space for the 15 rounds of the 1987 World Championship.

Peter Clifford reports on a closely fought season and Malcolm Bryan highlights all the action with his stunning photography.

Packed with special features and including coverage of US racing, detailed results and statistics, MOTOCOURSE is a must for all fans of this thrilling sport.

80 colour and 130 BW photographs
ISBN: 0-905138-48-1
● **Price: £19.95**

SAILING YEAR 1987-88

This new high-quality annual brings the ocean racing season to life in words and over 100 breathtaking colour pictures.

Aimed at the racing sailor – professional or amateur – SAILING YEAR covers all international races as well as the longer offshore competitions and smaller local events.

Technical and personality features, supported by a comprehensive results section, ensure that this will be an invaluable reference book for competitors and enthusiasts alike.

150 colour and 50 BW photographs
ISBN: 0-905138-50-3
● **Price: £19.95**

RALLYCOURSE 1987-88

Now in its sixth year, RALLYCOURSE is established as the world's premier rallying annual.

The championship struggle is retold in over 100 exciting colour photographs by Reinhard Klein and the words of leading journalist Mike Greasley.

Special features include detailed coverage of the Paris–Dakar rally and these are supported by comprehensive technical specifications, results, maps and stage times. RALLYCOURSE is the complete record of the rallying year.

120 colour and 30 BW photographs
ISBN: 0-905138-49-X
● **Price: £19.95**

THE GRAND PRIX DRIVERS

RACING HEROES FROM FANGIO TO PROST

Marlboro AUTOCOURSE

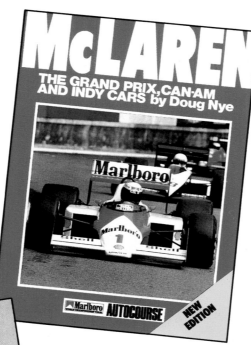

McLAREN: The Grand Prix, Can-Am and Indy Cars

by Doug Nye
Since publication of the McLaren marque history in 1984, the team has enjoyed three resoundingly successful seasons, winning three World Championships for Drivers and two Constructors' titles. Prompted by these spectacular achievements, Doug Nye's acclaimed McLaren story is being brought right up to date and will also include a selection of fresh colour and mono photographs.
21 colour and 150 BW photographs
ISBN: 0-905138-54-6
● **Price: £15.95**
Publication date: Spring 1988

THE GRAND PRIX DRIVERS

A unique record of all the great drivers, from the beginning of the World Championship in 1950 to the present day. Every Grand Prix winner is portrayed in a superb black-and-white photograph accompanied by a frank and informed appraisal by the journalist who knew him best. In addition, Maurice Hamilton, Nigel Roebuck, Alan Henry and Denis Jenkinson have selected their most highly rated drivers in an intriguing 'Top Ten' section.
24 colour and 130 BW photographs
ISBN: 0-905138-55-4
● **Price: £9.95**

GRAND PRIX IMAGES

Marlboro AUTOCOURSE

A fresh and original look at the glamour and excitement of Formula 1 presented in over 100 dramatic colour pictures from the sport's very best photographers – a fascinating insight into the multi-million dollar world of motor racing.
118 colour photographs
ISBN: 0-905138-52-X
● **Price: £12.95**

TECHNIQUES OF MOTOR CYCLE ROAD RACING

by Kenny Roberts
No-one is better qualified to write this book than triple motor cycle World Champion, Kenny Roberts. He shows how his success resulted not from sheer skill alone, but came also through careful planning and strategy, emphasising the importance of setting up the machine correctly, cornering style, slipstreaming, and personal physical and mental preparation.
16 colour and 130 BW photographs
ISBN: 0-905138-51-1
● **Price: £15.95**
Publication date: Spring 1988

GRAND PRIX CAR DESIGN AND TECHNOLOGY IN THE 1980s

by Alan Henry
Using photographs, line drawings and interviews with leading Formula 1 designers, Alan Henry reveals the inside technical story behind the main turning points of Grand Prix car design over the past 25 years. Covered in particular detail is the era from 1977 to 1987, when the acceleration of technical development probably outstripped that of any other decade in motor racing history.
16 colour and 130 BW photographs
ISBN: 0-905138-53-8
● **Price: £16.95**
Publication date: Spring 1988

EXISTING TITLES, ALSO AVAILABLE

JACKIE STEWART'S PRINCIPLES OF PERFORMANCE DRIVING
ISBN: 0-905138-43-0 ● Price: £14.95

THE AUTOCOURSE HISTORY OF THE GRAND PRIX CAR 1966-85
by Doug Nye
ISBN: 0-905138-37-6 ● Price: £19.95

THE ART & SCIENCE OF MOTOR CYCLE ROAD RACING
by Peter Clifford
ISBN: 0-905138-35-X ● Price: £12.95

FERRARI: THE GRAND PRIX CARS
by Alan Henry
ISBN: 0-905138-30-9 ● Price: £14.95

BRABHAM: THE GRAND PRIX CARS
by Alan Henry
ISBN: 0-905138-36-8 ● Price: £14.95

Not only did Randy Mamola demonstrate that he and the Dunlop tyres were an unbeatable combination in the rain but by the end of the season the pairing were threatening to eclipse the Michelin-shod riders in the dry as well. Dunlop certainly did enough to shake up the French company and the World Championship could well change hands again in 1988.

AND AFTER GARDNER?

Just occasionally a rider hits the Grand Prix scene who is obviously bound for greatness, a rider who doesn't seem to need a regular learning curve or the latest tyres and machinery. Kevin Magee was the revelation of 1987.

He rode in only three Grands Prix. In Japan he was impressive but was criticised for falling off too frequently; in Holland he astonished everyone by qualifying second but could not match that performance in the wet race; at Járama his performance was faultless and his place on the rostrum was well earned.

The Grand Prix performances are only half the story, for the Australian won the Suzuka Eight-hours, backed by Martin Wimmer. Although that was his most prestigious race win, earlier in the year he had claimed the Suzuka 200-kilometre race on the F1 Yamaha Genesis, using the same bike to win the Japanese round of the Formula 1 World Championship at Sugo. Marlboro Yamaha Australia team-mate Michael Dowson rode with Magee to reproduce their '86 success, winning the 1987 Castrol Six-hour race by four laps. Magee thus demonstrated that he can win on production bikes as well as on slick-shod Grand Prix and F1 machines.

It was not just that Magee won races but the manner in which he rode on all occasions that was so impressive. There is no-one who thinks more about racing than Martin Wimmer and he had plenty of time to consider just how well Magee was riding during their Japanese Endurance round.

'I have to say that Magee won the Eight-hour; all I did was ride and not screw up. We did nine sessions and he did six of them – that is like riding six Grands Prix. At the end of the race he was still doing the same times as he had done at the start and on tyres that had done the equivalent of four Grands Prix by that time.'

Of course Wimmer had noticed Magee before, at the Japanese Grand Prix and at Assen. 'When he set second-fastest qualifying time for the Dutch GP on tyres that were not brand new some people thought he must be crazy. I thought that perhaps it was not the right way to do it at the time but the way he rode at Suzuka I know he can ride fast however old the tyres are. The thing is that when the tyres are old they start to slide earlier, but in fact they are more predictable than new tyres and he makes use of this.'

After riding with him in Japan, Wimmer summed up many people's thoughts on Magee 'He should come Grand Prix racing because after a year of experience he will be able to ride just like Eddie and Randy. There are not many people who can but for sure he can do it.'

Wimmer's point about Magee's ability to ride on well-used tyres is an interesting one because Magee does not have the classic, deep dirt-track racing background of the Americans. He does, on the other hand, spend plenty of time riding motocross and that is his number one form of physical training. He also rides production machines and is well practised at sliding the big four-strokes on street tyres.

Strangely, apart from his great win with Dowson in the Castrol Six-hours, Magee has

certainly not dominated Australian racing. Between his appearances in Europe he has been beaten by old hands like Mal Campbell and Rob Phillis on production machines and superbikes, but he is obviously so at home on a Grand Prix 500 that he can mix it with the best in the world.

Magee has not exactly been brought up on Grand Prix 500s. His introduction to the YZR500 came in the Australian Swann Insurance Series at the end of 1986. He beat Rob McElnea on two occasions, which thrilled the crowd but did not gain universal praise. Kel Carruthers, who was in charge of the effort, pointed out that his passing manoeuvres were not really acceptable between team-mates who had no real opposition.

Magee was naturally keen to impress, and with the same thought uppermost in his mind he pushed hard from the start of practice when he made his Grand Prix debut in Japan. Three crashes in one meeting could not hide the fact that he was fast and what might have been a one-off ride quickly became a selection of two more Grands Prix with the Lucky Strike team fitted in between his commitments for the Australian Marlboro Yamaha team.

It was one of those commitments which could have finished his career completely, as he crashed during the Arai 500 at Bathurst at Easter and fractured his leg. It was a race he had won for Yamaha in '86 but Magee paid the price for a mistake at this road circuit bounded by trees and concrete walls.

Not only did he recover quickly but his self-confidence was not affected. The crash might just have made him a fraction more cautious without apparently slowing him down, because thereafter the crashing stopped. He won his next international race, the 200 km at Sugo on the 750 Genesis, and then arrived at Assen for his second Grand Prix. The speed at which he got to grips with the narrow circuit which so often catches out newcomers was remarkable. Second-fastest in practice, he failed to feature in the race after a nasty front-wheel slide nearly saw him follow Mamola into the sand pit, and he then struggled against a misting visor in the unfamiliar conditions.

There is no doubt that Magee's performances have been aided by his close association with Warren Willing – himself a very good rider in his time, and now an even better engineer. Willing translates Magee's comments into machine modifications that work and adds a wealth of riding experience. Willing found an old friend and fellow ex-rider to work alongside in the Lucky Strike Yamaha team as Phil Macdonald was allocated to Magee while Mike Baldwin was sidelined with injury. The two had raced against each other in the New Zealand Marlboro series in the late '70s as well as meeting in the US when Willing rode there.

Magee began his association with Australian Yamaha dealer Willing in the middle of '85 when in his first ride he joined Dowson to win the Denso 500. He had attracted the attention of Yamaha after some incredible giant-killing performances on several Ducatis run by enthusiastic dealer Bob Brown. Born on 16 July 1962, his first

_____ *by Peter Clifford*

Left: **Without a doubt, Kevin Magee was the most exciting find of the season. The young Australian gave a good indication of what can be expected from his full-scale attack on the World Championship in '88.**

Kevin Schwantz *(below)* **should have campaigned a full Grand Prix season in '87 after several outings in '86 but he was tied to a contract that restricted most of his racing to the USA. He developed into a much better Grand Prix rider than he had been the year before; if he continues to improve he will be a real threat on a more competitive Suzuki.**

Bottom: **At the end of 1986, Niall Mackenzie rode like a Grand Prix winner who only needed a better bike. In 1987, he had the bike but consistent results eluded him.**

David Goldman

Left: **Pier Francesco Chili may not have been quite as exciting as Magee but he attained a maturity that went well with his talent. He will make a solid and reliable Grand Prix performer under any conditions.**

Jean-Philippe Ruggia *(below)* **has the aggressive style that expresses the desperation of youth. His talent is beyond doubt but he needs guidance to succeed.**

successes came in an RD250LC series, like so many other of today's stars. Married and with a baby he lives in Horsham, Victoria, but '88 will see him on the World Championship trail for a full season. No-one would be wise to put a limit on what he might achieve in that first season.

Other riders do need that learning curve even though it may take them right to the top, as it did Gardner and Lawson before him. The latest hope to come out of France is Jean-Philippe Ruggia who started the year in great form and rode exceptionally well on his private Yamaha at Jerez to finish seventh. Unfortunately, the impossibility of racing a standard TZ250 Yamaha against the works machines meant that he did not score again until the French Grand Prix at Le Mans.

Though Ruggia seems to have raw talent his season was not beyond criticism: when he got the chance to ride Patrick Igoa's factory Yamaha while the regular Sonauto Gauloises rider was injured he went at it with rather too much aggression and crashed twice. His team have also been accused of making mistakes and have not been able to move beyond attitudes more suited to French club and national racing. His girlfriend was criticised for well-intentioned but misguided outspokenness and his father for tuning the TZ to a standstill. The Sonauto team hope to absorb him fully into their operation in '88 and that might provide him with a chance to become a consistent points scorer, especially as they hope to retain Igoa's '87 works bike for him to ride.

Further up the learning curve are Niall Mackenzie and Kevin Schwantz. Both were considered 'men most likely to' after the '86 season and both did fulfil at least some of that promise this season. Mackenzie starred in Japan and Austria but had more frustrations than he expected. He has the requisite riding ability but his style seems more suited to the 250 class where high corner speed is of more value than it is with a 500. He tried changing his style

and found that working at it detracted from the results. Next season should see him settle to a more appropriate style for both himself and the 500, hopefully suffering fewer problems than he did this year.

Kevin Schwantz had no such difficulties with his style and found racing the 500 suited him better than his more familiar superbike. He experienced fewer falls in Europe than whilst riding for Yoshimura back in the States, and he is unlikely to regret abandoning the four-strokes in favour of a full Grand Prix season which should see him regularly in the top six.

Pier Francesco Chili could also be a regular top six man in '88 so long as he can ride a four-cylinder and does not find that any harder to ride than the three which he took to very quickly. His second place in France was quite exceptional. One of Chili's few problems is his dislike for certain circuits, which he finds difficult to overcome.

YAMAHA FZ750. STILL AHEAD OF ITS TIME!

In future years, when observers look back on motorcycle development in the 1980s, one machine will stand out above the rest as the most significant step forward in motorcycle design of the decade – that machine will be the Yamaha FZ750.

And the reason is the Genesis concept. Rather than design an engine and chassis in isolation from each other, our engineers and designers adopted a totally new approach. An approach in which the chassis and engine positively enhance each other.

Central to the Genesis design is the forward inclined high-performance engine – a configuration developed to give a low centre of gravity, compact size and slim, aerodynamic profile. Utilising Yamaha's unique 5-valve per cylinder technology, the four cylinder power-plant produces tremendous power and torque, yet remains incredibly flexible at low speeds.

Complementing the high-performance engine, a slim box-section tube frame and aluminium swinging arm assure sure-footed handling and, together with the 39 mm diameter front forks and rising-rate Monocross rear suspension, enable the FZ to be taken to the limit with confidence.

Genesis design and worldwide racing successes including the Daytona 200 have assured the FZ750 of a place in the motorcycle history books. When you experience one, you'll understand why!

YAMAHA
A TRADITION OF PERFECTION.

THE HEAT

QXR is a totally new kind of oil from Duckhams, <u>specially developed for high performance engines — and high performance drivers.</u>

QXR is the outcome of a unique refining process that "cracks" the molecular structure of the base oil giving it a purity and a <u>viscosity index conventional technology could never achieve (and a price conventional oils could never justify).</u>

As a result, *QXR* has <u>better cooling properties at higher temperatures</u> than ordinary oils, and doesn't break down under the <u>stress of continuous hard driving.</u> At the same time it has a low-drag formulation that <u>protects your engine at low temperatures and during cold starts.</u>

QXR has been tested on and off the track, in all kinds of engine. In one torture test generating <u>turbo temperatures of 900° centigrade,</u> *QXR* maintained higher <u>oil pressures</u> than any other leading mineral or synthetic oil tested.

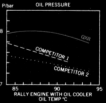

So if you have a red-hot engine, get some *QXR* under the bonnet. <u>Fast.</u>

OIL PRESSURE (P/bar)

QXR

COMPETITOR 1

COMPETITOR 2

85   90   95
RALLY ENGINE WITH OIL COOLER
OIL TEMP °C

HIGH PERFORMANCE **QXR** *ENGINE PROTECTION*

DEVELOPED TO A STANDSTILL

There was a time when a motor cycle and sidecar meant a solo machine with an attached 'chair'. Even racing machines were built like that and when Nortons and then BMWs dominated the class, ridden by men like Eric Oliver and Denis Jenkinson, Wilhelm Noll and Fritz Cron, there was a very close relationship between solos and sidecars.

That changed gradually as modifications like dustbin fairings (which were also adopted by solos but then outlawed) made the sidecars vary both mechanically and visually. Naturally, the extreme side forces experienced by the cornering outfit are distributed in an entirely different way from a leaning solo, which led to variations in frame and suspension construction as sidecars were first modified and then completely designed from scratch.

Without the solo's ground clearance problems, outfits were built lower and riding positions were adapted accordingly. Tyres increased in width because putting more rubber on the road helped to accommodate greater acceleration, braking and cornering forces.

Sidecars changed so much more than solos for two reasons. The regulations allowed more fully enclosing fairings, and the sidecar is more like a four-wheel car than a two-wheel motor cycle in the way that it corners.

Logically, therefore, sidecar design has followed that of cars more than solo motor cycle design, and only the FIM's regulations have prevented the building of three-wheel cars. The sport had actually gone a long way in that direction before it was hauled back by the FIM when the regulations were revised in 1979, a year in which two separate championships were held.

The more restricted sidecar class was continued and the rule dictating direct connection between handlebar and front wheel means that the rider still leans forward rather than sitting back behind a steering wheel as in a car.

Of course, there is one important distinction separating sidecars from three-wheeled racing cars: a sidecar carries two people and has a continuously changing weight distribution as the passenger moves around. While the passenger redistributes his weight to increase the load on one wheel or another, the setting up of a sidecar will never be quite as scientific as a Formula 1 car.

Prior to 1979's stricter regulations, there had been a period of great and frequent change in which a variety of ideas and designs appeared that were either great successes or conspicuous failures. All these made sidecar builders do a lot of thinking, but since then there has been, apparently, almost total stagnation. Today, the class is dominated by one chassis manufacturer to a greater extent than any other category in the sport.

While Seymaz, Windle and Busch build very good outfits, it is Louis Christen and his LCRs who led sidecar racing to its current position and who continues to dominate the results. With Steve Webster, Egbert Streuer, Rolf Biland and Alain Michel all starting the 1987 season with LCR chassis, there was little doubt that the

championship would remain with the Swiss marque and equally little chance that a single Grand Prix would be won by anyone else. Next year will probably be the same.

Not only do the top stars use the same outfit, but three also employ the same Krauser engine. This is the powerplant Yamaha would have built had they carried on with an across-the-frame production racing four. The Japanese continued with the twin-cylinder 250 and changed to crankcase reed-valve induction. The Krauser is a four-cylinder version of the 250 Yamaha, even incorporating Yamaha cylinders and internals.

The Krauser engine made its debut in 1986 and suffered from several problems which were sorted out before the start of the 1987 championship. As well as proving more powerful than the Yamaha engine, it has also been more reliable, mainly because of the crankcases which have increased the durability of the Yamaha internals, as Steve Webster's father Mick points out. 'The Krauser cases are aluminium instead of magnesium, and though they are heavier they are denser, stiffer and more robust. We use the same cranks as we did in the Yamaha but these cases do not flex, so the cranks last longer. The old Yamaha cases used to flex so much that they would split between the two middle cylinders and some people used to bolt a bridge across between the two middle cylinder heads to stop the cases flexing so much at that point. The gearboxes also used to break off the Yamahas but we haven't had any problems with the Krauser.'

The crank is not exactly the same as the old Yamaha because in the Krauser the ignition is mounted on the right-hand end of the crank instead of on a separate shaft behind the crank on the left-hand side of the engine. This means that the right-hand crank web has to be changed to carry the ignition rotor. The Krauser water pump has been moved to the position of the ignition on the Yamaha powerplant. The rest of the internals are all of Yamaha manufacture, and the gears etc. stand up very well.

Steve Webster insists that the reed-valve engine did not perform as he expected. 'I thought that all reed-valve engines were tractable and I thought the Krauser would drive like the old 750, but it is not like that at all. It has quite a sharp power band and at first I found it more difficult to drive than the Yamaha which revved from 9.5 to 12,500 rpm. The Krauser makes all its power between 10 and 12, though it will pull from 9. Inside the rev band, the Krauser is stronger but you have to be careful with the gearchanges so that the engine does not drop out of the power band.'

Webster and Hewitt started the year with a distinct advantage over the other top teams. From the beginning of the year their engine was running better than the others because they were the quickest to follow Yamaha's development of the 250 cc unit. 'We ordered '87 TZ250 spares because we wanted to fit the bigger reeds and carb rubbers', said Mick Webster. 'There just weren't any in Britain. I suppose Yamaha were surprised with the demand for spares as they had only sold a few 250s. In fact, we had to

The universal sidecar layout: engine bolted to the side of the monocoque; exhaust pipes pointing forward; passenger pan behind the rear wheel with monocoque side-spar at right angles to main member.

Above: **Like all the top sidecar runners, Alain Michel places his faith in the Swiss-built LCR chassis.**

borrow reeds and carb rubbers from solo riders Bosworth and Patrickson so that we could get on with testing.'

Webster and Hewitt's success in obtaining the new parts meant that at the Spanish and German Grands Prix they were racing with the '87 reeds and 38 mm flat-slide carbs while the opposition were trying to get their engines sorted out. After a season of work, though, Mick is not convinced that big reeds are the ultimate answer. 'The right sort of small reeds are just as good if not better; the quality and the way they work is probably more important than the size.'

Sorting out the reed-valve engines was not without its difficulties and the Websters ran into that old bugbear of the sidecar racer: fuel supply. 'Fuel supply causes more problems than anything else and everyone has their own idea on how to deal with it', states Steve. 'I have found vacuum pumps the best. I run two for safety, connected to the back of the crankcase. I have a jet in the return line to restrict the flow and no header tank. Every time I have tried to run a header tank I have had problems with fuel surge.

'I had some wrong information when we got the reed-valve engine. I had been told that vacuum pumps would not work because of the reed-valve induction direct into the cases. Before we ran the outfit I spent three days trying to rig up an electric fuel pump system, then found out

that vacuum pumps do work, so I threw the lot away. The advantages of the vacuum pump system are that it is simple and, of course, it responds to engine demand. The faster the engine runs the faster the pump works and the more fuel it supplies.'

Naturally, sorting out a chassis that works and a reliable, fast engine is only part of the battle in winning the championship. Between the outfit and the road are the tyres. 'We have had excellent service from the engineers, particularly George Cole', asserts Steve Webster. 'I can suggest that a tyre needs modifying and two weeks later he comes back with something new to try. We have five different rear tyres to use most of the time but I normally use the A10 compound which is pretty bullet-proof. The rear takes a lot of stick from wheelspin but they are pretty predictable. When they start to go off you get a vibration as though the wheel has gone out of balance, and with the Avons if you take it easy for a few laps it will come back. I have never actually blistered a tyre, but then I often run a harder tyre than most.'

No other racing vehicle has gained such universal respect as the LCR chassis; Egbert Streuer explained why: 'The handling is fair, it never throws you off if you don't do anything stupid. It is predictable and reliable and not difficult to sort out the handling and suspension.

I think the Busch chassis is good and occasionally it might have an advantage but I have never been close to it in the LCR. It would be interesting to see one of the top crews in a Busch.'

Streuer is the only one of the top four not using the Krauser engine and he started the year with the old Yamaha powerplant before building his own crankcase reed-induction engine when he realised that the Krauser had the edge. He has done Yamaha's development work for them. 'I didn't want the expense of buying new Krauser engines so I had a good look at the old Yamaha and decided that I could build a reed engine myself. I made the reed-valve adapter box from one piece of aluminium and use Honda 250 reeds, although almost any reeds will fit. It has give an improvement in acceleration because it is stronger from 10 to 11,500 rpm. I use Hummel cylinders with no power valves and I will be doing some more testing for Hummel in the winter, and I have some ideas for different exhaust pipes.'

Streuer carried out a considerable amount of bench testing himself when looking for more power. While the Websters had to do their testing at the circuit, Biland enlisted the help of Harold Bartol when he found himself behind in the power race. 'I started working for Rolf at Assen', Bartol remembers. 'I worked on cylinders, heads and exhaust pipes. We use '87 Yamaha cylinders

43

Peter Clifford

John McKenzie

Rolf Biland's Krauser engine in situ. The rear suspension is controlled by a White Power unit and the loads are taken by the corners of the monocoque. The engine's gearbox oil is cooled by a radiator, lying temporarily on top of the carburettors.

The crankcase reed-valve induction from the four Mikuni carburettors can be seen in this view of Steve Webster's Krauser engine. Unlike the Yamaha engine, this has the ignition on the right-hand end of the crank.

and I sorted out the 38 mm DellOrto carbs. I took off the special computer ignition system because it was causing more trouble than it was worth and we have been using the standard Yamaha system. I only started mid-season, so had no time for bench testing – we did all our testing at the track. I have tried to get more power and stretch the power band so it runs from 8.5 to 12.5.'

Alain Michel did his own work, as always, and he is developing his own engine-tuning business, 'AM Energie'. 'We worked on the Krauser engine through the winter and I thought that we would start the year with a considerable advantage over the others. I was mistaken because we were only a little way ahead. We tried many different reed valves but the Yamaha ones are the best, the most consistent. We had to wait a bit long for the '87 Yamaha parts and that delayed things for us.'

Michel agrees with Streuer about the value of the LCR chassis. 'They are predictable and reliable. The LCR chassis is the best because Louis knows what he is doing and the chassis has been developed by the best riders. I would like to build my own chassis; I have ideas but it doesn't make economic sense. The LCR costs about SFr28,000 and I would need about four times that much to develop my own chassis. I used to work with the Seymaz through '78, '79 and '80, and I think that sometimes we had the best chassis, but we lost so much time in development work. I was working on the chassis and lost time which I should have spent working on the engine. I would need to employ about ten people to do everything properly; it is impossible for me to develop a chassis and the engine as

well as race in the same season.'

Steve Webster has similar feelings about chassis development. 'I would like to get a totally different machine. It would be interesting, but I think that Rolf has lost a lot of championships spending time testing instead of racing.'

Nevertheless, Biland does not intend to ease off on his development work, and he has planned a busy winter. 'I want to try changing the bore and stroke of the Krauser engine and do some experimentation with fuel injection and a new ignition system. The chassis will probably remain the same but I want to do some work in the wind tunnel on the fairing. I made a mistake with this year's and made the radiator hole too big. I am not sure if this year's fairing has improved the top speed. I will find that out in the wind tunnel this winter; I do know it is much lighter.'

So Biland has plans for engine work and no-one seems prepared to attempt a radical alteration to the chassis. Louis Christen does not see himself making any major changes in the near future. 'Sidecars have now got to the same stage as solos: they work reasonably well and I do not think there will be any great changes in the near future – the FIM rules prevent any great developments. It is the same in Formula 1 car racing; they have not made any great changes for the last five years. We have steering and braking systems that work and we cannot do much with the steering system because of the regulations that say we have to have a direct connection between the handlebars and the front wheel. Because of this, we are limited with the steering geometry because the rider has no

mechanical advantage over the wheel like he would if there was a steering wheel and geared linkage as in a car.

'This year I did try moving the sidecar wheel forward a little on Biland's outfit because he thought he needed it, but since he has got more power from the engine it has gone back to the same place as everyone else. I could do more work with the aerodynamics but I do not see the advantage in that for myself; I will leave it up to the drivers. I could replace the aluminium monocoque, which is riveted and bonded together, with a complete carbon-fibre chassis, but it would be much more expensive and would only save three or four kilos.'

The sport's technical stagnation through lack of effective opposition to the LCRs is not necessarily bad for competition. The resultant stability has made life less expensive for participants. Christen has now built more than 70 outfits and the latest 55 have all been made the same. Because of that, the teams do not have to replace them every year. It is enough to refurbish the previous year's machines by rebuilding or replacing suspension units and replacing the rose joints which take the high load concentrations and become fatigued. Christen can even repair badly crash-damaged chassis by replacing bent or creased monocoque panels.

Not only can an outfit be kept by a team for several seasons but it can also have a good resale value. Christen does not foresee any mechanical problems for the class, especially now that the Krauser engines are available to replace ageing Yamaha powerplants. He sees the difficulties lying in other areas. 'I think sidecar racing has a good future but it is difficult to get enough races in the FIM calendar. Nationally, we do not have enough new drivers starting the sport in Switzerland and Germany. Each year we only have three to five new riders starting and there is little chance of finding a new World Champion out of them. In comparison, there are about fifty new solo riders each season.

'The biggest problem for beginners is that when they start they have to use virtually the same machinery as the top Grand Prix riders – there is nothing less – and you know that if Biland has problems with his outfit then the new riders are going to have trouble. Formula 2 could be a good idea, but the regulations are not very clever and they are very expensive.'

There seems no reason for the LCR domination of sidecar racing to be broken. Even the non-LCR machines are very similar and there is no immediate sign that anyone is likely to find a significant edge over Louis Christen. After many years of rapid development that have seen sidecars transformed so fundamentally in comparison to solos, the class's stability seems set to continue. At least the mechanical similarity has produced some good close racing this year, with any of the top four looking a possible race winner on each occasion. Some new blood at the front would be welcome, and perhaps new men would bring in new ideas. However, they are unlikely to have the time or money to be race winners as well as machine developers.

VERY CLEVER, TREVOR.

GRIPPING STUFF. TREVOR NATION ON A PRODUCTION FZR 750 SETS NEW ISLE OF MAN
LAP RECORD. 111.64 MPH ON PIRELLI TYRES. NATURALLY.

NOT VERY CLEVER, TREVOR.

GRIPPING FINISH? 24 SECONDS IN THE LEAD, AND YOU RUN OUT OF FUEL AT THE FINISH.
STILL, THIRD PLACE CERTAINLY DESERVES CONGRATULATIONS.

PIRELLI

GRIPPING STUFF

The BMW K100RS. To get near the same quality in a car would cost you at least £39,500 more

IF IT WERE A CAR IT WOULD COST £45,000.

But one thing's for certain, with a 0 to 60 time of 3·8 secs, you still won't get near the bike.

THE ULTIMATE RIDING MACHINE

WCRSMM

TRUST BELSTAFF

LEADERS

There's only one choice when you're a winner.

Only one name you can be sure of for Quality, Performance and Protection. One name that stands for Style. Belstaff—the choice of leaders!

Left to right:
Mark Phillips in Classique,
Mick Grant in Trialmaster Professional,
Keith Huewen in Mach I Racing Suit,
Steve Parrish in Tourmaster

Belstaff
The Only One!

The NSR500 engine laid bare. The four carburettor rubbers, moulded in pairs, are taped over. The cylinders have all been removed and the rods of cylinders 2 and 4 can be seen protruding. The angle between the gudgeon pins would appear to be close to 180°. The small end of no. 1 cylinder's rod can just be seen as a lump in the engine stand next to the protruding cylinder stud, whilst the no. 3 rod is out of sight and near the bottom of its stroke. The compact nature of the design is clear with very little room between the transfer ports of the lower cylinders.

Below: The YZR 500 Yamaha frame denuded. The frame may look identical to the '86 version but it has been strengthened around the steering head; riders reported that it felt more accurate going into corners.

Peter Clifford

Peter Clifford

Wayne Gardner
494.6 cc NSR 500 Honda

Engine: 54 mm x 54 mm, water-cooled, four-cylinder two-stroke, crankcase reed-valve induction; five transfer ports and electrically controlled variable-height exhaust port; one piston ring; needle roller big ends and needle roller small ends; one pressed crank, five roller bearings; dry clutch with seven friction and seven steel plates, six springs. *Gearbox:* six-speed, alternative ratios for all gears; drum selection. *Carburettors:* 34 mm or 35 mm cylindrical-slide Keihin.
Frame: Honda twin-spar rectangular-section aluminium tube, taper roller head bearings; triangulated aluminium swing arm, needle roller bearings; 'Pro-Link' rear suspension, one Showa unit, coil-spring plus nitrogen pressure, adjustable damping; Showa forks, coil-springs, oil-damped, adjustable, mechanical-hydraulic anti-dive. *Wheels:* Honda cast-magnesuim, commonly used sizes 3.5 in. x 17 in. front and 5.5 in. or 6.0 in. x 17 in. rear. *Tyres:* Michelin. *Brakes:* two Honda steel discs front (320 mm) and one Honda carbon-fibre rear (190 mm); Nissin calipers; Nissin pads. *Plugs:* NGK 9.5. *Gearbox and engine oil:* Shell.

Pier Francesco Chili
499 cc NS500 Honda

Engine: 62.6 mm x 54 mm, water-cooled, three-cylinder two-stroke, reed-valve induction; five transfer and one bridged exhaust port and mechanically controlled variable-volume exhaust pipes; one plain piston ring; roller big ends and needle roller small ends; one pressed crank, one ball and three roller bearings each; dry clutch with seven friction and seven steel plates, six springs. *Gearbox:* six-speed, six possible ratios for first and sixth gears, seven for second, nine for third and fourth, and eight for fifth; drum selection. *Carburettors:* 36 mm cylindrical-slide Keihin.
Frame: Honda twin-spar rectangular-section aluminium tube, taper roller head bearings; box-section aluminium swing arm, needle roller bearings; 'Pro-Link' rear suspension, one Showa unit, coil-spring plus nitrogen pressure, oil damping, adjustable; Showa forks, coil-springs, oil-damped, adjustable, mechanical-hydraulic anti-dive. *Wheels:* Marvic cast-magnesium alloy, commonly used sizes 3.5 in. x 17 in. front and 5.5 in. x 17 in. rear. *Tyres:* Michelin. *Brakes:* two Honda steel discs front (310 mm) and one Honda steel rear (215 mm); Nissin calipers; Nissin pads. *Plugs:* NGK. *Gearbox and engine oil:* Castrol.

Eddie Lawson
498 cc YZR 500 Yamaha

Engine: 56 mm x 50.6 mm, water-cooled, four-cylinder two-stroke; crankcase reed-valve induction; five transfer and three exhaust ports; one plain piston ring; roller big ends and needle roller small ends; two pressed cranks, four roller bearings each; dry clutch with five friction and six steel plates, six springs. *Gearbox:* six-speed, alternative ratios for all gears; drum selection. *Carburettors:* 34 mm or 35 mm flat-slide Mikuni.
Frame: Yamaha twin-spar fabricated box-section aluminium, taper roller head bearings; box-section aluminium swing arm, needle roller bearings; lower end-linked rear suspension, one Öhlins unit, coil-spring plus nitrogen pressure, oil damping, adjustable; Yamaha forks, coil-springs, oil-damped, adjustable. *Wheels:* Marvic, commonly used sizes 3.5 in. x 17 in. front and 5.5 in. x 17 in. rear. *Tyres:* Michelin. *Brakes:* two Brembo steel discs front (320 mm) and one Yamaha rear (220 mm); Brembo aluminium calipers front, Nissin rear; Brembo and Nissin pads. *Plugs:* NGK. *Gearbox and engine oil:* Castrol.

The Elf4 used a similar front suspension system to Elf3 but was built around the 4-cylinder Honda instead of the older triple. The swinging arm moved to the left of the front wheel and the rear suspension was modelled on Honda's Pro-Link but with a single swing arm on the left-hand side.

The Fior 500, as raced by Marco Gentile, Hervé Guilleux and Thierry Rapicault. Using RS500 Honda engines, the Fiors were often the most competitive of the private entrants but still had to battle hard to get into the points, although Gentile eventually succeeded. The fabricated aluminium frame loops over the top of the engine to carry the pivot points for the double wishbone front suspension. There are three radiators, one in front of the petrol tank and two low down either side of the front lower cylinder. The machine is interesting but the handling often proved rather too exciting.

The 500 Suzuki, with the bank of Mikuni carbs across the front of the crankcase, looks just like a Yamaha or a Cagiva but employs a different method of connecting the water hoses to the cylinder heads. The Mikuni carbs on the Yamaha and the Cagiva are identical but the Suzuki units differ in several respects, most obviously in the actuating mechanism for the slides. Nevertheless, all three units are similar, having flat slides and the bodies being cast in pairs.

Kenny Irons
498 cc XR75 Suzuki

Engine: 56 mm x 50.6 mm. water-cooled, four-cylinder two-stroke; crankcase reed-valve induction; seven transfer and one exhuast port; one plain piston ring; needle roller big ends and needle roller small ends; two pressed cranks, two ball and two needle roller bearings each; dry clutch with eight friction and nine steel plates, six springs. *Gearbox:* six-speed, six possible ratios for first four gears, five for fifth and sixth; drum selection. *Carburettors:* 36 mm flat-slide Mikuni.

Frame: Suzuki twin-spar fabricated box-section aluminium, taper roller head bearings in adjustable angle inserts; fabricated aluminium swing arm, needle roller and shims; adjustable rocker arm rear suspension, one Showa unit, coil-spring, oil damping, adjustable; Showa forks, coil-springs, oil-damped, externally adjustable. *Wheels:* Marvic, commonly used sizes 3.5 in. x 17 in. front and 5.5 in. x 17 in. rear. *Tyres:* Michelin. *Brakes:* two cast-iron Lockheed discs front (310 mm) and one carbon-fibre rear (210 mm); Lockheed aluminium calipers; Ferodo pads. *Plugs:* ND. *Gearbox and engine oil:* Shell.

The 500 Cagiva. This is the 1987 model, called the V587, with all four carbs in line instead of staggered as in the original version. This engine has a much narrower angle between the cylinders (56°) than the older Cagiva (90°).

Although the Cagiva design has obviously been heavily influenced by Yamaha, one major difference is that while the Yamaha cranks are geared together to run in opposite directions, the cranks in the Cagiva are both geared onto the clutch like the original V-four Yamaha and like the current Suzuki.

The water pump is mounted on the right-hand engine cover and takes its drive from the upper crank. The cylinders have guillotine exhaust valves, electrically driven; and a special ignition system, produced by Magneti Marelli, which did not use generator coils but drained a battery, was replaced by a better Japanese system for the last half of the season.

Engineer Alain Chevallier stated that the bike weighed 124 kg with water and oil but no fuel. 'It produces 148 bhp and the spread of power is the big improvement over the old engine because that had no flexibility, but the power that we have below 9000 rpm is still not good', admitted the Frenchman. He left the Cagiva team at the end of the season, feeling frustrated by the lack of response to his suggestions.

Henk Keulemans

Above: **Loris Reggiani and Dutch engineer Dolf van der Woude stand behind their Grand Prix-winning Aprilia. Der Woude said he was surprised how little work was needed to make the Rotax engine competitive. Unfortunately, the old Rotax reliability spoilt much of the season and Aprilia hatched plans to work with the Austrian factory on producing a new V-twin for '88.**

Sito Pons stands behind the Campsa NSR250 Honda. The gearbox internals have been removed and you can just see the right-hand end of the primary drive gear peeking out of the side cover below the water pump housing. The clutch takes the drive directly from that gear on the right-hand end of the crank. The input shaft uses the smaller of the two bearings on the far side of the case, the larger being for the output shaft *(top right).*

The NSR250 Honda, as raced by Carlos Cardus, displays the rear Showa unit fitted as standard; on Toni Mang's machine, however, this was replaced by a White Power unit. Despite being similar in layout to the '86 NSR, the rear subframe now unbolts and the frame has been completely redesigned in detail using new extrusions for the main frame rails and swing arm *(above right).*

Loris Reggiani
249.6 cc Aprilia
Engine: 54 mm x 54.5 mm, water-cooled, twin-cylinder two-stroke; five transfer and one exhaust port, vacuum-operated exhaust valve used when raining; one plain piston ring; needle roller big ends and needle roller small ends; two pressed cranks, two roller bearings; dry clutch with five friction and six steel plates, six springs. *Gearbox:* six-speed, six possible ratios for first and second gears, four for third and sixth, two for fourth, three for fifth; drum selection. *Carburettors:* 38 mm or 38.5 mm flat-slide Dell'Orto.
Frame: Aprilia twin-spar fabricated box-section aluminium; taper roller head bearings with spherical seating; aluminium swing arm, roller bearings; rocker arm rear suspension, single Öhlins unit, coil-spring, oil damping, adjustable for both compression and rebound; Marzocchi forks, coil-springs, oil-damped, adjustable rebound damping. *Wheels:* Tecno Magnesia, commonly used widths 3.25 in. and 3.5 in. x 17 in. front and 4.5 in. x 17 in. rear. *Tyres:* Michelin. *Brakes:* two Brembo cast-steel discs front (280 mm) and one Zanzani aluminium rear (200 mm); Brembo aluminium calipers; Ferodo pads. *Plugs:* Bosch WOCS7. *Gearbox and engine oil:* Elf.

Toni Mang
247.3 cc RS250R Honda
Engine: 54 mm x 54 mm, water-cooled, twin-cylinder two-stroke; crankcase reed-valve induction; electrically controlled variable-height exhaust port; one plain piston ring; needle roller big ends and needle roller small ends; one pressed crank, three ball bearings; dry clutch, five springs. *Gearbox:* six-speed, alternative ratios for all gears; drum selection. *Carburettors:* two 38 mm cylindrical-slide Keihin.
Frame: twin extruded spars with machined sections in addition, aluminium; caged ball head bearings; box-section aluminium swing arm, needle roller bearings; 'Pro-Link' rear suspension, one White Power unit, coil-spring, oil damping, adjustable; Showa forks, coil-springs, oil-damped, adjustable. *Wheels:* PVM cast-magnesium, commonly used sizes 3.25 in. x 17 in. front and 4.5 in. x 17 in. rear. *Tyres:* Michelin. *Brakes:* twin Nissin steel discs front (270 mm) and one Nissin steel rear (190 mm); Nissin aluminium calipers; Nissin pads. *Plugs:* NGK 10.5. *Gearbox and engine oil:* Castrol.

Stéphane Mertens
247.3 cc Sekitoba
Engine: 54 mm x 54 mm, water-cooled, twin-cylinder two-stroke; disc-valve induction; five transfer and three exhaust ports; one plain piston ring; needle roller big ends and needle roller small ends; two pressed cranks, three ball bearings each; dry clutch with six friction and six steel plates, six springs. *Gearbox:* six-speed, two possible ratios for first two gears; drum selection. *Carburettors:* 37.2 mm cylindrical-slide Dell'Orto.
Frame: Armstrong twin-spar, carbon-fibre composite, taper roller head bearings; box-section carbon-fibre composite swing arm, needle roller bearings; 'Pro-Link'-style rear suspension, one White Power unit, coil-spring, oil damping, adjustable; White Power forks, coil-springs, oil-damped, adjustable. *Wheels:* Marvic, commonly used widths 3.5 in. x 17 in. front and 4.5 in. x 18 in. rear. *Tyres:* Dunlop. *Brakes:* two Lockheed cast-iron discs front (260 mm) and one Brembo steel rear (220 mm); Lockheed aluminium calipers front, Brembo rear; Lockheed and Brembo pads. *Plugs:* NGK 10.5. *Gearbox and engine oil:* Castrol.

Right: **Martin Wimmer's YZR250 Yamaha remained very much like the 1986 model but incorporated a new ignition system only employing the lower crank. The machine lacked the speed of the Hondas but proved to have superior handling, making it competitive on occasions. It was very hard work to match the Honda's drive out of the turns, however.**

Kel Carruthers tried Keihin carbs on the 250 Yamaha in mid-season before Mikuni came up with some revised instruments of their own. The Keihins were over-the-counter flat-slide aluminium carburettors *(below).*

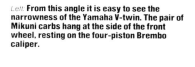

Left: **From this angle it is easy to see the narrowness of the Yamaha V-twin. The pair of Mikuni carbs hang at the side of the front wheel, resting on the four-piston Brembo caliper.**

Martin Wimmer
249 cc Yamaha

Engine: 56 mm x 50.6 mm, water-cooled, twin-cylinder two-stroke; crankcase reed-valve induction; five transfer and three exhaust ports; one plain piston ring; roller big ends and needle roller small ends; two pressed cranks, two roller bearings each; dry clutch with five friction and six steel plates, six springs. *Gearbox:* six-speed, alternative ratios for all gears; drum selection. *Carburettors:* 34 mm flat-slide Mikuni.

Frame: Yamaha, twin-spar fabricated box-section aluminium, taper roller head bearings; box-section aluminium swing arm, needle roller bearings; lower end-linked rear suspension, one Öhlins unit, coil-spring plus nitrogen pressure, oil damping, adjustable; Yamaha forks, coil-springs, oil-damped, adjustable. *Wheels:* Marvic, commonly used sizes 3.5 in. x 16 in. front and 4.5 in. x 17 in. rear. *Tyres:* Michelin. *Brakes:* two Brembo steel discs front (320 mm) and one Yamaha rear (220 mm); Brembo aluminium calipers front, Nissin rear; Brembo and Nissin pads. *Plugs:* NGK. *Gearbox and engine oil:* Castrol.

The Armstrong-framed Sekitoba looked good all year but the team was held back by engine problems and Stéphane Mertens' lack of development experience. Similar in principle to the carbon-fibre frame used on the Rotax-engined Armstrong in recent years, the Sekitoba uses a Pro-Link-style rear suspension instead of the unit being in tension and mounted under the engine.

Peter Clifford

August Auinger
124.7 cc Castrol MBA

Engine: 44 mm x 41 mm, water-cooled, twin-cylinder two-stroke; disc-valve induction; ten transfer and three exhaust ports; one plain piston ring; needle roller big ends and needle roller small ends; one pressed crank, two ball and two roller bearings; dry clutch with six friction and six steel plates, six springs. *Gearbox:* six-speed, three possible ratios for all gears; drum selection. *Carburettors:* 32 mm cylindrical-slide Dell'Orto.

Frame: sheet aluminium monocoque, taper roller head bearings; triangulated chrome-moly swing arm, taper roller bearings; cantilever rear suspension, one Öhlins unit, coil-spring, oil damping, adjustable; Marzocchi forks, coil-springs, oil-damped, adjustable. *Wheels:* Marvic, commonly used sizes 2.15 in. x 17 in. front and 2.5 in. x 18 in. rear. *Tyres:* Dunlop. *Brakes:* one Brembo cast-steel disc front (280 mm) and one Bartol carbon-fibre rear (200 mm); Brembo aluminium calipers; Ferodo and Bartol pads. *Plugs:* Champion. *Gearbox and engine oil:* Castrol.

Pier Paolo Bianchi
124.7 cc MBA Elit

Engine: 44 mm x 41 mm, water-cooled, twin-cylinder two-stroke; disc-valve induction; six transfer and three exhaust ports; one plain piston ring; needle roller big ends and needle roller small ends; one pressed crank, four ball bearings; dry clutch with seven friction and seven steel plates, five springs. *Gearbox:* six-speed, four possible ratios for each gear; drum selection. *Carburettors:* 29 mm cylindrical-slide Mikuni.

Frame: MBA twin-loop alloy steel, taper roller head bearings; triangulated box-section aluminium swing arm, plain bearings; cantilever rear suspension, one Marzocchi unit, coil-spring, oil damping, adjustable for compression and rebound; Marzocchi forks, coil-springs, oil-damped, adjustable for both compression and rebound. *Wheels:* Marvic, commonly used widths 2.0 in. front and 2.25 in. rear. *Tyres:* Dunlop. *Brakes:* two Zanzani aluminium discs front (230 mm) and one Zanzani aluminium rear (200 mm); Brembo aluminium calipers; Brembo pads. *Plugs:* Champion. *Gearbox and engine oil:* Castrol.

Domenico Brigaglia
124.7 cc Ducados

Engine: 44 mm x 41 mm, water-cooled, twin-cylinder two-stroke; disc-valve induction; eight transfer and three exhaust ports; one plain piston ring; needle roller big ends and needle roller small ends; one pressed crank, four ball bearings; dry clutch with seven friction and seven steel plates, six springs. *Gearbox:* six-speed, three possible ratios for first and third gears, five for second and fifth, four for fourth and sixth; drum selection. *Carburettors:* 30 mm cylindrical-slide Dell'Orto.

Frame: LCR sheet aluminium monocoque, taper roller head bearings; triangulated chrome-moly swing-arm, taper roller bearings; cantilever rear suspension, one Öhlins unit, coil-spring, oil damping, adjustable; Forcha Italia forks, coil-springs, oil-damped, adjustable. *Wheels:* Marvic, commonly used sizes 1.8 in. x 18 in. front and 2.25 in. x 18 in. rear. *Tyres:* Michelin. *Brakes:* one Disacciati cast-steel disc front (260 mm) and one Bartol carbon-fibre rear (230 mm); Brembo aluminium calipers; Ferodo pads. *Plugs:* Champion NS 502. *Gearbox and engine oil:* Elf.

Fausto Gresini
124.7 cc Garelli

Engine: 44 mm x 41 mm water-cooled, twin-cylinder two-stroke; disc-valve induction; six transfer and one exhaust port; one plain piston ring; needle roller big ends and needle roller small ends; one pressed crank, four ball bearings; dry clutch with seven friction and seven steel plates, five springs. *Gearbox:* six-speed, three possible ratios for each gear; drum selection. *Carburettors:* 29 mm cylindrical-slide Dell'Orto.

Frame: sheet aluminium monocoque, taper roller head bearings; box-section aluminium swing arm, taper roller bearings; twin-shock rear suspension, two White Power units, coil-springs, oil damping, adjustable; White Power forks, coil-springs, oil-damped, adjustable. *Wheels:* Campagnolo, commonly used sizes 1.85 in. x 18 in. front and 2.5 in. x 18 in. rear. *Tyres:* Michelin. *Brakes:* two Zanzani aluminium discs front (220 mm) and one Zanzani aluminium rear (220 mm); Brembo aluminium calipers; Brembo pads. *Plugs:* Champion. *Gearbox and engine oil:* Total.

Peter Clifford

Far left: **Paolo Casoli's LCR-framed MBA, as tuned by Jörg Moller. The strength of the frame is obvious, and with the exhaust pipes removed the engine is scarcely visible. The clutch and one carb can be seen, but the cylinder is hidden by the ignition coil.**

Harald Bartol and August Auinger work on the much-modified MBA. Towards the end of the season the pair agreed that there would be no point in continuing with the 125 class for '88 and decided to acquire a 250 *(left).*

Jorge Martínez
79.6 cc Derbi

Engine: 48 mm x 44 mm, water-cooled, single-cylinder two-stroke; disc-valve induction; four transfer and one exhaust port; one plain piston ring; needle roller big end and needle roller small end; pressed crank, two ball bearings; dry clutch with four friction and five aluminium plates, four springs. *Gearbox:* six-speed, four possible ratios for first to sixth gears; drum selection. *Carburettor:* 34 mm cylindrical-slide Dell'Orto.
Frame: Derbi four main tube triangulated alloy steel spine, taper roller head bearings; box-section alloy steel swing arm, needle roller bearings; con rod and rocker arm rear suspension, one White Power unit, coil-springs, oil damping, adjustable; White Power forks, coil-springs, oil-damped, non-adjustable. *Wheels:* Marvic, commonly used sizes 1.85 in. x 16 in. front and 1.85 in. x 18 in. rear. *Tyres:* Michelin. *Brakes:* two Zanzani aluminium discs front (220 mm) and one Zanzani aluminium rear (200 mm); Brembo aluminium calipers; Brembo pads. *Plug:* Champion. *Gearbox and engine oil:* Motul.

Jörg Seel
79.8 cc Seel

Engine: 46.5 mm x 47 mm, water-cooled, single-cylinder two-stroke; disc-valve induction; six transfer and one exhaust port; one plain piston ring; needle roller big end and needle roller small end; one pressed crank, one ball and one roller bearing; dry clutch with four friction and five steel plates, eight springs. *Gearbox:* six-speed, three possible ratios for first and second gears; drum selection. *Carburettor:* 34 mm cylindrical-slide Dell'Orto.
Frame: twin-spar fabricated box-section aluminium, taper roller head bearings; triangulated box-section aluminium swing arm, ball bearings; one underslung shock rear suspension, one White Power unit, coil-spring, oil damping, adjustable; Marzocchi forks, coil-springs, oil-damped, adjustable, mechanical anti-dive. *Wheels:* PVM, commonly used sizes 1.6 in. x 16 in. front, 2.0 in. x 18 in. rear. *Tyres:* Michelin. *Brakes:* one Bogl & Braun cast-steel disc front (260 mm) and one Zanzani aluminium rear (220 mm); Brembo aluminium calipers; Brembo pads. *Plug:* Champion. *Gearbox and engine oil:* Castrol.

Stefan Dörflinger
79.6 cc Krauser

Engine: 49 mm x 42.5 mm, water-cooled, single-cylinder two-stroke; disc-valve induction; six transfer and three exhaust ports; one plain piston ring; needle roller big end and needle roller small end; pressed crank, one ball and one roller bearing; dry clutch with five friction and six steel plates, six springs. *Gearbox:* six-speed, three or four possible ratios for each gear; drum selection. *Carburettor:* 34 mm flat-slide Mikuni.
Frame: LCR sheet aluminium monocoque, taper roller head bearings; box-section chrome-moly swing arm, plain bearings; rocker arm rear suspension, one Öhlins unit, coil-spring, oil damping, adjustable; Ceriani forks, coil-springs, oil-damped, adjustable for compression and rebound. *Wheels:* Marvic, commonly used sizes 1.85 in. x 16 in. front and 1.85 in. x 18 in. rear. *Tyres* Michelin. *Brakes:* one Bogl & Braun cast-iron disc front (220 mm) and one Zanzani aluminium rear (180 mm); Brembo aluminium calipers; Mozzi Motor pads. *Plug:* Champion N502. *Gearbox and engine oil:* Shell.

Luis M. Reyes
79.6 cc Huvo Casal

Engine: 48 mm x 44 mm, water-cooled, single-cylinder two-stroke; disc-valve induction; six transfer and three exhaust ports; one plain piston ring; needle roller big end and needle roller small end; one pressed crank, two ball bearings; dry clutch with five friction and five steel plates, five springs. *Gearbox:* six-speed, four possible ratios for all six gears; drum selection. *Carburettor:* 34 mm cylindrical-slide Dell'Orto.
Frame: triangulated tubular chrome-moly, taper roller head bearings; extruded aluminium swing arm, needle roller bearings; rocker arm rear suspension, one White Power unit, coil-spring, oil damping, adjustable; White Power forks, coil-springs, oil-damped, non-adjustable. *Wheels:* Campagnolo, commonly used sizes 2.0 in. x 16 in. front and 2.25 in. x 18 in. rear. *Tyres:* Michelin. *Brakes:* two Zanzani aluminium discs front (220 mm) and one Zanzani aluminium rear (190 mm); Brembo aluminium calipers; Brembo pads. *Plug:* Champion. *Gearbox and engine oil:* Campsa.

Henk Keulemans

Steve Webster
498 cc LCR Krauser
Engine: 56 mm x 50.6 mm water-cooled, four-cylinder two-stroke, crankcase reed-valve induction; seven transfer and three exhaust ports; one plain piston ring; roller big ends and needle roller small ends; four pressed cranks, two needle roller bearings each; dry clutch with seven friction and seven steel plates; six springs. *Gearbox:* six-speed, three possible ratios for first three gears; drum selection. *Carburettors:* 38 mm flat-slide Mikuni.
Chassis: LCR sheet aluminium monocoque, riveted and Araldited; wishbone rear suspension, Koni unit, coil-spring, oil damping, adjustable; parallelogram front suspension, Koni unit, coil-spring, oil damping, adjustable; no sidecar suspension. *Wheels:* Ronal, 13 in. diameter; commonly used widths 8.2 in. front, 10 in. rear and 9 in. sidecar. *Tyres:* Avon. *Brakes:* cast-iron all round; ventilated 254 mm front, 240 mm rear and side; Lockheed calipers; Ferodo pads. *Plug:* NGK B10F.V. *Gearbox and engine oil:* Silkolene.

Rolf Biland
498 cc LCR Krauser
Engine: 56 mm x 50.6 mm, water-cooled, four-cylinder two-stroke; crankcase reed-valve induction; eight transfer and three exhaust ports; one plain piston ring; roller big ends and needle roller small ends; four pressed cranks, two needle roller bearings each; dry clutch with seven friction and seven steel plates, six springs. *Gearbox:* six-speed, three possible ratios for first three gears; drum selection. *Carburettors:* 36 mm cylindrical-slide Dell'Orto.
Chassis: LCR sheet aluminium monocoque, riveted and Araldited, adjustable; wishbone rear suspension, White Power unit, coil-spring, oil damping, adjustable; parallelogram front suspension, White Power unit, coil-spring, oil-damped adjustable; no sidecar suspension. *Wheels:* BBS, 13 in. diameter, commonly used widths 9 in. front, 11 in. or 12 in. rear and 10 in. sidecar. *Tyres:* Yokohama. *Brakes:* cast-iron all round, ventilated 254 mm front, 240 mm rear and side; Lockheed calipers; Mintex pads. *Plugs:* NGK B10EGV. *Gearbox and engine oil:* Wintershall.

Egbert Streuer
498 LCR Yamaha
Engine: 56 mm x 50.6 mm, water-cooled, four-cylinder two-stroke; crankcase reed-valve induction; six transfer and three exhaust ports; one plain piston ring; roller big ends and needle roller small ends; two pressed cranks, four needle roller bearings each; dry clutch with seven friction and seven steel plates, six springs. *Gearbox:* six-speed, three possible ratios for first three gears; drum selection. *Carburettors:* 38 mm cylindrical-slide Mikuni.
Chassis: LCR sheet aluminium monocoque, riveted and Araldited, adjustable; wishbone rear suspension, Koni unit, coil-spring, oil damping, adjustable; parallelogram front suspension, Koni or Bilstein unit, coil-spring, oil-damped, adjustable; no sidecar suspension. *Wheels:* Ronal, 13 in. diameter; commonly used widths 9 in. front, 10 in. rear and sidecar. *Tyres:* Yokohama. *Brakes:* cast-iron all round, ventilated 254 mm front, 240 mm rear and side; Lockheed calipers; Tormos pads. *Plugs:* Champion N84. *Gearbox and engine oil:* Bel Ray.

Alain Michel
498 cc LCR Krauser
Engine: 56 mm x 50.6 mm, water-cooled, four-cylinder two-stroke; crankcase reed-valve induction; seven transfer and three exhaust ports; one plain piston ring; roller big ends and needle roller small ends; four pressed cranks, two needle roller bearings each; dry clutch with seven friction and seven steel plates, six springs. *Gearbox:* six-speed, three possible ratios for first three gears; drum selection. *Carburettors:* 38 mm flat-slide Mikuni.
Chassis: LCR sheet aluminium monocoque, riveted and Araldited, adjustable; wishbone rear suspension, Koni unit, coil-spring, oil damping, adjustable; parallelogram front suspension, Koni or Bilstein unit, coil-spring, oil-damped, adjustable; no sidecar suspension. *Wheels:* Gotti, 13 in. diameter; commonly used widths 9 in. front, 11 in. or 12 in. rear and 10 in. sidecar. *Tyres:* Avon. *Brakes:* cast-iron all round, ventilated 254 mm front, 240 mm rear and side; Lockheed calipers; Mintex pads. *Plugs:* Champion N82. *Gearbox and engine oil:* Elf.

Henk Keulemans

Egbert Streuer tests a single Hummel cylinder on his specially converted reed-valve induction engine. Streuer does his own engine testing and uses the single cylinder to prove the worth of his ideas before going to the race track _(above and left)_.

Far left: **Alain Michel's** fairing is removed to reveal the classic LCR layout with the Krauser engine bolted to the side of monocoque.

Peter Clifford

Faced with limited opposition, the factory Suzuki dominated the championship. Furthermore, logical refinement made it faster, more reliable and better handling.

Dominique Sarron, Jean-Louis Battistini, Jean-Michel Mattioli
748 cc Honda RVF750
Engine: 70 mm x 48.6 mm, water-cooled four-stroke V4 based on VFR750; gear-driven dohc operating four valves per cylinder. *Maximum power:* 130+ bhp at 12,500 rpm. *Carburettors:* 34 mm CV Keihin. *Ignition:* self-generating. *Clutch:* wet multi-plate. *Gearbox:* six-speed.
Frame: fabricated box-section aluminium using motor as stressed member; bolt-on rear subframe; one-side aluminium swing arm with inboard disc and dished wheel; Showa monoshock and 41 mm telescopic forks, all adjustable for spring pre-load and compression and rebound damping. *Wheels:* HRC, 17 in x 3.5 in. front, 17 in. x 5.5 in. rear. *Tyres:* Michelin radial. *Brakes:* two floating discs with four-piston calipers front, one disc with twin-piston caliper rear. *Plugs:* NGK. *Oil:* Elf. *Weight:* 370.4 lb/168 kg with oil and water.

Hervé Moineau, Bruno le Bihan, Jean-Louis Tournadre
749 cc Suzuki GSX-R750
Engine: 70 mm x 48.7 mm, oil-cooled across-the-frame four-cylinder four-stroke based on GSX-R750; chain-driven dohc operating four valves per cylinder. *Maximum power:* 135 bhp at 12,000 rpm. *Carburettors:* 34 mm flat-slide Mikuni. *Compression ratio:* 12:1. *Ignition:* Suzuki battery-powered CDI. *Clutch:* dry multi-plate. *Gearbox:* six-speed.
Frame: reinforced box-section aluminium cradle with bolt-on rear subframe; full-floater rising-rate rear suspension, Showa unit, adjustable for spring pre-load and compression and rebound damping; Showa 41 mm forks, adjustable for spring pre-load and compression and rebound damping. *Wheels:* Marvic, 17 in. x 3.5 in. front, 17 in. x 5.5 in rear. *Tyres:* Michelin radial. *Brakes:* two floating discs with Nissin four-piston calipers front, one floating disc with twin-piston caliper rear. *Plugs:* NGK. *Oil:* CCJ GS. *Weight:* 348.3 lb/158 kg.

Pierre-Etienne Samin, Thierry Crine, Pierre Bolle
748 cc Kawasaki GPX750
Engine: 68 mm x 51.5 mm, water-cooled across-the-frame four-cylinder four-stroke based on GPX750; chain-driven dohc operating four valves per cylinder. *Maximum power:* 135 bhp at 11,500 rpm. *Carburettors:* 34 mm Keihin. *Compression ratio:* 12.3:1. *Ignition:* electronic powered by alternator. *Clutch:* wet multi-plate. *Gearbox:* six-speed.
Frame: rounded tubular aluminium frame with bolt-together upper and lower sections and bolt on rear subframe; Uni-Trak rising-rate rear suspension, White Power unit, adjustable for spring pre-load and compression and rebound damping; White Power upside-down forks, internal pre-load and damping adjustments. *Wheels:* Marvic, 17 in. x 3.5 in. front, 17 in. x 5.5 in. rear. *Tyres:* Michelin radial. *Brakes:* two floating discs with four-piston AP Lockheed calipers front, one disc with twin-piston caliper rear. *Plugs:* Champion. *Oil:* Igol. *Weight:* 357.2 lb/162 kg.

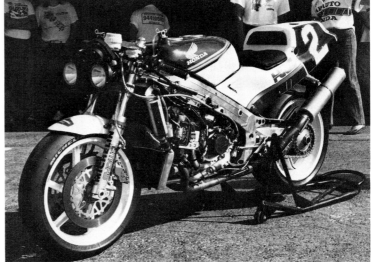

Christian Sarron, Patrick Igoa, Jean-Philippe Ruggia
749 cc Yamaha YZF750 Genesis
Engine: 68 mm x 51.6 mm, water-cooled across-the-frame four-cylinder four-stroke based on FZ750; chain-driven dohc operating five valves per cylinder. *Maximum power:* 130+ bhp at 12,000 rpm. *Carburettors:* 36 mm downdraught Mikuni. *Compression ratio:* 12.5:1. *Ignition:* Yamaha CDI. *Clutch:* dry multi-plate. *Gearbox:* six-speed.
Frame: fabricated beam-section aluminium with bolt-on rear subframe; one-sided swing arm with rising-rate rear suspension, Öhlins unit, adjustable for spring pre-load and compression and rebound damping; 41 mm forks adjustable for spring pre-load and compression and rebound damping. *Wheels:* Marvic, 17 in. x 3.5 in. front, 17 in. x 5.5 in. rear. *Tyres:* Michelin radial. *Brakes:* two floating discs with four-piston Nissin calipers front, one disc with Nissin caliper rear. *Plugs:* NGK. *Oil:* Motul. *Weight:* 339.5 lb/154 kg.

Geoff Fowler, Mat Oxley, Vesa Kultalahti
749 cc Harris Yamaha
Engine: 68 mm x 51.6 mm, water-cooled across-the-frame four-cylinder four-stroke based on FZ750, chain-driven dohc operating five valves per cylinder. *Maximum power:* 108 bhp at 10,500 rpm. *Carburettors:* 36 mm CV Mikuni. *Compression ratio:* 11.5:1 *Ignition:* CDI. *Clutch:* wet multi-plate. *Gearbox:* six-speed.
Frame: fabricated Harris beam-section aluminium with bolt-on rear subframe; rising-rate rear suspension, Öhlins unit, adjustable for spring pre-load and compression and rebound damping; Yamaha 41 mm forks, adjustable for spring pre-load and rebound damping. *Wheels:* Dymag, 17 in. x 3.5 in. front, 17 in. x 5.5 in. rear. *Tyres:* Michelin radial. *Brakes:* two floating discs with Lockheed four-piston calipers front, one disc with Brembo twin-piston caliper rear. *Plugs:* NGK. *Oil:* Castrol. *Weight:* 396.8 lb/180 kg.

The Bimota Yamaha *(top),* ridden by Flameling, van der Wal and Brand, was very similar to the F1 World Championship-winning machine but lacked the factory backing to make it competitive against the Suzukis.

Factory Hondas made few appearances but were still better than anything else *(centre).*

Above: Kawasaki showed increased interest in the series: Godier and Genoud ran a modified road bike prior to a possible full factory effort for '88.

RIDERS' CIRCUIT REPORT

	Possible score	JAPAN Suzuka	SPAIN Jerez	WEST GERMANY Hockenheim	ITALY Monza	AUSTRIA Salzburg	YUGOSLAVIA Rijeka	NETHERLANDS Assen	FRANCE Le Mans	GREAT BRITAIN Donington Park	SWEDEN Anderstorp	CZECHOSLOVAKIA Brno	SAN MARINO Misano	PORTUGAL Járama	BRAZIL Goiania	ARGENTINA Buenos Aires
1. Safety																
a) Natural safety of circuit	20	10	14	14	13	5	16	18	12	17	14	19	16	15	18	10
b) Temporary safety provisions	20	12	15	14	10	17	10	15	18	15	15	12	18	5	18	5
c) Clerk of Course	10	9	8	8	2	9	4	9	9	2	7	8	10	4	8	8
d) Marshals	10	2	6	8	9	8	4	9	8	9	5	5	9	4	4	6
e) First aid	10	4	9	2	6	9	4	8	6	8	5	8	8	5	6	5
Total	70	37	52	46	40	48	38	59	53	51	46	52	61	33	54	34
2. Facilities																
a) Paddock size	10	8	9	9	0	6	3	8	8	9	3	7	8	2	8	6
b) Paddock amenities	10	7	8	7	4	6	7	5	5	8	2	3	9	4	7	2
c) Sanitary arrangements	10	7	5	7	0	5	8	9	6	5	8	6	9	5	2	4
d) Paddock security	10	9	7	3	2	2	8	7	7	7	4	2	0	1	8	0
e) General working conditions	10	8	8	8	0	7	8	7	6	7	4	6	8	5	7	0
Total	50	39	37	34	6	26	34	36	32	36	21	24	34	17	32	12
3. Organisers' co-operation																
a) Circuit owners	10	10	8	9	3	8	9	9	7	10	8	7	7	9	9	0
b) Promoters	5	5	4	4	1	2	4	4	4	5	4	4	1	2	5	0
c) Organisers	5	5	3	4	1	2	4	4	4	4	2	2	2	1	5	0
Total	20	20	15	17	5	12	17	17	15	17	16	13	10	12	19	0
4. Spectator facilities																
a) Viewing	10	8	9	8	5	9	9	7	6	8	6	8	5	7	8	7
b) Facilities	10	8	5	8	3	4	2	7	4	6	5	8	3	2	4	4
Total	20	16	14	16	8	13	11	14	10	14	11	16	8	9	12	11
5. Location and scheduling																
a) Circuit location, travel hassle	10	5	5	7	7	7	4	7	7	4	3	1	7	5	0	0
b) Practice timing, race schedule	10	8	4	5	2	4	5	3	5	7	4	2	1	4	8	2
Total	20	13	9	12	9	11	9	10	12	11	7	3	8	9	8	2
6. Media																
a) Press facilities (Photo/reporting)	10	9	7	7	5	6	1	6	5	9	5	6	7	1	7	1
b) TV coverage (quality and volume)	10	8	6	7	8	8	6	8	8	8	3	5	8	8	6	4
Total	20	17	13	14	13	14	7	14	13	17	8	11	15	9	13	5
GRAND TOTAL	200	142	140	139	81	124	116	150	135	146	109	119	136	89	138	64
RANKING		3rd	4th	5th	14th	9th	11th	1st	8th	2nd	12th	10th	7th	13th	6th	15th
1986 Ranking (by country)		–	4[1]	1[2]	11	5	6	2	10[5]	3[6]	7	–	8	–	–	
1985 Ranking (by country)		–	11[1]	1	9[3]	3	8	4	12	2[6]	6	–	5	–	–	–
1984 Ranking (by country)		–	12[1]	3[2]	6[4]	4	10	2	5[5]	1[6]	9	–	7[3]	–	–	–

Notes: 1, Járama; 2, Nürburgring; 3, Mugello; 4, Misano; 5, Paul Ricard; 6, Silverstone.

Compiled from views expressed by regular GP riders throughout the season.

COMMENTS ON CIRCUITS
(IN RANK ORDER)

1
HOLLAND
ASSEN

Assen has twice been runner-up in the circuit rankings and this year, for the first time, takes the number one position.
The organisers at Assen always make every effort to accommodate the wishes of the teams and riders and, despite annual problems with the weather, the meeting still attracts the largest crowd in Europe. The organisers continue to invest money in their circuit and facilities and it should not be long before the Assen venue becomes a true 'closed circuit', safe from government interference.

2
GREAT BRITAIN
DONINGTON PARK

For an inaugural Grand Prix, the Donington event was superb. Donington would have taken first place in our survey had it not been for the way that the Clerk of the Course tried to bully teams and riders.
Improvements promised for the 1988 event should keep Donington in contention for the number one position.

3
JAPAN
SUZUKA

Never has there been a Grand Prix at which such an attempt was made to accommodate the views of the teams and riders in the way the meeting was run. The hospitality extended by the organisers was unprecedented and made this event one to which all teams will be glad to return.
Only the dangerous nature of the Suzuka circuit prevented the Japanese event from taking the number one place in our survey, despite the fact that it suffers from the problems associated with Grands Prix outside of Europe.
The Japanese have promised to modify the circuit in the interests of safety for 1988 and this will make the event a very hard one to beat.

Decaying old Monza – a classic circuit but let down by facilities and organisation that are 30 years out of date. Run-off in several areas is minimal and the parkland trees make modification difficult.

4
SPAIN
JEREZ

Three of the top four circuits in our survey, including this one, are new to Grand Prix racing. This has a lot to do with the attitude of the newer organisers in our sport, who compare favourably with some of the traditional luddites who have been organising for years and are stuck in their ways.
The teams were welcomed to this splendid venue and, despite a few shortcomings with the organisation and facilities, the teams came away feeling well satisfied with the event.
Unfortunately the Spanish Grand Prix reverts to Járama in 1988.

5
WEST GERMANY
HOCKENHEIM

This event has been a past winner of our survey, but the 1987 version did not live up to former standards. Organisation, normally a good feature of German events, seemed to fall apart at this year's meeting, and this was reflected in the way the races were run, in paddock security and so on.
Next year, the German Grand Prix moves to the Nürburgring and it is fairly certain that the event will move back up the charts.

6
BRAZIL
GOIANIA

Yet another new event, and in a different continent, that features in the top half of our survey. Goiania is blessed with a fine circuit, well suited to motor cycle racing. The organisers went out of their way to make the teams welcome, a fact which helped to mitigate the problems experienced with flights and carriage of the motor cycles.
The Brazilian event is another to which the teams will look forward to returning in 1988.

7
SAN MARINO
MISANO

The San Marino event has risen one place in the rankings and would have been higher had it not been for the excellent new events in 1987.
The facilities at Misano have been transformed in the last year and are now some of the best encountered at any circuit. Unfortunately, the San Marino organisers are unable to arrange satisfactory security measures. Overbearing and aggressive towards competitors with genuine passes, they are completely lax with general security and allow every lout and his dog into the paddock to harass and steal from the teams.

8
FRANCE
LE MANS

This French circuit has leapt up the rankings due to a significant improvement both in facilities and track safety. Equally, the organisers of the event have chosen to co-operate with riders and now take considerable pains to accommodate their views in the running of the meeting.
Le Mans is now the preferred circuit in France, being probably safer and certainly better run than the Paul Ricard event.

9
AUSTRIA
SALZBURG

Once again, the Salzburg event passed without a rider being seriously injured and everyone breathed an annual sigh of relief. Criticism of the safety at other venues is difficult to justify when Salzburg is retained on the Grand Prix calendar.
The organisers of the event do try very hard to improve their facilities on limited budgets. However, the imposition of five classes plus two support races was too much for the circuit and its facilities. Every aspect of the 1987 meeting suffered, which pushed the circuit back down the rankings.

10
CZECHOSLOVAKIA
BRNO

This venue would have been higher up the rankings had the circuit and facilities actually been finished by the time the teams arrived for the event.
It was patently obvious that it was fortunate that the Grand Prix happened at all, as, whilst the track was finished, many of the other installations were not ready. Equally, the lack of experience of the officials in operating at the new circuit showed through.
The organisers at Brno have shown themselves willing to listen to the teams' suggestions and this circuit should see an improvement in 1988.

11
YUGOSLAVIA
RIJEKA

The Yugoslavs were, as usual, keen to co-operate with the teams and to make the best of the limited budget within which they operate. Enormous improvements are promised for 1988 in both facilities and race track. Is this connected with the activity in Czechoslovakia and Hungary?
Certainly the enlargement of the paddock is long overdue and essential.

12
SWEDEN
ANDERSTORP

How much longer, it might be asked, can this event remain in the World Championship calendar? The Swedes who organise the event are charming and friendly, but the circuit becomes a little tattier each year and the paddock and general facilities are out of the Stone Age.

13
PORTUGAL
JÁRAMA

The Spanish organisers of this 'Portuguese' event made a good effort at trying to run an efficient Grand Prix, but unfortunately failed. Some of the old practices, like scrutineering every day, dictatorial decisions by the Clerk of the Course and a still-unimproved and small paddock, helped this event slip down the rankings.

14
ITALY
MONZA

Combine the prehistoric facilities at Monza with the confrontational organisation tactics of Mr Flammini and an inept and arrogant Clerk of the Course, and you have the recipe for the worst Grand Prix in Europe.
It is rumoured that the Monza facilities will be improved before next year's race. If not, it would be hard to understand continued sanctioning of the event by the FIM.

15
ARGENTINA
BUENOS AIRES

Although it is difficult to envisage any event capable of keeping Monza off the bottom ranking, the Argentinians succeeded in Buenos Aires.
An unmitigated disaster from start to finish, the meeting will be remembered for a race track that was basically sound but completely unprepared, non-existent organisation and a penny-pinching promoter who blamed everyone and everything for his own shortcomings.
The teams are unanimous in never wanting to return to Buenos Aires under similar conditions.

Colorsport

Martin Wimmer and Wayne Gardner won the Moët et Chandon trophies for their cumulative practice performances throughout the season.

The Trophée Moët Moto Vitesse has been devised to identify and reward those riders in the prestigious 500 and 250 cc categories who set the pace during official qualifying for Grands Prix. Points were awarded at each championship round, with five points going to the pole-position winner, four points for the man qualifying second, down to a single point for fifth place on the grid.

The final points tables at the end of the 1987 season were as follows:

500 cc

Pos.	Rider	Points	Prize money awarded
1	Wayne Gardner	66	FFr40,000
2	Eddie Lawson	51	FFr25,000
3	Randy Mamola	29	FFr15,000
4	Tadahiko Taira	17	FFr10,000
5	Niall Mackenzie	15	FFr10,000
6	Christian Sarron	14	
7	Shunji Yatsushiro	9	
8	Freddie Spencer	7	
9	Rob McElnea	6	
10 =	Ron Haslam	5	
10 =	Kevin Magee	5	
12	Kevin Schwantz	1	

250 cc

Pos.	Rider	Points	Prize money awarded
1	Martin Wimmer	37	FFr25,000
2	Carlos Lavado	25	FFr20,000
3 =	Dominique Sarron	20	FFr15,000
3 =	Anton Mang	20	FFr10,000
5	Jacques Cornu	19	FFr10,000
6 =	Loris Reggiani	18	
6 =	Reinhold Roth	18	
8	Luca Cadalora	16	
9	Patrick Igoa	13	
10 =	Juan Garriga	9	
10 =	Masahiro Shimuzu	9	
12	Carlos Cardus	8	
13	Sito Pons	6	
14	Masaru Kobayashi	3	
15 =	Masumitsu Taguchi	2	
15 =	Jean-François Baldé	2	

PROMOTERS OF MOTORCYCLE SPORT

The Highlight – The 1987 British Grand Prix at Donington

In 1987, Two Four Sports promoted at Donington Park:
The British Grand Prix, The World TT Formula 1 Championship,
The World Endurance Championship, The European Championships
and the TransAtlantic Challenge.

 are Consultants to . . .

Ron Haslam

Niall Mackenzie

Steve Webster/Tony Hewitt

GUESS WHICH PERFORMANCE TYRES HAVE NOW LEFT THE REST IN THE SHADE?

BRITAIN'S BEST SELLING PERFORMANCE TYRES

METZELER

GRANDS PRIX · 1987

Grand Prix of
JAPAN

The first Grand Prix of the season brought a host of new names. It was a story of Magee and Mackenzie, Shimuzu and Bridgestone, and the unfamiliar pairing of Mamola and Dunlop. The closed season generated a host of questions: would Spencer regain the form of '85, could Mackenzie really cope with the power of the NSR and would the new V-four Honda be a better bike than the rather second-rate NSR of 1986? Had Yamaha just rested on their laurels and hoped to maintain the position of top 250 and 500 machines or had they done their homework? Could Lawson maintain the desire and determination that had already taken him to two World Championships? He said he was still improving and, if that was true, wouldn't it take him out of reach of everyone else — or would this be Gardner's year, with a better bike and more experience than he had had in 1986?

Preceding the Japanese Grand Prix had been Speed Week at Daytona and the Two Plus Four International at Suzuka. In freezing cold damp conditions, Niall Mackenzie walked off with the Japanese event, demonstrating that he knew what he was doing on the new NSR. Second was another new bike, the V-four Suzuki, in the hands of Kenny Irons.

Irons, another of the riders who had been through the hard school of Yamaha RD 350 racing in England, had proved himself one of the best riders in England by winning the '86 Superstocks series. Yet he had negligible Grand Prix experience and only got the number one place as Suzuki GP rider because no-one else wanted it.

Through the winter, Suzuki chased first Mackenzie then de Radiguès, Roche, Baldwin and Merkel. Suzuki were either naïve or they were used by riders who said 'Yes, I'll ride for you' while privately adding 'unless something better comes along'. It didn't help that they lost the Skoal Bandit sponsorship when the American company decided to play things cool in a climate of mouth cancer scares and legal battles. That left the team without enough cash to pull a Cagiva-style 'offer you can't refuse' stunt and lost them de Radiguès and Roche to the Italian company. They also failed to lever Baldwin away from Roberts; even though he had been impressed when he rode the Suzuki in Japan during the winter.

The lack of Skoal Bandit money left the British-based Heron Suzuki Team without the freedom to do as they pleased with engines bought from the factory. They became the factory team run with money from Japan and hence had to do as they were told, which included running the factory aluminium twin-spar chassis instead of their own 1987 version of the successful carbon-fibre honeycomb.

Suzuki looked good at the Two Plus Four, however, with Irons finishing second to Mackenzie, even if some way behind. The factory asked Irons what the placing meant to him. 'Absolutely nothing', he replied. 'The bike is still just too slow.' He tried to impress upon them that the result was achieved simply because the conditions favoured the tractable engine and did not

punish its sad lack of top-end power. That problem had been with the V-four since it was first tested by Dave Petersen, Mal Campbell and Niall Mackenzie in Europe at the end of the previous season.

Honda started the year by winning at Daytona, thanks to Wayne Rainey and Kork Ballington, but the factory were probably more concerned by Freddie Spencer's crash in practice which injured his shoulder. Cracked bones and torn ligaments kept him from racing but the doctor's report suggested he would be fully fit for the first GP of the season. The Honda factory were not the only people who knew that medical predictions counted for little as far as Spencer was concerned. If he did not feel 100 per cent fit he would not be riding.

There was also doubt at Daytona about Spencer's overall fitness, for he looked noticeably chubbier. The good news was that the nerve trouble in his wrist that ruined his '86 season had apparently cleared up at last. Everyone hoped that Spencer would be fully fit for the start of the '87 season. Even arch-rival Eddie Lawson

said he hoped that was so. 'Every year people say things like "he only won because Freddie was not there", or something like that, and it makes me mad enough to want to go back and win again. I was riding better than ever at the end of '86 and I still think I can improve. I may not have been as good as Freddie in the past, but I think I am now, and I hope he doesn't have some kind of wrist problem because I am prepared to go and race him wheel to wheel. I hope he is prepared to do the same.'

Lawson was perhaps a little less enthusiastic after he had tested the latest YZR 500 at Jerez in Spain before the Japanese Grand Prix. He found that few things had been changed on the 500 apart from a conspicuously larger radiator. The frame was stronger, which Rob McElnea considered to be a big improvement, but Lawson feared that the minor changes to power, carburation and suspension would be insufficient to cope with the rumoured much-improved Honda.

Tadahiko Taira had made the switch to the 500 category, joining McElnea and Lawson on the Marlboro V-fours, but he could not test at Jerez having crashed in Japan and injured his knee. His place alongside Martin Wimmer had been taken by 125 cc World Champion Luca Cadalora, who was easing cautiously into the squad but only able to test a 1986 250 at Jerez because there was just one '87 bike (one of the 500s sent from Japan for the exercise).

Unlike the 500s, the 250 Yamahas were not going to come up against completely new Hondas. Instead, the competition would be refined versions of the '86 machines in the hands of Toni Mang, Sito Pons, Dominique Sarron, Jacques Cornu, Reinhold Roth and Carlos Cardus. Wimmer hoped that the biggest improvement in his results after a season of pole positions and disappointing finishes would come from the switch to clutch starts rather than from any vast improvement in his machinery. The traditional push start was dropped after a show of fairly typical rider apathy, reflected in a vote where the majority of slips showed a preference for clutch starting, but where the greatest number of riders failed to vote at all.

There was more pre-season testing than ever before, and more injuries. Lavado did himself a power of no good at home in Venezuela when he broke his ankle and wrist. The ankle was usable by the time he got to Suzuka but the wrist was still in a very sad state.

Lavado was the worst hit, but Pons, Wimmer, Cadalora, Garriga and Mang had all fallen before a race was started. It all helped to add to the tension of the 250 and 500 cc exponents assembled in Japan for what was to be the best-organised event that anyone could remember — the first Japanese Grand Prix since 1967.

The tension was red hot by the start of Grand Prix week, but that contrasted sharply with the weather which was cold and damp. The beginning of the week was dismal indeed, but by the time free practice started on Thursday it was dryer. The sensation was Mackenzie; it did not take long for stories of smooth speed and an

incredible angle of lean to circulate through the pits. Pit atmosphere in Japan is different: a pleasant little café sits in the middle of the circuit, which is surrounded by Hondaland — a mini Disneyland with restaurants and cafés as well as a hotel. This all contributed to a similarly sociable atmosphere to that found in the usual collection of caravans and motorhomes at European events.

The talk over coffee was of Mackenzie and it continued as timed practice started. The British rider was immediately fastest ahead of Gardner and Kevin Magee — the Australian making his Grand Prix debut on a works Yamaha. Magee had come to the attention of the factory while riding for the Australian Marlboro Yamaha team. He and Michael Dowson won the Castrol six-hour on the FZ750 Yamaha and then finished second in the Suzuka eight-hour. From the pair of them, Yamaha chose Magee to be given the big break when they let him ride a YZR500 alongside Rob McElnea in the Swann series at the end of '86. McElnea won the series, but Magee took two of the six races off him and Yamaha took notice.

A win in the four-stroke race at the Two Plus Four sealed matters for Magee, so an '86 500 was upgraded for him to ride in the Grand Prix, even though commitments to the Australian team would prevent him from riding anything like a full season in Europe. Would this be a one-off then? 'It will be if I finish 27th', grinned the Australian. That seemed unlikely, judging from his performance from the start of practice.

Suzuka is a tricky and threatening circuit; safety precautions had been improved for the GP yet there remained high-speed sections with little run-off. It obviously favoured those with plenty of experience, and that was reflected in those first practice times; Shunji Yatsushiro made up the top four ahead of Suzuka first-timers McElnea and Lawson.

The main Japanese hope for a home win in the 500 class was Tadahiko Taira, but he had fallen from a bicycle while training and hurt his shoulder, so, with that added to his knee injury, he was feeling rather second-hand. Surprisingly, he was not in the Marlboro Yamaha colours, wearing instead the all-blue livery of Tech 21, a Japanese cosmetics company, who feature him in their television adverts and sponsor him in other Japanese events like the Suzuka eight-hour.

Taira had made a great start to his Japanese build-up when, before his testing crash, he was reported to have broken the Yamaha test track lap record on the new YZR500. Interestingly, that had been using Dunlop tyres, although, like the rest of the Marlboro team, he was contracted to Michelin for the Grands Prix. That seemed to suggest that Dunlop were likely to provide a major threat, having joined forces with Kenny Roberts' Lucky Strike team after Baldwin and Mamola had tested them at Laguna Seca in mid-January.

However, that threat did not seem to mat-erialise in practice at Suzuka, as Baldwin, with all his Suzuka experience, was behind Sarron

Randy Mamola (left) had the right tyres, the skill and the determination to make everyone else look like novices at wet-weather riding.

In his Grand Prix debut, Kevin Magee leads Ron Haslam and Niall Mackenzie (below). All three were to fall but Magee had already impressed people with his speed in this first ride and will surely return to ride in more Grands Prix in 1988.

and only ninth-fastest, while Mamola lay eleventh behind Norihiko Kinoshita on a works NSR500. That was after the first session and things did not improve greatly over the four periods, for as Mamola climbed to eighth Baldwin dropped to eleventh, stating that his Suzuka experience (including two eight-hour wins) was of little benefit. 'The crucial corners where you can make up so much time are the long climbing corners and these are so different on a two-stroke that you have to rethink the way you ride the circuit.'

The Spencer threat never materialised because after four laps of timed practice he pulled in and was forced to end his Suzuka campaign. 'I had the shoulder X-rayed before I left America and the bone was well on its way to being healed. The muscles caused some trouble on Thursday but the more I rode the better I got and I thought that that improvement would continue. Unfortunately it didn't, and as soon as I got on the bike on Friday I had trouble. At first I thought the throttle was sticking and called at the pits to have it checked. There was nothing wrong with the throttle, though; the trouble was that the stiffness in the shoulder was stopping me from closing it properly. I was so keen to start the season but I am sure the shoulder will get better with rest and I will be fully fit to ride in Spain.'

Injury could have put several other riders on the sidelines as there were some heavy falls in practice. Magee escaped with a shaking, crashing twice from the Yamaha, and McElnea hit an armco barrier hard when he fell from the Marlboro bike behind the pits on Saturday morning. The 'S' section there has little run-off and the bike slid into the sponge cushion, knocking it out of the way just as Rob arrived and smacked into unforgiving steel. Knocked unconscious, McElnea remembers nothing of the accident and was a doubtful starter until a brain scan showed no residual effects. A good night's rest made him feel a good deal fitter.

That Saturday session also claimed Roger Burnett, who badly damaged his '86-model NSR, as well as Mackenzie and Gardner. The young Scot fell while trying to get used to the front Michelin radial which is harder to work with on the brakes than is the cross-ply preferred by Mackenzie. That fall occurred going into the long spoon corner and he was unhurt. Gardner was slightly less fortunate after his heavier fall

leaving the corner when the rear tyre let go, gripped and fired him over the bars. He twisted his ankle and needed pain-killing injections the next day before the race. Lawson stayed upright when the Yamaha tried to eject him in the same spot a few minutes later. 'If I was Barry Sheene I might tell you how I saved it, but in fact I was just damned lucky.'

Lawson was using the same cool and measured approach that made his campaign so effective through '86, and in the final session he quickened his pace as he got more used to the track and the bike started to work for him. He slipped in a time ahead of Gardner and within seven-tenths of Mackenzie's impressive best.

All the practice on a cool but dry circuit was to matter little on race day as it dawned dark and wet. The morning warm-up session was the only chance many of the regular Grand Prix men had to see what Suzuka was like in the wet.

250 cc

A dark grey day and a very damp circuit greeted the 250 cc competitors as they huddled on the grid for the first clutch start of the season. There was little chance of the sun coming out yet the track conditions could have gone either way. With no more rain even the cold wind that was blowing would have produced a dry line after a few laps, yet it was clear that more rain was in the clouds.

The choice of tyres was going to be critical and almost everyone had a different solution. As the conditions varied, most combinations between soft slicks and rain tyres offered some advantage at some point in the race.

The way Masaru Kobayashi rode seemed to take little account of the conditions because he set off on the Ajinomoto-entered works NSR250 Honda at a pace that no-one could match — not even his team-mate Masahiro Shimuzu, who had been fastest in practice. One difference between the two was that Kobayashi was using Bridgestone tyres whereas Shimuzu employed Dunlops.

Kobayashi's tyres were soft compound slicks with a light pattern of grooves cut into them. They warmed quickly and worked well as there was not a great deal of standing water on the surface. Although Dominique Sarron led off

the line Kobayashi passed him in the first corner, the Frenchman being unable to match his pace as he held off both Alan Carter on the Moriwaki Honda and Shimuzu.

Carter was determined to do well in this one-off ride for Moriwaki, using the works engine in the special twin-spar frame and classic twin-shock rear suspension. Carter did not rate the handling, but in the wet that was likely to be less of a handicap. He tried hard but eventually fell on lap 14 after slipping back to sixth place.

Kobayashi started to open up an advantage and was four seconds ahead after only three laps as Sarron, Shimuzu and Masumitsu Taguchi battled for second. Likewise, they were pulling away from the fifth-place battle led by Carter with Sito Pons, Jean-Philippe Ruggia and Patrick Igoa hard on his heels.

By lap 5 Shimuzu had shaken off Sarron and tried to close on the race leader, cutting his advantage to three seconds, but Kobayashi saw the danger and matched his pace. Taguchi continued to swap places with Sarron, with Jacques Cornu forcing his way into fifth place after a slow start. Reinhold Roth was also on the move; by lap 9 he had made his way into seventh place behind Cornu and Pons.

The rain started to fall more heavily and the track got considerably wetter as the race passed the half-way mark. Kobayashi had extended his lead to nearly six seconds over Shimuzu who was more badly affected by the rain as his Dunlop intermediate tyres did not work as well in the rain as Mamola's full wets were to do. Sarron held third but Taguchi was still close and well clear of Pons and Roth.

Cornu slid out on lap 10, a victim of the worsening conditions. 'I realised that the rain was getting heavier', said the tall Swiss ace later, 'so I slowed and started braking earlier for the corners. Then Roth came past going much quicker than I was and just as I thought he must crash I was sliding up the road.' Ruggia fell on the same lap and, like Cornu, was unhurt. He had been holding tenth place just behind Martin Wimmer, the latter struggling all through the race to show the form that had put him second on the grid.

Wimmer benefited from other riders' mistakes and the next to go was Dominique Sarron, out of third place on lap 12. He was furious with himself and his absence left the first three well strung out. Kobayashi had an eight-second lead over Shimuzu who was well clear of Taguchi. It was a Japanese benefit, but as the rain continued to fall the threat would come from the fourth-place group of Roth, Carter and Pons. Unfortunately, Carter was to fall before much longer, but Pons and Roth closed rapidly on the Japanese and the situation was slightly confused by Keiji Tamura who unlapped himself thanks to his full rain tyres finding the right conditions at last. Kobayashi did well not to be put off by him on the second-to-last lap when passed by the man who actually finished twelfth.

On lap 14, Pons and Roth swept past Taguchi who then lost ground to Wimmer, Igoa, Garriga and Mang — all GP experts capable of keeping going for the full distance. Shimuzu was more determined, but Pons and Roth got the better of him on lap 17 and at one point all three were side by side as the Japanese tried to fight back and hold on to the rostrum position.

There was no catching Kobayashi; despite the standing water being thrown up in large plumes of spray by his cut slicks, he had an almost 30-second advantage over the Europeans behind. He did well to maintain his own pace as the rain made his tyres unsuitable.

Roth had to follow Pons across the line. 'I lined up to make a move on the last lap, but I had a slick on the back with an intermediate on the front. When I tried to drive past Sito the bike just went sideways and I had to let him take second.'

Masaru Kobayashi demonstrates that even a 250 in the wet requires a good deal of strength and body weight movement to flick from left to right through a chicane. Terra sponsor the Ajinomoto team, their soft drink cans featuring a racing machine.

Below: **Erv Kanemoto had work to do, but it was not looking after Freddie Spencer. The triple World Champion could only stand and watch as team-mate Mackenzie put the new NSR500 on pole.**

Suzuki on lap 1 and Keiji Konishita dropped his NSR500 Honda two laps later. At the same time, Didier de Radiguès retired his Cagiva at the pits not wishing to risk a fall on his insufficiently recovered shoulder. Kenny Irons did not last much longer on his Suzuki, pulling out with water in the ignition.

More dramatic was Lawson's arrival in the pit lane at the end of the initial lap, having already run off the track and been lucky to stay upright on the grass whilst leaving the last left-hander that heads back towards the start-and-finish. The Marlboro Yamaha team had chosen intermediate tyres for what turned out to be full wet conditions, so the bike was sliding wildly. Lawson swapped tyres in the pits and rejoined the field half a lap down with the idea of seeing how much time he could make up on the field. McElnea persevered for a while with the intermediates but found that rolling back the throttle going into the corner was enough to make the back tyre slide. He pulled in to retire on lap 5.

Lawson stayed out until lap 8 but he, too, retired when informed by his pit board that he was not making up ground on the leaders. As things turned out, that was a mistake. However, no-one could have foreseen that, of the top ten when Lawson pulled in, six would crash before the end of the race. Gustav Reiner made a similar mistake and also pulled in, considering the conditions too risky.

Out front Mamola had a 19-second lead by half-way through the 22 laps, but this was over team-mate Mike Baldwin who had relegated Gardner to third. Baldwin and Mamola were the only Dunlop-shod Grand Prix regular works riders in the race and it was obvious that the Michelins could not offer the same grip. Baldwin was actually beginning to close on Mamola and had an 11-second advantage over

Gardner, who, in turn, was 10 seconds clear of Sarron; Haslam, Mackenzie, Magee and Yatsushiro were close behind.

Magee was having problems with the 500 Yamaha as, for some reason (perhaps water in the carburettors or electrics), the power band was getting narrower and narrower. With the engine refusing to run cleanly low down, the bike was getting more and more difficult to ride. It eventually spat him off on lap 15. On the same circuit, Sarron slid to earth at the same corner that claimed his younger brother in the 250 race. Yatsushiro only lasted half a lap more before he, too, went down, hurting his shoulder.

That left Mamola leading, but Baldwin was closing on him at the rate of nearly two seconds a lap. With six laps to go Baldwin remained 16 seconds behind, however, and looked unlikely to catch his team-mate. In third place, Gardner was on his own and riding at a comfortable speed in front of Haslam and Mackenzie.

The fact that the Lucky Strike Yamahas were well ahead of the field did not mean they were cruising, as Mamola later reported. 'I didn't think that the bike would finish: it almost stopped – I don't know why – it felt as if the engine had seized, but it kept going. There was something wrong with it, though, because it would not pull the gears. I am glad it was a Yamaha so it kept going. The Dunlop tyres were great and when I came in after the sighting lap, tyre engineer Peter Ingley said that the tyres were warmer than after a practice session, so I realised that I could go hard from the first lap.'

Water was getting at the electrics and Baldwin was having the same trouble, giving this as the cause of his fall on lap 19 'I was not trying that hard and not accelerating. I think the engine might have tightened or something because the back end just slid away.' That left Mamola with a 30-second advantage over Gardner, who was ignoring his injured ankle. 'I had pain-killing injections in it before the race. It is not something I like to do, but it was either that or probably not ride.'

The drama was not over because third place still had to be decided between Mackenzie and Haslam. The Scot was leading as he went onto the last lap, but he knew that Haslam was on his tail. The Englishman slid off trying to get on the power early to line up a passing manoeuvre, but while he ran and picked up the Elf team Honda Mackenzie pressed on unaware of what had happened behind. Going into the spoon corner – the one that had claimed him in practice – he slid to earth.

Those last-lap falls promoted to third Takumi Ito (one of the Suzuki test riders) on the new V-four, having benefited from Dunlop tyres. Pier Francesco Chili came in a good fourth on the Gallina Honda triple. Haslam made it across the line fifth after trying to retake Chili on the last half-lap, only to find that his front brake lever was inaccessible. Tadahiko Taira was sixth after a steady but personally disappointing race and Raymond Roche even claimed a point for the Cagiva, being the last man not to be lapped by Mamola.

500 cc

Ron Haslam and Wayne Gardner did get their new NSR500 Hondas into the lead briefly as the pack charged away from what was now a very wet starting grid. Randy Mamola was right behind them, and while for the first mile Haslam seemed to be stretching an advantage, Mamola was soon past Gardner and closing on the Englishman. Half-way round the first lap Mamola splashed his way into the lead and from that point the race winner was never in doubt.

The Lucky Strike team had a little more than an inkling that they might be on to a good thing when Mamola was eight seconds a lap faster than anyone else in the morning warm-up session, the only wet practice of the week. They found it hard to believe such a margin was possible, but they were left in no doubt as soon as the race started and the Californian started easing away from the rest of the field at over two seconds a lap whilst obviously taking no risks.

Gardner held second but Haslam had dropped back, being passed by Sarron, Magee and Yatsushiro. The fallers started going down early: Masaru Mizutani fell from the new

Suzuka International Racing Course, 3.67354-mile/5.91198-km circuit

500 cc

22 laps, 80.82 miles/130.6 km

Place	Rider	Nat.	Machine	Laps	Time & speed	Practice time	Grid
1	Randy Mamola	USA	Yamaha	22	57m 22.889s 84.505 mph/ 135.998 km/h	2m 16.403s	8
2	Wayne Gardner	AUS	Honda	22	58m 05.278s	2m 15.354s	3
3	Takumi Ito	J	Suzuki	22	58m 14.183s	2m 20.691s	22
4	Pier Francesco Chili	I	Honda	22	58m 43.242s	2m 19.779s	17
5	Ron Haslam	GB	Honda	22	58m 45.839s	2m 16.586s	9
6	Tadahiko Taira	J	Yamaha	22	59m 01.569s	2m 15.396s	5
7	Hiroyuki Kawasaki	J	Yamaha	22	59m 02.955s	2m 18.097s	13
8	Roger Burnett	GB	Honda	22	59m 31.147s	2m 20.528s	21
9	Shinji Katayama	J	Yamaha	22	59m 39.220s	2m 20.264s	19
10	Raymond Roche	F	Cagiva	22	59m 51.069s	2m 17.951s	12
11	Norio Iobe	J	Honda	21	57m 48.856s	2m 20.800s	23
12	Hisashi Yamana	J	Suzuki	21	57m 51.674s	2m 23.283s	29
13	Simon Buckmaster	GB	Honda	21	58m 22.197s	2m 25.525s	32
14	Wolfgang von Muralt	CH	Suzuki	21	58m 40.829s	2m 24.268s	30
15	Esko Kuparinen	SF	Honda	21	59m 47.878s	2m 28.659s	33
	Niall Mackenzie	GB	Honda	21	DNF	2m 14.433s	1
	Mike Baldwin	USA	Yamaha	18	DNF	2m 17.094s	11
	Shunji Yatsushiro	J	Honda	15	DNF	2m 15.377s	4
	Kevin Magee	AUS	Yamaha	14	DNF	2m 15.414s	6
	Christian Sarron	F	Yamaha	14	DNF	2m 16.728s	10
	Alessandro Valesi	I	Honda	13	DNF	2m 21.194s	25
	Susumu Shimada	J	Suzuki	11	DNF	2m 21.833s	27
	Gustav Reiner	D	Honda	9	DNF	2m 20.162s	18
	Eddie Lawson	USA	Yamaha	8	DNF	2m 15.075s	2
	Rob McElnea	GB	Yamaha	5	DNF	2m 16.294s	7
	Kenny Irons	GB	Suzuki	4	DNF	2m 20.876s	24
	Norinhiko Fujiwara	J	Yamaha	4	DNF	2m 20.365s	20
	Marco Gentile	I	Fior	3	DNF	2m 22.324s	28
	Keiji Kinoshita	J	Honda	2	DNF	2m 18.607s	16
	Didier de Radiguès	B	Cagiva	2	DNF	2m 21.303s	26
	Masaru Mizutani	J	Suzuki	0	DNF	2m 18.529s	14
	Osamu Hiwatashi	J	Honda		DNS	2m 18.538s	15
	Freddie Spencer	USA	Honda		DNS	2m 24.481s	31

Fastest lap: Mamola, 2m 34.602s, 85.540 mph/137.663 km/h.
Lap record: Tadahiko Taira, J (Yamaha), 2m 18.2s, 97.59 mph/157.06 km/h (1986).

World Championship: 1 Mamola, 15; 2 Gardner, 12; 3 Ito, 10; 4 Chili, 8; 5 Haslam, 6; 6 Taira, 5; 7 Kawasaki, 4; 8 Burnett, 3; 9 Katayama, 2; 10 Roche, 1.

250 cc

20 laps, 73.47 miles/118.24 km

Place	Rider	Nat.	Machine	Laps	Time & speed	Practice time	Grid
1	Masaru Kobayashi	J	Honda	20	51m 15.600s 85.997 mph/ 138.399 km/h	2m 19.659s	3
2	Alfonso Pons	E	Honda	20	51m 42.613s	2m 20.595s	8
3	Reinhold Roth	D	Honda	20	51m 43.151s	2m 20.579s	7
4	Masahiro Shimuzu	J	Honda	20	51m 54.718s	2m 18.724s	1
5	Martin Wimmer	D	Yamaha	20	52m 06.115s	2m 18.849s	2
6	Juan Garriga	E	Yamaha	20	52m 17.021s	2m 21.155s	11
7	Patrick Igoa	F	Yamaha	20	52m 23.273s	2m 20.343s	6
8	Anton Mang	D	Honda	20	52m 35.679s	2m 21.151s	10
9	Masumitsu Taguchi	J	Honda	20	52m 46.490s	2m 19.683s	4
10	Takayoshi Yamamoto	J	Yamaha	20	53m 41.662s	2m 23.068s	20
11	Toshihiro Wakayama	J	Yamaha	20	53m 47.432s	2m 24.954s	29
12	Keiji Tamura	J	Yamaha	20	53m 48.254s	2m 22.934s	18
13	Luca Cadalora	I	Yamaha	19	51m 21.627s	2m 22.442s	15
14	Harald Eckl	D	Honda	19	51m 34.033s	2m 22.268s	14
15	Jean-François Baldé	F	Honda	19	51m 34.823s	2m 24.182s	25
16	Guy Bertin	F	Honda	19	51m 35.903s	2m 24.739s	27
17	Hiroo Takemura	J	Honda	19	52m 11.933s	2m 25.166s	31
18	Jean-Michel Mattioli	F	Honda	19	52m 37.150s	2m 25.010s	30
19	Maurizio Vitali	I	Garelli	19	53m 23.879s	2m 23.879s	23
20	Bruno Bonhuil	F	Honda	19	53m 03.596s	2m 25.875s	33
	Alan Carter	GB	Honda	13	DNF	2m 22.126s	13
	Dominique Sarron	F	Honda	11	DNF	2m 20.087s	5
	Jacques Cornu	CH	Honda	10	DNF	2m 21.120s	9
	Jean-Philippe Ruggia	F	Yamaha	10	DNF	2m 23.042s	19
	Donnie McLeod	GB	Honda	10	DNF	2m 24.455s	26
	Shosuke Kita	J	Honda	10	DNF	2m 22.763s	16
	Hideshi Tomita	J	Honda	9	DNF	2m 24.063s	24
	Fausto Ricci	I	Honda	9	DNF	2m 26.319s	35
	Carlos Cardus	E	Honda	7	DNF	2m 25.339s	32
	Kevin Mitchell	GB	Yamaha	4	DNF	2m 24.926s	28
	Manfred Herweh	D	Honda	3	DNF	2m 23.574s	22
	Stéphane Mertens	B	Honda	2	DNF	2m 22.882s	17
	Virginio Ferrari	I	Honda	1	DNF	2m 25.880s	34
	Hiroshi Okumura	J	Yamaha		DNS	2m 21.227s	12
	Yoshihisa Hasegawa	J	Yamaha		DNS	2m 23.112s	21
	Carlos Lavado	YV	Yamaha		DNS	2m 34.813s	36

Fastest lap: Kobayashi, 2m 19.687s, 94.674 mph/152.363 km/h (record).
Previous record: Carlos Lavado, YV (Yamaha), 2m 20.4s, 94.62 mph/152.27 km/h (1986).

World Championship: 1 Kobayashi, 15; 2 Pons, 12; 3 Roth, 10; 4 Shimuzu, 8; 5 Wimmer, 6; 6 Garriga, 5; 7 Igoa, 4; 8 Mang, 3; 9 Taguchi, 2; 10 Yamamoto, 1.

Left: **During practice in Suzuka, Niall Mackenzie looks behind and sees no-one even close to him. That was not hard to deal with, yet it surprised him as he did not feel he was making a superhuman effort. While still as friendly as ever, his new responsibilities naturally prompted a new seriousness.**

Didier de Radiguès *(above)* **was slowly recovering from a winter shoulder injury. Alain Chevallier was already wondering what he had let himself in for when he signed to take care of the Cagivas.**

Top: **HB's Dieter Stappert was obviously happy with Roth's performance and, with that success and Mackenzie's tremendous promise, HB were building well on Lavado's championship win of 1986 after some lean years with Suzuki.**

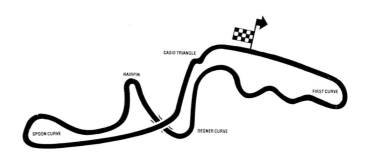

Gran Premio de
ESPAÑA

The season's second race presented riders with another new Grand Prix circuit to get to grips with. However, this was a very different prospect compared to Suzuka. The sunshine and warmth could not have been more of a contrast, except when the chill wind blew out of the north east, dragging the cold all the way from distant Siberia. It was a long way and the teams knew only too well how distant was this corner of Europe, for most had driven the full width of France and Spain. In Spain, the limited motorway network did little to help.

At the most westerly European GP circuit, the sun rose late in the paddock and the organisers adopted the usual Spanish habit of not hurrying to make an early start on anything. The result was that practice ran until late afternoon, leaving mechanics to work far into the night. Most people were unused to shops opening in the afternoon at about four o'clock or restaurants which often did not get going until nine at night.

The circuit itself is good, though already rippled in places thanks to the Formula 1 cars. It is also less safe than it should be, for while there is plenty of run-off going into the corners (required by the cars), the concrete barriers come close to the tarmac on the exit. The pit facilities, as well as the press room and hospitality boxes, are far superior to Járama, but the crowd was expected to be smaller as there is no nearby centre of population to compare with Madrid.

Yamaha had done their pre-season testing at Jerez, but Honda waited until the weekend before the race to let their 500s loose on the circuit. Spencer was absent, his shoulder still causing trouble, and HRC were not impressed. Mackenzie crashed: again, the reason was the Michelin radial. 'In the corner the radial offers good grip and stability, but because of my riding style I have a problem going in. I like to brake deep and, when I do, the front end starts to judder. I prefer to use the cross-ply, but I know that will not last the distance here and I am going to have to get on with the radial.'

Haslam and Sarron also favoured the cross-ply and were not prepared to make the change at any price. While Michelin had a few problems with some of their riders, Dunlop's men, Mamola and Baldwin, were experiencing difficulties.

Well down in practice, it was not obvious if the tyres were simply not working or if the suspension was not matched to tyres or bikes or riders. Of the top teams, they were the only ones not to have tested at Jerez; Dunlop engineer Peter Ingley admitted that they were up against it. 'We have a combination of problems. We have too little track time at this circuit and we have not worked with the Yamaha since we won the World Championship in '84. We have to match the tyre to the bike, the rider and the suspension, but we will get there.'

The Lucky Strike Team realised that they needed more track time to sort out their problems and Erv Kanemoto needed longer to relate to Mackenzie and to help him get the best from the machine. It would have helped if Spencer had been there as he and Kanemoto still have a very special relationship. If Spencer's absence upset Kanemoto he didn't show it, but the normally inscrutable Japanese were beginning to exhibit signs of frustration, especially as two perfectly good NSR500s remained unused. 'Mr Spencer's is just a spares truck at the moment', declared HRC director Shinichi Oguma. 'The problem is that all the spares we have made for the beginning of the season will soon be useless. We have learnt things at Suzuka and we will learn things here and we make modifications which make the older parts out of date. It is very expensive to go on making spares for a rider that does not use them. When I return to Japan after this weekend I will have a meeting with Mr Fukui and a Director from the Honda Motor Company, and we will have to decide what will have to be done with Mr Spencer's machines.' Oguma confirmed that Spencer was still being paid even though he did not ride.

HRC were certainly no longer dependent on Spencer on a standard NSR because the special Elf version would not be ready till later. From the outset, Honda had said they could not deliver an engine before January, and it was to take Elf some time to design and build the machine around the powerplant.

Riding the NSR for the Elf team brought things together for Haslam. It was the first time he had been on a competitive machine since 1985 when he rode for Honda Britain. He had not been happy with that team and said his riding had suffered. He found happiness with Serge Rosset and the Elf squad but the three-cylinder Elf could not compete against the best Yamahas and four-cylinder Hondas.

At last things were right. 'I like riding in this team and everything is much better for me – the team, my personal life; I feel much better. I have yet to find the limit of the four, though, and at first honestly it was a bit frightening, but I am getting used to it. I am also looking forward to the new Elf. I think the Elf was an easier machine to ride. That was with the three-cylinder engine in it and I don't know how it will work with the four, but one good thing is we will be using Michelin tyres and I think last year's Elf was held back a little by the Dunlops.'

Haslam may have been content, but Lawson was not, ending the first timed practice in fourth place with Gardner leading from Mackenzie and McElnea. 'It is very hard work here, the track is narrow and you have to use every inch of road from white line to white line. There are quite a few bumps and one in the middle of the fast right behind the pits that could easily make you lose the front if you don't watch out.'

In the second session both Lawson and McElnea moved in front of Gardner and Mackenzie, and Taira took over fifth place, saying that although he had missed the pre-season test session there were plenty of tracks like this in Japan so it was easy enough for him to get to grips with it.

Things got serious in the third session with Lawson going even quicker and Gardner inching ahead of McElnea. The latter admitted that the edge had been taken off his riding by the fall in Japan: 'I just don't feel I am riding as well as I did when I came here for the test at the beginning of the year.'

Kel Carruthers had been working on both the 250 and 500 Yamahas after the Japanese Grand Prix, where it had been obvious that Honda had turned the tables on them since the end of '86 when both the 500 and 250 YZRs were significantly the better machines. Through 1986, when he had charge of the 250 as well as the 500 Marlboro Yamahas, Carruthers had adopted the system of trying engine-tuning ideas on the 250 before the 500. 'Martin is such a good test rider that it makes life easier for me. He can tell if what I have done is an improvement or not, and of course I only have to make the changes to two cylinders to see if it works before I have to modify four cylinders for the 500. There are things that work on the 250 but not on the 500, but generally I have an idea what can be taken from one and used on the other.' Having the 250s to work on may have been an advantage but it all added to the workload. 'I have been working till twelve at

night every day since the bikes arrived at Bergamo from Japan, and since we got to the track it has been worse. I was up till four yesterday morning trying something on the 500 and I am not sure if it worked or not. One thing is, it is almost impossible to get all the bikes done the same, but if something is an advantage I work through them all eventually so that Rob and Eddie have the same as Martin and Luca. But Taira's men seem to do pretty much their own thing.'

In the 250 class the Marlboro Yamahas were well ahead of the Hondas and although Wimmer topped the table after three sessions he was less than half a second quicker than Luca Cadalora. The Italian was confident about the pace he was going although he doubted that it would be easy to improve on his performance. He surprised himself by cutting almost a second off his time in the final session.

125 cc

Domenico Brigaglia led on the first lap riding the AGV MBA, but while he had a piece of road to himself ex-World Champion Fausto Gresini on the all-powerful Garelli was in the middle of a second-place battle just behind. Gresini had his hands full holding off his new team-mate Bruno Casanova as well as the second black-and-splodge coloured MBA of Paolo Casoli. Quickly into fifth place came Pier Paolo Bianchi on his MBA, ahead of the star of the race Ezio Gianola on a single-cylinder Honda.

Riding for Honda Italia, Gianola had been promised a prototype works 125 single by HRC as a test bed for '88 when the rules would change. The new machine would not be ready before mid-season and until then the Italian had to make do with an old single that used the CR125 motocross engine as they had done for about ten years. The

Right: **Those old endurance adversaries Patrick Igoa and Dominique Sarron battle it out. Sarron's extra year of Grand Prix experience told in the end.**

Martin Wimmer *(below)* **was obviously glad to be back on the rostrum after a bare '86 season. Garriga, on the other hand, seems to be reflecting on why he came third instead of first . . . tyres, bike, or rider?**

team had expected something a little special from Honda and were shocked to find that the bike had wire wheels when they unpacked the crate.

Considering the whole project a joke they took it testing at Misano and were suprised how quickly Gianola could lap on it. With cast wheels fitted they arrived at Jerez and after Gianola qualified sixth team manager Carlo Florenzano commented, 'Either we have the best rider in the world or the other teams have been wasting their time developing twin-cylinder engines.'

In fact, the team were under no illusions that at circuits like Hockenheim and Monza, Gianola would be up against it, but at the moment they were enjoying his performance, marvelling at the angle of lean and the mid-corner speed he maintained. He quickly established himself in sixth place but was caught on lap 7 by August Auinger who had made a mess of the start and had been 14th on the first lap.

Brigaglia's slender advantage disappeared on lap 8 as he was caught by Gresini and Casoli, having dropped Casanova in the meantime. Brigaglia still held the lead but could not rest for a moment. Although he did not realise it, Gresini was merely playing a waiting game and took the lead on the final circuit. Brigaglia chased him across the line pulling away from Casoli, with Casanova a now-distant fourth.

Bianchi had been caught and passed by Auinger but the temperature of the Bartol MBA had been on the rise and as it lost power Auinger dropped back, being passed by Gianola on the run-in to the flag. Willy Pérez, Jean-Claude Selini and Thierry Feuz were fighting for the last points and on the final lap both Selini and Pérez fell at the last corner, leaving Feuz to take eighth, and Selini remounted to cross the line fourteenth.

80 cc

Aspar Martínez represented the best chance of a Spanish victory and the World Champion did not disappoint his fans. Gerhard Waibel led at the end of the initial lap on the Krauser, but Martínez was right in his slipstream and took a turn in front for

the second circuit before giving Luis Reyes a chance on the Autisa. The crowd loved it, but Reyes, who had suffered suspension problems all through practice, could not hang on to the lead as the Derbis proved too good.

Martínez took the lead on lap 6 and from that moment was never troubled. It became a Derbi benefit as Alex Creville took over second and Julian Miralles eased past Waibel and then Reyes into third.

Stefan Dörflinger had crashed out of sixth place on lap 4 and neither Manuel Herreros nor Ian McConnachie were ever in the hunt for the lead.

500 cc

Lawson won the drag race to the first corner and settled into a rhythm that looked as though it should give him fifteen points. He had, after all, been fastest in practice and with a clear road in front of him could repeat his domination of '86. When Gardner took the lead on lap 3 it was a little surprising, but perhaps he was riding on the wild side, perhaps Lawson was happy to follow and let the Australian wear himself and the tyres out. That seemed a cosy enough scenario until one realised that Gardner was slowly but very certainly extending his lead. It was not by much at first, but when the gap had grown to 2.3 seconds after eight laps, Lawson seemed to realise he was not going to be able to hold the NSR. A lap later, he had slipped a further second behind and then another seven-tenths as Gardner made quick work of passing some tail-enders.

Lap 10 had come and gone, with Gardner four seconds clear and the third-place battle that had been joined between Haslam and Mackenzie was a further twelve seconds astern. The possibility of a three-way struggle for the lead had disappeared on lap 6 when Rob McElnea went for a mighty tumble after passing Haslam into third. Frustrated for several laps trying to get past the Honda, McElnea had eventually squeezed through and set off in a rush to catch Lawson and Gardner. He highsided himself getting on the power too early and did a handstand on the Marlboro Yamaha

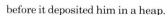

before it deposited him in a heap.

Lawson chased Gardner while Mackenzie looked for some way past Haslam, but the most exciting contest was that for fifth as Kevin Schwantz worked wonders with the Suzuki, keeping it ahead of Pier Francesco Chili's three-cylinder Honda, the Yamahas of Sarron, Mamola, Baldwin and Taira, and the four-cylinder Honda of Yatsushiro.

Baldwin had started well down but was advancing rapidly when the unthinkable happened and his Yamaha's gearbox packed up on lap 12. Schwantz still headed the group but had to work very hard to keep Chili at bay as Sarron started to work at finding his way past both of them. Mamola retained a position as an interested observer just behind, whilst Yatsushiro seemed to be succeeding in holding off Taira.

Sarron overdid it on lap 25. Brake troubles, he said, had made him squeeze the lever deep into the

corner and the front end tucked under. Gardner had extended his lead to 13 seconds and, with a fastest lap of 1m 51.08s, had proved Lawson wrong in his post-practice assertion that the race could not be run at that speed.

Lawson freely admitted after the race that he was surprised both by the way Gardner rode and by the pace of the Honda, which seemed to have the Yamaha beaten everywhere. Gardner ended the thirty laps with 23 seconds in hand, Haslam keeping Mackenzie at bay to take a comfortable third. The Scot said that every time he increased the pace to have a look at passing the Elf Honda, Haslam had a little in reserve, and with his own bike on the limit he had to be content with his first points of the year and fourth place.

Schwantz gave the Suzuki team a great boost by riding into fifth place; team-mate Kenny Irons, however, had crashed at the beginning of the race. Mamola was happy to be presented with

sixth place when Chili crashed at the last corner (he remounted to cross the line eleventh, just behind Richard Scott making his Grand Prix debut on an RS500 Honda). Scott ended up in the points because, as well as Chili's last-corner error, Gustav Reiner made the same mistake. Scott had been chasing Reiner and Roger Burnett for the last point, but when Burnett went to lap Wolfgang von Muralt going into the final corner Reiner was caught out as the Swiss moved over. Taira was seventh, having dived inside Yatsushiro on lap 27, complaining subsequently that the water temperature was way up and the engine just got slower and slower.

Even Gardner was surprised by the manner in which he had won. 'The plan was to try and stick with Eddie for most of the race and try and pass him near the end if I could. I was surprised that I could get by him so easily and more surprised that I could get away without trying too hard.'

250 cc

It was always possible that with the adoption of the clutch start, riders would shoot off the line before the lights turned green. To keep an eye on this, each row of the grid has a marshal to see if anyone moves too early. On this occasion Paul Lewis jumped the start from the last qualifying position. It was no accident. 'I found the 250 harder to ride than the 500 – not physically but mentally. In practice, riders would come past and I did not know who they were, I had no idea who to follow. In the race I decided that I had to get up the front from the start because even if I was penalised later I would be able to show everyone I could run at the front and make my point.'

Unfortunately for Lewis, things did not work out for him and he never did make it to the front of the field. That position was held by Toni Mang, but not for long. Riding hard from the

Kevin Schwantz and Kenny Irons (right) sit it out in the Suzuki truck during a lull in practice. The bike was more suited to the circuit but they were hardly overwhelmed by its power.

Far right: One of the biggest transporters and a huge road racing balloon were of little advantage to Carlos Cardus who was injured and unable to ride. Angel Nieto was not thrilled; Alan Carter offered his services but the team needed a Spaniard and the bikes remained unused after the first session.

Gresini slipstreamed Brigaglia and waited for the right moment to pass (below).

start, he threw the Rothmans Honda away on the second lap – making it two falls in one meeting, in addition to his testing crash at Jerez at the beginning of the season. Mang has never been a faller, but said this time he was caught out by the switch to Michelins and misjudging the speed he could go from the start.

That left Cadalora to lead from Cornu, Garriga, Ruggia and Wimmer. Jean-Philippe Ruggia had impressed everyone with his ninth-place qualifying position just behind Carlos Lavado and in front of Dominique Sarron, being almost alone in riding a production Yamaha in a field dominated by ten works bikes.

There was nothing that Cornu could do to hold on to the leading Yamaha and the Swiss was forced to turn his attention rearwards as Wimmer approached. By lap 5 the German was second and Cornu was coming under pressure from Garriga. Some way behind there was a private French battle between Igoa and Sarron, whilst Ruggia did his best to hold off Roth.

It was not easy for Wimmer to close on Cadalora as the latter had almost five seconds' advantage when the German moved into second on lap 6. As Cadalora had suggested after practice, although Wimmer's experience told in the end as he kept up a superbly smooth pace and set the fastest lap of the race on his ninth circuit, it was not until lap 17 of the 25 that Wimmer was right on his team-mate's tail. After the race, Wimmer pointed out just how hard it had been

and what a great rider the young Italian had already become. Garriga was a lonely third, having tried to hang on to Wimmer but feeling that his tyres were not as good as those of the two leaders, even though all were using Michelins. Sarron and Igoa were now contesting fourth having caught Cornu on lap 10.

Wimmer finally assumed the lead on lap 20 and opened just enough of an advantage over Cadalora to put out of his mind any possible last-lap manoeuvres. The Italian later claimed that he was thrilled just to be second.

Garriga's feelings as he stepped onto the rostrum in third place mingled pleasure at being there and frustration that he had not done better in front of his home crowd. Sarron proved that Igoa still has a little to learn about Grand Prix racing by squeezing him out of fourth and Ruggia finished seventh behind Cornu after a fight that had continued to the last lap.

Sito Pons and Carlos Lavado were uncharacteristically out of the action in ninth and tenth places. Pons completed the race in great pain having damaged his hand badly in a practice fall. It would have prevented him from running had it not been for his determination to compete at his own Grand Prix. Lavado was still recovering from his broken collarbone and wrist, complaining that everything hurt and he could not ride properly. Nevertheless, he hoped he would be well enough to ride in the German Grand Prix.

Sidecars

Steve Webster and Tony Hewitt said that they greatly enjoyed the race because for once they were able to pull past Rolf Biland and Kurt Waltisperg on the straight and wave at them. Both outfits had the Krauser engines and although Biland had put in a blistering lap to take pole position, once the race started he could not repeat that performance consistently. Despite setting the fastest lap of the race, he soon ran into brake trouble.

The race started as a three-team struggle, including World Champions Egbert Streuer and Bernard Schnieders, but Webster held the lead and by lap 4 Streuer was beginning to drop back with the ignition problems that would cause his retirement on lap 9. On the seventh lap, Biland took the lead and made a big effort to get away from the British crew, but there was no way Webster would let him get very far in front and they recaptured the lead on lap 10.

The two outfits had pulled well clear of Alain Michel and Jean-Marc Fresc, who in turn had little trouble staying in front of the Zurbrügg brothers and Bayley and Nixon. Biland stopped at the pits with his brakes shot completely on lap 15. He preferred to pull out rather than limp round and try to collect a point or two. That gave Webster a comfortable lead over Michel and the sting had very much gone out of the tail of the race.

Gran Premio de España, 26 April/statistics

Circuito Permanente de Jerez, 2.621-mile/4.218-km circuit

500 cc

30 laps, 78.63 miles/126.54 km

Place	Rider	Nat.	Machine	Laps	Time & speed	Practice time	Grid
1	Wayne Gardner	AUS	Honda	30	56m 02.07s 84.193 mph/ 135.495 km/h	1m 50.99s	2
2	Eddie Lawson	USA	Yamaha	30	56m 25.62s	1m 50.69s	1
3	Ron Haslam	GB	Honda	30	56m 51.16s	1m 52.13s	6
4	Niall Mackenzie	GB	Honda	30	56m 52.76s	1m 51.01s	3
5	Kevin Schwantz	USA	Suzuki	30	57m 12.56s	1m 53.57s	11
6	Randy Mamola	USA	Yamaha	30	57m 14.88s	1m 53.45s	9
7	Tadahiko Taira	J	Yamaha	30	57m 16.28s	1m 52.09s	5
8	Shunji Yatsushiro	J	Honda	30	57m 20.33s	1m 52.59s	7
9	Roger Burnett	GB	Honda	30	57m 42.11s	1m 55.23s	17
10	Richard Scott	NZ	Honda	30	57m 47.11s	1m 54.56s	15
11	Pier Francesco Chili	I	Honda	30	57m 58.07s	1m 53.46s	10
12	Marco Gentile	CH	Fior	29	56m 39.66s	1m 55.43s	19
13	Thierry Rapicault	F	Fior	29	56m 58.41s	1m 55.53s	20
14	Alessandro Valesi	I	Honda	29	57m 02.86s	1m 54.84s	16
15	Simon Buckmaster	GB	Honda	29	57m 13.32s	1m 56.83s	25
16	Daniel Amatriain	E	Honda	29	57m 33.28s	1m 56.40s	23
17	Wofgang von Muralt	CH	Suzuki	29	57m 45.06s	1m 56.42s	24
18	Bruno Kneubühler	CH	Honda	29	58m 01.30s	1m 58.09s	26
19	Maarten Duyzers	NL	Honda	28	56m 07.14s	1m 58.68s	28
20	Louis-Luc Maisto	F	Honda	28	56m 07.64s	1m 58.36s	27
21	Tony Carey	IRL	Suzuki	26	56m 46.75s	2m 02.01s	30
	Gustav Reiner	D	Honda	29	DNF	1m 55.31s	18
	Christian Sarron	F	Yamaha	24	DNF	1m 53.16s	8
	Mike Baldwin	USA	Yamaha	12	DNF	1m 53.94s	12
	Fabio Biliotti	I	Honda	9	DNF	1m 56.09s	22
	Gerold Fischer	D	Honda	9	DNF	2m 00.36s	29
	José Parra	E	Suzuki	9	DNF	2m 03.98s	31
	Raymond Roche	F	Cagiva	6	DNF	1m 54.53s	14
	Rob McElnea	GB	Yamaha	5	DNF	1m 51.44s	4
	Didier de Radiguès	B	Cagiva	1	DNF	1m 55.69s	21
	Kenny Irons	GB	Suzuki	1	DNF	1m 54.18s	13
	Larry Moreno Vacondio	YV	Suzuki		DNQ	2m 09.32s	

Fastest lap: Gardner, 1m 51.08s, 84.942 mph/136.701 km/h (record).
Previous record: Massimo Messere, I (Honda), 1m 57.18s, 80.52 mph/129.58 km/h (1986).

World Championship: 1 Gardner, 27; **2** Mamola, 20; **3** Haslam, 16; **4** Lawson, 12; **5** Ito 10; **6** Taira, 9; **7** Chili and Mackenzie, 8; **9** Schwantz, 6; **10** Burnett, 5; **11** Kawasaki, 4; **12** Yatsushiro, 3; **13** Katayama, 2; **14** Roche and Scott, 1.

250 cc

25 laps, 65.53 miles/105.45 km

Place	Rider	Nat.	Machine	Laps	Time & speed	Practice time	Grid
1	Martin Wimmer	D	Yamaha	25	47m 41.00s 82.449 mph/ 132.668 km/h	1m 52.38s	2
2	Luca Cadalora	I	Yamaha	25	47m 42.68s	1m 52.20s	1
3	Juan Garriga	E	Yamaha	25	47m 53.39s	1m 53.68s	3
4	Dominique Sarron	F	Honda	25	48m 03.35s	1m 54.36s	10
5	Patrick Igoa	F	Yamaha	25	48m 08.88s	1m 53.97s	4
6	Jacques Cornu	CH	Honda	25	48m 17.65s	1m 54.01s	5
7	Jean-Philippe Ruggia	F	Yamaha	25	48m 19.65s	1m 54.53s	9
8	Reinhold Roth	D	Honda	25	48m 19.94s	1m 54.02s	6
9	Alfonso Pons	E	Honda	25	48m 22.93s	1m 55.06s	14
10	Carlos Lavado	YV	Yamaha	25	48m 49.20s	1m 54.41s	8
11	Guy Bertin	F	Honda	25	48m 54.83s	1m 56.11s	21
12	Jochen Schmid	D	Yamaha	25	48m 55.72s	1m 55.82s	18
13	Maurizio Vitali	I	Garelli	25	49m 06.14s	1m 54.79s	11
14	Jean-Michel Mattioli	F	Honda	25	49m 12.37s	1m 55.07s	15
15	Manfred Herweh	D	Honda	25	49m 17.03s	1m 56.97s	29
16	Stefano Caracchi	I	Honda	25	49m 17.26s	1m 56.68s	25
17	Harald Eckl	D	Honda	25	49m 26.04s	1m 55.64s	17
18	Stéphane Mertens	B	Armstrong	25	49m 28.28s	1m 55.84s	19
19	Massimo Matteoni	I	Honda	25	49m 28.61s	1m 56.34s	23
20	Alain Bronec	F	Honda	25	49m 30.94s	1m 57.42s	34
21	Jean Foray	F	Yamaha	25	49m 32.73s	1m 57.36s	33
22	Philippe Pagano	F	Honda	25	49m 33.79s	1m 57.28s	31
23	René Delaby	LUX	Yamaha	25	49m 35.90s	1m 56.80s	26
24	Hervé Duffard	F	Honda	25	49m 38.42s	1m 57.25s	30
25	Paul Lewis	AUS	EMC	25	50m 30.65s	1m 57.48s	36
	Alberto Rota	I	Honda	14	DNF	1m 56.35s	24
	Donnie McLeod	GB	EMC	8	DNF	1m 54.92s	12
	Loris Reggiani	I	Aprilia	7	DNF	1m 54.98s	13
	Fausto Ricci	I	Honda	5	DNF	1m 57.48s	35
	Bernard Hänggeli	CH	Yamaha	4	DNF	1m 55.20s	16
	Juan Lopez	E	Yamaha	3	DNF	1m 57.32s	32
	Siegfried Minich	A	Honda	2	DNF	1m 56.92s	27
	Bruno Bonhuil	F	Honda	1	DNF	1m 56.93s	28
	Anton Mang	D	Honda	1	DNF	1m 54.24s	7
	Xavier Cardelus	AND	Kobas	0	DNF	1m 55.88s	20
	Ezio Gianola	I	Honda		DNS	1m 56.28s	22
	Fernando Gonzalez	E	Honda		DNQ	1m 57.86s	
	Juan Bravo	E	Honda		DNQ	1m 58.07s	
	Robin Appleyard	GB	Honda		DNQ	2m 00.84s	
	Ivan Palazzese	YV	Yamaha		DNQ	2m 03.60s	
	Carlos Cardus	E	Honda		DNQ	2m 17.07s	

Fastest lap: Wimmer, 1m 53.08s, 83.440 mph/134.284 km/h (record).
Previous record: Cees Doorakkers, NL (Yamaha), 1m 56.00s, 81.341 mph/130.905 km/h (1987)

World Championship: 1 Wimmer, 21; **2** Kobayashi and Garriga, 15; **4** Pons, 14; **5** Roth, 13; **6** Cadalora, 12; **7** Igoa, 10; **8** Shimuzu and Sarron, 8; **10** Cornu, 5; **11** Ruggia, 4; **12** Mang, 3; **13** Taguchi, 2; **14** Yamamoto and Lavado, 1.

125 cc

22 laps, 57.66 miles/92.80 km

Place	Rider	Nat.	Machine	Laps	Time & speed	Practice time	Grid
1	Fausto Gresini	I	Garelli	22	43m 25.97s 79.655 mph/ 128.192 km/h	1m 57.96s	2
2	Domenico Brigaglia	I	AGV	22	43m 26.31s	1m 57.59s	1
3	Paolo Casoli	I	AGV	22	43m 28.99s	1m 58.69s	3
4	Bruno Casanova	I	Garelli	22	44m 01.34s	1m 59.62s	5
5	Pier Paolo Bianchi	I	MBA	22	44m 09.22s	1m 59.61s	4
6	Ezio Gianola	I	Honda	22	44m 27.43s	1m 59.70s	6
7	August Auinger	A	MBA	22	44m 27.84s	1m 59.93s	7
8	Thierry Feuz	CH	LCR	22	44m 53.20s	2m 02.48s	17
9	Claudio Macciotta	I	MBA	22	44m 57.60s	2m 01.37s	9
10	Mike Leitner	A	MBA	22	45m 07.08s	2m 03.33s	21
11	Johnny Wickström	SF	Tunturi	22	45m 07.56s	2m 03.50s	22
12	Hubert Abold	D	Honda	22	45m 16.20s	2m 01.43s	10
13	Jean-Claude Selini	F	MBA	22	45m 39.52s	2m 01.44s	11
14	Ivan Troisi	YV	MBA	22	46m 09.23s	2m 03.75s	24
15	Paul Bordes	F	MBA	21	43m 34.59s	2m 02.87s	19
16	Jussi Hautaniemi	SF	LCR	21	43m 38.27s	2m 03.62s	23
17	Fernando Gonzalez	E	Cobas	21	43m 38.56s	2m 05.64s	34
18	Robin Milton	GB	MBA	21	43m 41.60s	2m 04.82s	28
19	Jacques Hutteau	F	MBA	21	43m 49.75s	2m 05.43s	33
20	Joaquin Alos	E	MBA	21	43m 52.22s	2m 05.48s	35
21	Robin Appleyard	GB	MBA	21	43m 52.44s	2m 05.21s	32
22	Peter Baláž	CS	MBA	21	43m 52.86s	2m 04.36s	26
23	Håkan Olsson	S	Starol	21	44m 32.92s	2m 05.01s	30
24	Thomas Møller-Pedersen	DK	MBA	21	44m 54.76s	2m 04.32s	27
25	Bady Hassaine	DZ	MBA	20	44m 11.66s	2m 05.95s	36
26	José Fombuena	E	MBA	19	43m 56.70s	2m 05.11s	31
	Willy Pérez	RA	Zanella	21	DNF	2m 02.36s	15
	Heinz Litz	D	MBA	17	DNF	2m 04.29s	25
	Gastone Grassetti	I	MBA	16	DNF	2m 02.40s	16
	Christian le Badezet	F	MBA	12	DNF	2m 04.98s	29
	Olivier Liegeois	B	Assmex	10	DNF	2m 02.09s	12
	Lucio Pietroniro	B	MBA	10	DNF	2m 01.10s	8
	Manuel Hernandez	E	Beneti	9	DNF	2m 03.18s	20
	Andrés Marin Sánchez	E	Ducados	6	DNF	2m 02.18s	13
	Esa Kytölä	SF	MBA	1	DNF	2m 02.72s	18
	Adolf Stadler	D	MBA		DNF	2m 02.25s	14
	Hans Spaan	NL	MBA		DNQ	2m 05.99s	
	Wilco Zeelenberg	NL	MBA		DNQ	2m 06.00s	
	Daniel Mateos	E	MBA		DNQ	2m 06.54s	
	Antonio Oliveros	E	MBA		DNQ	2m 06.66s	
	Allan Scott	USA	EMC		DNQ	2m 07.55s	
	Juan Munoz	E	MBA		DNQ	2m 07.63s	
	Manfred Braun	B	MBA		DNQ	2m 08.94s	
	Javier Navarro	E	MBA		DNQ	2m 10.71s	

Fastest lap: Brigaglia, 1m 56.92s, 80.700 mph/129.873 km/h (record).
Previous record: Manuel Hernandez, E (Beneti), 2m 01.42s, 77.710 mph/125.062 km/h (1987).

World Championship: 1 Gresini, 15; **2** Brigaglia, 12; **3** Casoli, 10; **4** Casanova, 8; **5** Bianchi, 6; **6** Gianola, 5; **7** Auinger, 4; **8** Feuz, 3; **9** Macciotta, 2; **10** Leitner, 1.

80 cc

18 laps, 47.18 miles/75.92 km

Place	Rider	Nat.	Machine	Laps	Time & speed	Practice time	Grid
1	Jorge Martinez	E	Derbi	18	37m 16.36s 75.944 mph/ 122.219 km/h	2m 02.79s	1
2	Alex Criville	E	Derbi	18	37m 17.28s	2m 03.55s	3
3	Julian Miralles	E	Derbi	18	37m 17.70s	2m 04.34s	5
4	Gerhard Waibel	D	Krauser	18	37m 17.89s	2m 04.34s	4
5	Luis M. Reyes	COL	Autisa	18	37m 21.38s	2m 03.13s	2
6	Manuel Herreros	E	Derbi	18	37m 46.71s	2m 05.41s	8
7	Ian McConnachie	GB	Krauser	18	38m 17.61s	2m 06.51s	11
8	Richard Bay	D	Krauser	18	38m 20.39s	2m 06.02s	9
9	Josef Fischer	A	Krauser	18	38m 36.31s	2m 07.93s	16
10	Hubert Abold	D	Krauser	18	38m 41.40s	2m 05.28s	7
11	Juan Ramon Bolart	E	Krauser	18	38m 43.17s	2m 06.98s	13
12	Francisco Torrontegui	E	Krauser	18	38m 47.44s	2m 10.36s	23
13	Felix Rodriguez	E	Cobas	18	38m 53.59s	2m 07.72s	15
14	Paolo Priori	I	Krauser	18	39m 02.56s	2m 11.00s	26
15	Jörg Seel	D	Krauser	18	39m 04.07s	2m 11.49s	27
16	Salvatore Milano	I	Krauser	18	39m 12.46s	2m 09.85s	22
17	Javier Arumi	E	Autisa	17	37m 17.08s	2m 10.72s	25
18	Wilco Zeelenberg	NL	Krauser	17	37m 18.28s	2m 08.18s	17
19	Raimo Lipponen	SF	Krauser	17	38m 11.91s	2m 09.32s	20
20	Joaquin Alos	E	Yamaha	17	38m 17.21s	2m 13.63s	32
21	Thomas Engl	D	Yamaha	17	38m 18.76s	2m 12.70s	30
22	Serge Julin	B	Krauser	17	39m 04.42s	2m 15.32s	36
23	Reiner Koster	CH	Krauser	17	39m 04.85s	2m 14.62s	33
24	Chris Baert	B	Seel	15	37m 23.37s	2m 13.58s	31
	René Dünki	CH	Krauser	13	DNF	2m 09.09s	19
	Javier Debon	E	Autisa	11	DNF	2m 10.62s	24
	Hernando Sande E. Silva	P	Huvo	10	DNF	2m 15.24s	35
	Günter Schirnhofer	D	Krauser	8	DNF	2m 06.69s	12
	Paul Bordes	F	Krauser	8	DNF	2m 09.56s	21
	José Saez	E	Huvo	6	DNF	2m 14.64s	34
	Rainer Kunz	D	Krauser	4	DNF	2m 06.50s	10
	Juan Esteve	E	Autisa	4	DNF	2m 11.71s	28
	Stefan Dörflinger	CH	Krauser	3	DNF	2m 04.73s	6
	Stuart Edwards	GB	Huvo	2	DNF	2m 15.80s	37
	Theo Timmer	NL	Krauser	2	DNF	2m 11.88s	29
	Alexandre Barros	BR	Autisa	1	DNF	2m 07.18s	14
	Hans Spaan	NL	Honda		DNS	2m 08.85s	18
	Elias Durendez	E	Autisa		DNQ	2m 16.42s	
	Dennis Batchelor	GB	Krauser		DNQ	2m 17.26s	
	Javier Navarro	E	Huvo		DNQ	2m 25.26s	
	Jean-François Verdier	F	Derbi		DNQ	2m 30.67s	

Fastest lap: Criville, 2m 01.68s, 77.543 mph/124.793 km/h (record).
Previous record: Luis M. Reyes, COL (Autisa), 2m 05.91s, 74.939 mph/120.602 km/h (1986).

World Championship: 1 Martinez, 15; **2** Criville, 12; **3** Miralles, 10; **4** Waibel, 8; **5** Reyes, 6; **6** Herreros, 5; **7** McConnachie, 4; **8** Bay, 3; **9** Fischer, 2; **10** Abold, 1.

Sidecars

22 laps, 57.66 miles/92.80 km

Place	Driver & passenger	Nat.	Machine	Laps	Time & speed	Practice time	Grid
1	Steve Webster/	GB	LCR-	22	42m 29.02s	1m 53.36s	2
	Tony Hewitt	GB	Yamaha		81.433 mph/		
					131.053 km/h		
2	Alain Michel/	F	LCR-	22	43m 14.29s	1m 53.85s	3
	Jean-Marc Fresc	F	Krauser				
3	Alfred Zurbrugg/	CH	LCR-	22	43m 25.37s	1m 55.80s	7
	Martin Zurbrugg	CH	Yamaha				
4	Derek Bayley/	GB	LCR-	22	43m 34.00s	1m 56.83s	8
	Bryan Nixon	GB	Krauser				
5	Steve Abbott/	GB	Windle-	22	43m 37.63s	1m 57.91s	11
	Shaun Smith	GB	Yamaha				
6	Derek Jones/	GB	LCR-	22	44m 13.25s	1m 56.88s	9
	Simon Birchall	GB	Yamaha				
7	Markus Egloff/	CH	LCR-	22	44m 23.88s	1m 54.28s	4
	Urs Egloff	CH	Yamaha				
8	Yoshisada Kumagaya/	J	LCR-	22	44m 24.98s	1m 58.95s	14
	Brian Barlow	GB	Yamaha				
9	René Progin/	CH	Seymaz-	21	42m 32.20s	1m 58.71s	12
	Yves Hunziker	CH	Yamaha				
10	Masato Kumano/	J	LCR-	21	43m 15.26s	2m 01.35s	19
	Andreas Racke	D	Yamaha				
11	Dennis Bingham/	GB	LCR-	21	43m 23.37s	1m 59.91s	16
	Julia Bingham	GB	Yamaha				
	Rolf Steinhausen/	D	Busch	18	DNF	1m 55.71s	6
	Bruno Hiller	D					
	Barry Brindley/	GB	LCR-	17	DNF	1m 57.17s	10
	Grahame Rose	GB	Yamaha				
	Vince Biggs/	GB	LCR-	15	DNF	2m 01.47s	21
	Laurie Genova	GB	Yamaha				
	Rolf Biland/	CH	Krauser	14	DNF	1m 52.08s	1
	Kurt Waltisperg	CH					
	Gary Thomas/	GB	LCR-	12	DNF	2m 01.42s	20
	Geoff White	GB	Yamaha				
	Theo van Kempen/	NL	LCR-	9	DNF	1m 58.86s	13
	Gerardus de Haas	NL	Yamaha				
	Egbert Streuer/	NL	LCR-	8	DNF	1m 54.95s	5
	Bernard Schnieders	NL	Yamaha				
	Ivan Nigrowski/	F	Seymaz-	8	DNF	2m 00.12s	17
	Frédéric Meunier	F	Yamaha				
	Wolfgang Stropek/	A	LCR-	2	DNF	1m 59.88s	15
	Hans-Peter Demling	A	Krauser				
	Bernd Scherer/	D	LCR-		DNS	2m 00.39s	18
	Wolfgang Gess	D	Yamaha				
	Erwin Weber/	D	LCR-		DNQ	2m 01.71s	
	Eckart Rosinger	D	Yamaha				
	Pascal Laratte/	F	LCR-		DNQ	2m 03.54s	
	Jacques Corbier	F	Yamaha				
	Judd Drew/	GB	BLR-		DNQ	2m 06.43s	
	Chris Plant	GB	Yamaha				
	Billy Gallros/	S	LCR-		DNQ	2m 07.97s	
	Auden Nordli	S	Yamaha				

Fastest lap: Biland, 1m 53.58s, 83.073 mph/133.693 km/h (record).
No previous record.

World Championship: 1 Webster, 15; **2** Michel, 12; **3** Zurbrugg, 10; **4** Bayley, 8; **5** Abbott, 6;
6 Jones, 5; **7** Egloff, 4; **8** Kumagaya, 3; **9** Progin, 2; **10** Kumano, 1.

Tony Hewitt gets the weight in the right place as Steve Webster opens the throttle on their way to a most impressive sidecar win using their new Krauser engine *(above).*

Hardly needing to get behind the screen for the ultra-short straights at Jerez, Gardner *(right)* **gets ready to brake for the next tight turn. The circuit offered no respite and a fast lap demanded white line to white line accuracy.**

Grosser Preis von
DEUTSCHLAND

Eddie Lawson strolled out to the startline and happened to gaze up at the blue, cloud-patched sky where a glider wafted from one thermal to another. It looked like perfect peace viewed from the preparatory tumult of the 500 grid. He would rather have been flying in that glider or driving his new speedboat back home in California – almost anything other than riding the Yamaha. It was not that the double World Champion had suddenly grown weary or afeared of combat by motor cycle, but that he as champion was forced to fight with an unequal weapon, with a stave against Gardner's broad sword.

The realisation that his task was impossible had come to Lawson only after the final practice session. At lunch before the Saturday afternoon period the Californian was in a buoyant mood. 'I think Kel has found a few things, the new fairing and radiators plus the old cylinders seem to be working and we have picked up some of the lost speed. It is not as fast as the Hondas but close enough for us to have a race and that is all I need. I compared it with Yatsushiro's bike and I think that is one of the fastest Hondas, and though I couldn't pass him I could at least get alongside, so I think it is possible to win here now and at Monza as well.'

Yatsushiro's bike may not have been running well in that morning session or it may no longer have been the fastest Honda because Lawson got a shock that afternoon when Gardner took a big enough chunk off his practice time to make it look as though he had missed out one of the chicanes.

Gardner was as pleased with the way things were going as Lawson was disillusioned. The Australian was not displeased by Freddie Spencer's absence from the Honda throng. Gardner did not need the ex-World Champion's presence to beat the Yamahas and to have him riding was likely to dilute the Honda effort rather than support Wayne. Spencer had tried to ride and in fact had come to Hockenheim early, on the Tuesday before race week, just for a press conference and free practice day. He insisted that he was fit and still determined to win the championship, and pointed out that discussion over his fitness to ride in Spain was meaningless as only he could decide that.

He had also tried to ride at home in America. 'The problem was I had no endurance. I tried riding a dirt bike and I could only go maybe five minutes. Now it is still only twenty minutes but I am working up to it. When I am riding the race bike it still hurts; the main problem is in my back not in the shoulder I broke – that is all right. I know I saw doctors in Japan who said things would soon be better, good enough to ride, but then I saw my own doctors in the US and they do not believe in that. It is up to the individual and I am the only one who can determine when I am fit to ride. Our doctors are getting away from the idea of punishing people, because otherwise in twenty years from now there will be people who can't get out of bed or can't walk. In '84 it was a foot problem and you can kind of get round that, but with my wrist and my shoulder they had to take time. It is frustrating for me too.

'I tried to ride in Suzuka, but it was a real bad mistake and three weeks was way too soon, and I was certain that I was not going to race again until I was fully fit. It is just too dangerous: the bikes have become so powerful that you cannot ride them unless you are fit. Ten years ago, or even five or six years ago, you could get away with more. Now, to race at the top you need all your strength. If I was on a 250 it would be a lot different. I have ridden both; I know. If I felt I could finish a race I would ride, but in Japan after two laps I could not even hold my arm up. Even up to a week ago I could not work properly. I had muscle spasms and everything because that Daytona crash is the hardest I have ever hit the ground . . . and I have been doing it for a long time.'

It seemed that one of those to suffer most from Spencer's absence from the race tracks over the previous twelve months was Erv Kanemoto, and an obvious question was 'Had their relationship suffered?'

'Erv and I are friends first and team-mates second. You would have to ask him how he feels, but the way he tells me – and I believe he is being honest – it has been tough on all of us and that is why I have worked so hard to come back and why I have flown here just for one day. I am certainly not going to quit. I am glad Erv has had Niall to work with so he could keep going, but I could not predict the Daytona accident. If that had not happened we would have been racing as normal.'

With reference to Mr Oguma's observations in Spain that the spares were being wasted when they were not being used, Spencer said that as far as he was concerned if he wasn't riding the spares were not being used and he was going to use them now that he was back in action. 'I have the same bike here that I had at Suzuka. I haven't got the same parts that Wayne and Niall have got right now but I will ride whatever motor cycle they give me; it won't make any difference to me. Because everyone says, "well, he has got the greatest stuff". I don't care; give them the greatest stuff, I'll race them anyway. At Daytona, Bubba Shobert put my race engine in and said it was slower than his. I race what the factory gives me; I have never asked for anything special. The bikes now are all the same. If Wayne is leading the championship and he gets special equipment, then fine; if I take the lead, fine. I'm not going to complain about it, I'm just going to go out and race.'

If there was any suggestion that the season had been lost as far as winning the World Title was concerned, Spencer was quick to emphasise that, in his opinion, there was everything still to go for. 'At the moment I am 27 points behind in the championship but the object for me is to win the championship. If it comes to the end of the year and we are fighting with the Yamahas, then of course we are all Honda riders and you have to do what you have to do then. I am a professional and I would not jeopardize his winning the championship.

'In '83 I was leading with 25 points but we had one mistake in Austria when the crankshaft broke. That is a good example of how it can dissipate, and Kenny beat me a few times in the middle there and that is what made the championship so close. Twenty-seven points is a good lead but the circuits that are coming up I like – they are the faster circuits.'

It had been just about a year since Spencer raced regularly, so had his confidence evaporated? 'I believe inside that I am as prepared as I have ever been, both mentally and physically. I went out today and the conditions were not good, but the times were good and the bike is better than it was and it steers good. These conditions showed that it is good, so that gives me confidence in the machine. I am not going into this race believing that it is a sure win. I know that it will be tougher than it has been, but of course I always go out with the idea of winning if I can.'

Nine days later everything went sour again for Spencer in the first practice period for the Grand Prix. This was an untimed session on Thursday and, as is customary, it was being used by all as a shakedown to get initial suspension and jetting settings. Spencer completed the practice, but not without incident.

'On the East curve, the fast right-hander at the far end of the circuit, I was going into it at the very end of practice and we had got the bike running good and I was feeling pretty good. I think we were about second-quickest on unofficial timing, and as I went into the corner and was coming down I caught my knee on the ground. When it caught it pulled the plastic knee protector down and it bent under and cut into me. It hurt a little when I did it and I slowed down. By the time I came into the pits it had stopped hurting and I talked for about fifteen

Always the clown, Jacques Cornu (left) plays to the gallery as Toni Mang gives him a shot on the mouth. Reinhold Roth deserved his place on the rostrum for overcoming his broken collarbone and riding so well.

minutes with Erv, and then I felt it was a little sticky.

'We went back to the motorhome and pulled my leathers off. We could see it was cut and at first we thought it might just need stitches, but then I went to the track hospital and they said I had to go to the hospital because it was worse. At the hospital they put it in plaster so that I cannot move it and will not get an infection in it. If something needs to be done, surgery or whatever, I would like to get it done in the next couple of days; I guess it depends on the extent. It does hurt and this morning I could not bend it. Recovery could be pretty fast or it could take a little longer – we should know for sure at the beginning of next week.

'It is only bad luck. I have hit my knee before but I have never had the protection in there. The protection is supposed to stop you hurting yourself. It is difficult and disappointing but I am certainly not going to give up.'

Spencer's was only the first of several injuries that were to have an important effect on the championship. The worst period was Saturday when Mike Baldwin was thrown off the Lucky Strike Yamaha as it seized approaching the first chicane, the fastest part of the course. He was flown to hospital by helicopter suffering from concussion, compressed vertebrae, and a badly injured right hand and left leg, both of which required operations.

Although Baldwin could not remember much about what happened in his fall it seems that the leg and hand injuries were sustained when he was hit by Pier Francesco Chili as he lay in the chicane escape road. The Italian was slipstreaming Ron Haslam and when the British rider sat up as he saw the yellow flags, Chili had to swerve to avoid him and ran down the escape road.

Baldwin said it was the sharpest seizure he had ever experienced. 'My first bike seized in the stadium section and before I got on the other bike the mechanics put in the biggest jets they had in the box. I did several laps with my hand on the clutch but it seemed all right, and then, as I started to concentrate on going fast, "snap" it bit me.

'The doctor said I have to keep the pin in my hand for eight weeks and there is no way I can use it or shorten the time.' In no time there were rumours of a replacement for Baldwin, Kiwi Richard Scott's name coming at the top of the list. He had obviously impressed the team with the way he rode his private Honda into tenth place in Spain.

The next most serious injury affected Martin Wimmer, leading the World Championship at the time. He fell from his Marlboro Yamaha at the Sachs curve in the stadium section and tore the ligaments of the little finger of his right hand and his left ankle. He could have raced with the finger injury but the ankle required an operation because he had broken the malleolus of the tibia as well as the fibula. (The malleolus is the bony projection that is important to ankle movement.)

'Hans Lindner fell in front of me and I slowed down in case there was any oil on the track. I started wondering why he had fallen off and I went wide. I wasn't concentrating and I accelerated, not thinking that I was on the non-power-valve bike with the narrower power band. The back slid round without me even realising what was happening.'

With Wimmer out, Reinhold Roth might have been favourite but he had also crashed at the same corner in the same session. A broken collarbone was suspected but Roth lied and said it was only cracked. He then raced and had an operation at nine o'clock on Sunday evening to pin the broken collarbone.

As if that was not enough, Sito Pons slid off and although the bike was hardly damaged the unlucky Spaniard injured his right hand once more. Luca Cadalora was luckier and escaped unhurt when he dropped his 250 Yamaha.

80 cc

From the first lap the three fastest men in practice, Gerhard Waibel, Stefan Dörflinger and Jorge Martínez, were in control and bound to decide the result between them. In fourth place, Ian McConnachie could not hold the leaders in sight and admitted later that he was just not feeling on form at all. He had trouble getting the bike to handle or go as well as his own bike had the year before.

McConnachie did succeed in getting away from the fifth-place battle where Manuel Herreros on the second Derbi had his work cut out trying to defend his position against Luis Reyes on the Autisa, Jörg Seel on the Seel and Mandy Fischer on his private Krauser. There were five others behind them, all equally determined to aim for the points.

The race for the lead was perhaps the best of the day with all three looking possible victors, but Dörflinger later complained that he had chosen the wrong gearing. 'It was all wrong for the last chicane and on the last lap I tried to go in there real fast to make up time and use the taller gear, but I nearly lost the front end completely so had to settle for third.'

Waibel led into the stadium and although Martínez had a look at a way past, the German left him no room and won his second 80 cc at the Hockenheimring in a row. McConnachie was a distant fourth and Herreros led home the next group. Fischer had retired on lap 10 whilst Reyes dropped back to twelfth with a suspected carburation fault, having lost ground suddenly on lap 8 during a challenge against Herreros for fifth.

125 cc

Once more this was to be Auinger versus the Italians. With Gresini nearly a second quicker than anyone else in practice the ex-champion was obviously favourite. There was still plenty to keep the crowd entertained, however, as Gresini, Brigaglia and Auinger headed the field at the end of lap 1. There was a cheer from the crowd the second time round as Auinger headed the pack into the stadium, but Gresini slipped past on the brakes before the Sachs curve. Right behind were Bianchi and Casanova, making it a four-man group splitting away from the rest.

Brigaglia had to work hard for most of the race trying to hold off Andrés Marín Sánchez on the Ducados. They contested fifth while sixth saw a three-way fight between Jussi Hautaniemi, Thierry Feuz and Adolf Stadler.

Bianchi found the speed of the leading men too

much and by lap 8 had lost their slipstream. All the same, he was a secure fourth, and with eleven of the fourteen laps run Brigaglia got away from Sánchez. In the final four laps, Gresini made his point and pulled away, leaving Auinger to beat off Casanova. The Austrian later pointed out that he had been wrongly geared.

Ezio Gianola provided plenty of entertainment as he passed riders by the handful in the infield, even though he was a lap behind having called into the pits on the third lap.

250 cc

Manfred Herweh completed a disastrous Grand Prix and a dispiriting start to the season by being unable to join the grid thanks to a broken plug lead. Through practice a string of engine failures had proved costly in time and money, yet Herweh had qualified eleventh. He was cursing his fortune as a Honda RS privateer for the first time after years with Rotax just as the Austrian company seemed to have produced something special for the '87 season. Reggiani showed the engine's potential by putting the Aprilia in fifth place on the grid only to have it stop after three laps while he was in third place and right behind Mang and Cornu (who had led from the start).

While Reggiani toured back to the pits on one cylinder thanks to some plastic from the fuel tank which had lodged in a carburettor, Sarron took over third place to make it a Honda benefit. Cadalora was the first of the Yamahas in fourth

place ahead of Cardus, Lavado, Roth, Pons and Garriga.

Mang had the race under control. The old master knew exactly what he had to do and paced himself precisely, a two-second gap after five laps became five seconds after nine laps, while behind him Cornu and Sarron were more concerned with each other. It was not obvious to the observer but Sarron was having a hard time even staying with Cornu. 'I don't know what was wrong with the front tyre. Almost from the start it was sliding going into the corners. I tried to accommodate it by slowing more going in and accelerating earlier, but in the end the front slid away as I accelerated through the Sachs curve.' Sarron crashed out of a rostrum position for the second time* in three Grands Prix and was obviously furious with himself. After failing to restart the Rothmans Honda he turned and was about to walk across the track in front of Igoa, but was stopped by a marshal.

That was lap 13 of 16, and Cornu was handed an easy second place, 8½ seconds behind Mang. The crowd had their attention on the superb battle for third between Lavado, Roth, Cardus, Cadalora and Pons, while Garriga had slipped to a distant eighth, still well in front of Igoa.

Roth had worked himself into a position where he could challenge for third place and when he came into the stadium at the head of the group on lap 14 there was a huge cheer from the crowd, who appreciated the problems he was having with his shoulder even if they did not realise that Cardus was also struggling against the pain of

his injured knee. There was no cheer when the Spaniard appeared in front a lap later, but Roth kept the partisan crowd happy by being in front when it mattered.

He was quick to point out that he could only take third because his bike was so fast. 'At first I had to brake very early for the chicanes but after a while I realised that I could brake a little later if a braced myself against the tank. Cornering was still a problem but what I lost there I made up for on the straights.'

Mang also admitted that the convincing victory was not entirely his own doing. 'The bike was fast and I would be lying if my win was not made easier by my rivals' crashes.' In fifth place, Cadalora excited everyone with his infield riding, diving inside and out, passing the faster Hondas on his Marlboro Yamaha. No respecter of reputations the young Italian passed Lavado on the last few corners to relegate the World Champion to sixth on the HB Yamaha.

500 cc

Perhaps Lawson's thoughts about going gliding lingered as he chased Gardner's Honda ineffectively from the first lap. Haslam made his customary fast getaway and held second for the first lap but Lawson was soon past and faced with only the disappearing Honda in front. The Australian already had a three-second advantage at the end of lap 1 and was able to increase that at will by up to one and half seconds per lap.

Lawson pulled away from the Elf Honda comfortably enough, leaving Haslam to concern

The Rothmans Honda begins to materialise out of the haze, yet its pursuers are barely distinguishable blobs of colour still accelerating from the last chicane. While Gardner sits up and brakes for the stadium section, Lawson, Haslam, Sarron, Mamola and McElnea slipstream each other. It only took him a couple of laps to get this far ahead.

himself with Sarron. Mamola, with brake problems, made a hesitant start and had to adapt his style to them to secure fourth place before he could consider advancing.

In sixth place the second and third Marlboro Yamahas of McElnea and Taira had little trouble pulling away from the HB Hondas of Chili and Mackenzie, but Shunji Yatsushiro on his Rothmans Honda looked to be more of a threat. The Japanese ace had started badly down in fifteenth place but soon got to grips with things and by lap 8 had passed the HB bikes. By lap 10 he was in the midst of the Taira/McElnea battle, but his progress got little attention as the eyes of the crowd were following the drama at the head of the field.

Gardner's lead had grown to a handsome nine seconds by lap 7, but suddenly the Honda faltered. The broad sword was flawed: an electrical failure had caused the exhaust valve to close, so preventing the engine from revving. Lawson closed rapidly, his Bell helmet masking a broad grin. Gardner remained tucked behind the screen but the potent Honda was flaccid, the flat exhaust note leaving no-one in doubt about the cause of Gardner's reversal.

As Gardner slipped rearwards, Sarron followed and then retired with clutch failure. It had taken too much punishment off the startline thanks to the tall Hockenheim gearing. That left Lawson with a very comfortable ten-second lead over Mamola, who, by lap 12 of the 19, had worked around his brake troubles and passed Haslam. Yatsushiro was up to fourth but crashed on lap

15 as he closed on Mamola and Haslam, and tried to do too much too quickly. He took a nasty fall going onto the start-and-finish straight and suffered concussion.

By that time, Taira had opened up enough of a gap over McElnea to be sure of fourth and the only interest remaining was the contest for sixth between Chili and Mackenzie. The Scot was beaten to the line and said later that he was 'embarrassed to be on a works bike', having found the high-speed circuit hard work.

Gardner stuck grimly to the task, riding the Honda hard round the corners – almost too hard in fact, as he nearly lost it leaving the Sachs curve on lap 17 – but was rewarded with a single point for tenth as he managed to keep in front of Bruno Kneubühler and Didier de Radigues. De Radigues, with his injured shoulder, did what he could to keep the Cagiva flag flying after Roche retired on lap 5 with gear-selection problems.

The home crowd expected fireworks from Gustav Reiner on the last lap after the German had hounded Roger Burnett for the entire race, just as he had in Spain. Gustav held back, though, and took the two points for eighth instead of risking a repeat of the last-corner débâcle at Jerez.

Sidecars

The fact that Rolf Biland failed to qualify knocked the German-speaking interest out of the race. The ex-World Champion had struck trouble in every practice session and, with the engine running out of steam at the top end, Biland had

convinced himself it was a carburation problem. Later he found out the trouble was with the ignition. 'It was my fault; I just chased after one thing. It felt just like carburation but in fact the chip in my electronic ignition system was giving completely the wrong advance curve.'

Biland's non-appearance on the grid made things a good deal easier for the front-row teams of Webster and Hewitt, Michel and Fresc, and Streuer and Schnieders.

Michel effectively put himself out of contention for a win with his start, which was a disaster. As he later pointed out, clutch starts may be fine for the solos but the sidecars use the same clutches and have to drag a heavier machine and two people off the line. At the end of lap 1 he was 13th yet amazingly it took him only until lap 5 to get through to third, passing Steinhausen and Hiller who later retired.

Webster took over from the first-lap leader Streuer, but it was not until lap 9 that he started to pull away. The British crew had been half a second quicker than the reigning champions in practice, but Streuer found some extra speed for the race and pressed them most of the way. Even when Webster did get clear Streuer was able to come back to threaten him over the last two laps and there was less than a second in it at the flag.

The most exciting battle was for fourth as van Kempen and de Haas tried to fight off Abbott and Smith and Bayley and Nixon. On lap 12, Derek Bayley and Bryan Nixon crashed unhurt. It was to be their last Grand Prix as they were to have a far worse accident in the Isle of Man TT.

500 cc

19 laps, 80.15 miles/128.98 km

Place	Rider	Nat.	Machine	Laps	Time & speed	Practice time	Grid
1	Eddie Lawson	USA	Yamaha	19	40m 21.64s 119.146 mph/191.746 km/h	2m 06.55s	3
2	Randy Mamola	USA	Yamaha	19	40m 34.99s	2m 08.39s	8
3	Ron Haslam	GB	Honda	19	40m 35.54s	2m 07.03s	5
4	Tadahiko Taira	J	Yamaha	19	40m 42.23s	2m 08.83s	11
5	Rob McElnea	GB	Yamaha	19	40m 50.78s	2m 08.07s	6
6	Pier Francesco Chili	I	Honda	19	41m 07.43s	2m 08.51s	9
7	Niall Mackenzie	GB	Honda	19	41m 07.73s	2m 08.38s	7
8	Roger Burnett	GB	Honda	19	41m 16.40s	2m 09.52s	13
9	Gustav Reiner	D	Honda	19	41m 16.86s	2m 09.13s	12
10	Wayne Gardner	AUS	Honda	19	41m 37.36s	2m 04.77s	1
11	Bruno Kneubühler	CH	Honda	19	41m 43.92s	2m 11.51s	19
12	Didier de Radiguès	D	Cagiva	19	41m 44.90s	2m 11.34s	18
13	Richard Scott	NZ	Honda	19	41m 57.61s	2m 12.76s	24
14	Fabio Biliotti	I	Honda	19	41m 58.00s	2m 09.86s	14
15	Donnie McLeod	GB	Suzuki	19	42m 06.52s	2m 10.99s	16
16	Fabio Barchitta	I	Honda	18	40m 24.20s	2m 13.38s	28
17	Ari Rämö	SF	Honda	18	40m 25.08s	2m 13.18s	26
18	Marco Papa	I	Honda	18	40m 30.82s	2m 11.23s	17
19	Daniel Amatriain	E	Honda	18	40m 35.93s	2m 15.80s	35
20	Simon Buckmaster	GB	Honda	18	40m 44.29s	2m 15.00s	32
21	Gerold Fischer	D	Honda	18	40m 46.76s	2m 14.76s	31
22	Maarten Duyzers	NL	Honda	18	40m 54.78s	2m 14.42s	30
23	Steve Manley	GB	Suzuki	18	41m 00.13s	2m 15.86s	36
24	Georg-Robert Jung	D	Honda	18	41m 00.41s	2m 15.52s	34
25	Helmut Schütz	D	Honda	18	41m 31.26s	2m 15.22s	33
	Shunji Yatsushiro	J	Honda	14	DNF	2m 07.00s	4
	Marco Gentile	CH	Fior	14	DNF	2m 12.03s	22
	Christian Sarron	F	Yamaha	13	DNF	2m 06.49s	2
	Michael Rudroff	D	Honda	12	DNF	2m 16.26s	38
	Thierry Rapicault	F	Fior	10	DNF	2m 12.36s	23
	Kenny Irons	GB	Suzuki	6	DNF	2m 11.76s	20
	Raymond Roche	F	Cagiva	5	DNF	2m 08.79s	10
	Esko Kuparinen	SF	Honda	5	DNF	2m 16.12s	37
	Manfred Fischer	D	Honda	2	DNF	2m 11.87s	21
	Silvo Habat	YU	Honda	1	DNF	2m 14.02s	29
	Mike Baldwin	USA	Yamaha		DNS	2m 10.80s	15
	Alessandro Valesi	I	Honda		DNS	2m 12.82s	25
	Josef Doppler	A	Honda		DNQ	2m 16.28s	
	Peter Schleef	D	Yamaha		DNQ	2m 16.46s	
	Louis-Luc Maisto	F	Plein-Pot		DNQ	2m 16.72s	
	Wolfgang von Muralt	CH	Suzuki		DNQ	2m 16.76s	
	Rolf Äljes	D	Suzuki		DNQ	2m 18.16s	
	Hans Klingebiel	D	Suzuki		DNQ	2m 18.37s	
	Chris Bürki	CH	Honda		DNQ	2m 18.89s	
	Gerhard Vogt	D	Suzuki		DNQ	2m 19.23s	
	Henny Boermann	NL	Assmex		DNQ	2m 19.30s	
	Pavol Dekánek	CS	Suzuki		DNQ	2m 21.39s	
	Tony Carey	IRL	Suzuki		DNQ	2m 26.38s	
	Andreas Leuthe	L	Honda		DNQ	2m 26.46s	
	Larry Moreno Vacondio	YV	Honda		DNQ	2m 28.44s	
	Bohumil Stasa	CS	Honda		DNQ	2m 41.49s	

Fastest lap: Gardner, 2m 05.50s, 121.001 mph/194.732 km/h (record).
Previous record: Freddie Spencer, USA (Honda), 2m 09.16s, 117.58 mph/189.23 km/h (1982).

World Championship: 1 Mamola, 32; **2** Gardner, 28; **3** Lawson, 27; **4** Haslam, 26; **5** Taira, 17; **6** Chili, 16; **7** Mackenzie, 12; **8** Ito, 10; **9** Burnett, 8; **10** Schwantz and McElnea, 6; **12** Kawasaki, 4; **13** Yatsushiro, 3; **14** Katayama and Reiner, 2; **16** Roche and Scott, 1.

250 cc

16 laps, 67.49 miles/108.62 km

Place	Rider	Nat.	Machine	Laps	Time & speed	Practice time	Grid
1	Anton Mang	D	Honda	16	36m 05.60s 112.196 mph/180.561 km/h	2m 13.46s	2
2	Jacques Cornu	CH	Honda	16	36m 14.09s	2m 14.51s	3
3	Reinhold Roth	D	Honda	16	36m 14.74s	2m 13.33s	1
4	Carlos Cardus	E	Honda	16	36m 14.87s	2m 16.17s	10
5	Luca Cadalora	I	Yamaha	16	36m 15.21s	2m 15.75s	8
6	Carlos Lavado	YV	Yamaha	16	36m 15.35s	2m 14.68s	4
7	Alfonso Pons	E	Honda	16	36m 15.91s	2m 18.30s	16
8	Juan Garriga	E	Yamaha	16	36m 30.25s	2m 15.74s	7
9	Patrick Igoa	F	Yamaha	16	36m 55.63s	2m 17.43s	13
10	Maurizio Vitali	I	Garelli	16	37m 11.16s	2m 17.05s	12
11	Hans Lindner	A	Honda	16	37m 12.39s	2m 20.01s	37
12	Stéphane Mertens	B	Honda	16	37m 12.91s	2m 19.46s	30
13	Andreas Preining	A	Rotax	16	37m 13.55s	2m 19.25s	28
14	Helmut Bradl	D	Honda	16	37m 13.55s	2m 18.25s	15
15	Jean-François Baldé	F	Defi	16	37m 24.94s	2m 19.91s	35
16	Engelbert Neumair	A	Helten	16	37m 28.27s	2m 19.53s	31
17	Konrad Hefele	D	Honda	16	37m 28.91s	2m 20.07s	38
18	Jean Foray	F	Chevallier	16	37m 29.43s	2m 19.14s	27
19	René Delaby	B	Yamaha	16	37m 29.72s	2m 18.93s	25
20	Bruno Bonhuil	F	Honda	16	37m 33.92s	2m 19.79s	33
21	Josef Hutter	A	Honda	16	37m 34.48s	2m 18.35s	18
22	Jean-Michel Mattioli	F	Honda	16	37m 38.33s	2m 19.12s	26
23	Harald Eckl	D	Honda	16	37m 39.09s	2m 18.40s	19
24	Jean-Philippe Ruggia	F	Yamaha	16	37m 47.99s	2m 18.68s	21
25	Alberto Rota	I	Honda	16	37m 48.24s	2m 19.57s	32
	Hermann Holder	D	Seufert	15	DNF	2m 18.91s	24
	Guy Bertin	F	Honda	14	DNF	2m 18.82s	23
	Dominique Sarron	F	Honda	12	DNF	2m 15.50s	6
	Ezio Gianola	I	Honda	9	DNF	2m 19.98s	36
	Donnie McLeod	GB	EMC	9	DNF	2m 18.77s	22
	Jean-Louis Guignabodet	F	MIG	6	DNF	2m 19.38s	29
	Gary Cowan	GB	Honda	5	DNF	2m 18.61s	20
	Loris Reggiani	I	Aprilia	4	DNF	2m 15.42s	5
	Stefan Klabacher	A	Schafleitner	1	DNF	2m 18.32s	17
	Xavier Cardelus	AND	Kobas	1	DNF	2m 19.90s	34
	Jochen Schmid	D	Yamaha	1	DNF	2m 18.03s	14
	Martin Wimmer	D	Yamaha		DNS	2m 15.85s	9
	Manfred Herweh	D	Yamaha		DNS	2m 16.91s	11
	Bernard Hänggeli	CH	Yamaha		DNQ	2m 20.26s	
	Alain Bronec	F	Honda		DNQ	2m 20.45s	
	Rainer Gerwin	D	Bakker		DNQ	2m 20.58s	
	Herbert Besendörfer	D	Honda		DNQ	2m 20.62s	
	Urs Lüzi	CH	Honda		DNQ	2m 20.83s	
	Stefano Caracchi	I	Honda		DNQ	2m 21.04s	
	Frank Wagner	D	Honda		DNQ	2m 21.40s	
	Massimo Matteoni	I	Honda		DNQ	2m 21.43s	
	Nigel Bosworth	GB	Yamaha		DNQ	2m 21.45s	
	Herbert Hauf	D	Honda		DNQ	2m 21.46s	
	Reinhard Strack	D	Honda		DNQ	2m 21.68s	
	Nedy Crotta	CH	Armstrong		DNQ	2m 21.83s	
	Hervé Duffard	F	Honda		DNQ	2m 21.93s	
	Fausto Ricci	I	Honda		DNQ	2m 22.60s	
	Kevin Mitchell	GB	Honda		DNQ	2m 23.02s	
	Siegfried Minich	A	Honda		DNQ	2m 23.16s	
	Ivan Palazzese	YV	Honda		DNQ	2m 24.00s	
	Rudi Gächter	CH	Yamaha		DNQ	2m 24.10s	
	Roland Busch	D	Honda		DNQ	2m 24.48s	
	Robin Appleyard	GB	Honda		DNQ	2m 25.03s	
	Tony Rogers	GB	Yamaha		DNQ	2m 28.64s	

Fastest lap: Lavado, 2m 14.06s, 113.275 mph/182.298 km/h (record).
Previous record: Hans Lindner, A (Rotax), 2m 18.45s, 109.68 mph/176.51 km/h (1986).

World Championship: 1 Roth, 23; **2** Wimmer, 21; **3** Pons, Garriga, Cadalora and Mang, 18; **7** Cornu, 17; **8** Kobayashi, 15; **9** Igoa, 12; **10** Shimuzu, Sarron and Cardus, 8; **13** Lavado, 6; **14** Ruggia, 4; **15** Taguchi, 2; **16** Yamamoto and Vitali, 1.

Left: **Sarron's bike has fallen but Cornu continues towards second place on the Parisienne Honda.**

Right: **Hello and goodbye ... Freddie Spencer made one of his comebacks at Hockenheim but before anyone could get used to him being around he left again, injured once more. How does he get insurance?**

Far right: **McElnea leads Chili, Taira and Roche. He had a steady ride, not inspired but it helped him on the road back from a low level of confidence after Suzuka and Jerez.**

125 cc

14 laps, 59.06 miles/95.04 km

Place	Rider	Nat.	Machine	Laps	Time & speed	Practice time	Grid
1	Fausto Gresini	I	Garelli	14	33m 40.31s 105.231 mph/ 169.352 km/h	2m 24.75s	1
2	August Auinger	A	MBA	14	33m 44.21s	2m 25.65s	2
3	Bruno Casanova	I	Garelli	14	33m 45.32s	2m 25.76s	4
4	Pier Paolo Bianchi	I	MBA	14	33m 58.49s	2m 25.69s	3
5	Domenico Brigaglia	I	AGV	14	34m 13.10s	2m 26.50s	5
6	Andrés Marin Sánchez	E	Ducados	14	34m 15.73s	2m 28.66s	7
7	Thierry Feuz	CH	LCR	14	34m 39.24s	2m 28.15s	6
8	Jussi Hautaniemi	SF	LCR	14	34m 40.18s	2m 34.00s	31
9	Adolf Stadler	D	MBA	14	34m 43.98s	2m 31.42s	19
10	Lucio Pietroniro	B	MBA	14	34m 44.31s	2m 30.84s	14
11	Mike Leitner	A	Bartol	14	34m 44.44s	2m 30.99s	15
12	Willy Pérez	RA	Zanella	14	34m 51.70s	2m 29.74s	10
13	Johnny Wickström	SF	Tunturi	14	34m 52.32s	2m 29.77s	11
14	Paul Bordes	F	MBA	14	34m 53.19s	2m 31.61s	20
15	Olivier Liegeois	B	Assmex	14	34m 53.52s	2m 29.46s	9
16	Ivan Troisi	YV	MBA	14	35m 10.94s	2m 31.83s	21
17	Norbert Peschke	D	LCR	14	35m 16.68s	2m 29.04s	8
18	Peter Sommer	CH	Hussaut	14	35m 23.92s	2m 31.15s	16
19	Håkan Olsson	S	Starol	14	35m 35.60s	2m 32.46s	25
20	Ton Spek	NL	MBA	14	35m 35.61s	2m 33.83s	30
21	Robin Milton	GB	MBA	14	35m 35.90s	2m 33.76s	29
22	Robert Zwidl	A	MBA	14	36m 01.49s	2m 34.99s	36
23	Fernando Gonzales	E	Cobas	14	36m 02.87s	2m 32.19s	23
24	Thomas Møller-Pedersen	DK	MBA	13	33m 41.62s	2m 34.06s	32
25	Robin Appleyard	GB	MBA	13	33m 54.14s	2m 33.32s	27
26	Ezio Gianola	I	Honda	12	35m 31.60s	2m 30.01s	12
	Bady Hassaine	DZ	MBA	11	DNF	2m 34.82s	35
	Alfred Waibel	D	Waibel	8	DNF	2m 31.22s	17
	Hubert Abold	D	Honda	5	DNF	2m 34.09s	33
	Esa Kytölä	SF	MBA	3	DNF	2m 32.97s	26
	Karl Dauer	A	MBA	3	DNF	2m 32.03s	22
	Jean-Claude Selini	F	ABF	3	DNF	2m 31.41s	18
	Dirk Hafeneger	D	MBA	2	DNF	2m 34.69s	34
	Jarmo Piepponen	SF	MBA	2	DNF	2m 35.04s	37
	Christian le Badezet	F	MBA	1	DNF	2m 32.21s	24
	Peter Baláž	CS	MBA	1	DNF	2m 33.71s	28
	Paolo Casoli	I	AGV		DNS	2m 30.80s	13
	Janez Pintar	YU	MBA		DNQ	2m 35.23s	
	Gastone Grassetti	I	MBA		DNQ	2m 35.25s	
	Jacques Hutteau	F	MBA		DNQ	2m 35.27s	
	Erich Zürn	D	MBA		DNQ	2m 35.42s	
	Wilco Zeelenberg	NL	Casal		DNQ	2m 35.53s	
	Claudio Macciotta	I	MBA		DNQ	2m 35.83s	
	Ernst Himmelsbach	D	MBA		DNQ	2m 35.96s	
	Jan Eggens	NL	LCR		DNQ	2m 36.61s	
	Ian McConnachie	GB	MBA		DNQ	2m 37.41s	
	Wilhelm Lücke	D	MBA		DNQ	2m 38.54s	
	Helmut Hovenga	D	Seel		DNQ	2m 38.84s	
	Allan Scott	USA	EMC		DNQ	2m 39.91s	
	Heinz Litz	D	MBA		DNQ	2m 40.60s	
	José Grau	E	MBA		DNQ	2m 40.90s	
	Steve Mason	GB	MBA		DNQ	2m 41.09s	
	Klaus Huber	D	MBA		DNQ	2m 42.22s	
	Gary Dickinson	GB	MBA		DNQ	2m 43.21s	
	Robert Hmeljak	YU	MBA		DNQ	2m 44.61s	
	Manuel Hernandez	E	Benetti		DNQ	2m 44.83s	
	Manfred Braun	B	MBA		DNQ	2m 49.52s	
	Uwe Mahl	D	Rimotu		DNQ	2m 55.89s	

Fastest lap: Gresini, 2m 22.45s, 106.603 mph/171.561 km/h.
Lap record: Luca Cadalora, I (Garelli), 2m 22.14s, 106.837 mph/171.937 km/h (1986).

World Championship: 1 Gresini, 30; **2** Brigaglia and Casanova, 18; **4** Auinger, 16; **5** Bianchi, 14; **6** Casoli, 10; **7** Feuz, 7; **8** Gianola and Sánchez, 5; **10** Hautaniemi, 3; **11** Macciotta and Stadler, 2; **13** Leitner and Pietroniro, 1.

80 cc

11 laps, 46.40 miles/74.67 km

Place	Rider	Nat.	Machine	Laps	Time & speed	Practice time	Grid
1	Gerhard Waibel	D	Krauser	11	28m 08.32s 98.940 mph/ 159.228 km/h	2m 32.47s	1
2	Jorge Martinez	E	Derbi	11	28m 08.55s	2m 33.63s	3
3	Stefan Dörflinger	CH	Krauser	11	28m 08.87s	2m 32.83s	2
4	Ian McConnachie	GB	Krauser	11	28m 51.70s	2m 36.13s	4
5	Manuel Herreros	E	Derbi	11	29m 06.33s	2m 36.19s	5
6	Jörg Seel	D	Seel	11	29m 06.48s	2m 39.90s	16
7	Heinz Paschen	D	Casal	11	29m 06.96s	2m 40.09s	17
8	Günter Schirnhofer	D	Krauser	11	29m 07.22s	2m 39.72s	14
9	Michael Gschwander	D	Seel	11	29m 07.48s	2m 41.23s	18
10	Ralf Waldmann	D	ERK	11	29m 12.93s	2m 38.15s	9
11	Alexandre Barros	BR	Arbizu	11	29m 19.35s	2m 39.89s	15
12	Luis M. Reyes	COL	Autisa	11	29m 19.89s	2m 36.37s	6
13	Hubert Abold	D	Krauser	11	29m 21.39s	2m 39.66s	12
14	Paolo Priori	I	Krauser	11	29m 23.26s	2m 38.63s	10
15	Bert Smit	NL	Minarelli	11	29m 42.80s	2m 43.41s	27
16	Juan Ramon Bolart	E	Cobas	11	29m 42.95s	2m 39.69s	13
17	René Dünki	CH	LCR	11	30m 11.84s	2m 43.60s	30
18	Wilco Zeelenberg	NL	JVM	11	30m 12.48s	2m 43.60s	29
19	Jos van Dongen	NL	Krauser	11	30m 12.87s	2m 44.26s	36
20	Alojz Pavlic	YU	Seel	11	30m 38.16s	2m 43.03s	26
21	Károly Juhász	H	Krauser	10	28m 20.27s	2m 37.17s	7
22	Serge Julin	B	Casal	10	28m 48.75s	2m 43.73s	31
	Richard Bay	D	Ziegler	10	DNF	2m 42.51s	24
	Josef Fischer	A	Krauser	9	DNF	2m 38.11s	8
	Reiner Scheidhauer	D	Seel	8	DNF	2m 39.60s	11
	Salvatore Milano	I	Krauser	8	DNF	2m 42.30s	23
	Raimo Lipponen	SF	Krauser	8	DNF	2m 41.84s	21
	Stefan Prein	D	HRC	7	DNF	2m 42.62s	25
	Paul Bordes	F	RB	6	DNF	2m 44.00s	33
	Thomas Engl	D	ESCH	6	DNF	2m 42.24s	19
	Rainer Kunz	D	LCR	5	DNF	2m 42.05s	22
	Peter Öttl	D	Krauser	5	DNF	2m 44.17s	35
	Felix Rodriguez	E	Cobas	1	DNF	2m 45.00s	37
	Francisco Torrontegui	E	Arbizu	1	DNF	2m 43.96s	32
	Janez Pintar	YU	Eberhardt	0	DNF	2m 43.51s	28
	Theo Timmer	NL	JVM		DNS	2m 41.77s	20
	Matthias Ehinger	D	LCR		DNS	2m 44.10s	34
	Hans Koopman	NL	Ziegler		DNQ	2m 45.22s	
	Reiner Koster	CH	LCR		DNQ	2m 45.33s	
	Stuart Edwards	GB	Casal		DNQ	2m 45.41s	
	Hagen Klein	D	Hess		DNQ	2m 45.67s	
	Stefan Bragger	CH	FFR		DNQ	2m 46.11s	
	Jacques Bernard	B	Huvo		DNQ	2m 46.35s	
	Roland Busch	D	Keifer		DNQ	2m 46.47s	
	Chris Baert	B	Seel		DNQ	2m 47.19s	
	Michael Knipp	D	Casal		DNQ	2m 50.68s	
	Petra Gschwander	D	Casal		DNQ	2m 51.43s	
	Olivier Friedrich	D	Ziegler		DNQ	2m 51.48s	
	Terho Kauhanen	SF	Casal		DNQ	3m 01.21s	
	Erich Reuberger	A	Hummel		DNQ	3m 57.63s	

Fastest lap: Martinez, 2m 31.23s, 100.414 mph/161.601 km/h.
Lap record: Stefan Dörflinger, CH (Krauser), 2m 30.72s, 100.755 mph/162.149 km/h (1986).

World Championship: 1 Martinez, 27; **2** Waibel, 23; **3** Criville and McConnachie, 12; **5** Herreros, 11; **6** Miralles and Dörflinger, 10; **8** Reyes, 6; **9** Seel, 5; **10** Paschen, 4; **11** Bay and Schirnhofer, 3; **13** Fischer and Gschwander, 2; **15** Abold and Waldmann, 1.

Sidecars

14 laps, 59.06 miles/95.04 km

Place	Driver & passenger	Nat.	Machine	Laps	Time & speed	Practice time	Grid
1	Steve Webster / Tony Hewitt	GB GB	LCR- Yamaha	14	31m 56.10s 110.954 mph/ 178.563 km/h	2m 15.67s	1
2	Egbert Streuer / Bernard Schnieders	NL NL	LCR- Yamaha	14	31m 57.02s	2m 16.14s	3
3	Alain Michel / Jean-Marc Fresc	F F	LCR- Krauser	14	32m 19.16s	2m 15.85s	2
4	Theo van Kempen / Gerardus de Haas	NL NL	LCR- Yamaha	14	32m 54.37s	2m 17.75s	5
5	Steve Abbott / Shaun Smith	GB GB	Windle- Yamaha	14	32m 54.77s	2m 20.56s	10
6	René Progin / Yves Hunziker	CH CH	Seymaz- Yamaha	14	33m 24.68s	2m 19.76s	9
7	Masato Kumano / Markus Fahrni	J CH	LCR- Yamaha	14	33m 28.47s	2m 21.72s	11
8	Pascal Larratte / Jacques Corbier	F F	LCR- Yamaha	14	33m 38.12s	2m 23.09s	15
9	Yoshisada Kumagaya / Brian Barlow	J GB	Windle- Yamaha	14	33m 42.88s	2m 26.04s	21
10	Fritz Stölzle / Hubert Stölzle	D D	LCR- Yamaha	14	33m 45.63s	2m 23.41s	17
11	Erwin Weber / Eckart Rösinger	D D	LCR- Yamaha	14	33m 51.66s	2m 22.78s	14
12	Luigi Casagrande / Adolf Hänni	CH CH	LCR- Yamaha	14	34m 08.53s	2m 23.17s	16
13	Barry Brindley / Grahame Rose	GB GB	Windle- Yamaha	14	34m 23.26s	2m 26.09s	22
14	Alfred Heck / Marlow Sturm	D D	LCR- Yamaha	13	32m 44.83s	2m 29.33s	29
15	Herbert Prügl / Christian Parzer	A A	Homa	13	32m 49.68s	2m 27.41s	27
16	Egon Schons / Andreas Schröder	D D	LCR- Yamaha	13	33m 14.84s	2m 30.57s	31
17	Christian Graf / Kurt Rothenbühler	CH CH	LCR- Yamaha	13	33m 32.73s	2m 26.73s	24
18	Reinhard Link / Walter Link	D D	LCR- Yamaha	13	34m 12.73s	2m 30.14s	30
	Derek Bayley / Bryan Nixon	GB GB	Windle- Krauser	11	DNF	2m 19.02s	6
	Rolf Steinhausen / Bruno Hiller	D D	Eigenbau	10	DNF	2m 19.24s	7
	Gary Thomas / Geoff White	GB GB	LCR- Yamaha	8	DNF	2m 26.88s	25
	Dennis Bingham / Julia Bingham	GB GB	LCR- Yamaha	8	DNF	2m 24.63s	19
	Derek Jones / Simon Birchall	GB GB	LCR- Yamaha	7	DNF	2m 24.36s	18
	Ivan Nigrowski / Frédéric Meunier	F F	Seymaz- JPX	7	DNF	2m 27.27s	26
	Bernd Scherer / Wolfgang Gess	D D	BSR- Eigenbau	6	DNF	2m 21.88s	12
	Marcus Egloff / Urs Egloff	CH CH	LCR- Seel	6	DNF	2m 19.73s	8
	Clive Stirrat / Simon Prior	GB GB	BLR- Yamaha	6	DNF	2m 28.46s	28
	Graham Gleeson / Peter Brown	NZ GB	Cagiva	2	DNF	2m 25.80s	20
	Wolfgang Stropek / Hans-Peter Demling	A A	LCR- Krauser	1	DNF	2m 26.53s	23
	Alfred Zurbrugg / Andreas Racke	CH D	LCR- Yamaha	1	DNF	2m 16.53s	4
	Ray Gardner / Tony Strevens	GB GB	LCR- Yamaha		DNS	2m 22.74s	13
	Dave Hallam / Robert Parker	GB GB	LCR- Yamaha		DNQ	2m 31.19s	
	Judd Drew / Chris Plant	GB GB	BLR- Yamaha		DNQ	2m 32.14s	
	Rudolf Reinhard / Karin Sterzenbach	D D	LCR- Yamaha		DNQ	2m 32.54s	
	Walter Eggerstorfer / Max Meyer	D D	LCR- Yamaha		DNQ	2m 33.15s	
	Axel von Berg / Wolfgang Riedl	D D	Busch		DNQ	2m 33.22s	
	Franz Wagner / David-Burcin Baydar	D D	Windle- Yamaha		DNQ	2m 34.17s	
	Vince Biggs / Laurie Genova	GB AUS	LCR- Yamaha		DNQ	2m 35.38s	
	Rolf Biland / Kurt Waltisperg	CH CH	Krauser		DNQ	2m 36.20s	
	Werner Kraus / Oliver Schuster	D D	LCR- Yamaha		DNQ	2m 41.53s	

Fastest lap: Webster, 2m 15.57s, 112.104 mph/180.268 km/h.
Lap record: Rolf Biland/Kurt Waltisperg, CH/CH (Krauser), 2m 14.61s, 112.814 mph/181.556 km/h (1986).

World Championship: 1 Webster, 30; **2** Michel, 22; **3** Abbott and Streuer, 12; **5** Zurbrugg, 10; **6** Bayley and van Kempen, 8; **8** Progin, 7; **9** Jones, Kumagaya and Kumano, 5; **12** Egloff, 4; **13** Larratte, 3; **14** Stölzle, 1.

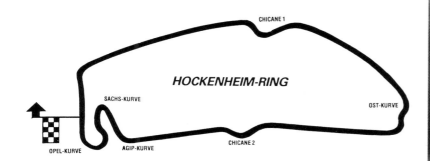

HOCKENHEIM-RING

CHICANE 1
SACHS-KURVE
OST-KURVE
OPEL-KURVE
AGIP-KURVE
CHICANE 2

Both Roth and Wimmer sustained injuries during practice. The HB rider *(right)* **bravely took third place in the 250 cc race despite a broken collarbone, but Wimmer non-started after damaging his hand and ankle** *(far right).*

Below: **Concentration . . . no more thoughts of gliders, of the new boat waiting at home in California . . . nothing but the tarmac for 40 minutes and 21.64 seconds.**

Gran Premio delle
NAZIONI

Wayne Gardner admitted he was enjoying life. 'Every time I see a Yamaha I wait for a straight and blast past it, just to remind them how I felt last year.' He had at last admitted that the Honda was superior. It may have been a small admission but it was significant now because of the professional shield Gardner was erecting around him. That professionalism produced quotes like, 'I wasn't really trying; I could have gone faster but there were some other riders in the way', or 'I was surprised I went so quickly.' As Dave Petersen recalled, referring to his days as Superbike Champion in South Africa, 'I used to say that after a practice lap where I had bounced off every kerb and lost the front or the back on every corner.'

Gardner was strengthening this aura of unbeatability by distancing himself from the masses. He was a man apart, in his Spencer-sized motorhome, yet he remained very approachable in a directly professional manner,

friendly even, and always ready to give interviews or opinions on how things were going. Yet the views and opinions seemed too well considered and offered for the most part with little feeling, as though Gardner had his mind so firmly fixed on winning the championship that the real man from Wollangong would remain hidden until the championship was won.

None the less, the facade could not always be maintained, and it vanished after hours and in front of his mechanics. Before timed practice started in Monza his team let their hair down and, like the others, Gardner got drunk. He had a hangover for two days but he still performed faultlessly. The Australian still had some way to go before distancing himself as far from normal paddock life as Freddie Spencer had done.

Now Spencer had distanced himself from Grand Prix life so completely that he was not there at all, despite familiar rumours of his arrival being fuelled by the summoning of the

Newell from Belgium. The hired hand drove through the night, but the bus stood unused in the paddock as Spencer once more stayed away, to confound HRC. Honda had thought they would save money by not sending his technicians from Japan until Spencer was actually at the race track. Thus they had stayed at home until he was sighted at Hockenheim, then jumped on the first available flight. Their arrival coincided with his departure to the States. As it was too expensive for them to return to Japan only to fly on to Monza for the following weekend, they waited, this time in vain.

Honda had Gardner and needed no-one else as long as the bike was reliable. Finding what had caused the NSR to lose power so disastrously in Germany led to some sleepless nights for the mechanics as nothing seemed to be physically wrong with the machine. After the race in Germany the exhaust valve that had remained shut for the second half of the race opened and

closed perfectly. Checked electrically the control box and motor appeared faultless, and certainly nothing mechanical had been broken.

For the first practice session Gardner was sent out on the bike just as it had been raced the previous weekend, and still nothing showed up. Eventually, the electronics were returned to Japan for further investigation and the team was left with the rather unsatisfactory conclusion that they could do no more than cross their fingers and hope it would not happen again.

That apart, Gardner was obviously pleased with the way the season was going, and not only because the bike was fast. 'It is handling very well. In fact, we have no problems and I am riding the bike at Monza just as we raced it at Hockenheim – no changes to the suspension at all – and that just shows what a good bike this year's is. With the old one we were always changing the suspension and never got it right; hardly anything we did had the effect it should have had.'

With Mike Baldwin and Martin Wimmer in hospital their teams had spare machines available. Names were bandied around with indecent haste for the ride on the Lucky Strike bike, but it seemed more likely that Wimmer's machines would remain unused until his return – possibly as early as Austria.

Surprisingly, it was Wimmer who was temporarily replaced for the Italian Grand Prix, so Massimo Messere had the use of one of his machines. The choice of Messere, the European Champion, surprised many and served little purpose. He was unlikely to be fast enough to generate publicity for the sponsors or to help test the machines for Cadalora. In the end, the unfortunate Italian fell off in the final session, broke his shoulder and could not race.

While the Lucky Strike team tried to get around the restriction placed on them by the sponsorship contract, which stated both riders were to be American, Kenny Roberts took a short step out of retirement to take part in Grand Prix practice for the first time since 1983. He rode during Friday's practice and recorded the thirteenth-fastest time in his single session. It was the third session for all the other riders and he was sixth-fastest compared with their first session times.

Roberts was not there merely to impress: he was helping Mamola test the Dunlop tyres in the absence of injured Mike Baldwin. 'I was not trying for a fast time, and I wasn't interested in where I'd qualify. I went out to help with the test programme and I am not trying to prove that I can still go faster than the other guys.

'It was kind of neat to be on a racing bike again. At first I couldn't see the braking markers. It takes time for your eyes and brain to adjust to the perspective of rushing along at 300 km/h. By the end of the session I could see where I was going.'

Roberts only did the single session and other riders took the opportunity to see what the old master could teach them. 'It was like a Kenny Roberts riding school out there', reported Gardner. 'Half the field were following him.'

'He came past when I was warming up some tyres', said Lawson, 'and he wasn't hanging around. He had the back end squirming good out of the second Lesmo and into the next chicane he really flicked her in. There is no doubt he can still do it.'

Roberts had no intention of racing, though. 'There is no way you can race unless you are 100 per cent fit and I am not, so I just wouldn't be able to keep the pace up for the whole race.' Speculation about what sort of time Roberts might do with a full day of practice remained just guesswork because he watched from the pit wall as Lawson tried to get closer to Gardner's best time. In the last fifteen minutes of practice Lawson put in a big effort and got within six-tenths of Gardner's lap, only to have the Australian axe nearly a second off his previous best.

125 cc

Run on Saturday this might have been Bruno Casanova's chance to show that he was equal to Garelli team-mate Fausto Gresini, as the younger team member was fastest in practice by two-tenths of a second. But the ex-champion was to prove that it takes more than a quick lap time to win a Grand Prix.

Like many others, Auinger has cause to be thankful for clutch starts and no longer has races spoilt by being slow off the line. This time he led at the end of the initial lap with Bianchi tucked into his slipstream and the two Garellis just astern.

Everyone changed places through a hectic lap 2 and Domenico Brigaglia brought the AGV MBA into the picture. Gresini took the lead from Bianchi, Casanova, Brigaglia and Auinger, but they were not getting away from the rest of the field because Andrés Marín Sánchez, Jussi Hautaniemi and Lucio Pietroniro tagged on to their tail.

Gresini continued to lead with Casanova and Auinger following his every move. As usual, their pace was too much for the rest of the field and even with the good slipstreaming possibilities at Monza, Brigaglia and company lost touch on lap 5. Once that happened the leading trio quickly pulled away and Brigaglia was able to leave Sánchez and Bianchi to fight it out for the rest of the race.

Hautaniemi got the better of Pietroniro after six laps and the pair of them had lonely rides to the finish. They were both well ahead of newcomer Corrado Catalano, who spent almost the entire race in ninth place, having pulled away from Adi Stadler. The German slipped back to be consumed by a four-way battle for the last point, and on the concluding lap Olivier Liegeois did just enough to get tenth.

Casanova put in a fastest lap over half a second quicker than his practice time and shaved over a second off Gresini's lap record, but the team captain could obviously lead at will and Casanova could do no more than follow him across the line with Auinger third.

Right: **Mamola tells Roberts and Sinclair. No-one is more lucid in their description of what happens to them on a racing motor cycle and no-one knows better what to do with the information than those who listen.**

Niall Mackenzie prepares for action.

80 cc

Monza should have seen McConnachie return to his 1986 form. He had been amazing through the chicanes that season but now that form eluded him. 'I always found the chicanes easy. I don't ride round them using all the road; I just go from one apex to the next in almost a straight line and flick it round the corner. But I still am not very happy with the bike and I just can't ride like I did last year.' To make things worse, the British rider fell off in the Sunday morning warm-up session and later suspected that the bike must have sucked in some dirt because it would not run properly in the race; he retired on lap 3.

At the front of the field it was business as usual, with the red Derbis against the white Krausers. At first it was Waibel, Martínez and Herreros, but Dörflinger was climbing quickly through the field after making a mess of the start. By lap 3 he was fifth, with Jörg Seel who had made some of the early running still in front of him. It took Dörflinger until lap 6 to get right with the leaders and the foursome then put on a

good display for the crowd.

The pace was fierce and Waibel very nearly lost his Krauser completely, forcing him to take to the grass at the Parabolica. He did well to regain control, getting back on the track in a distant eleventh place. From that point, Aspar looked to hold an advantage over Dörflinger and Herreros, with three men contesting fourth – Hubert Abold, Seel and Károly Juhász from Hungary. Waibel never really recovered from the excursion onto the grass and could only claim a single point by getting the better of Ascareggi and Zeelenberg on the final lap.

250 cc

The '86 race had been a classic two-man struggle between Mang and Lavado that was decided only on the last corner as the German virtually forced Lavado to back off by swinging in front of him as the pair approached the Parabolica.

Mang can be a hard man to ride with and this year seven men contested the lead, even if the final lap was decided between just Mang and Roth in apparent fairness. Carlos Cardus led initially, only to have his Ducados Honda seize on lap 2. It ran again but he had dropped well behind and it required a lot of work to get back in the points.

The commentator hardly noticed because he was shouting 'Loris! Loris!' as Reggiani took the lead on the Aprilia on lap 3. The crowd loved it and the commentator had them jumping up and down as he described every move their hero made. There was a groan as Roth took over with Sarron behind, and the Italian slipped to third ahead of Mang, Cornu, Pons and Lavado.

It was not long before Reggiani was in front again, however, and after lap 6 the commentator was screaming that he had recorded a new 'record de la pista'. The spectators were thrilled and the commentator neglected to mention later that Sarron improved on this time.

Roth was once more enjoying having a fast bike and even though his shoulder was still painful it had at least been operated on after the German Grand Prix and was a good deal stronger. For the most part he was able to keep Reggiani back in second place, but the lead changed frequently. Mang was in front on lap 9 when a groan came from the loudspeakers . . . Reggiani had cruised to a halt with ignition failure.

Understandably, Reggiani was inconsolable; after all, it was Italy – Monza – and he had been leading on an Italian machine even if it did have an Austrian motor. At first he shut himself in his motorhome but later commented that he must be one of the most unlucky riders. He certainly seemed a candidate, having suffered injury and disappointment so many times.

The commentator settled down to report matters of marginal interest as Mang led Roth, Sarron and Cornu. Pons and Lavado were always in the picture but just weren't able to get among the leading four. The World Champion later complained that he could not pass any of the Hondas out of their slipstream, even when he

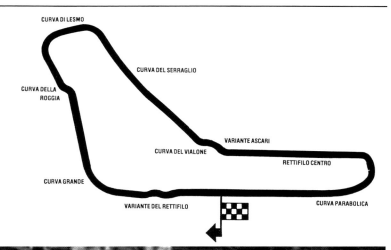

came out of the corner faster, yet they could pass him without even using his slipstream.

By lap 10, Cardus had climbed back to seventh and passed Igoa on the Sonauto Gauloises Yamaha. Behind him Maurizio Vitali on the Garelli (growing more impressive by the week) was locked in battle with Guy Bertin, working wonders with a private Honda.

Well out of the picture was Luca Cadalora on the Marlboro Yamaha. He was obviously struggling and down in eleventh place, only just able to beat Stefano Caracchi on the Rotax-engined Gazzaniga.

As the 18-lap race ran towards its close, Mang and Roth continued to swap places at the head of the field, but Sarron and Cornu were right behind and the Frenchman especially looked capable of threatening their lead. He was probably considering that it was better to get some points for third place than risk his third fall of the season. He had at least found the Honda a much better proposition with a 3.25 inch front rim than he had with the standard 3.5. He blamed the wide rim for his fall in Germany, which prompted him to copy Mang's move to the narrower wheel that gave the front tyre a better profile.

Mang was in front at the flag, with Roth saying he would not force things and would win a Grand Prix when the time came. Cornu had to settle for fourth, finding the other Hondas fast; even though Lavado was fifth half-way round the last lap, Pons passed him before the line, putting Hondas in the first five places.

500 cc

Despite the grim outlook, Lawson was determined to do what he could to stop Gardner and, like team-mate McElnea, took the trouble to pull into the pits half-way through the morning warm-up session so that he could swap the front tyre round and make sure it was scrubbed on both sides. Gardner probably did the same thing, being fully aware that Monza has few left-handers so the tyre would require working on that side if you wanted to push it hard everywhere from the first lap.

Pushing the psychology a little further, the Californian had a tyre warmer fitted to the front after the sighting lap to make sure the rubber was well warmed through even before the warm-up lap got under way. This was a slight risk to have taken as the regulations forbid any work on the machine between the sighting and warm-up laps. Lawson's idea was to see if he could push Gardner hard enough in the opening few laps so that he would make a mistake.

Lawson realised that he was not going to win a straight race with Gardner if the pattern of practice was followed. The Australian was equally aware of the situation, so he didn't get drawn into first-lap battle. He waited while Haslam led off the line and Lawson took the lead on the first lap, then he calmly motored past the Yamaha and set about providing himself with a comfortable lead as Lawson settled down to accept second.

Haslam was fast at first but quickly dropped

back, stiff and sore from a practice crash that ended with the Elf Honda landing on top of him. While Haslam slipped to seventh behind Taira, third became the most exciting struggle of the race between Mamola, Sarron and McElnea.

The all-Yamaha battle was an evenly matched affair although both Sarron and McElnea claimed that Mamola's bike had the edge. Mamola held on to third while McElnea and Sarron swapped places just behind him and Taira began to close in. At one point Haslam looked in danger of being absorbed by the eighth-place contest between Chili, Roche and Mackenzie, but half-way through the race he overcame his discomfort and started to advance again.

One of the best rides came from Kevin Schwantz who had been left struggling with a semi-welded clutch on the line. 'The bike was gassed up so bad that it took a whole lap to clear. Then it was good, though – as fast as anything I came across except Mackenzie's four.'

Yatsushiro pulled out after only five laps, still affected by the concussion he had suffered at Hockenheim, whilst twelfth was being fought over by the usual pairing of Gustav Reiner and Roger Burnett until the Hein Gericke Honda stopped on lap 18.

Gardner was happy to extend his lead by half a second or a few tenths depending on how much trouble the back-markers were; Lawson just had to suffer the frustration. Taira was among the third-place battle by lap 14, and as he had closed on them without apparent difficulty it seemed reasonable that he might get through. He tried, but just as Haslam also arrived to make it a five-way contest the Japanese ran off the track at the last chicane and dropped well behind in

seventh place.

That broke up the group a little. McElnea was on Mamola's tail, with Sarron and Haslam a few lengths behind. Coming onto the last lap McElnea realised what he had to do. 'The only place I could pass him with a slim chance of being in front at the flag was at the last chicane. I knew that he would pass me again down the back straight but I could get in front at the Parabolica even if he would then probably pass me again on the run-in to the line.

'I went inside him at the first left-hander then drove round the longer right. As I flicked it into the last left onto the back straight there was Randy on the inside. He hit my leg and I went off-line. It took me a second to get the bike straight and then Ron and Christian went past on each side. I had a big outbraking duel with Ron at the end of the straight and got past but I couldn't catch Christian before the line.'

Mamola fell hard and was mildly concussed, but said it was just part of racing. 'I guess two guys can't fit through that corner together. When Rob came past on the inside going in he then drifted wide and I went to go around him on the right-hand and was right there when he came across going out. I almost saved it, but by the time I got the bike under control I was heading for some bales. I put my weight back trying to stay on the bike when it hit but it stopped dead and threw me the length of this motorhome.'

The fall and even the concussion did not keep Mamola down for long. He bounced back that evening, larking around way into the night throwing fire crackers and shouting 'Marlboro' at the top of his voice. It wasn't only McElnea he kept awake.

Gran Premio delle Nazioni, 24 May/statistics
Autodromo Nazionale di Monza, 3.604-mile/5.800-km circuit

500 cc

24 laps, 86.50 miles/139.20 km

Place	Rider	Nat.	Machine	Laps	Time & speed	Practice time	Grid
1	Wayne Gardner	AUS	Honda	24	44m 04.81s 117.733 mph/ 189.473 km/h	1m 48.66s	1
2	Eddie Lawson	USA	Yamaha	24	44m 20.47s	1m 49.89s	2
3	Christian Sarron	F	Yamaha	24	44m 37.27s	1m 50.64s	5
4	Rob McElnea	GB	Yamaha	24	44m 37.30s	1m 50.65s	6
5	Ron Haslam	GB	Honda	24	44m 37.36s	1m 50.53s	4
6	Tadahiko Taira	J	Yamaha	24	44m 45.29s	1m 50.35s	3
7	Pier Francesco Chili	I	Honda	24	45m 06.70s	1m 50.87s	7
8	Kevin Schwantz	USA	Suzuki	24	45m 07.00s	1m 51.53s	12
9	Raymond Roche	F	Cagiva	24	45m 10.81s	1m 52.24s	13
10	Niall Mackenzie	GB	Honda	24	45m 11.07s	1m 51.40s	9
11	Roger Burnett	GB	Honda	24	45m 37.87s	1m 52.77s	14
12	Manfred Fischer	D	Honda	23	44m 14.85s	1m 51.49s	11
13	Richard Scott	NZ	Honda	23	44m 15.96s	1m 52.88s	15
14	Bruno Kneubühler	CH	Honda	23	44m 27.65s	1m 54.21s	22
15	Massimo Broccoli	RSM	Honda	23	44m 27.77s	1m 55.47s	28
16	Marco Papa	I	Honda	23	44m 36.85s	1m 54.87s	26
17	Fabio Barchitta	RSM	Honda	23	44m 38.25s	1m 55.72s	29
18	Alessandro Valesi	I	Honda	23	44m 54.86s	1m 54.45s	23
19	Vittorio Gibertini	I	Suzuki	23	45m 53.23s	1m 55.88s	32
20	Fabio Biliotti	I	Honda	22	44m 35.14s	1m 53.11s	18
21	Vittorio Scatola	I	Paton	22	44m 38.60s	1m 55.91s	33
22	Esko Kuparinen	SF	Honda	22	45m 16.62s	1m 57.29s	36
	Randy Mamola	USA	Yamaha	23	DNF	1m 50.93s	8
	Didier de Radiguès	B	Cagiva	19	DNF	1m 53.63s	19
	Gustav Reiner	D	Honda	17	DNF	1m 52.91s	16
	Gerold Fischer	D	Honda	14	DNF	1m 56.86s	34
	Marco Marchesani	I	Suzuki	9	DNF	1m 55.08s	27
	Marco Gentile	CH	Fior	4	DNF	1m 54.01s	21
	Shunji Yatsushiro	J	Honda	4	DNF	1m 51.48s	10
	Wolfgang von Muralt	CH	Suzuki	3	DNF	1m 54.86s	25
	Daniel Amatriain	E	Honda	3	DNF	1m 55.79s	30
	Thierry Rapicault	F	Fior	2	DNF	1m 54.62s	24
	Andreas Leuthe	LUX	Honda	1	DNF	1m 57.60s	37
	Kenny Irons	GB	Suzuki	0	DNF	1m 53.94s	20
	Kenny Roberts	USA	Yamaha		DNS	1m 52.99s	17
	Simon Buckmaster	GB	Honda		DNS	1m 55.86s	31
	Maarten Duyzers	NL	Honda		DNS	1m 57.03s	35
	Leandro Becheroni	I	Honda		DNQ	1m 57.73s	
	Josef Doppler	A	Honda		DNQ	1m 57.75s	
	Steve Manley	GB	Suzuki		DNQ	1m 57.77s	
	Alan Jeffery	GB	Suzuki		DNQ	1m 57.98s	
	Christoph Bürki	CH	Honda		DNQ	1m 59.36s	
	Tony Carey	IRL	Suzuki		DNQ	2m 09.09s	
	Larry Moreno Vacondio	YV	Suzuki		DNQ	2m 09.70s	

Fastest lap: Gardner, 1m 49.00s, 119.030 mph/191.560 km/h (record).
Previous record: Mike Baldwin, USA (Yamaha), 1m 49.31s, 118.693 mph/191.017 km/h (1986).

World Championship: 1 Gardner, 43; **2** Lawson, 39; **3** Mamola and Haslam, 32; **5** Taira, 22; **6** Chili, 17; **7** McElnea, 14; **8** Mackenzie, 13; **9** Ito and Sarron, 10; **11** Schwantz, 9; **12** Burnett, 8; **13** Kawasaki, 4; **14** Roche and Yatsushiro, 3; **16** Katayama and Reiner, 2; **18** Scott, 1.

125 cc

18 laps, 64.87 miles/104.40 km

Place	Rider	Nat.	Machine	Laps	Time & speed	Practice time	Grid
1	Fausto Gresini	I	Garelli	18	37m 23.63s 104.089 mph/ 167.514 km/h	2m 04.07s	2
2	Bruno Casanova	I	Garelli	18	37m 23.79s	2m 03.82s	1
3	August Auinger	A	MBA	18	37m 24.12s	2m 05.20s	5
4	Domenico Brigaglia	I	AGV	18	37m 50.84s	2m 05.11s	4
5	Pier Paolo Bianchi	I	MBA	18	37m 56.76s	2m 04.63s	3
6	Andrés Marín Sánchez	E	Ducados	18	37m 57.50s	2m 06.12s	7
7	Jussi Hautaniemi	SF	MBA	18	38m 03.90s	2m 05.87s	6
8	Lucio Pietroniro	B	MBA	18	38m 10.31s	2m 06.39s	8
9	Corrado Catalano	I	MBA	18	38m 36.04s	2m 09.94s	20
10	Olivier Liegeois	B	MBA	18	38m 42.38s	2m 08.57s	14
11	Mike Leitner	A	MBA	18	38m 42.77s	2m 07.42s	12
12	Johnny Wickström	SF	Tunturi	18	38m 44.37s	2m 08.88s	15
13	Gastone Grassetti	I	MBA	18	38m 45.99s	2m 08.56s	13
14	Adolf Stadler	D	MBA	18	38m 46.12s	2m 06.68s	9
15	Jean-Claude Selini	F	ABF	18	38m 54.67s	2m 09.13s	17
16	Willy Pérez	RA	Zanella	18	38m 55.63s	2m 07.14s	10
17	Jacques Hutteau	F	MBA	18	39m 10.01s	2m 08.99s	16
18	Claudio Macciotta	I	MBA	18	39m 10.49s	2m 09.29s	18
19	Håkan Olsson	S	Starol	17	37m 29.99s	2m 10.64s	27
20	Fernando Gonzalez	E	Kobas	17	37m 30.37s	2m 10.57s	25
21	Esa Kytölä	SF	MBA	17	37m 30.71s	2m 09.91s	19
22	Ivan Troisi	YV	MBA	17	37m 46.92s	2m 10.63s	26
23	Christian le Badezet	F	MBA	17	37m 47.30s	2m 10.35s	23
24	Marco Cipriani	I	MBA	17	37m 58.67s	2m 12.85s	34
25	Thomas Møller-Pedersen	DK	MBA	17	37m 59.17s	2m 11.70s	33
26	Hubert Abold	D	Honda	17	37m 59.80s	2m 11.06s	28
27	Stefano Bianchi	I	MBA	17	38m 07.26s	2m 10.48s	24
28	Peter Baláž	CS	MBA	17	39m 02.12s	2m 11.55s	32
	Norbert Peschke	D	LCR	12	NC	2m 10.02s	21
	Thierry Feuz	CH	LCR	17	DNF	2m 07.28s	11
	Flemming Kistrup	DK	MBA	8	DNF	2m 11.08s	29
	Karl Dauer	A	MBA	7	DNF	2m 13.00s	35
	Robin Milton	GB	MBA	7	DNF	2m 11.10s	30
	Gianluciano Garagnani	I	MBA	4	DNF	2m 13.22s	36
	Emilio Cuppini	I	MBA	0	DNF	2m 11.35s	31
	Peter Sommer	CH	MBA		DNS	2m 10.24s	22
	Paul Bordes	F	MBA		DNQ	2m 10.33s	
	Ezio Gianola	I	Honda		DNQ	2m 11.66s	
	Robin Appleyard	GB	MBA		DNQ	2m 13.31s	
	Ian McConnachie	GB	MBA		DNQ	2m 13.80s	
	Fernando Hernandez	E	Beneti		DNQ	2m 14.29s	
	Bady Hassaine	DZ	MBA		DNQ	2m 14.49s	
	Allan Scott	USA	EMC		DNQ	2m 15.04s	

Fastest lap: Casanova, 2m 03.15s, 105.353 mph/169.549 km/h (record).
Previous record: Fausto Gresini, I (Garelli), 2m 04.57s, 104.153 mph/167.618 km/h (1986).

World Championship: 1 Gresini, 45; **2** Casanova, 30; **3** Brigaglia and Auinger, 26; **5** Bianchi, 20; **6** Casoli and Sánchez, 10; **8** Feuz and Hautaniemi, 7; **10** Gianola, 5; **11** Pietroniro, 4; **12** Macciotta, Stadler and Catalano, 2; **15** Leitner and Liegeois, 1.

250 cc

18 laps, 64.87 miles/104.40 km

Place	Rider	Nat.	Machine	Laps	Time & speed	Practice time	Grid
1	Anton Mang	D	Honda	18	35m 10.63s 110.648 mph/ 178.070 km/h	1m 56.74s	6
2	Reinhold Roth	D	Honda	18	35m 10.83s	1m 56.31s	2
3	Dominique Sarron	F	Honda	18	35m 11.19s	1m 56.79s	7
4	Jacques Cornu	CH	Honda	18	35m 11.41s	1m 56.51s	4
5	Alfonso Pons	E	Honda	18	35m 16.15s	1m 57.74s	12
6	Carlos Lavado	YV	Yamaha	18	35m 16.33s	1m 56.34s	3
7	Carlos Cardus	E	Honda	18	35m 26.23s	1m 57.05s	8
8	Patrick Igoa	F	Yamaha	18	35m 33.08s	1m 56.62s	5
9	Maurizio Vitali	I	Garelli	18	35m 41.11s	1m 57.50s	10
10	Guy Bertin	F	Honda	18	35m 41.43s	1m 59.03s	16
11	Luca Cadalora	I	Yamaha	18	35m 56.01s	1m 57.21s	9
12	Stefano Caracchi	I	Rotax	18	35m 56.37s	1m 58.67s	14
13	Hans Lindner	A	Honda	18	35m 56.71s	1m 59.35s	19
14	Donnie McCleod	GB	EMC	18	35m 56.81s	1m 59.32s	18
15	Stéphane Mertens	B	Sekitoba	18	36m 00.68s	1m 59.06s	17
16	Andreas Preining	A	Rotax	18	36m 00.91s	1m 59.73s	25
17	Jean-Philippe Ruggia	F	Yamaha	18	36m 01.39s	1m 58.98s	15
18	Manfred Herweh	D	Honda	18	36m 18.75s	1m 59.54s	23
19	Massimo Matteoni	I	Honda	18	36m 18.86s	1m 59.84s	26
20	Harald Eckl	D	Honda	18	36m 20.01s	1m 59.45s	22
21	Jochen Schmid	D	Yamaha	18	36m 20.44s	2m 00.28s	32
22	René Delaby	LUX	Yamaha	18	36m 34.62s	2m 00.17s	30
23	Marcellino Lucchi	I	Honda	18	36m 34.79s	1m 59.64s	24
24	Urs Luzi	CH	Honda	18	37m 00.13s	2m 00.81s	34
25	Josef Hutter	A	Honda	18	37m 00.92s	2m 00.14s	29
26	Graham Singer	I	Rotax	17	35m 14.29s	2m 00.83s	36
	Loris Reggiani	I	Aprilia	8	DNF	1m 55.69s	1
	Juan Garriga	E	Yamaha	7	DNF	1m 57.73s	11
	Jean-Michel Mattioli	F	Honda	7	DNF	1m 59.37s	20
	Bruno Bonhuil	F	Honda	6	DNF	2m 00.01s	28
	Nedy Crotta	CH	Rotax	3	DNF	2m 00.83s	35
	Ivan Palazzese	YV	Yamaha	1	DNF	1m 59.43s	21
	Fabrizio Pirovanno	I	Yamaha	1	DNF	2m 00.61s	33
	Jean-Louis Guignabodet	F	MIG	1	DNF	2m 00.24s	31
	Jean-François Baldé	F	Defi	0	DNF	1m 58.05s	13
	Marcello Iannetta	I	Yamaha	0	DNF	1m 59.95s	27
	Gary Cowan	IRL	Honda		DNQ	2m 00.91s	
	Jean Foray	F	Chevallier		DNQ	2m 01.00s	
	Andrea Borgonovo	I	Honda		DNQ	2m 01.65s	
	Alberto Rota	I	Honda		DNQ	2m 01.81s	
	Hervé Duffard	F	Honda		DNQ	2m 02.20s	
	Alain Bronec	F	Honda		DNQ	2m 02.34s	
	Andrea Brasini	I	Honda		DNQ	2m 02.36s	
	Oscar Furlan	I	Yamaha		DNQ	2m 02.38s	
	Philippe Pagano	F	Honda		DNQ	2m 03.54s	
	Kevin Mitchell	GB	Yamaha		DNQ	2m 03.37s	
	Fausto Ricci	I	Honda		DNQ	2m 03.70s	
	Renzo Colleoni	I	Honda		DNQ	2m 03.66s	
	Tony Rogers	GB	Yamaha		DNQ	2m 03.80s	
	Engelbert Neumair	A	Rotax		DNQ	2m 02.90s	
	Claudio Antonellini	I	Honda		DNQ	2m 04.02s	
	Paolo Aita	I	Honda		DNQ	2m 04.47s	
	Manuel Gonzalez	E	Yamaha		DNQ	2m 05.19s	
	Janez Pintar	YU	Honda		DNQ	2m 05.43s	
	Gilberto Gambelli	I	Honda		DNQ	2m 06.26s	
	Robin Appleyard	GB	Honda		DNQ	2m 06.80s	
	Massimo Sirianni	I	Yamaha		DNQ	2m 08.63s	

Fastest lap: Sarron, 1m 55.75s, 112.089 mph/180.389 km/h (record).
Previous record: Alfonso Pons, E (Honda), 1m 57.16s, 110.741 mph/178.220 km/h (1986).

World Championship: 1 Roth, 35; **2** Mang, 33; **3** Cornu, 25; **4** Pons, 24; **5** Wimmer, 21; **6** Garriga, Cadalora and Sarron, 18; **9** Kobayashi and Igoa, 15; **11** Cardus, 12; **12** Lavado, 11; **13** Shimuzu, 8; **14** Ruggia, 4; **15** Vitali, 3; **16** Taguchi, 2; **17** Yamamoto and Bertin, 1.

80 cc

13 laps, 46.85 miles/75.40 km

Place	Rider	Nat.	Machine	Laps	Time & speed	Practice time	Grid
1	Jorge Martinez	E	Derbi	13	28m 47.31s 97.646 mph/ 157.146 km/h	2m 10.39s	1
2	Manuel Herreros	E	Derbi	13	28m 58.51s	2m 13.15s	5
3	Stefan Dörflinger	CH	Krauser	13	28m 58.64s	2m 11.01s	2
4	Hubert Abold	D	Krauser	13	29m 15.54s	2m 15.37s	6
5	Jörg Seel	D	Seel	13	29m 17.55s	2m 17.20s	11
6	Károly Juhász	H	Krauser	13	29m 19.19s	2m 15.51s	7
7	Paolo Priori	I	Krauser	13	29m 35.62s	2m 18.13s	13
8	Gunter Schirnhofer	D	Krauser	13	29m 48.45s	2m 17.16s	10
9	Luis M. Reyes	COL	Autisa	13	29m 53.35s	2m 15.73s	8
10	Gerhard Waibel	D	Krauser	13	30m 10.73s	2m 11.15s	3
11	Giuseppe Ascareggi	I	BBFT	13	30m 12.21s	2m 19.48s	20
12	Wilco Zeelenberg	NL	Casal	13	30m 12.82s	2m 18.35s	14
13	Felix Rodriguez	E	Cobas	13	30m 27.84s	2m 20.56s	22
14	Raimo Lipponen	SF	Krauser	13	30m 27.95s	2m 19.00s	18
15	Richard Bay	D	Ziegler	13	30m 38.27s	2m 17.82s	12
16	Rainer Kunz	D	Ziegler	13	30m 43.54s	2m 18.78s	16
17	Mario Stocco	I	Faccioli	13	30m 47.47s	2m 21.63s	25
18	Serge Julin	B	Casal	13	30m 47.56s	2m 21.95s	27
19	Mario Scalinci	I	UFO	13	30m 59.61s	2m 24.87s	30
20	Reiner Koster	CH	LCR	13	31m 05.57s	2m 21.90s	26
21	Jos van Dongen	NL	Krauser	12	28m 57.36s	2m 20.64s	23
22	René Dünki	CH	LCR	12	29m 08.45s	2m 20.24s	21
23	Chris Baert	B	Seel	12	29m 10.34s	2m 21.01s	24
24	Claudio Granata	I	Autisa	12	29m 18.59s	2m 24.92s	31
	Josef Fischer	A	Krauser	7	DNF	2m 16.19s	9
	Francisco Torrontegui	E	Arbizu	7	DNF	2m 18.99s	17
	Vincenzo Saffiotti	I	UFO	6	DNF	2m 26.25s	32
	Alexandre Barros	BR	Arbizu	3	DNF	2m 19.06s	19
	Stuart Edwards	GB	Casal	3	DNF	2m 26.44s	33
	Ian McConnachie	GB	Krauser	1	DNF	2m 13.12s	4
	Juan Ramon Bolart	E	Krauser	1	DNF	2m 18.36s	15
	Thomas Engl	D	ESCH	1	DNF	2m 23.42s	29
	Paul Bordes	F	RB		DNS	2m 23.03s	28
	Nicola Casadei	I	Unimoto		DNQ	2m 29.47s	
	Salvatore Milano	I	Krauser		DNQ	2m 31.50s	
	Francesco Fantini	I	RB		DNQ	2m 32.96s	

Fastest lap: Martinez, 2m 10.05s, 99.764 mph/160.554 km/h (record).
Previous record: Ian McConnachie, GB (Krauser), 2m 10.90s, 99.117 mph/159.513 km/h (1986).

World Championship: 1 Martinez, 42; **2** Waibel, 24; **3** Herreros, 23; **4** Dörflinger, 20; **5** Criville and McConnachie, 12; **7** Seel, 11; **8** Miralles, 10; **9** Abold, 9; **10** Reyes, 8; **11** Schirnhofer, 6; **12** Juhász, 5; **13** Paschen and Priori, 4; **15** Bay, 3; **16** Fischer and Gschwander, 2; **18** Waldmann, 1.

Grosser Preis von
ÖSTERREICH

Niall Mackenzie found out something important before practice started at the Austrian Grand Prix. 'Hold on with both hands.' That sounds simple, even banal, but Mackenzie spent his formative racing years on Rotax-powered machines where the threat of seizure remained in the back of the mind and the left hand stayed poised over the clutch. Using the left hand solely for holding on to the handlebar was an untried notion.

Mackenzie discovered the advantage in using both hands to lever the 500 around when he went testing in Rijeka on the Tuesday and Wednesday after Monza. It was hard work, two long days of riding from ten in the morning until eight in the evening, but the Scot was certain it had been worthwhile. 'The best thing I ever did', he said, rejoining McElnea, McLeod and the rest who were having a few days of rest and recuperation at Lago di Garda in Italy before driving up to Austria. 'I didn't want to go riding after Monza because I was fed up. I didn't feel good on the bike and the last thing I wanted to do was spend two days riding it, but I am glad I did. I sorted a lot of things out and I ended up lapping at close to the same time that Randy did to get on pole position last year. I found that I needed a narrower front rim; it is the same thing that Dominique found with the 250 and we didn't have a narrow rim so he lent me one of his. It really improved the way the bike goes through the corner. I had had trouble with it running wide coming out of the turn and I couldn't get the power on because it was going in the wrong direction. With the narrower rim it just seems to stick on line and without trying any harder I went quicker.

'I was so used to having to hold my left hand over the clutch on the Rotax that I have never been used to gripping both bars hard. I tried it at Rijeka and it makes so much difference where you have to pull on the left-hand bar, like coming out of the left-hander at the end of the circuit before the start-and-finish and getting the bike to turn into the right-hander.' After what he considered were disastrous rides in Germany and Italy, Mackenzie's normally buoyant personality was rising again. In future, he would let Erv look after the engine and make sure it would not seize, while he would concentrate on pointing the bike in the right direction.

For Erv the improvement was a great relief. 'I felt I was letting him down because I could not sort the bike out to make it work the way it should. I guess for so long I have worked with Freddie and instinctively I know what needs to be done, we hardly have to discuss it. With Niall things are new and we have to have time to work together before we understand each other that well.'

Mackenzie's return to form did not come to light in the first practice session because it was wet and Randy Mamola headed the table from Gardner and Lawson. The second Lucky Strike rider, Richard Scott, was fourth, making his debut as a temporary replacement for the injured Mike Baldwin.

Scott had been testing in Yugoslavia at the same time as Mackenzie but with quite different results. The New Zealander had crashed the YZR500 after 27 laps of practice in Rijeka and it was a heavy fall that left Scott badly bruised and shaken. His Arai helmet had been pushed against his face, breaking a tooth. Either through coincidence or the shape of his head, this was the second time he had been injured in this way, a crash at Oulton Park in '86, leaving him with a badly cut lip.

The Lucky Strike bike was in even worse shape, having carried on after dumping Scott and cartwheeled to total destruction. However the wet practice that started the Austrian Grand Prix gave Scott a chance to ease back into things, and it also gave Ron Haslam the chance to try out the new Elf 4 prototype.

The new bike performed well, even though it had not turned a wheel until it arrived in Austria. The bike should have been built over the winter but had to wait until Honda could supply the NSR engine around which it was to be constructed. Even the mock-up that Honda sent to Annemasse early in the year proved to be of very limited use. Serge Rosset explained that there were so many differences between the mock-up and the real engine that almost every significant part of the machine had subsequently to be redesigned.

Based on the ideas developed around the three-cylinder centre-hub-steering machine raced so well by Haslam in '86, the 1987 version shared no common parts and in fact the front swing arm on the latest machine ran to the left of the front wheel instead of the right.

Elf's reason for backing a Grand Prix team was publicity, and they did not consider that just having their name on the side of a factory NSR provided the right kind of exposure. The Elf 4 has been developed to show the company's technological bent, but while Haslam looked certain to finish in the top four of the World Championship, if not the top three, it seemed a shame to consign him to a period of development with the Elf 4 mid-season which was bound to lose him points.

The standard factory NSR was obviously the best machine on the track in the 500 class and Yamaha were struggling to match its performance. Some of the top Yamaha factory technicians had come to the Salzburgring to see how the bikes were shaping up and Eddie Lawson wasted no time in telling them that the best thing they could do with the YZR was to take it back to Japan and put it into the crusher. Carruthers did not speak quite so strongly but bemoaned the lack of progress made in getting more power. The Japanese always maintain that the current year's parts must be better than the previous year's, yet Carruthers had been employing the shorter 1986 con rods and older cylinders that gave better acceleration even if they lost a little on top speed.

The Lucky Strike team had been hard at work as well and not only had Mike Sinclair been performing similar juggling acts with old and new parts plus modifying what he could to coax the best out of the engine, but the team had employed the services of British designer John Mocket to produce new fibreglass components. They started with a more enclosed seat, which was used in Spain, and Austria saw the debut of a new fairing with a very rounded nose that could use the wide 1987 radiator that previously had been wedded to the blunt factory fairing with the huge side ducts.

Although no wind tunnel work had been done, it looked as though the Mocket-designed fairing ought to have lower drag than the original factory unit, especially as great care had been taken with the outfall from the radiator. The alternative was to use the factory radiator and fairing issued just in time for the German GP, or the huge ducted fairing which might or might not have been causing a loss of top speed – no-one had done sufficient back-to-back testing to be absolutely sure. The Lucky Strike Team's next idea was to improve on Yamaha's airbox design, but testing that would take time.

Fairing experimentation was not limited to the 500 class and Rolf Biland had a new fairing for his LCR Krauser outfit that he claimed weighed only 12 kg and was 18 kg lighter than the original. Apart from that, the fairing also included a wing in the other side radiator duct that should provide some downforce. The fairing was to be used with a complete belly pan, but while always keen to try new things Biland was happier with the fact that he had discovered what had failed in Germany and resulted in him failing to qualify.

'It was the special ignition system I have. For some reason it was developing completely the wrong advance curve and it made the engine perform as though it was running lean and so I kept chasing problems with the carburation and the fuel supply. It was my fault; I was blind to the idea that it could have been anything else. Once we tried a standard Yamaha system it was perfect. I will be using the special system again but only when it is fitted with a new chip.'

Biland was struggling but the other two top teams using the Krauser engine were very much enjoying the engine's power and reliability, as Alain Michel pointed out. 'It is the first time in my career that I have had an engine that is as fast or faster than the opposition. Normally they pass me on the straights and I have to try and get back on the brakes, but now I can pass some of them because we have been able to put a lot of our experience with the Yamaha engines into the Krauser because it uses so many Yamaha parts. The advantage is that the Krauser crankcases are so well made that they make the engine more reliable. There are never any surprises when you open the cases, they do not rub together and the crank bearings do not chatter.'

After two wet periods of practice the first dry session saw World Champions Egbert Streuer and Bernard Schnieders top the table ahead of Michel and Jean-Marc Fresc, while Biland and Webster both struggled in the first dry period only to get their act together in the final practice period.

With the first practice periods wet or at least

This is the way the 250 race was run for much of its distance: Mang holds on to the slenderest lead while Pons, Roth, Cardus, Cornu and Sarron swap places behind. Cadalora battled hard to keep up and was able to pass the others only with the most aggressive riding. In the end, he paid the price for trying to keep an underpowered Yamaha in company with the Hondas.

damp it was not surprising to see Mamola on top of the table as he had demonstrated on previous occasions the superiority of the Dunlop wets and his ability to use them. Most expected him to slip down the table on Saturday in the dry, but although Gardner was indeed quickest, Mamola was right behind him. It was the first time in the season that he had secured a place on the front row of the grid and it was due to an improvement in his relationship with the Dunlop tyres that stemmed from an accumulation in the track time and a conversation the Californian had with the Dunlop tyre engineer at lunchtime on Saturday.

'I am a second quicker than I was last year and I was quite comfortable at that speed. It has been good for testing tyres here and we have had everything on the bike from full wets to slicks. Today in the dry every tyre we put on was an improvement. I was quite happy after this morning's practice but I knew I had made a few mistakes and Peter Ingley the tyre technician said that I should soon be braking all the way into the corner. Sure enough I was doing it in the afternoon in the long right-hander at the end of the circuit round the paddock. I did two laps with Wayne Gardner, and the Honda gets out of the corners better but on top speed the Yamaha is maybe a bit better.'

Mamola was obviously at home through the high-speed sweeps of the Salzburgring and said he liked the track. Gardner held the opposite view and considered the circuit dangerous and to be treated with the greatest respect, even with the changes made before the '86 event.

One of those changes was the inclusion of a chicane at the end of the start-and-finish straight that took away the sixth-gear right-hander with no run-off. The exit of the chicane unfortunately pointed the riders back at the armco on the right of the track, but the addition of some concrete at the edge of the track on the exit effectively widened the circuit for '87 and gave the riders a straight run out of the chicane well away from the armco. It probably knocked a second off the lap times.

After missing the German Grand Prix because of his practice crash and then sitting out the Italian GP, Martin Wimmer returned to the fray at the Salzburgring on the Thursday. After the first two periods of untimed training he was satisfied that he had made the right decision. Eighteen days after breaking the tibia and fibula of his left leg he was riding a racing motor cycle again. 'Some people have said I am crazy but in fact I have thought very carefully about this and have discussed it with my doctors. They say that riding the bike and walking on the leg will not hinder the healing process and it was just up to me to see if I could ride the bike.'

Wimmer has had the gear lever swapped from the left to the right side of the 250 Marlboro Yamaha and the injured foot which has been plated and screwed now operates only the rear brake. 'I never use the rear brake normally but I could still do so in an emergency. Obviously it is difficult to swap over the gearchange after riding so long but I have been practising on a road bike and have found it no problem. My advantage is that because I never use the rear brake my right foot is not programmed to do anything so I only have to teach it to change gear; I don't have to make it forget braking.

I have only come to race to try and score some points for the championship. I have already missed two races and if I also missed this race and Yugoslavia I think I could say goodbye to the championship. If I had been too slow in unofficial practice and did not think I could improve I would have gone home straight away but I was pleased with the way things went. If I am not in the top fifteen qualifiers or close to it I will not start because I just need some championship points – one would be worth it. I realise that even if I can race here Yugoslavia will be harder. There are more corners and it is a left-hand circuit which makes it harder on my left foot. I hope that by Assen I will be fully fit.'

By qualifying tenth Wimmer satisfied his own criteria and surprised those who thought that the compounded problems of the injury and the swapping over of controls, plus the fact that he was not riding the fastest machine, might have prevented him from being in contention for a point.

80 CC

Gerhard Waibel made his intention clear from lap 1 when he forced his works Krauser up to the front, but championship leader Aspar Martinez was instantly on his tail with the red Derbi. The two soon pulled clear of the second-place battle, which was more involved. At first Hungarian Károly Juhász was right in the thick of things but lasted for only eight impressive laps. By lap 4 ex-World Champion Stefan Dörflinger had worked his way up to third place after a poor start, passing Manuel Herreros, Mandy Fischer and Juhász.

Once Dörflinger had got past he tried to close on the leading duo but never really got them in sight. He held a lonely third place until lap 14 when the Krauser was obviously slowing. He slipped back and stopped on lap 16. 'The nut on the end of the primary gear came undone. The bike started misfiring on about lap 6; up till then I was catching the leaders. Then it just got worse and eventually it wrecked the oil seal and I had to stop', reported Dörflinger later.

The third-place group was closing on Martinez and Waibel over the last few laps, led by Herreros by the smallest margin from Fischer, McConnachie, Spaan and Abold. Martinez had the answer and held on to win from Waibel, with the next group crossing the line in a bunch, and the last place on the rostrum going to Herreros.

125 CC

What in previous years had been one of the most closely contested classes with as many as eight riders fighting for the lead had become rather uninteresting. The Garelli pair won once again despite the earnest attempts of Paolo Casoli on the AGV MBA and August Auinger on his Bartol MBA. Ex-Champion Fausto Gresini

maintained his 100 per cent record and stretched his lead in the title chase. He allowed team-mate Bruno Casanova to lead for several laps but when it came near to the flag Gresini just increased the pace and won by a comfortable margin.

Initially, though, there was a four-man train of machines slipstreaming up the hill behind the pits as Auinger and Casoli tried to keep the faster Garellis in sight. On lap 7 Auinger suddenly dropped back and once the Garellis had broken clear it was impossible to match their lap times without the aid of their slipstream. Bartol later said that Auinger's bike had mysteriously lost power, probably because of a partial ignition failure.

On the last lap, Auinger raised a huge cheer from the crowd as he tried to repass Casoli for third place, but the AGV MBA had enough power to keep the Italian in front and he crossed the line three-tenths of a second ahead of the local hero.

Domenico Brigaglia, obviously hindered by the broken ankle he suffered in practice, did well to climb through the field into fifth place on the second of the AGV MBAs. He beat Andrés Marín Sánchez on the Ducados and Adi Stadler on the MBA after a long fight.

Half-way through the 22-lap race the ambulance had to come onto the circuit when Ezio Gianola crashed at the back of the paddock. Fortunately he was not seriously hurt. It should have dawned on him that trying to race the single-cylinder Honda against the twins at a horsepower circuit like the Salzburgring was an impossible task.

250 cc

Those who watched this classic 250 battle came away with the idea that either Toni Mang or Loris Reggiani should be World Champion. Reggiani was very unlikely to, having scored in so few rounds and with the reliability of the Rotax engine a constant problem. Mang, on the other hand, was working his way back into strong contention after his mistake in Spain. Just as important as the fifteen points that Mang collected for the win was the way that he did it.

The four-times World Champion used all his experience to maintain a punishing pace, even though he was in front of the field with no-one to aim at. The pack behind had him to chase and plenty of opportunities to slipstream but either they spent too much time passing and repassing each other or they just could not match his speed.

Looking at the fastest laps put up by the top five, Mang was in fact the slowest but presumably the most consistent. The fastest lap was put up by Cardus who finished fifth, whilst the second slowest of the five was Reggiani who was still the hero of the hour because of the way he pulled through the field.

'I was hit on the startline'. recalled the Italian later. 'It made me drop the clutch and the bike almost stalled. I staggered off the line and my team say I was 22nd going up the hill on the first lap. I was catching up and then Cadalora crashed in front of me and I must have lost a couple of seconds avoiding him.'

At the end of the first lap it was Sito Pons who led before being overtaken by fellow Spaniard Carlos Cardus. Mang hit the front on lap 3 and, despite the efforts of others such as Reinhold

Ron Haslam is out on his own as he sweeps through the curve at the bottom of the hill behind the pits. The barriers are an ever-present threat here, for even when protected by straw bales they are unyielding.

almost every corner only to be blown off on the straights. Cadalora was sliding past Cornu and Cardus in the middle of the S-bend before the main straight where most riders would have been prepared to follow, but in the end it did not pay off.

It was not until lap 14 that Mang's advantage over Roth or Pons looked anything like a significant gap. At first he just held a lead of 1.5 seconds but then inched away further until by lap 20 he was four seconds in front, just as Reggiani moved through the pack and into second place.

Although there were only four laps left, Reggiani might have been expected to make some impression on Mang's lead considering the rate at which he had been advancing, but of course once in front of the group he lost the advantage of their slipstream and was far too distant to pick up Mang's. The Aprilia was not fast enough for Reggiani to get a secure second but he did enough during the final circuit to make sure there was no chance of Roth passing him on the way to the line.

A mere second covered Reggiani to Cornu as they flashed under the chequered flag with Sarron only two-tenths adrift, complaining that his Honda had been running poorly throughout. There was then a 20-second gap to Lavado who once more gave his mechanics a graphic description of just how useless his bike had been.

Another long interval separated Lavado from the ninth-place battle, which was resolved in favour of Stéphane Mertens on the Armstrong-framed Honda ahead of Martin Wimmer on the Marlboro Yamaha. Wimmer was delighted with his single point and said that it was as good as winning, being the hardest point he had ever scored. He might have been ninth and indeed set himself up in a position to pass Mertens coming out of the last corner on the run-in to the flag but missed a gear coming onto the straight. He said it was the only gear he had missed all race.

Wimmer was obviously coping successfully with his broken ankle and finger, but Yamaha had another two men placed on the injury list after the race. Cadalora was concussed, but Patrick Igoa had a suspected broken leg and hip after misjudging his braking and going straight on at the new chicane on the eighth lap.

500 cc

The Salzburgring has been good to Yamaha and, with two wins and two second places in his four years of Grand Prix racing, it has been a source of a large number of World Championship points for Eddie Lawson. His batting average in Austria took a nose dive when he retired from the race after only two laps with the Yamaha running on two or three cylinders.

There was another prepared to carry the gauntlet for Yamaha, though, and Randy Mamola led after passing Ron Haslam – quickest off the line as usual. Gardner slotted himself into third place with Niall Mackenzie fourth ahead of Roger Burnett, Pier Francesco Chili and Christian Sarron.

Rob McElnea made a poor start: his Marlboro Yamaha struggled to get off the line and took a complete lap before it ran properly at all. Thereafter it improved and was strong enough for him to start climbing through the pack. From thirteenth place on lap 2 he passed Richard Scott who was battling against the stiffness and pain caused by his two recent falls. By lap 4 McElnea was tenth and closing on the fifth-place battle.

At the head of the field Gardner had taken the lead, but Mamola and Mackenzie were still chasing hard. Haslam had slipped to a more distant fourth with Burnett still heading the pack and keeping Sarron, Chili, Raymond Roche and Shunji Yatsushiro behind him.

The interesting contest behind could not distract the attention from the three men up front. As Gardner failed to get away from Mamola and Mackenzie, the struggle became breathtaking. It was fairly obvious that the Rothmans Honda had the power advantage over the Lucky Strike Yamaha but, remembering Gardner's stated dislike of the circuit, it was understandable to see Mamola climbing all over him. There was no point in Gardner sticking his neck out as he knew he had the answer in his right wrist. As these two battled together, Mackenzie shadowed them and even passed Mamola though he never put a wheel in front of Gardner.

'I thought about trying for the lead,' admitted Mackenzie later, 'but there was no point in pushing my luck, and towards the end my front tyre was not giving me as good grip as it had at the beginning and I had been making up time going into the corners.' Mackenzie was obviously back to the form he had shown in Japan, comfortably, unhurriedly keeping his HB NSR500 in contest until two-thirds of the way through the race when the fading front tyre meant he could not recover ground he had lost in passing back-markers.

That last third of the race did not see Mamola's effort tailing off, though, and the more he was frustrated by the Honda's speed the more determined he became. He was prepared to squeeze past Gardner anywhere there was an opening and that included ducking out of his slipstream at the top of the hill and flashing past the Honda as the pair flicked left and right between the armco barriers.

Mamola later explained that by keeping his bike leant over in a long arc going up the hill he could build up enough revs to make better speed before he had to straighten up. Coming upright, the contact patch moves to the centre of the tyre which was a much larger radius and effectively a higher gearing ratio. Keeping the bike leaned over lowered the overall gearing and made the Yamaha pull better up the hill. There are not too many circuits with a curved straight that allow that tactic to be used.

No matter where Mamola overtook him, Gardner was able to power past again, so it was a very frustrated California who took second place on the rostrum. In the end, Mamola made a minor mistake on the brakes at the west end of the circuit and with a one-second advantage

Roth and Pons, he defended his position with his usual determination. Yet, for the first half of the race he looked no more likely to be the winner than did anyone else from the top six (Roth, Pons, Cardus, Dominique Sarron and Jacques Cornu).

It was a totally Honda-dominated event, for by half-distance Reggiani had yet to make an impression on the top six and the most threatening Yamaha rider, Luca Cadalora, had crashed on lap 11, giving himself a nasty concussion. Carlos Lavado could not match his promising practice lap that put him second on the grid behind Mang after the second of only two dry sessions. Lavado went slower in the race while everyone else except Mang went faster.

Lavado had made a poor start and even when he worked his way through the field and chased Reggiani to get onto the tail of the leaders, all he could do was try and hang on. It was frustrating for the Yamaha star who refused to be drawn into riding at eleven-tenths to make up for an underpowered machine.

That was precisely what led to Cadalora's fall as the Italian passed the faster Hondas on

Alexander Savel

going onto the last lap Gardner was safe, though he pressed on and increased that before taking the chequered flag.

Mackenzie was ecstatic with third and Haslam slightly disappointed that he let them get away. He reported that his bike lacked something in speed but it kept him well up in the championship as Lawson had failed to score.

McElnea crossed the line fifth after a fine ride from that dismaying start. He had little trouble getting through the field although for a while it looked as though Sarron would tail him all the way to the finish. In the end the Frenchman had to give up complaining of suspension problems as well as a slow engine, so the Sonauto Yamaha was sixth ahead of Yatsushiro and Burnett.

Sidecars

In the best sidecar race of the season so far Rolf Biland and Kurt Waltisperg won by three and a half seconds from Egbert Streuer and Bernard Schnieders, with Alain Michel and Jean-Marc Fresc third. Championship leaders Steve Webster and Tony Hewitt came fourth after spinning on the last lap as they tried to pass Michel.

The four outfits had been changing places all the way, with early leader Webster being passed by Biland on lap 4. Michel took his turn to lead on lap 5 but could not get away as all the top four except Streuer significantly improved on their practice times.

Biland was back in front by lap 7 and the leading four had pulled well clear of the field led by Rolf Steinhausen and Bruno Hiller. Biland held the lead for a few laps but Streuer, who had been on the tail of the group, was working his way through. Just as Biland seemed to have opened up a slight advantage on lap 9, the Dutchman moved into second place and closed the gap. On lap 11 the outfit bearing the number one plate took over the lead, albeit briefly, and Steinhausen retired at the pits leaving Wolfgang Stropek to contest fifth place with Masato Kumano.

Streuer's effort brought more speed from Biland and he started to open up a slight advantage over the reigning champion who still had Michel and Webster on his tail. Michel saw that they were losing ground to the Swiss so he passed Streuer and tried to catch Biland. He set the fastest lap of the race in the process but never completely made up the deficit. Webster and Streuer were swapping places behind and at one point Webster ran into the back of Michel as the three outfits jostled for position.

Biland kept up the pressure and put in the fastest lap on the second-to-last lap while Streuer passed Michel and made the final circuit his fastest to take second. Michel was third after Webster overdid it trying to close in the final mile. 'I just got a bit carried away', said Webster. Passenger Hewitt takes up the story: 'We spun round coming into the long right-hander and then we were going backwards with the brakes full on. When he seemed to have it under control he turned the bars and spun us straight again. I think the crowd enjoyed it.'

Sidecar train: Webster heads Michel and Streuer in their pursuit of Biland.

Grosser Preis von Österreich, 7 June/statistic
Salzburgring, 2.636-mile/4.243-km circuit
500 cc

29 laps, 76.44 miles/123.05 km

Place	Rider	Nat.	Machine	Laps	Time & speed	Practice time	Grid
1	Wayne Gardner	AUS	Honda	29	39m 57.89s 114.71 mph/ 184.733 km/h	1m 21.46s	1
2	Randy Mamola	USA	Yamaha	29	40m 00.26s	1m 21.77s	2
3	Niall Mackenzie	GB	Honda	29	40m 11.10s	1m 22.77s	6
4	Ron Haslam	GB	Honda	29	40m 17.26s	1m 22.98s	9
5	Rob McElnea	GB	Yamaha	29	40m 22.26s	1m 22.57s	5
6	Christian Sarron	F	Yamaha	29	40m 32.10s	1m 22.96s	7
7	Shunji Yatsushiro	J	Honda	29	40m 42.07s	1m 22.50s	4
8	Roger Burnett	GB	Honda	29	40m 54.52s	1m 23.55s	12
9	Tadahiko Taira	J	Yamaha	29	40m 54.86s	1m 23.04s	10
10	Pier Francesco Chili	I	Honda	29	40m 55.09s	1m 22.97s	8
11	Richard Scott	NZ	Yamaha	29	41m 09.82s	1m 24.03s	15
12	Didier de Radiguès	B	Cagiva	29	41m 16.35s	1m 24.66s	17
13	Fabio Biliotti	I	Honda	28	40m 35.90s	1m 25.70s	20
14	Wolfgang von Muralt	CH	Suzuki	28	40m 36.56s	1m 25.57s	19
15	Alessandro Valesi	I	Honda	28	40m 44.43s	1m 25.89s	21
16	Karl Truchsess	A	Honda	28	40m 51.14s	1m 25.94s	22
17	Simon Buckmaster	GB	Honda	28	40m 51.93s	1m 27.62s	28
18	Manfred Fischer	D	Honda	28	40m 52.54s	1m 26.26s	24
19	Gerold Fischer	D	Honda	28	41m 22.08s	1m 26.36s	25
20	Hervé Guilleux	F	Fior	28	41m 25.06s	1m 25.98s	23
21	Silvo Habat	YU	Yamaha	27	39m 58.15s	1m 27.67s	29
22	Maarten Duyzers	NL	Honda	27	40m 03.97s	1m 27.98s	33
23	Georg-Robert Jung	D	Honda	27	40m 06.41s	1m 27.74s	30
24	Steve Manley	GB	Suzuki	27	40m 17.01s	1m 28.30s	34
25	Rudolf Zeller	A	Honda	27	40m 50.04s	1m 29.71s	37
	Marco Gentile	CH	Fior	23	DNF	1m 25.48s	18
	Michael Rudroff	D	Honda	19	DNF	1m 27.33s	26
	Franz Kaserer	A	Suzuki	18	DNF	1m 29.59s	36
	Christoph Bürki	CH	Honda	14	DNF	1m 27.61s	27
	Kenny Irons	GB	Honda	12	DNF	1m 23.86s	14
	Raymond Roche	F	Cagiva	11	DNF	1m 23.39s	11
	Andreas Leuthe	LUX	Honda	8	DNF	1m 28.65s	35
	Gustav Reiner	D	Honda	5	DNF	1m 23.71s	13
	Bruno Kneubühler	CH	Honda	5	DNF	1m 24.24s	16
	Helmut Schütz	D	Honda	2	DNF	1m 27.75s	31
	Eddie Lawson	USA	Yamaha	1	DNF	1m 21.83s	3
	Sepp Doppler	A	Honda	1	DNF	1m 27.85s	32
	Dietmar Marehardt	A	Homa		DNQ	1m 31.67s	
	Fabio Barchitta	RSM	Honda		DNQ	1m 49.87s	

Fastest lap: Yatsushiro, 1m 20.46s, 117.89 mph/189.843 km/h (record).
Previous record: Eddie Lawson, USA (Yamaha), 1m 22.40s, 115.186 mph/185.374 km/h (1986).
World Championship: 1 Gardner, 58; **2** Mamola, 44; **3** Haslam, 40; **4** Lawson, 39; **5** Taira, 24; **6** Mackenzie, 23; **7** McElnea, 20; **8** Chili, 18; **9** Sarron, 15; **10** Burnett, 11; **11** Ito, 10; **12** Schwantz, 9; **13** Yatsushiro, 7; **14** Kawasaki, 4; **15** Roche, 3; **16** Katayama and Reiner, 2; **18** Scott, 1.

Alexander Savel

Rob McElnea *(above)* rode well but the disastrous first lap left him no chance of catching the first four.

Left: After scoring a World Championship point in Italy, Richard Scott found the Salzburgring circuit more challenging.

250 cc

24 laps, 63.26 miles/101.83 km

Place	Rider	Nat.	Machine	Laps	Time & speed	Practice time	Grid
1	Anton Mang	D	Honda	24	35m 01.18s 108.35 mph/ 174.471 km/h	1m 26.36s	1
2	Loris Reggiani	I	Aprilia	24	35m 06.64s	1m 26.76s	3
3	Reinhold Roth	D	Honda	24	35m 06.86s	1m 27.20s	7
4	Sito Pons	E	Honda	24	35m 07.15s	1m 27.46s	9
5	Carlos Cardus	E	Honda	24	35m 07.37s	1m 27.12s	5
6	Jacques Cornu	CH	Honda	24	35m 07.64s	1m 26.77s	4
7	Dominique Sarron	F	Honda	24	35m 07.87s	1m 27.35s	8
8	Carlos Lavado	YV	Yamaha	24	35m 28.37s	1m 26.67s	2
9	Stéphane Mertens	B	Sekitoba	24	35m 44.21s	1m 27.88s	13
10	Martin Wimmer	D	Yamaha	24	35m 44.43s	1m 27.47s	10
11	Juan Garriga	E	Yamaha	24	35m 44.71s	1m 27.70s	11
12	Hans Lindner	A	Honda	24	35m 51.56s	1m 28.05s	14
13	Engelbert Neumair	A	Rotax	24	35m 53.46s	1m 28.68s	20
14	Jean-François Baldé	F	Defi	24	35m 53.73s	1m 28.22s	16
15	Wilhelm Hörhager	A	Honda	24	35m 54.94s	1m 28.84s	22
16	Guy Bertin	F	Honda	24	35m 55.22s	1m 29.16s	25
17	Manfred Herweh	D	Honda	24	36m 06.69s	1m 28.55s	19
18	Maurizio Vitali	I	Garelli	24	36m 07.00s	1m 28.09s	15
19	Donnie McLeod	GB	EMC	24	36m 07.46s	1m 28.88s	23
20	Jochen Schmid	D	Yamaha	24	36m 07.91s	1m 29.39s	30
21	Helmut Bradl	D	Honda	24	36m 08.10s	1m 28.37s	18
22	Jean-Philippe Ruggia	F	Yamaha	24	36m 08.37s	1m 29.70s	35
23	Josef Hutter	A	Honda	24	36m 08.74s	1m 29.30s	28
24	Thomas Bacher	A	Rotax	24	36m 08.97s	1m 28.76s	21
25	Jean-Michel Mattioli	F	Honda	24	36m 09.24s	1m 29.55s	32
26	Stefan Klabacher	A	Rotax	24	36m 11.11s	1m 28.29s	17
27	Harald Eckl	D	Honda	24	36m 11.50s	1m 29.28s	27
28	Gary Cowan	IRL	Honda	24	36m 14.26s	1m 29.25s	26
29	Urs Lüzi	CH	Honda	24	36m 14.53s	1m 29.32s	29
30	Urs Jucker	CH	Yamaha	23	35m 03.47s	1m 29.54s	31
31	Siegfried Minich	A	Honda	23	35m 03.79s	1m 29.62s	33
	René Delaby	LUX	Yamaha	19	DNF	1m 29.79s	36
	Luca Cadalora	I	Yamaha	10	DNF	1m 27.15s	6
	Ivan Palazzese	YV	Yamaha	10	DNF	1m 28.88s	23
	Patrick Igoa	F	Yamaha	7	DNF	1m 27.82s	12
	Konrad Hefele	D	Honda	2	DNF	1m 29.62s	34
	Alberto Rota	I	Honda		DNQ	1m 29.80s	
	Kevin Mitchell	GB	Yamaha		DNQ	1m 29.85s	
	Andreas Preining	A	Rotax		DNQ	1m 30.11s	
	Jean Foray	F	Chevallier		DNQ	1m 30.16s	
	Werner Felber	A	Rotax		DNQ	1m 30.61s	
	Stefano Caracchi	RSM	Rotax		DNQ	1m 30.80s	
	Bernard Hänggeli	CH	Yamaha		DNQ	1m 31.37s	
	Fausto Ricci	I	Honda		DNQ	1m 31.80s	
	Alain Bronec	F	Honda		DNQ	1m 32.12s	

Fastest lap: Cardus, 1m 26.39s, 109.8 mph/176.812 km/h (record).
Previous record: Martin Wimmer, D (Yamaha), 1m 27.18s, 108.871 mph/175.210 km/h (1986).

World Championship: 1 Mang, 48; **2** Roth, 45; **3** Pons, 32; **4** Cornu, 30; **5** Sarron and Wimmer, 22; **7** Cadalora, Cardus and Garriga, 18; **10** Igoa and Kobayashi, 15; **12** Lavado, 14; **13** Reggiani, 12; **14** Shimuzu, 8; **15** Ruggia, 4; **16** Vitali, 3; **17** Mertens and Taguchi, 2; **19** Bertin and Yamamoto, 1.

125 cc

22 laps, 57.99 miles/93.35 km

Place	Rider	Nat.	Machine	Laps	Time & speed	Practice time	Grid
1	Fausto Gresini	I	Garelli	22	33m 57.20s 102.43 mph/ 164.955 km/h	1m 32.20s	3
2	Bruno Casanova	I	Garelli	22	33m 58.82s	1m 32.16s	2
3	Paolo Casoli	I	AGV	22	34m 14.67s	1m 32.14s	1
4	August Auinger	A	MBA	22	34m 14.98s	1m 32.37s	4
5	Domenico Brigaglia	I	AGV	22	34m 49.10s	1m 34.82s	10
6	Andrés Marin Sánchez	E	Ducados	22	34m 54.65s	1m 34.99s	13
7	Adolf Stadler	D	MBA	22	35m 08.20s	1m 33.81s	6
8	Thierry Feuz	CH	MBA	22	35m 16.68s	1m 34.07s	7
9	Johnny Wickström	SF	Tunturi	22	35m 16.89s	1m 36.01s	18
10	Willy Pérez	RA	Zanella	22	35m 17.10s	1m 34.55s	8
11	Olivier Liegeois	B	Assmex	22	35m 17.38s	1m 34.88s	11
12	Mike Leitner	A	Bartol	22	35m 17.61s	1m 35.19s	14
13	Ivan Troisi	YV	MBA	22	35m 30.09s	1m 37.40s	29
14	Flemming Kistrup	DK	MBA	22	35m 33.07s	1m 36.54s	21
15	Peter Sommer	CH	Supeso	21	34m 03.62s	1m 36.91s	22
16	Jean-Claude Selini	F	MBA	21	34m 05.99s	1m 36.33s	20
17	Esa Kytölä	SF	MBA	21	34m 06.45s	1m 37.03s	23
18	Karl Dauer	A	MBA	21	34m 36.23s	1m 37.15s	25
19	Fernando Gonzales	E	Cobas MBA	21	34m 36.70s	1m 37.92s	34
20	Robert Zwidl	A	MBA	21	34m 36.95s	1m 36.24s	19
21	Robin Milton	GB	MBA	21	34m 38.15s	1m 37.56s	30
22	Håkan Olsson	S	MBA	21	34m 38.38s	1m 37.15s	24
23	Christian le Badezet	F	MBA	21	34m 38.86s	1m 37.31s	27
24	Hubert Abold	D	Honda	21	35m 11.93s	1m 37.76s	33
25	Thomas Møller-Pedersen	DK	MBA	21	35m 22.00s	1m 37.68s	32
26	Helmut Hovenga	D	Seel	20	34m 55.11s	1m 35.89s	17
	Lucio Pietroniro	B	MBA	21	DNF	1m 34.71s	9
	Norbert Peschke	D	Seel	18	DNF	1m 35.60s	15
	Ton Spek	NL	MBA	7	DNF	1m 38.27s	36
	Ezio Gianola	I	Honda	7	DNF	1m 37.17s	26
	Alexander Eschig	A	MBA	7	DNF	1m 37.97s	35
	Peter Baláž	CS	MBA	2	DNF	1m 37.38s	28
	Jussi Hautaniemi	SF	MBA	2	DNF	1m 34.88s	12
	Pier Paolo Bianchi	I	MBA	1	DNF	1m 32.81s	5
	Gastone Grassetti	I	MBA		DNS	1m 35.71s	16
	Dirk Hafeneger	D	MBA		DNS	1m 37.66s	31
	Paul Bordes	F	MBA		DNQ	1m 38.27s	
	Jacques Hutteau	F	MBA		DNQ	1m 38.43s	
	Karl Bubenicek	A	MBA		DNQ	1m 38.52s	
	Alfred Waibel	D	Waibel		DNQ	1m 38.72s	
	Allan Scott	USA	EMC		DNQ	1m 38.88s	
	Alfred Gangelberger	A	MBA		DNQ	1m 39.39s	
	Marco Cipriani	I	MBA		DNQ	1m 39.55s	
	Robin Appleyard	GB	MBA		DNQ	1m 39.72s	
	Werner Schmied	A	Rotax		DNQ	1m 40.76s	
	Robert Hmeljak	YU	MBA		DNQ	1m 40.94s	
	Heinz Pristavnik	A	MBA		DNQ	1m 43.63s	
	Manfred Braun	B	MBA		DNQ	1m 44.85s	
	Manuel Hernandez	E	Beneti		DNQ	1m 46.43s	
	Gerd Kafka	A	Kazuo		DNQ	2m 13.47s	

Fastest lap: Gresini, 1m 30.58s, 104.72 mph/168.633 km/h (record).
Previous record: Ezio Gianola, I (MBA), 1m 32.28s, 100.67 mph/162.01 km/h (1986).

World Championship: 1 Gresini, 60; **2** Casanova, 42; **3** Auinger, 34; **4** Brigaglia, 32; **5** Bianchi and Casoli, 20; **7** Sánchez, 15; **8** Feuz, 10; **9** Hautaniemi, 7; **10** Stadler, 6; **11** Gianola, 5; **12** Pietroniro, 4; **13** Catalano, Macciotta and Wickström, 2; **16** Leitner, Liegeois and Pérez, 1.

80 cc

17 laps, 44.81 miles/72.13 km

Place	Rider	Nat.	Machine	Laps	Time & speed	Practice time	Grid
1	Jorge Martinez	E	Derbi	17	28m 12.31s 95.29 mph/ 153.422 km/h	1m 45.30s	1
2	Gerhard Waibel	D	Krauser	17	28m 13.20s	1m 46.51s	4
3	Manuel Herreros	E	Derbi	17	28m 44.22s	1m 45.95s	3
4	Josef Fischer	A	Krauser	17	28m 44.62s	1m 49.28s	11
5	Ian McConnachie	GB	Krauser	17	28m 44.83s	1m 49.88s	13
6	Hans Spaan	NL	Casal	17	28m 45.16s	1m 48.07s	6
7	Hubert Abold	D	Krauser	17	28m 45.54s	1m 48.72s	9
8	Alexandre Barros	BR	Casal	17	29m 12.39s	1m 48.01s	5
9	Luis M. Reyes	E	Autisa	17	29m 12.62s	1m 48.45s	8
10	Juan Ramon Bolart	E	Krauser	17	29m 14.05s	1m 50.58s	14
11	Michael Gschwander	D	Seel	17	29m 21.23s	1m 51.74s	18
12	Ralf Waldmann	D	Erk	17	29m 23.86s	1m 50.90s	15
13	Richard Bay	D	Ziegler	17	29m 33.35s	1m 51.66s	17
14	Theo Timmer	NL	Casal	17	29m 40.50s	1m 52.62s	24
15	Heinz Paschen	D	Casal	17	29m 43.12s	1m 51.16s	16
16	Wilco Zeelenberg	NL	Casal	17	29m 43.58s	1m 52.12s	21
17	Matthias Ehinger	D	Krauser	17	29m 52.02s	1m 52.95s	25
18	Peter Öttl	D	Krauser	17	29m 52.30s	1m 51.75s	19
19	Alojz Pavlic	YU	Seel	17	29m 53.31s	1m 52.56s	23
20	Francisco Torrontegui	E	Arbizu	17	29m 55.86s	1m 55.39s	32
21	Reiner Koster	CH	Kroko	16	28m 24.96s	1m 53.68s	29
22	Bert Smit	NL	Minarelli	16	28m 25.22s	1m 53.67s	28
23	Jos van Dongen	NL	Krauser-Hummel	16	28m 27.65s	1m 55.98s	36
24	Chris Baert	B	Seel	16	28m 43.54s	1m 55.96s	35
25	Hans Koopman	NL	Ziegler	16	28m 46.50s	1m 55.92s	34
26	Serge Julin	B	Casal	16	29m 39.19s	1m 49.87s	12
	Stefan Dörflinger	CH	Krauser	16	DNF	1m 45.76s	2
	Paul Bordes	F	RB	14	DNF	1m 56.26s	37
	Raimo Lipponen	SF	Krauser	9	DNF	1m 55.87s	33
	Rainer Kunz	D	Kroko	9	DNF	1m 54.51s	31
	Károly Juhász	H	Krauser	8	DNF	1m 48.16s	7
	Janez Pintar	YU	Eberhardt	4	DNF	1m 52.35s	22
	Günther Schirnhofer	D	Krauser	4	DNF	1m 53.12s	26
	Sepp Bader	D	Auer	3	DNF	1m 53.75s	30
	Jean-Marc Velay	F		1	DNF		38
	Jörg Seel	D	Seel	1	DNF	1m 53.52s	27
	Paolo Priori	I	Krauser		DNS	1m 48.88s	10
	René Dünki	CH	Krauser		DNS	1m 51.79s	20
	Otto Machinek	A	H&M		DNQ	1m 59.05s	
	Thomas Engl	D	GPE		DNQ	2m 00.64s	
	Mika-Sakari Komu	SF	Eberhardt		DNQ	2m 00.79s	
	Stuart Edwards	GB	Casal		DNQ	2m 01.06s	
	Erich Reuberger	A	Hummel		DNQ		

Fastest lap: Waibel, 1m 37.45s, 97.34 mph/156.745 km/h (record).
Previous record: Ian McConnachie, GB (Krauser), 1m 38.25s, 96.604 mph/155.496 km/h (1986).

World Championship: 1 Martinez, 57; **2** Waibel, 36; **3** Herreros, 33; **4** Dörflinger, 20; **5** McConnachie, 18; **6** Abold, 13; **7** Criville, 12; **8** Seel, 11; **9** Fischer, Miralles and Reyes, 10; **12** Schirnhofer, 6; **13** Juhász and Spaan, 5; **15** Paschen and Priori, 4; **17** Barros and Bay, 3; **19** Gschwander, 2; **20** Bolart and Waldmann, 1.

Sidecars

22 laps, 57.99 miles/93.346 km

Place	Driver & passenger	Nat.	Machine	Laps	Time & speed	Practice time	Grid
1	Rolf Biland/ Kurt Waltisperg	CH CH	LCR-Krauser	22	32m 15.43s 107.80 mph/ 175.916 km/h	1m 27.33s	3
2	Egbert Streuer/ Bernard Schnieders	NL NL	LCR-Yamaha	22	32m 18.90s	1m 26.94s	1
3	Alain Michel/ Jean-Marc Fresc	F F	LCR-Krauser Elf	22	32m 19.89s	1m 28.14s	5
4	Steve Webster/ Tony Hewitt	GB GB	Yamaha	22	32m 30.97s	1m 27.23s	2
5	Wolfgang Stropek/ Hans-Peter Demling	A A	LCR-Krauser	22	33m 19.68s	1m 30.37s	12
6	Masato Kumano/ Markus Fahrni	J CH	Toshiba Tec	22	33m 19.90s	1m 29.77s	8
7	Alfred Zurbrügg/ Simon Birchall	CH GB	LCR-Yamaha	22	33m 27.48s	1m 29.25s	6
8	Derek Jones/ Brian Ayres	GB GB	LCR-Seel	22	33m 27.77s	1m 30.41s	13
9	Pascal Larratte/ Jacques Corbier	F F	LCR-Yamaha	22	33m 34.02s	1m 31.57s	19
10	Theo van Kempen/ Gerardus de Haas	NL NL	LCR-Yamaha	22	33m 35.02s	1m 30.17s	10
11	Barry Brindley/ Grahame Rose	GB GB	Windle-Yamaha	22	33m 35.29s	1m 31.36s	16
12	Markus Egloff/ Urs Egloff	CH CH	LCR-Seel	22	33m 37.13s	1m 27.89s	4
13	Bernd Scherer/ Wolfgang Gess	D D	BSR-Yamaha	21	32m 17.70s	1m 31.28s	15
14	Luigi Casagrande/ Adolf Hänni	CH CH	LCR-Yamaha	21	32m 46.13s	1m 31.46s	17
15	Gary Thomas/ Geoff White	GB GB	LCR-Yamaha	21	32m 46.51s	1m 32.26s	21
16	Graham Biggs/ Vince Biggs	AUS AUS	LCR-Yamaha	21	33m 12.46s	1m 32.33s	22
17	Dennis Bingham/ Julia Bingham	GB GB	LCR-Yamaha	20	33m 29.32s	1m 31.74s	20
	Graham Gleeson/ Peter Brown	NZ NZ	LCR-Cagiva	15	DNF	1m 30.37s	11
	Yoshisada Kumagaya/ Brian Barlow	J GB	Windle-Yamaha	12	DNF	1m 31.52s	18
	Steve Abbott/ Shaun Smith	GB GB	Windle-Yamaha	11	DNF	1m 29.60s	7
	Rolf Steinhausen/ Bruno Hiller	D D	Eigenbau	10	DNF	1m 29.81s	9
	René Progin/ Yves Hunziker	CH CH	Seymaz	7	DNF	1m 30.59s	14
	Werner Kraus/ Oliver Schuster	D D	LCR		DNQ	1m 32.50s	
	Erwin Weber/ Eckart Rösinger	D D	LCR-Sams		DNQ	1m 32.82s	
	Fritz Stölzle/ Hubert Stölzle	D D	LCR-Yamaha		DNQ	1m 33.12s	
	Hans Hügli/ Andreas Räcke	CH CH	Sigwa		DNQ	1m 33.65s	
	Ivan Nigrowski/ G. Loreille	F F	Seymaz		DNQ	1m 33.81s	
	Egon Schons/ Thomas Schröder	D D	Yamaha		DNQ	1m 36.56s	
	Herbert Prügl/ Christian Parzer	A A	Homa-LCR		DNQ	1m 39.89s	

Fastest lap: Michel, 1m 26.56s, 109.58 mph/176.465 km/h (record).
Previous record: Egbert Streuer/Bernard Schnieders, NL/NL (LCR-Yamaha), 1m 28.39s, 107.380 mph/172.811 km/h (1986).

World Championship: 1 Webster, 38; **2** Michel, 32; **3** Streuer, 24; **4** Biland, 15; **5** Zurbrügg, 14; **6** Abbott, 12; **7** Kumano, 10; **8** van Kempen, 9; **9** Bayley and Jones, 8; **11** Progin, 7; **12** Stropek, 6; **13** Kumagaya and Larratte, 5; **15** Egloff, 4; **16** Stölzle, 1.

Grand Prix de
YOUGOSLAVIE

The Yugoslavs do not appear to have much to be happy about, except that they are not quite shut behind the Iron Curtain. Their status as 'have nots', compared to others in the Grand Prix world, means that they want whatever they might be able to get. The first signs of this are the kids that line the approach roads demanding stickers or 'tickets', which seems to be their idea of an international word. Unfortunately, it does not stop with the kids – some of the adults who work at the circuit now demand something like a T-shirt before they will co-operate.

Not everyone is like that and some try very hard to work with the Grand Prix circus. An example of this was the early meeting between representatives of the riders and the marshals in an attempt to iron out some of the problems with the very poor marshalling of previous years. Over-use of the waved blue flag and incorrect use of the yellow flags were both mentioned and Randy Mamola, speaking for the 500 cc men, was very diplomatic yet got his message across by referring to these failings as though they had been noticed at other Grands Prix as well.

One important point aimed directly at the local men was the request not to have a marshal with a red flag stand in the middle of the track before the first corner immediately the chequered flag had been held out to end a practice session or race, as flag marshals had so nearly been run down in the past. After the point was made, the marshals concerned said they would wait until the next lap before going out with the red flag. Come practice, however, all this was forgotten and again there were nearly collisions which would have left a flattened marshal.

Little has been done to improve the very rudimentary pits at Rijeka and the tarmac paddock is too small. However, all that will change for '88 – not because the circuit owners have come to realise that it needs doing but because the government wants a Formula 1 car Grand Prix at the circuit. To get that, the whole pits complex and paddock will have to be rebuilt, involving the levelling of a large hill behind the present pits.

The track itself has always been a great test of man and machine, but unfortunately the F1 cars are likely to make the bumpy surface far worse. Even with the present surface it caught out a good number of the top men and all fell hard. Three of the top 500 campaigners were missing from the grid by the time Sunday afternoon came and Freddie Spencer continued a run of extraordinary misfortune.

After being expected so many times over the preceding season and a half, it was a real surprise to see bike no. 19 being warmed up for practice and a somewhat plump-looking Spencer walking out of the Newell to get on it. In the first untimed session the official time-keepers had their equipment running and recorded Spencer fastest, but most team clocks had Rob McElnea slightly faster on the Marlboro Yamaha.

When timed practice officially got under way on Friday, Spencer was still fourth-quickest behind Gardner, Mamola and Mackenzie. Spencer rode fewer laps than anyone in the top ten,

slipping back into the old routine of only doing a few laps in a quick burst to register a fast time. Many riders stay out on the circuit for almost twice his number of laps, pushing harder and harder as they try to shave that fraction of a second off their time.

Spencer's tactics had worked well in previous years but, on this occasion and only with the advantage of hindsight, one might suggest it was a mistake. With so few racing miles under his belt he would have been better off spending time on the machine, but then the knee injury suffered at Hockenheim was still troubling him and he looked fairly exhausted after only completing ten laps in the session.

Back in the Newell he used his physiotherapy black box – the 'Electro Acuscope' – so that he could treat his knee himself. By passing current through the knee it helped reduce the swelling that had kept him out of action since striking his knee in Germany.

'The knee is perhaps 70-80 per cent right and it is hard to predict if it is going to work through the race or not, but I am going to try. That is what has kept me from riding at the last two GPs. Every time I tried to ride a street bike at home the knee would swell up and I wouldn't be able to move it. Then the fluid would have to be drained.'

The ex-World Champion looked a touch overweight and unfit, as he had at Daytona, but said that the increase in body mass was due to the weight training he had been doing. 'I was at my lightest when I rode the 250 but then I was consciously keeping my weight down. Now I have been building up my body strength for the 500. Obviously I haven't been able to train normally while I had the shoulder injury and then the knee so I don't know how well I will get on racing, but we will have to wait and see.'

Spencer never did get to test his knee or shoulder over race distance because ten minutes before the end of the Saturday morning session the red-and-white Honda went missing. Mamola pulled into the pits and told a worried Erv Kanemoto that Spencer was OK, but in fact his collarbone was broken. He had been trying to go round the outside of a slower rider and got off onto the dirt. He was under control until the front wheel hit a hole then the bike went down. 'I was sliding along and got away from the bike. I had almost come to a stop when I rolled over once and that did my collarbone. It is broken in exactly the same place as it was at Daytona.'

Claudio Costa, doctor to the Grand Prix riders, X-rayed Spencer's shoulder in the *Clinica Mobile*. He said that the break was very unusual for a rider in that it was a clean break at right angles to the bone, which was why it had taken so long to heal after Daytona and was still not strong. If Spencer did not have an operation to plate it he would be unable to race until the very end of the season.

Before flying back to America, Spencer did make it plain that there was no way this would be the end of his racing career and he would be back racing in Grands Prix as soon as he was fit. Despite missing so much of '86 and '87, Spencer

After his early-season injuries, World Champion Carlos Lavado was back on top in Yugoslavia.

Kel Edge

In a three-way battle for the lead Mamola
and Lawson pressure Gardner.

has age on his side, still being younger than Kenny Roberts was when he started his serious GP campaign.

For Kanemoto it was the second harsh blow of the weekend and left him without any rider as Niall Mackenzie was already nursing a broken ankle after a fall early in the second session. 'After the first practice I was very pleased because I had not been trying too hard and I got a good time that put me third, even though I only had a couple of clear laps because there was a lot of traffic and that makes a big difference to your lap time at Rijeka. I did stay out for most of the session, though, and did a fair number of laps and when we looked at the front tyre it was obvious that it might not last the full race distance.

'So we decided that I should try a harder front tyre that afternoon and I did a couple of laps to get it warm. It felt fine so I decided to go for a faster lap, but at the first tight right-hander it just tucked under on me and I slid into the straw bales in front of the armco. I thought I had just twisted the ankle and walked back to get on the other bike but after a lap on that the ankle was too painful and I realised I had done something to it. When Dr Costa X-rayed it he found a crack in the ankle and it swelled up so much there was no way I could ride again.'

That put both of Kanemoto's men out of the running. Shonichi Oguma, the director of HRC who seems closest to the road racing and who has a personal interest in Mackenzie and Spencer as well as Japanese hope Yatsushiro, seemed particularly hard hit by the unfortunate run of events. Rumours from their camp suggested that, Oguma had defended Spencer against criticism from within HRC for some time and was under some pressure since Honda lost both 250 and 500 titles in '86. Those rumours concluded that, because of his internally unpopular support of Spencer and the lack of success last season, Oguma had been passed over in the latest round of HRC promotions.

Fate had not finished with Honda yet and it almost kicked their 1987 500 Championship hopes in the teeth in that Saturday morning session when Gardner also fell. 'It really shook me because one moment I was riding round well off the pace doing 34s instead of 30s and the next moment I was on the ground. I guess I must have chosen the wrong tyre.'

The Australian was fortunate to escape with a nasty scrape and a twist to his right hand. Yamaha were also bitten at Rijeka: McElnea was not as lucky as Gardner when he was highsided and ended up with a badly broken little finger on his right hand. McElnea was determined to race if he could and he was better off than Christian Sarron who suffered a nasty bang to his head when he crashed the Sonauto Gauloises Yamaha. With quite a bad case of concussion there was no question of him riding.

The stack of crashed machinery under the team's awning grew even bigger when Jean-Philippe Ruggia, the temporary stand-in for injured Patrick Igoa, crashed twice in practice. The injury list was looking pretty sad, for

Richard Scott was decidedly off-colour after his two recent falls, and Luca Cadalora had decided to sit things out. He had found that his judgement was being affected by his Austrian race crash when he had tried to ride in the first practice period.

People were falling off in all classes and Gerhard Waibel crashed the factory 80 cc Krauser on Friday morning. The smallest capacity class finally got the chance to test Michelin radials and Stefan Dörflinger and Manuel Herreros were the first to have a go on the new tyres on Saturday morning.

That was not the only interesting thing to happen in the 80 cc category because World Champion and Derbi team leader Aspar Martínez took Dörflinger's works Krauser out for a couple of laps while both his machines were being worked on.

80 cc

World Champion Jorge Martínez gained an advantage in his first lap on the works Derbi and never lost it. Initially, second place was held by his team-mate and fellow Spaniard Manuel Herreros. He did a perfect job of keeping at bay the Krauser squad headed by Stefan Dörflinger and Gerhard Waibel while Martínez extended his lead.

It took the third Krauser man, Ian McConnachie, until lap 4 to get into fifth place after being ninth on lap 1. On lap 6 of the 17 Dörflinger made a break for it, got away from Herreros and tried in vain to catch Martínez. That left Herreros attempting to defend third from Waibel and McConnachie, and for the next five laps the three were often side by side or arguing over the same line through a corner.

That battle resolved itself in favour of McConnachie, who got away on lap 12 to a secure third place, leaving Herreros and Waibel to battle all the way to the line. In spite of the Spaniard forcing Waibel to give way going into the first corner of the last lap and leading all the way round the final circuit, it was the German who won the run-in to the finish.

The struggle for sixth was every bit as good, with Hans Spaan, Hubert Abold and Jörg Seel swapping places at every turn almost to the flag. The fight for the last two points places between Alexandre Barros and Juan Ramon Bolart also kept the spectators entertained, and all in all the race was very entertaining.

250 cc

Carlos Lavado was a second faster than anyone else in practice and didn't even have to stretch himself that far in the race. Yugoslavia is one of the fairest tests of riding talent in the calendar, if any one track can possibly be representative, and Lavado is simply King of Rijeka. In '86 he was obviously faster than anyone yet crashed totally unnecessarily. The year before that he had drawn praise from Freddie Spencer by pushing him hard when the Honda was so obviously a superior machine.

This time, he made no mistake and if the Hondas had a significant advantage over Lavado's HB Yamaha he did not allow it to show. If anyone else deserved Lavado's heroic mantle it was Loris Reggiani for the way he rode the Aprilia into second place ahead of Roth and Cornu on the leading Hondas. Then Martin Wimmer could also place a claim on it as he belied his broken ankle to beat both Sarron and Mang out of fifth place.

In what was in all respects an exciting race, Sito Pons led into the first corner on the Campsa Honda with Mang on his tail and just in front of Sarron, Wimmer and Cardus. Despite the clutch start and his pole position, Lavado was only ninth. Pons held the advantage as those behind swapped places and Mang dropped to fourth before making the first challenge to the Spaniard for the lead.

When Mang took the lead on the second lap and stayed there for four circuits it looked possible that he could settle in for a Salzburgring-like win, except for the fact that Lavado was advancing and by lap 5 was third behind Cornu.

Mang had not finished a race at Rijeka since he stopped riding the Kawasaki so he was not expecting great things at what he considered to be his bogey circuit. On lap 6 he gave up the lead to Cornu and was immediately passed by Lavado. With Roth right behind him, the four men had a slight advantage over Sarron and Pons who were being passed by Reggiani on his way through from a mediocre start that had him tenth on the first lap.

Once he lost the lead Mang seemed to run out of steam. Even though he put in his fastest time on lap 11 he slipped back through the field. 'I could just hold that pace in the lead for a few laps but it was dangerous and I did not want to take the risk. I eased off and I think the others were prepared to take more chances.'

Cornu was soon ousted by Lavado and had his work cut out to stay in front of Roth. While the Swiss rode hard through the corners, he lost out on the straights to Roth's Honda. His team seemed ready to blame his weight and stature, perhaps wanting to forget the advantage Roth enjoyed with Sepp Schlögl working on his HB Honda.

By lap 10 the true outline of the race was evolving. Lavado was ahead and cautiously building on a three-second lead. Roth and Cornu traded places in second while Mang had been caught and passed by Reggiani. He would then spend most of the rest of the race clashing fairings with Sarron while Wimmer watched from a discreet distance.

Pons had worked his way back to eighth and was coming under strong pressure from Ivan Palazzese who was riding as well as he did when he won 125 cc races and getting back to the form he had shown when he was second to Venemotos team-mate Lavado at Assen in '83. After that his performances seemed to drop off but now he was back on a very rapid-looking production Yamaha. Palazzese and Pons also had Juan Garriga and Jean-Philipppe Ruggia to contend with, and the sparks flew all the way to lap 26 when the stiff

Kel Edge

and sore Ruggia was the unlucky one who missed out on a point.

While Lavado inched away, Reggiani took second place on lap 15 but Roth was able to counter-attack and get past the Italian once more. It was not until the final three of the 26 laps that there was daylight between the two bikes and even at the flag Reggiani was only a second ahead. There was still less of a gap between Roth and Cornu as the Swiss lost out on the approach to the line.

Wimmer watched the twin Rothmans Hondas of Sarron and Mang fight for fifth. Sarron subsequently complained that Mang's tactics were too forceful; it was not the first time that the German had received such criticism. When a particularly heavy clash between the two left Sarron some way off line Wimmer closed in.

He passed the Frenchman on lap 21 and, once able to deal with Mang on his own, he considered passing was a reasonable risk. So he moved into fifth place on lap 24 and Mang had no answer. It was six points and another personal triumph for Wimmer.

500 cc

Randy Mamola and Ron Haslam had a drag race to the first corner which Mamola won and for the first lap the Californian led while Gardner moved into second, pushing Haslam to third just ahead of Lawson and Chili.

Gardner hit the front on lap 2 and it was natural to expect the championship leader to start pulling away. He was chased by Mamola and Lawson with Haslam just about holding on as the foursome started to open a gap over Chili, Gustav Reiner, Tadahiko Taira, Raymond Roche and Rob McElnea.

Gardner did not get away immediately, but then he could afford to be cautious and make sure everything was working perfectly – practice and the preceding races had showed he had the upper hand. Slowly, but perceptibly, Lawson and Mamola lost ground until by lap 8 the Honda was nearly two seconds in front. The two Yamahas had in turn dropped Haslam, who was having rear suspension problems severe enough to set the NSR off in some wild gyrations.

Behind Haslam, Chili lost some of the advantage his great start had given him as he was swallowed up by McElnea, Roche and Reiner, with Taira a little in arrears but still well ahead of Richard Scott, who was to come under pressure from Shunji Yatsushiro. Chili later complained that the shoulder he injured in his '86 Silverstone fall had unusually caused problems, presumably because of the very demanding nature of the circuit.

Gardner never quite made the two-second buffer because Lawson, shadowed by Mamola, started to cut his advantage metre by metre. By lap 12 it had fallen to less than a second and the next time round they were on his tail once more. 'I found that my injured right hand went dead during the race', said Gardner later. 'I could not work the throttle and brake properly. I found I was grabbing too much throttle in a hurry and I had to ease off and wait for the feeling to come back into the hand.'

So on lap 13 Gardner had Lawson and Mamola climbing all over him. The commentator got quite excited, shouting in Serbo Croat as Lawson briefly put the Marlboro Yamaha ahead of the Rothmans Honda. Gardner's reply was swift and assured, although he could not break away again immediately. The effort he was putting in was evident: black marks on the road marked his passing and several ended with a curl, indicating an abrupt end that sent the rider out of the saddle and fighting for control.

Gardner won those battles and the long fight with Lawson that faded as the Californian had abused his tyres by lap 20. He was later to complain that the carburation problems ·that had upset them all through practice made the bike hard to ride, refusing to run below 8000 rpm. In '86, when Lawson walked off with the same race, he reported that it was the only time all season that the bike had carburated perfectly.

Kel Edge

500 cc

30 laps, 77.7 miles/125.04 km

Place	Rider	Nat.	Machine	Laps	Time & speed	Practice time	Grid
1	Wayne Gardner	AUS	Honda	30	46m 30.64s 100.17 mph/ 161.305 km/h	1m 30.70s	1
2	Randy Mamola	USA	Yamaha	30	46m 33.07s	1m 31.69s	2
3	Eddie Lawson	USA	Yamaha	30	46m 45.86s	1m 31.76s	3
4	Ron Haslam	GB	Honda	30	47m 00.96s	1m 32.74s	8
5	Raymond Roche	F	Cagiva	30	47m 14.35s	1m 32.80s	9
6	Pier Francesco Chili	I	Honda	30	47m 15.08s	1m 32.80s	10
7	Tadahiko Taira	J	Yamaha	30	47m 22.31s	1m 33.01s	12
8	Shunji Yatsushiro	J	Honda	30	47m 30.14s	1m 32.70s	7
9	Richard Scott	NZ	Yamaha	30	47m 30.40s	1m 33.41s	13
10	Kenny Irons	GB	Suzuki	30	47m 43.70s	1m 34.10s	16
11	Roger Burnett	GB	Honda	30	47m 55.73s	1m 34.67s	19
12	Fabio Biliotti	I	Honda	30	48m 01.28s	1m 34.56s	18
13	Alessandro Valesi	I	Honda	29	46m 53.39s	1m 34.33s	17
14	Wolfgang von Muralt	CH	Suzuki	29	46m 55.35s	1m 35.14s	21
15	Bruno Kneubühler	CH	Honda	29	47m 11.20s	1m 36.25s	24
16	Simon Buckmaster	GB	Honda	29	47m 11.56s	1m 37.66s	27
17	Fabio Barchitta	RSM	Honda	29	47m 14.15s	1m 35.86s	23
18	Massimo Broccoli	RSM	Honda	29	47m 28.35s	1m 35.15s	22
19	Andreas Leuthe	LUX	Honda	29	47m 41.86s	1m 37.75s	32
20	Hervé Guilleux	F	Fior	29	47m 43.70s	1m 37.68s	30
21	Gerold Fischer	D	Honda	29	47m 44.67s	1m 37.44s	28
22	Georg-Robert Jung	D	Honda	29	47m 59.97s	1m 36.48s	25
23	Marco Gentile	CH	Fior	28	47m 01.32s	1m 35.04s	20
24	Dimitrios Papandreou	GR	Suzuki	28	47m 44.96s	1m 39.61s	35
	Louis-Luc Maisto	F	Plein Pot	27	DNF	1m 38.70s	34
	Gustav Reiner	D	Honda	23	DNF	1m 33.42s	14
	Rob McElnea	GB	Yamaha	18	DNF	1m 32.50s	6
	Pavol Dekánek	CS	Suzuki	11	DNF	1m 38.00s	33
	Silvo Habat	YU	Honda	5	DNF	1m 37.71s	31
	Helmut Schütz	D	Honda	5	DNF	1m 37.54s	29
	Vittorio Scatola	I	Paton	2	DNF	1m 36.87s	26
	Freddie Spencer	USA	Honda		DNS	1m 31.94s	4
	Niall Mackenzie	GB	Honda		DNS	1m 32.30s	5
	Christian Sarron	F	Yamaha		DNS	1m 32.87s	11
	Didier de Radiguès	B	Cagiva		DNS	1m 33.57s	15
	Tony Carey	IRL	Suzuki		DNQ	1m 46.96s	

Fastest lap: Gardner, 1m 32.00s, 101.28 mph/163.096 km/h.
Lap record: Eddie Lawson, USA (Yamaha), 1m 31.78s, 101.586 mph/163.487 km/h (1985).

World Championship: 1 Gardner, 73; **2** Mamola, 56; **3** Lawson, 49; **4** Haslam, 48; **5** Taira, 28; **6** Chili and Mackenzie, 23; **8** McElnea, 20; **9** Sarron, 15; **10** Burnett, 11; **11** Ito and Yatsushiro, 10; **13** Roche and Schwantz, 9; **15** Kawasaki, 4; **16** Scott, 3; **17** Katayama and Reiner, 2; **19** Irons, 1.

Mamola passed Lawson on the brakes at the end of the start-and-finish straight going on to lap 22 but he was unable to pressurise the Australian in quite the same way and slowly a gap opened up that was over a second by lap 23 of the 30. Lawson dropped behind Mamola by a similar amount and the drama had gone out of the race for the lead.

Haslam held on to his fourth place and by this point Roche had secured fifth ahead of Chili as Gustav Reiner crashed out of a certain sixth place. That fifth-place battle had been exciting, particularly until lap 19 when Rob McElnea crashed soon after getting to the head of what had been a four-man pack.

McElnea had the front wheel slide away from him at the end of the back straight and ended a pretty disastrous meeting for him. 'I don't understand why it tucked under. I was trying to get away from Roche but I didn't think I was braking too hard.' It is possible that the injured finger upset the feel in his hand.

Chili had managed to keep clear of Taira on the third of the Marlboro Yamahas, who was never seriously threatened by Scott on the Lucky Strike bike. The New Zealander had enough to worry about from behind as he was overhauled at the end of the race by Yatsushiro on the Rothmans Honda. By passing Roger Burnett on Gardner's '86 machine half-way through the race, Kenny Irons scored his first World Championship point with tenth place. He threw some light on how hard it must have been for Gardner to do battle with Mamola on that bike twelve months before by commenting that the bike steered so sluggishly that 'it required a crane to get it through the corners.'

Fifth was a great result for Cagiva and their new engine, representing the best performance put up by a European manufacturer since MV pulled out of racing. Even then, Roche pointed out that the bike was '10 kg too heavy and short of 10 horsepower'.

Above: **Gardner's win kept him comfortably ahead of Lawson and Mamola in the title race.**

Almost inevitably, the 80 cc race went to champion Martínez on the works Derbi.

250 cc

26 laps, 67.34 miles/108.368 km

Place	Rider	Nat.	Machine	Laps	Time & speed	Practice time	Grid
1	Carlos Lavado	YV	Yamaha	26	41m 24.76s 99.50 mph/ 157.007 km/h	1m 33.15s	1
2	Loris Reggiani	I	Aprilia	26	41m 29.71s	1m 34.43s	3
3	Reinhold Roth	D	Honda	26	41m 30.66s	1m 34.65s	6
4	Jacques Cornu	CH	Honda	26	41m 30.92s	1m 34.20s	2
5	Martin Wimmer	D	Yamaha	26	41m 33.92s	1m 34.70s	7
6	Dominique Sarron	F	Honda	26	41m 35.95s	1m 34.54s	5
7	Anton Mang	D	Honda	26	41m 36.62s	1m 34.44s	4
8	Sito Pons	E	Honda	26	41m 50.29s	1m 34.91s	9
9	Juan Garriga	E	Yamaha	26	41m 50.49s	1m 35.17s	11
10	Ivan Palazzese	YV	Yamaha	26	41m 50.85s	1m 34.81s	8
11	Jean-Philippe Ruggia	F	Yamaha	26	41m 51.10s	1m 35.22s	13
12	Maurizio Vitali	I	Garelli	26	42m 16.68s	1m 35.59s	14
13	Manfred Herweh	D	Honda	26	42m 18.55s	1m 35.18s	12
14	Stéphane Mertens	B	Sekitoba	26	42m 31.68s	1m 36.97s	24
15	Hans Lindner	A	Honda	26	42m 33.90s	1m 36.17s	16
16	Donnie McLeod	GB	EMC	26	42m 34.27s	1m 36.39s	17
17	Guy Bertin	F	Honda	26	42m 34.89s	1m 36.60s	18
18	Jean-François Baldé	F	Defi	26	42m 42.43s	1m 36.86s	22
19	Kevin Mitchell	GB	Yamaha	26	42m 45.97s	1m 36.88s	23
20	Harald Eckl	D	Honda	26	42m 46.41s	1m 36.72s	20
21	Marcellino Lucchi	I	Honda	26	42m 46.56s	1m 37.26s	28
22	Urs Lüzi	CH	Honda	26	42m 46.88s	1m 37.20s	26
23	René Delaby	LUX	Yamaha	26	42m 59.13s	1m 37.15s	25
24	Jochen Schmid	D	Yamaha	26	42m 59.55s	1m 36.67s	19
25	Jean Foray	F	Chevallier	25	41m 45.88s	1m 38.47s	33
26	Alain Bronec	F	Yamaha	25	41m 56.55s	1m 39.24s	35
27	Zdravko Leljak	YU	Honda	24	42m 34.45s	1m 40.55s	36
	Bruno Bonhuil	F	Honda	18	DNF	1m 36.78s	21
	Josef Hutter	A	Honda	16	DNF	1m 38.38s	32
	Massimo Matteoni	I	Honda	13	DNF	1m 37.43s	29
	Jean-Michel Mattioli	F	Honda	11	DNF	1m 35.92s	15
	M. Sraj	YU	Honda	9	DNF	1m 41.28s	37
	Siegried Minich	A	Honda	6	DNF	1m 38.48s	34
	Carlos Cardus	E	Honda	6	DNF	1m 34.92s	10
	Gary Cowan	IRL	Honda	5	DNF	1m 37.20s	27
	Jean-Louis Guignabodet	F	MIG	5	DNF	1m 37.82s	31
	Luca Cadalora	I	Yamaha		DNS	1m 37.73s	30
	D. Stankovic	YU	Yamaha		DNQ	1m 41.42s	
	Massimo Sirianni	I	Yamaha		DNQ	1m 41.78s	
	I. Sola	YU	MBA		DNQ	1m 42.32s	
	N. Marmaras	GR	Yamaha		DNQ	1m 46.19s	

Fastest lap: Lavado, 1m 34.09s, 99.03 mph/159.473 km/h.
Lap record: Carlos Lavado, YV (Yamaha), 1m 33.43s, 99.72 mph/160.599 km/h (1986).

World Championship: 1 Roth, 55; **2** Mang, 52; **3** Cornu, 38; **4** Pons, 35; **5** Lavado, 29; **6** Wimmer, 28; **7** Sarron, 27; **8** Reggiani, 24; **9** Garriga, 20; **10** Cadalora and Cardus, 18; **12** Igoa and Kobayashi, 15; **14** Shimuzu, 8; **15** Ruggia, 4; **16** Vitali, 3; **17** Mertens and Taguchi, 2; **19** Bertin, Palazzese and Yamamoto, 1.

80 cc

17 laps, 44.03 miles/70.856 km

Place	Rider	Nat.	Machine	Laps	Time & speed	Practice time	Grid
1	Jorge Martinez	E	Derbi	17	29m 10.37s 90.49 mph/ 145.730 km/h	1m 41.09s	1
2	Stefan Dörflinger	CH	Krauser	17	29m 17.27s	1m 41.48s	2
3	Ian McConnachie	GB	Krauser	17	29m 25.27s	1m 44.98s	10
4	Gerhard Waibel	D	Krauser	17	29m 31.98s	1m 44.22s	6
5	Manuel Herreros	E	Derbi	17	29m 32.15s	1m 43.60s	3
6	Hubert Abold	D	Krauser	17	29m 49.55s	1m 44.10s	5
7	Jörg Seel	D	Seel	17	29m 50.19s	1m 44.60s	8
8	Hans Spaan	NL	Casal	17	29m 58.19s	1m 43.93s	4
9	Juan Ramon Bolart	E	Krauser	17	30m 18.91s	1m 45.77s	11
10	Alexandre Barros	BR	Casal	17	30m 19.10s	1m 46.22s	14
11	Mario Stocco	I	Faccioli	17	30m 42.05s	1m 47.19s	16
12	Rainer Kunz	D	Ziegler	17	30m 49.32s	1m 46.02s	12
13	Alojz Pavlic	YU	Seel	16	29m 10.88s	1m 46.18s	13
14	Reiner Koster	CH	Kroko	16	29m 22.96s	1m 49.37s	23
15	Richard Bay	D	Ziegler	16	29m 23.44s	1m 47.34s	17
16	Janez Pintar	YU	Eberhardt	16	29m 24.16s	1m 48.26s	20
17	Jos van Dongen	NL	Krauser-Hummel	16	29m 24.35s	1m 48.29s	21
18	Serge Julin	B	Casal	16	29m 27.37s	1m 49.89s	25
19	Paul Bordes	F	RB	16	29m 27.60s	1m 49.24s	22
21	Hagen Klein	D	Hess	16	29m 46.57s	1m 49.50s	24
21	Brane Rokavec	YU	Seel	16	30m 57.86s	1m 54.02s	30
22	Francisco Torrontegui	E	Arbizu	15	30m 25.70s	1m 46.22s	14
	Luis M. Reyes	E	Autisa	9	DNF	1m 44.28s	7
	Theo Timmer	NL	Casal	8	DNF	1m 47.63s	18
	Zdravko Matulja	YU	Ziegler	6	DNF	1m 49.95s	26
	Stuart Edwards	GB	Casal	6	DNF	1m 53.70s	29
	Josef Fischer	A	Krauser	1	DNF	1m 44.61s	9
	Wilco Zeelenberg	NL	Casal		DNS	1m 46.30s	15
	Johann Auer	D	Auer		DNS	1m 51.81s	27
	Felix Rodriguez	E	Casal		DNS	1m 52.45s	28
	Giuliano Tabanelli	I	UFO		DNQ	1m 58.55s	
	S. Vasic	YU	Sever		DNQ	2m 00.60s	
	Zdravko Leljak	YU	Sever		DNQ	2m 00.78s	
	M. Nervo	YU	Sever		DNQ	2m 01.19s	
	U. Tomanovic	YU	Sever		DNQ	2m 02.71s	
	Miroslav Lesicki	YU	Sever		DNQ	2m 02.99s	

Fastest lap: Martinez, 1m 41.23s, 91.93 mph/148.225 km/h.
Lap record: Jorge Martinez, E (Derbi), 1m 40.16s, 93.087 mph/149.808 km/h (1986).

World Championship: 1 Martinez, 72; **2** Waibel, 44; **3** Herreros, 39; **4** Dörflinger, 32; **5** McConnachie, 28; **6** Abold, 18; **7** Seel, 15; **8** Criville, 12; **9** Fischer, Miralles and Reyes, 10; **12** Spaan, 8; **13** Schirnhofer, 6; **14** Juhász, 5; **15** Barros, Paschen and Priori, 4; **18** Bay and Bolart, 3; **20** Gschwander, 2; **21** Waldmann, 1.

Grote Prijs van NEDERLAND

How things had changed in one year since Lawson dominated the Dutch TT practice in '86 and set a target that no-one could match, even if you took the official timing when private clocks had the Californian a second faster yet. Lawson crashed out on the first lap of that race and joked this season that he would not waste everyone's time and would just lay the bike down on the first corner.

A year later everything was turned around completely and Lawson was outpaced in practice but rode a perfectly measured race to win. What shook things in practice was not the way Gardner acquired his now-customary advantage but the fact that Lawson was pushed out of second place by a virtual newcomer, Kevin Magee, riding in only his second Grand Prix. After crashing three times in that meeting it was easy to criticise him for over-enthusiasm and think that his riding would have to be more

restrained if he was to stay aboard. The critics must have nodded knowingly when Magee crashed at home in Australia during the Easter Bathurst meeting and broke his leg.

Unrestrained Magee may have been in Japan, and he certainly lacked 500 cc experience, having ridden only in the three Swann series events in late '86 when he beat McElnea twice in six short races and finished second to him in the series. All newcomers make mistakes and Magee learnt fast and never put a foot wrong at Assen. Despite disappointment in Japan and injury at home, he maintained that innate confidence in his own ability that is a formidable resource in so many champions.

Belief in your ability is no good if it is misplaced, but to watch Magee play with the 500 Yamaha like it was a familiar dirt bike that he could turn, slide and wheelie at will left little doubt that he has the requisite ability.

Like all Assen newcomers Magee found the circuit narrow but he quickly got down to some impressive times and he was thirteenth-fastest after the first session, while Lawson led from Chili who was fast confirming his position as one of the men of '87. If thirteenth was good, fourth for Magee in session two was sensational, with only Lawson, Mamola and Gardner ahead.

The third session was damp yet that hardly slowed the Australian at all and he was the quickest man on Friday morning even though he was new to the Dunlop tyres as well as the circuit. The afternoon became an Australian benefit with Gardner in crushing form and Magee putting every other Yamaha rider in the shade while Lawson battled after seizing his best engine early in the final period and slipped to third.

Magee was using basically a 1986-specification Yamaha as he had done at Suzuka, but this time

it was supplied and maintained by the Lucky Strike team who were obviously considering his services for their 1988 line-up. The bike was not in Lucky Strike colours because of Magee's commitment to the Australian Marlboro Yamaha at home.

With Baldwin still injured, Richard Scott continued to ride as a replacement but was still fighting to find form after his accidents in Yugoslavia and Austria. He was getting into his stride at Assen and was placed eleventh after three sessions but dropped to fourteenth in the end and slipped off when he left the track and could not control the Yamaha on wet grass.

Niall Mackenzie did the same thing and neither rider needed the extra tap to their confidence. Mackenzie was down in eleventh place still troubled by his Yugoslav ankle injury and wearing one of McElnea's boots Wimmer-fashion to protect it. McElnea seemed to be struggling with his broken finger and had gained little by spending a week at Willi Dungl's clinic in Austria with Mackenzie. McElnea saved the day with an inspired couple of laps right at the end of the final session to jump from tenth to fifth just behind Ron Haslam and ahead of Christian Sarron. The Frenchman said things were improving slowly after his Yugoslav accident though on Thursday he had been very concerned that he would be unable to race. 'I cannot pick a line properly; I dare not go near the white lines because I do not trust my judgement.' Not only did the Frenchman have problems with his riding but his personal life was upset by his estrangement from girlfriend Karen.

Team-mate Patrick Igoa made his comeback after his horrific Salzburgring accident and had a painful ride with his healing hip injury.

There were plenty of falls in Holland too, with Fabio Biliotti breaking his ankle and possibly his scafoid when he crashed his 500 Honda, and Gustav Reiner wrenched his hip when he crashed his Hein Gericke Hondas twice in five minutes. After falling from one bike he got back to the pits only to rush out and fall off the other while the tyres were still cold.

Eternally unlucky, Loris Reggiani broke two bones in his foot without even falling off the Aprilia. Another rider crashed in front of him and his foot was hit by the machine as he rode past; it also tore the carburettors off the Rotax. 'No, I am not unlucky,' said the Italian. 'It hit me so hard I thought it had taken my foot off. I should be able to ride at the French GP.' Fellow Italian Maurizio Vitali crashed the 250 Garelli and broke a finger.

80 cc

Aspar Martínez started by charging into the lead on the works Derbi and was never headed, while the opposition either struggled or crashed behind him. At the end of twelve laps team-mate Manuel Herreros was second ahead of ex-champion Stefan Dörflinger on the Krauser. His team-mates Gerhard Waibel and Ian McConnachie had both fallen though McConnachie remounted to come home eighth.

Waibel looked a threat to Martínez early on but by lap 4 the championship leader had opened a visible advantage that the German could not recover. The third-place struggle was the most exciting, with Herreros under pressure from McConnachie, Dörflinger, Jörg Seel on his father's machine, Luis Reyes on the Autisa and Alex Barros on the Arbizu.

On lap 7, Seel crashed and broke his collarbone. The seventeen-year-old has been riding well all season, especially considering his age, and only rode in his first race the weekend after last year's Dutch TT. Though his father, Horst Seel, builds the machine only Jörg works on it.

That fall split up the group and for a short period McConnachie had an advantage in third place ahead of Dörflinger and Herreros. A lap later he had thrown it all away, as had Waibel his second place, and the Krauser challenge was effectively cut from three to two as Dörflinger tried to hold Herreros at bay. The Krauser was losing power, though, and Dörflinger later said that it had been sick since lap 3. That explained why he could not match his practice performance and on the final circuit Herreros made it a Derbi one-two. Barros fell on lap 9 but remounted to finish 22nd.

250 cc

Cornu seems to be one of those riders who either clicks into gear at a Grand Prix or will be below par for the entire weekend. He is not helped by the fact that either his size and weight are a significant disadvantage on a 250 or his bikes are not very fast. This time his best machine seized in the morning warm-up session and though he led from the start he was soon relegated to second as the faster Hondas took over. First to get in front was Reinhold Roth on the HB machine, followed by Sito Pons on the Campsa bike and then Carlos Cardus on the Ducados entry who survived being hit by Dominique Sarron at the chicane on the end of the first lap. The Frenchman ended up in the dirt and out of the race.

Mang was ninth at the end of lap 1 after a sluggish start where he thought many others jumped the lights. He did not stay back for long. A lap later he was sixth just behind Carlos Lavado and by the fifth circuit he was right behind Pons and Roth and challenging them for the lead.

Those three moved ahead of Cardus and Cornu with a tight bunch behind in which Stéphane Mertens led Juan Garriga, Lavado, and old Venemotos team-mate Ivan Palazzese – for the second time in as many Grands Prix making a big impact on his private TZ250. Patrick Igoa and Martin Wimmer joined that pack after slow starts.

Mang took the lead on lap 6 but it was not until lap 9 that he opened up any kind of substantial advantage. Once clear of Roth and Pons he was obviously going to win as neither could make any impression. Roth broke free of Pons who had found his machine no match for those of the two

Germans but he was well clear of fellow Spaniard Cardus.

Cornu's fifth place was not so secure because that group behind him were catching up and Wimmer, who was in the middle of the pack, suddenly jumped to the front as Igoa, Mertens and Lavado tried to out-brake each other into the 90-degree right-hander at the end of the back straight. Mertens crashed and ended up 13th, while the other two also lost ground.

Both Wimmer and Palazzese managed to beat Cornu to the line. 'I was lucky that those in front collided because it gave me the chance to catch Cornu', said Wimmer. 'I was a gear higher than everyone else through one section so I held back and passed him there just as he looked over his shoulder. I would have done better but I made a bad start. I don't know what went wrong but I had to use the clutch twice to get away.'

125 cc

The least inspiring race of the day was as usual a Garelli benefit, perhaps a sign that many teams are already thinking of single-cylinder development. Ex-title holder and championship leader Fausto Gresini led team-mate Bruno Casanova, and neither Paolo Casoli nor August Auinger on the MBAs could offer any sort of challenge.

At first Casoli was close while Casanova had the lead but Gresini was playing games and on lap 3 increased the pace enough to drop Casoli. Auinger thought his rear chain was jumping the sprocket because the engine was making a strange noise as he changed gear so he tried shifting early and it seemed to go away. That left him with no chance of catching Casoli but at least he finished the race.

Even the lower places were decided early as Pier Paolo Bianchi secured himself fifth ahead of Mike Leitner who at least had to do a bit of work to get away from Corrado Catalano. The only real interest was the race-long battle for eighth between Andrés Marín Sánchez, Jean-Claude Selini and Thierry Feuz.

500 cc

The grey day got greyer as the 500 race approached, fine drops of rain fell, but with the track substantially dry and Assen having a reputation for good predictable grip everyone was fitted with slicks for the start. Haslam made his jump off the line closely pursued by Mamola, Gardner and McElnea. Haslam held the lead for the first lap from Mamola while Roche shot through to third half-way round the first circuit.

As Mamola chased Haslam into the chicane before the start-and-finish straight the front wheel of the Yamaha tucked under and he was down sliding across the grass. 'I remembered last year that the marshals did not let Eddie restart so I was right back on the bike and riding it out of the dirt as soon as I could while I could see the marshals running towards me.'

Magee felt the front end tuck under as he pitched the Yamaha into the same turn but saved it and held on to seventh place. The drama

From the start, Egbert Streuer had the advantage over Steve Webster, and the British outfit's misfire ensured that the Dutch crew were never seriously threatened.

Like several others, Niall Mackenzie (below) discovered that a slick-shod 500 does not handle well on wet grass.

gave Haslam a 1.4s lead over Gardner and McElnea, while Lawson had made ground quickly passing Roche and de Radiguès to take fourth.

It looked to the Clerk of the Course watching at the startline as though the fine rain had already wetted the circuit. After he had seen Mamola fall he stopped the race.

Mamola's luck was in because as the race had run such a short distance it was restarted afresh and he could have used another bike. In fact the first machine was quickly repaired while the start was delayed. The light rain stopped as soon as the race did but, as the riders lined up for the second start, the conditions were precisely the same as at the first.

No-one could risk wet tyres because if the track dried they would not last the distance. Starting on slicks the riders knew that the Clerk of the Course was bound by FIM regulations to stop the race if the rain made the track dangerous for untreaded tyres.

In a fine mist of precipitation the race started again and, true to form, Haslam again took charge with Mamola once more second ahead of Gardner and Lawson fifth but cutting his way to the front in a ruthless fashion. By half-way round the first lap he was pushing aside Mamola to take second while Roche was threatening Gardner for third.

Completing lap 1 there was another incident at the chicane and this time Mamola and Roche came together. Although the cause of the collision is not certain the result was that Roche crashed out of the race while Mamola was able to recover, only losing enough time to drop him to seventh just behind Magee.

The race pattern quickly developed with Lawson and Gardner chasing Haslam who said later that he should have had a bigger lead in the opening laps except that he, too, had had a slide at the chicane. Fourth was McElnea ahead of Taira, Magee, Mamola and de Radiguès.

Lawson went inside Haslam at the Strubben to take the lead but certainly did not pull away, and even when Gardner went by two laps later Haslam was still trying to ride round the outside of both. McElnea was a good fourth, although he might soon come under pressure from Sarron who had charged through to fifth after a slow start. Taira held sixth from Magee who looked very reserved, obviously not sure how much grip was available after his early slide. Likewise Mamola was not making up ground and the rain was getting heavier.

By half-way round lap 6 the leaders were touring, having taken the decision amongst themselves that the track was getting too wet for them to continue on slicks. Lawson later explained how they had come to an agreement. 'We were riding side by side and I looked across at Wayne and he signalled "no way" and shut the throttle. So did I and so did Ron.' Obviously the thought had been in the minds of those following because they all eased off and toured back to the pits in line astern. Confusion reigned

Right: **Another win for Gresini, followed home by the lapped Appleyard (36) and second-placed Casanova.**

Below: **Martínez – the man they all look up to in the 80 cc class.**

for a moment as it was clearly a case of the tail wagging the dog and some riders were so far behind that they did not even see the leading twenty or so tour into the pits. Buckmaster, Kneubühler and six others went past to start their seventh lap and only then did the Clerk of the Course put out the red flag.

That left a degree of confusion over whether or not the eight should be credited with an extra lap, but the rules clearly state that when a race is stopped the results are taken from the previous lap and everyone had crossed the finish line at the end of lap 6 even though many had done so in the pit lane.

As it was, the results were taken from the end of lap 5, the thinking being that the red flag was shown at the end of lap 6, but in fact the leaders never saw the flag and had they continued would not have done so until the end of lap 7. The result after five laps was the only reliable one because the timing beams do not work in the pit lane and the overall race result had to be calculated on total time.

Bad luck for Buckmaster and co., but the rules did not really cover a decision made by the riders. While no-one can criticise them for taking a safety-oriented decision like that and none of them had anything to gain by it, the organisation all but fell apart because of it. There can be no rules that are flexible enough to cover all such eventualities so riders really have to be controlled by the Clerk of the Course with the hope that he has the wisdom to act properly.

With five laps counting, the rest of the twenty laps were to be completed in a separate race. The track remained wet this time and the announcement was made that under no circumstances would the race be stopped again.

With the finishing times for the first race rather than the order being important, Mamola was left with a 13.5s deficit to Gardner. Lawson was just two-tenths behind the Australian and an equal distance ahead of Haslam.

The riders used a variety of cut slick and intermediate tyres, and the pack shot off the line in a cloud of spray, with Gardner ahead of Haslam, Lawson and Mamola. The Lucky Strike man knew what his task entailed and cut straight through to lead on lap 1 with Lawson second and Gardner third while Haslam had been pushed straight back to sixth behind Burnett and de Radiguès.

Mamola quickly opened up a lead and later he would say that in the opening laps his choice of cut slick tyres was perfect with the rear giving him particularly good drive. Haslam was soon back up to fourth by lap 3 but then went straight on at the end of the front straight and dropped down to twelfth.

The race settled to Mamola forcing his way clear of Lawson and Gardner with the Marlboro Yamaha gaining the upper hand after a couple of laps. McElnea was a lonely fourth while Burnett looked good in fifth just ahead of de Radiguès, Irons, Haslam and Sarron.

Lawson had pulled well clear of Gardner but then took to the same slip road as Haslam had used and he had to pull away from the Australian once more.

That meant that Mamola had more than recovered his first race deficit when on lap 10 he matched Lawson's mistake and braked too hard at the end of the front straight, locked the wheel and had to take to the slip road while he recovered control. 'I got the bike turned around and heading back up the slip road as Lawson came down to the corner. I was heading straight towards him and could just imagine him muttering "dumb son of a b . . ." as he saw that I had screwed up. I just got back on the track as he made the turn.'

From lap 10 Lawson was in front with Mamola tailing him, but it looked as though he had settled for second, accepting that he could not reopen the necessary time gap over the Marlboro Yamaha. Though he could not beat Lawson he was still in front of Gardner and on the last lap Mamola put in a big effort to gain the 13.5s he needed to steal second from the Australian. The fact that it meant finishing in front of Lawson just suited the Lucky Strike rider's sense of drama and he dived past on the final circuit leaving him no more room than was absolutely essential.

On his way to the rostrum Lawson said he was lucky to get the overall victory. 'I had the wrong tyres on because we needed full wets once the rain really started coming down. Every time I touched the throttle it went sideways and I lucked out when Randy went down the slip road. I had already been down it once and I thought I would never catch him till he did the same thing. It is easy enough to do: with all that rain and spray about it is hard to see the brake markers.'

The crowd loved Mamola's performance, particularly the last-lap effort, but he had not gained enough over the Rothmans Honda so ended the day third. McElnea was fourth after a lonely race when he might have been able to beat Mamola had he been informed about their relative time difference, for he had a seven-second advantage over the Californian going into the second leg but finally finished three and a half seconds behind on total time, deprived of a place on the rostrum once more.

Haslam was a good fifth, but it could have been so much better considering the opening laps of the first two races. De Radiguès had had by far his best ride of the season and so had Burnett, who finished behind him. Solid performances, too, from Irons and Chili, with Magee getting a single point for tenth which was hardly what he had come to expect after practice. 'There was so much spray and water running down the inside of my visor that I could not see from one corner to the next. I decided to pull in and cruised for half a lap but then realised I could still get one point so I carried on.'

Mackenzie had pulled out when he realised that he would not finish in the points, not wanting to risk his injured ankle. Sarron was forced out with engine trouble on lap 18, the Sonauto Gauloises Yamaha had been going slower and slower through the race. Richard Scott crashed at the first corner when he ran wide in the spray and slipped over on the grass.

Sidecars

Not surprisingly the crowd had got a little fed up with the delays in the 500 race after sitting all day getting soaked but they loved the sidecar race run in the same wet conditions as the second leg of the 500. It was a perfect demonstration by Egbert Streuer and Bernard Schnieders, and championship leaders Steve Webster and Tony Hewitt were just pleased to finish second after their Krauser LCR misfired all the way through. Alain Michel and Jean-Marc Fresc had to work very hard for third after being balked on the line.

The French ace, who is closest to Webster in the championship, thought about protesting after the race. 'Streuer did not play the game. When he pulled up on the startline after the warm-up lap he pulled across a little so that he was in front of me leaving me no room to go through. I started faster than he did and would have run into him had I not almost stopped again. That ruined my start so I was way behind. I thought of protesting but that is not my way. I will have a word with Egbert later.'

Michel was down in twelfth place at the end of the first lap while Rolf Steinhausen and Bruno Hiller were ahead of Rolf Biland and Kurt Waltisperg. Michel advanced all the time and by the end of lap 7 was up to fifth behind Steinhausen who had been relegated by Biland. It took the French ace until lap 15 of the 16 to get past into third but the effort was well worth it as he stays in front of Streuer in the championship and in touch with Webster.

Grote Prijs van Nederland, 22/27 June/statistics
Circuit van Drenthe, Assen, 3.812-mile/6.134-km circuit

500 cc

20 laps, 76.24 miles/122.68 km

Place	Rider	Nat.	Machine	Laps	Time & speed	Practice time	Grid
1	Eddie Lawson	USA	Yamaha	20	50m 12.91s 91.03 mph/ 146.585 km/h	2m 14.07s	3
2	Wayne Gardner	AUS	Honda	20	50m 19.58s	2m 12.33s	1
3	Randy Mamola	USA	Yamaha	20	50m 25.90s	2m 14.64s	7
4	Rob McElnea	GB	Yamaha	20	50m 29.34s	2m 14.31s	5
5	Ron Haslam	GB	Honda	20	50m 51.22s	2m 14.27s	4
6	Didier de Radiguès	B	Cagiva	20	50m 56.25s	2m 15.16s	10
7	Roger Burnett	GB	Honda	20	50m 58.14s	2m 16.80s	13
8	Kenny Irons	GB	Suzuki	20	51m 16.00s	2m 17.51s	17
9	Pier Francesco Chili	I	Honda	20	51m 54.33s	2m 15.88s	12
10	Kevin Magee	AUS	Yamaha	20	52m 13.02s	2m 14.01s	2
11	Ray Swann	GB	Honda	20	52m 36.17s	2m 19.74s	27
12	Simon Buckmaster	GB	Honda	20	53m 07.93s	2m 20.05s	31
13	Marco Gentile	CH	Fior	20	53m 16.52s	2m 18.46s	20
14	Shunji Yatsushiro	J	Honda	20	53m 32.28s	2m 17.33s	15
15	Fabio Barchitta	RSM	Honda	20	53m 34.79s	2m 20.88s	36
16	Gerold Fischer	D	Honda	20	53m 37.12s	2m 21.02s	37
17	Steve Manley	GB	Suzuki	20	54m 28.75s	2m 19.78s	29
18	Tadahiko Taira	J	Yamaha	19	51m 18.66s	2m 14.74s	9
19	Silvo Habat	YU	Honda	19	51m 43.38s	2m 20.20s	33
20	Hervé Guilleux	F	Honda	18	50m 10.51s	2m 18.94s	23
21	Bruno Kneubühler	CH	Honda	18	51m 46.31s	2m 19.95s	30
22	Daniel Amatriain	E	Honda	18	54m 12.33s	2m 20.09s	32
	Christian Sarron	F	Yamaha	18	DNF	2m 14.60s	6
	Karl Truchsess	A	Honda	14	DNF	2m 19.57s	25
	Niall Mackenzie	GB	Honda	12	DNF	2m 15.43s	11
	Mark Phillips	GB	Suzuki	11	DNF	2m 19.52s	24
	Rob Punt	NL	Suzuki	11	DNF	2m 20.49s	34
	Manfred Fischer	D	Honda	9	DNF	2m 18.33s	19
	Alan Jeffery	GB	Suzuki	6	DNF	2m 18.59s	21
	Wolfgang von Muralt	CH	Suzuki	6	DNF	2m 17.50s	16
	Richard Scott	NZ	Yamaha	5	DNF	2m 16.84s	14
	Henk van der Mark	NL	Honda	5	DNF	2m 19.73s	26
	Alessandro Valesi	I	Honda	1	DNF	2m 18.66s	22
	Raymond Roche	F	Cagiva	1	DNF	2m 14.74s	8
	Marco Papa	I	Honda		DNS	2m 17.90s	18
	Koos van Leyen	NL	Suzuki		DNS	2m 19.77s	28
	Fabio Biliotti	I	Honda		DNS	2m 20.83s	35
	Maarten Duyzers	NL	Honda		DNQ	2m 21.51s	
	Andreas Leuthe	LUX	Honda		DNQ	2m 21.75s	
	Henny Boerman	NL	Assmex-Honda		DNQ	2m 23.25s	
	Josef Doppler	A	Honda		DNQ	2m 31.52s	
	Larry Moreno Vacondio	I·	Suzuki		DNQ	2m 17.48s	

Fastest lap: Lawson, 2m 16.05s, 100.79 mph/162.311 km/h.
Lap record: Wayne Gardner, AUS (Honda), 2m 14.28s, 102.185 mph/164.450 km/h (1986).

World Championship: 1 Gardner, 85; **2** Mamola, 66; **3** Lawson, 64; **4** Haslam, 54; **5**McElnea and Taira, 28; **7** Chili, 25; **8** Mackenzie, 23; **9** Burnett and Sarron, 15; **11** Ito and Yatsushiro, 10; **13** Roche and Schwantz, 9; **15** de Radiguès, 5; **16** Irons and Kawasaki, 4; **18** Scott, 3; **19** Katayama and Reiner, 2; **21** Magee, 1.

80 cc

12 laps, 45.74 miles/73.61 km

Place	Rider	Nat.	Machine	Laps	Time & speed	Practice time	Grid
1	Jorge Martinez	E	Derbi	12	31m 02.52s 88.35 mph/ 142.274 km/h	2m 34.28s	2
2	Manuel Herreros	E	Derbi	12	31m 24.93s	2m 37.72s	8
3	Stefan Dörflinger	CH	Krauser	12	31m 25.98s	2m 32.83s	1
4	Luis M. Reyes	E	Autisa	12	31m 38.72s	2m 37.64s	7
5	Julian Miralles	E	Derbi	12	31m 40.11s	2m 37.88s	9
6	Károly Juhász	H	Krauser	12	31m 44.09s	2m 41.90s	27
7	Hubert Abold	D	Krauser	12	31m 48.34s	2m 37.55s	6
8	Ian McConnachie	GB	Krauser	12	32m 10.82s	2m 34.67s	3
9	Peter Öttl	D	Krauser	12	32m 12.96s	2m 40.92s	18
10	Günther Schirnhofer	D	Krauser	12	32m 28.24s	2m 41.86s	26
11	Reiner Scheidhauer	D	Seel	12	32m 36.16s	2m 40.79s	17
12	Heinz Paschen	D	Casal	12	32m 36.75s	2m 41.64s	23
13	Stefan Prein	NL	Casal	12	32m 37.15s	2m 41.82s	25
14	René Dünki	CH	Krauser	12	32m 39.30s	2m 40.96s	19
15	Reiner Koster	CH	Kroko	12	32m 39.73s	2m 41.58s	22
16	Bert Smit	NL	Minarelli	12	32m 42.77s	2m 40.24s	16
17	Janez Pintar	YU	Eberhardt	12	32m 43.72s	2m 42.89s	30
18	Wilco Zeelenberg	NL	Casal	12	32m 52.61s	2m 43.62s	33
19	Ralf Waldmann	D	Seel	12	32m 55.50s	2m 39.30s	14
20	Jos van Dongen	NL	Krauser	12	32m 55.74s	2m 43.71s	35
21	Rainer Kunz	D	Ziegler	12	33m 11.98s	2m 38.88s	12
22	Alexandre Barros	BR	Arbizu	12	33m 15.36s	2m 38.49s	11
23	Theo Timmer	NL	Casal	12	33m 21.30s	2m 42.81s	29
24	Alojz Pavlic	YU	Seel	11	31m 29.84s	2m 42.99s	31
	Hans Spaan	NL	Casal	11	DNF	2m 39.23s	13
	Gerhard Waibel	D	Krauser	8	DNF	2m 35.60s	4
	Raimo Lipponen	SF	Krauser	8	DNF	2m 41.36s	21
	Jörg Seel	D	Seel	6	DNF	2m 38.17s	10
	Kees Besseling	NL	Special	6	DNF	2m 43.02s	32
	Richard Bay	D	Ziegler	6	DNF	2m 41.81s	24
	Alejandro Criville	E	Derbi	5	DNF	2m 36.16s	5
	Paolo Priori	I	Krauser	5	DNF	2m 42.09s	28
	Josef Fischer	A	Krauser	5	DNF	2m 40.96s	20
	Lionel Robert	F	SPR	4	DNF	2m 44.25s	36
	Mario Stocco	I	Faccioli	2	DNF	2m 43.64s	34
	Juan Ramon Bolart	E	Krauser	1	DNF	2m 39.44s	15
	Jacques Bernard	B	Huvo		DNQ	2m 44.39s	
	Serge Julin	B	Casal		DNQ	2m 44.98s	
	Thomas Engl	D	Esch-GPE		DNQ	2m 45.14s	
	Stuart Edwards	GB	Casal		DNQ	2m 45.19s	
	Chris Baert	B	Seel		DNQ	2m 45.21s	
	Hans Koopman	NL	Ziegler		DNQ	2m 45.31s	
	Adrie Nijenhuis	NL	Casal		DNQ	2m 45.47s	
	Paul Bordes	F	RB		DNQ	2m 46.15s	
	Dennis Batchelor	GB	Krauser		DNQ	2m 50.15s	
	Otto Machinek	A	H&M		DNQ	2m 51.14s	
	Francisco Torrontegui	E	Arbizu		DNQ	2m 53.89s	
	Mika-Sakari Komu	SF	Eberhardt		DNQ	3m 02.02s	

Fastest lap: Martinez, 2m 33.89s, 89.11 mph/143.496 km/h.
Lap record: Ian McConnachie, GB (Krauser), 2m 30.79s, 90.997 mph/146.445 km/h (1986).

World Championship: 1 Martinez, 87; **2** Herreros, 51; **3** Waibel, 44; **4** Dörflinger, 42; **5** McConnachie, 31; **6** Abold, 22; **7** Reyes, 18; **8** Miralles, 16; **9** Seel, 15; **10** Criville, 12; **11** Fischer and Juhász, 10; **13** Spaan, 8; **14** Schirnhofer, 7; **15** Barros, Paschen and Priori, 4; **18** Bay and Bolart, 3; **20** Gschwander and Öttl, 2; **22** Waldmann, 1.

250 cc

18 laps, 68.62 miles/110.41 km

Place	Rider	Nat.	Machine	Laps	Time & speed	Practice time	Grid
1	Anton Mang	D	Honda	18	41m 47.20s 98.45 mph/ 158.537 km/h	2m 19.08s	2
2	Reinhold Roth	D	Honda	18	41m 53.65s	2m 19.48s	5
3	Sito Pons	E	Honda	18	42m 00.34s	2m 19.23s	4
4	Carlos Cardus	E	Honda	18	42m 14.34s	2m 19.71s	7
5	Martin Wimmer	D	Yamaha	18	42m 21.24s	2m 19.91s	8
6	Ivan Palazzese	YV	Yamaha	18	42m 21.56s	2m 21.33s	18
7	Jacques Cornu	CH	Honda	18	42m 21.89s	2m 19.09s	3
8	Juan Garriga	E	Yamaha	18	42m 22.16s	2m 19.97s	9
9	Patrick Igoa	F	Yamaha	18	42m 26.59s	2m 20.51s	11
10	Carlos Lavado	YV	Yamaha	18	42m 33.19s	2m 18.65s	1
11	Manfred Herweh	D	Honda	18	42m 37.17s	2m 20.55s	12
12	Guy Bertin	F	Honda	18	42m 40.07s	2m 21.19s	16
13	Stéphane Mertens	B	Sekitoba	18	42m 45.25s	2m 19.60s	6
14	Donnie McLeod	GB	EMC	18	42m 45.47s	2m 20.96s	15
15	Luca Cadalora	I	Yamaha	18	42m 46.19s	2m 20.24s	10
16	Hans Lindner	A	Honda	18	42m 51.36s	2m 22.05s	23
17	Xavier Cardelus	AND	Cobas	18	42m 53.92s	2m 20.60s	14
18	Jochen Schmid	D	Yamaha	18	42m 54.13s	2m 21.33s	17
19	Harald Eckl	D	Honda	18	42m 54.49s	2m 22.80s	27
20	Alberto Puig	E	Cobas	18	42m 54.74s	2m 22.72s	26
21	Jean-Michel Mattioli	F	Honda	18	42m 55.27s	2m 21.34s	19
22	Cees Doorakkers	NL	Honda	18	42m 56.06s	2m 22.38s	24
23	Urs Lüzi	CH	Honda	18	42m 56.31s	2m 23.17s	29
24	Patrick van der Goorbergh	NL	Honda	18	42m 59.91s	2m 22.61s	25
25	Jean Foray	F	Chevallier	18	43m 12.25s	2m 21.95s	22
26	Jean-Philippe Ruggia	F	Yamaha	18	43m 19.47s	2m 21.93s	21
27	Gary Cowan	IRL	Honda	18	43m 32.47s	2m 23.39s	31
28	René Delaby	LUX	Yamaha	18	43m 36.43s	2m 23.51s	33
29	Massimo Matteoni	I	Honda	18	43m 36.70s	2m 22.88s	28
30	Andreas Preining	A	Rotax	18	44m 11.50s	2m 23.81s	36
	Siegfried Minich	A	Honda	15	DNF	2m 23.69s	35
	Kevin Mitchell	GB	Yamaha	7	DNF	2m 23.43s	32
	Stefano Caracchi	RSM	Honda	4	DNF	2m 21.38s	20
	Nedy Crotta	CH	Rotax	1	DNF	2m 23.56s	34
	Dominique Sarron	F	Honda		DNS	2m 20.56s	13
	Rob Orme	GB	Yamaha		DNS	2m 23.35s	30
	Nigel Bosworth	GB	Yamaha		DNQ	2m 23.82s	
	Gerard van der Wal	NL	Rotax		DNQ	2m 23.99s	
	Josef Hutter	A	Honda		DNQ	2m 24.33s	
	André Stamsnijder	NL	Honda		DNQ	2m 24.43s	
	Jean-François Baldé	F	Defi		DNQ	2m 24.57s	
	Mar Schouten	NL	Honda		DNQ	2m 24.79s	
	Jean-Louis Guignabodet	F	MIG		DNQ	2m 25.04s	
	Rudi Gächter	CH	Yamaha		DNQ	2m 27.57s	
	Albert Jacmin	B	Rotax		DNQ	2m 29.68s	

Fastest lap: Mang, 2m 17.75s, 99.55 mph/160.308 km/h (record).
Previous record: Martin Wimmer, D (Yamaha), 2m 19.07s, 98.665 mph/158.786 km/h (1986).

World Championship: 1 Mang and Roth, 67; **3** Pons, 45; **4** Cornu, 42; **5** Wimmer, 34; **6** Lavado, 30; **7** Sarron, 27; **8** Cardus, 26; **9** Reggiani, 24; **10** Garriga, 23; **11** Cadalora, 18; **12** Igoa, 17; **13** Kobayashi, 15; **14** Shimuzu, 8; **15** Palazzese, 6; **16** Ruggia, 4; **17** Vitali, 3; **18** Mertens and Taguchi, 2; **20** Bertin and Yamamoto, 1.

125 cc

16 laps, 60.99 miles/98.14 km

Place	Rider	Nat.	Machine	Laps	Time & speed	Practice time	Grid
1	Fausto Gresini	I	Garelli	16	39m 00.97s 93.73 mph/ 150.928 km/h	2m 25.62s	2
2	Bruno Casanova	I	Garelli	16	39m 01.26s	2m 25.34s	1
3	Paolo Casoli	I	AGV	16	39m 34.67s	2m 26.67s	3
4	August Auinger	A	MBA	16	39m 42.86s	2m 26.94s	4
5	Pier Paolo Bianchi	I	MBA	16	39m 57.15s	2m 28.15s	7
6	Mike Leitner	A	MBA	16	40m 02.56s	2m 27.80s	6
7	Corrado Catalano	I	MBA	16	40m 12.67s	2m 29.92s	14
8	Andrés Marin Sánchez	E	Ducados	16	40m 17.01s	2m 29.79s	10
9	Jean-Claude Selini	F	MBA	16	40m 19.25s	2m 29.86s	12
10	Thierry Feuz	CH	MBA	16	40m 20.32s	2m 29.56s	9
11	Johnny Wickström	SF	Tunturi	16	40m 26.79s	2m 29.81s	11
12	Adolf Stadler	D	MBA	16	40m 27.09s	2m 30.62s	16
13	Olivier Liegeois	B	Assmex	16	40m 34.05s	2m 31.44s	19
14	Ezio Gianola	I	Honda	16	40m 46.65s	2m 31.58s	21
15	Norbert Peschke	D	Seel	16	40m 47.34s	2m 32.11s	26
16	Håkan Olsson	S	Starol	16	40m 47.59s	2m 32.90s	29
17	Claudio Macciotta	I	MBA	16	41m 01.47s	2m 31.45s	20
18	Peter Sommer	CH	Supeso	16	41m 10.92s	2m 30.97s	18
19	Manuel Hernandez	E	Beneti	16	41m 19.98s	2m 30.92s	17
20	Esa Kytölä	SF	MBA	16	41m 20.40s	2m 31.58s	22
21	Robin Appleyard	GB	MBA	16	41m 44.39s	2m 34.37s	36
22	Fernando Gonzales	E	Cobas	15	39m 01.88s	2m 33.67s	31
23	Peter Baláž	CS	MBA	15	40m 07.58s	2m 33.72s	34
	Gastone Grassetti	I	MBA	15	DNF	2m 31.63s	24
	Jan Eggens	NL	LCR-EGA	9	DNF	2m 34.31s	35
	Robin Milton	GB	MBA	6	DNF	2m 33.72s	32
	Anton Straver	NL	MBA	6	DNF	2m 32.36s	27
	Jussi Hautaniemi	SF	MBA	4	DNF	2m 29.86s	13
	Christian le Badezet	F	MBA	4	DNF	2m 32.82s	28
	Paul Bordes	F	MBA	3	DNF	2m 33.43s	30
	Heinz Litz	D	MBA	3	DNF	2m 33.72s	33
	Domenico Brigaglia	I	AGV	1	DNF	2m 27.26s	5
	Ivan Troisi	YV	MBA	1	DNF	2m 31.59s	23
	Willy Pérez	RA	Zanella	1	DNF	2m 30.00s	15
	Alfred Waibel	D	MBA		DNS	2m 31.78s	25
	Lucio Pietroniro	B	MBA		DNS	2m 29.19s	8
	Thomas Møller-Pedersen	DK	MBA		DNQ	2m 34.85s	
	Hubert Abold	D	Honda		DNQ	2m 34.90s	
	Dirk Hafeneger	D	MBA		DNQ	2m 35.15s	
	Hans Spaan	NL	MBA		DNQ	2m 36.31s	
	Allan Scott	GB	EMC		DNQ	2m 36.57s	
	Karl Dauer	A	MBA		DNQ	2m 37.14s	
	Wilco Zeelenberg	NL	Casal		DNQ	2m 37.81s	
	Helmut Hovenga	D	MBA		DNQ	2m 39.06s	
	Boy van Erp	NL	MBA		DNQ	2m 39.09s	
	Alain Kempener	B	MBA		DNQ	2m 39.59s	
	Michael McGarrity	IRL	MBA		DNQ	2m 42.69s	

Fastest lap: Gresini, 2m 24.02s, 92.25 mph/153.323 km/h (record).
Previous record: Fausto Gresini, I (Garelli), 2m 26.43s, 93.209 mph/150.005 km/h (1986).

World Championship: 1 Gresini, 75; **2** Casanova, 54; **3** Auinger, 42; **4** Brigaglia, 32; **5** Casoli, 30; **6** Bianchi, 26; **7** Sánchez, 18; **8** Feuz, 11; **9** Hautaniemi, 7; **10** Catalano, Leitner and Stadler, 6; **13** Gianola, 5; **14** Pietroniro, 4; **15** Macciotta, Selini and Wickström, 2; **18** Liegeois and Pérez, 1.

Sidecars

16 laps, 60.99 miles/98.14 km

Place	Driver & passenger	Nat.	Machine	Laps	Time & speed	Practice time	Grid
1	Egbert Streuer/	NL	LCR-	16	41m 13.86s	2m 19.04s	2
	Bernard Schnieders	NL	Yamaha		88.69 mph/		
					142.821 km/h		
2	Steve Webster/	GB	Yamaha	16	41m 37.61s	2m 19.54s	3
	Tony Hewitt	GB					
3	Alain Michel/	F	LCR-	16	41m 45.79s	2m 20.52s	5
	Jean-Marc Fresc	F	Krauser Elf				
4	Rolf Biland/	CH	Krauser	16	41m 54.32s	2m 18.11s	1
	Kurt Waltisperg	CH					
5	Rolf Steinhausen/	D	RS-	16	42m 13.41s	2m 22.04s	7
	Bruno Hiller	D	Yamaha				
6	Alfred Zurbrügg/	CH	LCR-	16	42m 23.34s	2m 21.87s	6
	Simon Birchall	GB	Yamaha				
7	Steve Abbott/	GB	Windle-	16	42m 32.21s	2m 23.48s	13
	Shaun Smith	GB	Yamaha				
8	Bernd Scherer/	D	BSR-	16	42m 51.23s	2m 24.16s	14
	Wolfgang Gess	D	Yamaha				
9	Barry Brindley/	GB	Windle-	16	43m 05.65s	2m 23.38s	12
	Grahame Rose	GB	Yamaha				
10	Theo van Kempen/	NL	LCR-	16	43m 21.15s	2m 24.61s	16
	Gerardus de Haas	NL	Yamaha				
11	Masato Kumano/	J	Yamaha	16	43m 21.20s	2m 22.91s	8
	Markus Fahrni	CH					
12	Wolfgang Stropek/	A	LCR-	16	44m 40.60s	2m 25.33s	18
	Hans-Peter Demling	A	Krauser				
13	Fritz Stölzle/	D	LCR-	15	41m 19.61s	2m 24.79s	17
	Hubert Stölzle	D	Yamaha				
14	René Progin/	CH	Seymaz	15	41m 33.51s	2m 22.97s	10
	Yves Hunziker	CH					
15	Gary Thomas/	GB	LCR-	15	41m 55.82s	2m 26.10s	20
	Geoff White	GB	Yamaha				
	Derek Jones/	GB	LCR-	9	DNF	2m 23.26s	11
	Brian Ayres	GB	Seel				
	Markus Egloff/	CH	LCR-	7	DNF	2m 20.03s	4
	Urs Egloff	CH	Seel				
	Pascal Larratte/	F	LCR-	7	DNF	2m 22.97s	9
	Jacques Corbier	F	Yamaha				
	Yoshisada Kumagaya/	J	Windle-	6	DNF	2m 24.39s	15
	Brian Barlow	GB	Yamaha				
	Graham Gleeson/	NZ	LCR-	6	DNF	2m 25.42s	19
	Peter Brown	NZ	Cagiva				
	Erwin Weber/	D	LCR-		DNQ	2m 26.12s	
	Eckart Rösinger	D	Sams				
	Dennis Bingham/	GB	LCR-		DNQ	2m 26.37s	
	Julia Bingham	GB	Yamaha				
	Graham Biggs/	AUS	LCR-		DNQ	2m 28.93s	
	P. Kramer	AUS	Yamaha				
	Ivan Nigrowski/	F	Seymaz		DNQ	2m 29.17s	
	G. Loreille	F					
	Hans Hügli/	CH	Sigwa		DNQ	2m 30.30s	
	Andreas Racke	CH					

Fastest lap: Streuer, 2m 32.07s, 90.18 mph/145.212 km/h.
Lap record: Rolf Biland/Kurt Waltisperg, CH/CH (Krauser), 2m 20.27s, 97.821 mph/157.428 km/h (1986).

World Championship: 1 Webster, 50; **2** Michel, 42; **3** Streuer, 39; **4** Biland, 23; **5** Zurbrügg, 19; **6** Abbott, 16; **7** Kumano and van Kempen, 10; **9** Bayley and Jones, 8; **11** Progin, 7; **12** Steinhausen and Stropek, 6; **14** Kumagaya and Larratte, 5; **16** Egloff, 4; **17** Scherer, 3; **18** Brindley, 2; **19** Stölzle, 1.

Didier de Radiguès, on the Bastos Cagiva, found his style was still being inhibited by his shoulder injury.

Right: **Toni Mang slices across the nose of Reinhold Roth on his way to winning the Dutch TT. Mang's assertive style contrasted with that of Roth, who had begun to realise that his plan of riding for points might not provide him with the World Championship at the end of the season as Mang seemed unlikely to repeat the mistake he made at Jerez.**

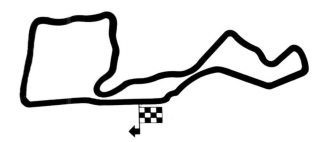

Grand Prix de
FRANCE

Paul Ricard makes one think of long summer evenings, cicadas and barbecues. Le Mans is more likely to provide rain and cold, and even though the centre of the old town is pleasant the circuit is nowhere near the class of Ricard, so each alternate year at Le Mans is a comparative let-down.

True to form, the good weather in which everyone set up camp at Le Mans soon deteriorated. The best day of practice was Thursday and the untimed sessions were dry as many riders had their first chance to try the new chicanes built in the hope of getting the Formula 1 Grand Prix to the Bugatti circuit.

Most accepted something had to be done about the ultra-fast right-hander at the end of the start-and-finish straight, though the chicane could have been better designed as it produced a dangerous approach and an exit that projected man and machine towards the barrier that stands right on the track's edge. If it was an improvement it was because accidents were likely to be at slower speeds.

The second chicane that changed the course where there used to be a very fast left-hander at the back of the pits was unnecessary, but at least it improved the approach to the next right-hander. It meant that with no fast corners remaining the track is rather uninteresting and even less of a Grand Prix circuit.

Toni Mang, for one, protested that Le Mans was too slow, too boring and too bumpy. The Sarron brothers were not likely to complain for that would hardly endear them to their home crowd. Besides,who would complain about being in pole position? With Dominique fastest on the 250 Rothmans Honda and Christian ahead of the rest of the 500 field with the Sonauto Gauloises Yamaha,the family scored a unique double.

The fast times were all recorded on Saturday after a day of rain on Friday but unlucky Tadahiko Taira did not get that far having crashed off the Marlboro Yamaha on Thursday when the bike seized at the end of the start-and-finish straight. He suffered displaced vertebrae in his neck, cracked shoulder and ribs as well as an injured forearm. Not surprisingly he took no more part in the proceedings that weekend but at the end of the meeting flew back to Japan hoping to compete in the Suzuka Eight-hour race.

Both Taira and Martin Wimmer had been in Japan prior to Le Mans testing the eight-hour bike and there were strong rumours that they had also tried a new 250 parallel twin. The bike was said to be a new production racer similar to the existing model in layout but with the carburettors mounted on the front of the engine and rearward-facing exhaust pipes.

That would make it half a V-four 500, but split horizontally instead of vertically as in the works 250 V-twin. That made sense as such an engine would have better breathing and exhaust flow than the current parallel twin but be cheaper to make than the V. Another possiblity was that the new engine might be a completely new powerplant, a prototype with perhaps a three- instead of four-bearing crank to reduce running

friction. Doubled up as a new V-four it would cut the crank bearing number from eight to six and reduce the Honda's advantage.

Wimmer would say nothing about whatever he might have ridden in Japan except that the Endurance bike had the normal left-footed gearchange and he had re-adapted to it without any problems. The injured ankle was almost fully healed with virtually normal movement.

Back to form, Wimmer was second-fastest at the end of practice and in a confident mood. 'The bike is good and I feel great. I am looking forward to a good result because we have found something a bit extra for the bike in the race.'

Wimmer was one of the few top men not to fall in the very slippery sessions on Friday and said he was lucky. 'The front wheel locked up when I braked and the handlebars turned right round before I got off the brakes and it came back again.' Not so fortunate were Toni Mang, Carlos Cardus, Sito Pons, Jean-Philippe Ruggia and Manfred Herweh. Carlos Lavado and Juan Garriga both crashed twice and the Spaniard ended up with a broken bone in his hip that sent him back to Barcelona for specialist treatment. There were few fallers in the 500 class, though Pier Francesco Chili slipped off the HB Gallina Honda on Friday in the wet.

One man who always excels in wet conditions is August Auinger, but he did not even get to Le Mans having crashed the 125 Bartol MBA at the Salzburgring the week before at a national meeting. The bike seized at the top of the hill behind the pits and Auinger was thrown off, breaking several vertebrae in his back. A body cast would make sure he was out of action for some time, probably until the very end of the season.

During wet practice it was obvious that the circuit was very slippery, particularly the old surface rather than the new chicanes. Even the Dunlop-shod Lucky Strike Yamahas were battling for grip and Mamola did not dominate in the rain as he had done throughout the season. He tried the usual cross-ply rain tyre and a radial but the latter was no good at all and the lack of grip seemed to demonstrate that no-one could make a tyre to cope with the track surface.

Sarron ended the wet day fastest but with a time recorded at the end of the afternoon session when the track was drying and he was the first man to go out on a slick-shod machine. Some riders like Gardner and Mackenzie were a little slower to risk unpatterned tyres and their lap times suffered.

Brother Dominique was only third-fastest in the 250 class after the wet Friday because Stéphane Mertens got inspired on the Sekitoba. After a frustrating season, some testing since Assen had borne fruit. A day at Donington Park helped get the suspension sorted out and the bike was fitted with the upside-down White Power forks. Several days in Austria at the Salzburgring demonstrated that the engine problems that had plagued the team since day one had been solved, though no single thing could be said to have caused them.

A combination of air box design, power valve

motor mounting and other engine settings caused by differences between the Armstrong-framed machine and the standard NSR works bikes seemed to be the cause and were gradually sorted out, but meanwhile half the season had passed the team by. They would have been far better off had they had the services of the experienced and sensitive Donnie McLeod as originally intended.

McLeod continued to ride for the EMC team and hoped that Harris Performance Products could soon produce the new frame he wanted, as Joe Ehrlich had decided to accede to his requests for the redesigned frame geometry that he had wanted since the beginning of the year. Until the new frame arrived he could do no more than qualify in the top twenty.

McLeod had not ridden the factory Suzuki since Hockenheim and they did seem to be making some progress with the machine as Kevin Schwantz made one more transatlantic hop to ride alongside Kenny Irons. Irons had also had a day testing at Donington and after a season of engine problems at last had a chance to do a bit of work with the steering and suspension. 'We improved things quite a bit in one day and I am now using the narrower 3.25 front rim which helps going into the corners.'

Schwantz also said that the bike was getting better. 'Now it revs from 8500 to 11,500 or 12,000 when before it would stop at about 11,200. It is also stronger from the bottom of the rev band, although jetting is still very critical and on top speed we are a bit down.'

There was a lot of work being done in the Elf camp as well and the team had announced that Ron Haslam would race the Elf 4 for the first time at Le Mans. That was the plan, but by chance the planned debut was at a circuit that uncovered the machine's weakness in the worst possible way. Le Mans places a premium on braking performance and the Elf's Lockheed front brake system was playing up.

The single huge caliper on the centrally mounted disc was developed specially for the new machine using a similar layout to some of Lockheed's car racing calipers, but it was giving Haslam some problems. 'It is very difficult to control the braking force with the lever force. At first the brake bites but then goes away again and you have to change the lever force all the time.'

The team had been so committed to the idea of using the prototype that Haslam hardly looked at the standard NSR until Saturday when Rosset realised that they were up against a brick wall until Lockheed could provide some answers. He calculated that Haslam was losing three-tenths of a second every time he had to use the brake hard. At that point the NSR was wheeled out and he qualified fifteenth – hardly his usual position – and he was to suffer in the race not only because he started from well back but because he had not been able to set up the NSR. He is not the sort of rider to go berserk on a bike with which he is unhappy.

Haslam was not the only man with brake problems, as Steve Webster and Tony Hewitt

Mamola and Dunlop 'strike lucky'. The wet weather was cause for celebration in the Roberts team as Randy used his superior wets to dominate the 500 race.

Chili was fast getting a reputation as a great wet-weather competitor and seemed to be taking over Sarron's mantle. The Frenchman admitted he had made the wrong choice of tyres, whereas the Italian had obviously made use of the kinder power characteristics provided by the three-cylinder engine.

had juddering brakes on their LCR outfit. On checking they found that the discs had warped and needed to be replaced. Braking problems carried over to the race but did not prevent the British pair from qualifying second. Rolf Biland and Kurt Waltisperg were quickest by nearly a full second while Alain Michel and Jean-Marc Fresc recorded an identical time to Webster and Hewitt. After a poor start to the year Biland was obviously well on his way back to the sort of form that had deserted him for most of the time in recent seasons.

125 cc

If the first race of the day was to be representative then it was to be a day of crashes. In fact there were more fallers in the 125 cc race than any other and in different places. Surprisingly, considering their wet practice performance, most of the 250 riders stayed upright, the 500s that hit trouble did so on the brakes, but the 125s slid off because of too high a corner speed or because they got on the power too early.

The 125 riders know that they have to keep the corner speed up because they cannot expect the engine to make up for lost speed in a hurry. They are not used to having trouble with rear-wheel slides under acceleration so perhaps that is why they were caught out in this way.

Championship leader Fausto Gresini hit the front right from the start. He and Ezio Gianola, who finished a superb second on the well-outdated single-cylinder Honda, were just about the only riders not to make a mistake in the pouring rain.

Gresini's team-mate, Bruno Casanova, was a close second, with Paolo Casoli a good third, but both went off the track on lap 3, giving Pier Paolo Bianchi second place. But he fell a lap later, leaving Gianola second, a position he never relinquished. Casanova rejoined the race to hold third place well behind Gianola and he was wise enough not to try and close on his fellow Italian.

For much of the race Casanova had his work cut out to stay in front of Mike Leitner but eventually he pulled clear. Lucio Pietroniro, who normally goes well in wet conditions, fell on lap 5 and could not continue. That gave sixth place to Johnny Wickström, who later came under pressure from Olivier Liegeois until the Belgian crashed on lap 15, though he was able to remount and continue in eighth place. Paolo Casoli, who had himself pulled the bike out of the straw bales after his earlier crash, managed to take fifth from Wickström on lap 17.

250 cc

Reinhold Roth had planned to go through the season picking up second and third places and accruing enough points to finish well up in the championship if not to win it. It must have dawned on him that while Mang kept finishing races and ahead of him he was not going to end up as World Champion. He could not rely on Mang crashing again as he had done in Jerez.

Roth stated publicly that he has the greatest

respect for Mang as a rider, but luck played into the HB rider's hands at Le Mans in several ways. It started with the rain, as with great rides at Silverstone in '86 and Suzuka at the beginning of this season Roth had demonstrated his wet-weather riding ability beyond doubt. Mang has also had good rides in the rain but not recently. He seems to be one of those riders who either clicks into gear when the track is wet or is off form.

From early in the 250 race Mang was obviously going to be no match for Roth and hence would lose his equal position with him at the head of the table. The final stroke of luck as far as Roth was concerned was provided by Jacques Cornu who torpedoed the Rothmans Honda and knocked it out of the race altogether. The result: Roth 15, Mang 0.

Roth extended his lead steadily from lap 1. Carlos Cardus was quickly into second place, displacing Mang who had then to do battle with Wimmer, Sarron, Herweh and Pons. Sarron had started from pole position but later said he made a mistake choosing the right-hand side of the track to start from. 'That used to be the best side but now with the new chicane it is not and I lost some places going into the chicane. Later in the first lap I was hit by Mertens as he crashed and that put me further back. From there I knew that it would be hard work and though I got into second there was no chance of catching Roth.'

Cardus did well. After attracting the reputation for crashing rather too often, his ride was particularly noteworthy in the tricky conditions. The multi-rider battle for third continued but Wimmer slipped back, finding no traction from the rear tyre he had patterned himself. As Wimmer went in one direction Sarron went the other, leaving the group to pass Cardus under brakes at the hairpin going on the start-and-finish straight ending lap 9.

Pons was fourth but was soon absorbed once more by a battle with Mang, Herweh plus Cornu and Spanish newcomer Rosa de la Puig on his Cobas. Better known at home as a trials rider he was using great throttle control to find grip.

Behind this group and closing all the time were Loris Reggiani and Hans Lindner, while Wimmer had slipped to thirteenth just ahead of Donnie McLeod who would have been better placed but for a trip down a slip road on lap 7.

During the second half of the 24-lap race there was no change in the leading three bar the fact that Sarron moved well ahead of Cardus who could not chase him, not least because his knee injury still troubled him severely.

Pons sorted himself out into second place and the group broke up, but only in the last few laps. Cornu had taken himself and Mang out of the action on lap 16, as Herweh later explained. 'I saw Cornu brake and lose control. He must have let go of the brakes and run straight into the back of Toni.' Mang's bike had a large hole punched in the seat and Cornu's temperature gauge ended up wedged in the Rothmas Honda.

That left Pons leading Puig, Herweh, Reggiani and Lindner, but on lap 20 Puig slid off at the hairpin and remounted to finish eleventh

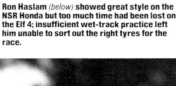

Ron Haslam *(below)* showed great style on the NSR Honda but too much time had been lost on the Elf 4; insufficient wet-track practice left him unable to sort out the right tyres for the race.

without his right footrest. Andreas Preining should have been tenth but he ran out of petrol on the last lap and gave the last point to Wimmer, while McLeod was a good ninth, almost catching Jean-Philippe Ruggia on the run-in to the line.

500 cc

For once Haslam did not feature at the start, coming as he did from well down the grid. That gave the other fast starter, Mamola, an uncontested run into the lead. Gardner held second from Lawson, Sarron, Chili and Yatsushiro. On lap 2 Gardner slipped to fifth while Lawson slipped off. 'I braked at the downhill hairpin and the front just went away and we were sliding down the road', said Lawson simply.

No-one was surprised to see Mamola take a commanding lead, even though he had not been so dominating in wet practice. The important thing was the way he had approached the race, throwing his weight about, loud, boisterous and building himself into a mood determined to win.

Sarron was second ahead of Chili but the French ace later said he had made the wrong choice of tyres. 'I did not use the tyre that had given me the fast practice time in the wet and that was a mistake. I also had a misfire every time I tried to accelerate out of the corner.'

Gardner joined Chili and Sarron in a three-way battle for second and got in front of them on lap 7 before realising that in the conditions he was well advised to take things easy as he suffered diabolical wheelspin out of every turn.

As Gardner dropped back Chili took second from Sarron, while down in fifth place Niall Mackenzie was being passed by Ron Haslam, on his way through after a careful start. After being passed by Haslam, Mackenzie was then overtaken by Kenny Irons. Heron Suzuki team-mate Kevin Schwantz slipped off at the last hairpin as he completed lap 1. Remounting at the rear of the field he started to battle forward despite the lack of a right footrest.

Rob McElnea lay ninth after ten laps ahead of Roger Burnett. As he moved forward Mackenzie and Yatsushiro joined battle in front of him for seventh place as Irons closed on Haslam. By lap 16, with Mamola romping away in the lead, Sarron was having another go at Chili. Gardner was a lonely fourth well ahead of Haslam, who was being threatened by Irons. Three men – Yatsushiro, Mackenzie and McElnea – were chasing seventh, with Burnett a distant tenth and soon to come under pressure from Schwantz.

With Mamola cruising and his only problem being to maintain concentration, Chili had finally dispensed with the attentions of Sarron by lap 20. Irons passed Haslam and closed rapidly on Gardner but on lap 21 went straight on after locking up the front wheel. That put him back behind Haslam. On that lap McElnea crashed. His gearbox had started playing up, changing of its own accord. It caused him to lose ground on lap 16, but he was once more closing rapidly on Yatsushiro and Mackenzie when it jumped from third to second as he accelerated away from the new chicane at the back of the

Kenny Irons (left) was in good form both in practice and the race. For the first time, people began to take notice of him as although Schwantz was still faster it became obvious that the British rider was improving.

Dominique Sarron (below) had more track time on the revised circuit than anyone, but a bad start put an end to his chances of winning.

circuit. This time he was dumped on the ground.

There was not much excitement up front and Chili obviously had the measure of Sarron by the last third of the race. Haslam was closing on Gardner but later told the Australian that when he realised who it was in front he eased off, not wishing to stick his neck out just to take a couple of points away from a fellow Honda rider. Schwantz passed Burnett and almost caught Yatsushiro who had been dropped by Mackenzie in the closing laps.

Mamola wheeled over the finishing line emphasising his total domination of the event and the grip provided by the rear tyre. As the rest of the field accelerated past the chequered flag all they got was wheelspin and a fishtail from the machine. When Mamola later complained that he was tired of Dunlop getting all the credit for his wet-weather wins he should have been shown a film of the race.

'There are other riders that could beat me in the rain but it depends on the attitude you go into the race with. Lawson could beat me and he went

into the race as determined as I did but unfortunately he crashed. Chili lapped within half a second of my time so there was nothing wrong with his tyres. I think I could have won on Michelins today.'

Taking nothing away from Mamola's superb skill as a wet-weather rider, he was leading the race from lap 1 and had no chance to see just how much trouble the others were getting into just accelerating in a straight line.

Sidecars

There was no stopping Rolf Biland and Kurt Waltisperg on their Krauser LCR and even when Egbert Streuer and Bernard Schnieders moved into second place on lap 13 the result was never in doubt. Steve Webster and Tony Hewitt kept their championship hopes going well by pushing Alain Michel and Jean-Marc Fresc out of third place on lap 16.

Biland was in pole position on the grid and took the lead from the first lap with Webster

second. The British crew had suffered from brake problems all through practice and though second on the grid were almost a second slower than Biland. They chased hard from the start but things got out of hand and three times during the race they ran off the track. On lap 3 they lost second to Michel while Streuer was still fourth ahead of Brindley and Rose who threatened the World Champion briefly on lap 4 before themselves being passed by Jones and Ayres.

Streuer started to work harder in the second half of the race while local men Larratte and Corbier spun their LCR outfit into the Egloff crew knocking them out of eighth place behind Kumagaya and Barlow.

Webster had repassed Michel but on lap 9 Streuer caught up, making it a three-way battle, and the British crew were suddenly pushed back to fourth by one of their off-track excursions. That left Michel second, but on lap 13 Streuer made his big effort and relegated Michel to third. Webster then forced the Frenchman into fourth on lap 16.

Grand Prix de France, 19 July/statistics
Circuit Bugatti, Le Mans, 2.635-mile/4.240-km circuit

500 cc

29 laps, 76.42 miles/122.96 km

Place	Rider	Nat.	Machine	Laps	Time & speed	Practice time	Grid
1	Randy Mamola	USA	Yamaha	29	58m 43.50s 78.50 mph/ 126.430 km/h	1m 43.95s	7
2	Pier Francesco Chili	I	Honda	29	59m 17.68s	1m 44.82s	12
3	Christian Sarron	F	Yamaha	29	59m 24.14s	1m 42.38s	1
4	Wayne Gardner	AUS	Honda	29	59m 27.69s	1m 42.97s	2
5	Ron Haslam	GB	Honda	29	59m 33.75s	1m 45.66s	15
6	Kenny Irons	GB	Suzuki	29	59m 49.52s	1m 43.91s	6
7	Niall Mackenzie	GB	Honda	29	60m 17.03s	1m 43.14s	4
8	Shunji Yatsushiro	J	Honda	29	60m 22.35s	1m 44.47s	11
9	Kevin Schwantz	USA	Honda	29	60m 22.89s	1m 43.84s	5
10	Roger Burnett	GB	Honda	29	60m 41.37s	1m 45.30s	14
11	Marco Gentile	CH	Fior	28	59m 30.85s	1m 45.86s	16
12	Manfred Fischer	D	HG Hanau	28	59m 50.86s	1m 47.00s	20
13	Simon Buckmaster	GB	Honda	28	59m 51.12s	1m 48.53s	26
14	Silvo Habat	YU	Honda	28	60m 40.67s	1m 49.26s	29
15	Maarten Duyzers	NL	Honda	27	59m 23.93s	1m 49.20s	28
16	Vittorio Scatola	I	Paton	27	59m 53.75s	1m 47.96s	23
17	Daniel Amatriain	E	Honda	27	60m 19.32s	1m 48.62s	27
18	Daniel Pauget	F	Honda	27	60m 27.69s	1m 52.33s	36
19	Rachel Nicotte	F	Suzuki	27	60m 54.11s	1m 49.37s	31
20	Ian Pratt	GB	Suzuki	27	60m 57.80s	1m 51.88s	35
21	Alan Jeffery	GB	Suzuki	26	60m 07.91s	1m 49.71s	32
22	Louis-Luc Maisto	F	Honda	26	60m 27.23s	1m 48.42s	25
	Fabio Barchitta	RSM	Honda	23	DNF	1m 48.17s	24
	Rob McElnea	GB	Yamaha	19	DNF	1m 44.26s	9
	Didier de Radiguès	B	Cagiva	17	DNF	1m 45.15s	13
	Wolfgang von Muralt	CH	Suzuki	13	DNF	1m 46.16s	17
	Kees van der Endt	NL	Honda	13	DNF	1m 50.39s	33
	Andreas Leuthe	LUX	Honda	11	DNF	1m 49.31s	30
	Ari Rämö	SF	Honda	10	DNF	1m 51.74s	34
	Alessandro Valesi	I	Honda	9	DNF	1m 47.10s	21
	Bruno Kneubühler	CH	Honda	6	DNF	1m 47.32s	22
	Hervé Guilleux	F	Fior	5	DNF	1m 46.92s	19
	Raymond Roche	F	Cagiva	3	DNF	1m 43.99s	8
	Richard Scott	NZ	Yamaha	2	DNF	1m 44.27s	10
	Gustav Reiner	D	Honda	2	DNF	1m 46.38s	18
	Eddie Lawson	USA	Yamaha	2	DNF	1m 43.13s	3
	Rolf Aljes	D	Suzuki		DNS	1m 53.23s	37
	Ray Swann	GB	Honda		DNS	1m 54.73s	38
	Stelio Marmaras	GR	Suzuki		DNQ	1m 57.50s	

Fastest lap: Mamola, 1m 59.29s.
Previous circuit record: Christian Sarron, F (Yamaha), 1m 33.92s, 100.986 mph/162.521 km/h (1985).

World Championship: 1 Gardner, 93; **2** Mamola, 81; **3** Lawson, 64; **4** Haslam, 60; **5** Chili, 37; **6** McElnea and Taira, 28; **8** Mackenzie, 27; **9** Sarron, 25; **10** Burnett, 16; **11** Yatsushiro, 13; **12** Schwantz, 11; **13** Ito, 10; **14** Irons and Roche, 9; **16** de Radiguès, 5; **17** Kawasaki, 4; **18** Scott, 3; **19** Katayama and Reiner, 2; **21** Magee, 1.

250 cc

24 laps, 63.24 miles/101.76 km

Place	Rider	Nat.	Machine	Laps	Time & speed	Practice time	Grid
1	Reinhold Roth	D	Honda	24	49m 46.33s 76.66 mph/ 123.452 km/h	1m 46.71s	3
2	Dominique Sarron	F	Honda	24	50m 01.88s	1m 46.58s	1
3	Carlos Cardus	E	Honda	24	50m 08.27s	1m 48.09s	11
4	Sito Pons	E	Honda	24	50m 14.45s	1m 47.90s	10
5	Manfred Herweh	D	Honda	24	50m 17.22s	1m 47.80s	8
6	Hans Lindner	A	Honda	24	50m 21.01s	1m 49.50s	24
7	Loris Reggiani	I	Aprilia	24	50m 28.88s	1m 47.85s	9
8	Jean-Philippe Ruggia	F	Yamaha	24	50m 33.04s	1m 48.87s	15
9	Donnie McLeod	GB	EMC	24	50m 33.40s	1m 48.88s	16
10	Martin Wimmer	D	Yamaha	24	50m 59.17s	1m 46.69s	2
11	Alberto Puig	E	Cobas	24	51m 06.88s	1m 49.10s	17
12	Hervé Duffard	F	Honda	24	51m 12.05s	1m 50.19s	30
13	Urs Lüzi	CH	Honda	24	51m 16.11s	1m 50.04s	27
14	Andreas Preining	A	Rotax	24	51m 19.83s	1m 51.24s	34
15	Luca Cadalora	I	Yamaha	23	50m 10.78s	1m 49.47s	23
16	Gary Cowan	IRL	Honda	23	50m 14.90s	1m 51.45s	35
17	Bruno Bonhuil	F	Honda	23	50m 29.26s	1m 49.88s	26
18	Nedy Crotta	CH	Armstrong	23	50m 33.85s	1m 51.07s	32
19	René Delaby	LUX	Yamaha	23	50m 51.46s	1m 50.91s	31
20	Engelbert Neumair	A	Rotax	23	51m 02.17s	1m 51.19s	33
21	Christian Boudinot	F	Fior	22	50m 48.86s	1m 49.15s	20
22	Alain Bronec	F	Honda	21	50m 50.54s	1m 50.12s	28
	Jochen Schmid	D	Yamaha	21	DNF	1m 49.15s	19
	Harald Eckl	D	Honda	16	DNF	1m 49.25s	21
	Anton Mang	D	Honda	15	DNF	1m 47.25s	4
	Jacques Cornu	CH	Honda	15	DNF	1m 47.63s	5
	Jean-Michel Mattioli	F	Honda	13	DNF	1m 48.83s	14
	Carlos Lavado	YV	Yamaha	10	DNF	1m 47.66s	7
	Stefano Caracchi	RSM	Honda	10	DNF	1m 49.59s	25
	Ivan Palazzese	YV	Yamaha	9	DNF	1m 49.14s	18
	Patrick Igoa	F	Yamaha	9	DNF	1m 47.66s	6
	Jean Foray	F	Chevallier	9	DNF	1m 50.12s	29
	Jean-François Baldé	F	Honda	7	DNF	1m 49.33s	22
	Guy Bertin	F	Honda	5	DNF	1m 48.79s	13
	Stéphane Mertens	B	Sekitoba	1	DNF	1m 48.74s	12
	Didier Bordeaux	F	Yamaha		DNQ	1m 51.66s	
	Marcellino Lucchi	I	Honda		DNQ	1m 51.94s	
	Bernard Hänggeli	CH	Yamaha		DNQ	1m 52.04s	
	Urs Jucker	CH	Yamaha		DNQ	1m 52.04s	
	Jean-Louis Guignabodet	F	MIG		DNQ	1m 52.29s	
	Richard Gauthier	F	Yamaha		DNQ	1m 52.54s	
	Bruno Sparza	F	Honda		DNQ	1m 52.62s	
	Alberto Rota	I	Honda		DNQ	1m 52.78s	
	Etienne Quartararo	F	Honda		DNQ	1m 53.16s	
	Siegfried Minich	A	Honda		DNQ	1m 53.50s	
	Michel Galbit	F	JBB		DNQ	1m 54.25s	
	Fausto Ricci	I	Honda		DNQ	1m 54.42s	
	Philippe Pagano	F	Yamaha		DNQ	1m 54.65s	
	Juan Garriga	E	Yamaha		DNQ	2m 06.64s	

Fastest lap: Roth, 2m 2.81s.
Previous circuit record: Freddie Spencer, USA (Honda), 1m 39.10s, 95.708 mph/154.026 km/h (1985).

World Championship: 1 Roth, 82; **2** Mang, 67; **3** Pons, 53; **4** Cornu, 42; **5** Sarron, 39; **6** Cardus, 36; **7** Wimmer, 35; **8** Lavado, 30; **9** Reggiani, 28; **10** Garriga, 23; **11** Cadalora, 18; **12** Igoa, 17; **13** Kobayashi, 15; **14** Shimuzu, 8; **15** Ruggia, 7; **16** Herweh and Palazzese, 6; **18** Lindner, 5; **19** Vitali, 3; **20** McLeod, Mertens and Taguchi, 2; **23** Bertin and Yamamoto, 1.

125 cc

22 laps, 57.97 miles/93.28 km

Place	Rider	Nat.	Machine	Laps	Time & speed	Practice time	Grid
1	Fausto Gresini	I	Garelli	22	47m 37.84s 73.43 mph/ 118.252 km/h	1m 52.48s	1
2	Ezio Gianola	I	Honda	22	48m 20.76s	1m 56.80s	13
3	Bruno Casanova	I	Garelli	22	48m 33.34s	1m 52.76s	2
4	Mike Leitner	A	MBA	22	48m 43.61s	1m 55.90s	8
5	Paolo Casoli	I	AGV	22	48m 57.33s	1m 54.35s	3
6	Johnny Wickström	SF	MBA	22	49m 15.80s	1m 56.90s	15
7	Domenico Brigaglia	I	AGV	22	49m 22.50s	1m 57.06s	17
8	Olivier Liegeois	B	Assmex	22	49m 34.36s	1m 56.76s	12
9	Gastone Grassetti	I	MBA	22	49m 48.98s	1m 57.07s	18
10	Flemming Kistrup	DK	MBA	22	49m 57.19s	1m 57.07s	19
11	Adolf Stadler	D	MBA	21	48m 13.72s	1m 55.78s	7
12	Willy Pérez	RA	Zanella	21	48m 21.13s	1m 56.56s	11
13	Allan Scott	USA	EMC	21	48m 54.22s	2m 01.00s	36
14	Håkan Olsson	S	Starol	21	49m 01.09s	1m 57.69s	21
15	Ivan Troisi	YV	MBA	21	49m 24.43s	1m 58.27s	25
16	Michel Escudier	F	MBA	21	49m 40.89s	1m 58.54s	26
17	Denis Longueville	F	MBA	21	49m 54.01s	2m 00.26s	31
18	Andrés Marin Sánchez	E	Ducados	20	48m 07.93s	1m 55.22s	4
19	Laurent Chapeau	F	MBA	19	49m 05.82s	2m 00.49s	34
	Claudio Macciotta	I	MBA	16	DNF	1m 59.83s	29
	Thomas Møller-Pedersen	DK	MBA	15	DNF	2m 00.31s	32
	Paul Bordes	F	MBA	11	DNF	1m 59.98s	30
	Ian McConnachie	GB	MBA	8	DNF	1m 59.68s	28
	Jacques Hutteau	F	MBA	7	DNF	1m 58.03s	23
	Pier Paolo Bianchi	I	MBA	6	DNF	1m 55.78s	6
	Christian le Badezet	F	MBA	6	DNF	1m 57.82s	22
	Bady Hassaine	DZ	MBA	6	DNF	1m 56.84s	14
	Lucio Pietroniro	B	MBA	5	DNF	1m 56.46s	10
	Thierry Feuz	CH	MBA	2	DNF	1m 56.22s	9
	Gilles Payraudeau	F	MBA	2	DNF	1m 58.77s	27
	Jean-Claude Selini	F	MBA	2	DNF	1m 57.19s	20
	Corrado Catalano	I	MBA	2	DNF	1m 55.60s	5
	Esa Kytölä	SF	MBA	2	DNF	1m 58.13s	24
	Robin Appleyard	GB	MBA	1	DNF	2m 00.40s	33
	Fernando Gonzales	E	Cobas	1	DNF	2m 00.74s	35
	Jussi Hautaniemi	SF	MBA		DNS	1m 56.91s	16
	Robin Milton	GB	MBA		DNQ	2m 01.01s	
	Pascal Serra	F	Honda		DNQ	2m 01.23s	
	Jan Eggens	NL	EGA		DNQ	2m 01.48s	
	Philippe Souliez	F	MBA		DNQ	2m 01.59s	
	Hans Spaan	NL	MBA		DNQ	2m 02.17s	
	Helmut Hovenga	D	Seel		DNQ	2m 02.99s	
	Steve Mason	GB	MBA		DNQ	2m 07.02s	
	Peter Sommer	CH	Supeso		DNQ	2m 28.11s	
	Alexandre Laranjeira	P	Yamaha		DNQ	2m 28.22s	
	Dave Brown	GB	MBA		DNQ	2m 31.71s	

Fastest lap: Gresini, 2m 8.11s..
Previous circuit record: Ezio Gianola. I (Garelli), 1m 45.08s, 90.261 mph/145.260 km/h.

World Championship: 1 Gresini, 90; **2** Casanova, 64; **3** Auinger, 42; **4** Brigaglia and Casoli, 36; **6** Bianchi, 26; **7** Sánchez, 18; **8** Gianola, 17; **9** Leitner, 14; **10** Feuz, 11; **11** Hautaniemi and Wickström, 7; **13** Catalano and Stadler, 6; **15** Liegeois and Pietroniro, 4; **17** Grassetti, Macciotta and Selini, 2; **20** Kistrup and Pérez, 1.

Ezio Gianola (left) was in tremendous form. The Honda single had acquired a new cylinder and exhaust pipe from the factory and, while the engine's tractability was useful, the twins still had a speed advantage; Gianola simply out-rode everyone except Gresini.

Reinhold Roth (right), a gentleman and upholder of the spirit of competition, demonstrated that he could use Michelin tyres to dominate the 250 race much as Mamola used Dunlops in the 500.

Sidecars

22 laps, 57.97 miles/93.28 km

Place	Driver & passenger	Nat.	Machine	Laps	Time & speed	Practice time	Grid
1	Rolf Biland/ Kurt Waltisperg	CH CH	LCR-Krauser	22	45m 47.15s 76.39 mph/ 123.017 km/h	1m 47.72s	1
2	Egbert Streuer/ Bernard Schnieders	NL NL	LCR-Yamaha	22	46m 01.95s	1m 49.91s	5
3	Steve Webster/ Tony Hewitt	GB GB	Yamaha	22	46m 03.22s	1m 48.63s	2
4	Alain Michel/ Jean-Marc Fresc	F F	LCR-Krauser Elf	22	46m 15.39s	1m 48.63s	3
5	Derek Jones/ Brian Ayres	GB GB	LCR-	22	46m 58.02s	1m 51.07s	8
6	Yoshisada Kumagaya/ Brian Barlow	J GB	Windle-Yamaha	22	47m 19.20s	1m 53.46s	13
7	Theo van Kempen/ Gerardus de Haas	NL NL	LCR-Yamaha	22	47m 23.36s	1m 53.35s	12
8	Steve Abbott/ Shaun Smith	GB GB	Windle-Yamaha	22	47m 26.21s	1m 53.72s	15
9	Alfred Zurbrügg/ Simon Birchall	CH GB	LCR-Yamaha	22	47m 36.47s	1m 51.44s	9
10	Bernd Scherer/ Wolfgang Gess	D D	BSR-Yamaha	22	47m 38.79s	1m 53.90s	16
11	Wolfgang Stropek/ Hans-Peter Demling	A A	LCR-Krauser	22	47m 57.23s	1m 54.20s	17
12	René Progin/ Yves Hunziker	CH CH	Seymaz	21	45m 49.94s	1m 53.53s	14
13	Pascal Larrate/ Jacques Corbier	F F	LCR-Yamaha	21	46m 14.48s	1m 51.47s	10
14	Ray Gardner/ Tony Strevens	GB GB	LCR-Yamaha	21	46m 17.62s	1m 54.99s	21
15	Graham Gleeson/ Peter Brown	NZ NZ	LCR-Cagiva	21	46m 51.87s	1m 54.66s	19
16	Ivan Nigrowski/ Michel Charpentier	F F	Seymaz	21	47m 10.92s	1m 55.50s	23
17	Jean-Louis Millet/ Claude Debroux	F F	Seymaz	21	47m 47.41s	1m 54.92s	20
18	Dennis Bingham/ Julia Bingham	GB GB	LCR-Yamaha	20	46m 46.38s	1m 55.47s	22
	Luigi Casagrande/ Adolf Hänni	CH CH	LCR-Yamaha	18	DNF	1m 57.18s	24
	Henri Golemba/ Alain-Robert Barillon	F F	LCR	13	DNF	1m 57.46s	25
	Barry Brindley/ Grahame Rose	GB GB	Windle-Yamaha	12	DNF	1m 52.81s	11
	Markus Egloff/ Urs Egloff	CH CH	LCR-Seel	8	DNF	1m 49.88s	4
	Masato Kumano/ Markus Fahrni	J CH	LCR-Yamaha	8	DNF	1m 50.95s	7
	Fritz Stölzle/ Hubert Stölzle	D D	LCR-Yamaha	7	DNF	1m 54.65s	18
	Rolf Steinhausen/ Bruno Hiller	D D	Eigenbau	5	DNF	1m 50.83s	6
	Jacques Heriot/ Jean-Luc Sage	F F	Seymaz		DNQ	1m 57.53s	
	Amadeo Zini/ Carlo Sonaglia	I I	LCR-Yamaha		DNQ	1m 57.60s	
	Clive Stirratt/ Peter Prior	GB GB	Yamaha		DNQ	1m 57.78s	
	P. Loreille/ G. Loreille	F F	Seymaz		DNQ	1m 58.00s	
	Billy Gällros/ Auden Nordli	S S	Yamaha		DNQ	1m 58.03s	
	Erwin Weber/ Eckart Rösinger	D D	Sams		DNQ	1m 58.18s	
	Gary Thomas/ Geoff White	GB GB	LCR-Yamaha		DNQ	1m 58.69s	
	Judd Drew/ Christopher Plant	GB GB	Yamaha		DNQ	1m 58.94s	
	John Evans/ Geoff Wilbraham	GB GB	LCR		DNQ	2m 00.57s	

Fastest lap: Webster, 2m 02.63s.
Previous circuit record: Egbert Streuer/Bernard Schnieders, NL/NL (LCR-Yamaha), 1m 39.50s, 95.323 mph/153.407 km/h (1985).

World Championship: 1 Webster, 60; **2** Streuer, 51; **3** Michel, 50; **4** Biland, 38; **5** Zurbrügg, 21; **6** Abbott, 19; **7** Jones and van Kempen, 14; **9** Kumano and Kumagaya, 10; **11** Bayley, 8; **12** Progin, 7; **13** Steinhausen and Stropek, 6; **15** Larratte, 5; **16** Egloff and Scherer, 4; **18** Brindley, 2; **19** Stölzle, 1.

SHELL OILS
BRITISH
Grand Prix

Gardner was certainly favourite to win. Despite being beaten in Holland and France when rain made it prudent to take things easy there was every chance that he would get back to his winning ways if the British weather was kind. He had done as many laps of Donington Park as most, though the new section was a factor strange to almost everyone.

The universal feeling typified by Gardner's comment was that the track lengthening required to bring the circuit up to minimum Grand Prix distance had spoilt it. 'I don't like the new hairpins; they are too tight for a 500 and when you want to set the bike up for the rest of the circuit it is no good for the hairpins so you end up with a compromise.' Toni Mang added his criticism of the new hairpins. 'They are bumpy and that makes things very difficult for throttle control. You can have bumps on fast corners and the back wheel will run over them all right; it might step out but it will keep going in the right direction. On slow corners it is more sudden and there is no time to find control.'

The old circuit had been a flowing series of curves with only the single chicane before the start-and-finish to break the rhythm. Now, with a tighter chicane plus two hairpins, one-quarter of the track was all stop and go.

It was a shame things worked out that way and once more car requirements were at least partly to blame because the chicane was to have been a fast curve. However, that would have meant cars arriving at the hairpin at 200 mph with insufficient room to stop in the event of a brake failure.

On the other hand the circuit looked beautiful and Donington Park had done a great job of getting the paddock and track facilities up to standard with extra power and water outlets and even washing machines for the competitors to use. Such things are really appreciated and with first class press facilities and marshalling the event was a great success. It did not look as though the Grand Prix would be going back to Silverstone for some time.

On the Tuesday of practice week, Mike Trimby and Wayne Gardner went with Luigi Brenni to inspect Brands Hatch with a view to homologating it for a World Championship event. The circuit was not homologated but Brenni said he would grant a provisional licence once he had seen plans for a number of safety improvements.

Unofficial practice started on Thursday but Raymond Roche did not make it to the circuit having been involved in a car crash on his way from the East Midlands airport only five miles from the track. He suffered facial injuries and two broken bones in his hand and would miss the Swedish as well as the British Grand Prix.

Wayne Gardner headed the times that day but when timed practice officially got under way on Friday Niall Mackenzie was on top of the table with the HB Honda, although Gardner equalled his time later in the session. 'I have done quite well here on the 250 and 350 Armstrongs,' said Mackenzie, 'but I never went well in practice. I am feeling quite confident, though, because at last my foot is not causing me any trouble and I

can even run on it a bit now. I feel that I would have been able to carry on riding like I did in Austria but for my foot and although things did not go that well in France I learnt a lot about riding in the wet, how important it is to get the bike upright quickly to get the power on.'

Everyone went quicker that afternoon and Mackenzie dropped behind Gardner and Kenny Irons moved up to fourth behind Lawson and ahead of Mamola. Roger Burnett was doing better than he had all season on the 1986 ex-Gardner NSR500 Honda. 'It helps that I know the track and I know how the bike should handle here. Most of the year I have being going to tracks I did not know much about and on a bike that was hard to work with. Here at least I know how it should be.'

In the afternoon he slipped from fifth to seventh but that evening took Patrick Igoa for a lap in the car to show him the good line. Even though Igoa had done plenty of laps on an endurance bike there was obviously plenty he could learn because next day he jumped from fourth to first on the Sonauto Gauloises Yamaha. He said that Burnett had been able to help a lot with picking the right line through the sweeping curves.

Roth was second ahead of Mang and Stéphane Mertens who was getting to grips with the Armstrong-framed Rotax. Wimmer, who had led the first session, had slipped to fifth by Saturday morning. He climbed to third ahead of Mang that afternoon. He was happy that the circuit suited the Yamahas. 'I think the Hondas have trouble because the front wheels tend to tuck under on some of the corners. It is a pity about the new section because they have better acceleration. If it was not for that we would be a second better off.' After the race Wimmer was to express the opinion that of the Honda riders only Mang had the handling sorted out so that the bike worked well down the notorious Craner Curves, yet Wimmer was still taking yards out of everyone there. He too was feeling fully fit at last and had discarded the special left boot and right-hand gearchange.

His confidence had been helped by his win in the Suzuka Eight-hour, though he was the first to admit that he owed victory to partner Kevin Magee. 'I have to say that Magee won the Eight-hour – all I did was ride and not screw up. We did nine sessions and he did six of them: that is like riding six Grands Prix. At the end of the race he was still doing the same times as he had done at the start and on tyres that had done the equivalent of four Grands Prix by that time.

'I remember when he set second-fastest qualifying time for the Dutch GP on tyres that were not new, people thought he must be crazy. I thought that perhaps it was not the right way to do it at the time but the way he rode at Suzuka I know he can ride fast however old the tyres are. When the tyres are old they start to slide earlier but in fact they are more predictable than new tyres and he uses that. He should come Grand Prix racing because after a year of experience he will be able to ride just like Eddie and Randy. There are not many people who can do it but for

sure he can.

'It was only my second race on that sort of bike and there is not much practice time to get used to a bike that is completely different to my 250. I knew before I went that I would not be that fast. I was happier in the race than I was in practice and the only people who were faster were the works Hondas so I just rode at what I knew was my limit. I think the mistake that Campbell and Sarron made was trying to go as fast as Mackenzie and Gardner; that is why they crashed.

'Magee won the race because he pushed the Japanese rider Takayoshi so hard that he just could not keep it up and he made a mistake. At least the win has done a lot for my confidence and I feel strong now for Grand Prix racing.'

Mertens slipped to sixth behind Sarron in that final session and Jean-François Baldé was an impressive seventh on the Rotax-engined DEFI. There had been little doubt all season that he could still ride given the right machinery and it was strange to see the number 5 on a private bike. The next Rotax was Loris Reggiani's Aprilia in tenth place, just behind Lavado. During practice on Saturday, he tried Öhlins upside-down forks in his Aprilia for the first time, which were of the same type as those used by Anders Andersson in his Formula 1 Suzuki.

Gardner continued to go quicker through the final day of practice and so hung on to pole position. Even when Lawson cut a full second off his time the Australian remained in front by three-quarters of a second. Mamola ended up ahead of Mackenzie and Sarron, with Haslam taking sixth once he had swapped from the Elf 4 to the NSR. After braking problems kept Ron Haslam from riding the Elf at Le Mans, Lockheed produced a carbon-fibre front disc in time for Donington. At first, the usual carbon-fibre delay was a problem but after a couple of sessions of practice that was sorted out. Haslam reported that the braking was then good br' required a great deal of lever pressure and he would not be able to keep it up for the 30-lap race.

McElnea was seventh and then came Spencer making his fourth attempt in one year to start in a Grand Prix. 'The main problem is lack of time on the bike. They have kept making changes to it through the season, so the times I have ridden it it has never been the same twice. I have been concentrating on one bike trying to get that sorted out.

'I will not know if I am fit to race until it is over but I am certainly fit to ride. I feel I just have to get into a rhythm and then I will be OK. I have been running, weight training, swimming and exercising to get ready for this, and I feel good, but Boris Becker said on the TV the other day that he was not "match tough" and that is how I feel.

'At least riding here will be easier than it would have been in Yugoslavia – there is nowhere tougher than that. I felt confident that I could come here and get up to speed but it is that extra second that makes all the difference and that is the hard part. For me to ride at or over 100 per cent everything has to be just right. My 100

Lawson waited in the final session while
exhaust pipes and jets were changed,
Agostini offered encouragement.

per cent is fast and really demanding so it may not be possible right away.

'I would love to have come here and won straight away; that is the ideal scenario but I guess it is not really practical to think like that. The most important thing is to think of the rest of the season and the six races that come after this.'

One rider who was not fit was Mike Baldwin who found his injured hand was not good enough when he tested the Lucky Strike Yamaha at Donington the week before the Grand Prix. It looked as though Richard Scott would be retained for the rest of the season while Baldwin might need another operation.

Scott's first job at Donington was to test a new airbox system that completely enclosed the carburettors. The factory Yamahas have a baffle system to separate carb intake air from radiator air but this goes a step further with a moulding that should create increased intake pressure.

On the left-hand side of the fairing is a large air duct leading to a passage which turns left through a grill and across the front of the carbs. They are enclosed in a fibreglass box.

A plastic tube leads from the right-hand side of the box to a digital pressure gauge mounted on the top of the rev counter. This showed that intake pressure was up but no increase in power was determined at Donington and the box was not used in the race.

The new fairing also had a duct in the right-hand side to take air through one of the older, narrower radiators that had been extended in an 'L' shape down the right-hand side for more cooling area.

125 cc

The two Garellis had been close many times during the season but this time they got a little too close as Gresini was hit early in the race by team-mate Bruno Casanova who had been fastest in practice by over half a second and looked as though he might press his team leader hard in the race. From the start the two Italians set off with fellow-countryman Pier Paolo Bianchi on his MBA right behind.

Bianchi was in a determined mood and mixed with the Garellis as the three pulled away from Andrés Marín Sánchez on the Ducados and Corrado Catalano on the Team Italia MBA. Domenico Brigaglia was well down in eleventh place on the first lap but quickly started to cut his way through the field.

Bianchi tried hard but slowly slipped behind the two Garellis as the speed advantage told. Casanova and Gresini swapped places but, with Casanova leading his team-mate by just a yard as they went onto lap 9, Casanova had the front end slide away as he flicked the little machine into the downhill left-hander at Craner Curves (the first left-hander on the circuit and a corner that has caught out so many good riders at Donington).

While Casanova walked back to the pits, Gresini continued with a handsome lead over

Bianchi and his only worry was pain from the left ankle where Casanova had bounced off him. He kept shaking his foot between gearchanges. Brigaglia had worked his way into third but after a good ride was forced to retire as his gearchange mechanism fell apart on lap 16.

That left Jean-Claude Selini to take third well ahead of Johnny Wickström who had pulled through from a poor start and Ezio Gianola had another great ride on the Honda single. Catalano crashed out of fourth place with one lap to go.

250 cc

Jean-François Baldé made reasonable use of his second-row position but Manfred Herweh did better from the third rank and was just in front of the Frenchman as they braked for the chicane on lap 1. Baldé's left handlebar hit the Honda's seat, smashing the fibreglass. Herweh was able to continue, but Baldé could not get his bar straight and had to retire at the pits. McLeod

had been well placed just behind them but the collision put him way back at the tail of the field.

Sarron led by a small margin from Wimmer, Roth, Cardus, Mang, Mertens, Gary Cowan and Herweh, who had not been slowed at all by the incident. Mertens only got as far as the old hairpin on lap 2 when the front end tucked under. That just about matched his first-lap crash in France; despite machinery coming right, the unfortunate Belgian was hitting an all-time low as he tried to make up for the disastrous early-season mechanical problems.

Roth took the lead on the second lap but Mang was working his way forward and was in front by lap 4 as Roth, Wimmer and Sarron pulled away from the rest of the field briefly. The gap did not get established because Reggiani was at the front of the next bunch and soon put Cornu, Cardus and Igoa back in touch while Cadalora battled a little to get on terms. He had not taken well to Donington Park and a practice fall did not help his confidence. Herweh was way ahead

of the rest of the privateers in tenth place, leading Vitali, Lavado and Pons.

Through laps 5 to 10 Mang tried earnestly to stretch his advantage but found it was not possible to maintain the speed. 'The back tyre got too hot and started sliding so I had to slow down.' By lap 8 Reggiani had worked his way to the front of the second-place group and he closed on Mang followed by Roth, Wimmer, Sarron, Igoa and Cornu.

By lap 14 the Italian was right with Mang and, together with Wimmer, challenged for the lead. It was great entertainment and things got even more exciting as a three-way battle became a six-man conflict. Then Reggiani broke free and opened a slight lead. By lap 20 of the 26 he was over a second ahead of Mang but his right forearm was so tired from the braking effort of three dead-stop corners that he started to lose ground. He had been making up ground on the brakes but now he suffered in the same area.

In contrast Mang was picking up the pace

Webster was prepared to do what was necessary to beat Biland, and Hewitt kept his end up, but at the end of the day it was Biland's engine that faltered.

Below: Taira slides the Marlboro Yamaha onto the straight. Shaking off the effects of his Le Mans crash, he set the fastest lap of the race and would have been a serious contender for the lead but for a disastrous first two laps.

once more. 'When Roth passed me and Igoa was just behind I realised that the pace was too slow and the rear tyre had cooled so I could go faster.' Chased by Wimmer, Mang closed once more on Reggiani and tailed him onto the last lap.

The Italian still thought he could win. 'The Aprilia was faster than the Yamahas but not as fast as the Honda. I thought that he would come past on the straight on the last lap but if he did not I would win. Then he came past on the brakes into the chicane and there was nothing I could do.' Mang actually ran wide at the right-hand hairpin but, as Reggiani started to accelerate up the inside, the back wheel slid and he fell back a little. He and Wimmer could only chase Mang across the line.

Earlier on, Wimmer had thoughts of winning. 'When Loris and I were still behind Toni and catching I thought I could win, but when I got behind the Honda I realised there was no chance. It was just too fast and if I passed he would just come by me again.' Wimmer's team-

mate, Cadalora, had retired on lap 21 with a tooth broken off the primary drive gear. The technicians suggested that the crashes and resulting shocks to the primary drive must have taken their toll because it was not a common fault.

Sarron, with brake problems, had dropped back to ninth behind Cardus, who also had a swollen forearm. Lavado had crashed at Craner Curves on lap 9 just as he had got away from Pons in tenth place. McLeod recovered well from that first-lap drama but though he caught the four-man battle for tenth place he could only get past Ruggia and Vitali in time, so it was Herweh who got the point ahead of Caracchi.

80 CC

With a 36-point lead over team-mate Manuel Herreros, who had crashed and broken his collarbone in the morning warm-up session, it was little more than a formality for Martínez to win the World Championship.

Martínez on the Derbi led from the start, although Stefan Dörflinger caused some excitement by charging through to take the lead briefly on lap 2. After being over half a second quicker than ex-champion Dörflinger in practice, Martínez was able to grab the lead back by lap 4. From the first lap, British hope McConnachie was fifth behind Jörg Seel who was bouncing back after breaking his collarbone at Assen.

The field soon started to spread out and as Martínez opened up his lead Dörflinger pulled away from the third-place battle. That was a heated contest between Krauser team-mates Gerhard Waibel and Ian McConnachie which lasted until lap 10 when the German started to drop behind. Seel was locked in battle with Luis Reyes on the Autisa up to the end of the race, with the Dutchman holding the advantage. On lap 12, Dörflinger pulled into the pits with gear selection problems and that presented second to McConnachie.

Martínez romped home to an easy win and the World title with almost twice as many points as Waibel.

500 CC

Freddie Spencer had not forgotten how far he could push the tyres on the first lap. He leapt from the second row of the grid into the lead. Haslam came from a similar position into second place leaving Lawson to take third ahead of Gardner, de Radiguès, Mackenzie, Mamola and Sarron.

Taira had blown the start and then almost ran off the track on the first lap trying to make up for it. Having lost ten seconds on the initial lap, he later reckoned that he regressed another five on lap 2 while he recovered his composure. That put him down in 21st place behind Gustav Reiner who had also made a mess of the first lap and would later retire when his Honda went onto two cylinders.

Lawson had eased himself into second place by lap 3 but the pace was still fairly casual and Spencer was enjoying a small lead. On lap 4 he ran wide going into Coppice Corner that leads onto the main straight. He later said he felt the back wheel lock up.

Lawson took the lead while Spencer regained the racing line, having been passed by Haslam, Gardner and Sarron. Mamola also went past and a lap later Spencer went straight on at the chicane and retired. When he got off the bike he said that the engine had seized. Later, a Honda spokesman said that the rear brake had locked on but the mechanics could not find the problem.

With Lawson in front the pace increased, but it was never comparable to the practice times and Gardner was more than a second off the time he had posted in training. In fact it was Taira who set the new lap record, going more than a second quicker than his twelfth-place practice time.

Lawson admitted later that he quite expected Gardner to come past. The Australian was

Bianchi (8) was in great form and pushed Gresini hard early on, even though the machinery made it an unequal struggle.

Martínez *(below)* **was obviously in a class of his own, the Derbi proving a much better machine than the Krauser through the season.**

having trouble with his rear tyre and when Lawson started to get away on lap 13 it was Mamola who took up the chase, even though the Californian knew he could not catch the World Champion. 'At first I thought I could win. It was no problem to go past Wayne and I would have had a go at Eddie but then my arm started to pump up so that by the time I took over second I was already in trouble. I was going nowhere because I could not control the throttle; I was grabbing at it instead of opening it slowly and I had to ease off.'

By lap 19 Gardner was back in second place and though he was then two and half seconds behind Lawson that gap soon closed as the leader ran into some back-markers. 'I never saw a blue flag being shown', said Lawson later. 'They were so slow and they didn't know I was coming.'

The blue flag is not normally used at motor cycle races in Britain and that has not affected Grands Prix much in the past because the wide open spaces of Silverstone leave so much room for passing. At Donington the opposite is true and round several sections there is only a single fast line.

By lap 23 of the 30, Gardner was right on Lawson's tail again and then for several laps they were side by side. 'The closest he came to getting past was at the chicane', said Lawson later. 'He tried to come round the outside as I went into the left-hander and I just stuck to my line going into the right, thinking he will have to go across the grass if he wants to get in front. I needed to stay in front because getting around him again would have been tough.'

Then the pair ran into some more back-markers and this time they worked to Lawson's advantage. With an open road, Lawson could open up a second a lap over Gardner who resigned himself to second well ahead of Mamola. Sarron was a distant fourth, slowing in the second half exhausted by flu'. 'I could only watch my board and defend the distance to the next rider', said the Frenchman.

The next rider was Mackenzie who had suffered over the first few laps. 'I don't have the confidence to go fast from the start and I had a couple of rear-wheel slides that made me slow down.' However, he was never challenged by de Radiguès, who had passed Haslam on lap 24 as the British rider slowed having chosen the wrong tyre.

At that point McElnea was fighting for the same place, but it was an unequal struggle. He had warped a disc early in the race and the front wheel juddered and tried to tuck under if he held the brakes on while going into a corner. The brakes faded badly with rapid pad wear and finally gave up altogether with a lap to go. He shot up the escape road at the chicane and then toured back to the pits, determined to change the Brembos for Lockheeds before Sweden.

Haslam was almost overhauled by Taira on the last lap and the last two points places went to Burnett and Irons. Both had brake troubles and were frustrated that they could not do better. Yatsushiro was eleventh ahead of Chili who said

it was a bad race with too many problems to mention, not the least of which was his very sore leg that had been bent back when he smacked it on a curb in Saturday morning practice.

Sidecars

Steve Webster and Tony Hewitt gave a tremendous boost to their sidecar World Championship hopes when they won the 24-lap event from World Champions Egbert Streuer and Bernard Schnieders. They battled for much of the race with ex-champions Rolf Biland and Kurt Waltisperg in their similar Krauser LCR outfit, but when the Swiss were forced into the pits at the end of lap 21 the race was theirs.

'It was a strange race', said Webster later. 'I was prepared to stick behind Rolf until near the end of the race, but he seemed to want to slow the race down. We would get in front and he then passed us again and slowed down. I think he wanted Streuer to be able to catch us and get in front of us so we got less points for the championship – either that or he was worried about his tyres. I think I could have gone faster

at the end if it had needed it, but then Rolf retired.'

Biland stopped with a seized engine after 20 of the 24 laps and Alain Michel and Jean-Marc Fresc had halted after only four laps with the same problem. 'The weather changed so much', said Michel. 'As the air pressure changed, the carburation got weaker. Mine should have been all right and Rolf's nearly lasted the distance, but the pressure kept changing. Larratte's engine seized the same way.'

Third were Rolf Steinhausen and Bruno Hiller. They were well placed from the start and defended their lonely position all the way, ahead of Derek Jones and Brian Ayres who were passed on lap 22 by Alfred Zurbrügg and Simon Birchall on their way through from a bad start that had left them at the back of the field on the first lap.

The liveliest battle was that for eighth between the two Japanese drivers, Yoshisada Kumagaya and Masato Kumano, and their passengers Brian Barlow and Markus Fahrni. Kumagaya crossed the line first but not before some fibreglass had been exchanged, and some cross words followed after the race.

Shell Oils British Grand Prix, 2 August/statistics

Donington Park Race Circuit, 2.5-mile/4.02-km circuit

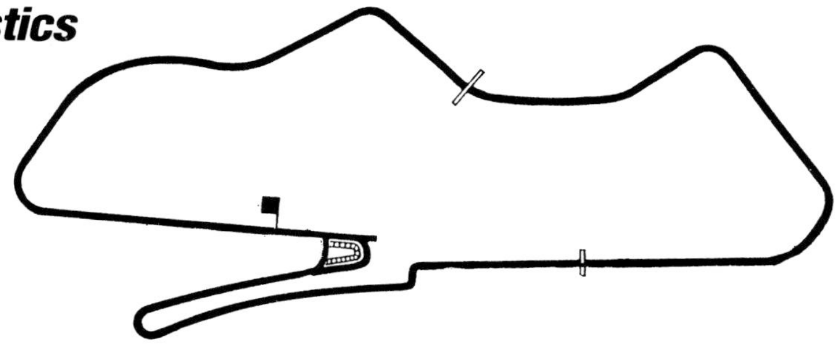

500 cc

30 laps, 75 miles/120.69 km

Place	Rider	Nat.	Machine	Laps	Time & speed	Practice time	Grid
1	Eddie Lawson	USA	Yamaha	30	50m 09.77s 89.70 mph/ 144.35 km/h	1m 39.05s	2
2	Wayne Gardner	AUS	Honda	30	50m 14.38s	1m 38.29s	1
3	Randy Mamola	USA	Yamaha	30	50m 24.69s	1m 39.11s	3
4	Christian Sarron	F	Yamaha	30	50m 31.21s	1m 39.44s	5
5	Niall Mackenzie	GB	Honda	30	50m 34.41s	1m 39.26s	4
6	Didier de Radiguès	B	Cagiva	30	50m 41.31s	1m 39.95s	9
7	Ron Haslam	GB	Honda	30	50m 41.70s	1m 39.47s	6
8	Tadahiko Taira	J	Yamaha	30	50m 42.74s	1m 40.43s	12
9	Roger Burnett	GB	Honda	30	50m 45.73s	1m 40.00s	11
10	Kenny Irons	GB	Suzuki	30	51m 01.91s	1m 39.95s	10
11	Shunji Yatsushiro	J	Honda	30	51m 17.35s	1m 40.74s	13
12	Pier Francesco Chili	I	Honda	30	51m 25.73s	1m 41.26s	15
13	Richard Scott	NZ	Yamaha	30	51m 31.21s	1m 40.77s	14
14	Marco Gentile	CH	Honda	30	51m 33.20s	1m 42.37s	19
15	Fabio Biliotti	I	Honda	30	51m 33.89s	1m 42.38s	20
16	Wolfgang von Muralt	CH	Suzuki	29	50m 22.51s	1m 41.70s	17
17	Bruno Kneubühler	CH	Honda	29	50m 22.77s	1m 43.86s	29
18	Hervé Guilleux	F	Fior	29	50m 25.87s	1m 43.85s	28
19	Alessandro Valesi	I	Honda	29	50m 37.35s	1m 42.92s	23
20	Joey Dunlop	GB	Honda	29	50m 54.04s	1m 42.97s	24
21	Louis-Luc Maisto	F	Plein-Pot	29	50m 54.35s	1m 44.18s	32
22	Alan Irwin	GB	Honda	29	51m 06.32s	1m 44.58s	34
23	Maarten Duyzers	NL	Honda	29	51m 08.76s	1m 44.59s	36
24	Fabio Barchitta	RSM	Honda	29	51m 11.79s	1m 43.96s	31
25	Silvo Habat	YU	Honda	28	50m 23.78s	1m 44.46s	33
26	Henny Boerman	NL	Assmex	28	50m 31.23s	1m 44.58s	35
	Rob McElnea	GB	Yamaha	29	DNF	1m 39.70s	7
	Simon Buckmaster	GB	Honda	23	DNF	1m 43.79s	27
	Roger Marshall	GB	Suzuki	22	DNF	1m 41.70s	16
	Gustav Reiner	D	Honda	16	DNF	1m 42.52s	22
	Andy McGladdery	GB	Honda	15	DNF	1m 43.32s	25
	Mark Phillips	GB	Suzuki	14	DNF	1m 42.40s	21
	Steve Henshaw	GB	Suzuki	12	DNF	1m 43.88s	30
	Manfred Fischer	D	Honda	7	DNF	1m 43.50s	26
	Ray Swann	GB	Honda	6	DNF	1m 42.25s	18
	Freddie Spencer	USA	Honda	4	DNF	1m 39.85s	8
	Alan Jeffery	GB	Suzuki		DNQ	1m 44.99s	
	Andreas Leuthe	LUX	Honda		DNQ	1m 49.91s	
	Ian Pratt	GB	Suzuki		DNQ	1m 50.51s	
	Dennis Ireland	GB	Suzuki		DNQ	2m 06.98s	

Fastest lap: Taira, 1m 39.37s, 90.57 mph/145.73 km/h (record).
Previous record (outright): Wayne Rainey, USA (Honda), 1m 42.61s, 87.71 mph/141.13 km/h (1987).

World Championship: 1 Gardner, 105; **2** Mamola, 91; **3** Lawson, 79; **4** Haslam, 64; **5** Chili, 37; **6** Mackenzie and Sarron, 33; **8** Taira, 31; **9** McElnea, 28; **10** Burnett, 18; **11** Yatsushiro, 13; **12** Schwantz, 11; **13** de Radiguès, Irons and Ito, 10; **16** Roche, 9; **17** Kawasaki, 4; **18** Scott, 3; **19** Katayama and Reiner, 2; **21** Magee, 1.

250 cc

26 laps, 65 miles/104.60 km

Place	Rider	Nat.	Machine	Laps	Time & speed	Practice time	Grid
1	Anton Mang	D	Honda	26	44m 54.26s 86.85 mph/ 139.76 km/h	1m 42.75s	4
2	Loris Reggiani	I	Aprilia	26	44m 54.42s	1m 43.14s	9
3	Martin Wimmer	D	Yamaha	26	44m 55.69s	1m 42.48s	3
4	Jacques Cornu	CH	Honda	26	44m 57.74s	1m 43.22s	10
5	Reinhold Roth	D	Honda	26	44m 58.67s	1m 42.43s	2
6	Patrick Igoa	F	Yamaha	26	44m 59.17s	1m 42.21s	1
7	Sito Pons	E	Honda	26	45m 16.09s	1m 43.56s	11
8	Carlos Cardus	E	Honda	26	44m 22.75s	1m 44.11s	20
9	Dominique Sarron	F	Honda	26	45m 26.77s	1m 42.77s	5
10	Manfred Herweh	D	Honda	26	45m 48.57s	1m 43.74s	13
11	Stefano Caracchi	RSM	Honda	26	45m 48.80s	1m 43.99s	17
12	Donnie McLeod	GB	EMC	26	45m 49.27s	1m 43.98s	16
13	Maurizio Vitali	I	Garelli	26	45m 49.30s	1m 43.89s	15
14	Jean-Philippe Ruggia	F	Yamaha	26	45m 49.80s	1m 44.02s	18
15	Gary Cowan	IRL	Honda	26	45m 58.10s	1m 44.29s	23
16	Jean-Michel Mattioli	F	Honda	26	45m 58.39s	1m 43.80s	14
17	Alain Bronec	F	Honda	26	45m 59.17s	1m 44.68s	26
18	Harald Eckl	D	Honda	26	45m 59.88s	1m 44.36s	24
19	Kevin Mitchell	GB	Yamaha	26	46m 07.92s	1m 45.14s	32
20	Guy Bertin	F	Honda	26	46m 12.55s	1m 44.60s	25
21	Hans Lindner	A	Honda	26	46m 17.58s	1m 45.00s	31
22	Jochen Schmid	D	Yamaha	26	46m 23.51s	1m 44.26s	22
23	Patrick van der Goorbergh	NL	Honda	26	46m 25.67s	1m 44.85s	27
24	Andy Machin	GB	Rotax	26	46m 29.36s	1m 44.85s	28
25	Bernard Hänggeli	CH	Yamaha	26	46m 37.58s	1m 44.94s	30
26	Rob Orme	GB	Yamaha	25	45m 04.87s	1m 45.34s	34
27	Hervé Duffard	F	Honda	25	45m 12.45s	1m 45.45s	36
28	Christian Boudinot	F	Fior	25	46m 07.36s	1m 44.22s	21
	Nigel Bosworth	GB	Yamaha	25	DNF	1m 45.43s	35
	Luca Cadalora	I	Yamaha	21	DNF	1m 43.63s	12
	Ivan Palazzese	YV	Yamaha	18	DNF	1m 44.10s	19
	René Delaby	LUX	Yamaha	16	DNF	1m 44.92s	29
	Marcellino Lucchi	I	Honda	8	DNF	1m 45.23s	33
	Carlos Lavado	YV	Yamaha	8	DNF	1m 43.13s	8
	Jean-François Baldé	F	Defi	2	DNF	1m 42.90s	7
	Stéphane Mertens	B	Sekitoba	1	DNF	1m 42.84s	6
	Bruno Bonhuil	F	Honda		DNQ	1m 45.51s	
	Eddie Laycock	GB	EMC		DNQ	1m 45.59s	
	Gerard van de Wal	NL	Assmex		DNQ	1m 45.68s	
	Jean Foray	F	Yamaha		DNQ	1m 45.75s	
	Urs Lüzi	CH	Honda		DNQ	1m 45.96s	
	Steve Patrickson	GB	Yamaha		DNQ	1m 45.94s	
	Ian Newton	GB	Honda		DNQ	1m 46.16s	
	Carl Fogarty	GB	Honda		DNQ	1m 46.47s	
	Takayoshi Yamamoto	J	Honda		DNQ	1m 46.51s	
	Cees Doorakkers	NL	Honda		DNQ	1m 47.13s	
	Siegfried Minich	A	Honda		DNQ	1m 47.20s	

Fastest lap: Wimmer, 1m 42.28s, 87.99 mph/141.58 km/h (record).
Previous record: Alberto Rota, I (Honda), 1m 45.47s, 85.12 mph/136.99 km/h (1986).

World Championship: 1 Roth, 88; **2** Mang, 82; **3** Pons, 57; **4** Cornu, 50; **5** Wimmer, 45; **6** Sarron, 41; **7** Reggiani, 40; **8** Cardus, 39; **9** Lavado, 30; **10** Garriga, 23; **11** Igoa, 22; **12** Cadalora, 18; **13** Kobayashi, 15; **14** Shimizu, 8; **15** Herweh and Ruggia, 7; **17** Palazzese, 6; **18** Lindner, 5; **19** Vitali, 3; **20** McLeod, Mertens and Taguchi, 2; **23** Bertin and Yamamoto, 1.

125 cc

24 laps, 60 miles/96.55 km

Place	Rider	Nat.	Machine	Laps	Time & speed	Practice time	Grid
1	Fausto Gresini	I	Garelli	24	43m 54.50s 81.98 mph/ 131.93 km/h	1m 47.74s	2
2	Pier Paolo Bianchi	I	MBA	24	44m 14.11s	1m 49.87s	6
3	Jean-Claude Selini	F	MBA	24	44m 35.65s	1m 50.26s	9
4	Johnny Wickström	SF	Tunturi	24	44m 43.49s	1m 50.85s	13
5	Ezio Gianola	I	Honda	24	44m 49.15s	1m 50.86s	14
6	Gastone Grassetti	I	MBA	24	45m 00.25s	1m 51.07s	17
7	Lucio Pietroniro	B	MBA	24	45m 00.84s	1m 50.18s	8
8	Jussi Hautaniemi	SF	MBA	24	45m 00.94s	1m 51.07s	16
9	Robin Milton	GB	MBA	24	45m 02.42s	1m 53.73s	27
10	Ivan Troisi	YV	MBA	24	45m 06.60s	1m 51.58s	21
11	Flemming Kistrup	DK	MBA	24	45m 23.68s	1m 49.86s	5
12	Olivier Liegeois	B	Assmex	24	45m 32.42s	1m 50.99s	15
13	Thierry Feuz	CH	MBA	24	45m 32.56s	1m 50.30s	10
14	Willy Pérez	RA	Zanella	24	45m 33.15s	1m 51.14s	18
15	Michael McGarrity	IRL	MBA	23	44m 06.90s	1m 53.86s	28
16	Fernando Gonzalez	E	Cobas	23	44m 23.04s	1m 54.00s	29
17	Jacques Hutteau	F	MBA	23	44m 38.05s	1m 54.54s	32
18	Thomas Møller-Pedersen	DK	MBA	23	44m 41.63s	1m 54.63s	33
19	Christian le Badezet	F	MBA	23	44m 43.19s	1m 54.09s	31
20	Mark Carkeek	GB	Scitsu	23	44m 47.50s	1m 55.35s	35
21	Allan Scott	USA	EMC	23	44m 49.51s	1m 53.60s	25
22	Hubert Abold	D	Krauser	23	44m 56.56s	1m 53.71s	26
23	Chris Galatowicz	GB	Honda	23	45m 10.88s	1m 54.06s	30
24	Paul Bordes	F	MBA	23	45m 15.12s	1m 53.47s	24
25	Steve Mason	GB	MBA	22	44m 48.57s	1m 55.69s	36
26	Robin Appleyard	GB	MBA	21	44m 45.16s	1m 54.93s	34
	Corrado Catalano	I	MBA	23	DNF	1m 49.45s	3
	Adolf Stadler	D	MBA	18	DNF	1m 50.47s	12
	Domenico Brigaglia	I	AGV	16	DNF	1m 50.16s	7
	Esa Kytölä	SF	MBA	13	DNF	1m 53.12s	23
	Peter Sommer	CH	Supeso	9	DNF	1m 53.00s	22
	Bady Hassaine	DZ	MBA	8	DNF	1m 51.14s	19
	Bruno Casanova	I	Garelli	8	DNF	1m 47.01s	1
	Andrés Marín Sánchez	E	Ducados	6	DNF	1m 50.42s	11
	Mike Leitner	A	MBA	4	DNF	1m 49.75s	4
	Håkan Olsson	S	Starol		DNS	1m 51.50s	20
	Doug Flather	GB	Honda		DNQ	1m 55.77s	
	Garry Dickinson	GB	MBA		DNQ	1m 56.17s	
	Ken Beckett	GB	MBA		DNQ	1m 56.48s	
	Reg Lennon	GB	Morbidelli		DNQ	1m 58.64s	
	Tim Salveson	GB	MBA		DNQ	2m 00.40s	
	Dave Browns	GB	MBA		DNQ	2m 04.90s	

Fastest lap: Gresini, 1m 48.24s, 83.14 mph/133.77 km/h (record).
Previous record: Jean-Claude Selini, F (MBA), 1m 51.60s, 80.64 mph/129.75 km/h (1987).

World Championship: 1 Gresini, 105; **2** Casanova, 64; **3** Auinger, 42; **4** Bianchi, 38; **5** Brigaglia and Casoli, 36; **7** Gianola, 23; **8** Sánchez, 18; **9** Wickström, 15; **10** Leitner, 14; **11** Selini, 12; **12** Feuz, 11; **13** Hautaniemi, 10; **14** Pietroniro, 8; **15** Grassetti, 7; **16** Catalano and Stadler, 6; **18** Liegeois, 4; **19** Macciotta and Milton, 2; **21** Kistrup, Pérez and Troisi, 1.

80 cc

18 laps, 45 miles/72.41 km

Place	Rider	Nat.	Machine	Laps	Time & speed	Practice time	Grid
1	Jorge Martinez	E	Derbi	18	34m 20.99s 78.60 mph/ 126.48 km/h	1m 52.32s	1
2	Ian McConnachie	GB	Krauser	18	34m 38.27s	1m 52.98s	3
3	Gerhard Waibel	D	Krauser	18	34m 41.40s	1m 54.54s	6
4	Luis M. Reyes	E	Autisa	18	35m 01.47s	1m 55.45s	9
5	Jörg Seel	D	Seel	18	35m 01.74s	1m 54.67s	7
6	Josef Fischer	A	Krauser	18	35m 22.92s	1m 56.03s	12
7	Günther Schirnhofer	D	Krauser	18	35m 27.25s	1m 56.87s	14
8	Hubert Abold	D	Krauser	18	35m 30.65s	1m 55.88s	11
9	Paolo Priori	I	Krauser	18	35m 35.52s	1m 56.28s	13
10	Jacques Bernard	B	Huvo	18	35m 35.98s	1m 57.36s	16
11	Heinz Paschen	D	Casal	18	36m 07.14s	1m 57.62s	20
12	René Dünki	CH	Krauser	18	36m 07.38s	1m 57.74s	21
13	Alojz Pavlic	YU	Seel	18	36m 07.97s	1m 58.82s	23
14	Serge Julin	B	Casal	18	36m 09.68s	1m 57.26s	15
15	Theo Timmer	NL	Casal	17	34m 28.42s	1m 57.41s	18
16	Lionel Robert	F	SPR	17	34m 39.85s	2m 01.76s	30
17	Reiner Koster	CH	Kroko	17	34m 46.34s	1m 58.86s	24
18	Paul Bordes	F	RB	17	35m 04.65s	2m 00.52s	27
19	Thomas Engl	D	Esch GPE	17	35m 05.13s	2m 00.18s	26
20	Dennis Batchelor	GB	Krauser	17	35m 07.09s	2m 02.28s	32
21	Doug Flather	GB	Wicks	17	35m 38.73s	2m 03.48s	33
22	Stuart Edwards	GB	Casal	17	35m 44.09s	2m 02.21s	31
23	Steve Lawton	GB	Eberhardt	16	34m 29.86s	2m 06.92s	35
24	John Cresswell	GB	Lusuardi	16	34m 32.05s	2m 05.88s	34
	Stefan Dörflinger	CH	Krauser	12	DNF	1m 52.96s	2
	Jos van Dongen	NL	Krauser	11	DNF	1m 58.91s	25
	Wilco Zeelenberg	NL	Casal	6	DNF	1m 57.58s	19
	Steve Mason	GB	Huvo	6	DNF	2m 00.95s	29
	Hans Spaan	NL	Casal	5	DNF	1m 54.10s	4
	Juan Ramon Bolart	E	Krauser	5	DNF	1m 55.88s	10
	Francisco Torrontegui	E	Casal	5	DNF	1m 57.41s	17
	Chris Baert	B	Seel	3	DNF	1m 58.48s	22
	Károly Juhász	H	Krauser	1	DNF	1m 54.44s	5
	Richard Bay	D	Ziegler	1	DNF	2m 00.55s	28
	Manuel Herreros	E	Derbi		DNS	1m 55.43s	8

Fastest lap: Martinez, 1m 52.44s, 80.04 mph/128.78 km/h (record established).

World Championship: 1 Martinez, 102; **3** Waibel, 54; **3** Herreros, 51; **4** McConnachie, 43; **5** Dörflinger, 42; **6** Reyes, 26; **7** Abold, 25; **8** Seel 21; **9** Miralles, 16; **10** Fischer, 15; **11** Criville, 12; **12** Schirnhofer, 11; **13** Juhász, 10; **14** Spaan, 8; **15** Priori, 6; **16** Barros and Paschen, 4; **18** Bay and Bolart, 3; **20** Gschwander and Ottl, 2; **22** Bernard and Waldmann, 1.

Sidecars

24 laps, 60 miles/96.55 km

Place	Driver & passenger	Nat.	Machine	Laps	Time & speed	Practice time	Grid
1	Steve Webster/ Tony Hewitt	GB GB	Yamaha	24	41m 14.69s 87.28 mph/ 140.45 km/h	1m 40.62s	2
2	Egbert Streuer/ Bernard Schnieders	NL NL	LCR- Yamaha	24	41m 37.96s	1m 42.49s	4
3	Rolf Steinhausen/ Bruno Hiller	D D	Eigenbau	24	41m 48.46s	1m 43.56s	6
4	Alfred Zurbrügg/ Simon Birchall	CH GB	LCR- Yamaha	24	42m 25.52s	1m 43.64s	7
5	Derek Jones/ Brian Ayres	GB GB	LCR- Seel	24	42m 26.73s	1m 44.28s	11
6	Steve Abbott/ Shaun Smith	GB GB	Windle- Yamaha	24	42m 26.87s	1m 43.97s	8
7	Barry Brindley/ Grahame Rose	GB GB	Yamaha	24	42m 41.75s	1m 44.15s	10
8	Yoshisada Kumagaya/ Brian Barlow	J GB	Windle- Yamaha	23	41m 27.29s	1m 45.45s	14
9	Masato Kumano/ Markus Fahrni	J CH	Toshiba	23	41m 27.74s	1m 45.58s	16
10	Ivan Nigrowski/ Michel Charpentier	F F	Seymaz	23	42m 03.69s	1m 47.10s	23
11	Jean-Louis Millet/ Claude Debroux	F F	Seymaz	23	42m 10.54s	1m 46.07s	18
12	Billy Gällros/ Auden Nordli	S S	Yamaha	22	42m 11.23s	1m 47.52s	24
	Dennis Bingham/ Julia Bingham	GB GB	LCR- Yamaha	21	DNF	1m 46.91s	21
	Rolf Biland/ Kurt Waltisperg	CH CH	LCR- Krauser	20	DNF	1m 40.23s	1
	Markus Egloff/ Urs Egloff	CH CH	LCR- Seel	19	DNF	1m 44.12s	9
	Pascal Larratte/ Jacques Corbier	F F	LCR- Yamaha	19	DNF	1m 43.50s	5
	Christian Graf/ Kurt Rothenbühler	CH CH	LCR- Yamaha	16	DNF	1m 47.61s	25
	Theo van Kempen/ Gerardus de Haas	NL NL	LCR- Yamaha	11	DNF	1m 45.29s	12
	Wolfgang Stropek/ Hans-Peter Demling	A A	LCR- Krauser	10	DNF	1m 45.98s	17
	Bernd Scherer/ Wolfgang Gess	D D	BSR- Yamaha	5	DNF	1m 45.56s	15
	Alain Michel/ Jean-Marc Fresc	F F	LCR- Krauser Elf	4	DNF	1m 42.22s	3
	Ray Gardner/ Tony Strevens	GB GB	LCR- Yamaha	3	DNF	1m 46.23s	19
	René Progin/ Yves Hunziker	CH CH	Seymaz	2	DNF	1m 45.30s	13
	Tony Baker/ John Hennigan	GB GB	Baker- Yamaha	2	DNF	1m 47.04s	22
	Gary Thomas/ Geoff White	GB GB	LCR- Yamaha		DNS	1m 46.76s	20
	Werner Kraus/ Oliver Schuster	D D	LCR		DNQ	1m 47.62s	
	Dave Hallam/ Steve Parker	GB GB	LCR- Yamaha		DNQ	1m 48.65s	
	Clive Stirrat/ Simon Prior	GB GB	BLR- Yamaha		DNQ	1m 48.99s	
	Mick Boddice/ Donny Williams	GB GB	Yamaha		DNQ	1m 49.79s	
	Graham Gleeson/ Peter Brown	NZ NZ	LCR- Cagiva		DNQ	1m 49.95s	
	John Evans/ Geoff Wilbraham	GB GB	BLR- Yamaha		DNQ	1m 50.10s	
	Gary Knight/ Phil Coombes	GB GB	Yamaha		DNQ	1m 50.31s	
	Judd Drew/ Christopher Plant	GB GB	BLR- Yamaha		DNQ	1m 50.38s	
	George Hardwick/ Carl Fieldhouse	GB GB	Yamaha		DNQ	1m 51.00s	

Fastest lap: Webster, 1m 41.71s, 88.48 mph/142.36 km/h (record).
Previous record: Derek Bayley/Bryan Nixon, GB/GB (Yamaha), 1m 45.61s, 85.22 mph/136.552 km/h (1986).

World Championship: 1 Webster, 75; **2** Streuer, 63; **3** Michel, 50; **4** Biland, 38; **5** Zurbrügg, 29; **6** Abbott, 24; **7** Jones, 20; **8** Steinhausen, 16; **9** van Kempen, 14; **10** Kumagaya, 13; **11** Kumano, 12; **12** Bayley, 8; **13** Progin, 7; **14** Brindley and Stropek, 6; **16** Larratte, 5; **17** Egloff and Scherer, 4; **19** Nigrowski and Stölzle, 1.

In another stirring 250 battle Toni Mang
(above) **once again emerges victorious.**

Photo: David Goldman

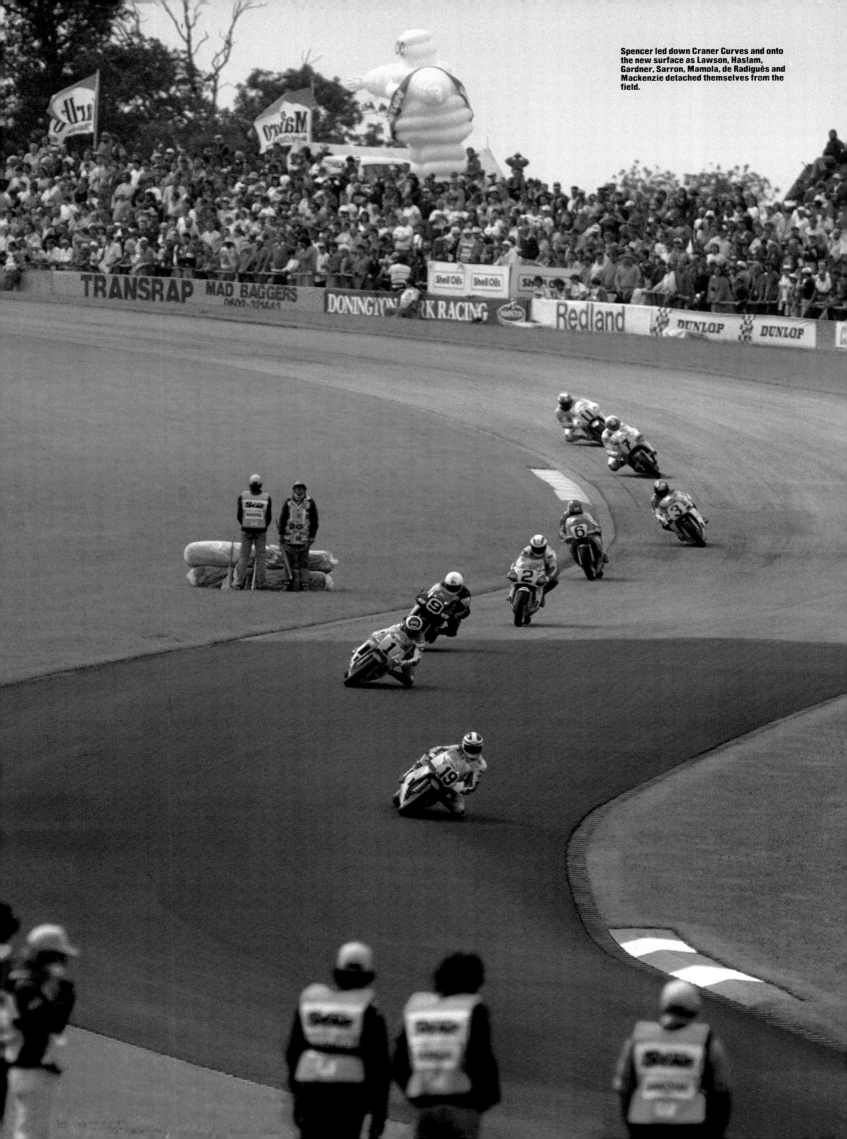

Spencer led down Craner Curves and onto the new surface as Lawson, Haslam, Gardner, Sarron, Mamola, de Radiguès and Mackenzie detached themselves from the field.

SWEDISH
TT

Theories abound, but when the flag drops that all stops. Theories in the air at Anderstorp included the idea that Spencer's return was the best thing that could have happened to Yamaha. The reasoning was that Gardner would be more upset than anyone else by being beaten by the triple World Champion, so he would be forced to decide between pushing harder to beat Spencer and ignoring him because he presented no threat to his World Championship.

During the first three practice sessions, and indeed well into the fourth, that notion seemed to be supported by the facts, because Spencer led the field. While Lawson was in contention, Gardner was fourth, after being seventh at the end of two sessions.

In the last minutes of the final session, however, Gardner kicked those theories into touch with a single lap at 1m 35.72s – a tenth of a second quicker than Lawson and over half a second better than Spencer.

It was not as big a practice lead as he had held at other times in the season but he was still on pole. The next day, he won the race very much as he pleased, which followed the pattern established during the season.

If Gardner *was* upset by Spencer's return it did not show at all. He had taken time to get to the top of the table because it had taken time to get the Honda sorted out: the track is very hard on suspension because its bumps suggest the suspension should be soft, while the long, banked corners require harder springing to withstand the compression.

Even in that final session Gardner blasted round for just one quick lap instead of the string

he normally manages, and said he had some more ideas to try during the untimed warm-up session on Saturday morning. It is not surprising that his team were pleased with the final outcome. They collected him from his motorhome in the paddock that evening and took him out for a drink – nothing riotous, but they know what makes him tick and an evening out keeps his mind off the race ahead. Gardner works best after winding down with his team rather than through monastic, solitary preparation.

Perhaps it was Lawson who was more affected by Spencer's return. The old needle was certainly back, pushed deeper by so many people speculating where Spencer might have finished in the British Grand Prix had he not had that mysterious mechanical problem early on. In Sweden, Lawson seemed more interested in beating Spencer than Gardner, even though when it came to the race he concentrated on the Australian ahead.

Why does so much controversy surround Spencer? So many theories and so many unsubstantiated 'facts' abound that no-one is ever sure of the truth. What did happen at Donington? Many of the stories floating around Anderstorp implied there was nothing wrong with the bike. The mechanics had stripped the brakes and then the engine, for the first time outside Japan, and nothing was wrong. Had a stone lodged momentarily between disc and caliper? Had Spencer made a mistake and imagined the mechanical failure or made it up altogether? Or had the locking rear brake problem simply not shown up when the unit was taken apart? As usual with Spencer, fifty people

had fifty different theories.

Well away from the heady heights of the $300,000 motorhomes, the World Championship was being decided in the less rarefied atmosphere of the sidecar class. After the first wet session, when Barry Brindley and Graham Rose had headed the table with their Fowler Yamaha, it was down to the usual four crews to fight it out for places on the front row.

At the end of four sessions, 1.5s separated Webster on pole from Michel in fourth place, but of more importance for the championship was Streuer's third place behind Biland. If the race finished like that Webster would be champion.

Streuer had succeeded in making his home-converted crankcase reed-valve Yamaha work well but it was still not quite as good as the three Krauser engines around him. Certainly he did not enjoy the speed advantage he had often had during his three championship-winning years.

With one round remaining, things were naturally a little tense in the Webster and Hewitt camp, who were now so close that they only needed to score three points more than Streuer to clinch the title. They could not afford any repeat of the previous year's Anderstorp mechanical failure. Mick Webster had looked after the outfit for almost the entire season, although he missed one race while on holiday. Dennis Trollope had looked after the outfit on that occasion, but Trollope also came to Sweden and wanted to help, even though the Websters preferred to work alone. Thankfully such troubles did not affect performance on the track, and the machine ran as faultlessly as it had done for almost the entire season.

Pier Francesco Chili fights for grip with
Roberto Gallina's HB Honda *(above)*.

Eddie Lawson was certain that Luca Cadalora
had ridden harder than anyone in the 250 race
(left).

While mechanical difficulties are still fairly common in the sidecar class they rarely affect the works machines in either the 250 or 500 categories. One of the few 250 teams to be smitten by problems was Sito Pons' Campsa Honda équipe, suffering a recurrence of their Monza seizing saga when the NSR250 had stopped five times. In Anderstorp, the bike seized on the final day of practice, then again in the Saturday morning warm-up. For the race it managed the trick twice, firstly on the opening lap, though continuing to run, only to stop completely on the last lap. Toni Mang's team manager Dave Peterssen said Pons' bike always seemed to be fitted with far smaller jets than they were using. Mang's bike continued to be fast, always vying with Reinhold Roth's as the fastest of the Hondas which continued to be a good deal quicker than the Yamahas.

Lavado qualified way down in twelfth place and said that he would not win another Grand Prix this year on his machine but Martin Wimmer was more hopeful in fifth place on the grid just behind Patrick Igoa. Team-mate Luca Cadalora was on pole an incredible 0.94s faster than second man Carlos Cardus, despite the Marlboro Yamaha clearly being less fast in a straight line.

There was some confusion over the final session on Friday because it was extended from forty to fifty minutes. Unfortunately, only about

half the teams got to hear about the change. Some then protested that the times from the final ten minutes should not count. The first time sheets issued included the full fifty minutes and Mang was second-fastest but when the ten minutes was axed he dropped to 13th.

That did not bother the team unduly, for he had shown that he could go as fast as necessary and was unlikely to be held up greatly by his poor position on the third row of the grid between Lavado and Sarron. On the second row were a couple of privateers, Manfred Herweh on the RS250 Honda and Donnie McLeod on the Pepsi EMC. Both had demonstrated through the year that they deserved better machinery, as had Jean-François Baldé and Ivan Palazzese on occasions. Jean-Philippe Ruggia was struggling to recapture the form he had shown early in the season before being given the chance to ride the V-twin YZR in Yugoslavia.

Mang had voiced the opinion at the end of '86 that it was a waste of time and effort having too many factory machines. Just the top three or four who had proved themselves should have the best bikes, putting them comfortably in front. A

year later he seemed to be having little trouble dealing with the other five Hondas and an equal number of Yamahas.

Over dinner at the Rothmans bus on Friday evening, Dave Peterssen had Toni run through a little experiment, something that Roberto Gallina had taught him the previous season. It simply entails sitting with a stopwatch in your hands, eyes shut and timing yourself over an imaginary lap, a mind's eye lap. Toni had never tried it before yet lapped in just over 1m 40s, as he had in that final, disallowed ten minutes of practice.

250 cc

Dry but dull, Saturday presented good racing conditions and Reinhold Roth leapt into the lead on the HB Honda. Half-way round the first lap he had an almost one-second lead over Cardus, McLeod and Sarron with Cadalora fifth ahead of Mang. Roth stretched his advantage to two, then almost three, seconds as Mang moved into second place. Nevertheless, the pace was not all that hot, in the high 1m 41s range.

Mang cut Roth's advantage gradually until he took over on lap 8, but Roth was not letting him go and upped the pace a little. He regained the lead on lap 10, with Mang still second and now ahead of Cornu and Cadalora. Wimmer had just taken fifth from Cardus and, like Reggiani who

was not far behind, was moving threateningly through the field. Also advancing was Lavado after being only 17th on lap 1.

By lap 14 there was a group of six fighting for the lead, led by Mang but with the others climbing over each other to get to him. Lavado continued to make progress and was about to oust Cardus from seventh. Sarron, meanwhile, had his work cut out to stay ahead of the ninth-place battle with Vitali, Pons, McLeod and Igoa.

It was obvious that no-one at the front had an advantage and Cadalora was passing where there seemed to be too little room, as he had through much of the season – maybe not downright dangerous but certainly hair-raising. It was Mang and Roth who were most often trading places for the lead, but Cadalora took his shot as well before being blown off down the straight.

'That Yamaha was so fast,' remarked Lawson sarcastically, watching from the top of the paddock grandstand, 'he would be a second in front going onto the straight and they would just pull up behind him, go around and away. He just outrode them so bad.'

Although those three spent their time leading, Reggiani and Wimmer both looked strong contenders for the win because of the way they had progressed through the field. Reggiani took third from Cadalora on lap 18 as Wimmer weighed up how he could get through the bunch. Reggiani made a mistake the next lap and was the first to be passed by Wimmer, who was determined that his progress should be certain and that no-one once passed would retake him.

He passed Cornu at the end of the main straight but ran a little wide coming out of the tight right-hander. That gave Cornu the idea of getting back underneath him as they headed for the next right onto the start-and-finish straight. Cornu had a look up the inside but realised that he could not make it. He braked and started to ease to the left to fall in behind Wimmer just as the Yamaha rider was curving in. A touch became inevitable, but such things happen and quite often both parties get away with it. This was not one of those occasions. Cornu's left handlebar caught Wimmer's seat, yanking the bar forward and making the front wheel turn right, in turn forcing Cornu's Honda to fall into the Yamaha which took both machines straight off the track, locked together.

The first Wimmer knew of it was when his bike was pushed upright and propelled off the circuit. Cornu tried to bail out, but just as he climbed back off the seat and was at the furthest distance from Wimmer's front wheel, it dug into the sponge protecting the barrier and flicked the Swiss rider over the bikes and along the wall. He was lucky that the angle of impact was along rather than into the wall, yet the speed was enough to dislocate and break his hip, ending his season there and then.

Wimmer was shocked by the incident and his chin was gashed. He was in pain because his crutch had been forced into the petrol tank and something on the bike almost broke his leg, but fortunately he was protected by his boots,

reinforced and sporting shin guards since his Hockenheim accident.

He later insisted on seeing an amateur home video of the crash some six times in freeze-frame to assure himself that it was in no way his fault. 'Two of these is more than enough for one year. You could break your neck in an accident like that,' he said, and it did not take much perception to realise that he was thinking about quitting, for a moment at least.

Mang still led by the narrowest of margins from Cadalora, Roth and Reggiani, the latter being just far enough behind not to lose time through the crash. It only took him two laps to catch right up to the leading trio, while Lavado had got to fifth after setting the fastest lap of the race but could progress no further because his bike started to mischange.

Though Cadalora, Reggiani and even Sarron had also lapped under 1m 40s, Mang had not. He was consistently fast, just above the 1m 40s mark, and nodded to his pit indicating that he knew what he had to do to win. There was some confusion on laps 22 and 23 as the ambulances carrying Wimmer and Cornu drove round the circuit to the exit. Anderstorp looks bad in such circumstances with no service road.

Mang was later to accuse Cadalora of passing under the yellow flag and would almost certainly have protested had the Italian finished in front of him. After that, Mang was shaking his head as he passed the pits. With Cadalora in front he was unsure how to make certain of victory.

With two laps to go he was in front again, with Cadalora second and Roth third, as he was later to point out at the post-race press conference. 'Those last two laps from Toni were perfect; any rider could learn something from watching him.'

Up to that point, both Roth and Cadalora also thought they could win but Mang just opened up about four-tenths of a second as he went down the back straight ahead of Cadalora and Roth for that final time. That left the two riders to try and make it up at the end of the straight, as Roth also remembered. 'Cadalora went for the inside of Toni so I could only go outside. I braked late, ran a little wide and, after using second gear out of that corner for 24 laps, this time I needed first and it spun round and threw me off.'

Roth collected himself together and eventually crossed the line eleventh, but Mang had sprinted home ahead of Cadalora to gain 15 points and take the championship lead by 9. Roth made those comments in front of Mang and said that with such a lead the experienced Mang would be hard to beat. Roth was seen not only as a great rider but a genuine sportsman. It was the first race in which he had failed to score. Both he and Mang had one fall apiece, though Mang had hit the ground a second time when torpedoed by Cornu in France. Roth had finished in the top three on seven occasions but Mang had now won six races. No-one else was even close.

125 cc

Sunday was equally dull and perhaps more threatening, with black clouds rolling across the

rough airstrip in the clearing that doubles as a Grand Prix circuit. As usual there were noises about the lack of television coverage and rumours that this would be the last Swedish Grand Prix. Swedish television is so disinterested in motorsport that they do not even get excited about Formula 1, where they have a first class driver. An outside company had to be hired to film this Grand Prix with the result that the pictures were much more expensive than the usual Eurovision feed.

That was of little concern to the 125 field as they lined up with Champion-elect Fausto Gresini in pole position. For once it was not team-mate Bruno Casanova but AGV MBA man Paolo Casoli who took second, with his team-mate, Domenico Brigaglia, fourth. Mike Leitner had qualified ninth on his MBA but behind Ezio Gianola on the single-cylinder Honda who had crashed early in practice.

Gresini was well over a second quicker than

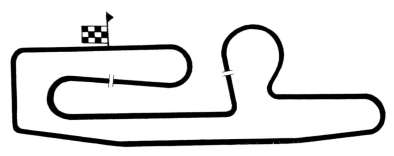

The traditional dunking for Steve Webster and Tony Hewitt.

anyone else so it was hardly surprising that he casually took the lead from Pier Paolo Bianchi at the end of the first lap. Casanova had struggled off the line in eighth place behind Gianola but was up to fifth by lap 2 as Casanova had a go at challenging the leading Garelli.

Gresini dallied for two laps before using a few more revs and easing himself into a more comfortable lead. By lap 5 he was disappearing, while his team-mate had secured third. Bianchi was left to fight with Andrés Marín Sánchez on the Ducados, Johnny Wickström on the Tunturi and Leitner.

At that point, lone female competitor Taru Rinne, the 18-year-old from Turku in Finland, crashed her ex-Jussi Hautaniemi LCR MBA out of 20th place. She was unhurt. Domenico Brigaglia had been very slow away and by lap 5 had only just passed the ninth-place battle between Gianola and Lucio Pietroniro.

With Gresini in boring isolation at the front, things were warming up behind. Casoli's second was looking less secure as he was being caught, not only by Casanova but also Bianchi, Marín Sánchez, Wickström, Leitner and Brigaglia, who were moving very quickly.

Casanova was still the strongest threat to Casoli and after shadowing him through laps 9 and 10 finally got past and, a few laps later, away. By lap 15 Bianchi was still holding his own against Brigaglia and Wickström while Marín Sánchez and Leitner had been dropped. At that point Gianola slipped off the Honda towards the end of the long, looping right-hander approaching the pit straight. He walked back to the pits as, two laps later, Casoli fell heavily on his way into the same bend. The second man was not so lucky, injuring his mouth as he hit the ground face first.

At the same time Marín Sánchez had found another burst of speed and in two laps had caught and passed Brigaglia, Bianchi and Wickström. This broke up the third-place group and only Brigaglia could match the Spaniard's new-found pace. The Brigaglia/Marín Sánchez contest was the only interest that remained, and when the Ducados rider made a mistake on lap 21 going into the left-hander leading onto the pits straight, that gave Brigaglia all the help he needed to take third behind the two Garellis.

500 cc

No-one was impressed with the start. 'I saw the starter walk off the grid, then suddenly the lights were red and green', said Spencer later. 'I had stabbed it into gear and let the clutch out but I did not have enough 'Rs' on and it just crawled off the line.'

Haslam was not caught out, however, and from the second row of the grid went into the first corner side-by-side with Lawson and on a better line. Gardner was right behind them and so were McElnea and Mackenzie, with Spencer about 10th, stuck behind Burnett and Mamola but ahead of Taira who was the slowest of all those off the front row.

Haslam had two laps to make the most of his

start but Gardner was soon into gear and took over the lead while Lawson struggled with a front tyre that refused to work. 'It was just sliding away from me and I had to back it down. Later, when the fuel went down and the bike got lighter, the tyre warmed up and worked a little better; at least I could predict the slide and feel it, but it was still there.'

While Lawson struggled and could not pass Haslam (who would later say his bike was the fastest in the race), McElnea hung back behind Lawson waiting for him to make a move and unwilling to spoil anything by diving in front of his team leader. Mackenzie, of course, had no such qualms and passed first McElnea, then, on lap 4, Lawson. Before he could get past Haslam, Mamola took them both, looking the fastest rider out of the six-man pack contesting second which had Spencer at its tail.

It was entertaining, that battle for second, but meanwhile Gardner was stretching his lead. Five seconds on lap 6 became eight and a half seconds on lap 11, and clearly Mamola was going to make no impression. Haslam was still third ahead of Lawson, Mackenzie, Spencer and McElnea.

McElnea had made his break and passed Lawson on lap 8. 'I decided I had to try and get past Eddie, but at the end of the back straight the engine stalled and I braked hard. I felt sure it had seized and as I let the clutch out the wheel was locked. I got round the corner and bumped it and it started again but I was back behind Freddie.'

Lawson was finally on the move and by lap 13 was in front of Mamola and lapping fractionally faster than Gardner, who had that healthy eight-second lead. With Mamola third the contest was hottest for fourth, with Mackenzie leading Haslam, Spencer and McElnea, but both Mackenzie and Haslam were having trouble with the front tyre folding under. Both insisted on using the cross-ply, as does Sarron and Burnett, while Gardner, Lawson, McElnea and Spencer employed the radial.

Sarron had crashed on lap 2 entering the long right-hander before the pits. Once more he landed on his head and suffered concussion. His helmet showed damage in the same place as with his two previous falls this season. Yatsushiro had fallen on lap 1 and Taira had been forced off the track as they had a confused braking match with Sarron at the end of the back straight.

Taira was climbing up from last place but by half-way through the 30-lap race he was still 15th. A lap later McElnea had passed Spencer and then went under Haslam into the pits corner as the Elf man went under back-marker Ray Swann. There was little room but all three must have breathed in because they made it.

On lap 18, Mackenzie made a small mistake and that helped McElnea get onto his tail. The Marlboro Yamaha rider would later point out that, while his bike was no match for the supposedly similar machines ridden by Lawson and Mamola, it was on a par with Mackenzie's Honda, which meant the HB bike must have been the slowest NSR on the track.

Back in eighth place, de Radiguès was having

a lonely ride on the Cagiva. It had not been inspiring in practice and during the warm-up the ignition system had started to play up. The team only had two of their new Japanese systems and one had failed at Donington, so they had nothing to replace it. He remained well ahead of the ninth-place battle where initially Burnett had been held up a little by Chili until they were both caught by Irons. Chili fell on lap 18, breaking two bones in his foot, and Irons managed to stay ahead of Burnett. After failing to score in the first five races of the year he had collected points steadily in the second five.

With seven laps to go Lawson had cut Gardner's lead to under seven seconds but the Australian was well aware of the position and, by this point in the season, he was used to defending his advantage. Mamola was a distant third, some four seconds in front of McElnea who ran out of time before he got close enough to challenge.

Haslam put in a little extra effort over the last two laps to make sure he secured sixth ahead of Spencer, saying that once more he felt short of testing time on the NSR. Spencer said he was glad the race was over and that while most of his body had stood up well, the right forearm had proved weak and had affected his braking.

Sidecars

The World Championship hinged on Steve Webster and Tony Hewitt scoring three more points than Streuer and Schnieders, so when the Dutch outfit slowed with gearbox problems with five laps remaining while holding third place, the title was almost in the bag. All Webster had to do was cruise to second after his race-long battle with Biland, but, being a competitive sort, he wanted to clinch the championship with a win. Like the Roberts/Spencer duel four years before and the Roth/Mang effort only a day earlier, it all hinged on those last two corners.

Webster braked early and on the outside, planning to come back under Biland between the two right-handers. He made his move but, as he started to draw alongside, the Swiss ex-champions saw what was happening and moved across to slam the door. The British crew had their sidecar wheel fairing crushed by the leading machine. With one hand Hewitt grabbed the broken fibreglass and shook the other fist angrily at Biland as they crossed the line second to claim the World title.

'That was not very gentlemanly', was Webster's restrained statement as he climbed the rostrum. The fury was in his eyes. Biland claimed it was a justifiable, if not totally fair, method of winning. He offered to repair the damage and will probably not be very proud of the incident upon reflection.

It was a shame the race ended that way because it had been a first class duel between the two outfits after they dropped early leader Streuer by lap 7. Alain Michel and Jean-Marc Fresc had started slowly but passed Rolf Steinhausen and Bruno Hiller on the seventh lap and then started to close on Streuer.

Swedish TT, 8/9 August/statistics
Anderstorp Circuit, 2.505-mile/4.031-km circuit

500 cc

30 laps, 75.14 miles/120.93 km

Place	Rider	Nat.	Machine	Laps	Time & speed	Practice time	Grid
1	Wayne Gardner	AUS	Honda	30	48m 46.36s 92.44 mph/ 148.768 km/h	1m 35.72s	1
2	Eddie Lawson	USA	Yamaha	30	48m 48.56s	1m 35.82s	2
3	Randy Mamola	USA	Yamaha	30	49m 06.29s	1m 36.86s	5
4	Rob McElnea	GB	Yamaha	30	49m 07.52s	1m 36.88s	6
5	Niall Mackenzie	GB	Honda	30	49m 16.02s	1m 37.40s	10
6	Ron Haslam	GB	Honda	30	49m 20.76s	1m 36.98s	7
7	Freddie Spencer	USA	Honda	30	49m 22.12s	1m 36.38s	3
8	Didier de Radiguès	B	Cagiva	30	49m 29.00s	1m 37.13s	9
9	Kenny Irons	GB	Suzuki	30	49m 33.09s	1m 37.72s	11
10	Roger Burnett	GB	Honda	30	49m 37.59s	1m 38.22s	14
11	Richard Scott	NZ	Honda	30	50m 05.23s	1m 38.13s	13
12	Fabio Biliotti	I	Honda	30	50m 21.68s	1m 38.94s	16
13	Tadahiko Taira	J	Yamaha	30	50m 22.38s	1m 36.57s	4
14	Bruno Kneubühler	CH	Honda	29	49m 27.45s	1m 39.74s	17
15	Manfred Fischer	D	Honda	29	49m 29.54s	1m 41.44s	22
16	Peter Sköld	S	Honda	29	49m 32.35s	1m 41.58s	23
17	Simon Buckmaster	GB	Honda	29	49m 32.69s	1m 41.97s	27
18	Fabio Barchitta	RSM	Honda	29	49m 33.45s	1m 41.65s	25
19	Louis-Luc Maisto	F	Honda	29	49m 36.64s	1m 41.58s	24
20	Maarten Duyzers	NL	Honda	29	49m 51.81s	1m 42.00s	28
21	Marco Gentile	CH	Fior	29	50m 10.38s	1m 39.85s	18
22	Ray Swann	GB	Honda	29	50m 23.43s	1m 41.82s	26
23	Ari Rämö	SF	Honda	28	49m 12.25s	1m 45.42s	31
24	Gerold Fischer	D	Honda	28	49m 49.18s	1m 44.55s	30
25	Geir Hestmann	N	Suzuki	27	49m 46.40s	1m 47.26s	34
	Alessandro Valesi	I	Honda	27	DNF	1m 40.20s	21
	Pier Francesco Chili	I	Honda	18	DNF	1m 37.97s	12
	Pavol Dekánek	CS	Suzuki	17	DNF	1m 46.33s	32
	Wolfgang von Muralt	CH	Suzuki	13	DNF	1m 40.06s	20
	Peter Lindén	S	Honda	10	DNF	1m 43.23s	29
	Claus Wulff	DK	Honda	8	DNF	1m 46.46s	33
	Christian Sarron	F	Yamaha	1	DNF	1m 37.07s	8
	Hervé Guilleux	F	Fior	1	DNF	1m 39.94s	19
	Shunji Yatsushiro	J	Honda	0	DNF	1m 38.59s	15

Fastest lap: Gardner, 1m 36.37s, 93.65 mph/150.582 km/h (record).
Previous record: Eddie Lawson, USA (Yamaha), 1m 36.59s, 93.36 mph/150.25 km/h (1986).

World Championship: 1 Gardner, 120; **2** Mamola, 101; **3** Lawson, 91; **4** Haslam, 69; **5** Mackenzie, 39; **6** Chili, 37; **7** McElnea, 36; **8** Sarron, 33; **9** Taira, 31; **10** Burnett, 19; **11** de Radiguès and Yatsushiro, 13; **13** Irons, 12; **14** Schwantz, 11; **15** Ito, 10; **16** Roche, 9; **17** Kawasaki and Spencer, 4; **19** Scott, 3; **20** Katayama and Reiner, 2; **22** Magee, 1.

250 cc

25 laps, 62.65 miles/100.78 km

Place	Rider	Nat.	Machine	Laps	Time & speed	Practice time	Grid
1	Anton Mang	D	Honda	25	42m 09.70s 89.11 mph/ 143.412 km/h	1m 40.75s	13
2	Luca Cadalora	I	Yamaha	25	42m 09.99s	1m 39.02s	1
3	Loris Reggiani	I	Aprilia	25	42m 11.75s	1m 40.64s	9
4	Carlos Lavado	YV	Yamaha	25	42m 15.10s	1m 40.71s	12
5	Dominique Sarron	F	Honda	25	42m 15.58s	1m 40.79s	14
6	Carlos Cardus	E	Honda	25	42m 15.85s	1m 39.96s	2
7	Patrick Igoa	F	Yamaha	25	42m 16.30s	1m 40.14s	4
8	Maurizio Vitali	I	Garelli	25	42m 24.82s	1m 40.65s	10
9	Donnie McLeod	GB	EMC	25	42m 25.95s	1m 40.64s	8
10	Jean-François Baldé	F	Defi	25	42m 32.53s	1m 41.57s	19
11	Reinhold Roth	D	Honda	25	42m 38.84s	1m 40.49s	7
12	Stefano Caracchi	RSM	Honda	25	42m 44.56s	1m 41.25s	17
13	Harald Eckl	D	Honda	25	42m 44.85s	1m 41.69s	20
14	Jean-Michel Mattioli	F	Honda	25	42m 45.24s	1m 41.05s	16
15	Hans Lindner	A	Honda	25	43m 10.34s	1m 42.80s	23
16	Alain Bronec	F	Honda	25	43m 10.70s	1m 42.94s	26
17	Urs Lüzi	CH	Honda	25	43m 11.23s	1m 43.39s	31
18	Guy Bertin	F	Honda	25	43m 11.50s	1m 41.86s	22
19	René Delaby	LUX	Yamaha	25	43m 11.77s	1m 42.83s	25
20	Andreas Preining	A	Rotax	25	43m 45.65s	1m 43.00s	27
21	Christian Boudinot	F	Fior	25	43m 48.89s	1m 43.10s	28
22	Kevin Mitchell	GB	Yamaha			1m 44.36s	38
23	Jean Foray	F	Yamaha			1m 43.36s	30
24	Patrick van der Goorbergh	NL	Honda			1m 42.81s	24
25	Jochen Schmid	D	Yamaha	24	42m 30.34s	1m 43.45s	33
	Alfonso Pons	E	Honda	24	DNF	1m 41.47s	18
	Jacques Cornu	CH	Honda	18	DNF	1m 39.99s	3
	Martin Wimmer	D	Yamaha	18	DNF	1m 40.22s	5
	Ivan Palazzese	YV	Yamaha	18	DNF	1m 40.80s	15
	Stéphane Mertens	B	Sekitoba	18	DNF	1m 40.69s	11
	Manfred Herweh	D	Honda	15	DNF	1m 40.29s	6
	Hervé Duffard	F	Honda	15	DNF	1m 43.43s	32
	Takayoshi Yamamoto	J	Yamaha	13	DNF	1m 43.74s	35
	Jean-Philippe Ruggia	F	Yamaha	9	DNF	1m 41.84s	21
	Markku Kivi	SF	Yamaha	5	DNF	1m 44.17s	37
	Bobby Issazadhe	S	Honda	2	DNF	1m 43.97s	36
	Bruno Bonhuil	F	Honda	2	DNF	1m 43.18s	29
	Gerard van der Wal	NL	Assmex	2	DNF	1m 43.50s	34
	Cees Doorakkers	NL	Honda		DNQ	1m 44.78s	
	Siegfried Minich	A	Honda		DNQ	1m 45.05s	
	Håkan Olsson	S	Rotax		DNQ	1m 45.06s	
	Per Jansson	S	Yamaha		DNQ	1m 45.29s	
	Eilert Lundstedt	S	ESW-MBA		DNQ	1m 45.39s	
	Harri Kallio	SF	Yamaha		DNQ	1m 49.44s	

Fastest lap: Lavado, 1m 39.49s, 90.63 mph/145.860 km/h (record).
Previous record: Anton Mang, D (Honda), 1m 41.64s, 88.72 mph/142.78 km/h (1985).

World Championship: 1 Mang, 97; **2** Roth, 88; **3** Pons, 57; **4** Cornu and Reggiani, 50; **6** Sarron, 47; **7** Wimmer, 45; **8** Cardus, 44; **9** Lavado, 38; **10** Cadalora, 30; **11** Igoa, 26; **12** Garriga, 23; **13** Kobayashi, 15; **14** Shimuzu, 8; **15** Herweh and Ruggia, 7; **17** Palazzese and Vitali, 6; **19** Lindner, 5; **20** McLeod, 4; **21** Mertens and Taguchi, 2; **23** Baldé, Bertin and Yamamoto, 1.

125 cc

23 laps, 57.52 miles/92.71 km

Place	Rider	Nat.	Machine	Laps	Time & speed	Practice time	Grid
1	Fausto Gresini	I	Garelli	23	40m 25.58s 84.50 mph/ 137.603 km/h	1m 44.45s	1
2	Bruno Casanova	I	Garelli	23	41m 02.80s	1m 46.00s	3
3	Domenico Brigaglia	I	AGV	23	41m 07.68s	1m 46.72s	4
4	Andrés Marín Sánchez	E	Ducados	23	41m 09.94s	1m 46.84s	7
5	Johnny Wickström	SF	Tunturi	23	41m 17.06s	1m 46.82s	6
6	Pier Paolo Bianchi	I	MBA	23	41m 22.59s	1m 46.73s	5
7	Mike Leitner	A	MBA	23	41m 29.75s	1m 47.12s	9
8	Lucio Pietroniro	B	MBA	23	41m 42.64s	1m 47.23s	10
9	Gastone Grassetti	I	MBA	23	41m 51.28s	1m 48.28s	13
10	Esa Kytölä	SF	MBA	23	41m 52.30s	1m 48.68s	17
11	Jean-Claude Selini	F	MBA	23	41m 56.50s	1m 48.29s	14
12	Håkan Olsson	S	Starol	23	41m 58.70s	1m 49.26s	21
13	Bady Hassaine	DZ	MBA	23	42m 10.82s	1m 49.55s	22
14	Thierry Feuz	CH	LCR	23	42m 15.08s	1m 51.42s	31
15	Robin Milton	GB	MBA	23	42m 15.42s	1m 50.52s	26
16	Christian le Badezet	F	MBA	22	40m 26.85s	1m 51.16s	30
17	Thomas Møller-Pedersen	DK	MBA	22	40m 44.92s	1m 48.83s	18
18	Allan Scott	USA	EMC	22	40m 49.49s	1m 50.93s	29
19	Peter Sommer	CH	Supeso	22	41m 01.77s	1m 49.17s	20
20	Jacques Hutteau	F	MBA	22	41m 03.05s	1m 50.83s	28
21	Reijo Rosnell	SF	MBA	22	41m 13.38s	1m 50.14s	24
22	Frede Jensen	DK	MBA	22	41m 16.13s	1m 52.39s	32
23	Peter Baláž	CS	MBA	22	41m 50.74s	1m 50.61s	27
	Adolf Stadler	D	MBA	22	DNF	1m 47.89s	11
	Jussi Hautaniemi	SF	MBA	22	DNF	1m 47.96s	12
	Ivan Troisi	YV	MBA	22	DNF	1m 48.35s	16
	Willy Pérez	RA	Zanella	22	DNF	1m 48.30s	15
	Paolo Casoli	I	AGV	16	DNF	1m 45.67s	2
	Ezio Gianola	I	Honda	14	DNF	1m 47.10s	8
	Fernando Gonzales	E	Cobas-MBA	10	DNF	1m 50.46s	25
	Robin Appleyard	GB	MBA	6	DNF	1m 53.31s	33
	Flemming Kistrup	DK	MBA	5	DNF	1m 49.16s	19
	Taru Rinne	SF	MBA	4	DNF	1m 49.79s	23

Fastest lap: Gresini, 1m 43.79s, 86.88 mph/139.817 km/h (record).
Previous record: Luca Cadalora, I (Garelli), 1m 45.01s, 85.88 mph/138.21 km/h (1986).

World Championship: 1 Gresini, 120; **2** Casanova, 76; **3** Brigaglia, 46 **4** Bianchi, 43; **5** Auinger, 42; **6** Casoli, 36; **7** Sánchez, 26; **8** Gianola, 23; **9** Wickström, 21; **10** Leitner, 18; **11** Selini, 12; **12** Feuz and Pietroniro, 11; **14** Hautaniemi, 10; **15** Grassetti, 9; **16** Catalano and Stadler, 6; **18** Liegeois, 4; **19** Macciotta and Milton, 2; **21** Kistrup, Kytölä, Pérez and Troisi, 1.

Sidecars

23 laps, 57.52 miles/92.71 km

Place	Driver & passenger	Nat.	Machine	Laps	Time & speed	Practice time	Grid
1	Rolf Biland/ Kurt Waltisperg	CH CH	LCR-Krauser	23	38m 52.02s 88.93 mph/ 143.123 km/h	1m 39.51s	2
2	Steve Webster/ Tony Hewitt	GB GB	Yamaha	23	38m 53.52s	1m 39.28s	1
3	Alain Michel/ Jean-Marc Fresc	F F	LCR-Krauser	23	39m 00.60s	1m 40.17s	4
4	Rolff Steinhausen/ Bruno Hiller	D D	Eigenbau	23	39m 21.73s	1m 40.57s	5
5	Alfred Zurbrügg/ Simon Birchall	CH GB	LCR-Yamaha	23	39m 34.39s	1m 40.86s	6
6	Pascal Larratte/ Jacques Corbier	F F	LCR-Yamaha	23	39m 56.39s	1m 43.47s	16
7	Masato Kumano/ Markus Fahrni	J CH	LCR-Yamaha	23	39m 57.45s	1m 42.10s	8
8	Wolfgang Stropek/ Hans-Peter Demling	A A	LCR-Krauser	23	40m 10.00s	1m 42.76s	14
9	Markus Egloff/ Urs Egloff	CH CH	LCR-Seel	23	40m 23.74s	1m 41.39s	7
10	René Progin/ Yves Hunziker	CH CH	Seymaz	23	40m 24.12s	1m 43.42s	15
11	Bernd Scherer/ Wolfgang Gess	D D	BSR-Yamaha	22	38m 58.41s	1m 44.03s	16
12	Egbert Streuer/ Bernard Schnieders	NL NL	LCR-Yamaha	22	39m 01.34s	1m 39.91s	3
13	Ivan Nigrowski/ Frédéric Meunier	F F	Seymaz	22	39m 16.58s	1m 45.78s	18
14	Egon Schons/ Thomas Schröder	D D	Yamaha	21	39m 40.42s	1m 49.68s	22
	Yoshisada Kumagaya/ Brian Barlow	J GB	Yamaha	22	DNF	1m 42.63s	12
	Derek Jones/ Brian Ayres	GB GB	LCR-Seel	17	DNF	1m 42.37s	9
	Barry Brindley/ Grahame Rose	GB GB	Yamaha	10	DNF	1m 42.57s	11
	Billy Gällros/ Auden Nordli	S S	Yamaha	9	DNF	1m 48.54s	21
	Theo van Kempen/ Gerardus de Haas	NL NL	LCR-Yamaha	8	DNF	1m 42.74s	13
	Steve Abbott/ Shaun Smith	GB GB	Windle-Yamaha	7	DNF	1m 42.40s	10
	Graham Gleeson/ Peter Brown	NZ NZ	LCR-Cagiva	7	DNF	1m 46.77s	19
	Erwin Weber/ Eckart Rösinger	D D	LCR-Sams	3	DNF	1m 46.82s	20

Fastest lap: Biland, 1m 39.59s, 90.54 mph/145.713 km/h (record).
Previous record: Steve Webster/Tony Hewitt, GB/GB (LCR-Yamaha), 1m 40.27s, 89.94 mph/144.74 km/h (1986).

World Championship: 1 Webster, 87; **2** Streuer, 63; **3** Michel, 60; **4** Biland, 53; **5** Zurbrügg, 35; **6** Abbott and Steinhausen, 24; **8** Jones, 20; **9** Kumano, 16; **10** van Kempen, 14; **11** Kumagaya, 13; **12** Larratte, 10; **13** Stropek, 9; **14** Bayley and Progin, 8; **16** Brindley and Egloff, 6; **18** Scherer, 4; **19** Nigrowski and Stölzle, 1.

Grand Prix
C. S. S. R.

In his first race at the new Brno circuit Eddie Lawson finished 13th. It was a race for Porsches and he was a guest celebrity. Martin Wimmer also competed, having taken part in a couple of events before and arranged the drive for Lawson.

It was a good idea: take a look at the track the weekend before the Grand Prix started. It should at least have given the two men a slight advantage for the first practice sessions as hardly anyone else had seen the track before. On reflection, though, Lawson considered that, if anything, his advance knowledge worked against him. 'The track is so simple anyone can learn which way it goes in five laps, and the cars were sliding so much it gave me the idea that the track surface was slippery. That took a while to work out of my mind.'

Reinhold Roth agreed with that latter point for he had ridden at an international the weekend before Donington, along with Loris Reggiani, Hans Lindner and a few others. Then the surface had been so slippery that riders were using intermediate tyres to get grip.

Roth said it certainly worked against him and, with the second day of timed practice still to go, he blamed it for his fourth place behind Wimmer, Sarron and Mang. 'It was better that I had no test here before because at the back of my mind for the first three practice sessions I have thought that the track is slippery. I know it isn't and tomorrow that will be out of my brain. I am sure I can go faster, but I think that Martin's time is about the limit for a 250.'

Indeed, Wimmer had impressed everyone with his time of 2m 12.29s because it was almost a second quicker than Sarron and the Frenchman, for one, was not sure he could match it. 'At the moment I have tyre patter front and rear, and I am going to have to sort that out if I am going to go any quicker.'

Sarron did sort out the suspension problem, found a new line on a couple of corners and produced a better time than Wimmer. On Saturday morning his time of 2m 12.2s put him on pole, but that afternoon he was credited with a 2m 11.62s. 'My team did not get me at that time and I think it is very unlikely that I went that fast but I was still in pole position anyway.'

Wimmer was not particularly upset at losing pole because he was still very competitive but he had thought he could go even quicker after setting pole time on the first day. He considered that a change of internal gearbox ratios might be the key to an even faster time even though most of the opposition were sure he had gone as fast as was practicably possible. 'I have an idea for a different gearbox that might not work but if it did I would be half a second faster.'

It did not work but at least the Yamaha was proving as competitive as the Hondas, and Wimmer knew why. 'The Hondas tend to suffer with the front end tucking under going into the downhill corners and the only one who has his bike sorted out is Mang.' The Rothmans Honda rider had made more alterations to his machine than anyone else, changing the steering geometry with different fork yokes, and as well as making

a new connecting link for the rear suspension the team had also adopted a White Power rear suspension as a replacement for the standard Showa.

Mang did not feature at all in practice, however, and having set only one pole position all year it was obviously not important to him. He concentrated on getting the bike sorted out for the race and putting together a string of practice laps at a pace he could manage in racing conditions rather than just a single flash in the pan effort for a good grid position that he could never repeat.

He was using his experience to the full and yet he remained keen to learn, as team manager Dave Peterssen pointed out: 'If I had won four World Championships and had been racing as long as he has I think I would act as if I knew everything, but he doesn't. He is always ready to listen to new ideas and to try different things.' This receptiveness could be the secret of Mang's long period at the top of the sport for, as engines, tyres and suspension have changed, he has continued to learn rather than insist on using the ideas that worked on last year's bike or the gearing that worked the last time he raced at a certain circuit.

Mang said he was spending most of his time working with the suspension and the track was changing with every session. 'The track is hard on suspension. The old circuit was the same: as practice goes on the grip gets better and that puts more load on the suspension and gives us more problems.'

Another reason for Mang not starring in practice was that he did not like the circuit. 'It is designed by computers; the corners are stupid and every one is the same and none of them are fast.' It was a feeling shared by many, for even though the track looked exciting with great changes of elevation and superb spectator bankings, the corners were tight and of constant radius. It still looked a much more interesting facility than the Nürburgring where the wooded hills had been flattened to build the new circuit.

Loris Reggiani also found the track uninteresting but, as usual, his was the fastest non-Japanese machine. In the interests of simplicity, they had dropped the Öhlins front forks they had been experimenting with. 'I was sure that they were better and stiffer but I found them so different to use that having one bike with Marzocchi forks and one with Öhlins was no good to me. Every time I swapped from one to the other it would take me four or five laps to get used to the other forks. We will try the Öhlins again when we have time to do more testing with two bikes using the same forks.'

Practice produced several falls and Carlos Lavado broke the same collarbone that he had injured in the first round at Suzuka. He also injured his hand, and that just about rounded off a frustrating season for the World Champion who only showed his best form in Yugoslavia.

In the 500 class the Yamahas were equally competitive, with Taira swiftly getting to grips with the circuit. 'The track is quite like the ones we have at home and no-one else has raced here

before so they do not have an advantage over me. It has taken me time this year to get used to riding the 500 in the Grands Prix because it is so different to the 250 but now I am happier with the bike.'

Lawson was certainly *not* happy, complaining that the old carburation problem was as bad as ever. He admitted frankly that he did not think he could match Taira's practice time, so getting close to Gardner was likely to be out of the question. The Australian, on the other hand, had little to trouble him and was very relaxed about the situation. His nearest rival remained Randy Mamola, who had never been able to beat him in a straight dry race.

That was set to change because Dunlop had produced a new rear tyre for Mamola (still numbered KR108) which, for an 18 inch rim, had a 3.75 x 7.25 aspect ratio and was of a completely new construction. Peter Ingley said that it had been designed earlier in the season – back at Monza in the paddock – but it was some time before they decided to make the new design. Some work had been done with Cornu on the rear 250 tyre, and ten versions of the 500 tyre in two different compounds were shipped to Czechoslovakia for testing. It was intended that

the new construction would form the basis of their 1988 tyres. Ingley wanted to prove the idea now because he had ceased to believe in off-season testing, maintaining that riders could rarely be persuaded to go fast enough to give meaningful results.

The tyre seemed to offer something right from the start, although it was not perfect and created some pattering problems. It also seemed a little out of step with the front which had been so good all season. Nevertheless, it was a very good first test and Dunlop knew where they wanted to go next.

80 cc

Aspar Martínez already had the World Championship in the bag but ex-champion Stefan Dörflinger had some consolation for his second defeat in as many years by taking a fine win in an interesting race that produced some rapid changes of fortune.

Spaniard Martínez led on lap 1 by a slender margin from Gerhard Waibel on the first of the Krausers. By lap 2, another Krauser had taken the lead, with Ian McConnachie riding. While Waibel dropped back, Martínez and Dörflinger chased McConnachie.

Total domination is the way to describe Wayne Gardner's win. He had to try hard but was never likely to be caught.

When the British rider ran wide on lap 4, Dörflinger led from Martínez, but a lap later McConnachie was back in front and looked able to pull away. He started to get clear, but then Martínez and Dörflinger closed in again. This time, as they put the pressure on McConnachie, he crashed on the exit from the all-important right-hander that dictated speed up the long hill before the last corner and the start-and-finish straight. Later, he said he thought the suspension unit had given up because he did not try any harder on that lap than previously.

He pulled the wrecked fairing off the bike and restarted but could only finish eleventh. With Martínez put off-line because he was close when McConnachie fell, Dörflinger was able to take the lead and, once in front, defended his position well.

In the closing stages, Waibel looked as though he had lost third to the second Derbi (Manuel Herreros, who had started badly and was not in the top ten until lap 4). Then, coming out of the final corner, Waibel had the better line and shot past the Derbi to secure his place on the rostrum.

250 cc

Reinhold Roth got one of his great starts on the HB Honda, with Dominique Sarron, Toni Mang, Sito Pons and Loris Reggiani behind. Mang was quick to take the lead and made a nonsense of the practice times. Wimmer never got the chance to show what he could do as a pin came out of the gearchange mechanism and he retired at the end of the first lap. This pin has come out of a 250 gearbox once before, but when checked normally the pin is impossible to remove and in all the time the same part has been used in a 500 gearbox it has never come out.

Reggiani was soon forcing his way forward and, together with Sarron, he challenged Mang for the lead. It was Sarron who got past first but then Reggiani took his turn to lead. There was nothing in it between the members of the leading group and they traded places every few hundred yards. Roth, meanwhile, slipped back to fifth ahead of Cadalora and Urs Lüzi (having his first ride on the works Parisienne in the absence of injured Jacques Cornu).

The fact that Reggiani had a brief run at the head of the field gave Mang an advantage because the Aprilia started to leak oil and as it

sprayed over his pursuers, Mang suffered least from the hazard. Sarron later said he could hardly see for the oil covering his screen and visor. Reggiani felt oil on his boot and then his rear tyre and pulled out on lap 8, leaving Mang to lead from Pons. Sarron, Roth, Cadalora and the rest dropped back a little.

Pons made a brave attempt to hang on to Mang, but he had not been able to do so all year – perhaps because he did not have his NSR working as well as Mang's. It took Mang four laps to rid himself completely of Pons so, by lap 11, he was getting away, while the third-place battle that had included Sarron, Roth, Cadalora, Lüzi, Cardus and Igoa began to break up, as Cardus was inspired to pull away from Sarron.

Once Pons had lost Mang, he was quickly caught by Cardus and Sarron. Mang increased his lead slowly but steadily, gaining anything from three to six-tenths of a second per lap. Fifth place was being fought over by Roth, Cadalora and Lüzi, while Igoa had dropped back and Ivan Palazzese held a secure ninth ahead of Juan Garriga. Donnie McLeod was 11th, finding that his front tyre gave almost no grip right from the start.

Mang extended his lead to four seconds, but with three laps to go the contest for second got hotter. Cadalora latched on to the tail of the three-man group behind Cardus, Pons and Sarron. On the final lap, Pons led Cardus and

Sarron up to the last left and right 'S' to the finish line, but both Spaniards made a mess of the final corner and let Sarron through to claim 12 points.

Cadalora was fifth, saying he made his big effort too late, and for the second week running Roth crashed on the last lap. 'Going into the long right-hander at the bottom of the circuit Lüzi hesitated and I thought I could get past on the inside, but as I tried he turned in and he touched my front wheel.' Roth remounted but was passed by Igoa, Palazzese and Garriga before the finish line. He still finished tenth and denied McLeod a point.

Mang said after the race that the crosswinds were a real problem on the downhill sections as they threatened to wash the front wheel away. He had not stuck his neck out, but just maintained a good pace and suddenly found himself getting away from the rest. It was another great ride from the front where he had judged the pace perfectly. The team had swapped engines from one machine to the other after the Sunday morning warm-up session because while one engine was faster that bike could not be made to handle as well as the other.

125 cc

The race was decimated by a first-lap crash which brought down five riders on their way towards the second corner. Those who never completed the first lap were Domenico Brigaglia, Johnny Wickström, Willy Pérez, Olivier Liegeois and Mike Leitner. That left a big hole in mid-field.

It probably made little difference to Fausto Gresini, however, who won his second World

Championship with a 100 per cent record of eight straight wins on the factory Garelli. Again, he was never troubled once he passed Pier Paolo Bianchi on the MBA on the second lap.

It took Garelli number two rider Bruno Casanova until lap 4 to work his way into fourth place, getting the better of Bianchi and Andrés Marín Sánchez on the Ducados. Bianchi stopped on lap 6 leaving Sánchez to finish a lonely third well ahead of the most interesting battle of the race.

Ezio Gianola had yet another brilliant ride on the single-cylinder Honda, successfully defending his position against four other men on the twin-cylinder machines. He was fourth ahead of Lucio Pietroniro, Ivan Troisi, Claudio Macciotta and Esa Kytölä, with whom he had been fighting all the way.

Gianola never led the group but played his hand perfectly and with only three riders, Troisi, Pietroniro and Gianola, together on the last lap, Gianola won by pure riding skill over the final circuit. He said later that there was no way he could have ridden like that all race but he was prepared to stick his neck out for the final lap and see what he could do. As Honda will use his machine as the basis of next year's production bike for the new 125 single-cylinder Grand Prix class, it should provide some exciting racing.

Bady Hassaine finished ninth and scored his first-ever World Championship points even though he has been racing in Grands Prix since the beginning of the Eighties.

500 cc

Wayne Gardner produced a perfect ride on the Rothmans Honda and led from lap 1. Eddie Lawson was unable to give chase and later said he ran into exactly the same trouble that he had

Stan Perec

The huge crowd appreciated the superb new Brno facility.

Inset **Eddie Lawson does not often get out of shape but chasing Gardner requires an extraordinary effort.**

suffered in Sweden: the front tyre refused to work over the opening laps, forcing him to ease off and let Taira past. Only when the tyre had warmed sufficiently could he press on again.

For the first couple of laps, all three Marlboro Yamahas were grouped behind Gardner, but McElnea found that his rear tyre was not offering any grip and just rolling the throttle off going into the corners was enough to set the bike sliding. Soon, he started to slip back and later pointed out that he had to choose between slowing down or falling off. 'It was very disappointing, because for once my bike seemed as fast as Ed's – we were side by side going up the hill away from the first corner.'

Gardner quickly started to pull away and after only three laps had a healthy advantage. By lap 4, Taira had passed Lawson and as they broke away from the pack Mamola and Sarron passed McElnea.

Spencer was not looking especially impressive, being passed by Mackenzie on lap 4, but no-one knew that he had lost a contact lens on the warm-up lap. It is incredible that he managed to continue, as his judgement must have been completely destroyed by the imbalance in his vision. He has needed corrective eyewear since the age of eight.

Taira was pulling away from Lawson, who looked as though he might soon come under pressure from Mamola, but then the Lucky Strike rider made a mistake and ran up the pit entrance road. 'I hit a neutral and couldn't make the turn', reported Mamola, who was lucky enough to be able to turn the bike round and go across the dirt strip onto the circuit, losing only four places.

Mackenzie was also progressing and catching Sarron who was having trouble with his rear suspension. He passed him on the brakes going

into the last 'S' section to complete lap 9, and at that point Mamola was just thinking about repassing Spencer who was still behind McElnea in seventh place.

On lap 11 Lawson got back in front of Taira, but by then Gardner had a five-second advantage. Mamola had made his way past Spencer and McElnea, but on lap 13 Spencer went straight on, just as Mamola had done, and continued up the pit entrance road. He went a little further than the Californian had and had to back up before he could turn and regain the circuit. That dropped him to 12th, just in front of Richard Scott and Ron Haslam, the latter having his first race on the Elf 4.

Gardner's lead slipped a little as Lawson increased the pace; the Australian was not having an easy time of it. 'One of the front discs warped. They are the same as we used last year and the bike is faster and I am going into the corners harder, so I guess they are just not up to it. The rear tyre also started going off so I had to take things as easy as I could. I couldn't get away from Eddie any more but at least I held on to the lead.'

By lap 15 Mamola had caught Sarron; in only one lap he passed the Frenchman and Mackenzie to the cheers of the crowd. Lawson nibbled away at Gardner's advantage but it never seemed very likely that he could catch the Australian in the time remaining, even though the pressure caused Gardner to ride a little raggedly a couple of times.

In the closing stages, Shunji Yatsushiro made great progress after being down in 14th place at the beginning of the race. He finally passed Sarron on the last lap. Rob McElnea only just managed to hold on to eighth ahead of Pier Francesco Chili, while Roger Burnett scored the last point.

Sidecars

Rolf Biland repeated his Swedish Grand Prix win and this time new World Champions Steve Webster and Tony Hewitt could not chase them to the flag. A fading rear tyre gave the British crew trouble and they were passed by ex-champions Egbert Streuer and Bernard Schnieders on lap 16 of the 18.

'I did not expect the race pace to be so hot,' admitted Webster, 'so I put on a soft rear tyre and by half-way through the race it had gone.' Webster had chased Biland hard for the first six laps but, with the Swiss ace a second faster than anyone else in practice, the Englishman was always up against it.

Alain Michel and Jean-Marc Fresc finished fourth after a disastrous first corner. 'We made a good start', recalled Michel. 'Then, when we got to the first corner, I saw that Brindley, who was in front of us, had thrown his passenger out at the start. He could not go round the corner properly and I was stuck behind while everyone else went round the outside.'

That left Michel to work his way back up from seventh on lap 2. His fourth place means he has the same points as Biland in the championship, but because of Biland's greater number of wins the Swiss driver is third behind Streuer. Michel must wear number three next year: 'I do not care about three or four I just want that number one.'

Grand Prix ČSSR, 23 August/statistics
Autodromo Brno, 3.35-mile/5.394-km circuit

500 cc

24 laps, 80.4 miles / 129.45 km

Place	Rider	Nat.	Machine	Laps	Time & speed	Practice time	Grid
1	Wayne Gardner	AUS	Honda	24	51m 52.17s 92.99 mph/149.748 km/h	2m 07.58s	1
2	Eddie Lawson	USA	Yamaha	24	51m 54.04s	2m 08.36s	3
3	Tadahiko Taira	J	Yamaha	24	52m 09.22s	2m 07.86s	2
4	Randy Mamola	USA	Yamaha	24	52m 11.23s	2m 09.67s	9
5	Niall Mackenzie	GB	Honda	24	52m 22.49s	2m 09.24s	7
6	Shunji Yatsushiro	J	Honda	24	52m 33.06s	2m 09.84s	11
7	Christian Sarron	F	Yamaha	24	52m 33.33s	2m 08.76s	5
8	Rob McElnea	GB	Yamaha	24	52m 36.44s	2m 09.09s	6
9	Pier Francesco Chili	I	Honda	24	52m 36.69s	2m 10.66s	13
10	Roger Burnett	GB	Honda	24	52m 45.10s	2m 11.32s	14
11	Freddie Spencer	USA	Honda	24	52m 57.80s	2m 08.51s	4
12	Didier de Radiguès	B	Cagiva	24	52m 59.62s	2m 09.99s	12
13	Richard Scott	NZ	Yamaha	24	53m 14.75s	2m 09.76s	10
14	Ron Haslam	GB	Elf	24	53m 52.10s	2m 11.68s	15
15	Massimo Broccoli	I	Honda	24	53m 53.78s	2m 14.08s	22
16	Fabio Barchitta	RSM	Honda	24	53m 54.73s	2m 14.11s	23
17	Simon Buckmaster	GB	Honda	23	52m 15.38s	2m 14.69s	26
18	Gerold Fischer	D	Honda	23	53m 49.16s	2m 16.85s	29
19	Rudolf Zeller	A	Honda	23	53m 51.68s	2m 18.70s	31
20	Sepp Doppler	A	Honda	23	53m 54.17s	2m 21.57s	35
21	Claus Wulff	DK	Honda	22	52m 00.71s	2m 21.04s	33
22	Vincenzo Cascino	I	Suzuki	22	52m 22.71s	2m 17.89s	30
23	Pavol Dekánek	CS	Honda	22	52m 36.18s	2m 19.78s	32
24	Larry Moreno Vacondio	YV	Suzuki	22	53m 48.46s	2m 21.38s	34
25	Dietmar Marehardt	D	Suzuki	21	54m 00.32s	2m 21.77s	36
	Marco Gentile	CH	Fior	21	DNF	2m 12.64s	17
	Alessandro Valesi	I	Honda	12	DNF	2m 14.01s	21
	Ray Swann	GB	Honda	10	DNF	2m 14.28s	24
	Kenny Irons	GB	Suzuki	9	DNF	2m 12.14s	16
	Bruno Kneubühler	CH	Honda	6	DNF	2m 13.61s	19
	Karl Truchsess	A	Honda	6	DNF	2m 13.15s	18
	Hervé Guilleux	F	Fior	4	DNF	2m 15.63s	28
	Fabio Biliotti	I	Honda	3	DNF	2m 14.33s	25
	Raymond Roche	F	Cagiva	2	DNF	2m 09.51s	8
	Wolfgang von Muralt	CH	Suzuki	1	DNF	2m 13.88s	20
	Silvo Habat	YU	Honda	1	DNF	2m 14.77s	27
	Imrich Majoroš	CS	Suzuki		DNQ	2m 22.37s	
	Harry Heutmekers	D	Suzuki		DNQ	2m 23.52s	
	Marien Troliga	CS	Suzuki		DNQ	2m 24.14s	
	P. Hlavatka	CS	Honda		DNQ	2m 24.98s	
	Gerhard Vogt	D	Suzuki		DNQ	2m 35.78s	

Fastest lap: Gardner, 2m 08.20s, 94.06 mph/151.470 km/h (record).
Previous record: not available.

World Championship: 1 Gardner, 135; **2** Mamola, 109; **3** Lawson, 103; **4** Haslam, 69; **5** Mackenzie, 45; **6** Taira, 41; **7** Chili and McElnea, 39; **9** Sarron, 37; **10** Burnett, 20; **11** Yatsushiro, 18; **12** de Radiguès, 13; **13** Irons, 12; **14** Schwantz, 11; **15** Ito, 10; **16** Roche, 9; **17** Kawasaki and Spencer, 4; **19** Scott, 3; **20** Katayama and Reiner, 2; **22** Magee, 1.

125 cc

18 laps, 60.3 miles/97.09 km

Place	Rider	Nat.	Machine	Laps	Time & speed	Practice time	Grid
1	Fausto Gresini	I	Garelli	18	41m 57.22s 86.22 mph/138.856 km/h	2m 16.59s	1
2	Bruno Casanova	I	Garelli	18	42m 09.28s	2m 18.12s	2
3	Andrés Marín Sánchez	E	Ducados	18	42m 43.04s	2m 19.98s	5
4	Ezio Gianola	I	Honda	18	42m 52.59s	2m 21.71s	10
5	Lucio Pietroniro	B	MBA	18	42m 52.93s	2m 20.80s	8
6	Ivan Troisi	YV	MBA	18	42m 53.20s	2m 21.71s	11
7	Claudio Macciotta	I	MBA	18	43m 05.36s	2m 23.03s	16
8	Esa Kytölä	SF	MBA	18	43m 06.77s	2m 21.66s	9
9	Bady Hassaine	DZ	MBA	18	43m 17.78s	2m 24.49s	26
10	Thierry Feuz	CH	MBA	18	43m 25.96s	2m 23.88s	22
11	Håkan Olsson	S	Starol	18	43m 39.22s	2m 23.30s	18
12	Norbert Peschke	D	Seel	18	43m 41.31s	2m 24.06s	24
13	Jean-Claude Selini	F	MBA	18	43m 41.64s	2m 23.84s	21
14	Marco Cipriani	I	MBA	18	43m 57.20s	2m 24.34s	25
15	Jacques Hutteau	F	MBA	18	43m 57.45s	2m 25.66s	33
16	Robin Milton	GB	MBA	18	44m 01.34s	2m 24.04s	23
17	Robin Appleyard	GB	Ceba	18	44m 06.06s	2m 25.38s	31
18	Karl Dauer	A	MBA	18	44m 06.27s	2m 26.24s	36
19	Alfred Gangelberger	A	MBA	17	41m 57.72s	2m 24.92s	28
20	Taru Rinne	SF	MBA	17	42m 09.54s	2m 26.36s	37
21	Thomas Møller-Pedersen	DK	MBA	17	43m 25.16s	2m 25.99s	35
	Flemming Kistrup	DK	MBA	15	DNF	2m 25.58s	32
	Gastone Grassetti	I	MBA	12	DNF	2m 21.83s	19
	August Auinger	A	MBA	11	DNF	2m 23.04s	17
	Allan Scott	USA	EMC	10	DNF	2m 23.80s	20
	Christian le Badezet	F	MBA	9	DNF	2m 24.94s	29
	Pier Paolo Bianchi	I	MBA	5	DNF	2m 19.01s	3
	Adolf Stadler	D	MBA	5	DNF	2m 25.30s	30
	Hubert Abold	D	Honda	3	DNF	2m 25.85s	34
	Peter Sommer	CH	MBA	1	DNF	2m 24.71s	27
	Mike Leitner	A	MBA	0	DNF	2m 22.31s	13
	Olivier Liegeois	B	Assmex	0	DNF	2m 22.41s	14
	Willy Pérez	RA	Zanella	0	DNF	2m 22.69s	15
	Johnny Wickström	SF	Tunturi	0	DNF	2m 20.57s	7
	Domenico Brigaglia	I	AGV	0	DNF	2m 19.11s	4
	Corrado Catalano	I	MBA		DNS	2m 20.15s	6
	Paul Bordes	F	MBA		DNQ	2m 26.90s	
	Fernando Gonzales	E	Cobas		DNQ	2m 27.81s	
	Alexander Eschig	A	MBA		DNQ	2m 27.88s	
	Wilco Zeelenberg	NL	Casal		DNQ	2m 29.78s	
	W. Glawaty	D	MBA		DNQ	2m 32.85s	
	Jiří Safránek	CS	MBA		DNQ	2m 34.40s	
	Bogdan Nikolov	BG	MBA		DNQ	2m 29.19s	
	Ladislav Polák	CS	MBA		DNQ	2m 30.58s	

Fastest lap: Casanova, 2m 18.18s, 87.26 mph/140.53 km/h (record).
Previous record: not available.

World Championship: 1 Gresini, 135; **2** Casanova, 88; **3** Brigaglia, 46; **4** Bianchi, 43; **5** Auinger, 42; **6** Casoli and Sánchez, 36; **8** Gianola, 31; **9** Wickström, 21; **10** Leitner, 18; **11** Pietroniro, 17; **12** Feuz and Selini, 12; **14** Hautaniemi, 10; **15** Grassetti, 9; **16** Catalano, Macciotta, Stadler and Troisi, 6; **20** Kytölä and Liegeois, 4; **22** Hassaine and Milton, 2; **24** Kistrup and Pérez, 1.

250 cc

21 laps, 70.35 miles/113.27 km

Place	Rider	Nat.	Machine	Laps	Time & speed	Practice time	Grid
1	Anton Mang	D	Honda	21	47m 09.56s 89.49 mph/ 144.117 km/h	2m 13.02s	5
2	Dominique Sarron	F	Honda	21	47m 12.99s	2m 11.62s	1
3	Carlos Cardus	E	Honda	21	47m 13.26s	2m 13.74s	11
4	Alfonso Pons	E	Honda	21	47m 13.54s	2m 12.83s	4
5	Luca Cadalora	I	Yamaha	21	47m 13.89s	2m 13.25s	8
6	Urs Lüzi	CH	Honda	21	47m 19.24s	2m 13.88s	12
7	Patrick Igoa	F	Yamaha	21	47m 27.32s	2m 13.17s	7
8	Ivan Palazzese	YV	Yamaha	21	47m 32.55s	2m 13.92s	14
9	Juan Garriga	E	Yamaha	21	47m 47.63s	2m 14.11s	16
10	Reinhold Roth	D	Honda	21	47m 50.20s	2m 13.17s	6
11	Donnie McLeod	GB	EMC	21	47m 53.51s	2m 14.00s	15
12	Maurizio Vitali	I	Garelli	21	48m 02.42s	2m 14.44s	17
13	Jean-Michel Mattioli	F	Honda	21	48m 02.81s	2m 13.92s	13
14	Stéphane Mertens	B	Sekitoba	21	48m 06.42s	2m 15.06s	19
15	Hans Lindner	A	Honda	21	48m 06.71s	2m 15.69s	23
16	Xavier Cardelus	AND	Cobas	21	48m 07.57s	2m 15.99s	28
17	Bernard Hänggeli	CH	Yamaha	21	48m 10.49s	2m 16.33s	32
18	René Delaby	LUX	Yamaha	21	48m 11.94s	2m 15.30s	20
19	Harald Eckl	D	Yamaha	21	48m 25.62s	2m 15.03s	18
20	Gary Cowan	IRL	Honda	21	48m 26.09s	2m 15.92s	26
21	Guy Bertin	F	Honda	21	48m 39.28s	2m 16.31s	31
22	Massimo Matteoni	I	Honda	21	48m 39.58s	2m 15.82s	24
23	Bruno Bonhuil	F	Honda	21	48m 43.46s	2m 16.47s	33
24	Stefan Klabacher	A	Rotax	21	49m 11.28s	2m 16.98s	35
25	Engelbert Neumair	A	Yamaha	21	49m 16.54s	2m 16.10s	29
26	Kevin Mitchell	GB	Honda	19	48m 50.29s	2m 17.10s	36
	Thomas Bacher	A	Yamaha	16	DNF	2m 15.97s	27
	Jean-Philippe Ruggia	F	Yamaha	12	DNF	2m 15.47s	21
	Josef Hutter	A	Honda	10	DNF	2m 16.20s	30
	Jean-François Baldé	F	Defi	10	DNF	2m 15.52s	22
	Manfred Herweh	D	Honda	8	DNF	2m 13.30s	9
	Loris Reggiani	I	Aprilia	8	DNF	2m 12.82s	3
	Christian Boudinot	F	Fior	8	DNF	2m 16.79s	34
	Andreas Preining	A	Yamaha	4	DNF	2m 17.18s	37
	Alain Bronec	F	Honda	3	DNF	2m 15.83s	25
	Martin Wimmer	D	Yamaha	1	DNF	2m 12.29s	2
	Carlos Lavado	YV	Yamaha		DNS	2m 13.72s	10
	Nedy Crotta	CH	Armstrong		DNQ	2m 17.39s	
	Alberto Rota	I	Honda		DNQ	2m 17.81s	
	Gilberto Gambelli	I	Yamaha		DNQ	2m 18.10s	
	Siegfried Minich	A	Honda		DNQ	2m 18.23s	
	Takayoshi Yamamoto	J	Yamaha		DNQ	2m 18.34s	
	Jean Foray	F	Honda		DNQ	2m 18.37s	
	Hervé Duffard	F	Honda		DNQ	2m 18.43s	
	Jean-Louis Guignabodet	F	Rotax		DNQ	2m 18.74s	
	Rüdi Gächter	CH	Yamaha		DNQ	2m 19.25s	
	Jan Bartůněk	CS	Yamaha		DNQ	2m 21.40s	
	Heinz Simantke	D	Rotax		DNQ	2m 23.38s	
	Dario Marchetti	I	Yamaha		DNQ	2m 24.28s	
	Imrich Majoroš	CS	Yamaha		DNQ	2m 32.59s	
	Marian Srna	CS	Yamaha		DNQ	2m 33.11s	
	G. Chrounopoulos	GR	Yamaha		DNQ	2m 41.75s	

Fastest lap: Cardus, 2m 12.25s, 91.18 mph/146.831 km/h (record).
Previous record: not available.

World Championship: 1 Mang 112; **2** Roth, 89; **3** Pons, 65; **4** Sarron, 59; **5** Cardus, 54; **6** Cornu and Reggiani, 50; **8** Wimmer, 45; **9** Lavado, 38; **10** Cadalora, 36; **11** Igoa, 30; **12** Garriga, 25; **13** Kobayashi, 15; **14** Palazzese, 9; **15** Shimuzu, 8; **16** Herweh and Ruggia, 7; **18** Vitali, 6; **19** Lindner and Lüzi, 5; **21** McLeod, 4; **22** Mertens and Taguchi, 2; **24** Baldé, Bertin and Yamamoto, 1.

80 cc

14 laps, 46.9 miles/75.52 km

Place	Rider	Nat.	Machine	Laps	Time & speed	Practice time	Grid
1	Stefan Dörflinger	CH	Krauser	14	34m 14.23s 82.18 mph/ 132.34 km/h	2m 24.28s	3
2	Jorge Martinez	E	Derbi	14	34m 23.59s	2m 24.28s	2
3	Gerhard Waibel	D	Krauser	14	34m 38.83s	2m 26.45s	7
4	Manuel Herreros	E	Derbi	14	34m 39.07s	2m 28.09s	8
5	Jörg Seel	D	Seel	14	34m 40.91s	2m 26.41s	5
6	Luis M. Reyes	E	Autisa	14	35m 10.37s	2m 26.31s	4
7	Josef Fischer	A	Krauser	14	35m 10.68s	2m 28.61s	9
8	Juan Ramon Bolart	E	Krauser	14	35m 11.20s	2m 30.32s	18
9	Theo Timmer	NL	Casal	14	35m 12.47s	2m 29.25s	13
10	Günther Schirnhofer	D	Krauser	14	35m 14.63s	2m 30.36s	19
11	Ian McConnachie	GB	Krauser	14	35m 23.02s	2m 23.86s	1
12	Hans Spaan	NL	Casal	14	35m 40.72s	2m 28.88s	11
13	Serge Julin	B	Casal	14	35m 45.20s	2m 31.69s	23
14	Chris Baert	B	Seel	14	35m 48.13s	2m 31.89s	25
15	Michael Gschwander	D	Seel	14	35m 50.20s	2m 31.57s	22
16	Heinz Paschen	D	Casal	14	36m 03.68s	2m 35.19s	34
17	Jos van Dongen	NL	Krauser	14	36m 04.02s	2m 33.57s	29
18	Mario Stocco	I	Faccioli	14	36m 04.07s	2m 35.35s	35
19	Wilco Zeelenberg	NL	Casal	14	36m 11.64s	2m 31.82s	24
20	Thomas Engl	D	GPE	14	36m 42.91s	2m 33.59s	30
21	Stefan Brägger	CH	Casal	14	36m 48.29s	2m 35.69s	37
22	Paul Bordes	F	RB	13	34m 48.43s	2m 35.04s	33
	Kees Besseling	NL	Derbi	11	DNF	2m 30.31s	17
	Alexandre Barros	BR	Casal	9	DNF	2m 26.44s	6
	Reiner Koster	CH	Kroko	9	DNF	2m 32.92s	26
	Francisco Torrontegui	E	Casal	9	DNF	2m 33.35s	28
	Rainer Kunz	D	Kroko	8	DNF	2m 32.97s	27
	Felix Rodriguez	E	Cobas	8	DNF	2m 34.68s	32
	Ralf Waldmann	D	Seel	6	DNF	2m 31.31s	21
	Károly Juhász	H	Krauser	6	DNF	2m 30.02s	16
	Raimo Lipponen	SF	Krauser	5	DNF	2m 35.51s	36
	Peter Öttl	D	Krauser	4	DNF	2m 30.75s	20
	René Dünki	CH	Ziegler	4	DNF	2m 29.60s	14
	Richard Bay	D	Ziegler	2	DNF	2m 33.79s	31
	Paolo Priori	I	Krauser	1	DNF	2m 30.00s	15
	Hubert Abold	D	Krauser	0	DNF	2m 29.10s	12
	Bogdan Nikolov	BG	Krauser		DNS	2m 28.70s	10
	Otto Krmíček	CS	Casal		DNQ	2m 41.58s	
	Stuart Edwards	GB	Casal		DNQ	2m 43.88s	
	Eduard Klimek	CS	RB		DNQ	2m 44.10s	
	Nicola Casadei	I	Krauser		DNQ	2m 44.48s	
	Zbyněk Havrda	CS	Casal		DNQ	2m 46.59s	
	Kvetoslav Samák	CS	Casal		DNQ	2m 50.55s	

Fastest lap: Dorflinger, 2m 24.02s, 83.73 mph/134.831 km/h.
Lap record: not available.

World Championship: 1 Martinez, 114; **2** Waibel, 64; **3** Herreros, 59; **4** Dörflinger, 57; **5** McConnachie, 43; **6** Reyes, 31; **7** Seel, 27; **8** Abold, 25; **9** Fischer, 19; **10** Miralles, 16; **11** Criville and Schirnhofer, 12; **13** Juhász, 10; **14** Spaan, 8; **15** Bolart and Priori, 6; **17** Barros and Paschen, 4; **19** Bay, 3; **20** Gschwander, Öttl and Timmer, 2; **23** Bernard and Waldmann, 1.

Sidecars

18 laps, 60.3 miles/97.09 km

Place	Driver & passenger	Nat.	Machine	Laps	Time & speed	Practice time	Grid
1	Rolf Biland/ Kurt Waltisperg	CH CH	LCR- Krauser	18	39m 49.39s	2m 10.05s	1
2	Egbert Streuer/ Bernard Schnieders	NL NL	LCR- Yamaha	18	40m 06.85s	2m 11.15s	2
3	Steve Webster/ Tony Hewitt	GB GB	LCR- Yamaha	18	40m 11.43s	2m 11.18s	3
4	Alain Michel/ Jean-Marc Fresc	F F	LCR- Krauser	18	40m 22.79s	2m 11.89s	4
5	Markus Egloff/ Urs Egloff	CH CH	LCR	18	40m 47.49s	2m 12.64s	5
6	Masato Kumano/ Markus Fahrni	J CH	Toshiba	18	40m 47.79s	2m 13.37s	7
7	Alfred Zurbrügg/ Simon Birchall	CH GB	LCR- Yamaha	18	40m 51.75s	2m 13.73s	8
8	Derek Jones/ Brian Ayres	GB GB	Seel	18	40m 58.01s	2m 14.66s	11
9	Steve Abbott/ Shaun Smith	GB GB	Windle- Yamaha	18	40m 58.68s	2m 15.11s	12
10	Pascal Larratte/ Jacques Corbier	F F	LCR- Yamaha	18	41m 05.77s	2m 14.27s	9
11	René Progin/ Yves Hunziker	CH CH	Seymaz	18	41m 17.53s	2m 15.89s	15
12	Theo van Kempen/ Gerardus de Haas	NL NL	LCR- Yamaha	18	41m 17.76s	2m 15.29s	13
13	Bernd Scherer/ Wolfgang Gess	D D	BSR- Yamaha	18	41m 32.64s	2m 15.33s	14
14	Fritz Stölzle/ Hubert Stölzle	D D	LCR- Yamaha	18	41m 37.04s	2m 17.16s	19
15	Yoshisada Kumagaya/ J. Wilson	J GB	Windle- Yamaha	18	41m 38.54s	2m 17.45s	20
16	Jean-Louis Millet/ Claude Debroux	F F	Seymaz	18	41m 54.08s	2m 18.31s	23
17	Graham Gleeson/ Peter Brown	NZ NZ	LCR- Cagiva	18	42m 00.64s	2m 16.15s	16
18	Erwin Weber/ Eckart Rösinger	D D	LCR- Sams	18	42m 10.37s	2m 16.97s	18
19	Dennis Bingham/ Julia Bingham	GB GB	LCR- Yamaha	17	39m 58.01s	2m 19.74s	25
20	Gary Thomas/ A. Murray	GB GB	Yamaha	17	40m 27.69s	2m 19.41s	24
21	Herbert Prügl/ Christian Parzer	A A	Homa- LCR	17	41m 08.97s	2m 20.59s	27
22	Judd Drew/ Christopher Plant	GB GB	BLR- Yamaha	17	41m 36.28s	2m 22.36s	29
23	Hans Hügli/ Adolf Hänni	CH CH	Sigma	15	40m 56.37s	2m 20.04s	26
	Ivan Nigrowski/ Frédéric Meunier	F F	Seymaz	17	DNF	2m 17.50s	21
	Wolfgang Stropek/ Hans-Peter Demling	A A	LCR- Krauser	12	DNF	2m 14.31s	10
	Rolf Steinhausen/ Bruno Hiller	D D	Eigenbau	7	DNF	2m 12.82s	6
	Egon Schons/ Thomas Schröder	D D	Yamaha	7	DNF	2m 23.66s	30
	Dave Hallam/ Steve Parker	GB GB	Windle- Yamaha	2	DNF	2m 22.18s	29
	Billy Gällros/ Håkan Olsson	S S	LCR- Yamaha	2	DNF	2m 18.24s	22
	Barry Brindley/ Grahame Rose	GB GB	Yamaha	0	DNF	2m 16.38s	17

Fastest lap: Webster, 2m 11.44s, 91.74 mph/147.736 km/h.
Lap record: not available.

Final Sidecar World Championship points: see pages 198–200.

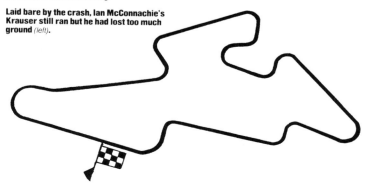

Above: **Kurt Waltisperg is not looking where he is going and concentrates on balance while Rolf Biland does the driving.**

Laid bare by the crash, Ian McConnachie's Krauser still ran but he had lost too much ground *(left)*.

Gran Premio di
SAN MARINO

It was a relief to get across the border and out of Czechoslovakia. Few waited for Monday – the desire to be in a free country sent most to the three-hour queues to get through the border checks on Sunday night.

The weather that had held so well fell apart as the teams drove through Austria and into northern Italy. At one point the autostrada was closed by a landslip and other roads not used by the continental travellers were washed away completely. Yet, by the time the Adriatic coast loomed into view, the sun was out and the sky blue.

Lifting spirits rose further on sight of the Misano paddock. For so long a cramped and filthy hole, it had been completely resurfaced and fitted with clean, new toilets and showers, as well as having been provided with a generous distribution of power and water points. Could this be something to do with seventeen 1987 Grands Prix vying for sixteen places on the 1988 calendar and Misano's position as reserve? If they had not been so unreasonable for so long, the Misano organisers would probably not have needed to fight to get off the reserve bench.

Representatives of the South American Grands Prix in Brazil and Argentina were in Misano to sort out details and questions pertaining to the shipping of teams and so on – which was just as well because there had been few confirmations of flights and freighting, with rumours circulating that the events might not take place.

That might just have been wishful thinking on behalf of the Rothmans Honda teams of Wayne Gardner and Toni Mang, who would have just about wrapped up the championships there and then had the final two races been cancelled.

Nevertheless, the races *were* going ahead, so while each was in the position of having a very healthy lead each knew that anything could still happen. Mang had the added advantage that his nearest rival, Reinhold Roth, had been forced to undergo an operation on his shoulder – the consequence of re-breaking the Hockenheim collarbone when he fell on the last lap in Czechoslovakia.

Carlos Lavado did similar damage to his Suzuka shoulder but, as he was not even thinking about World Championships, saw no reason to rush back into action in Italy. He turned up at the circuit, none the less, showing off his new baby girl and promising to be back in action at Jarama.

Mr Oguma, director of HRC, made one of his Grand Prix visits and in passing said he realised that if Lavado had been 'in good condition' all season they would not have had such an easy time of it in the 250 class. 'Winning the 250 Championship is very important for us because we sell a lot of 250 machines and sales are very much related to racing success. We do not sell a replica of the 500, but that class is important for prestige.' He also stated that while Honda were conscious of criticism that they were putting too many works bikes into the 250 class, Honda would continue to field enough machines to counter the threat from Yamaha.

He also announced that the leasing system would continue; while all the factory 250s were leased in '87, Ron Haslam's 500 was a leasing deal with the remainder being run by HRC with outside sponsorship. The same riders were to be retained in '88 but the only one that already had a contract was Freddie Spencer who was entering the third term of a three-year deal.

It is interesting to reflect that Spencer's three-year contract was signed after he had won the 250 and 500 class double in '85, when Honda must have congratulated themselves on securing his services for three straight seasons. One can imagine how their feelings must have altered as Spencer was unable to complete a single race through '86 and suffered continuing problems well into '87. Throughout this time, they had still to pay him at the rate agreed when he was double World Champion.

Elf had agreed to continue through 1988, using Haslam to ride their experimental machine. That meant they would be availing themselves of a similar leasing contract, although at an increased price for two NSR500s and a spare engine of US$500,000 and $300,000 for a 250. That sum was supposed to include a season's spares but, as the 250 teams soon found out, another $50,000 had to be allowed for extra engine spares and the minimum of crash repairs.

The Elf deal was slightly different as they only used a single standard NSR, and that stayed firmly under wraps as practice started in Italy because it was the firm intention to use the Elf 4, as they had in Czechoslovakia.

There the single front disc had been replaced with twin steel units using twin Lockheed calipers, one pointing forward and one aft of the vertical steering arm. Ray Bailey explained that they had experienced two problems with the single carbon disc. Firstly, it had been made from the same material as the Formula 1 car disc and that had an operating temperature starting at 400°C. It takes a long time to get up to that temperature on a bike and the lag and inconsistency make it unusable. A disc was then produced in a different material that was consistent at a lower temperature but that disc lacked power. The response was to replace the original 304 mm diameter disc with one as large as the wheel would take – about 330 mm.

Getting this disc made was causing a delay and meanwhile the twin-disc arrangement was being used with its attendant weight penalty. Haslam had little chance to do any serious testing at Misano because after four laps of official practice on Friday morning he crashed. 'I had just run in the brake pads, pistons and tyres and started to go a bit faster when the back end came round on me. It fair spat me off, higher than the motorhome. My leg came down with a slap and that broke my ankle.'

Not only was Haslam injured but the Elf 4 was badly damaged. While that was worked on for the following day the NSR was unwrapped so that he could try and ride that afternoon. He succeeded but said it was very painful; he could not shift his weight from one side to the other and just sticking his knee out into the airstream

twisted the ankle enough to make it unbearable.

Obviously Haslam was going to be well out of contention no matter what he rode, but as practice unfolded it became clear that it was not a good track for the NSR500 Hondas. Gardner had often been below par during the first day of practice but this time he never got on top of it and ended up nearly two-tenths slower than he had in 1986 on the older NSR that had been so much slower at most circuits.

Spencer was a fraction slower than Gardner in sixth place and complaining that the characteristics of the engine were wrong for him. 'The power band is too wide so when the rear tyre breaks away it slides too far.' Spencer's style required a narrow band so that when he spun the rear wheel and turned the bike through the corner by sliding the back end the engine would

there were two problems. One was braking into the corners, where the Honda is not as stable as the old Suzuki, and the other is accelerating, where the Honda has so much power it is so aggressive and hard to ride.'

Mackenzie also raised the gearing and found one second for Saturday but Honda must have wondered what they had to do because only a year before Gardner had been complaining that the power band was too narrow because the bike had been designed for Spencer. Could they really be expected to provide a different engine for each rider?

Mackenzie was only just in front of Roger Burnett on Gardner's old machine while Shunji Yatsushiro was twelfth on the '87 model. They had been pushed down by Didier de Radiguès on the Cagiva and some less charitable souls suggested that the Italian stopwatches might have been tuned to put the home-grown machine in the top ten. The Cagiva squad were struggling somewhat, and Raymond Roche lay thirteenth on the second machine ahead of Kenny Irons who was suffering further woes.

Suzuki were actually in a worse state than they had been a year before. In 1986 they had a man on the front row and the prospect of a more competitive machine for the coming season. A year on, that new bike had not proved itself to be a possible winner so a star rider would be hard to find for it; just as they had lost Mackenzie to Honda, this time the rumours were equally strong that they would lose Kevin Schwantz to the Marlboro Yamaha team.

The Marlboro team's strength would almost certainly be cut from five to four, and, with the rumours about Schwantz and Agostini's stated intention to find a second rider who could win Grands Prix, Rob McElnea's position was looking distinctly shaky.

McElnea qualified fourth behind team-mate Tadahiko Taira while Eddie Lawson cut over half a second off his time in the final session to jump onto pole. He did not realise he had managed it after the usual carburation troubles in practice, and as he did a plug chop on the back straight and coasted to a halt he thought practice had ended too early. 'I was just getting to feel good out there and they hung out the chequered flag. We had so much trouble with the carburation and it took so long to get it sorted that we ran out of time.'

That final lap was still sufficient to boost him above Mamola who had led throughout practice using a new Dunlop tyre that had first been tried in Yugoslavia. At Brno there had been a few problems with chattering but a revised sidewall design for Misano proved to be the answer. Mamola was enjoying a superb drive on the Lucky Strike Yamaha whereas the Hondas and even the Michelin-shod Yamahas were wheelspinning and moving sideways. 'The front tyre has been great all along,' enthused Mamola, 'at last we have a rear that is just as good.'

It was Yamaha's day in the 250 class as well because in the final session Luca Cadalora just kept himself ahead of Marlboro Yamaha team-mate Martin Wimmer. In company with Loris

run out of steam before the bike came so far round that he lost control. With the engine running out of revs the rear tyre would grip again gradually without that yank that kicks the rider over the bars.

Almost inevitably, any attempt to control the slide on the throttle eventually produces that sudden hook-up of the rear tyre that kicks the rider out of the saddle. Gardner had been fighting them all season but has always ridden like that and got away with it. Spencer could do it but some nasty moments in practice at Misano reminded him how chancy it was and he realised something had to be changed.

It was not practical to make the power band narrower overnight without losing power so he decided to raise the gearing. This was hardly the ideal solution because it made the bike impossible

to ride in the classic Spencer style but it did enable him to drive out of the slower corners in safety as the rear tyre was not lighting up hard at all.

Mackenzie needed the same modification after he found himself slower than he had been on the Suzuki in '86 when he had qualified third with a time of 1m 20.13s. A year later he was tenth-quickest with a time of 1m 20.67s. 'I was very disappointed,' said Mackenzie. 'I expected to do well in Misano because I had gone well on the Suzuki and with a better bike and more horsepower I thought I would be well up. When practice began I wondered what was wrong but when I realised that Wayne and Freddie also had problems that made things a little easier. After the first day, though, I was a second and a half slower than I was a year ago and I realised

Inset: **Erv Kanemoto and Niall Mackenzie try to work out how the NSR can be made to work like the old Suzuki.**

Getting to the front of the pack, Luca Cadalora directs his attention to passing Sito Pons.

Reggiani on the Aprilia they were the only ones to get under 1m 22s.

But it was not a trouble-free practice for the Marlboro Yamaha team because to get the little V-twins to work they were run very close to the mark on carburation. That resulted in detonation and holed pistons, including one for Martin Wimmer in the Sunday morning warm-up, which meant he had to start the race with the spare engine and something of an estimation about the carburation. As one might expect, Carruthers' calculations were not far out but the concern affected Wimmer.

'This is very different to the situation in Jerez. There I knew I would win, everything was worked out. Now I have had problems with the bike this morning and I do not even know if it will finish the race and that is not good for the head.'

80 cc

On the second of the works Derbis, Manuel Herreros rode a superbly judged race and fought off the three Krausers to win as his team leader and World Champion Aspar Martínez retired at the pits on lap 9.

Herreros took the lead from fast-starting Giuseppe Ascareggi a third of the way round the first lap, but Martínez was right on his tail. Just as the two Derbis looked as though they could command the race Martínez ran wide . . . the engine had started to play up and he dropped back to ninth.

That left Herreros still leading but with the Krausers of Ian McConnachie, Gerhard Waibel and Stefan Dörflinger right behind him. Luis Reyes joined them by the fifth lap and the five machines swapped places at every turn, with McConnachie making a concerted effort to lead.

Martínez was on his way back, though, and had caught the leading group on lap 7. He cut through quickly and was challenging for second behind McConnachie when the Derbi failed again and he was forced to retire at the pits.

With his leader gone it was important that Herreros should win to make sure of Derbi's Manufacturers' World Title, so he forced his way to the front again. Reyes retired when the Autisa boiled over and Herreros was forced to swap places with Dörflinger as they began to leave McConnachie and Waibel behind.

Over the last five of the twenty-two laps, Herreros managed to get away from Dörflinger. On the final lap, McConnachie dived inside Waibel at the second-to-last corner and, despite having to take to the grass as the pair clashed fairings leaving the final bend, crossed the line in front by half a wheel.

125 cc

World Champion Fausto Gresini did not even have Garelli team-mate Bruno Casanova to contend with as he maintained his 100 per cent record, for when both fell independently in the final practice session Casanova came off worse with torn ligaments in his ankle and could not ride. Despite great pain from his injured knee,

Four-cylinder speed overcomes Chili's triple as Gardner sweeps past down the back straight on the first lap.

August Auinger on the Bartol MBA was second after a monumental slide on the second-to-last lap dropped AGV rider Paolo Casoli from a certain second to third.

Pier Paolo Bianchi on the MBA led from the start but there was nothing in it at the end of the first lap as Casoli and Gresini climbed all over him. Andrés Marín Sánchez on the Ducados and Auinger were fourth and fifth, with Lucio Pietroniro on his MBA and Ezio Gianola on the single-cylinder Honda just behind.

Casoli led briefly but Gresini soon cleared off and Casoli established his second place while Bianchi started to come under pressure from Auinger. That went on until lap 20 when Bianchi retired. Domenico Brigaglia had climbed to fifth on the second AGV but he, too, stopped on lap 18.

For the remainder of the race the excitement lay with the struggle for fourth between Sánchez, Pietroniro and Gianola. That reached its climax on the last corner, where all three collided. Gianola came through unscathed while Pietroniro survived a trip on the grass to finish sixth. Sánchez crashed but picked the bike up and pushed it across the line a minute later, yet still took seventh place because everyone else had been lapped.

250 cc

Carruthers had raised the needle jets on the V-twins to get rid of the detonation that had holed a piston on Martin Wimmer's Marlboro Yamaha during the morning warm-up. He warned Cadalora that a similar alteration would mean he would have to rev the engine hard before the start to keep it clean.

The young Italian only got it half right. He revved the engine as he arrived back on the line from the warm-up but then let the engine speed fall as he waited for the start. That was enough to load up the crankcases with too much fuel so when the lights changed to green he was left to struggle away from pole position as the rest of the field screamed past and into the first corner. Depending on who you speak to, he was either dead last or second from it into that first corner.

Reinhold Roth managed to forget about his injured shoulder long enough to lead on the first lap but with fifteen riders all within one second of Cadalora's practice time it was obviously going to be a hard-fought race. Reggiani was second on lap 1 but then took the lead as Roth kept himself ahead of Sarron, Wimmer, Pons, Mang and Cardus.

Cadalora was already on the attack, but, relative to the leaders, his progress hardly seemed important. Nevertheless, by lap 5 of the 30 he was 14th and those in front were still virtually in a single group.

The one man who had started to make some distance over the others was Reggiani, who inched ahead while Roth still held second. If there was one man who might be able to stem Reggiani's advance it was surely Mang, and by the fifth lap he was third and challenging Roth.

Mang got to the front of the group briefly but could not get clear to chase after Reggiani. He

was soon passed by Roth once more as Cadalora closed on what had become a ten-man chain fighting for second, with Garriga and Palazzese apparently having the most trouble hanging on to the tail of it.

By half-way through the race Reggiani had an eight-second lead, as Mang took second once more from Roth, Pons, Wimmer and Sarron. Cadalora was right in the middle of the group by this time, ahead of Mertens, Herweh, Garriga and Palazzese.

'I never thought it was possible to pass so many people in one race,' said Cadalora later. 'When I caught up to the tail of the group I saw that Loris was not in it and I realised he must be leading by a long way. I think that if I had got a good start I could have raced with him but ifs and buts do not count in racing.'

By lap 20 Cadalora was challenging Mang for second and using every inch of road to do it. A lap later he was in front of the championship leader and starting to pull away, but Reggiani was by then ten seconds in front and time would run out before the Aprilia could possibly be caught.

With five laps left, Wimmer made an attempt to secure third but, having got past Mang and Sarron, he made a mistake on the brakes and ran wide. 'The Hondas were too good on acceleration and that mistake ruined my chance to get away,' said Wimmer later.

That left the battle for third to be fought between Pons, Sarron and Mang, and Sarron thought he had his tactics worked out. 'I was going to pass Pons on the last lap, but then Mang tried to pass me and Pons got away a little and I could not catch him before the flag.' Mang missed a gear leaving the final corner and slipped behind Wimmer.

500 cc

The 500 was never going to offer quite the excitement of the 250 race but it was none the less a fascinating struggle of Yamaha against Honda, Dunlop against Michelin and Lawson against Mamola while Gardner fought Taira.

Lawson led from lap 1 and when McElnea and Taira slotted in behind it looked like a Marlboro freight train in front, but Chili had also made a great start representing HB, with Lucky Strike and Rothmans in the form of Mamola and Gardner right behind.

The three-cylinder fell back on lap 2 and Chili came under the scrutiny of Spencer and de Radiguès while Mamola and Gardner moved ahead and closed on the leading trio.

Lawson was forging ahead as lap 3 saw Mamola pass Taira. McElnea was having a touch of front tyre trouble as experienced by Lawson in Sweden and Czechoslovakia. He eased off and was passed by Mamola on the fourth lap. From there, the two Californians were clear to fight their own battle while Gardner closed in on Taira and McElnea.

McElnea had suffered front wheel slides on the first two laps. Having eased the pace the problem went away, but after being passed by

Taira and Gardner the desire to fight back got the better of him. As he pressed on, the front tucked under one more time and down he went. Two years running, fourth in practice, a possible third in the race . . . then a crash.

He was not the only faller. Chili and Spencer had gone missing on lap 4 and in the same incident de Radiguès dropped to 14th. Chili hit the rear of Spencer's machine but the details are not altogether clear. Spencer passed Chili down the back straight but, according to the Italian, as soon as Spencer got in front he put the brakes on about fifty metres earlier than expected and Chili ran into the back of the NSR.

Chili puts the blame on Spencer but de Radiguès was alongside Chili and, according to Burnett who saw the incident from some way behind, it looked as though Chili collided with de Radiguès while side by side and then ran into the back of Spencer. So did the Italian try to repass Spencer only to hit the Cagiva, not realising that de Radiguès had pulled up alongside?

De Radiguès regained the circuit while Chili bundled down the tarmac at high speed, scraped his back and broke his finger. Spencer went off the track fighting for control but finally ran out of room and crashed. He was knocked out for several minutes but left hospital the next day.

That left a gap in the field and fifth place was contested by Yatsushiro, Burnett, Sarron and Mackenzie. In ninth place was de Radiguès, but he retired at the pits on lap 14 complaining that the Cagiva was running poorly. Roche had already stopped with the other bike when the clutch failed.

On lap 10 of the 35, Mamola took the lead from Lawson whilst Gardner took second from Taira. Lawson tried, unsuccessfully, to hang on to the Lucky Strike machine. 'Round the fast lefts onto the back straight he was just motoring away while my rear tyre was sliding and I was playing with the throttle trying to keep it on the track.'

Mamola inched away and Gardner similarly got the better of Taira, but with a nine-second gap to Lawson the Australian was never likely to challenge the leading Yamahas. For the rest of the race that battle for fifth produced the excitement as each rider tried to get in front, but Yatsushiro held the advantage for most of the time.

When it came to passing back-markers – and several were lapped twice – things got hairy. Vittorio Scatola on the Paton was almost punted off the circuit as Yatsushiro and Mackenzie went underneath him going into the last two left-handers on lap 29. Unfortunately, the Italian machine only completed one more lap because it had already started to lose its cooling water.

Fifth place was decided on the final lap, with Yatsushiro doing well to hang on, Burnett passing Mackenzie, leaving Sarron eighth. In ninth was Gustav Reiner, disgusted with the fact that he had been lapped on his way to two points. Tenth place was taken by Marco Gentile, scoring the first World Championship point for the Fior. He was presented with that by Richard Scott who ran off the track and fell as he chased Reiner with nine laps to go.

Gran Premio di San Marino, 30 August/statistics
Autodromo Santamonica, Misano, 2.167-mile/3.488-km circuit

500 cc

35 laps, 75.85 miles/122.08 km

Place	Rider	Nat.	Machine	Laps	Time & speed	Practice time	Grid
1	Randy Mamola	USA	Yamaha	35	46m 35.85s 98.25 mph/ 157.193 km/h	1m 19.24s	2
2	Eddie Lawson	USA	Yamaha	35	46m 39.81s	1m 18.99s	1
3	Wayne Gardner	AUS	Honda	35	47m 10.68s	1m 19.89s	5
4	Tadahiko Taira	J	Yamaha	35	47m 17.56s	1m 19.48s	3
5	Shunji Yatsushiro	J	Honda	35	47m 37.60s	1m 20.56s	12
6	Roger Burnett	GB	Honda	35	47m 38.04s	1m 20.52s	11
7	Niall Mackenzie	GB	Honda	35	47m 38.22s	1m 20.46s	10
8	Christian Sarron	F	Yamaha	35	47m 38.54s	1m 20.19s	7
9	Gustav Reiner	D	Honda	34	46m 50.29s	1m 21.36s	16
10	Marco Gentile	CH	Fior	34	47m 07.43s	1m 21.27s	15
11	Daniel Amatriain	E	Honda	34	47m 20.41s	1m 22.09s	20
12	Alessandro Valesi	I	Honda	34	47m 31.63s	1m 22.14s	21
13	Fabio Barchitta	RSM	Honda	34	47m 40.76s	1m 22.77s	25
14	Ray Swann	GB	Honda	34	47m 49.77s	1m 22.85s	27
15	Bruno Kneubühler	CH	Honda	34	47m 49.95s	1m 22.36s	23
16	Manfred Fischer	D	Honda	33	46m 37.56s	1m 23.23s	29
17	Marco Papa	I	Honda	33	46m 41.71s	1m 22.51s	24
18	Simon Buckmaster	GB	Honda	33	46m 59.23s	1m 24.13s	31
19	Romolo Balbi	I	Honda	33	47m 15.82s	1m 24.89s	34
20	Karl Truchsess	A	Honda	33	47m 26.23s	1m 25.19s	36
21	Marco Marchesani	I	Suzuki	32	46m 40.22s	1m 24.33s	33
	Vittorio Scatola	I	Paton	30	DNF	1m 22.77s	26
	Richard Scott	NZ	Honda	26	DNF	1m 22.30s	22
	Vittorio Gibertini	I	Suzuki	23	DNF	1m 22.89s	28
	Fabio Biliotti	I	Honda	17	DNF	1m 22.02s	18
	Didier de Radiguès	B	Cagiva	14	DNF	1m 20.36s	9
	Kenny Irons	GB	Suzuki	10	DNF	1m 20.98s	14
	Leandro Becheroni	I	Honda	10	DNF	1m 24.31s	32
	Wolfgang von Muralt	CH	Suzuki	9	DNF	1m 23.37s	30
	Massimo Broccoli	RSM	Honda	8	DNF	1m 21.59s	17
	Rob McElnea	GB	Yamaha	6	DNF	1m 19.63s	4
	Ron Haslam	GB	Honda	5	DNF	1m 22.04s	19
	Silvo Habat	YU	Honda	5	DNF	1m 24.99s	35
	Raymond Roche	F	Cagiva	5	DNF	1m 20.79s	13
	Pier Francesco Chili	I	Honda	3	DNF	1m 20.24s	8
	Freddie Spencer	USA	Honda	3	DNF	1m 19.93s	6
	Ari Rämö	SF	Honda		DNQ	1m 25.62s	
	Joseph Doppler	A	Honda		DNQ	1m 25.64s	
	Claus Wulff	DK	Honda		DNQ	1m 26.02s	
	Gerold Fischer	D	Honda		DNQ	1m 26.34s	
	Andreas Leuthe	LUX	Honda		DNQ	1m 26.40s	
	Larry Moreno Vacondio	YV	Suzuki		DNQ	1m 26.78s	
	Vincenzo Cascino	RCH	Honda		DNQ	1m 26.95s	
	Thierry Rapicault	F	Fior		DNQ	1m 29.82s	
	Georg-Robert Jung	D	Honda		DNQ	1m 31.85s	

Fastest lap: Mamola, 1m 18.98s, 99.4 mph/158.987 km/h (record).
Previous record: Eddie Lawson, USA (Yamaha), 1m 20.20s, 97.287 mph/156.569 km/h (1986).

World Championship: 1 Gardner, 145; **2** Mamola, 124; **3** Lawson, 115; **4** Haslam, 69; **5** Mackenzie and Taira, 49; **7** Sarron, 40; **8** Chili and McElnea, 39; **10** Burnett, 25; **11** Yatsushiro, 24; **12** de Radiguès, 13; **13** Irons, 12; **14** Schwantz, 11; **15** Ito, 10; **16** Roche, 9; **17** Kawasaki, Reiner and Spencer, 4; **20** Scott, 3; **21** Katayama, 2; **22** Gentile and Magee, 1.

250 cc

30 laps, 65.01 miles/104.64 km

Place	Rider	Nat.	Machine	Laps	Time & speed	Practice time	Grid
1	Loris Reggiani	I	Aprilia	30	41m 21.58s 94.88 mph/ 151.800 km/h	1m 21.93s	3
2	Luca Cadalora	I	Yamaha	30	41m 29.47s	1m 21.78s	1
3	Alfonso Pons	E	Honda	30	41m 32.64s	1m 22.59s	14
4	Dominique Sarron	F	Honda	30	41m 33.00s	1m 22.03s	4
5	Martin Wimmer	D	Yamaha	30	41m 33.76s	1m 21.90s	2
6	Anton Mang	D	Honda	30	41m 33.90s	1m 22.40s	12
7	Juan Garriga	E	Yamaha	30	41m 34.11s	1m 22.25s	8
8	Manfred Herweh	D	Honda	30	41m 35.05s	1m 22.73s	15
9	Reinhold Roth	D	Honda	30	41m 35.27s	1m 22.08s	5
10	Patrick Igoa	F	Yamaha	30	41m 35.63s	1m 22.23s	7
11	Maurizio Vitali	I	Garelli	30	41m 35.84s	1m 22.26s	9
12	Ivan Palazzese	YV	Yamaha	30	41m 40.65s	1m 22.16s	6
13	Stéphane Mertens	B	Sekitoba	30	41m 40.91s	1m 22.33s	10
14	Urs Lüzi	CH	Honda	30	41m 49.24s	1m 23.10s	19
15	Donnie McLeod	GB	EMC	30	41m 55.02s	1m 22.88s	16
16	Jean-Michel Mattioli	F	Honda	30	41m 55.45s	1m 22.94s	17
17	Marcellino Lucchi	I	Honda	30	42m 09.80s	1m 22.56s	13
18	Guy Bertin	F	Honda	30	42m 09.97s	1m 23.46s	22
19	Marcello Iannetta	I	Yamaha	30	42m 10.30s	1m 23.97s	28
20	Fausto Ricci	I	Honda	30	42m 11.90s	1m 23.46s	23
21	Jean-Philippe Ruggia	F	Yamaha	30	42m 12.12s	1m 23.58s	25
22	Massimo Matteoni	I	Honda	30	42m 17.57s	1m 23.25s	20
23	René Delaby	LUX	Yamaha	30	42m 25.92s	1m 23.47s	24
24	Harald Eckl	D	Honda	30	42m 30.52s	1m 23.40s	21
25	Christian Boudinot	F	Fior	30	42m 36.67s	1m 24.03s	29
26	Bruno Bonhuil	F	Honda	30	42m 43.42s	1m 24.10s	32
27	Gary Cowan	IRL	Honda	29	41m 29.01s	1m 23.79s	26
28	Alberto Rota	I	Honda	29	41m 29.64s	1m 24.20s	33
29	Renzo Colleoni	I	Honda	29	42m 09.47s	1m 24.34s	34
	Jean Foray	F	Chevallier	20	DNF	1m 24.05s	30
	Stefano Caracchi	RSM	Honda	16	DNF	1m 22.97s	18
	Jochen Schmid	D	Yamaha	11	DNF	1m 24.10s	31
	Carlos Cardus	E	Honda	10	DNF	1m 22.37s	11
	Jean-François Baldé	F	Defi	9	DNF	1m 23.84s	27
	Andrea Brasini	I	Honda	6	DNF	1m 24.48s	36
	Antônio Neto	BR	Honda		DNS	1m 24.38s	35
	Bernard Hänggeli	CH	Honda		DNQ	1m 24.59s	
	Graham Singer	I	Rotax		DNQ	1m 24.62s	
	Xavier Cardelus	AND	Cobas		DNQ	1m 24.86s	
	Kevin Mitchell	GB	Yamaha		DNQ	1m 24.89s	
	Hans Lindner	A	Honda		DNQ	1m 25.11s	
	Engelbert Neumair	A	Rotax		DNQ	1m 25.13s	
	Takayoshi Yamamoto	J	Yamaha		DNQ	1m 25.20s	
	Nedy Crotta	CH	Honda		DNQ	1m 25.38s	
	Hervé Duffard	F	Honda		DNQ	1m 27.28s	
	Janez Stefanec	YU	Honda		DNQ	1m 27.32s	
	Jean-Louis Guignabodet	F	Honda		DNQ	1m 30.52s	

Fastest lap: Cadalora, 1m 21.82s, 95.91 mph/153.469 km/h (record).
Previous record: Carlos Lavado, YV (Yamaha), 1m 22.20s, 94.905 mph/152.734 km/h (1986).

World Championship: 1 Mang, 117; **2** Roth, 91; **3** Pons, 75; **4** Sarron, 67; **5** Reggiani, 65; **6** Cardus, 54; **7** Wimmer, 51; **8** Cornu, 50; **9** Cadalora, 48; **10** Lavado, 38; **11** Igoa, 31; **12** Garriga, 29; **13** Kobayashi, 15; **14** Herweh, 10; **15** Palazzese, 9; **16** Shimizu, 8; **17** Ruggia, 7; **18** Vitali, 6; **19** Lindner and Lüzi, 5; **21** McLeod, 4; **22** Mertens and Taguchi, 2; **24** Baldé, Bertin and Yamamoto, 1.

125 cc

28 laps, 60.68 miles/97.66 km

Place	Rider	Nat.	Machine	Laps	Time & speed	Practice time	Grid
1	Fausto Gresini	I	Garelli	28	38m 36.20s 90.89 mph/ 146.375 km/h	1m 25.04s	1
2	August Auinger	A	MBA	28	39m 04.34s	1m 26.58s	5
3	Paolo Casoli	I	AGV	28	39m 19.05s	1m 25.34s	2
4	Ezio Gianola	I	Honda	28	39m 42.26s	1m 27.30s	8
5	Mike Leitner	A	EMCO	28	39m 48.85s	1m 27.44s	9
6	Lucio Pietroniro	B	MBA	28	39m 48.85s	1m 26.73s	6
7	Andrés Marin Sánchez	E	Ducados	28	40m 45.17s	1m 27.84s	12
8	Gastone Grassetti	I	MBA	27	38m 38.21s	1m 28.26s	16
9	Håkan Olsson	S	Starol	27	38m 39.23s	1m 28.67s	20
10	Norbert Peschke	D	Seel	27	38m 39.80s	1m 28.05s	14
11	Olivier Liegeois	B	Assmex	27	38m 40.51s	1m 27.95s	13
12	Jussi Hautaniemi	SF	MBA	27	38m 43.05s	1m 28.66s	19
13	Willy Pérez	RA	Zanella	27	38m 45.15s	1m 27.72s	10
14	Flemming Kistrup	DK	MBA	27	38m 55.91s	1m 29.00s	23
15	Bady Hassaine	DZ	MBA	27	38m 58.71s	1m 28.74s	21
16	Jean-Claude Selini	F	MBA	27	39m 03.53s	1m 28.63s	18
17	Claudio Macciotta	I	MBA	27	39m 10.02s	1m 29.77s	31
18	Stefano Bianchi	I	MBA	27	39m 13.91s	1m 29.66s	29
19	Robin Appleyard	GB	MBA	27	39m 14.35s	1m 30.27s	36
20	Jacques Hutteau	F	MBA	27	39m 14.60s	1m 30.20s	35
21	Ivan Troisi	YV	MBA	27	39m 19.68s	1m 27.78s	11
22	Luciano Garagnani	I	MBA	27	39m 20.65s	1m 29.54s	26
23	Emilio Cuppini	I	MBA	27	39m 20.91s	1m 28.99s	22
24	Manuel Hernandez	E	Benetti	27	39m 34.25s	1m 29.77s	30
25	Heinz Litz	D	MBA	27	39m 34.91s	1m 30.04s	34
26	Peter Sommer	CH	Supeso	26	38m 37.46s	1m 29.34s	25
	Marco Cipriani	I	MBA	17	38m 45.02s	1m 29.65s	27
	Pier Paolo Bianchi	I	MBA	20	DNF	1m 25.71s	4
	Domenico Brigaglia	I	AGV	18	DNF	1m 26.92s	7
	Allan Scott	USA	MBA	13	DNF	1m 29.16s	24
	Esa Kytölä	SF	MBA	11	DNF	1m 29.79s	32
	Hubert Abold	D	Honda	10	DNF	1m 29.66s	28
	Johnny Wickström	SF	Tunturi	9	DNF	1m 28.14s	15
	Adolf Stadler	D	MBA	7	DNF	1m 29.87s	33
	Thierry Feuz	CH	MBA	6	DNF	1m 28.31s	17
	Bruno Casanova	I	Garelli		DNS	1m 25.66s	3
	Robin Milton	GB	MBA		DNQ	1m 30.38s	
	Heinz Lüthi	D	MBA		DNQ	1m 30.73s	
	Paul Bordes	F	MBA		DNQ	1m 30.89s	
	Marco Pirani	I	Balen		DNQ	1m 30.93s	
	Roberto Dova	I	EMC		DNQ	1m 30.95s	
	Ian McConnachie	GB	MBA		DNQ	1m 31.01s	
	Taru Rinne	SF	MBA		DNQ	1m 31.21s	
	Nicolas Gonzalez	E	MBA		DNQ	1m 31.28s	
	Vincenzo Sblendorio	I	Mancini		DNQ	1m 31.33s	
	Karl Dauer	A	MBA		DNQ	1m 31.36s	
	Thomas Møller-Pedersen	DK	MBA		DNQ	1m 31.48s	
	Christian le Badezet	F	MBA		DNQ	1m 31.74s	

Fastest lap: Gresini, 1m 24.88s, 92.46 mph/147.936 km/h.
Lap record: August Auinger, A (Bartol), 1m 24.73s, 92.61 mph/148.174 km/h (1986).

World Championship: 1 Gresini, 150; **2** Casanova, 88; **3** Auinger, 54; **4** Brigaglia and Casoli, 46; **6** Bianchi, 43; **7** Sánchez, 40; **8** Gianola, 39; **9** Leitner, 24; **10** Pietroniro, 22; **11** Wickström, 21; **12** Feuz, Grassetti and Selini, 12; **15** Hautaniemi, 10; **16** Catalano, Macciotta, Stadler and Troisi, 6; **20** Kytölä and Liegeois, 4; **22** Hassaine, Milton and Olsson, 2; **25** Kistrup, Pérez and Peschke, 1.

80 cc

22 laps, 47.67 miles/76.74 km

Place	Rider	Nat.	Machine	Laps	Time & speed	Practice time	Grid
1	Manuel Herreros	E	Derbi	22	32m 05.36s 85.59 mph/ 136.958 km/h	1m 30.89s	2
2	Stefan Dörflinger	CH	Krauser	22	32m 09.04s	1m 30.98s	3
3	Ian McConnachie	GB	Krauser	22	32m 16.97s	1m 31.47s	4
4	Gerhard Waibel	D	Krauser	22	32m 16.98s	1m 33.30s	9
5	Jörg Seel	D	Seel	22	32m 30.77s	1m 33.88s	12
6	Giuseppe Ascareggi	I	BBFT	22	32m 31.86s	1m 32.87s	7
7	Alexandre Barros	BR	Arbizu	22	32m 32.43s	1m 33.54s	10
8	Hans Spaan	NL	Casal	22	32m 35.23s	1m 33.24s	8
9	Francisco Torrontegui	E	Cobas	22	33m 04.62s	1m 35.33s	20
10	Peter Öttl	D	Krauser	22	33m 04.93s	1m 34.57s	16
11	Salvatore Milano	I	Krauser	22	33m 05.24s	1m 34.18s	14
12	Károly Juhász	H	Krauser	22	33m 09.82s	1m 33.81s	11
13	Reiner Koster	CH	Kroko	22	33m 21.47s	1m 35.12s	19
14	Heinz Paschen	D	Casal	22	33m 34.71s	1m 36.93s	26
15	Theo Timmer	NL	Casal	22	33m 35.54s	1m 34.97s	17
16	Günther Schirnhofer	D	Krauser	21	32m 14.16s	1m 36.94s	27
17	Josef Fischer	A	Krauser	21	32m 21.64s	1m 34.15s	13
18	Wilco Zeelenberg	NL	Casal	21	32m 23.89s	1m 36.05s	24
19	Serge Julin	B	Casal	21	32m 27.09s	1m 36.68s	25
20	Otto Machinek	A	Krauser	21	32m 43.16s	1m 37.42s	30
21	Mario Stocco	I	Faccioli	21	32m 52.45s	1m 38.45s	33
22	Raimo Lipponen	SF	Krauser	21	33m 03.98s	1m 38.21s	32
23	Lionel Robert	F	Krauser	21	33m 46.06s	1m 38.66s	35
24	Rainer Kunz	D	Kroko	20	32m 41.84s	1m 35.63s	22
25	Chris Baert	B	Seel	20	33m 16.72s	1m 36.96s	28
	Hubert Abold	D	Krauser	12	DNF	1m 32.69s	5
	Paolo Priori	I	Krauser	12	DNF	1m 34.20s	15
	Luis M. Reyes	E	Autisa	11	DNF	1m 32.76s	6
	Jorge Martinez	E	Derbi	9	DNF	1m 29.58s	1
	Stuart Edwards	GB	Casal	9	DNF	1m 39.72s	37
	Juan Ramon Bolart	E	Krauser	7	DNF	1m 34.98s	18
	Paul Bordes	F	RB	5	DNF	1m 37.31s	29
	Mario Scalinci	I	Huvo	4	DNF	1m 38.45s	34
	Thomas Engl	D	Esch-GPE	2	DNF	1m 37.46s	31
	Giuliano Tabanelli	I	UFO	2	DNF	1m 39.20s	36
	René Dünki	CH	Krauser		DNS	1m 35.45s	21
	Richard Bay	D	Ziegler		DNS	1m 35.72s	23
	Felix Rodriguez	E	Cobas		DNQ	1m 42.16s	
	Paolo Scappini	I	Unimoto		DNQ	1m 42.79s	
	Nicola Casadei	I	Casal		DNQ	1m 42.85s	

Fastest lap: Herreros, 1m 30.00s, 86.64 mph/139.52 km/h.
Lap record: Pier Paolo Bianchi, I (Seel), 1m 29.65s, 87.018 mph/140.042 km/h (1986).

World Championship: 1 Martinez, 114; **2** Herreros, 74; **3** Waibel, 72; **4** Dörflinger, 69; **5** McConnachie, 53; **6** Seel, 33; **7** Reyes, 31; **8** Abold, 25; **9** Fischer, 19; **10** Miralles, 16; **11** Criville and Schirnhofer, 12; **13** Spaan, 11; **14** Juhász, 10; **15** Barros, 8; **16** Bolart and Priori, 6; **18** Ascareggi, 5; **19** Paschen, 4; **20** Bay and Öttl, 3; **22** Gschwander, Timmer and Torrontegui, 2; **25** Bernard and Waldmann, 1.

Gran Prêmio
MARLBORO *de*
PORTUGAL

A Portuguese Grand Prix in Spain? Well, it didn't seem to make that much sense but the FIM had given the Portuguese governing body a Grand Prix in repayment for the cost of running the congress. As the Portuguese were unable to run the race themselves, they sold the name to Járama who recognised the possibility of making a great deal of money as long as the date was well removed from the Spanish Grand Prix. Two trips to Spain were therefore necessary this year.

That is a fairly typical example of how the FIM run the sport and the fact that two countries were involved in running the GP provided a perfect excuse to pass the buck on numerous occasions. As usual at Járama, the meeting was rather a shambles but the racing is exciting and well worthwhile as the small track was packed with 80,000 spectators.

The circuit currently faces criticism for its bumps and Kevin Magee said that though he was used to such circuits at home in Australia it was not quite what he had expected from a Grand Prix track. Magee was having his third Grand Prix ride of the season and was just as impressive as he had been at the previous two. As the end of the season approached it was obvious that his future should be the subject of much discussion; whilst Kenny Roberts naturally wanted to extend Magee's association with the Lucky Strike team, the possibilities were restricted by the sponsor's requirement that riders should be American.

Because of that, Roberts had already agreed terms with Wayne Rainey for the '88 season, which almost certainly cut Baldwin out of the action. Roberts needed money from another source to finance a separate pair of machines for Magee. Fosters Lager had been mentioned but the latest news was that they were disinclined to try to match Swann Lager's involvement in the sport. Gardner had become a household name in Australia through a special Swann television advertisement that had just been released.

Assuming Roberts remained unable to find the extra cash, Magee's future was uncertain, though he wished to remain with Yamaha if practical and also wanted to make certain that Warren Willing would be able to join him in whatever team signed him for 1988. With McElnea out of favour at Marlboro, there was possibly a place for him there, although Kevin Schwantz had flown to Spain to speak to Agostini. There were rumours that the Texan was close to an agreement to join Lawson in that squad.

Schwantz should have been riding the Suzuki but, in an unprecedented move, the factory had recalled all its machines after the San Marino Grand Prix. The racing team was disbanded and the employees were forced to look for new jobs. At first it was assumed that the factory could no longer accept the lack of results, but there were wider reasons, which included dissatisfaction with Heron, the distributor for Suzuki cars and motor cycles in Britain.

Heron also ran the racing team, but seemed to be one of the losers in Suzuki's wide-ranging reorganisation. Suzuki Japan issued a letter that stated their firm intention to compete in '88 and thanked Heron for their help in the past. The letter's pointed reference to the past made it plain that the racing association with Heron was at an end.

Just how the team would be run in '88 and who might ride what machines was a mystery. Roberto Gallina said he had no intention of swapping back to Suzuki after his first year with Honda but he also wanted a four-cylinder for Chili to ride in '88 and if one was not forthcoming from Honda he might be tempted back to Suzuki.

The Lucky Strike team had Magee in action again at Járama, as well as Mike Baldwin, who was riding for the first time since his practice crash at Hockenheim. The arrival of Baldwin left no bike for Ricard Scott who had been riding in his stead.

Baldwin reported that his hand had by no means healed completely and he was still having trouble bending it even though the bones had mended. He said it was only good for between five and seven fast laps. Far from being depressed about that he was pleased to be back in action and declared that the Lucky Strike Yamaha had improved beyond comparison. 'It is great now, it works like a motor cycle', enthused Baldwin, who, like other Yamaha riders, had always found the carburation lacking.

Lawson was still finding his Yamaha carburation a pain in the backside and stopped after a few laps of Thursday afternoon's practice, parked the bike, before strolling across the pit lane to the barrier where he tapped the Japanese technician on the shoulder and told him exactly what he could do with his machine.

When timed practice began on Friday, Mamola was quickest ahead of Gardner and Magee. The Lucky Strike team had spent time testing the week before the Grand Prix so it was not surprising to see that they were quick from the start. Dunlop were also pleased with the progress being made with the latest tyres.

Peter Ingley was very impressed with Mamola as a tyre tester - a change in attitude from the Spanish Grand Prix at Jerez when he had found the feedback from Mamola and Baldwin confusing and contradictory. He said that nothing useful was learnt from that entire Grand Prix but, at the other end of the season, things were very different. 'Randy must have incredible concentration to be able to pick up the differences he can between tyres. He has spotted a difference in construction that is so small that you would think it was insignificant but it is very important and will make a lot of difference to the way we build the next batch of tyres. I think we have made a real breakthrough here', said Ingley.

Mamola managed to retain pole position all through practice, but Gardner was not far behind and all the top men were quick with little more than a second covering the fastest eight from Mamola to McElnea.

In the 250 class, practice was dominated by the Yamahas, with local hero Juan Garriga

leading from the start chased by Wimmer and then Igoa. Honda had to suffer the embarrassment of being pushed out of fourth place by Jean-François Baldé riding the wheels off the home-grown Rotax-engined Defi.

Baldé later complained that no matter what he did he could not get the appropriate help from Michelin. Although they eventually gave him a good tyre for the race (but still not the best), he could not obtain satisfactory tyres for the last two races of the season. Privately, he suspected Michelin of succumbing to influence from Honda in being denied tyres that would enable him to embarrass them further.

The tyre company's lot is never easy: the better tyres are produced in such small numbers that they will always disappoint riders with their priorities. Peter Ingley freely admitted that there were differences between the tyres used by the three Lucky Strike men. Magee's rear tyre would lose him half a second to Mamola yet be a second quicker than Baldwin. At the front of development it is just not possible to produce enough of

A curved black line shows where Gardner has put down rubber chasing Lawson and Mamola under the bridge.

the very latest for everyone. Company policies decided behind closed doors at both Michelin and Dunlop ensure that certain riders are given preferential treatment, either according to their expected performance or to pressure from the factories.

125 cc

There is no doubt about who dominated the championship, but Fausto Gresini lost the chance of writing his name into a special place in the record books. When he crashed the works Garelli on lap 11, it meant he had failed to complete a unique achievement of eleven GP wins in one season. The only riders to have won every Grand Prix are Frith, Surtees, Redman and Agostini, when there were fewer Grands Prix. Agostini took 11 wins, but that was out of 13 races.

When August Auinger crashed a lap later the race was handed to Paolo Casoli on the AGV MBA. Casoli's team-mate, Domenico Brigaglia, had led on the first lap, but Casoli was right behind and soon took over. Gresini held a cautious third and August Auinger had to pull through from seventh place on lap 1.

By lap 4, Gresini was right behind Casoli and a lap later Auinger had joined them. Casoli could not match their pace, so one lap further on Gresini led Auinger and they began to pull away. Auinger challenged the Italian hard, sweeping past on lap 10 as they raced over the hill under the Dunlop bridge. Gresini fell only a few corners later but Auinger was unaware and pressed on. Trying too hard to get away from his imagined opposition, he fell a lap later.

Casoli had no trouble cruising to victory ahead of Brigaglia and Lucio Pietroniro, with Mike Leitner fourth. Ezio Gianola was in the middle of another last-lap fairing-banging session, this time with Gastone Grassetti, which ended in Gianola's favour.

80 cc

The race meeting came to a complete halt after Aspar Martínez won and then went on to the slowing-down lap trailing a huge Spanish flag. He managed to reach the largest spectator banking, but there the track was blocked by fans and fireworks. He was lifted from his machine and carried shoulder high along the road in front of the spectator fencing. It was a celebration of his World Championship and his number two, Herreros, enjoyed a similar reception.

On lap 1, Ian McConnachie dived inside both Martínez and Herreros to take the lead and for the first seven laps Martínez and McConnachie traded the lead, joined by Waibel as Herreros dropped back.

The seventh lap saw McConnachie dive inside Martínez at the same hairpin as he had used on lap 1, but this time he did not get away with it as the front end slid away. The crowd loved every minute and, trailed by Waibel, Martínez slowed the pace a little as 17-year-old hero Alejandro

Right: **Gardner raises his backside a fraction to get a better aerodynamic shape as he attempts to stay ahead of Kevin Magee.**

Criville, riding the Derbi he uses in the European Championship, charged through from about 17th at the start.

By lap 15, Criville had risen to a close third, and then second as the two Derbis started to pull away from Waibel. On lap 18, however, the second Derbi seized and Criville stopped. It was two laps before the crowd finished their standing ovation.

As if that was not enough excitement for the crowd, Herreros then got a second lease of life and stole second from Waibel.

500 cc

The 500 cc contest had all the makings of a great race and the spectators were not disappointed. Mamola led from Lawson and Sarron, with Gardner only a yard behind them and ahead of McElnea, Magee and Burnett. Mackenzie had shot off the second row of the grid but found his way blocked. 'I got rolling before anyone else but then Lawson and Gardner moved together in front of me and I had to back off. It was all over then and I was well behind with a lot to do.'

Mamola led Lawson and Gardner away from the pack though Sarron tried to follow. McElnea was not about to try any heroics after his fall at Misano and slipped back. Magee took a little time to work out what pace was appropriate but then began to close on McElnea.

By lap 6 Mamola and Lawson were getting away from Gardner slightly but only momentarily. Magee passed McElnea as on lap 9 the leaders started lapping the woefully slow back-markers who should never have got into the same event. Mamola hesitated for a moment and decided on the outside line while Lawson passed on the inside. The slow man moved over to block Mamola, which let Gardner past as well.

Mamola lost 20 yards and was only just in front of Sarron but he was soon back in the groove. He chased Gardner and by lap 16 was back into second and looking at Lawson. By that point, Magee had passed Sarron who started to suffer from cramp in his wrist.

Gardner was clearly not going to feature in the battle for the win; his bike had slowed and though the temperature gauge read normal it had pumped out most of the water. As the 37-lap race ran into its second half Mamola was right on Lawson's tail and Magee had Gardner in his sights.

On lap 24 Mackenzie caught and passed McElnea. As the Scot ran wide exiting a tight right-hand hairpin, McElnea tried to accelerate out from underneath him. The HB Honda came back across the track heading for the next left-hander and neither rider saw each other. The two bikes collided and McElnea ended up as a heap on the floor. Mackenzie kept going and finished a distant sixth, realising that he could not catch Sarron in the time available.

Magee passed Gardner on lap 28 and next time around the younger Australian was second as Mamola had run off the track at the end of the start-and-finish straight. 'I was catching Eddie on the brakes but this time the back wheel came

off the ground and by the time it was down I was heading off the track for Madrid. I only just got the bike stopped before the fence and when I turned it round I was heading back up to the track as Magee and Gardner came down to the corner.'

It only took Mamola a couple of laps to get back past Gardner but it seems doubtful that he could have caught Magee had he not eased the pace on team orders. It was obvious that as far as Yamaha, and particularly the Lucky Strike Team, were concerned Mamola should finish second, but it must have been frustrating for Gardner who had waged a lone battle against two or three Yamahas all season.

It transpired that Gardner's Honda had seized on two cylinders when it lost most of the cooling water and it was surprising that it kept going at all. No certain cause was ever found for the failure and unusually the team were running the optional extra lower radiator.

250 cc

Yet another great 250 race and another that proved Toni Mang to be a great champion. He was only eighth-fastest in practice, yet remained unconcerned about being a second and a half slower than pole-position man Garriga.

Roth led off the line and stayed there for the first three laps while Mang worked his way from fourth to second and then into the lead on lap 4. Garriga had started a little slower and it was not until lap 5 that he eased Roth out of second place. Roth had said before the race that he only felt about 70 per cent fit with his injured shoulder and did not expect to be able to keep the pace up for the entire race.

Mang and Garriga started to ease away from the rest as Roth continued to feel pressure from Pons, Sarron and even Baldé, who was riding his heart out and trying to stay ahead of Wimmer and Igoa.

Garriga could never get the better of him and ran wide a couple of times as he tried a little too hard. He did not give up, but Mang's error-free riding made it impossible for Garriga to exact any kind of advantage.

On lap 17, Roth finally yielded third to Pons and then was overwhelmed by Igoa and Wimmer while Sarron was engaged in battle with Baldé. The third-place struggle did not ease up at all, and on lap 20 Pons was hounded by Roth, Igoa, Wimmer, Sarron and Baldé. It was Wimmer who made the break by securing third on lap 22. Igoa followed his advantage and Pons took fifth. Baldé had his hard work rewarded by claiming a fine sixth.

Mang's victory was perfect and he did not even realise he was champion until minutes after the race was over when he noticed that his team were wearing the World Champion T-shirts. That night there was an enormous party and at 6.0 a.m. Gardner was tapping Mang's knowledge on just what it took to win a championship. They were in Toni's motorhome: a lot of beer had been consumed but the information was still valuable.

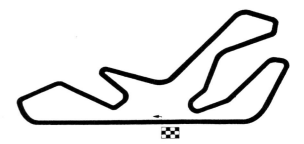

Sipping water, Mike Baldwin has time to
reflect on his return to racing. Járama was
the place where he first made an impact on
Grand Prix racing, but this time he maintained
a lower profile *(above)*.

Left: **Only when he saw his team wearing the
special T-shirts did Toni Mang realise that he
was World Champion.**

Below left: **De Radiguès and Roche were
promising but inconsistent on the Bastos
Cagivas.**

Grande Premio Marlboro de Portugal, 13 September/statistics

Circuito Permanente del Járama, 2.058-mile/3.312-km circuit

500 cc

37 laps, 76.15 miles/122.54 km

Place	Rider	Nat.	Machine	Laps	Time & speed	Practice time	Grid
1	Eddie Lawson	USA	Yamaha	37	55m 20.66s 82.50 mph/ 132.854 km/h	1m 28.14s	3
2	Randy Mamola	USA	Yamaha	37	55m 29.96s	1m 27.64s	1
3	Kevin Magee	AUS	Yamaha	37	55m 30.37s	1m 28.27s	5
4	Wayne Gardner	AUS	Honda	37	55m 39.90s	1m 27.91s	2
5	Christian Sarron	F	Yamaha	37	56m 02.35s	1m 28.26s	4
6	Niall Mackenzie	GB	Honda	37	56m 23.05s	1m 28.55s	7
7	Pier Francesco Chili	I	Honda	37	56m 35.04s	1m 29.65s	11
8	Shunji Yatsushiro	J	Honda	37	56m 47.59s	1m 30.03s	14
9	Ron Haslam	GB	Elf	36	55m 43.98s	1m 30.28s	16
10	Gustav Reiner	D	Honda	36	55m 53.94s	1m 30.71s	17
11	Bruno Kneubühler	CH	Honda	36	56m 35.60s	1m 32.36s	24
12	Wolfgang von Muralt	CH	Suzuki	36	56m 35.78s	1m 32.02s	23
13	Ray Swann	GB	Honda	36	56m 38.42s	1m 31.08s	22
14	Simon Buckmaster	GB	Honda	36	56m 48.39s	1m 33.08s	25
15	Henny Boerman	NL	Honda	35	56m 42.17s	1m 34.01s	27
16	Ian Pratt	GB	Suzuki	34	56m 36.31s	1m 37.13s	30
17	Gerhard Vogt	D	Suzuki	33	57m 04.67s	1m 39.85s	33
18	Vincenzo Cascino	RCH	Suzuki	32	55m 31.58s	1m 38.30s	32
	Didier de Radiguès	B	Cagiva	24	DNF	1m 29.96s	13
	Rob McElnea	GB	Yamaha	23	DNF	1m 28.74s	8
	Larry Moreno Vacondio	YV	Suzuki	21	DNF	1m 37.29s	31
	Roger Burnett	GB	Honda	17	DNF	1m 29.33s	10
	Raymond Roche	F	Cagiva	16	DNF	1m 29.31s	9
	Alessandro Valesi	I	Honda	15	DNF	1m 31.14s	19
	Marco Gentile	CH	Fior	14	DNF	1m 31.80s	21
	Fabio Biliotti	I	Suzuki	13	DNF	1m 30.14s	15
	Fabio Barchitta	RSM	Honda	13	DNF	1m 31.45s	20
	Christoph Bürki	CH	Honda	13	DNF	1m 36.49s	29
	Mike Baldwin	USA	Yamaha	10	DNF	1m 29.70s	12
	Tadahiko Taira	J	Yamaha	9	DNF	1m 28.43s	6
	Hervé Guilleux	F	Fior	8	DNF	1m 33.37s	26
	Daniel Amatriain	E	Honda	7	DNF	1m 30.88s	18
	Tony Carey	IRL	Suzuki	6	DNF	1m 40.54s	34
	Maarten Duyzers	NL	Honda		DNS	1m 34.70s	28

Fastest lap: Gardner, 1m 27.995s, 84.14 mph/135.500 km/h (record).
Previous record: Wayne Gardner, AUS (Honda), 1m 29.35s, 82.973 mph/133.532 km/h (1986).

World Championship: 1 Gardner, 153; **2** Mamola, 136; **3** Lawson, 130; **4** Haslam, 71; **5** Mackenzie, 54; **6** Taira, 49; **7** Sarron, 46; **8** Chili, 43; **9** McElnea, 39; **10** Yatsushiro, 27; **11** Burnett, 25; **12** de Radiguès, 13; **13** Irons, 12; **14** Magee and Schwantz, 11; **16** Ito, 10; **17** Roche, 9; **18** Reiner, 5; **19** Kawasaki and Spencer, 4; **21** Scott, 3; **22** Katayama, 2; **23** Gentile, 1.

80 cc

22 laps, 45.28 miles/72.86 km

Place	Rider	Nat.	Machine	Laps	Time & speed	Practice time	Grid
1	Jorge Martinez	E	Derbi	22	36m 38.69s 74.08 mph/ 119.304 km/h	1m 37.02s	1
2	Manuel Herreros	E	Derbi	22	36m 50.47s	1m 39.08s	3
3	Gerhard Waibel	D	Krauser	22	36m 51.09s	1m 39.72s	6
4	Hubert Abold	D	Krauser	22	37m 01.59s	1m 39.66s	5
5	Stefan Dörlinger	CH	Krauser	22	37m 04.18s	1m 39.03s	4
6	Jörg Seel	D	Seel	22	37m 11.54s	1m 39.94s	7
7	Juan Ramon Bolart	E	Krauser	22	37m 30.61s	1m 40.66s	13
8	Paolo Priori	I	Krauser	22	37m 35.46s	1m 42.65s	15
9	Julian Miralles	E	Derbi	22	37m 49.76s	1m 40.28s	10
10	Francisco Torrontegui	I	Arbizu	22	37m 58.06s	1m 42.22s	14
11	Hans Spaan	NL	Casal	22	38m 03.34s	1m 40.35s	11
12	Josef Fischer	A	Krauser	22	38m 18.21s	1m 42.72s	16
13	Reiner Koster	CH	Kroko	22	38m 19.63s	1m 44.87s	19
14	Günther Schirnhofer	D	Krauser	22	38m 21.48s	1m 44.12s	17
15	Wilco Zeelenberg	NL	Casal	21	37m 04.65s	1m 45.58s	22
16	Theo Timmer	NL	Casal	21	37m 20.27s	1m 45.28s	21
17	Lionel Robert	F	Krauser	21	37m 50.86s	1m 47.11s	29
18	Chris Baert	B	Seel	21	37m 51.01s	1m 46.64s	27
19	Raimo Lipponen	SF	Krauser	21	38m 02.09s	1m 46.43s	25
20	Juan Esteve	E	Autisa	21	38m 21.65s	1m 48.85s	30
21	Serge Julin	B	Casal	20	37m 09.84s	1m 44.32s	18
22	Joaquin Alos	E		20	37m 55.16s	1m 51.45s	32
23	Jacques Bernard	B		19	37m 08.38s	1m 46.56s	26
	Felix Rodriguez	E	Cobas	20	DNF	1m 45.66s	23
	Luis M. Reyes	E	Autisa	19	DNF	1m 40.02s	8
	Alexandre Barros	BR	Arbizu	19	DNF	1m 40.48s	12
	Alejandro Criville	E	Derbi	17	DNF	1m 38.60s	2
	Stuart Edwards	GB	Casal	9	DNF	1m 48.94s	31
	Ian McConnachie	GB	Krauser	8	DNF	1m 40.20s	9
	Paul Bordes	F	RB	3	DNF	1m 47.10s	28
	Javier Debon	E	Autisa	1	DNF	1m 46.18s	24
	José Saez	E	Autisa	1	DNF	1m 45.27s	20
	José Luis Sangrador				DNQ	1m 51.99s	
	Elias Durendez				DNQ	1m 55.06s	
	Severo Calleja				DNQ	1m 57.30s	
	Jean-François Verdier	F			DNQ	2m 05.77s	

Fastest lap: Martinez, 1m 37.528s, 75.92 mph/122.256 km/h (record).
Previous record: Jorge Martinez, E (Derbi), 1m 38.50s, 75.266 mph/121.128 km/h (1986).

Final 80 cc World Championship points: see pages 198-200.

There is a rider in there somewhere ... the end of the 80 cc race.

125 cc

28 laps, 57.62 miles/92.74 km

Place	Rider	Nat.	Machine	Laps	Time & speed	Practice time	Grid
1	Paolo Casoli	I	AGV	28	44m 23.15s 77.84 mph/ 125.36 km/h	1m 35.31s	5
2	Domenico Brigaglia	I	AGV	28	44m 32.04s	1m 34.80s	3
3	Lucio Pietroniro	B	MBA	28	44m 55.68s	1m 34.94s	4
4	Mike Leitner	A	EMCO	28	45m 23.95s	1m 36.43s	9
5	Ezio Gianola	I	Honda	28	45m 41.56s	1m 36.32s	8
6	Gastone Grassetti	I	MBA	28	45m 41.75s	1m 36.65s	12
7	Jean-Claude Selini	F	MBA	28	45m 51.07s	1m 37.02s	15
8	Adolf Stadler	D	MBA	28	45m 51.61s	1m 36.85s	14
9	Ivan Troisi	YV	MBA	28	45m 52.09s	1m 37.70s	20
10	Thierry Feuz	CH	MBA	28	45m 59.26s	1m 37.10s	17
11	Willy Pérez	RA	Tunturi	27	44m 38.88s	1m 37.93s	21
12	Håkan Olsson	S	Starol	27	44m 47.77s	1m 39.19s	29
13	Bady Hassaine	DZ	MBA	27	45m 01.11s	1m 38.11s	22
14	Allan Scott	USA	EMC	27	45m 04.04s	1m 38.99s	27
15	Robin Appleyard	GB	MBA	27	45m 16.41s	1m 37.10s	16
16	Manuel Hernandez	E	Benetti	27	45m 27.85s	1m 39.74s	30
17	Antonio Oliveros	E		27	45m 28.04s	1m 40.09s	33
18	Helmut Hovenga	D	MBA	26	44m 32.97s	1m 40.05s	32
19	Thomas Møller-Pedersen	DK	MBA	26	45m 37.43s	1m 40.68s	35
20	Paul Bordes	F	MBA	26	45m 48.81s	1m 39.79s	31
21	Robin Milton	GB	MBA	25	45m 32.52s	1m 38.84s	25
22	Jacques Hutteau	F	MBA	25	45m 07.19s	1m 36.21s	7
	Olivier Liegeois	B	Assmex	22	DNF	1m 37.49s	19
	Jussi Hautaniemi	SF	MBA	21	DNF	1m 38.69s	24
	Flemming Kistrup	DK	MBA	18	DNF	1m 36.60s	11
	Andrés Marín Sánchez	E	Ducados	17	DNF	1m 37.34s	18
	Heinz Lüthi	CH	Honda	17	DNF	1m 39.16s	28
	Christian le Badezet	F	MBA	17	DNF	1m 36.79s	13
	Johnny Wickström	SF	MBA	16	DNF	1m 34.38s	2
	August Auinger	A	MBA	10	DNF	1m 33.12s	1
	Fausto Gresini	I	Garelli	9	DNF	1m 38.24s	23
	Esa Kytölä	SF	MBA	9	DNF	1m 40.49s	34
	Nicolas Glez	E	Cobas	8	DNF	1m 36.56s	10
	Hubert Abold	D	Honda	7	DNF	1m 35.59s	6
	Pier Paolo Bianchi	I	MBA	3	DNF	1m 40.74s	36
	José Fombuena	E		3	DNF		
	Vicente Faubel				DNQ	1m 45.29s	
	Juan Miguel Munoz				DNQ	1m 45.69s	
	Daniel Mateos	E			DNQ	1m 45.81s	
	Javier Navarro				DNQ	1m 45.93s	
	Joaquin Alos	E			DNQ	1m 48.58s	

Fastest lap: Auinger, 1m 33.258s, 79.39 mph/133.258 km/h (record).
Previous record: Fausto Gresini, I (Garelli), 1m 35.47s, 77.654 mph/124.972 km/h (1986).

Final 125 cc World Championship points: see pages 198-200.

250 cc

31 laps, 63.80 miles/102.67 km

Place	Rider	Nat.	Machine	Laps	Time & speed	Practice time	Grid
1	Anton Mang	D	Honda	31	47m 31.33s 80.50 mph/ 129.632 km/h	1m 30.62s	8
2	Juan Garriga	E	Yamaha	31	47m 32.12s	1m 29.02s	1
3	Martin Wimmer	D	Yamaha	31	47m 35.93s	1m 29.80s	2
4	Patrick Igoa	F	Yamaha	31	47m 38.14s	1m 29.85s	3
5	Alfonso Pons	E	Honda	31	47m 40.26s	1m 30.80s	11
6	Jean-François Baldé	F	Defi	31	47m 46.04s	1m 30.15s	4
7	Reinhold Roth	D	Honda	31	47m 46.29s	1m 30.53s	7
8	Dominique Sarron	F	Honda	31	47m 52.76s	1m 30.62s	9
9	Luca Cadalora	I	Yamaha	31	47m 56.97s	1m 30.88s	13
10	Manfred Herweh	D	Honda	31	48m 11.17s	1m 30.84s	12
11	Stéphane Mertens	B	Sekitoba	31	48m 12.54s	1m 30.51s	6
12	Stefano Caracchi	RSM	Yamaha	31	48m 12.73s	1m 31.23s	15
13	Jean-Philippe Ruggia	F	Yamaha	31	48m 13.00s	1m 31.98s	22
14	Jean-Michel Mattioli	F	Honda	31	48m 13.76s	1m 31.38s	18
15	Maurizio Vitali	I	Garelli	31	48m 20.62s	1m 31.46s	19
16	Guy Bertin	F	Honda	31	48m 32.24s	1m 32.15s	25
17	Alberto Puig	E	Cobas	31	48m 41.06s	1m 32.29s	27
18	Alberto Rota	I	Honda	31	48m 45.10s	1m 32.13s	24
19	René Delaby	LUX	Yamaha	31	48m 47.54s	1m 32.62s	30
20	Bernard Hänggeli	CH	Honda	31	48m 49.81s	1m 32.92s	32
21	Alain Bronec	F	Honda	30	47m 53.42s	1m 33.57s	35
22	Christian Boudinot	F	Fior	30	47m 53.62s	1m 31.95s	21
23	Marcello Iannetta	I	Yamaha	30	48m 16.53s	1m 33.94s	34
	Bruno Bonhuil	F	Honda	26	DNF	1m 32.30s	28
	Jean Foray	F	Chevallier	26	DNF	1m 32.84s	31
	Donnie McLeod	GB	EMC	22	DNF	1m 31.30s	16
	Gerard van der Wal	NL	Assmex	17	DNF	1m 33.85s	36
	Urs Lüzi	CH	Honda	16	DNF	1m 31.76s	20
	Carlos Lavado	YV	Yamaha	13	DNF	1m 32.47s	29
	Carlos Cardus	E	Honda	9	DNF	1m 30.27s	5
	Xavier Cardelus	AND	Cobas	9	DNF	1m 32.26s	26
	Juan Lopez Mella	E	Yamaha	7	DNF	1m 33.27s	33
	Fausto Ricci	I	Honda	7	DNF	1m 31.32s	17
	Loris Reggiani	I	Aprilia	2	DNF	1m 30.76s	10
	Ivan Palazzese	YV	Yamaha	2	DNF	1m 31.11s	14
	Harald Eckl	D	Honda	1	DNF	1m 32.07s	23
	Antonio García	E			DNQ	1m 33.92s	
	Pedro Ortega				DNQ	1m 35.64s	
	Ruben del Rio	E			DNQ	1m 36.00s	
	Hervé Duffard	F	Honda		DNQ	1m 36.02s	
	Nicolas Glez	E			DNQ	1m 36.15s	
	Pedro Lozano				DNQ	1m 36.78s	

Fastest lap: Garriga, 1m 30.415s, 81.89 mph/131.874 km/h (record).
Previous record: Martin Wimmer, D (Yamaha), 1m 31.05s, 81.424 mph/129.53 km/h (1986).

World Championship: 1 Mang, 132; **2** Roth, 95; **3** Pons, 81; **4** Sarron, 70; **5** Reggiani, 65; **6** Wimmer, 61; **7** Cardus, 54; **8** Cadalora and Cornu, 50; **10** Garriga, 41; **11** Igoa, 39; **12** Lavado, 38; **13** Kobayashi, 15; **14** Herweh, 11; **15** Palazzese, 9; **16** Shimizu, 8; **17** Ruggia, 7; **18** Baldé and Vitali, 6; **20** Lindner and Lüzi, 5; **22** McLeod, 4; **23** Mertens and Taguchi, 2; **25** Bertin and Yamamoto, 1.

A whirlwind dragged rubbish high into the air as Lawson and Mamola fought for second. Once Lawson's fuel load was lightened and Mamola had seen the best of his tyres, second was bound to go to the departing champion.

Grande Prêmio do
B R A S I L

A Grand Prix should be remembered for the racing; the Brazilian Grand Prix might have been remembered for the fact that Wayne Gardner won his first World Championship. The truth is that most will remember Goiania for the social life, the holiday atmosphere that started as the bikes failed to arrive on the expected day and people began to wonder whether there would be a race at all.

It had already been a long season, the 250 title had been secured and the chances were that Gardner would take the 500. After a tough year in Europe the last thing the teams needed was to pack up everything and ship it to South America. The flights were long and delayed and cancelled. Some took six flights to get to Goiania and everyone was ready to let their hair down.

Most of the teams were staying in the same brand new hotel and it was a first class establishment. The place started to hum as soon as the room keys were handed out. The good life was helped by the exchange rate, which made everything cheap, and the girls were friendly – according to unconfirmed sources, they outnumbered the men locally at a ratio of between 5 and 12 to 1, depending on who you wished to believe.

As the Irish are the butt of English jokes and the Belgians bear the brunt of European humour, Goiania is in the state of Goya and is the subject of Brazilian derogatory remarks. That made them very proud to have the Grand Prix and keen to try and limit the effects of their below-par organisation. With attractions like a Grand Prix beauty contest judged by a panel of riders and the local discotheque, 'Zoom', everyone was soon hoping that the bikes would not turn up at all.

The crates arrive only a day late but, by then, the rhythm of the week had been established. Different things work for different people. Gardner had partied all year as a defence against the pressure but as he got closer to the championship his fuse grew shorter. Mamola is a party animal through and through and seems to need to expend considerable energy to avoid exploding. Lawson is different: he went to the disco once, for a full 15 minutes. He does not enjoy it unless he is drinking and he will not drink before a race: 'If I lost the race by half a second I would never know if that one late night had cost me first place.'

Each worked to his own plan and there is no doubt that the results of the race on Sunday were connected more to the Dunlop tyres that went missing than to who stayed out latest. Gardner might well have won with demoralising certainty in any case, but the absence of the latest-generation Dunlops took away any chance Mamola might have had to push him along. The only time that the Lucky Strike Yamaha has looked like winning a race in the dry came after the new tyre made its appearance in Czechoslovakia.

The latest versions of the new tyres landed in Rio only to go missing, so Mamola had no choice but to use the Japanese Dunlops that he last employed at Donington. Tyres were not the first

problem encountered in practice, though: before grip could be considered, the wheels would need to make contact with the road more than once every few feet.

The track was bumpy, old and cracked. It looked as though it had not been resurfaced since it was built in 1974. The layout was great, almost perfect as it combined safety with spectator visibility and a variety of corners with a pleasant change of elevation. The track had not been overused or rippled by F1 cars; it was simply old and caused a lot of problems for the frame and suspension systems.

Particularly telling were two corner exits leading to straights – one running behind the pits, the other being the main front straight. In those two places the bumps traversed under heavy acceleration caused the most frightening gyrations, and those who watched felt sure the worst-handling bikes (like that of Yatsushiro) would spit their riders into the dirt.

In fact, there were very few fallers. One was Pier Francesco Chili who lost the front end. 'I just tried a little harder and the front tyre skipped across the bumps.' The other was Rob McElnea who had the front end of the Marlboro Yamaha tuck under on him without serious injury.

Gardner's team had shipped in 1.5 tonnes of equipment and HRC had a total of 5.2 tonnes for their four 500 class riders. That was enough to enable the World Championship leader to get the NSR to work well by the end of practice after much experimentation with the suspension and particularly with the front forks. Gardner frightened his team by running off the track on one occasion, but he kept the Honda upright. 'I was catching Chili at the end of the straight and thinking about where to pass him. He isn't normally late on the brakes but while I was looking at him I missed my braking marker and ran out of track.'

Lawson said he also had the Yamaha working but was not able to go any quicker: '28.6 is as fast as I can go. If they lap any quicker than that in the race they are going to leave me. If I go any faster into the corners I push the front; if I get on the gas any harder the back slides, there is just no more grip. I can do that time for as many laps as it takes but I don't know how long the tyres will last out.' Lawson ended practice down in fifth place because he never got a clear lap on the bike that was working well. What peeved him a little was not that Shunji Yatsushiro chased him round in the final session but that, in doing so, the Japanese recorded a faster time.

After the morning warm-up session Freddie Spencer's girlfriend approached Erv Kanemoto with a message that Freddie wanted to speak to him. The ex-triple champion stated that he was having problems with his vision. He had lost three contact lenses in the course of one practice session and said that because the track was 800 metres above sea level the lenses were drying out. If he blinked, the lenses were flicked out. Spencer told Kanemoto that even when the lens was still in his eye its dryness caused it to cloud over, which was why he kept blinking.

Kanemoto accepted that Spencer should not ride and went on to look after Mackenzie. Spencer's bike had run better in practice, so the fibreglass, footrests and front forks were transferred to that machine from Mackenzie's bike. Before the race was over Spencer had left the circuit, and he had left the country before his team could see him again.

There was plenty of activity after the warm-up session, including furious work in the Elf pit where they were changing pistons and reed valves because Haslam had used the entire half-hour session to try and sort out a new front suspension unit. Serge Rosset had decided to swap units after the last official practice session because of their lack of success in making the existing unit work. It was a brave move but unfortunately it failed to provide the answer.

500 cc

For most of the season Gardner had dominated the class but things had slipped in the two most recent races. For those with short memories, however, he won the race at Goiania like a true champion, reminding everyone of his number one position for 1988. Lawson led off the line but Gardner was determined to get into the first corner ahead of him and from that moment the breathing space offered by the second-place squabble swiftly allowed him to open up a clear advantage.

Lawson was second but once more found the Yamaha unmanageable with a full tank of fuel. He did not complain specifically that the front tyre was sliding away as it had in Sweden and Czechoslovakia but that the bike was simply 'heavy and slow to turn into corners with a full tank of gas'.

He was tailed in the early laps very closely by Yatsushiro and Mamola. It even took them some time to get clear of de Radiguès who had been amongst them at the start and was then left to fight with Roche, Taira, Sarron and McElnea.

By lap 9 Gardner had opened up a 5-second lead but, by then, Lawson had started to flick the Yamaha in quicker and the gap did not greatly increase. Team-mate McElnea was not doing as well: flicked off by the Yamaha, he suffered another nasty fall, which took the skin off his right forearm and broke a bone in his hand. He could not hide the distress of a wretched end to a dismal meeting.

Roche had featured at the front early on but his rear brake broke up and he went off the road at the end of the main straight on lap 14, subsequently retiring. Gardner stretched his lead slowly while Mamola passed Lawson on lap 9 and held second until the rear tyre started to go away.

Lawson was back in front by lap 13 and Yatsushiro slipped back to a distant fourth. His bike was handling so wildly that it was surprising he could stay on it, and slowly he was caught by Sarron and de Radiguès. The three battled it out from lap 18 to lap 24, until Yatsushiro slipped behind in sixth place as de Radiguès tried to hold fourth from Sarron.

Below: **Mamola's spare bike stands in the pits while Gardner charges past on his way to another quick lap in the last moments of practice.**

Above: **Dominique Sarron concentrates hard.**

Arch-rivals Wayne Gardner and Eddie Lawson still have time to discuss the problems of getting their bikes to handle on the very bumpy circuit. They agreed that the problem seemed to lie in the choice of front fork springs.

Peter Clifford

Peter Clifford

Peter Clifford

Gardner said later that he had hoped to get a ten-second buffer but had to settle for six seconds. It was enough for safety and he defended it well as Lawson tried continually to chip away at it but without making an impression. Mamola never stood much of a chance after the good Dunlops had been lost *en route*.

The de Radiguès/Sarron fight went down to the flag with the Belgian holding on to take his best result of the year. Yatsushiro managed to keep ahead of Taira who said that the bike was never as fast as it had been in practice and just kept getting slower. Eighth was Mackenzie on Spencer's machine, having discovered that although the engine was faster than his own machine, the gearbox was all wrong for his very different riding style. Well behind him was Pier Francesco Chili, who had been involved in a lengthy contest with Mike Baldwin for ninth. The Italian eventually got the better of the Lucky Strike rider who was doing his best against his still-stiff wrist and some third-rate tyres after the best available had naturally gone to Mamola. Ron Haslam was out of the points and lapped on the Elf.

250 cc

Only a week after winning the Bol d'Or, which many observers described as a 24-hour Grand Prix, a 45-minute race seemed rather short to Dominique Sarron. He was determined that this should be no flag-to-flag battle between ten riders that had often characterised the 250 class race. He hit the front on lap 1 and set a pace that no-one else could match.

By lap 4, Mang had worked his way to the head of the second-place group, having passed Cardus, Roth, Wimmer, Pons, Cadalora, Lavado and Reggiani. Mang looked capable of chasing Sarron; he tried for a lap but found it impossible. 'As soon as I tried to catch him the tyres started

sliding and I had to slow down.' Mang saw no point in taking risks, for he had already won the championship.

The first to pass Mang was Cardus and he did chase Sarron hard. He might have been able to get in front of the Frenchman, but 'if onlys' do not count; before he could think about it, the Spaniard ran into trouble with his right forearm. The tendonitis has been bothering him all year and Cardus will have a winter operation on that as well as on the knee he injured in Japan.

The injury prevented him from controlling his braking and, after threatening Sarron on laps 8 to 11, he started to slip back. By that time, Pons had worked his way through the group and started to overhaul the fading Cardus. The second Spaniard was never going to have the laps he needed to catch Sarron, for the Frenchman was comfortably reeling off lap after lap at a consistently fast pace. Laps 13 and 14 were taken at under 1m 31s, then he settled at 1m 31s until lap 22 when he eased off by a second.

Mang continued to head the group with Wimmer right on his tail just ahead of Cadalora, Roth, Lavado and Reggiani (who was having overheating problems with the Aprilia). Behind them, Masahiro Shimuzu was on his own and finding it impossible to make up for his slow start.

Through the last three laps, Mang lost fourth place and Lavado had the helm briefly before being passed by Wimmer on the final circuit. The German opened up a lead of five machine lengths before the last corner, a long widening radius right-hander. Going in hard, he locked up the front end and slid off. Roth took fourth from Lavado, Cadalora and Mang.

Wimmer had not realised that it was the last lap. 'We were slipstreaming so close that all I could see was the bike in front. The last pit board I saw said seven laps to go and I thought we still had four or five to do. I would never have ridden like that on the last lap.'

Grande Premio do Brasil, 27 September/statistics

Goiania circuit, 2.359-mile/3.773-km circuit

500 cc

32 laps, 75.51 miles/120.736 km

Place	Rider	Nat.	Machine	Laps	Time & speed	Practice time	Grid
1	Wayne Gardner	AUS	Honda	32	47m 39.57s 95.50 mph/ 153.69 km/h	1m 27.36s	1
2	Eddie Lawson	USA	Yamaha	32	47m 44.76s	1m 28.62s	5
3	Randy Mamola	USA	Yamaha	32	47m 52.18s	1m 28.13s	2
4	Didier de Radiguès	B	Cagiva	32	48m 03.99s	1m 28.69s	6
5	Christian Sarron	F	Yamaha	32	48m 05.16s	1m 29.16s	10
6	Shunji Yatsushiro	J	Honda	32	48m 21.90s	1m 28.39s	4
7	Tadahiko Taira	J	Yamaha	32	48m 31.28s	1m 28.36s	3
8	Niall Mackenzie	GB	Honda	32	48m 36.26s	1m 30.00s	12
9	Pier Francesco Chili	I	Honda	32	48m 40.69s	1m 30.12s	13
10	Mike Baldwin	USA	Yamaha	32	48m 43.29s	1m 29.85s	11
11	Ron Haslam	GB	Honda	31	47m 53.93s	1m 30.64s	14
12	Marco Gentile	CH	Fior	31	48m 45.58s	1m 32.52s	15
13	Wolfgang von Muralt	CH	Suzuki	31	48m 47.89s	1m 33.27s	16
14	Vincenzo Cascino	RSM	Suzuki	29	48m 07.13s	1m 36.89s	17
15	Gerhard Vogt	D	Suzuki	29	49m 07.57s	1m 39.58s	18
	Raymond Roche	F	Cagiva	23	DNF	1m 29.14s	9
	Rob McElnea	GB	Yamaha	8	DNF	1m 28.84s	8
	Freddie Spencer	USA	Honda		DNS	1m 28.72s	7

Fastest lap: Gardner, 1m 28.79s, 96.62 mph/155.590 km/h (record).
Previous record: not available.

World Championship: 1 Gardner, 168; **2** Mamola, 146; **3** Lawson, 142; **4** Haslam, 71; **5** Mackenzie, 57; **6** Taira, 53; **7** Sarron, 52; **8** Chili, 45; **9** McElnea, 39; **10** Yatsushiro, 32; **11** Burnett, 25; **12** de Radiguès, 21; **13** Irons, 12; **14** Magee and Schwantz, 11; **16** Ito, 10; **17** Roche, 9; **18** Reiner, 5; **19** Kawasaki and Spencer, 4; **21** Scott, 3; **22** Katayama, 2; **23** Baldwin and Gentile, 1.

250 cc

27 laps, 63.71 miles/101.87 km

Place	Rider	Nat.	Machine	Laps	Time & speed	Practice time	Grid
1	Dominique Sarron	F	Honda	27	41m 22.22s 93.26 mph/ 150.08 km/h	1m 30.29s	1
2	Alfonso Pons	E	Honda	27	41m 25.66s	1m 31.41s	9
3	Carlos Cardus	E	Honda	27	41m 28.10s	1m 31.00s	4
4	Reinhold Roth	D	Honda	27	41m 34.92s	1m 31.39s	7
5	Carlos Lavado	YV	Yamaha	27	41m 35.01s	1m 30.74s	3
6	Luca Cadalora	I	Yamaha	27	41m 35.45s	1m 31.23s	5
7	Anton Mang	D	Honda	27	41m 36.60s	1m 31.30s	6
8	Loris Reggiani	I	Aprilia	27	41m 40.26s	1m 31.50s	10
9	Masahiro Shimuzu	J	Honda	27	41m 43.17s	1m 31.65s	12
10	Juan Garriga	E	Yamaha	27	41m 50.35s	1m 31.40s	8
11	Urs Lüzi	CH	Honda	27	42m 01.43s	1m 32.61s	15
12	Jean-François Baldé	F	Yamaha	27	42m 08.35s	1m 32.41s	14
13	Stéphane Mertens	B	Sekitoba	27	42m 08.52s	1m 31.54s	11
14	Patrick Igoa	F	Yamaha	27	42m 08.76s	1m 32.36s	13
15	Stefano Caracchi	RSM	Honda	27	42m 13.88s	1m 33.22s	17
16	Guy Bertin	F	Honda	27	42m 15.08s	1m 33.37s	19
17	Jean-Michel Mattioli	F	Honda	27	42m 36.56s	1m 33.14s	16
18	Jean Foray	F	Honda	27	42m 41.62s	1m 33.92s	20
19	Jean-Philippe Ruggia	F	Yamaha	27	42m 43.81s	1m 33.29s	18
20	Alberto Puig	E	Cobas	27	42m 54.48s	1m 35.04s	22
21	Bruno Bonhuil	F	Honda	26	41m 30.13s	1m 34.10s	21
22	Miguel Gonzales	YV	Yamaha	26	42m 28.25s	1m 37.53s	26
23	Luis Lavado	YV	Yamaha	26	42m 30.63s	1m 36.18s	25
24	Hervé Duffard	F	Honda	26	42m 32.85s	1m 35.58s	23
25	Eduardo Aleman	YV	Yamaha	25	42m 34.98s	1m 38.93s	29
	Martin Wimmer	D	Yamaha	26	DNF	1m 30.60s	2
	Sergio Granton	RA	Yamaha	22	DNF	1m 39.18s	30
	Raul Piloni	RA	Cobas	20	DNF	1m 43.46s	31
	Fernando Gonzales	E	Cobas	20	DNF	1m 38.76s	28
	Raul Calvelo	URU	Yamaha	5	DNF	1m 45.08s	32
	Alain Bronec	F	Honda	4	DNF	1m 35.67s	24
	Philippe Pagano	F	Yamaha	4	DNF	1m 37.82s	27

Fastest lap: Pons, 1m 31.25s, 93.95 mph/150.179 km/h.
Lap record: not available.

World Championship: 1 Mang, 136; **2** Roth, 103; **3** Pons, 93; **4** Sarron, 85; **5** Reggiani, 68; **6** Cardus, 64; **7** Wimmer, 61; **8** Cadalora, 55; **9** Cornu, 50; **10** Lavado, 44; **11** Garriga, 42; **12** Igoa, 39; **13** Kobayashi, 15; **14** Herweh, 11; **15** Shimuzu, 10; **16** Palazzese, 9; **17** Ruggia, 7; **18** Baldé and Vitali, 6; **20** Lindner and Lüzi, 5; **22** McLeod, 4; **23** Mertens and Taguchi, 2; **25** Bertin and Yamamoto, 1.

Wayne Gardner starts to open up a lead over Eddie Lawson and Raymond Roche early in the 500 race. Despite missing the apex here on two occasions, his championship rivals were unable to close on him *(above left).*

Early in the 250 race, Dominique Sarron was still trying to get away from Mang, Cardus, Wimmer, Roth, Pons and Cadalora. At this point it looked as though Mang might win but, with the championship his own and the bike not handling as well as he liked, the German let the Frenchman go.

Gran Premio de
ARGENTINA

The candles that had been burning at each end began to sag a little in the middle by the time the teams arrived in Buenos Aires. The Sunday night celebrations in Goiania had staggered on until it was time to get on the bus for the airport on Monday morning. Just to end things as they had begun, the organisers neglected to supply the bus they had promised, so a last-minute taxi dash became necessary to catch the flight.

Everyone knew that the bikes would not turn up on time in Argentina if they were going to arrive at all, but, with the teams spread out in hotels across Buenos Aires, the party spirit dissipated. Shopping became the major pastime, encouraged by an equally favourable exchange rate and some of the best clothes shopping in the world.

The exchange rate was good if you used the black market rate. Black market suggests covert exchange but in fact the rate was quoted in the financial section of each evening news and exchange could be made openly in any shop. The rate fluctuated slightly and the greedy were tempted by sharks propositioning in the street and offering a 5 per cent better rate.

The sharks succeeded in cheating at least three people out of several hundred dollars each by letting them count the wad of local currency but then doing a switch before the exchange so that the cash actually received by the duped party was a mere fraction of that expected.

The idea that rip offs were common gathered strength when Dunlop tried to reclaim their tyres from customs. In contrast to the previous week in Brazil, the tyres were there to be taken, but the customs authorities stated that because of the 1982 Falklands war it was illegal to import anything from Britain. The only tyres that Dunlop could lay their hands on were the 25 that had been shipped from Brazil on the bikes and spare wheels. These used covers were demounted and, with a bribe reputed to be $3000, these 25 were swapped for 25 new tyres from the bonded customs stores.

Michelin were also given a hard time by customs and more money changed hands before both tyre companies were ready for practice to start. As expected, the bikes arrived late. However, it was not the lack of machinery that actually held up practice but the circuit itself. The track used was the same as that employed in 1982 but with the addition of a chicane, intended to slow riders going into the fast left-hander onto the start-and-finish straight.

The chicane was still being built when practice should have started and it was the most Mickey-Mouse arrangement of concrete kerbs imaginable. No-one liked it; it was as tight as a trials section and dangerous as well.

Both World Championships had been decided and even second in the 250 class was unlikely to change, so the only interest lay in the struggle for second in the 500 class between Mamola and Lawson. The absence of real competition at the end of this long season probably robbed riders of enthusiasm for getting the meeting underway.

The riders' lack of enthusiasm was nothing compared with organiser Reinaldo Cozzani's lack of interest in safety or other rider and team requirements. Faced with the prospect of having no race at all, he was forced to concede the need for changes to the track. The loop before the start-and-finish was cut out, shortening the circuit and bringing it closer to the pits, and then redirecting the track through a bigger chicane that needed heavy straw-baling because of the proximity of the barriers. The track was far more bumpy than it had been in '82 and there was insufficient run-off for the fast right-hander onto the back straight. Lawson said it frankly frightened him but the departing World Champion also stated that there was no need to boycott the meeting. 'There are other places that are as bad. We should never have come here, we should never come here again but now we are here we should race. I am not saying anything to the other riders because I do not want to convince anyone to ride. If they did and got hurt I would feel bad about it. Of course I want to ride because I can still get second in the championship but that would not be important if I thought the track was unrideable.'

Mamola was one of those who thought the track *was* unrideable and was particularly voluble after free practice finally took place on Friday morning, over a day late, and after riders and mechanics had created the 'do it yourself' circuit out of straw-bales. Mamola's opinion was that the circuit was rubbish and the race should not be held. Together with other riders, he voted at a meeting between three possible circuits, and they agreed that the one they had used for the free practice was the best possibility. Nevertheless, the meeting voted 10:3 against racing at all, though there were several abstentions.

The team managers of IRTA met and decided that the event should go ahead so long as more straw-bales were made available, apparently confident that riders' lives would not be endangered by racing. The team managers' main fear was that if the race was cancelled they would never see the bikes again, for each had many hundreds of thousands of pounds worth of equipment to look after. With machines on lease from the factory it would have been an interesting point of liability had the bikes been lost in transit.

Losing the bikes may sound far-fetched but by this time there was a general awareness of the two-way bribery and corruption that operates in Argentina. Agostini recalled that in 1982, when there had been no problems, he had nevertheless been obliged to pay the airfreight before his team's machines were released from the airport in Europe, although this had, in theory, been paid by the organisers.

Mamola's antipathy to the meeting had nothing to do with the fact that, as matters stood, he would take second in the championship. He has always spoken from the heart whether or not it has been to his advantage and he honestly believed that the organiser's attitude was unacceptable and that to ride would run contrary to everyone's desire to see the sport progress.

More straw-bales were expected, but the time

for the first official 500 session came and went without any bales being delivered and without anyone even noticing that practice should have started. It had been rescheduled so many times that no-one missed it. A lone 250 going out for its first session brought the paddock to life and riders donned leathers as mechanics warmed up machines for a rather ragged start to the first timed session.

A second (or first, if you like) 500 session was run after the 250, followed by two 500 and three 250 sessions planned for Saturday. Even though he got going a little late, Martin Wimmer soon had the circuit down pat and was fastest on the Marlboro Yamaha. Half a second slower was Patrick Igoa on the Sonauto Gauloises, ahead of Honda men Carlos Cardus, Reinhold Roth, Dominique Sarron and Masahiro Shimuzu.

From the start, Shimuzu was closer to the pace than he had been in Brazil. The reason escaped

Peter Clifford

Lawson leads Gardner against the backdrop of Buenos Aires. The lake is part of the motor sports complex and one circuit variation encompasses it.

Inset: Bikes and empty crates wait for action while the organisers try to find a usable circuit.

him: he thought he was just doing the same as he had the previous week yet he was second-fastest to Roth in the next session and that moved him to fourth overall. He then topped the third session with a remarkable time that took pole position from Wimmer and became the talk of the pits.

Meanwhile, Gardner had started at the head of the 500 table and stayed there, with Lawson second ahead of first Niall Mackenzie and then Randy Mamola. In the fourth and final session Mamola moved ahead of Lawson whilst Mackenzie was fourth ahead of Shunji Yatsushiro who had fallen earlier and torn a finger nail from his left hand. It was painful but he wasn't intending to become a concert pianist, so the damage was not too serious. Wolfgang von Muralt was not so lucky when his Suzuki spat him over the highside. For a while he looked seriously hurt and was spitting up blood. That later subsided

but he was left with an injured ankle and a wrecked bike that prevented him from racing.

Another non-starter was Rob McElnea who thought he would try to ride with the still-swollen right hand but found he could not grip the bar well enough to work the throttle and brake. Costa had another look at the injury and confirmed his earlier diagnosis of a broken bone in the hand. Lawson was prepared to ride the no. 5 bike for a few laps wearing a jacket over his leathers so that McElnea could at least claim the SFr2000 for qualifying, but Agostini thought that was a bad idea. McElnea went back to Costa who cut off the light hand cast so that he could do just enough to qualify and then bandaged it up again.

McElnea, already ninth in the championship, was to lose that to Yatsushiro and see his no. 5 go to Niall Mackenzie who, like Shimuzu, had little idea why he was suddenly on the pace. 'I just feel

as though I am riding the same as last weekend, but here it is good enough while there I was well off the pace. The bike is running better but that does not seem to make that much difference.'

Mackenzie had the use of parts from Spencer's machines as the ex-triple champion had disappeared to Shrieveport before the race had been run in Goiania. Even Erv Kanemoto was at a loss to explain Spencer's absence from Argentina, for as Kanemoto watched Mackenzie in the Brazilian Grand Prix, Spencer was already on his way out of the country.

Kanemoto is as reticent as he is charming and much admired by all, but he cannot completely hide the fact that he is hurt by Spencer's comings and goings. As the situation unsettled Kanemoto, it was bound to affect Mackenzie, but in Argentina Erv was able to concentrate solely on the young Scot.

Kel Carruthers has always said he cannot

Right: **Masahiro Shimuzu was most definitely the star of the 250 race and after only three Grands Prix the Japanese champion will be a man to watch out for in '88.**

Coming through the chicane onto the start-and-finish straight, Shimuzu has a momentary advantage over Sarron, Pons, Roth, Cardus and Cadalora *(far right).*

Peter Clifford

understand why Erv puts up with so much from Spencer, and certainly Lawson's attitude to racing is a great deal easier to cope with. Unfortunately, Carruthers had to miss the weekend as he flew to Australia on hearing of a death in his family. The 500s were running well and his absence was not too disruptive but Wimmer had problems with the 250. Mechanics Trevor Morris and Colin Davies seemed to have cured a persistent misfire but they never found the actual cause and it returned in the race. It is just possible that Carruthers' experience would have uncovered the source of the malfunction before it turned a possible Wimmer victory into a disaster. Morris and Davies were unlucky not to sort it out for themselves; it was one of those frustrating misfires that proved elusive because of its inconsistency.

In the final practice session, Wimmer was determined to retake pole position from Shimuzu. He is a rider who always aims for a fast time in practice, going to the lengths of putting in the minimum amount of fuel only when he is ready to put on fresh tyres and go for a time. At the appropriate moment, Wimmer swapped wheels and transferred onto the one fast bike the fuel tank from the spare bike, which contained just enough petrol for a few laps. As soon as the spare tank was fitted, the engine began to misfire. It looked as though there could be a fuel blockage, so the tanks were swapped again, but without success. The plugs were swapped; again, there was no change. The battery was replaced . . . and the bike worked. By that point there was little practice left. 'I realised that I only had time for two laps. It had made me mad and I decided that one lap would warm the tyres up and then one lap would stuff the opposition.'

Wimmer must have been inspired because that final lap gave him back pole position; it was more than six-tenths quicker than his previous best and put Shimuzu second ahead of Carlos Lavado who had found over a second in that final session. Pons was fourth with Juan Garriga fifth on the Ducados Yamaha. Luca Cadalora brought a fourth Yamaha into the top ten, but they were to be nowhere near as competitive in the race. The riders were expecting that, because they needed a clear road to set a fast time, especially as the secret of a quick lap at Buenos Aires lies in having a good run through the right-hander onto the back straight. Wimmer said he was taking that in fifth while the Hondas were using fourth. Without a perfectly clear road, the Honda's superior power and speed held the advantage, allowing their riders to set a fast time with a less-than-perfect line.

250 cc

From pole position Wimmer started well, but Honda power buried him in the pack on the way down to the first corner. By the end of the first lap it was Dominique Sarron who led from Sito Pons and Loris Reggiani. Sarron fought hard to win his second Grand Prix in a row but there was no way he could pull away from the pack as he had in Goiania, and the Frenchman was chased hard by Pons, Shimuzu, Reggiani, Wimmer, Roth, Cardus, Cadalora and Garriga.

Shimuzu had been warned before the race that as a newcomer he might be bumped around a bit by the experienced hands if he became embroiled in a battle at the front of the field. Far from being put off by the idea, the quiet young Japanese was fascinated. 'How do they do that? I must find out.'

He soon discovered what it was like in the heat of battle, but he gave a great account of himself and was certainly not elbowed out. Neither wild nor desperate in the usual mould of young Japanese, he looked merely aggressive, controlled and very talented.

The leading pack of nine had quickly pulled away a little from the rest of the field. Both Carlos Lavado and Patrick Igoa had made mediocre starts and were suffering for it as they tried to make up ground. Gradually they succeeded as the pace of the front runners reduced somewhat, but Lavado found his bike slower than it had been in practice. Although Igoa struggled on and eventually caught the men in front he had abused his tyres so badly in the process that he was unable to make his way through the group.

Up front, no-one could extract a clear advantage, although Pons had taken over the lead from lap 3. He came under increasing pressure from Reggiani, who hit the front on lap 8 and clearly had the idea that the only way to win was to break away from the group. He tried harder and harder through laps 9, 10 and 11, before crashing on lap 12 when he locked up the front wheel going into the 180-degree left-hander at the back of the pits. Lawson was watching from the tower: 'He didn't even get to lean it over: he smoked the tyre and it tucked under while he was still going straight.'

That put Pons on the Honda in the lead ahead of similarly-mounted Sarron and Shimuzu with Martin Wimmer fourth on the Marlboro Yamaha ahead of Roth, Cardus, Cadalora and Garriga. Igoa was continuing to catch up, whereas Lavado had made a mistake and lost ground which put paid to his chances of joining the leaders.

Sarron was particularly hard on the brakes at the end of the back straight and got past Pons again on lap 13. Fourth was the highest Wimmer was able to reach because the Yamaha started to misfire and he slipped back, eventually to retire on lap 19 with a suspected power valve motor failure.

In his stead, Cadalora put the second Marlboro Yamaha amongst the leaders. By lap 19 the young Italian had passed Shimuzu to take third behind Pons; a lap later he was second and closing on Sarron who had briefly opened a small lead.

Cadalora was so quick through the right-hander onto the back straight that he could draw alongside and even pass Sarron down the straight but, as he approached the corner, he could not match the speed of the Honda, so Sarron was able to retrieve his lead several times on the brakes. Cadalora tried repeatedly but could not secure his claim to the lead. On lap 25 it looked as if he had succeeded, only to have Shimuzu steal the front position on the brakes in the same place.

The one place where Shimuzu had been making a mistake was the entry to that right-hander: by running in too quickly, he was too slow on the way out. Cadalora rocketed past and gained such an advantage that he held sway over the Japanese, with Sarron still back in third and Pons fourth. That quartet started to pull away from the rest, leaving Cardus to do battle with Roth, Garriga and Igoa.

With a clear road ahead and only two laps to go, Cadalora's claim on the first place now carried some weight, as Shimuzu, Pons and Sarron got in each other's way. That clear road was crucial to Cadalora's speed and on the second-to-last lap a mobile road block loomed ahead of him in the form of Alberto Puig, Bruno Bonhuil and Hervé Duffard who were engaged in their own private battle for 13th, completely unaware of what was approaching from behind.

Cadalora elbowed his way through but the time he lost proved crucial and it was Sarron who emerged first from the group. Cadalora's moment had passed and in the last remaining lap he could not retake the lead. Through the fast right and onto the back straight for the final

Peter Clifford

Frenchman had been relegated to fifth by Yatsushiro. Accelerating out of the 180-degree left-hander behind the pits on lap 10, Sarron's rear wheel let go and the blue Yamaha flicked him off just as it had several times before during '87. Doctors had warned him that landing on his head again could have serious consequences; fortunately, he was not thrown ballistically but was tossed in front of the bike, which then slid over his hand and broke a couple of bones.

The fall lost him his championship no. 6 to Taira, who was uninspired but comfortable in eighth place and ready to take the three points. Yatsushiro was unable to remain with Mamola who was increasing his pace. Nevertheless, the Japanese continued riding fast and consistently up to the flag.

Mamola's Lucky Strike Yamaha had been playing up in the early laps. 'It would not change cleanly from sixth to fifth and you should have seen my eyes bulge out of my head trying to get it stopped at the end of the straight. After about lap 10 it started to work and I could go quicker. I closed the gap on Gardner to three seconds and I could see he was having trouble with the tyre. A couple of times it got so loose I could see the side of the bike and then I knew I could beat him.'

It was not until lap 29 that Mamola actually went past and Gardner later said he allowed it. 'I didn't want Eddie to get no. 2 so I waved Randy past. If I had used the tyre I raced on in Brazil I could have won easily.'

Yatsushiro kept that lonely fourth well ahead of the battle for fifth which was the best of the race. Roche had held the position after a good start but by lap 18 he had been overhauled by Niall Mackenzie and Mike Baldwin, both riding well from poor starts.

Baldwin was first past Roche, but by lap 22 Mackenzie had powered in front of both of them – the pace of his advance made it look as though he might have a chance of catching Yatsushiro. The young Scot intended to, but failed. 'I had been trying hard and when I wanted to get away I found the front tyre pushed on a couple of corners and the bike ran wide.'

Roche was not dropped by the pair that had caught him. While Cagiva team-mate Didier de Radiguès had retired with a broken gear-selection mechanism, Roche fought back and both he and Baldwin passed Mackenzie once more before lap 30.

Baldwin had been of the opinion that his hand would last the distance, and even though he still did not have full movement in his wrist he was obviously finding the form that had made him no. 4 in '86. In the last-lap battle between himself and Roche, the Frenchman won by a whisker.

Lawson expressed surprise at the ease of his victory. His lap times were remarkably consistent and quicker than practice. Gardner had said before the race that he lacked the aggression he had felt before winning the championship and, not surprisingly, he had been winding down since clinching the title. Lawson might have remembered that he, too, had finished fourth in the last race of the season after claiming his first title, in 1984.

time, Sarron had a rear-wheel slide that lost him enough drive to allow Pons to ease past. Sarron looked to outbrake him up the inside into the last 180-degree right-hander. Cadalora lined himself up but had no chance of passing both on the white line. His move gave Shimuzu the room to go round the outside, so Hondas were able to monopolise the rostrum.

Cadalora was furious. 'The Hondas were so fast it was not even a contest.' Wimmer agreed with his team-mate, who had just eased him out of seventh place in the championship. 'We were faster than them everywhere but not on the straight.' The two Marlboro Yamahas had collided at one point, as witnessed by the scrape mark across Wimmer's right-rear number plate.

500 cc

The start was just one more organisational disaster. The starter was still standing on the grid when the lights flickered red and then green. Half the field left and perhaps it was unfortunate the gentleman was not run over. The race was red-flagged and a shortened version started half an hour later.

Mamola led off the line but to Lawson's amazement he then slowed. 'He reached up and adjusted the steering damper and I shot past',

said Lawson later. In truth, Mamola was probably adjusting the clutch as it refused to hook up completely.

That meant Lawson was able to lead into the first corner, with Gardner second ahead of Roche, Haslam, Mamola and Sarron. Mamola dived inside Haslam into the second corner and the British rider soon found that all the practice experimentation with a new front suspension unit flown in from France had not produced the desired effect, as he was forced to drop back.

Shunji Yatsushiro did not make a spectacular start but he was soon on the pace and catching Sarron and Mamola as first Haslam and then Roche fell behind. Lawson held the lead by a slender margin from Gardner and when the Californian got sideways coming out of the 180-degree left-hander behind the pits Gardner drew alongside and passed him. 'I only just held on', recalled Lawson. 'For a while I had a great view looking down on the front wheel.'

Gardner had a clear road but could not get away as his rear tyre was soon past its best. 'The Michelin guys asked me to try a tyre we had never raced on before because we wanted to test it for next year: it didn't last the distance.' By lap 7, Lawson was back in front and pulling away.

Sarron was having trouble hanging on to Mamoia who had taken second and by lap 9 the

Gran Premio de Argentina, 4 October/statistics

Buenos Aires, 2.146-mile/3.435 km circuit

500 cc

34 laps, 72.964 miles/116.79 km

Place	Rider	Nat.	Machine	Laps	Time & speed	Practice time	Grid
1	Eddie Lawson	USA	Yamaha	34	46m 38.25s 93.32 mph/ 150.272 km/h	1m 22.09s	3
2	Randy Mamola	USA	Yamaha	34	46m 49.64s	1m 21.79s	2
3	Wayne Gardner	AUS	Honda	34	46m 52.28s	1m 21.56s	1
4	Shunji Yatsushiro	J	Honda	34	47m 14.05s	1m 22.76s	5
5	Raymond Roche	F	Cagiva	34	47m 28.32s	1m 22.94s	7
6	Mike Baldwin	USA	Yamaha	34	47m 28.59s	1m 23.27s	8
7	Niall Mackenzie	GB	Honda	34	47m 29.40s	1m 22.76s	4
8	Tadahiko Taira	J	Yamaha	34	47m 52.65s	1m 24.05s	11
9	Pier Francesco Chili	I	Honda	33	46m 43.85s	1m 23.50s	10
10	Ron Haslam	GB	Honda	33	47m 39.99s	1m 24.23s	12
11	Marco Gentile	CH	Fior	32	47m 14.05s	1m 26.15s	13
12	Gerhard Vogt	D	Suzuki	30	47m 37.53s	1m 33.28s	17
13	Vincenzo Cascino	RCH	Suzuki	30	48m 12.32s	1m 29.21s	15
	Christian Sarron	F	Yamaha	9	DNF	1m 22.78s	6
	Didier de Radiguès	B	Cagiva	9	DNF	1m 23.30s	9
	Rob McElnea	GB	Yamaha		DNS	1m 31.97s	16
	Wolfgang von Muralt	CH	Suzuki		DNS	1m 26.51s	14

Fastest lap: not available.
Lap record: not available.

Final 500 cc World Championship points: see pages 198-200.

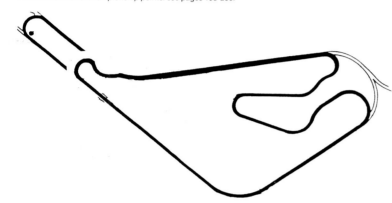

250 cc

30 laps, 64.38 miles/103.05 km

Place	Rider	Nat.	Machine	Laps	Time & speed	Practice time	Grid
1	Alfonso Pons	E	Honda	30	42m 56.52s 89.43 mph/ 144.002 km/h	1m 24.84s	4
2	Dominique Sarron	F	Honda	30	42m 56.71s	1m 25.63s	13
3	Masahiro Shimuzu	J	Honda	30	42m 56.99s	1m 24.51s	2
4	Luca Cadalora	I	Yamaha	30	42m 57.21s	1m 25.05s	8
5	Carlos Cardus	E	Honda	30	42m 58.77s	1m 25.10s	9
6	Reinhold Roth	D	Honda	30	43m 00.17s	1m 24.90s	6
7	Juan Garriga	E	Yamaha	30	43m 00.52s	1m 24.84s	5
8	Patrick Igoa	F	Yamaha	30	43m 00.82s	1m 25.62s	12
9	Carlos Lavado	YV	Yamaha	30	43m 21.82s	1m 24.80s	3
10	Stefano Caracchi	RSM	Honda	30	43m 35.75s	1m 25.27s	10
11	Guy Bertin	F	Honda	30	44m 02.76s	1m 27.14s	18
12	Jean-Michel Mattioli	F	Honda	30	44m 14.98s	1m 26.54s	17
13	Alberto Puig	E	Cobas	29	42m 59.88s	1m 27.78s	20
14	Bruno Bonhuil	F	Honda	29	43m 01.16s	1m 28.12s	22
15	Hervé Duffard	F	Honda	29	43m 02.65s	1m 27.85s	21
16	Luis Lavado	YV	Yamaha	29	43m 23.41s	1m 29.59s	26
17	Miguel Gonzalez	YV	Yamaha	29	44m 13.86s	1m 28.89s	24
18	Eduardo Aleman	YV	Yamaha	28	43m 24.93s	1m 30.77s	28
19	Raul Piloni	RA	Cobas	28	43m 37.32s	1m 32.29s	32
20	Nicolas Gonzalez	E	Yamaha	28	43m 37.89s	1m 32.86s	33
21	Philippe Pagano	F	Yamaha	27	43m 19.73s	1m 34.15s	34
22	Francisco Incorvaia	RA	Yamaha	27	44m 47.59s	1m 35.06s	35
23	Oscar Cobas	RA	Yamaha	26	43m 25.12s	1m 31.52s	30
	Urs Luzi	CH	Honda	22	DNF	1m 26.29s	16
	Martin Wimmer	D	Yamaha	19	DNF	1m 24.23s	1
	Stéphane Mertens	B	Sekitoba	18	DNF	1m 25.70s	14
	Jean-Philippe Ruggia	F	Yamaha	16	DNF	1m 26.12s	15
	Ricardo Bianco	RA	Yamaha	15	DNF	1m 31.78s	31
	Alfredo Rios	RA	Yamaha	12	DNF	1m 35.27s	36
	Loris Reggiani	I	Aprilia	11	DNF	1m 24.95s	7
	Jean Foray	F	Chevallier	2	DNF	1m 28.15s	23
	Anton Mang	D	Honda	1	DNF	1m 27.30s	19
	Alain Bronec	F	Honda	1	DNF	1m 30.04s	27
	Jean-François Baldé	F	Defi		DNS	1m 25.44s	11
	René Zanatta	RA	Yamaha		DNS	1m 28.93s	25
	Sergio Granton	RA	Yamaha		DNS	1m 31.36s	29
	Raul Calvelo	URU	Yamaha		DNQ	1m 36.61s	
	Claudio Incorvaia	RA	Yamaha		DNQ	1m 40.87s	

Fastest lap: not available.
Lap record: not available.

Final 250 cc World Championship points: see pages 198-200.

Below: **Sito Pons took his only win of the season and fought all the way for it.**

Opposite: **Season's shimmering sunset, slipping silently, silhouettes raconteur Roth's Römer's robust round rim.**

Peter Clifford

RIDERS ON THE STORM

by JOHN CUTTS, SuperBike Magazine

It was the TT's 80th birthday this year and there were more spectators present to celebrate it than at any time since Hailwood's famous comeback in 1978. With over 10,000 bikes and 40,000 visitors, the TT must be doing something right.

The pace of change in the Isle of Man is notoriously slow. The overburdened ferry service was worse than ever, although there were some encouraging innovations – Manx Radio TT broadcasting 18 hours a day exclusively for a TT audience was one of them. The course itself had been improved. The Sulby Straight had been resurfaced and was like a carpet compared to the bumpy ride of yesteryear. Quarry Bends had been opened out still further; May Hill was in better shape. These were small, sensible improvements probably worth five seconds a lap.

What the authorities can do nothing to influence is the weather. Contrary to popular opinion, the island's climate is neither severe nor extreme. It just rains a lot in June.

This year, the rain came down in buckets. The Manx have their own word for it – *fliaghey* – and it fell thick and fast from dark, stormy skies. When it wasn't *spittin'*, it was *mizzlin*. When the days weren't soft, they were fierce and terrible. Of course, the sun came out occasionally but over two weeks its performance was somewhat eclipsed by the rain.

Over the years, both riders and spectators have come to know that the weather can change around the course in minutes. This year, the rough weather set in for days. The 1987 TT races will largely be remembered for fast practice times and some appalling race weather. As always, though, come rain or shine there was plenty of fast and exciting closed-road racing to be seen.

Practice

The weather during practice week was near perfect. The local farmers bemoaned the lack of rain since nothing substantial had fallen on their fields for months, but to the newly arrived motor cycle fraternity the forecasted continuing fair weather was agreeable news. Racing conditions were mostly dry and bright. Even the 5.0 a.m. early risers were rewarded with clean roads and ideal visibility, and in the warmer evenings they could go still quicker.

Joey Dunlop set the trend on the first day. On Monday evening, riding the Honda VFR-based F1 machine, he shaved a second off his own F1 record at 116.5 mph, swapped immediately to his RS500 Senior bike and ran 115 mph. Fast times on the first day? Off the boat and straight on to the course, Dunlop was giving ample early evidence of his determination and status as King of the Roads. While the rest were reacquainting themselves with 37.7 miles of tar roads they hadn't seen for a year, Joey had already stuck a couple of big ones on to the leaderboard.

Tuesday evening saw him go still quicker on his F1 750 at 117.4 mph, but by then plenty of riders had their eye in. Phil Mellor, Trevor Nation and Roger Marshall had all clocked in under 20 minutes and Mellor, running 116 mph on his full

Kel Edge

house Suzuki GSX-R 1100 Senior mount, looked distinctly on form. He was consistently finding 15 seconds a lap over his previous best times.

On Thursday, during the only afternoon session of the week, Mellor fulfilled all his early promise by running a sensational 118.05 mph in 19m 10.8s. The time was just 4.4s off Dunlop's outright lap record and Mellor was suddenly elevated to the third-fastest man ever around the TT Mountain Course.

The time rocked the paddock and shook Honda. The real surprise was that Phil had been riding his F1 750 and not the abundantly more powerful and plain faster 1100 cc Senior bike. As is common when a record-breaking TT lap comes along, Mellor was completely unaware of his own fast time. He felt the lap had been no quicker than his previous 116 and simply didn't know where he had made those vital seconds. Everything had gone perfectly. The smaller bike might be fractionally quicker through the leafy, twisty sections but he knew the 1100 machine had horsepower and lively handling to spare and he wondered how much quicker he might go. Joey Dunlop wondered about it too.

In the other classes there were some notable leaderboard performances. Geoff Johnson, recruited to an enormous Mitsui Yamaha team (20 bikes for eight riders), topped both the big proddie classes. In the 1000 cc class he had run 112.2 mph on an FZR1000 while aboard the FZR750 he managed 110.6 mph. In the smallest of the four production classes, Barry Woodland had unofficially knocked the existing 250-400 cc record sideways with a lap of 104 mph on his FZR400, while in the 600 cc class, Honda CBR600s filled the first twelve places, led by Phil Armes at 105 mph.

A 350 Yamaha led both the F2 and Junior

classes, with Eddie Laycock and Steve Hislop both hitting the 110 mph mark. The sidecar times were split fairly closely between three experienced crews – Mick Boddice/Donny Williams, Warwick Newman/Eddie Yarker and Lowry Burton/Pat Cushnahan, all Yamaha 700 mounted and all on 104 mph.

Friday's final evening practice session was lost when heavy rain and thick fog descended. For a few competitors, the final session is important as a last chance to try, say, a rebuilt engine or different suspension. Although the weather was filthy and there seemed little point in going out, a surprising number of riders gathered, eager for a ride in the rain and the mist. At one stage the organisers announced that the waiting riders could have a closed-roads run, but only as far as Ramsey where travelling marshals would then escort them through the fog across the mountain. In the end, the skies turned black and the rain and fog set in with a vengeance, so the idea of even half a lap was abandoned. Storms raged all night. Only the local farmers celebrated the break in the weather.

Formula 1

Saturday dawned fresh and dry. By lunchtime the sun was out and everybody knew that the 226-mile World Championship race would start on time and be a slick-shod, heat and dust affair.

At 2.00 p.m. plus ten seconds, Joey Dunlop started at his customary no. 3 position and set off for a high-speed spin through the pretty countryside on closed roads. By Ballacraine on lap 1 he was reported to be ahead on the roads but slightly down on corrected time to Phil Mellor riding no. 10 at an interval of 30s. The first that Joey knew about the time difference was at the 13th Milestone when he got a signal telling him he was three seconds down. Something remarkable happened between the 13th and Glencrutchery Road at the end of that first lap. Dunlop started accelerating away on the tricky road to Ramsey at a hugely raised pace and he was rarely backing off the throttle. From the 13th onwards he was pulling back over a second a mile and Mellor had no answer to this dramatic raising of the wick. Through the quick and wooded sections as well as over the wide open spaces of the mountain, Dunlop forged ahead.

By the time he flashed through St Ninian's Crossroads to begin lap 2, he was 21s up and it had been announced that he'd run 116.4 mph from a standing start. Mellor had opened with 114.2 mph and while both stretched to a record-breaking 117 mph on the second lap, it was Joey who was always a shade quicker and obviously in control. He was reading his signals well and adjusting the pace accordingly. Racing against a considerable first-lap cushion, Mellor chased as hard as he knew how but Dunlop was ahead, alone and consolidating his lead. They took two fuel stops each but depot time was equal and Joey couldn't afford the luxury of a tyre change as in previous years. On his original Michelin

Kel Edge

Opposite: **Ten TT wins for Dunlop.**

Right: Adding a Junior TT win to his second place in the Formula 2, Eddie Laycock used Metzeler road tyres on the EMC in the tricky conditions and said they worked perfectly.

Just 17 seconds separated winner Steve Hislop from Laycock and Heath in the Yamaha-dominated Formula 2 race *(below right).*

Kel Edge

radials, he pulled away still further towards the end to win by 51s for his fifth consecutive TT F1 victory. He broke both lap and race records and was mighty tired and emotional afterwards. His VFR-based 750 had run perfectly after they'd reverted to early practice week suspension settings and Joey was unusually lavish in his praise for the bike.

For Honda, it was a most professional performance. All year, Joey had been struggling in the F1 World Championship but now, after a scorching ride on his favourite hunting ground, he led the World Championship.

Phil Mellor was an easy second and said afterwards that he had resolved to set off at his own pace and then raise it. He realised that he'd lost it on the first lap but simply had no answers to Joey's early burst and no complaints about his GSX-R. One spectacularly quick practice lap was rather different to a gruelling six-lapper, but Mellor gave it his best shot all the same.

Both Mellor and third-place man, Geoff Johnson, had their fastest-ever TT outings. Roger Marshall was fourth after being hampered early on by a GSX-R that wouldn't pull cleanly. The carburation didn't sort itself out until the last lap when Marshall was the fastest man at 115.3 mph.

Of the other championship contenders, Peter Rubatto was 7th, Glenn Williams 9th whilst Anders Andersson was out of the points at 12th. He would have collected a few points had his Suzuki's ignition not broken down on the last lap. Before that he had run 112.9 mph – not bad for a second-year visitor.

It was a hard race and the men up front were going for it all the way. But Yer Man had done it again and Honda had opened their F1 account at the most important date on the calendar.

Junior

The Junior race was run for 250 and 350cc two-strokes this year and proved a minor classic of the TT art. Practice had shown that on a dry course the 250s stood no chance. Their only tangible advantage over six laps was a single half-distance refuel against the thirstier 350s' two stops at the depots. But then a light rain fell over the entire course just before the start and tyre choice became yet another tricky variable.

By the time the first pair pushed away, the rain had stopped and the wind was about but the roads were wet everywhere. The surface was drying fast over the mountain yet it was still slippery and treacherous under the trees and anywhere the water could gather.

Steve Hislop led from the start on a 350 Yamaha wearing an intermediate front and a slick rear. The further he got round lap 1, the more the road dried out and he piled on the coals, pleased with his bike, his tyres and his ability to overhaul a lot of the early starters. Riding no. 28 at an interval of two minutes, he had a lot of traffic to clear.

By the end of lap 2 he was flying at 111.5 mph, by far the quickest man over the first 75 miles. His refuel confused things but by the fourth lap it

was clear cut. Hislop was two minutes ahead and sharing the road with the men who were behind him on time – Brian Reid and Eddie Laycock, both on 250 EMCs. The attentive crowds witnessed a fascinating dice as the three leaders threaded their way together around the course, racing each other and the clock.

The fifth time round saw the return of an ignition problem that had plagued Hislop in practice. The sparks began to falter. The two-minute advantage soon vanished as the bike began to sound sick and likely to expire. By Glen Helen he was parked and out of it.

Now Laycock saw his chance. He had made ground on Reid over the previous lap and on to the last they were just three seconds apart. It proved a fascinating struggle. Reid pulled away for sure but Laycock's starting interval was 30s and he could afford to let him go.

Laycock had prudently chosen to start the race on regular Metzeler road tyres rather than hand-cut slicks. It may have been a weird decision but he'd been battling through successfully enough up to this point. He lost sight of Reid on the run into Ramsey. While chasing Reid across the mountain Laycock survived a huge slide on his hot and shot road tyres through the notorious damp patches at the 33rd Milestone. The lights from Signpost Corner couldn't split them. Laycock got the win by five seconds from Reid in a thriller that went to the line.

Graeme McGregor was the first 350 home and Carl Fogarty was an excellent fourth on his 250 Honda. While Brian Reid muttered darkly about overgearing – a problem that really should have been eliminated in practice – Dubliner Laycock took the spoils. Considering his rubberwear, he deserved to qualify for some special award. Both men paid tribute to Steve Hislop as the fastest

rider on the course by a mile. But, as Brian Reid has reason to remember, every dog has his day ... eventually.

Sidecars

Held over two legs, the first victory went to Mick Boddice and Donny Williams, who led throughout the three laps, never stopped for fuel and crossed the line 30s ahead of husband-and-wife team, Dennis and Julia Bingham. It was the fourth TT victory for Boddice and the fourth runner-up spot for the Binghams who have never known what it's like to be first under the linen. The Binghams were never far behind but an exhaust mount fractured over the bumps of the final lap and Julia had good cause to lament being always the bruised bridesmaid, never the blushing if battered bride.

The second sidecar race went to Ulsterman Lowry Burton and Pat Cushnahan (700 Yamaha). Boddice/Williams had been close and with them on the roads until their outfit expired at Quarry Bends on the last. At the flag, Lowry Burton earned the distinction of becoming the oldest TT winner ever at 49, although he was still a mere boy compared to some of the ancient TT crews.

Dave Saville and Dave Hall were easily the first F2 350 outfit home in both races. However, the F2 class is also open to 1000 cc fours and in each race there was always one large capacity chair they couldn't get ahead of.

The overall two-leg aggregate victory went to Kenny Howles and Steve Pointer. The fastest lap of the two races went to Lowry Burton at 105.9 mph, so Jock Taylor's 1982 sidecar record of 108 mph remained untouched, possibly untouchable.

David Goldman

Kel Edge

Opposite: **Geoff Johnson demonstrated his TT experience once more by taking a fine win in the 750 Production race on his Yamaha. He also took second in the Senior TT and third in the Formula 1.**

Left: **A hard man to beat: Joey Dunlop was a double winner in the 1987 TT with the Formula 1 and 500 cc Hondas.**

Trevor Nation *(bottom)* **only stood on the rostrum once but tried hard all through race week.**

Below: **Lowry Burton and Pat Cashnahan on their 700 Yamaha won the second Sidecar TT and set the fastest lap of both races.**

Kel Edge

Kel Edge

Mez Mellor took second behind Dunlop in the Formula 1 race on the 750 Suzuki *(far right).*

Right: **Barry Woodland has accrued an enviable fund of TT knowledge, which doubtless contributed to his win in the 400 cc Production TT on his Yamaha.**

Formula 2

Wednesday was rained off so the F2 race was run on Thursday morning with the sun out and good conditions on the course.

No longer a World Championship class, the F2 was an odd affair, being a kind of rerun of the Junior but including a lot of Honda CBR600s. Practice had shown that the four-strokes stood no chance. The fastest of them had clocked 106 mph in practice while the two-stroke 350s were hitting 109 or 110 mph. In a six-lap race, the heat and the pace might claim more two-stroke retirements but it really wasn't likely that the fours would be in the hunt.

So it proved. The early leader was Brian Reid (350 Yamaha) but he was parked by Ramsey on the second with ignition failure and Steve Hislop on the same 350 Yam that had led the Junior was again stretching and picking up seconds everywhere. By the end of lap 2, Hislop had run a record-breaking 112.1 mph and held a 20s lead. He'd doubled that by the end of the third holding 40s over Graeme McGregor, with Eddie Laycock third.

Laycock had started cautiously, but once over the hump of half-distance he decided to raise the pace. Although Hislop led the fourth lap he lost a handful of seconds to his chasers. Laycock was now ahead of McGregor and closing the gap fast.

Somewhere out on the fifth lap, Steve Hislop started remembering how he'd lost the Junior while miles and minutes in the lead. Caution took hold and he started backing off. McGregor seized at Guthries which just left Laycock in flying pursuit.

The final lap saw 30s between them. By Ballaugh, it was down to around 20s, and Hislop's signallers implored him to get moving over the mountain. Two miles from home, Hislop was comfortably in the lead as he tired up Cronk-ny-Mona, a rising left-hander that tightens before the burst to Signpost. Hislop went in too quickly and the rear slick slid into the bank. He scared himself but survived to win the race by 17s from Laycock who ran the fastest lap of the race on the last of 112.3 mph. It was a just and well-deserved result for the pair of them.

Bob Heath, the visor king and 39-year-old holiday racer was third, his best-ever result and rolling proof that the TT is a mature game. The first 600 home belonged to Michael Seward who finished seventh. He had started with Dave Dean, another 600 man, and they stayed together for the whole race taking turns to lead with neither man able to break clear. The traffic made no difference and nor did the fuel stop. They were together on the same 100 yards of tarmac for the whole 226 miles. Seward's nerve held steady over the mountain and he beat his man by 1.8s over the line.

Production

As usual, the 750 and 250/400 cc race started with the bigger bikes departing first, which caused the usual problem of the 750 tail-enders getting in the way of the faster of the 250/400

men. It's bound to happen and the wise man (like Barry Woodland) asks for a higher starting number and a longer starting interval.

In the 750 race, Trevor Nation on an FZR had it in the bag, leading by 24s and hoisting the lap record to an almighty 111.6 mph by the end of the second lap when he refuelled. That wasn't to take on a full tank, of course, but a few litres – just to make sure he'd be able to go the distance. Somebody miscalculated. However much was put in, it wasn't enough. Nation recognised the tell-tale signs of an empty tank as he gunned it out of Creg-ny-Baa, less than four miles from the flag. He shut off immediately, knowing that he could coast down through Brandish and Hillberry saving what few drops of gas he had for Cronk-ny-Mona and Governors.

It didn't work out. Geoff Johnson (FZR) loitering forlornly in second was surprised to come upon Nation on the run down to Brandish and realised his chance – 20s in three miles against a man on a freewheeling motor cycle. In determined mood, Johnson cleared the spectators at Signpost Corner where he almost rode up the bank in his quest for the line. Johnson won by four seconds from a hard-chasing Brian Morrison (Suzuki GSX-R), with Nation third.

It was Yamaha's race for sure, with the tyre honours going to Avon (Johnson) and Pirelli (Nation). It also neatly completed Johnson's hat-trick of proddie TT wins, representing one apiece for Honda, Kawasaki and Yamaha.

The first Honda VFR over the line belonged to Nick Jefferies in sixth. Just for reference, the next one was 18th and belonged to Mr J. Dunlop of Ballymoney.

The race marked the return of Kawasaki UK to international production racing. They worked hard, prepared and practised hard, but they had no luck at all in the race. None of their three-man GPX 750 team made the top ten, although a fast privateer, Rob Haynes, brought one home in seventh.

The 250/400 cc class victory went, as the form predicted, to Barry Woodland on a Yamaha FZR400. Another veteran TT campaigner, mostly retired from racing now, Woodland had ridden the wheels off the 400 in practice and was the hottest favourite of the week. He made no mistakes in the race, whacking 33s off the lap record and establishing enough of a time advantage to take on a couple of litres of gas before the last.

Mat Oxley could afford no such luxury on his TZR250 and hard-charged, head behind the bubble all the way. Balked by the slower 750s, he had one memorable leap over Ballaugh Bridge some 20 mph faster than is considered safe. Oxley knew it was all to no avail though. He was the first 250 home, it's true, but Woodland won easily and Malcolm Wheeler on another FZR400 pipped Oxley by one second for the runner-up spot. The first eleven home all averaged over 100 mph. Race and lap records were savaged.

Road bikes on road tyres on real roads – the formula is irresistible, the proof is irrefutable. This year, Yamaha took the honours, most of the places, and hence all of the prestige.

David Goldman

Senior

Heavy rain fell all day on Friday with strong winds and dense hill fog covering the mountain road, so racing was postponed. By Saturday, the TT was running a day late and many spectators and racers were booked on ferries to go home, yet it was still raining and the mountain remained covered in fog.

After several false starts and inspections, there was a break in the weather at 2.0 p.m., so the organisers decided to run a reduced-length four-lap Senior instead of the scheduled production event. Almost from the start, weather conditions deteriorated rapidly. The rain came sweeping in and was bouncing high off the road. Fierce winds were gusting everywhere as the fog settled in over the mountain, reducing visibility between Guthries and the 33rd to near zero.

The first lap wasn't as bad as subsequent ones and Joey Dunlop, wearing intermediates on his RS500, made the most of the opportunity

to establish a lead. His opening lap was 105 mph. Phil Mellor was second at 103 mph, while Geoff Johnson, Trevor Nation, Roger Marshall and Andy McGladdery were the only other riders to lap above the ton.

From lap 2 onwards the event became a matter of survival rather than racing. Marshals' flags were out everywhere to warn of huge puddles and rivers of rainwater. The course was proving completely unpredictable: through one section the line would be fine, through the next and you were sideways. When you weren't sliding, you were aquaplaning. The wind could strike anywhere and kick you off line. In the mountain maelstrom, there were seven grim miles where it was impossible to see ahead.

Dunlop's RS500 triple was one of the few two-stroke entries. Most of the field consisted of Super One variations – 1100 cc road bike engines, overbored, moderately tuned and faster in a straight line than an RG500. Some of these bikes were geared for 190 mph and made their F1 counterparts look slow. In such appalling conditions, staying aboard these horsepower monsters called for delicate throttle control.

At the half-distance fuel stop, Dunlop still led but wanted to quit. He could see no point in going on; it was too dangerous. Honda officials persuaded him to continue.

Phil Mellor on a GSX-R1100 was actually closing the gap. Mellor wasn't stopping for gas until the end of the third lap and caught up with Joey on the road. By Sulby he was ahead and leading the race but Dunlop knew he could count on the time Mellor would lose in the pits.

Over Snaefell for the third time, Dunlop got back ahead. Visibility was at best 50 yards, but even at much-reduced speeds the winding road was impossible to see. Intimate course knowledge counted for everything, especially since no rider had experienced such appalling course conditions before.

Mellor never lost touch with Dunlop through the mountain mists. The pair of them were rushing upon back-markers, yet still Mellor hung on and by the time they'd reached the Creg and daylight, he was eager to get ahead before his fuel stop.

He never made it. Although wheel-to-wheel, Dunlop held him off and Mellor lost the line at The Nook approaching Governors and crashed hard. Victory went to Dunlop, the course expert. It was his tenth TT win and he won't want another like it. In terms of overall TT victories, only Mike Hailwood has now scored more.

Back in the paddock after the race, riders could be seen shivering in sodden leathers, glad it was all over and thankful they had survived. The 1000 cc production race was cancelled. The course was simply too dangerous and the riders had no desire to go out again in any event. The paddock degenerated into a sea of mud and the rain kept falling. For the first time in 80 years, the organisers were unable to complete the full TT programme... the rain had won. Fortunately, there were no brave losers.

A QUESTION OF TYRES

It was no great surprise that Wayne Rainey and Team Honda won the 1987 AMA National Championship Road Race Series. His ultimate victory had been expected. But what had not been expected was the transformation of Rainey from cool, all-conquering hero to struggling underdog in the course of the first US season with Superbike featured as the premier class (GP-style Formula 1 having been abandoned entirely). By the time the year was done, Rainey had lost more races than he had won and had taken his championship by a bare nine points, 143 to 134.

The spoiler in Rainey's perfect-start season was Kevin Schwantz.

Few people would have bet against Rainey and Honda when the season dawned at Daytona in Florida. Even Schwantz wasn't sure then that he and his Yoshimura-prepared Suzuki could win a race against Rainey, never mind the series championship. Rainey winning the first three races of the year reinforced the early-season idea that he was unbeatable, even though Schwantz had one problem or another as a plausible excuse at each of those early events.

But by the time the year ended at Sears Point in California, Schwantz had won five races to Rainey's three and had come close to the championship despite crashing while leading at two tracks. Rainey ended the season by publicly stating that his Honda VFR750F was inferior in handling to Schwantz's Suzuki GSX-R750; Rainey said that the balance of power had shifted from Honda to Suzuki at the racing year's mid-point.

The way Rainey saw it, Schwantz's Suzuki was visibly working better as the year progressed. Rainey figured that improvements in the machine made the difference, and he told reporters that it was frustrating to have to ride so hard with his bike fighting him and jumping around when Schwantz's Suzuki was running around the track as if it was on rails.

The turning point came at the fourth race of the year, on the tight, twisty Bryar Motorsports Park track in Loudon, New Hampshire. Schwantz could do no wrong, looking so smooth that his riding appeared effortless as he ran away from Rainey. Schwantz won that race and the one after, crashed while leading the next, then won another three in a row.

Rainey seemed tentative at times, uncomfortable. He told reporters that he always rode to win, that trying to win was the only way he could live with himself the week after a race, that gathering points for the championship was not his style. Yet, as the season wore on, there seemed to be less and less Rainey could do to counter Schwantz and the Suzuki.

There was more to it than met the eye. There was the question of tyres, Schwantz riding on Michelin radials and Rainey on Dunlop radials. In 1986 it had been the other way around: Schwantz on Dunlop, Rainey on Michelin. The two were often the only riders in a particular race using radial slicks. But Team Honda switched camps and made a deal with Dunlop after post-season testing. The reasoning, Team Honda

sources said, was that Dunlop, working exclusively with Honda, would give the team the best tyre it had, would pay close attention to the team's needs and deliver the best possible service. The fact that Michelin tyres had chunked underneath Rainey at Daytona and that Rainey crashed out of contention for the 1986 championship on a too-soft Michelin at Mid-Ohio encouraged the changeover.

Schwantz, on the other hand, tried Michelin radials on the Heron Suzuki RG500 in Europe late in 1986 and was convinced that the Michelins were far superior to the Dunlops; Schwantz wanted Michelins for 1987. Furthermore, Schwantz's personal contract with Dunlop conflicted with the Suzuki factory's GP Michelin deal, and Suzuki asked Yoshimura to change to Michelin for 1987. A deal was made.

Team Honda's initial belief in the superiority of the Dunlops faded when tyre problems cropped up at several races. As early as Daytona, Rainey and Honda team-mate Bubba Shobert were worrying about the feel of certain Dunlop front tyres. And when Rainey started losing in the later stages of the season, each loss documented in Honda press materials put the blame squarely on the shoulders of the Dunlops.

By the time the season was over, Rainey and Schwantz were convinced that the Michelins were better, and so were many top-running privateers. Michelin's introduction of for-sale 17-inch rear radials into US racing transformed racing grids into haves and have-nots by mid-season, the limiting factor being the supply of 5.50 x 17-inch wheels available for sale. Demand instantly outstripped supply, blowing all projections for the year out the window. At some races only used Michelins were available for privateer riders, and at others emergency air-freight shipments saw tyres arriving at the last possible moment. The Michelin racing tyre supply operation had the frenzied look of a short-order kitchen by season's end.

Supplies of Dunlop rear radials were better, but scarcely any of the 5.50 x 18-inch wheels needed for the Dunlops were available. Several privateers who had been with Dunlop for years had to change camps because it was easier to find a 17-inch wheel – without radials there was no chance to be competitive.

The idea that Schwantz's Suzuki had been changed and improved throughout the year turned out not to be the case. What changed was Schwantz's approach to riding, which was a direct result of what he had learnt whilst riding the RG500 in Grands Prix.

Even before the season started, Schwantz had a new, serious approach. He trained hard, shed what had been a growing good-time, party-down attitude, and looked to be deadly serious. To race Rainey, Schwantz knew he'd have to be in top form and would need to run hard and stay healthy – a combination that had eluded him throughout the 1986 season.

Schwantz looked good at Daytona, qualifying second-fastest to Freddie Spencer and inheriting pole position when Spencer crashed and was injured in the last qualifying session. Rainey

qualified third-fastest behind Schwantz.

Rainey took a cautious, go-for-the-finish approach and was running in second place when Schwantz fell on the 34th of 57 laps. Schwantz clipped a hay bale entering the back-straight chicane whilst diving underneath a lapped rider, the hay bale catching the Suzuki's front brake lever and sending Schwantz sprawling with a badly broken finger. Yoshimura's Japanese import, Satoshi Tsujimoto finished second, the only rider still on the lead lap, with Doug Polen third on a kit-equipped GSX-R750 with stock front forks and swing arm.

Schwantz left Daytona still uncertain that he could win.

Hilly Road Atlanta outside Atlanta, Georgia, was the next stop on the circuit, and it was lucky that Schwantz even got to race. His bike was underweight by half a pound; Tsujimoto's was several pounds light and he was disqualified after heat races. Polen, too, was light, and he also sat out the final. All that kept Schwantz in the race was a reasonable doubt about the accuracy of the AMA's scale, which seemed to read inconsistently.

The race was between Rainey and Schwantz; they traded first place several times, but when a fairing bracket broke and the Suzuki's fairing dragged entering a corner, Schwantz ran off the track and the race was effectively over. Rainey had two wins now, Schwantz a single second place. Shobert, who had crashed out at Daytona, finished third.

The dead-flat, fast road course at Brainerd, Minnesota, was the site of disaster and revelation for Yoshimura and for Schwantz. Disaster because Schwantz and Tsujimoto both fell as they entered turn one outrageously fast in Saturday practice. Schwantz was behind Rainey in lap times and was trying to run through turn one at full throttle, he explained later. He was passing a slower rider as he entered the turn, and a breeze was blowing. As his bike emerged from behind the slower rider's bike and was hit by the wind, Schwantz lost the front end and hit the pavement at what he later estimated as 160 mph. Tsujimoto, who was following Schwantz in the practice session, also crashed, for unexplained reasons (although marks on the pavement seemed to indicate that Tsujimoto did not hit Schwantz's bike or crash debris), and broke his neck. The injury ended Tsujimoto's US racing season.

Schwantz was materially uninjured, although he bruised over half his body and was suffering from pavement scrapes. However, the incident set him thinking hard about his approach to riding and about the fact that even when he pushed very hard entering corners, his lap times at Brainerd were slower than Rainey's.

Schwantz thought about something he'd learned riding the RG500 in Europe, a technique previously foreign to him, having been raised on Production bikes and Superbikes: the best way to enter a corner was to do all your downshifting with the bike upright while braking, concentrating on getting off the brakes early (instead of concentrating on braking as deeply

Honda was sure that in signing Wayne Rainey
(below) they had the championship wrapped up
before the season began. They were nearly
proved wrong.

Doug Polen *(right)* emerged as one of the
rising stars of the superbike series and
almost impossible to beat on the 600
production bikes.

AMA number one and fast becoming a great
road racer, Bubba Shobert *(below right)*.

177

Tom Riles

as possible), flicking the bike into the turn and accelerating around. The benefits included higher cornering and exit speeds, higher top speed on straightaways and increased smoothness. With the bike accelerating around the corners, the chassis loading stayed constant and suddenly the suspension worked better making the bike easier to ride.

Schwantz, bruises and scrapes and all, was suddenly close to two seconds a lap faster when it came time to race on Sunday. He lost the 60-mile race by five seconds, but suddenly it wasn't as hard to run that fast; his lap times were improved even though everything seemed easier. Shobert was third.

It all came together for Schwantz at Loudon, New Hampshire. It was easy, Schwantz said later. It was demoralising, said Rainey later. Schwantz led every lap, set a new lap record, won the race . . . and suddenly knew with certainty that yes, he could win, yes, he could beat Rainey. Schwantz would later describe the moment of crossing the finish line at Loudon as being the high point of his season. Rainey, meanwhile, was second, with Shobert third.

Schwantz followed up his win at Loudon with another at fast, tricky Road America in Elkhart Lake, Wisconsin. His bike was slower than Rainey's, and up the long front straight at Elkhart Rainey could gain what Schwantz later estimated was 17 lengths. But Schwantz could make up enough in various infield sections to negate that, and Rainey's blistering front tyre didn't help him at all. At the finish it was Schwantz by 15 seconds ahead of Rainey, Polen and Shobert.

Schwantz didn't win at Laguna Seca in California. Rainey didn't win, either. Shobert was the one to emerge victorious in the curious, two-segment race on the fast and scenic course. Schwantz won the first segment, shortened by crash-induced red flags; Rainey started the race at the back of the grid for allegedly jumping the start of a heat race. Schwantz started on the pole and led the whole way, whilst Rainey quickly reached second place but pitted one lap before the red flag with a blistered Dunlop rear tyre. He was credited with 12th place for the segment, Polen was second, Shobert third.

In the second segment, Schwantz led and Rainey gained, moving into second and taking over first when Schwantz came into turn nine (a 90-degree left-hander) and hit his knee on the inside curb, levering up his bike's front wheel, losing the front wheel, losing the back wheel and finally high-siding onto the ground. Shobert's first-segment third and his second-segment second (after Polen crashed) gave him the overall win, ahead of Jim Filice on a Yamaha FZR750 and Gary Goodfellow on a Suzuki Canada GSX-R750. Rainey's combined finishes were good for fifth overall; Schwantz was 13th overall.

But it was Schwantz as usual at Mid-Ohio Sports Car Course in Lexington, Ohio, winning by 13 seconds with Rainey second, Filice third, Shobert fourth.

And it was Schwantz again, at Memphis International Motorsport Park, a dragstrip with return roads in Memphis, Tennessee. Rainey was second, Shobert third, then Polen.

That brought the season down to the final race, at Sears Point Raceway in the hills of Sonoma, California. All Rainey needed was a single point (which is what 14th place pays in AMA events), even if Schwantz won. This time Schwantz was docked for allegedly jumping a heat race start, and Rainey started on the front row. Pundits declared there was no way Schwantz would be able to get through heavy traffic on the difficult Sears Point course and reach the leaders before the race ended.

It took Schwantz a handful of laps to take the lead and pull away, and he was well in front when first Polen and then Shobert crashed in separate incidents, causing the race to be stopped. At the restart, Schwantz quickly moved into first place and left, his riding looking smooth and effortless.

Rainey, frantic for his single point and the championship, finished sixth after an uncertain race spent in the company of riders he had never raced before and who therefore made him nervous. The race was nerve wracking for him, Rainey was to admit later, the longest race of his life, a race that seemed longer than all the other races of the season combined. His mind wandered at the forced conservative pace, and he thought of something different on every lap. But when it was over, Wayne Rainey was Superbike Champion.

Finishing behind Schwantz were Filice and Doug Chandler, with the final points order reading Rainey, Schwantz, Shobert, Polen.

And when the season's racing was done, the effect of currency exchange rates – the Japanese yen versus the US dollar – bore down. Team Honda had already started to contract with budget cutbacks. Rainey was released from the third year of his contract, to join Kenny Roberts' Team in 500 cc Grands Prix. Shobert would be carrying Team Honda's US banner in 1988.

Schwantz would also be in Europe, riding for the Suzuki factory. US Suzuki shuddered with budget cuts, too, and Yoshimura ended the year uncertain of what type of programme they would have or who would ride.

Private teams, like the Kosar Racing effort that backed Polen in 1987, faced equally uncertain futures. The volume of money available for chasing the premier championship in the US would undoubtedly shrink in 1988. There would be fewer paid rides, fewer works bikes, fewer sponsors, less support. Certainly the prospects at the end of 1987 were not what had been expected when the AMA dropped Formula 1 on the basis that Superbike racing would stimulate competition, reduce costs and help racing at America's top level flourish.

Meanwhile, in the absence of Formula 1, two classes showed great promise and intense competition. One, called Supersport, was open to 600 cc Production machines with minimal modifications allowed. Cam timing could be altered but stock camshafts had to be used; racing exhaust systems were legal and ignition

Wayne Rainey took second place at Mid-Ohio *(left)*.

Kevin Schwantz unleashes the power of the Yoshimura Suzuki. His riding was entertaining but errors meant that the championship stayed out of his reach.

Tom Riles

timing could be changed. But the bikes were to be standard in all other respects.

Honda CBR600 Hurricanes took over the class at the season's start and never relinquished their hold. Polen won eight of nine races and the series title, being the only rider to attend all nine rounds. Polen's single loss was to 21-year-old Thomas Stevens at Atlanta. Stevens finished second to Polen at six other races, didn't enter two, and finished second in points. But Stevens' performance on his Honda and on a GSXR1100 endurance bike attracted widespread attention; race observers were soon tipping him as the most exciting new American Superbike prospect since Schwantz was discovered racing a Yamaha FJ600 in 1984.

For close racing, though, it was impossible to beat the Castrol 250 GP class, formerly known as Formula 2. Four-times World Champion Kork Ballington of South Africa teamed with Briton Alan Carter on Bob MacLean's Team MacLean Honda RS250Rs with Michelin sponsorship, facing off former Formula 1 and Formula 2 champion Randy Renfrow on a Vance & Hines-sponsored RS250R running Dunlops. Three-times Formula 2 Champion Don Greene returned with his personal Honda, and Kenny Roberts introduced his Team Nordica Roberts effort with John Kocinski and Cal Rayborn III on Dunlop radials.

Kocinski, 19, came to Roberts' care and attention after a lacklustre 1986 season riding Yamaha Superbikes. Rayborn (son of late, great American Harley-Davidson rider, Cal Rayborn), started road racing on Production machines in local events in 1985 and gained attention with decent finishes in 1986. Putting Rayborn on a TZ250 was rather like throwing a non-swimmer into the deep end of a pool, but by season's end he had made a creditable showing and his riding had improved dramatically.

The star of Roberts' effort, however, was Kocinski, who moved to Modesto and entered a daily training programme with his mentor. Kocinski's duties in Modesto included maintaining a dirt track with a tractor and installing a sprinkler system for dry days, to hold down the dust. He learned much of what Roberts had to teach by riding lap after lap after lap of the dirt oval on a Honda XR100 – certainly an unusual road racing instruction method. He didn't miss home or family, Kocinski volunteered, when asked how he liked being uprooted from Little Rock, Arkansas and plunked down in a single boarding house room in California's Central Valley. All he cared about, Kocinski allowed, was racing, and he was willing to do anything to get to the top.

Roberts told Kocinski right away not to expect to beat Ballington in his first year. 'There's no way you're gonna beat Kork Ballington', Roberts said, in words that seared into Kocinski's brain, providing a drive he later admitted might not have been there.

At Daytona, Ballington won when Renfrow ran out of gas, despite Kork's last-lap crash, and it seemed probable that Kocinski never would beat his arch-rival. Kocinski was second at Daytona, and second to Renfrow at Road Atlanta, Ballington finishing fourth after run-ning off the track in the midst of a four-rider battle for first place on the last lap.

Ballington beat Renfrow and Carter at Brainerd, (Carter's debut) with Kocinski fourth. But at Loudon, Ballington, Carter and Renfrow all crashed, and John Kocinski won, beating Greene and Rayborn. Road America saw Kocinski beat Ballington heads up. It was Ballington versus Kocinski for the lead the entire way at Laguna, and when the pressure came down it was 36-year-old Ballington who erred, not rock-steady Kocinski. Ballington slid, got sideways, slid, and ran off the track, whereas Kocinski just won, neat and tidy.

Kocinski came from last to win the Mid-Ohio race, his bike having lost a cylinder intermittently due to a faulty CDI box sometimes closing a power valve at peak revs, and Ballington crashed. By the time Memphis came around, all Kocinski needed was a decent finish, and his conservative second to Renfrow, ahead of Carter and Ballington, gave him the title. Freed of that concern, Kocinski came to Sears Point ready to win, and did. Ballington, once again, was second.

Asked how it was that Kocinski turned around his season, Roberts said that Kocinski had learned to ride his Yamaha, that his lessons, which could not be learned overnight, had begun to sink in. Another year in the US and Kocinski would be ready for Europe, Roberts said, and he'd be a threat on a 250. Another year after that and he'd be ready for a 500, and he'd do fine. He's got time, said Roberts, because he's only 19.

Consider it fair warning.

Left: **John Kocinski learnt quickly from his own mistakes and Kenny Roberts' tutoring to win the 250 series handsomely.**

Kork Ballington (below) **used to be famous in Grand Prix racing for his faultless performances. However, mistakes in the US cost him the 250 championship.**

Devoted followers of the long-distance thrash didn't know quite how to react to Honda's winter announcement that they were to pull out of full-time endurance racing.

Depending on who you listened to it was either a blessing, because Honda's three-year domination of the sport was becoming stifling, or a disaster, because the withdrawal of the most prestigious team reflected badly on a series already beleaguered by the slump in the world's two-wheeler trade.

Hardly surprisingly, few riders bemoaned Honda's departure from the championship. The RS750s and RVF750s had proved invincible since they arrived on the scene in 1984. It seemed unlikely that anyone would have been able to stop them if they decided to go for a fourth title. But Honda had proved their point and felt it enough to enter teams in the three big crowd pullers of the endurance calendar – Le Mans, Suzuka and the Bol d'Or.

The news pleased no-one more than Suzuki endurance boss Dominique Meliand. Bludgeoned into defeat for three years running by the Hondas, Meliand at last saw the chance of another World title, his first since 1983. Despite lacking the machinery, riders and resources to beat Honda, he would have a relatively easy task in brushing aside the low-budget privateer teams that continue to make up endurance grids in the absence of factory Yamaha and Kawasaki squads.

Meliand retained the services of his top two riders from '86 – Bruno le Bihan and ex-World Champion Hervé Moineau, but third man Eric Delcamp was replaced by ex-250 World Champion Jean-Louis Tournadre, returning to two wheels after an abortive attempt at car racing.

24 Heures du Mans, 19 – 20 April

There was little talk of World titles at the Le Mans non-championship season-opener.

Instead, the paddock buzzed with vivid reports of the phenomenal speed of Honda's oval-piston NR750. The 32-valve V4 was making its race debut and had Honda factory officials smiling. After all the abuse and ridicule heaped onto the failed NR500 GP bike, here was moving proof that the oval-piston concept was workable.

Pushing out a realistic 155 bhp, the NR was piloted by Australian ace Mal Campbell and two journalists, Frenchman Gilbert Roy from *Moto Revue* and Japanese Ken Nemoto from *Riders Club*. Honda's inclusion of the two magazine testers illustrated that this was not intended to be an all-out attempt to win Le Mans but rather an exhibition of the bike's potential.

Yamaha meanwhile preferred not to get involved at all. They quietly refrained from entering the Genesis at Le Mans. After three humbling defeats at the hands of Honda in '86, Yamaha were gathering their forces for revenge, but the new Genesis wouldn't be ready until

Suzuka in July. The French Yamaha importers, Sonauto, however, blamed their non-appearance on the following weekend's Spanish GP. They stated they didn't want either Christian Sarron or Patrick Igoa (newly defected from Honda) to risk themselves so near to the second GP of the year. But, had Yamaha seriously considered they could have won Le Mans, then rest assured Sarron and Igoa would have ridden.

Campbell ended practice in second spot just behind the Honda of Dominique Sarron/Jean-Louis Battistini/Jean-Michel Mattioli. Campbell was convinced he could have snatched pole from the Rothmans-backed RVF if he had found a clear lap on the Bugatti track, which now boasted two tight chicanes.

Both chicanes drew nothing but criticism from riders. The first, installed to slow speeds through the Dunlop bridge curve, was blamed on the requests of car drivers. But a couple of months later at the 24-hour car race, the blame was laid firmly on the motor cyclists!

In bright sunshine it was Sarron who led from the start into the first chicane, rapidly setting up a lead that even slow-starting Campbell found it hard to eat into.

But Campbell's spirited attack in his first 24-hour race was in vain; without professional co-riders, the NR was unable to keep up the pressure and lay sixth after three hours with the leading quartet of Sarron, Gérard Coudray/Alex Vieira/Richard Hubin (Honda RVF), Moineau/le Bihan/Tournadre (Suzuki), and Pierre-Etienne Samin/Pierre Bolle/Thierry Crine (Kawasaki) all on the same lap.

A short while later the NR was out. A loosened big-end bolt had blocked an oil-way with its swarf, seizing a piston. Honda had fully realised that the bike might not last 24 hours but they were downhearted at such a rapid exit.

The disappearance of the NR at least made sure that Sarron and his co-riders would no longer have to contend with the embarrassment of being passed by Campbell, and by quarter-distance only Coudray's RVF was on the same lap. By midnight they looked comfortably in command after a Coudray crash put them three laps ahead.

But in the early hours the rain came and after Sarron lost six minutes making repairs to the rear brake, Moineau's Suzuki counter-attacked. Wet-weather ace le Bihan was sent out for particularly long stints and as dawn broke the Suzuki had a remarkable four-lap advantage. The lead alternated repeatedly as the track dried and the Honda was able to fight back on equal terms.

In the end, the RVF's superior speed told and Honda got the verdict by just over two laps. Coudray recovered from his fall to take third while Samin's semi-factory Kawasaki was fourth after he crashed in the night and had to leave his partners Bolle and Crine to carry on alone.

Estoril 1000 km, 10 May

The virtually empty Estoril paddock made a sharp contrast to the teeming paddock area at Le Mans. Few teams had bothered with the long, expensive and punishing journey across Spain and Portugal, despite the fact that this was the World Championship opener and the new track's first World title event.

Of course, all the top privateer teams turned up but it was difficult to see any of them giving Moineau and le Bihan a hard time after the Suzuki team's strong Le Mans showing.

The men most likely to were Frenchmen Patrice More and Bernard Chateau who had acquired an '86 factory Suzuki for the full season. It seemed all too obvious that the official Suzuki squad had provided this hardware to make sure that they had some competition, even if they ultimately held the upper hand.

As expected, it was More who gave chase to Moineau from the start, followed by the Bimota YB4 of Dutchmen Dirk Brand and Gerard Flameling. More, however, was having to ride his machine too hard to stay in touch with Moineau and he was soon slowed by a misfire which eventually forced his retirement.

That left Brand's Bimota, the Yamaha FZR of Team MCN's Mat Oxley/Geoff Fowler and the Swiss Honda VFR of Robbi Schläfi/Ulrich Kallen battling for runner's-up spot. The Swiss were soon in control, though, after first Fowler and then Brand ran out of petrol.

Team MCN's unscheduled stop dropped them to 16th and Brand, too, fell well down the leaderboard. But Fowler was riding brilliantly on Team MCN's modified roadster and, with 2½ hours to go, he had fought back to third spot with Brand and Frenchman Thierry Salles (Suzuki) in close attendance.

With Moineau's Suzuki safely in front and Schläfi comfortably second, the interest was settling on the third-place tussle when an unexpected rainstorm drenched the track just 90 minutes from the end.

Both the Suzuki and Honda were able to afford the luxury of stopping for wets but Brand, Salles and Oxley found themselves together on the soaking track on slicks. Only Brand made the wrong decision, calling into the pits for wets just before the track dried out again, while Oxley got ahead of Salles.

That left Team MCN to assert themselves in third as Salles slipped to fifth and Brand's costly tyre mistake dropped the Bimota to sixth.

Moineau and le Bihan, meanwhile, cruised home with a gaping lead of seven laps. Hopefully, it wasn't going to be that easy for the rest of the season.

By **MAT OXLEY**, *Performance Bikes*

WORLD ENDURANCE CHAMPIONSHIP

Donington Park 8 Hours, 24 May

World-class endurance racing returned to Britain for the first time since 1983, allowing Donington Park to stage a World Championship rehearsal for their first-ever bike GP.

The event started well, too, with Moineau's factory Suzuki down in third on the grid behind the Suzuki of Gérard Jolivet/Michel Simeon and Team MCN. Suzuki didn't lead right from the start either, but it wasn't long before Moineau used the factory bike's speed advantage to take the lead.

But, try as he might, Moineau couldn't stretch the gap and with two hours gone the Bimota of Brand and Flameling was closing. The heavy braking demands of the new Donington GP track meant that brake pads took particularly fierce punishment, and Brand crashed out at Redgate when his pads wore through to the metal. Although the Dutchman got going again, they called it a day after they realised a time penalty they had incurred for taking a short-cut back to the pits would make a good finish impossible.

That left Team MCN to take up the privateer gauntlet and after three hours Geoff Fowler had closed to within less than 30 seconds of Moineau. For the second race running, however, the Team MCN FZR ran dry just before a refuelling stop and Fowler was left with a short push-in. A faulty fuel valve was diagnosed but it was too late. Fowler had lost three laps pushing in and that was too much to make up on the Suzuki.

Jolivet and Simeon, meanwhile, stepped up the pressure in third, getting on the same lap as Team MCN who were being slowed by a sporadic misfire that had plagued them throughout practice. Despite their best efforts, the Franco-Belgian partnership were unable to close in sufficiently to mount a final attack.

Fowler was once again on top form, consistently lapping faster than the factory Suzuki and setting the fastest lap of the race to finish half a lap ahead of Jolivet and a further three laps ahead of Schläfi and Kallen.

Monza 6 Hours, 21 June

The Italians were also hosting a World Endurance round following a year's absence from the scene. And this time they had a reason for it: Bimota, already in with a chance of winning the World F1 Championship, entered their star duo of Virginio Ferrari and Davide Tardozzi aboard their beautiful FZ750-powered YB4.

Despite the factory Suzuki, the Italians had to be favourites for a win. They were on home ground and their bike was at least as good as the Suzuki, even though their engine was devoid of trick factory parts (despite pleas to Yamaha by Bimota race boss Frederico Martini).

Ferrari qualified in pole and led for all but the first few corners. It was interesting to see the Suzuki under real pressure again. Moineau and le Bihan refused to rise to the Bimota bait, however. They knew that the Italians were not intending to continue with the championship, so runner's-up spot would be as good as a win.

But as Ferrari led comfortably going into the second hour, the fortunes of four of the top privateer teams took a disastrous turn.

First the long Monza straights claimed the Suzuki engine of Patrice More. Just minutes later, Simeon also went out with a broken GSX-R engine. Within half an hour, Flameling crashed the Bimota he shared with Brand as he was forced off the track by a back-marker at the Parabolica. Flameling got going again but the team withdrew after they diagnosed gravel in the motor.

That left Schläfi and Team MCN as the two acknowledged top privateers to fight it out for the last rostrum position. But Schläfi crashed out when he hit a massive oil slick round the back of the track that claimed five other bikes.

All should have been easy for Team MCN from then on, but for the appearance of the very fast Harris GPX of Belgians Johan van Vaerenbergh and Eric de Doncker. An unnoticed sixth at Donington, their new machine was suddenly proving itself to be the best non-factory bike on the endurance grid.

For the latter half of the race the Belgians and Team MCN were separated by mere seconds until Oxley got oil on the back tyre in a pit stop and had to call into the pits for a tyre change. That gave third to the Belgians but Team MCN's troubles weren't over. Fowler crashed on a damp section of the track with just 20 minutes to go, completing the race sitting on the wildly bent subframe in sixth spot.

Ferrari and Tardozzi were triumphant by 1m 4s, averaging an impressive 106.9 mph. Suzuki weren't worried, though: their championship lead had extended to 15 points over Team MCN.

6 Stunden Motorrad Marathon Österreichring, 28 June

The Austrian round is traditionally the endurance circus's favourite non-24-hour race. The Österreichring, set high in the Austrian Tyrol, is beautiful, very fast and the restaurants in the area are excellent! The atmosphere is relaxed but race organisation is efficient.

For the first time in three races, Suzuki were back in pole position, with Brand's Bimota second on the grid and Team MCN third. Suzuki boss Meliand had not been happy with his riders' performance at Donington. True, the team had won and were easily leading the World Championship but their riding was becoming too 'safe'. They were beginning to be embarrassed by hard-riding privateers, desperate for success at any cost.

It was no surprise, then, that le Bihan led from the start and was already well out of touch by the end of the first lap, leaving the top privateers to flog it out among themselves.

Once more, the battle immediately behind the Suzuki turned into a war of attrition. Brand, Oxley and Simeon exchanged second place for the first hour until Brand was forced out of the running when his Bimota suffered an engine mount breakage that lifted the cylinder head and forced their retirement in a cloud of steam.

Two hours later Team MCN's FZR confirmed the mechanics' worst fears when a persistent trail of smoke from the oil breather heralded a broken valve. Oxley pushed the bike back to the pits but the Team were unable to carry on once the problem had been diagnosed.

That left Jolivet/Simeon in a relatively safe second spot. The privateer curse then struck them as well when their GSX-R750 threw a rod in the second half of the race.

That provided another chance for the Harris GPX of van Vaerenbergh and de Doncker to take advantage of their rivals' misfortune. Though they were riding well, the new privateer force in the World Championship couldn't make an impression on the leading Suzuki.

The intense Austrian heat had caught most of the endurance regulars by surprise, leaving the Honda VFR of locals Walter Oswald and Reinhold Gutzelnig to slot into third place just a lap behind the Belgians, a further four laps behind Moineau and le Bihan.

The only other World Championship contender, Schläfi's Swiss Honda VFR, scored fifth spot after losing several minutes from a first-lap crash.

Below: **Just one of Magee's brilliant rides was the Suzuka 8-hour victory on the Tech 21 Yamaha.**

Suzuka 8 Hours, 26 July

Every July the World Endurance Championship switches into a totally different gear when it travels to Japan. Very few of the full-time title chasers follow the series out east. Quite simply, they can't afford it and the Suzuka grid is instead filled mostly with well-heeled GP stars and immensely well-backed Japanese teams.

At Suzuka there are more factory squads than in the GPs and this race ranks only second to a World 500 crown in its importance to the Big Four Japanese manufacturers. A Suzuka win sells an awful lot of motor cycles in Japan.

The race is most important to Honda. They own the circuit: victory is expected; defeat is unimaginable.

This year, unbeaten since 1983, Honda fielded the same team that had won them a decisive victory in '86. Wayne Gardner and Dominique Sarron returned from their Rothmans GP duties to head qualifying from new GP hero Niall Mackenzie and partner Mal Campbell.

And it was Gardner who led in the early stages from Yoshimura Suzuki's Kevin Schwantz and the new Kawasaki GPX750 of Kork Ballington and Rob Phillis.

Soon the Honda established a commanding lead and only lost their advantage once in the first half of the race when the factory Yamaha Genesis of Kevin Magee and Martin Wimmer took over at the front for a brief spell. Then, just after half-way, Sarron crashed and rode the badly mangled Honda back to the pits. After several minutes repairing the damage, Gardner got back out in ninth place as the second Yoshimura Suzuki of Garry Goodfellow and Katsuro Takayoshi hit the front for the first time.

Honda's other factory entries were having no better luck. Mal Campbell had crashed his RVF out of the race while on line for a good result and Shunji Yatsushiro and Keiji Kinoshita were forced back into the pits when their RVF struck engine trouble.

New stars Goodfellow and Takayoshi, flying the Yoshimura Suzuki flag alone after Schwantz's first-hour demise, were desperately hanging onto their lead under immense pressure from the Genesis of Magee and Wimmer. The German was deputising for local hero Tadahiko Taira who had practised but was still unfit to race following his French GP injuries.

The situation remained the same up front for the rest of the race – Suzuki just leading from Yamaha. Gardner, meanwhile, had fought his way back up to seventh before Sarron crashed again with two hours to go. With no chance of a good finish, the duo decided to retire.

Kenny Roberts' protégés John Kocinski and Cal Rayborn were running well in third on another Genesis, whilst championship leaders Hervé Moineau and Bruno le Bihan varied their position from tenth to fourth in typical endurance style.

Suzuki looked to have the race wrapped up as darkness descended over the Suzuka track. But Takayoshi, out for the last session, was being caught at speed by Magee who had done 65 per cent of the riding in an effort to catch the Suzuki. It was all too much for the young Japanese. With Magee breathing down his neck, Takayoshi collided with a back-marker and crashed with just three laps to go.

He remounted but by then Magee had swept past to take the lead and, hardly believing his luck, the chequered flag.

The race itself made little difference to the World Championship, though. Moineau finished a very respectable fourth, his first Suzuka points in three years, while Belgian Johan van Vaerenbergh and Paul Ramon were a creditable seventh, making the trip with Kawasaki backing after impressing in Europe.

24 Heures du Liège, 15–16 August

Suzuki had by now gained a tight enough grip on the championship to allow them to field a second team at Spa who would not be held back by team orders.

With Moineau and le Bihan joined by Tournadre on the latest-spec factory GSX-R brought back from Suzuka, a three-man Belgian squad was assembled on the second factory Suzuki. Ex-World Champion Richard Hubin led the team completed by little Michel Simeon and Mark Simul.

The ride made Hubin a bit of a rarity in racing circles. In less than a year he'd ridden for three factory endurance teams with Honda, Yamaha and now Suzuki all glad to make use of his huge depth of endurance racing experience.

From the start, it was Hubin and old team-mate Moineau who immediately pulled away from the rest of the 55 starters. Sweeping through the fast curves that had robbed the Ardennes circuit of its July Grand Prix, Hubin got the upper hand and led the number one Suzuki after the first hour.

But without strength in depth the Belgian team dropped to second an hour later, only regaining the lead when Tournadre crashed after 2½ hours. Relegated to eighth place, Moineau and Co. were to crash twice more.

With the number one Suzuki out of the hunt, the battle for second was taken up by the top two privateer teams – the Belgian Harris Kawasaki and the Team MCN Yamaha, who were running their new Harris frame for the first time.

Team MCN had also signed up ex-Suzuki GP star Paul Lewis for his endurance debut. Lewis joined team regulars Geoff Fowler and Vesa Kultalahti after Mat Oxley broke a knee ten days before the race in a practice crash.

For the next five hours van Vaerenbergh, de Doncker and Paul Ramon swapped places with Fowler, Kultalahti and Lewis, with the little Australian often putting in faster lap times than the factory teams.

The battle continued into the night as Moineau's band worked their way back up to fourth place only to crash again. By midnight, Team MCN had established themselves firmly in second spot as the Kawasaki lost time with electrical problems and Moineau found himself back in third place with just one crash to go.

Then, with dawn just over the horizon, Lewis lost control of the Team MCN machine on the quickest corner of the track. Fighting a massive slide at almost 160 mph, Lewis was eventually thrown from the machine and miraculously escaped injury. Knocked unconscious, he was taken to the local hospital for a check-up, and Team MCN were unable to continue.

As Team MCN went out, van Vaerenbergh's Kawasaki showed its ever-improving form and fought back to overtake Moineau's Suzuki once more, finally taking a firm hold of second spot. There was no chance of them catching the leading Belgian Suzuki, though. Hubin, Simeon and Simul had run a perfect race and by the flag were an impressive eight laps ahead, with the number one Suzuki a further three laps in arrears.

Jerez 1000 km, 6 September

Moineau and le Bihan arrived at Jerez with a 30-point lead over the van Vaerenbergh Kawasaki. So long as the Frenchmen finished ahead of the Belgians in Spain, they would be the new World Champions.

Right from practice it seemed there was little chance of them being beaten. They qualified comfortably ahead of Team MCN's Geoff Fowler who was now partnered by ex-Bol d'Or winner and Suzuki factory teamster, Jean-Pierre Oudin. The Frenchman hadn't raced since '86 but, with Oxley still injured and Lewis and Kultalahti engaged in national races at home, he looked like being a good second man.

Against all the odds, the Suzuki wasn't leading at the end of the first hour. Instead, the less thirsty Yamahas of locals Jean-Miguel Pardo/André Garcia and Fowler/Oudin were ahead, with Moineau third.

An hour later, however, Suzuki were in first spot; with no other team coming within two seconds of their best lap time, they rapidly began to pull away from their pursuers.

The Spanish duo and Team MCN both dropped down the order now, the locals held up by less-than-perfect pit-work and Team MCN slowed by Oudin, who after such a long lay-off was not at his best. That gave the Belgian Kawasaki and Dutch Bimota a chance to make their charges.

After a luckless season, Dirk Brand and Dick Bemelman had qualified well at Jerez to claim second place on the grid, but the usual gremlins struck when they hit fuel pump problems in the first hour. Riding harder than ever, they were back up to eighth after two hours and from there on steadily gained on the leading pack.

Van Vaerenbergh and de Doncker were also pulling through after the Jerez debutants had made a slow start. It took them five hours to make the runner's-up spot, and from then on they were under increasing pressure from the Bimota, with Fowler also catching, followed closely by the ex-factory Suzuki of Patrice More and Bernard Chateau.

Moineau and le Bihan were able to watch this frenzied activity behind them without worry. Three laps ahead of the Kawasaki they were only concerned with avoiding crashing or breaking the motor to secure the championship.

Irregular lap bulletins meant that the protagonists in the fight for second place were actually a lot closer than they realised, and they were getting closer. Fowler was making a particularly hard last-hour charge and by the flag was just 20 seconds behind second-placed van Vaerenbergh, with the Bimota sandwiched between them.

For Suzuki it had been an easy championship win. At the Bol d'Or, though, they would have to work harder to prove their worth as the kings of endurance.

Bol d'Or, 19–20 September

All four factory teams arrived at Ricard to do battle for endurance racing's most prestigious prize. This was the first time since the capacity limit had dropped to 750 cc in 1984 that the Bol had played host to the Big Four on competitive machinery.

The fact that there were seven factory bikes entered didn't stop the race from being a two-way battle between the Rothmans Honda RVF750 of Dominique Sarron, Jean-Louis Battistini and Jean-Michel Mattioli and the Gauloises Yamaha Genesis of Christian Sarron, Patrick Igoa and Jean-Philippe Ruggia.

Yamaha had suffered four ignominious 24-hour defeats at the hands of the RVF and now they really felt they had the Genesis sufficiently well sorted to take their revenge. They'd already won the Suzuka 8 Hour and now the bike appeared for the first time in Europe with a single-sided swing arm, a vital factor in Honda's long-distance successes over the past 2½ years.

Christian Sarron eventually qualified his Yamaha on pole just ahead of little brother Dominique's RVF; for the third year running, the siblings lined up side by side for the Le Mans-style start.

The first ten laps turned out to be the best in endurance for years. As if they were starting a 45-minute GP, the two Sarrons swapped the lead every lap with hard-racing Alex Vieira on the Japauto Honda and first-lap leader, Pierre-Etienne Samin, on the rapid factory Kawasaki GPX.

Samin couldn't hold the pace, though, and had to let the first three go as they fought for prime spot in the nationally televised first hour's racing.

By the end of that first hour, the Yamaha had pulled out a tiny lead over the two Hondas, but it was Battistini who appeared out of the pits first. With four hours gone, Yamaha had again got back in front, a half-lap ahead of Sarron's Honda with the Japauto Honda of Gérard Coudray, Alex Vieira and Richard Hubin following behind a close third.

Honda, with little recent endurance experience behind them, were not their usual selves in the pits and that alone allowed Yamaha to continue to prise open the gap between the two teams.

Shortly after dusk, however, Yamaha made an appalling pit error. A last-second decision to change the rear tyre before the bike went out again went unnoticed by the mechanic operating the hydraulic one-sided stand. Just as the old rear wheel was thrown away from the bike, the stand was released and the whole bike crashed to the ground.

Honda were similarly embarrassed when just minutes later, their two machines both arrived together for a fill-up from the teams' shared quick-filler. The time gained when Yamaha messed up was promptly lost again.

By midnight, Yamaha had managed to pull out a lap's lead over the two Hondas, who were nevertheless still on the same lap. The remaining 80 teams were in a different race, Moineau's World Championship Suzuki as much as five laps behind in fourth place.

But Yamaha's lead wasn't enough to stop Honda regaining the advantage when Igoa had to pit for a new rear subframe and fairing that had been cracked by the Genesis's vibration. After the stop, Honda were 1m 30s ahead.

It took Yamaha almost two hours to whittle 30 seconds off that lead, and a further 45 minutes to close to within 20 seconds of the Honda. As the sun dawned over the rocky mountains around Paul Ricard, the two Sarrons were side by side, fighting for the lead.

Meanwhile, Coudray's Honda had gone out with a broken valve and both factory Kawasakis had been sidelined by ignition failure.

By breakfast time, Yamaha were a full lap ahead. Then at 10.45 they had to replace the rear subframe again and rejoined the track just 15 seconds ahead. Fifteen minutes later Sarron got a flat rear tyre on the Yamaha and pitted again, to give the Honda a one minute lead.

Yet, hard as they tried, Honda couldn't hold Yamaha's fight back to supremacy as Igoa closed on the Honda again. At 11.40, Igoa crashed the Genesis. The Yamaha needed new forks, radiator and fairing. Led tearfully from the pit, Igoa had handed Honda a three-lap lead.

Yamaha knew they'd lost but certainly weren't happy at taking second place in the best Bol d'Or since the old Honda/Yamaha battles of the early Eighties. Suzuki took third, a massive 12 laps behind the leaders, which proved to all that they'd only won the World title because there was no real competition.

EUROPEAN CHAMPIONSHIP

In the scintillating 250 cc European Championship class of 1987, the JJ Cobas concern took glory with their competent Spanish representative Javier Cardelus. His three dominant victories in Spain, Czechoslovakia and West Germany plus a second place in Holland have ensured that Cardelus is likely to be a very serious contender for Toni Mang's World title in 1988.

Cardelus was literally at home in the Jerez circuit as he scored a win in Round 1 from Dutchman Patrick van der Goorbergh, as Britain's Nigel Bosworth firmly established himself and the Keppel racing banner in the minds of their continental opposition. Unfortunately for van der Goorbergh and Bosworth, Spain was destined to be the high point for their season in the star-making series.

Swiss rider Bernard Hänggeli was fourth in Spain ahead of Cees Doorakkers of the Netherlands and a second Brit, Rob Orme.

Round 2 took the glamorous European Championship community to Donington Park for the British event. The amazingly quick Rotax-powered machine of Austrian Andreas Preining dominated practice, leaving him obviously confident of victory in the race. Victory was indeed his, but he was forced to work harder than anticipated when a gallant effort by Orme

almost scored a victory at Donington. Orme passed Preining as the pair began their final lap, but in hindsight it was the wrong move, 2.5 miles too early. Preining was able to use the Rotax capabilities to full advantage and he scored fifteen valuable points on British soil.

Van der Goorbergh took third with Hänggeli repeating his fourth place in Spain. Bosworth was fifth while young Steve Patrickson had worked very hard to take sixth place on the final lap. Much to his surprise, he was penalised one minute for jumping the start and relegated to 21st place. Champion-elect Cardelus had broken his collarbone a week before the Donington race yet still qualified; the pain far outweighed his courage, however, and he failed to score.

In an extraordinary third round at Austria's Salzburgring, Orme, van der Goorbergh and Preining all crashed, Hänggeli and Cardelus retired, leaving Austrian Stefan Klabacher to take victory at his home circuit on his exceptionally quick Austrian-built Rotax. Helmut Bradl on a Honda provided the German filling in the Austrian sandwich ahead of Engelbert Neumair,

Rotax-mounted, naturally. Wilhelm Horhager finished fourth (unusually, the Austrian rider rode a Honda), German Mitsui rider Jochen Schmid was fifth, while Bosworth struggled home in tenth spot.

The Most circuit in Czechoslovakia provided a second benefit race for Cardelus, winning from Neumair and a second JJ Cobas ridden by Spaniard Alberto Puig. Orme finished seventh but Bosworth was forced to retire with six laps to go after a petrol pipe came loose. Hänggeli finished just outside the points in 11th, Schmid opted for the Yugoslavian Grand Prix that weekend and unlucky van der Goorbergh crashed on the very first lap.

Assen Speed Week gave Schmid his only victory of the series, but he led home the formidable Cardelus, Neumair and Bradl. Bosworth was fifth and Andy Machin tenth on the Rotax. Puig struggled to start his Cobas and ran into the back of him, ruling both riders out of contention for a good score.

In his home round, Schmid was the recipient of Cardelus's revenge, being relegated to third place by fellow-countryman Bradl at the Hockenheimring. Cardelus had made sure of the title with this victory, for nearest rival Neumair could only finish 16th. Orme was 17th and

Bosworth 19th as the long straights of the German circuit revealed the truth about the European speed merchants.

The Mugello finale in Italy saw Bradl take advantage of the absence of Cardelus and Schmid to snatch victory from Italian Andreas Brasini on the Honda and Nedy Crotta, the latter piloting his Swiss Armstrong to a best-ever third. Bosworth crashed on the warm-up lap, breaking two bones in his foot, and Orme retired with serious engine trouble at half-distance – a practice spill had left the Raydel Yamaha rider with stitches in his arm before the race.

After four of the five 500 cc European Championship rounds, German Manfred Fischer had secured the title on his Hein Gericke Honda following wins at Donington Park in Britain and at Assen in Holland. Britain's Mark Phillips destroyed Fischer and his fellow contenders with a blistering victory in Spain on the Suzuki that saw Fischer second and Honda-mounted Italian Marco Papa third. Austrian Karl Truchsess was fourth and Daniel Amatriain of Spain fifth, both on exotic three-cylinder Honda machinery. Alan Jeffrey of Britain scored his only points of the series at Jerez with seventh place.

Phillips dominated practice at Donington Park but a crash in a Transatlantic Trophy race ruled the 'Captain' out with a serious arm injury. In a race featuring a strong British contingent, Fischer was pushed all the way to the finish by the pure grit of Steve Manley on his private Suzuki.

Three years after finishing fourth in the 500 cc class Steve Henshaw performed well on his Suzuki to take third ahead of a quartet of Hondas; Dutchman Henk van der Mark was fourth, Papa fifth, Maarten Duyzers of the Netherlands sixth, while Ari Rämö of Finland led home British riders Ian Pratt and Mike Lomas on Suzukis and John Brindley on an ageing Yamaha.

At Most in Czechoslovakia the talent of Amatriain shone through as he won from Truchsess with Fischer third, the German showing the consistency which eventually landed him the title. Van der Mark was fourth, Papa fifth and Duyzers sixth, but Phillips had held fourth place until the Padgett Suzuki seized, wrecking his chances of taking the title. With two rounds remaining, Fischer led Papa by fifteen points. The real interest concerned second place, however, for Amatriain was a single point adrift of Papa and just one ahead of Truchsess.

At Assen, for the Dutch round, Fischer took the title by his victory over Papa and van der Mark. Amatriain was fourth at Assen, leaving him in contention for second place overall. A fifth place for Truchsess meant he retained fourth on the championship scoreboard, whilst Mark Phillips struggled home in seventh place with a sick motor when earlier in the race he had looked set for victory.

At the Mugello circuit in Italy for the final round, Italian Massimo Broccoli gave the Cagiva concern victory. Fischer was absent, his title secure, but the fight for second place was still to be decided. Amatriain finished second but Papa was fourth giving him the overall runner's-up place by a point. Fabio Barchitta took third place on a Honda at his home round with yet another Italian Honda rider, Alberto Rota, fifth.

Although Fischer showed all the professionalism and consistency required to win a European title, he was also fortunate to have a very significant advantage: the backing of the giant Hein Gericke team.

The sidecar European Championship kicked off at Donington Park when British crew Ray Gardner and Tony Strevens stormed away to a comfortable victory over Tony Baker and John Hennigan. French pair Jean-Louis Millet and Claude de Broux were third in this Yamaha-dominated event. Seven British teams finished in the points at Donington, of whom German crew Fritz and Hubert Stölzle in fifth were to feature strongly in the final standings.

At the Most circuit the husband-and-wife team of Dennis and Julia Bingham took the fifteen points for their win over Swiss pair Luis Casagrande and Adolf Hänni and the Stölzle team. Millet was fourth, maintaining his series lead with the British Smith brothers, Barry and David, sixth. Casagrande was the victor at the Assen round, which meant the series lead passed to him jointly with the Binghams (following their runner's-up place in the Netherlands). The Stölzle team beat off Baker and Hennigan for third place at Assen with Gardner fifth and Millet sixth.

Millet had shown very competitive consistency and his win at the final round in Germany gave him the title from the Stölzle brothers after they finished third at Hockenheim. Toni and Kilian Wyssen from Switzerland split Millet and Stölzle in the fourth and final round. The Binghams' eighth place, however, was far from joyous and they finished third in the final standings – still enough to guarantee them a start with Millet and Stölzle in every sidecar Grand Prix during 1988.

In the fiercely contested 125 cc Championship, Spaniard Manuel Hernandez took an opening victory at Jerez on the Benetti but the interest lay with Adi Stadler. The MBA-mounted German held off Jean-Claude Selini for second place, while a JJ Cobas ridden by Fernando Gonzalez kept the single-cylinder Honda of Chris Galatowicz in fifth position.

At Donington Park, Corrado Catalano gave Stadler an exhibition as the Italian MBA star scored fifteen points. Stadler's second runner-up place seemed to suggest that his consistency might shine through in yet another European class of '87. Frenchman Gilles Payraudeau took third in the British round ahead of Danish rider Fleming Kistrup. Galatowicz was again fifth and revelling in the glory days surrounding his brave ride on the only Honda competing in the series.

The serious battle continued at the Salzburgring in Austria when Stadler scored his only victory of the year; nevertheless, Catalano made sure of the points by taking second place. German Seel rider Norbert Peschke arrived on the scene to follow Catalano home ahead of Payraudeau and Kistrup.

Peschke was in total control at Most as he stamped his authority over runner-up Catalano and third-placed Stadler. Fourth place went to Kistrup and fifth to first-round winner Hernandez.

The Netherlands hosted Round 5 and Jean-Claude Selini became the fifth different 125 cc winner as he led Waibel and Kistrup home. Stadler was fourth and Catalano lost his chance of championship victory as he reached the flag in a lowly ninth position.

Although Stadler was sixteen points clear and was now champion prior to Mugello, Catalano was keen to impress and won the final round from Italians Emilio Cuppini and Stefano Pennese. Selini finished fourth to guarantee his third place in the championship.

Hungary almost took a rare 80 cc title in the capable hands of Károly Juhász, but the Krauser star failed to repeat his winning rides at Most and the Salzburgring.

Spanish Derbi rider Julian Miralles was victor at Jerez from teenager Alex Criville – another Spanish Derbi star of the future – while German Günter Schirnhofer took a Krauser to third ahead of Juhász.

Juhász demonstrated his capability with his victory in Austria over Miralles and German Krauser rider Peter Öttl. Criville finished fourth to remain third in the championship.

The Most circuit provided the venue for Juhász's second victory and the series lead, but Miralles was third and only one point behind Juhász at the half-way stage. Second place in Czechoslovakia was West German Michael Gschwender on a Seel machine. Criville was fifth and showing astonishing consistency for a 17-year-old.

Criville was to take centre stage at Assen; his victory from Juhász and Miralles left nine points splitting the three of them, Juhász holding the advantage.

An identical result at Hockenhiem meant Juhász led Miralles by five points overall, and this second successive victory for Criville reduced Miralles' second-place advantage to just one point prior to the Mugello finale.

Miralles overhauled all opposition, however, by being first to the flag in Italy and taking the championship. Spaniard Francisco Torrontegui brought his Derbi into second place, aiding Miralles. Juhász could only manage fourth place behind Italian Giuseppe Ascareggi, while Criville's fifth position was enough to ensure that the three stars of the '87 series were all given a chance to prove themselves in the 1988 World Championship.

Twenty-two different makes of motor cycle scored points in the 1987 European Championship. No less than 135 competitors from 16 countries rode those machines to point-scoring positions.

The fact remains that the European Championship provides the natural breeding ground for Grand Prix competitors; the past season has proved to be no exception.

FORMULA 1 WORLD CHAMPIONSHIP

The Formula 1 World Championship dominance of five-times successive winner Joey Dunlop was obviously nearing an end when Honda announced their plans for 1987. With one eye on the future and the proposed World Superbike series, Honda took away the all-conquering RVF750 machine of 1986 in favour of a 'Superbike-style' model which Dunlop initially struggled with.

Early problems for Honda were noted by Formula 1 stalwarts Heron Suzuki. Their '87 hopes lay with the experienced double act of Paul Iddon and Roger Marshall.

Further opposition arrived on the increasingly colourful Formula 1 scene with the Italian Bimota-Yamaha concern. Their number one, Virginio Ferrari, was no stranger to the international stage, having been runner-up to Kenny Roberts in the 1979 500 cc World Championship. Fellow Italian Davide Tardozzi was the Bimota team choice to assist Ferrari in the campaign.

American Fred Merkel was also competing in World Formula 1 as a prelude to his World Superbike effort in 1988.

Suzuki were well represented with the Swedish team behind former endurance star Anders Andersson, contesting his second Formula 1 season.

The West German Suzuki machines were run by Ernst Gschwender and Klaus Caspers and the two private Bimota-Yamahas of Peter Rubatto and Klaus Klein were challenging the world under the Hein Gericke banner. British-based Kiwi Glenn Williams was campaigning a private Suzuki, as was Andy McGladdery, having twice finished fifth in the series over recent years.

The 1987 schedule was revised at an early stage in the season from a ten-round series to a best-ever eight-round series. The Imatra track in Finland did not meet the required safety standards and the FIM had no hesitation in withdrawing the Finnish permit. The Vila Real venue in Portugal was allocated a date in July for their round, but when the national general election caused the cancellation of an important Portuguese car event, the car event took over the Formula 1 date at Vila Real and the FIM refused to allow a change of date, leaving the organisers no option but to cancel their 1987 race. This left a calendar with the regular Italian, Dutch and German venues, first-ever trips to Japan and to Hungary, and the Donington Park final round, adding to the original two rounds of the inaugural 1977 Championship in the Isle of Man and Ireland controversially remaining.

The initial showdown of the Formula 1 contenders took place at the Misano circuit in Italy. The Skoal Bandit Heron Suzuki team were to draw first blood in the Italian sunshine. By lap 35 Iddon and Marshall were a massive 42s in front. However, Marshall was subjected to a constant rear-wheel slide and when he looked down he discovered oil covering the green-and-white livery of his leathers and his 750 cc machine. Marshall retired with a new lap record behind him, leaving Iddon to take victory by 20s. But the surprise package was in second place: 23-year-old American Fred Merkel on his privately-entered Honda. Merkel was overjoyed by his Italian debut.

'I was down on power against the factory teams and while they had sophisticated refuelling equipment I had a funnel and gas can', commented the Californian, who had made a late charge to beat Joey Dunlop by eight seconds. Fourth place was taken by West German Peter Rubatto on the semi-works Bimota-Yamaha. Talented British privateer Andy McGladdery and his home-built Suzuki followed Rubatto home to take fifth place. The Bimota team had a disastrous start to the series at their home round, Ferrari crashing on oil after 42 of the 75 laps and Tardozzi retiring with fuel pump trouble.

Round 2 set the scene for the best Formula 1 World Championship yet. The Hungaroring staged its first F1 motor cycle race and the competitors had mixed feelings about the surface after using intermediate tyres in the scorching conditions of the opening practice session. Joey Dunlop emphasised the problem by experiencing his first practice crash in four years.

The surface, luckily, had improved lap by lap in practice and come race day it was no longer a problem. The Hungarian round firmly established Ferrari and Tardozzi as serious candidates for the title.

Iddon and Marshall repeated the early-race tactics of Italy by opening a substantial lead but both were to crash out. Marshall said: 'I just lost the front end on the fast right-hander at the top of the circuit.' Marshall's words were to be echoed by Iddon: 'I had opened up such a leading margin when the front wheel just tucked in.' An obviously disappointed Iddon still held on to second place in the championship after Hungary. Ferrari and Tardozzi took full advantage of the Suzuki misfortune, although Tardozzi had caused problems for other riders on his charge to the front. He first took McGladdery out before Dunlop survived the Italian's fierce riding style two laps later.

Swede Anders Andersson took third place, making amends for his problems in Italy when a stone pierced his oil-cooler. Rubatto finished fourth in Hungary and took the series lead through his consistent finishing on the Hein Gericke Bimota. Jari Suhonen took his private Yamaha to a brave fifth place while World Champion Dunlop struggled down in eighth spot, hoping Round 3 in the Isle of Man would bring an answer to his Irish prayers.

Merkel never arrived in Hungary after a gearbox problem in Italy left him short of spares.

While most European riders preferred to stay at home, the rest of the Formula 1 convoy moved to the Isle of Man.

If 'Yer Maun' was going to lose his title it was definitely not going to be without a memorable fight, but naturally Dunlop won the Isle of Man round. In doing so, he established a new lap and race record. His margin over Suzuki TT draft Phil Mellor was 52s while third-place man Geoff Johnson was having his first encounter with the Loctite Yamaha in an excellent performance by the TT veteran. A disappointed Marshall came home fourth. 'The carburation was far from right and the bike just wasn't running well', said Marshall, who still managed to claim his first points of '87.

Dunlop was now in command, enjoying an eight-point championship margin over Rubatto who rode to a superb seventh and commented afterwards, 'Seventh was OK. I made some points; if conditions are bad here I prefer not to race.'

The Dutch TT provided the half-way point for the 1987 series. It was a race which will not be forgotten in the records of how Dunlop lost the title.

While Ferrari and Tardozzi fought out a personal battle for the lead, Marshall and Iddon sat behind the Italians, preferring to play a safer role in the background. Behind the Suzuki pair, Merkel was the subject of controversy as he had collided with Dunlop and the Rothmans Honda

The Bimota Yamaha *(opposite page)* **is a perfect example of what Formula 1 is all about – acquiring a roadgoing engine from Japan and putting it in the best-handling chassis that can be made.**

Right: **Suzuki tried hard to win the championship but Anders Andersson, Paul Iddon and Roger Marshall all had enough problems to keep them behind the Bimota.**

Reigning World F1 Champion Joey Dunlop *(below right)* **did not have the machinery or the backing from the factory he had enjoyed in the past.**

on the approach to the Assen chicane. Down went World Champion Dunlop, rising to his feet to wave a crowd-pleasing two-fingered gesture at the American. Some consolation for Dunlop came when Merkel was forced out, though still claiming, 'Dunlop ran into the side of me, it wasn't my fault.'

With the Italian dominance at the Dutch, Ferrari was on top of the world for the first time. None the less, Dunlop's position just two points behind him ensured the titanic tussle for honours would continue.

Round 5 was scheduled for the Ulster Grand Prix. Ferrari practised but then returned to Italy, not happy with the Dundrod venue, stating 'This circuit is too dangerous and not for my mentality.'

Atrociously wet conditions prior to the Formula 1 race left the officials in a very serious predicament; part of the 40-strong grid were willing to race while the rest were preparing to push their machines from the line.

The race was started but lasted only one lap before the worst happened. West German Klaus Klein crashed and lost his life on a circuit he had so much respect for.

Andy McGladdery had been injured during practice for the Ulster event; commenting after the ill-fated race: 'Formula 1 needs a representative like Mike Trimby in the GPs. When riders are sat on a grid they can't be expected to make decisions.'

Suzuki GB rider Paul Iddon told his version of events: 'I asked them not to start the race. They ignored me and said there was one minute to go.'

Paying tribute to his fellow-countryman, Peter Rubatto said, 'The Ulster Grand Prix is a bad memory. Klaus and I decided to change to rain tyres and then we started the race without a warm-up lap. Klaus just hit a very deep puddle. I lost my team-mate and a very good friend.'

As far as the championship was concerned, Dunlop had lost his one hope of regaining the crown. Victory in Ireland would have left him a very happy man.

As anticipated, Sugo produced nothing more than a domination by factory machinery. Aussie Kevin Magee piloted his Yamaha to victory with seven of the top ten finishers being Japanese. Anders Andersson took seventh place as sole European points-scoring representative. Unlucky Dunlop was twelfth while his rival Ferrari slid off after touching Dunlop's rear wheel following the Italian's fuel stop. Tardozzi and Iddon both suffered retirements, and Marshall lost his third place by crashing heavily, being very fortunate to escape unhurt. The top of the championship table remained the same.

The splendid Hockenheimring provided the venue for the penultimate round. For the third time in the 1987 Championship, Bimota were celebrating a Ferrari/Tardozzi winning performance. Third-placed Ernst Gschwender turned in his best ride on the Suzuki West Germany mount, but Dunlop was still not about to yield his title in haste. Showing his true character, the Irishman took fourth place ahead of a third Bimota ridden competently by local ace Bodo

Schmidt. Iddon eventually beat the Italian, with the Finn and the German breathing down his neck, to finish sixth.

Marshall was missing, having opted to neglect Hockenheim in favour of the televised Silverstone British Championship round. There were further problems for Andersson in Germany when his oil-cooler sprang a leak. 'From the start I could see something leaking', commented the luckless Andersson, who retired after two laps. Andersson wasn't the only rider suffering from the Swedish Suzuki trouble. 'Anders passed me on the opening lap and he sprayed oil all over my visor. I couldn't see anything and I lost fifteen places in one lap', reported Rubatto, who finished his home round in eleventh place.

The title chase was poised for the ultimate showdown seven days later at Donington Park. Dunlop desperately needed to put a ten-point difference between himself and Ferrari in the final round, but it was not to be.

The Team Suzuki Sweden mount in the capable hands of Anders Andersson led the race for eight of the forty laps. Iddon took over and from that moment the final race victory was to be decided privately between himself and Marshall, with Marshall knowing his fuel stop was quickly approaching while Iddon was prepared to risk 40 laps on a single tank. Behind the Suzuki pair, Andersson was being relegated

to an eventual fifth. Dunlop was on the charge after a poor start, reaching third spot on lap 10, but was then relegated for two laps by Fred Merkel prior to the American's fuel stop.

His usual cool, calm and collected self, 34-year-old Ferrari was paying his first visit to Donington Park since riding with a broken wrist in 1982 on an HB 500 cc Suzuki. Here, in 1987, he was lying fourth behind arch-rival Dunlop in this, the most important race of his fifteen-year career. As Merkel stormed out of the pit-lane and back into fourth place, in came Ferrari. A lightning stop saw him return to the action in eighth place. By the finish he had gained a further position which brought him the title.

A disappointed Marshall was runner-up to a jubilant Iddon who was ending the '87 campaign exactly how he started it, with victory, this time on home soil and on his 30th birthday.

Dunlop's hard-earned third place on the machine which had won the Bol d'Or seven days previously was not enough to prevent Ferrari and an excited Bimota concern taking their first title.

The closest Formula 1 World Championship since its conception in 1977 has emphasised that the future for World Championship events lies with the mighty roar of the four-stroke machinery, be it Formula 1 or Superbike, the former being favourite.

BRITISH NATIONAL RACING

Roger Marshall's march to innumerable race wins and his 11th and 12th domestic titles was, in one sense, the story of 1987, giving an air of consistency to National racing. But the 36-year-old Suzuki rider's domination hid another season of change in which the major trends of recent years were continued.

Production-based four-strokes have almost completely taken over the National scene. With no Honda Britain to contend with and with fewer privateers than ever riding Grand Prix-style 500 cc two-strokes, even the year's biggest races were left wide open to the big roadster-based four-strokes of Marshall and his cohorts.

The ultra-competitive 250 cc class continued to draw healthy grids but Gary Noel and Darren Dixon were just two for whom Kenny Irons' move from 250 cc struggles to Superstock stardom provided sufficient incentive to follow suit away from the real race bikes.

'The change to four-strokes and road-based

machines isn't something I'm in favour of but I think it's the way we've got to be looking if we're going to keep the scene healthy, simply on grounds of cost,' admitted the ACU's Colin Armes. 'I can see 500 cc Grand Prix bikes pricing themselves out of the market completely in the near future. They won't be available to anybody except factory riders.'

While the success of the British Grand Prix showed that there are still plenty of people who'll pay to watch top-line motor cycle racing, the lack of the biggest names in National meetings throughout the rest of the season was one reason why, once again, most promoters were lucky to draw a tenth of Donington's 50,000-plus GP crowd. It's a Catch-22 situation to some extent, for without big-name riders the spectators won't come, but without a guaranteed crowd the promoters won't risk making it worthwhile for the top riders to race.

Britain had five riders scoring points in 500 cc

Grands Prix in '87 but the factory stars appeared on home tarmac even less frequently than in recent years. 'Perhaps we should have a system like they do in Italy, where the top blokes have to ride in a certain number of National meetings to earn their licences', suggested Suzuki's long-serving Team Manager Rex White. The system is used in other continental countries, too, but White's Yamaha counterpart Steve Parrish was doubtful. 'The only way the top riders would appear is if the main sponsors like Shell and Castrol insisted on it', he said. 'The factories won't muck about doing National meetings otherwise.'

Even when the Grands Prix had finished there was no sign of the British factory men. 'We could have had the Elf out in one or two British meetings, and Burnett and Irons because they're finished for the year, but I don't think the promoters even rang them up,' said a disappointed Roger Marshall at Brands in October. 'The

Roger Marshall demonstrated that there is
plenty of life left in the wily old dog.

promoters have to make the effort to talk to the riders, and the riders have to make the effort to come.'

The sight of Messrs Burnett, Haslam, Irons, Mackenzie and McElnea clashing works-500 fairings would certainly give domestic racing a big boost if the problems of finance, date clashes and risk of injury could be overcome. If the full factory teams couldn't be persuaded to appear, Parrish's suggestion of late-season Superstock-type events featuring the top riders would be an alternative way of attracting crowds and creating interest in the sport. Britain's best riders are once again making an impression at world level. But if we only see them here once a year that's less likely to be true in a few years' time.

ACU British Championship and Shell Oils/ACU Superbike Championship

The 1987 British Championship produced some good racing but was no example of how the country's major race series should be organised. The format was confusingly changed once more – from last season's multi-round marathon to a truncated four-race affair in September and October. The late-season idea was to attract the aforementioned Grand Prix riders but it didn't have a chance: three of the four British rounds took place on the same day as, or the weekend before, the season's final 500 cc and 250 cc GP rounds in South America.

The ACU's major class throughout the season was the Shell Oils-backed Superbike Champion-ship. Formula 1 continued to thrive at world level but in Britain the class – whose capacity limit was dropped from 1000 cc to 750 cc 'for safety reasons' a few years ago, you'll recall – was axed and replaced by a Super One series that pitted 750 cc two-strokes against four-strokes of up to 1300 cc. Few people had believed that the old F1 litre bikes were too fast in any case so the Super One sounded quite promising. It was hoped that some of the old 998 cc dinosaurs would be dusted down again to take on the GP-style two-strokes and a newly-created breed of monsters based on the latest big-bore road bikes.

Unfortunately it rarely worked out like that. Advances in road bike technology would have meant a big struggle to make the old two-valve lumps competitive, and nobody bothered to try. The likes of Ray Swann and Mark Phillips put in the odd appearance on two-strokes between Grands Prix, but didn't take the British series seriously. And although both the Suzuki and Yamaha importer teams put together big-inch machines specifically for Super One, very few private riders did likewise.

That much was clear from the first round at Donington. Roger Marshall and Phil Mellor, their Suzukis an amalgam of GSX-R1100 roadster engine in last year's Formula 1 raceframe, diced for the lead, Marshall holding off a last-lap challenge to win by half a wheel's width. Keith Huewen dropped out with brake problems; Trevor Nation's similar FZR1000 Yamaha was never in contention in third. And behind

them Roland Brown, on a standard-framed GSX-R1100, motored past Ray Swann, Andy McGladdery and Jamie Whitham, all on 750 cc four-stroke Superstockers, to take fourth. There was barely another litre-plus bike in the race.

The Heron Suzuki team-mates broke away in Cadwell's second round, too, but instead of mounting a last-lap challenge Mellor crashed out at half-distance. Marshall won with ease while a hard-charging Colin Breeze led the Superstock hordes behind, taking second from Roger Hurst, John Lofthouse and Steve Chambers. At Knockhill, Marshall won again, with Mellor back in second ahead of Mark Phillips's RG500 and Paul Iddon's F1 World Championship-contending 750 cc Suzuki. Marshall may have lost his 100 per cent record at Snetterton, running on at the Esses before recovering to pip Ray Swann and his Honda RS500 for second, but Mellor's win still left the little Yorkshireman 18 points behind his team-mate in the championship.

Mallory Park saw the two-strokes get serious at last. With the British Grand Prix approaching, Marshall chose to try out the ex-Paul Lewis carbon-fibre Heron Suzuki RG500. He finished only fifth, after getting away almost last, but Mark Phillips won the race on his RG500 from Ray Swann's RS500 Honda triple and the four-stroke Suzukis of Mellor and Iddon.

Marshall was back on the 'Beast' and back on form in a great televised scrap at Thruxton, powering underneath Phillips to get the better of a three-way dice for the lead. Mellor, at the back of the trio, was a long way clear of Steve Henshaw's RG500. The same three riders broke clear at Scarborough and again Marshall took the win, just one of his five that weekend at Oliver's Mount. Mellor this time held off Phillips for second.

Just as at Thruxton, Marshall's big four-stroke had proved capable of beating the circuit's outright lap record. It was soon to be crowned champion, too. Torrential rain forced Silverstone's penultimate round to be cancelled and Marshall, 22 points ahead, won the title from the comfort of his caravan. He made sure by taking second at Brands, an RG500 wheel's width behind Mark Phillips, whose win secured third place, behind Mellor, in the championship. Roger Hurst, fourth at Brands behind Mark Farmer, ended the year fourth overall on his Superstocker.

It was a convincing display by the veteran Marshall, who seems to get faster every year. 'I think I'm riding better than ever,' he declared at Brands. 'I've broken practically every lap record when it's been dry and when you consider that Burnett and Gardner and I set them on Grand Prix machines I think that says it all.'

The big Suzuki had rather a lot to do with that, too. Powered by a near-standard road engine, the GSX-R put out around 135 bhp and provided plenty of entertainment. 'We nicknamed it "the Beast" and it really is a beast to ride because it smokes the back tyre out of corners and stands up on its back wheel – at Cadwell I looped it backwards and slid 167 yards and I'll never do that again,' Marshall recalled. 'It can be a bit of a

handful. You need a different technique: put it in too low a gear and it'll spit you over the handlebars. But I've really enjoyed riding the 1100; it's very entertaining and it's also very easy to set up.'

Most of all, it's a winner. Roger took his eighth official British Championship with equal aplomb, once again clinching the title without need of the Brands Hatch finale. At the soaking-wet Mallory opener he used all his experience to shadow Ray Swann's RS500 Honda, surging past out of the Devil's Elbow on the last lap to cross the line inches ahead. Jamie Whitham, on his Superstock Suzuki, held off Mark Phillips's RG500 for third.

Swann was again the damp danger-man at Silverstone, but once more Marshall held off the two-stroke triple. Keith Huewen finished third ahead of Terry Rymer and Gary Noel. Although Swann got ahead of Marshall at Donington, he couldn't stay there. The Luton rider crashed hard at the fast Starkey's Bridge bend. Marshall hit his bike, went onto the grass and came back on to pass Paul Iddon's F1 Suzuki and take the championship with his third win in a row.

Mark Phillips spoiled the 100 per cent record at Brands Hatch after a great dice that saw Marshall, for once, accept second. Ray Swann's third place gave him runner-up spot; Paul Iddon's fourth earned him that position overall, behind Whitham. The battle up front was again decided by less than a second. This year's 1300 cc British Championship might have been a story of too little, too late but the four rounds had produced some very close racing.

The 250 cc class saw plenty of action, too, and this one went all the way to the wire. Carl Fogarty splashed to victory in the first leg at Mallory, ahead of Irishman Gary Cowan and Kevin Mitchell. But Fogarty crashed his Honda in the next round, at Silverstone, and broke his leg. The experienced Donnie McLeod held off Lincoln's Andy Machin to win; Cowan again beat Mitchell, this time for third place, and inherited the championship lead.

The Donington race developed into a real battle between Machin, Cowan and Ian Newton. Newton eventually slowed, letting Steve Patrickson through for third place, while Machin pulled away to win. But Machin's no-score at Mallory, where he'd stopped with water in the carburettors of his Rotax engine, gave Cowan a seven-point lead going into the last round at Brands.

With the experience of a season's racing behind him the 23-year-old from Antrim, near Belfast, never looked like making a mistake. Donnie McLeod won the race to go third in the series; Cowan kept just ahead of Andy Machin to take second and became the new 250 cc Champion of Britain. 'I'd have preferred a few more rounds but this championship means everything to me – I really wanted to win it', said the delighted Cowan. 'At the start I reckoned I could do it if I could finish in the top three each time. Sometimes I could have gone for a win but I didn't want to risk it and it all worked out in the end.'

Cowan works as a fitter in a guided missile factory and has his sights set firmly on a career

in Grands Prix. 'Four-stroke racing seems to be the big thing in England now but I still believe that the cream of riders are on real Grand Prix machinery. I'm not tempted by Superstocks - it doesn't point riders in the direction of World Championship races,' he said. Cowan's Irish licence means that he, at least, will have no problem getting a ride on the Continent next near. For riders like Andy Machin, who was refused a place on the FIM grading list this season by the ACU committee, second place in the British Championship still meant no automatic place on the list for 1988.

While a four-stroke had dominated the Super-One series, the Super Two class - for 600 cc four-strokes and 350 cc two-strokes - had turned into a struggle between the pure 250 cc racing bikes and the road-based 350 cc Formula 2 two-strokes. Steve Williams won the last round for the F2s but generally it was the pure-bred 250s that had the upper hand.

Steve Patrickson won the first two rounds on his 250 Yamaha, beating Rob Orme and Kevin Mitchell at Donington and heading Andy Machin and Steve Hislop (on the leading 350) at Cadwell Park. Machin's charge started at Knockhill, where he won from Carl Fogarty (Honda 250) and Hislop, with Patrickson fifth. At Snetterton Machin won again on his Spondon-framed Rotax, beating Patrickson, Mitchell and Hislop to haul himself into contention.

Carl Fogarty could finish only fifth at Snetterton but, after rain had caused both the next two rounds to be restarted, the Blackburn rider won both, then came out on top again in the next round at Scarborough only to wreck his leg and his season in the British Championship round at Silverstone. Meanwhile, Steve Patrickson's consistency in finishing fourth, third and third at Mallory, Thruxton and Scarborough respectively had given the Shipley rider the championship lead.

Andy Machin, looking for a win at Oliver's Mount, had survived a frightening seizure on the Scarborough start/finish straight and lay second. With the Silverstone round abandoned, Machin, 14 points behind, knew that only a win at Brands would give him a chance. But the Lincoln rider struck trouble and was never in the hunt. Steve Patrickson kept cool and steered his Raydel Engineering 250 Yamaha to the title with a third place behind Williams and Rob Orme. The absent Fogarty retained his second place; Steve Hislop was the leading 350 cc rider in fourth.

Patrickson wasn't the only two-stroke man sweating on his championship chances in that final Brands Hatch meeting. World sidecar kings Steve Webster and Tony Hewitt lined up for the third and final British round knowing that they too could afford no mistake. The returning heroes had won both earlier rounds with little trouble. But the cancellation of Silverstone meant that both Yoshisada Kumagaya and Brian Barlow (second and third at Mallory and Donington) and Barry Brindley and Grahame Rose (who'd finished sixth and second), could

still pip them.

Webster and Hewitt made no mistake, of course, and took their third consecutive British title with yet another victory. They'd won every race they entered in Britain, and in 19 meetings worldwide hadn't once broken down. It was the perfect end to an outstanding year. 'Winning the first one's always the best but it's great to be British Champions again,' said a relieved Steve Webster. 'The short races here are quite a lot easier than the long GPs in hot countries but people like Brindley and Kumagaya were all capable of going very fast for those short distances. It could so easily have gone wrong.'

Tony Hewitt put the pair's success down to six years of steady progress. 'We're both keen to learn and we have learned a lot. This year we had the backing behind us and it all came together, so we've got to go out next season and prove it wasn't just a flash in the pan. I hope our World Championship will give British sidecar racing a boost - I know it did for us when we'd just started and Jock Taylor won a few years ago.'

MCN/EBC Brakes Superstock Championship

It was another good year for Superstock racing, with eight men surviving some fiercely competitive riding to take wins on three different makes of motor bike. The crowds loved it, and, by and large, so did the riders. But the thrills on the racetrack didn't always hide some equally bitter off-track confrontations which were perhaps inevitable given the championship's rules, drawn up to allow engine tuning within certain limits.

When Roger Hurst's Yamaha FZ750 was found to contain an illegal race-kit camshaft after he'd won a televised non-championship Superstock race at Cadwell Park, it became clear that the organisers' aim to strip the winning bike and one other from the top six in every round was not being carried out. Hurst, who'd won the Snetterton round earlier in the season, claimed a genuine mistake and said he'd been using the same engine all year. The incident emphasised the problem of stripping engines when riders often have another race on the same bike that weekend; or simply when they're in a hurry to go home.

However, the real problem did not concern obvious illegalities, but rather different people's interpretation of the rules. The Honda VFR750 Richard Scott had ridden to second place in the 1986 series contained a crankshaft cut in half and reweided to give a 360-degree firing arrangement, with cams and ignition modified to suit – against the rules, in some people's view. This year's regulations were changed to allow key standard parts to be 'otherwise modified', so the Honda was legal.

Yamaha's Keith Huewen (third behind Scott in '86) didn't like it and nor did Suzuki's Rex White. Suzuki protested and trimmed their official Superstock effort to one rider, Phil Mellor. The wily Huewen bit the bullet, joined Steve Parrish's Mitsui Loctite team alongside

Trevor Nation and set about making sure his own FZ750 was the fastest on the track. Honda UK, having announced their own team's withdrawal from racing, handed the 360-degree VFR to hardy Formula 1 campaigner Andy McGladdery.

But it was a little-known privateer, 19-year-old Terry Rymer, who showed the big names the way home by leading the Brands Hatch first round from start to finish. Huewen and Nation were second and third ahead of Ian Muir, like Rymer a south London boy out on his FZ750. Once again, the Superstocks had proved a star-maker, and once again there was a wide variety of machinery on show. Yamahas took the first four places but Phil Mellor beat Steve Chambers to fifth on his Suzuki. Behind them, McGladdery's Honda and Darren Dixon's Kawasaki GPX750. seventh and eighth respectively, meant that all four Japanese makes were in the points.

So Rymer had won on his local track, but how would he fare at bumpy, less-familiar Cadwell? After three days spent practising and a race stopped and run in two halves we had the answer - another win. The top four were again all on Yamahas, Roger Hurst taking second from Huewen and Colin Breeze. Mellor was fifth once more but starred at Donington's next round. He and Nation crossed the line so close together that they couldn't be split for the win. Huewen, in third, picked up more championship points; Rymer finished fourth to keep his overall lead.

If the Donington race was close, the next round at Knockhill in Scotland was even better. After an epic, multi-rider battle that could have gone any way, Andy McGladdery charged through to win from Mellor, Steve Chambers, Huewen and Ray Swann. It was Honda's first-ever Superstock win. Andy Mac looked like repeating it at Snetterton, too, when he came through the pack to lead with two laps remaining. But Roger Hurst, who'd crashed while in the leading bunch at Knockhill a week earlier, nipped past at the Esses and held on to take the flag. Behind McGladdery, the consistent Huewen, Gary Noel, Steve Chambers and Colin Breeze were all separated by a few yards.

Keith Huewen's third place had given him a slender half-way lead in the championship from Rymer, who could manage only eighth, and the Loctite Yamaha rider moved further ahead after winning Cadwell's sixth round. Pumped-up mentally and with his FZ750 ideally set up for the tight Cadwell track, Huewen led into the all-important first hairpin and never looked like being caught. Suzuki-mounted Jamie Whitham, back after an early-season injury, scratched round to second ahead of McGladdery, Roger Hurst and Huewen's Mitsui team-mate Trevor Nation.

Terry Rymer's sixth place meant he dropped to third place in the championship, but the south Londoner's flagging fortunes took a sharp upturn at Thruxton. Series leader Huewen hit tyre problems on the recently resurfaced track and McGladdery, his nearest challenger, was an injured spectator. Phil Mellor fought off Gary Noel to give Suzuki their first outright win of the

Phil Mellor enjoyed one of his best seasons ever.

series. And Rymer, third ahead of Nation and Keith Nicholls, overhauled Andy Mac and moved to within six points of Huewen's lead.

When Phil Mellor splashed into a handy lead in Mallory's next round, the Suzuki man looked set to move right into contention for the title. Then, with three laps to go, he threw his chances away at the hairpin. Jamie Whitham, who'd borrowed a spare bike from the Heron Suzuki team after wrecking his own in an earlier race, repaid them by taking the win and 15 points from Huewen. With Rymer a waterlogged non-finisher, Keith's second spot was still enough to open a 12-point gap with two rounds to go. Brian Morrison, third on the still-injured McGladdery's Honda, and Darren Dixon, fourth on a Kawasaki, made it four makes in the top four positions.

If the Mallory race was dramatic, it was nothing compared to the following round back at Cadwell Park. Yet another first-bend crash saw Keith Huewen and half a dozen other riders bite the dust at the 100 mph Coppice left-hander. Huewen's Yamaha was badly bent but the championship leader walked back to the grid, borrowed team-mate Trevor Nation's similar FZ750 and, ignoring the pain from his injured shoulder and ribs, stormed off to win the race and the series.

The victory capped a good year for the 30-year-old from Northamptonshire, whose Grand Prix career was wrecked by a Honda RS500 that wouldn't run right but who has never lost faith in his own ability. Property dealings have made Huewen financially secure but his racing ambition still burns strongly. 'I did the Superstocks this year because it fitted the bill, got me back in the frame, but next season I want to move on – back to World Championship level if the bikes and the set-up are right', he said. 'I'm good enough and I'm definitely not too old yet.

'Winning the Superstocks was the least I wanted to do this year but it hasn't been easy. At the beginning of the season the bike wasn't going too well and I was riding defensively to score some points; then at Cadwell I suddenly found myself leading the championship and from that point had to ride to conserve it', Huewen said. 'At most circuits I've been a second a lap quicker than Kenny Irons was last year and I've still had everyone breathing down my neck. Most people have caught up with the development of the bikes; they're all taken right to the edge of the rules now. But we've had a guy working full-time on our Yamahas and there was no faster bike in Superstock than my FZ750.'

The infamous 360-degree Honda was as fast as most but its year ended rather less gloriously. After McGladdery was injured, first Mark Phillips and then Brian Morrison were given rides on the Superstock VFR. And while champ Huewen cruised to fifth at Brands behind Whitham, Des Barry, Nation and Hurst – the latter snatching second in the series from Mellor and crash victim Rymer – the Honda exploded on the hill leading up to Druids. In a final, last-lap act of defiance it brought down not only Morrison but several other riders as well.

Despite breaking his collarbone in the penultimate round, Keith Huewen won the MCN Superstocks Championship on the Loctite Yamaha.

The Production Championships

While production-based machinery continued to take over from out-and-out racing bikes in almost all classes, pure production racing, using standard or near-standard bikes running on road tyres, was also enjoying a gradual increase in popularity. The suitability of modern machines and tyres for racing, straight out of the crate, means that even the best riders now have few qualms about having a go, especially when there's often quite generous prize money to be won.

Geoff Johnson is the acknowledged production bike expert at the Isle of Man TT, where racing on road bikes has really hit the big time in recent years. The twice Proddy TT winner took an early lead in the 1100 cc Metzeler series, winning Donington's first round on his Yamaha FZR1000 and taking second, behind the Suzuki of Ian Wilson, at Cadwell. Brian Morrison had crashed at Donington and finished only sixth at Cadwell but the Scot came back to win the next three rounds (Knockhill, Snetterton and Mallory) and draw level in the series with Johnson and the consistent Phil Mellor.

Mellor fought off a race-long challenge from Ian Wilkinson to win the next round at Thruxton. But Brian Morrison, third at the Hampshire track, won at Scarborough to close the gap to two points. Mellor kept in front by finishing second ahead of Geoff Johnson, who'd crashed at Thruxton, and Wilson.

An exciting climax to the season was spoiled first at soggy Silverstone, where the big proddy race was one of the many to be cancelled, and then at Brands where both series leader Mellor and Ian Wilson were forced to sit out the last round with injuries. Brian Morrison needed only a safe seventh place but raced off to take the championship with yet another win. Tony Thompson kept his Suzuki just ahead of the Yamaha of Johnson, whose third at Brands was enough to take that spot in the championship from Wilson. Suzukis had won the battle of the big road rockets, although the Yamaha FZR of David Pickworth and Colin Ward had earlier taken all three legs of the Pirelli-sponsored six-hour production endurance series.

The 750 cc Metzeler class was all over before Brands Hatch thanks to Phil Mellor, champion in both classes in 1986. The Suzuki rider won the first two rounds and then placed third, first, second, second and first in his next five races. A steady fourth place at streaming Silverstone was enough to give Mellor the championship and he rounded off the year with another second, behind Morrison, at Brands.

Ray Stringer's third at Brands was enough to give the Nuneaton rider second place in the series, ahead of Morrison and John Lofthouse. All rode Suzuki GSX-R750s, the lightweight Suzuki having seen off early Kawasaki challenges to monopolise what were generally full grids. The 1300 cc series attracted fewer entries and for next year the two classes will be combined (and a 600 cc four-stroke limit introduced).

Honda's new £8300 VFR750R road bike, an almost exact replica of the hugely successful RVF750 racer, will quite likely be a winner against the bigger machines. It's to be hoped that the new bike doesn't dominate too much, though. This year, a National production race could be won on a low-mileage GSX-R bought for about £3000. A new Honda, complete with the race pipe which next season will be allowed under mainland proddy rules, will cost almost three times as much. If that sum is what's needed for a competitive bike it won't be only production racing that suffers.

A Honda was certainly needed to win in the Honda/*Bike* CBR600 Challenge, which replaced last year's VF500 Cup as the method by which Honda sold plenty of middleweight fours (and even more fairings). The series was organised with dealer support and proved popular enough to need heats early in the season before the numbers took their toll and some of the less successful riders (and their sponsors) began to lose heart. At the front just seconds often covered all the finalists' race times. The identical red bikes – standard four-cylinder machines using road tyres but with racing pipes fitted – produced some fast and spectacular racing.

Eight different riders won the first eight rounds but only one of them could produce the consistency needed for the championship. While everyone around him soared and then fell, 35-year-old Geoff Johnson scored a top-four finish in all of the first seven rounds to take a massive 36-point lead in the series with three races to go. He pulled out of the Mallory downpour but in Silverstone's even wetter conditions Johnson was crowned Champion without having to turn a wheel. The cancelled race meant no-one could catch him and the Yorkshireman celebrated by winning the last round at Brands. Knockhill winner Eric McFarlane's fourth at Brands gave him second in the Challenge ahead of fellow-Scot Brian Morrison.

The Yamaha SBS/TZR 250 Challenge continued, after a year's break, the tradition of single-make scrapping upheld for so many years by Yamaha's RD350LC. Unfortunately, there was no return to the old system by which importers Mitsui provided the tools of destruction. Three riders dominated, their respective fortunes changing sharply during the course of the season.

Mike Edwards started the year well and looked a possible champion but crashed and missed crucial rounds through injury. Back to winning form by the Brands finale, he could manage only third in the series. Darren Dixon started just a little erratically, finishing crash-crash-win-crash-crash in the first five rounds after leading the lot. But by mid-season he'd got the winning knack, coming through to take second place in the championship.

The top two riders from all the countries with a Yamaha race series were invited to a late-season World Final at the Vallelunga circuit near Rome. Dixon produced a daring last-lap outbraking manoeuvre to take second place and end his season on a high note. But Leeds rider Gary Thrush, who had put together a season of faultless consistency to win the home TZR Challenge by a distance, crashed out at Vallelunga and then repeated the trick – this time on his own blue Yamaha – in the last British round at Brands Hatch.

Wayne Rainey and Kevin Schwantz set the annual Transatlantic on its way; both were clearly superior to any member of the British team.

It is just possible that when the Britain versus America motor cycle race series was dreamt up, back in the days of Triumph triples and open-face helmets, the contest was seen as a real team event. Old Country against New, Limeys versus Yanks, Union Jack against Stars and Stripes – unselfish tactical riding from fellow-countrymen pulling together to see off the foreign opposition.

The scene changes to Brands Hatch, Easter 1987. Transatlantic Race Two, final lap: Wayne Rainey flicks his gleaming factory Honda inside Kevin Schwantz to retake the lead at Druids hairpin and blasts down the hill, sound from the four-stroke Superbikes' exhausts echoing round the short circuit's natural bowl. The two have been neck and neck all race, chopping and changing the lead way ahead of the field. Now Schwantz is inches behind along the back straight and, as Rainey peels off for Clearways, hurls his Suzuki inside. The bikes crunch together and for moments are entangled.

Rainey comes out of it in front as Schwantz gets a wild slide, controls it and tries for the lead once more. Again he's shut out, and this time catches his knee on the grass, is pulled out of his seat . . . and has to settle for second as Rainey crosses the line to even the series at one victory apiece. It's awe-inspiring stuff, and the crowd love it, even if Rainey doesn't. 'What he did was dangerous – nobody needs to ride like that', he snarled afterwards.

This battle had nothing to do with any Anglo-American match race. This was Texan against Californian, Suzuki versus Honda, Michelin against Dunlop . . . American against American, with no quarter asked or given. 'We have pretty well the opposite in everything and we both have a point to prove', said Schwantz, defending his tactics by pointing to an equally violent Rainey-instigated fairing-bashing incident in the first leg. The fact that this was a team race appeared not to have occurred to either man.

Once again the Transatlantic series was providing some thrilling racing almost despite itself. Every year the format changes and every year one side or the other wins the Challenge by a street, the result of the team contest a foregone conclusion long before the end. But, somehow, every year a new star or an epic battle crops up to send the crowd home happy.

Last year's meeting, the first to adopt the four-stroke Superbike formula, belonged to newcomer Schwantz and American Superbike champ Fred Merkel. Now Merkel - champion for the third time running back home but since dropped by Honda USA, and bikeless - joined Messrs Lawson, Spencer, Mamola and Baldwin on the list of missing Americans. The British team included Ron Haslam but lost GP men McElnea, Mackenzie, Burnett and Irons, not to mention factory four-stroke riders Dunlop, Marshall and Iddon, abroad on F1 duty.

The strength in depth that had led to the British team's victory in 1986 had been weakened, despite the controversial drafting-in of New Zealander Richard Scott. Trevor Nation, Keith Huewen and Phil Mellor had the speed and experience to put alongside hungry youngsters like Mark Phillips and Roger Hurst, but the home riders' machinery was mostly little more than Superstock bikes with race carburettors and looked a bit sick in comparison to the well-sorted American Superbikes.

Bubba Shobert and Daytona winner Rainey uncrated factory Honda VFRs, Schwantz's Suzuki GSX-R was the machine on which he'd led the 200-miler before crashing, whilst Daytona third-placeman Doug Polen and the Canadian-based Gary Goodfellow and Michel Mercier arrived with finely honed bikes that may not have looked special but certainly didn't lack the go-faster bits. A favourite paddock pastime was estimating the value of Schwantz's Showa forks, with the bidding opening at £5000. 'You name it and we can have it', said Ottis Lance of his and Polen's millionaire sponsor's backing.

The series returned to Brands Hatch as its starting point. None of the American team had raced there before and for Bubba Shobert it would stay that way. A practice crash broke a finger, damaged an elbow and put the Texan on a plane back home. His team-mates had discovered that parts were broken or missing in

As usual, the Transatlantic Trophy produced a few new stars, amongst whom was Kiwi Gary Goodfellow. Here he dives inside Michel Mercier at Brands.

their crates, and British fuel was disagreeing with their bikes.

But Race One showed that the British would need more help than that. Schwantz stormed away, Rainey followed and caught him, and the pair opened up a huge lead. With two laps left Rainey challenged at Paddock, took the lead with a clash of fibreglass . . . then lost it again as Schwantz stormed back going into Druids. The Suzuki man held on to win and behind him the Americans cleaned up. The only members of the home team to make the top ten were Richard Scott, in fifth, and eighth-place Keith Huewen.

Druids hairpin was Schwantz's undoing in the second race, Rainey darting past on the last lap as his younger rival showed his relative inexperience by running wide. With the £100,000 nine-wins jackpot flashing before his eyes Schwantz made a desperate effort to get back but the last-bend dramatics weren't enough. Rainey's revenge was matched by Gary Goodfellow, who this time beat Mercier for third and by Doug Polen, who pushed best 'Brit' Scott down to sixth.

Having scored only 165 points against 246, the home team were already in trouble. Ron Haslam, on GP form the best rider on the track, had managed only 14th and 9th on a VFR Honda lacking power, brakes and handling. Huewen and Nation had first ridden their Yamahas the day before, so were still learning. In a better Race Three, Nation finished sixth and Huewen eighth, behind fourth-placed Scott. Schwantz won by inches from Rainey, whose compensation was breaking the circuit's absolute lap record. The match race was all but over; the battle between the two Americans just beginning.

Gary Goodfellow led briefly in the first of Donington's six races but the Schwantz/Rainey combination was soon past to fight it out in front. Rainey, 26 years old, benefiting from a US Superbike championship in 1983 and a stint in Kenny Roberts' 250 cc Grand Prix team, used this experience to shadow Schwantz before making his move two laps from home. While the Americans increased their points lead, Schwantz admitted he'd made a tactical error. But it was to be a mistake by his rival in the next race that would prove critical.

Transatlantic rain has often been the undoing (and unseating) of American riders and this year the British weather struck two laps into Race Five. Schwantz had fitted a cut front slick as storm clouds scudded over beforehand; the others were on slicks and in trouble. Goodfellow, Briton Mark Phillips and John Ashmead all crashed, the last two putting themselves in hospital and out of the meeting. Wayne Rainey stayed on board but at a price: he'd overdone the washing-up liquid on his visor the night before, and when the rain came his helmet filled with bubbles.

Schwantz won a shortened race from Richard Scott and Phil Mellor, with Americans fourth to seventh. Rainey spluttered home a soapy tenth, the first time he had been out of the first two, to trail the Suzuki man by 3½ points overall. With the Americans' lead a massive 142 points and Haslam having finally given up on a bike that had refused to run right all weekend, the match race was a much less close-fought affair.

Rainey again out-thought Schwantz to take a last-lap win in Race Seven, the consistent Goodfellow following up for another third place. But Wayne muffed the start of Race Eight – caught in the wrong gear and delayed by traffic as Schwantz streaked away into the distance. Rainey came through the field but couldn't catch Goodfellow who this time took second to leave Schwantz needing third place in the final leg to secure the top-scorer's £5000 prize.

He made it in a predictable anti-climax. Rainey won at a canter; behind him Schwantz took his time before securing second from Goodfellow. Huewen and Nation's fourth and fifth places couldn't stop the British team ending up fully 188 points adrift. Yet another one-sided Transatlantic series was over.

The Americans had come, seen and conquered, their fast and well-ridden Superbikes too good for the cheaper and often hastily prepared British machinery. On the track it had been every man for himself; now the Yanks could become a team. Drinks were drunk, the injured Ashmead was visited in hospital – they'd done it all for Uncle Sam. No doubt that's the way the Transatlantic has always been.

After one season supporting the Clubmen's Championships, the Motor Cycle Association moved up a peg for 1987, joining forces with the ACU in promoting the Star UK series.

The aim was to provide riders in six solo and two sidecar classes with a stepping stone to international and Grand Prix racing.

Welshman Steve Williams and Ian Burnett, from Humberside, dominated the 350 cc and Formula 2 classes.

When they lined up for the final at Donington Park, Burnett led Williams by two points in the 350 cc table. But he failed at the final hurdle and second place behind Ulsterman Gary Cowan took Williams to the title.

Although Williams won the opening F2 round at Thruxton, consistent hard riding by Burnett had taken him to a 20-point lead by the half-way stage. In the final race, Burnett finished fourth behind Williams, Steve Hislop and Eddie Laycock to raise his score to 80. However, he had to discard eight points – with the result that he and Williams shared the championship with 72 points apiece.

Cowan scored a 250/350 double at Thruxton but then hit the international trail, leaving Steve Patrickson and Andy Machin to fight for 250 cc honours. And what a battle they had – even racing to a dead heat at Carnaby.

Patrickson, from Yorkshire, finished second to Donnie McLeod and ahead of Machin at Donington to clinch the title by eight points.

After taking fifth at the first round (won by Steve Williams), Midlander Ray Stringer began a serious challenge in the 1300 cc division when he finished second after a tough battle with Mark Stone at Snetterton.

When he claimed third behind Mark Phillips and Jamie Whitham at Donington, Stringer earned his Star with a 19-point margin over Steve Henshaw.

Gary Buckle, Chris Galatowicz and Doug Flather were always in contention in the 125 class before finishing in that order.

Flather was also a contender in the 80 cc class but despite winning the final from Dennis Batchelor and John Cresswell, it was Cresswell who scooped the title, just two points clear of Batchelor.

Formula 2 sidecar campaigners Joe Heys and Peter Greetham won the first two rounds after tremendous battles with Eddy Wright and Ian Marchant. But their campaign faltered and despite Heys' win, with a lap record, at Carnaby, Wright and Marchant had edged into a five-point lead.

When Heys' machine failed to start at Cadwell, Wright snatched full points and the championship was in the bag.

The open sidecar class also produced some heart-stopping action. After a lowly ninth at Thruxton, Kenny Howles and Steve Pointer began their charge with a win ahead of Lindsay and Gary Hurst at a windswept Snetterton.

These two hard-riding teams were then locked in a fight to the finish but fourth place just behind Howles at Donington was good enough to secure the championship for the Hursts.

Craig Ryding won both the Junior and Lightweight races on his Yamaha-engined Kimocos.

The original terms of reference of the Manx Grand Prix (or Amateur TT as it was first known) are interesting to reflect upon 64 years after they were laid down. The definition of 'amateur' was accepted as being one who did not accept bonuses from firms supplying motor cycle accessories.

The terms were extended to exclude as competitors anybody in the motor cycle business – including dealers – and anyone who permitted himself to be used for advertising purposes. It may not have been ideal, but the system was the best that anyone could think of at the time. However, contrast that with present needs and it can easily be seen that the Manx Grand Prix has become considerably more liberal in its ideas.

So it was that nearly 400 riders paid £70 apiece to race in the 1987 meeting, where very few could truthfully say they had received absolutely nothing without payment. Indeed, the majority were persuaded by the organisers themselves to acknowledge such assistance by a direct reference to sponsorship in the programme. Such is progress.

Mixed weather conditions prevailed for the ten separate practice sessions held over a period of eight days. By the end, the fastest lap had been set by 26-year-old Brian Raynor, a married toolmaker from Grantham, Lincolnshire, who duly recognised the financial assistance he had received from Tony and Jayne Gilbert of KPS Racing, who had purchased a powerful 1000 cc four-stroke Yamaha for him to race.

But his lap at just over 106 mph was well off the outright Manx Grand Prix lap record set in 1986 by Mike Seward, and, with only one previous finish to his credit, there were many who said it was a fluke.

He was swift to deny it, pointing to other quick laps in other sessions. And he also claimed his record was only poor because of an unfortunate series of mechanical misfortunes. Nevertheless, 47th place on a single-cylinder Honda the year before was hardly sufficient to silence the cynics.

Race day was sunny and windy, with the prospect of a hotly contested event known as the Senior, though now it catered for machines of up to 1000 cc as against the previous ceiling of 500 cc.

Six laps of the 37¾-mile Snaefell Mountain Course totals 226.4 miles and Raynor was banking on just one refuelling stop, having specially enlarged his petrol tank.

Early practice leader Pete Beale from Milton Keynes led at the end of the first lap, averaging 106.64 mph, putting him 6.6 seconds ahead of top local rider Paul Hunt and 10.2 seconds up on Steve Dowey from Marske, Cleveland. Raynor was fourth, a further 10.8 seconds in arrears.

Hunt retired a quarter of the way round the second lap when the camshaft of his Kawasaki disintegrated. He later revealed the bike had not been running well from the start. Beale led still at the end of the second lap, improving to 107.27 mph and a two-lap average of 106.95. Raynor lapped at 108.59 to leapfrog Dowey, whose lap 2 speed was 106.96. At a quickening average for the race of 106.72 mph, he was then only 5.6 seconds behind Beale, with Dowey trailing by 8.2 seconds.

As the fuel load lightened for the first time, Raynor wound up the Yamaha and lapped at what was to prove the fastest of the entire MGP meeting. His third lap was done in 20m 38.2s, an average speed of 109.69 mph. Beale managed 107.49, but it wasn't enough to prevent him sacrificing the lead. At half-distance Raynor led by 25.4 seconds at 107.69 mph for the 113.2 miles.

Dowey maintained station, making it an all-Yamaha affair in the top three. Fourth was Kenny Harmer (Honda) from Charnock Richard, fifth Kevin Jackson (Suzuki) from Blackpool, and sixth Dave Sharratt (Suzuki) from Stafford.

The second half of the race saw Raynor settling to the renewed task of coping with a heavy fuel load and his pit stop was accounted for in his fourth-lap speed of 103.95 mph, reducing his race average to 106.73. Dowey was within two seconds at 103.86 but was 25.4 seconds behind overall at 106.20 mph. It pushed out Beale, who had been forced to stop a second time to take on petrol. Sharratt and Jackson switched places, whilst coming up well was Steve Hazlett from Ulster on a 350 cc Yamaha twin.

The final two laps of the race saw Raynor consolidate his position. He lapped at 108.59 and 107.71 mph to produce a final race average speed of 107.20, winning by 34.4 seconds from Dowey.

In doing so, he set a new race record by 34.2 seconds over previous holder, Grant Goodings, who had won the Senior the year before.

Dowey was 11.4 seconds clear of Beale, with Harmer, Sharratt and Jackson fourth, fifth and sixth respectively. Hazlett averaged 102.72 mph to take seventh spot against the more powerful four-cylinder machines.

There were 75 finishers out of 100 starters, firmly demonstrating the reliability of the modern generation of superbikes, many of which were being ridden straight from the crate.

The Junior and Lightweight races were both won by 26-year-old Longton labourer Craig Ryding on the Eddie Roberts-developed Yamaha-engined Kimoco machines. The Junior he won by 16.8 seconds from Hazlett, with Mark Linton third. The Lightweight was won by two minutes from Mick Robinson and Billy Craine.

The combined three-class race for newcomers featured a big-class win for Colin Gable from Andover, breaking the lap record by 52.6 seconds at 107.33 mph and the race record by an incredible 4m 10.8s at 105.23. Local rider Billy Craine won the 350 cc class and Ian Morris from Wirral the 250 cc class. Honeymooner Dave Pither repeated his 1984 500 cc Classic race win, averaging over 100 mph where the previous fastest lap had not been into three figures. Richard Swallow from Huddersfield won the 350 cc class, also at record speed.

500 cc World Championship

Position	Rider	Nationality	Machine	Japan	Spain	Germany	Italy	Austria	Yugoslavia	Holland	France	Great Britain	Sweden	Czechoslovakia	San Marino	Portugal	Brazil	Argentina	TOTAL
1	Wayne Gardner	AUS	Honda	12	15	1	15	15	15	12	8	12	15	15	10	8	15	10	**178**
2	Randy Mamola	USA	Yamaha	15	5	12	–	12	12	10	15	10	10	8	15	12	10	12	**158**
3	Eddie Lawson	USA	Yamaha	–	12	15	12	–	10	15	–	15	12	12	12	15	12	15	**157**
4	Ron Haslam	GB	Honda	6	10	10	6	8	8	–	6	6	4	5	–	–	2	1	**72**
5	Niall Mackenzie	GB	Honda	–	8	4	1	10	–	–	4	6	6	6	4	5	3	4	**61**
6	Tadahiko Taira	J	Yamaha	5	4	8	5	2	4	–	–	3	–	10	8	–	4	3	**56**
7	Christian Sarron	F	Yamaha	–	–	–	10	5	–	10	8	–	–	–	4	3	6	6	**52**
8	Pier Francesco Chili	I	Honda	8	–	5	4	1	5	2	12	–	–	2	–	4	2	2	**47**
9	Shunji Yatsushiro	J	Honda	–	3	–	–	4	3	–	3	–	–	5	6	3	5	8	**40**
10	Rob McElnea	GB	Yamaha	–	–	6	8	6	–	8	–	–	8	3	–	–	–	–	**39**
11	Roger Burnett	GB	Honda	3	2	3	–	3	–	4	1	2	1	1	5	–	–	–	**25**
12	Didier de Radiguès	B	Cagiva	–	–	–	–	–	–	5	–	5	3	–	–	–	8	–	**21**
13	Raymond Roche	F	Cagiva	1	–	–	2	–	6	–	–	–	–	–	–	–	–	6	**15**
14	Kenny Irons	GB	Suzuki	–	–	–	–	1	3	5	1	2	–	–	–	–	–	–	**12**
15=	Kevin Magee	AUS	Yamaha	–	–	–	–	–	–	1	–	–	–	–	–	10	–	–	**11**
15=	Kevin Schwantz	USA	Suzuki	–	6	–	3	–	–	–	2	–	–	–	–	–	–	–	**11**
17	Takumi Ito	J	Suzuki	10	–	–	–	–	–	–	–	–	–	–	–	–	–	–	**10**
18	Mike Baldwin	USA	Yamaha	–	–	–	–	–	–	–	–	–	–	–	–	–	1	5	**6**
19	Gustav Reiner	D	Honda	–	–	2	–	–	–	–	–	–	–	–	–	2	1	–	**5**
20=	Hiroyuki Kawasaki	J	Yamaha	4	–	–	–	–	–	–	–	–	–	–	–	–	–	–	**4**
20=	Freddie Spencer	USA	Honda	–	–	–	–	–	–	–	–	–	4	–	–	–	–	–	**4**
22	Richard Scott	NZ	Yamaha	–	1	–	–	–	2	–	–	–	–	–	–	–	–	–	**3**
23	Shinji Katayama	J	Yamaha	2	–	–	–	–	–	–	–	–	–	–	–	–	–	–	**2**
24	Marco Gentile	CH	Fior	–	–	–	–	–	–	–	–	–	–	–	–	1	–	–	**1**

250 cc World Championship

Position	Rider	Nationality	Machine	Japan	Spain	Germany	Italy	Austria	Yugoslavia	Holland	France	Great Britain	Sweden	Czechoslovakia	San Marino	Portugal	Brazil	Argentina	TOTAL
1	Anton Mang	D	Honda	3	–	15	15	15	4	15	–	15	15	15	5	15	4	–	**136**
2	Reinhold Roth	D	Honda	10	3	10	12	10	10	12	15	6	–	1	2	4	8	5	**108**
3	Alfonso Pons	E	Honda	12	2	4	6	8	3	10	8	4	–	8	10	6	12	15	**108**
4	Dominique Sarron	F	Honda	–	8	–	10	4	5	–	12	2	6	12	8	3	15	12	**97**
5	Carlos Cardus	E	Honda	–	–	8	4	6	–	8	10	3	5	10	–	–	10	6	**70**
6	Loris Reggiani	I	Aprilia	–	–	–	12	12	–	4	12	10	–	15	–	3	–	–	**68**
7	Luca Cadalora	I	Yamaha	–	12	6	–	–	–	–	–	12	6	12	2	5	8	–	**63**
8	Martin Wimmer	D	Yamaha	6	15	–	–	1	6	6	1	10	–	–	6	10	–	–	**61**
9	Jacques Cornu	CH	Honda	–	5	12	8	5	8	4	–	8	–	–	–	–	–	–	**50**
10	Carlos Lavado	YV	Yamaha	–	1	5	5	3	15	1	–	–	8	–	–	–	6	2	**46**
11	Juan Garriga	E	Yamaha	5	10	3	–	–	2	3	–	–	–	2	4	12	1	4	**46**
12	Patrick Igoa	F	Yamaha	4	6	2	3	–	–	2	–	–	5	4	4	1	8	3	**42**
13	Masahiro Shimuzu	J	Honda	8	–	–	–	–	–	–	–	–	–	–	–	–	2	10	**20**
14	Masaru Kobayashi	J	Honda	15	–	–	–	–	–	–	–	–	–	–	–	–	–	–	**15**
15	Manfred Herweh	D	Honda	–	–	–	–	–	–	–	6	1	–	–	3	1	–	–	**11**
16	Ivan Palazzese	YV	Yamaha	–	–	–	–	–	1	5	–	–	–	3	–	–	–	–	**9**
17	Jean-Philippe Ruggia	F	Yamaha	–	4	–	–	–	–	–	3	–	–	–	–	–	–	–	**7**
18=	Jean-François Baldé	F	Defi	–	–	–	–	–	–	–	–	–	1	–	5	–	–	–	**6**
18=	Maurizio Vitali	I	Garelli	–	–	1	2	–	–	–	–	–	3	–	–	–	–	–	**6**
20=	Hans Lindner	A	Honda	–	–	–	–	–	–	5	–	–	–	–	–	–	–	–	**5**
20=	Urs Lüzi	CH	Honda	–	–	–	–	–	–	–	–	–	5	–	–	–	–	–	**5**
22	Donnie McLeod	GB	EMC	–	–	–	–	–	–	2	–	2	–	–	–	–	–	–	**4**
23=	Stéphane Mertens	B	Sekitoba	–	–	–	2	–	–	–	–	–	–	–	–	–	–	–	**2**
23=	Masumitsu Taguchi	J	Honda	2	–	–	–	–	–	–	–	–	–	–	–	–	–	–	**2**
25=	Guy Bertin	F	Honda	–	–	–	1	–	–	–	–	–	–	–	–	–	–	–	**1**
25=	Stefano Caracchi	RSM	Honda	–	–	–	–	–	–	–	–	–	–	–	–	–	–	1	**1**
25=	Takayoshi Yamamoto	J	Yamaha	1	–	–	–	–	–	–	–	–	–	–	–	–	–	–	**1**

Past 500 cc World Champions

			(Wins/Races)
1949	Les Graham, GB	AJS	(2/6)
1950	Umberto Masetti, I	Gilera	(2/6)
1951	Geoff Duke, GB	Norton	(4/8)
1952	Umberto Masetti, I	Gilera	(2/8)
1953	Geoff Duke, GB	Gilera	(4/8)
1954	Geoff Duke, GB	Gilera	(5/8)
1955	Geoff Duke, GB	Gilera	(4/8)
1956	John Surtees, GB	MV-Agusta	(3/6)
1957	Libero Liberati, I	Gilera	(3/6)
1958	John Surtees, GB	MV-Agusta	(6/7)
1959	John Surtees, GB	MV-Agusta	(7/7)
1960	John Surtees, GB	MV-Agusta	(5/7)
1961	Gary Hocking, RSR	MV-Agusta	(7/10)
1962	Mike Hailwood, GB	MV-Agusta	(5/8)
1963	Mike Hailwood, GB	MV-Agusta	(7/8)
1964	Mike Hailwood, GB	MV-Agusta	(7/9)
1965	Mike Hailwood, GB	MV-Agusta	(8/10)
1966	Giacomo Agostini, I	MV-Agusta	(3/9)
1967	Giacomo Agostini, I	MV-Agusta	(5/10)
1968	Giacomo Agostini, I	MV-Agusta	(10/10)
1969	Giacomo Agostini, I	MV-Agusta	(10/12)
1970	Giacomo Agostini, I	MV-Agusta	(10/11)
1971	Giacomo Agostini, I	MV-Agusta	(8/11)
1972	Giacomo Agostini, I	MV-Agusta	(11/13)
1973	Phil Read, GB	MV-Agusta	(4/11)
1974	Phil Read, GB	MV-Agusta	(4/10)
1975	Giacomo Agostini, I	Yamaha	(4/10)
1976	Barry Sheene, GB	Suzuki	(5/10)
1977	Barry Sheene, GB	Suzuki	(6/11)
1978	Kenny Roberts, USA	Yamaha	(4/11)
1979	Kenny Roberts, USA	Yamaha	(5/12)
1980	Kenny Roberts, USA	Yamaha	(3/8)
1981	Marco Lucchinelli, I	Suzuki	(5/11)
1982	Franco Uncini, I	Suzuki	(5/12)
1983	Freddie Spencer, USA	Honda	(6/12)
1984	Eddie Lawson, USA	Yamaha	(4/12)
1985	Freddie Spencer, USA	Honda	(7/12)
1986	Eddie Lawson, USA	Yamaha	(7/11)

Past 350 cc World Champions

			(Wins/Races)
1949	Freddie Frith, GB	Velocette	(5/5)
1950	Bob Foster, GB	Velocette	(3/6)
1951	Geoff Duke, GB	Norton	(5/8)
1952	Geoff Duke, GB	Norton	(4/7)
1953	Fergus Anderson, GB	Guzzi	(3/7)
1954	Fergus Anderson, GB	Guzzi	(4/9)
1955	Bill Lomas, GB	Guzzi	(4/7)
1956	Bill Lomas, GB	Guzzi	(3/6)
1957	Keith Campbell, AUS	Guzzi	(3/6)
1958	John Surtees, GB	MV-Agusta	(6/7)
1959	John Surtees, GB	MV-Agusta	(6/6)
1960	John Surtees, GB	MV-Agusta	(2/5)
1961	Gary Hocking, RSR	MV-Agusta	(4/7)
1962	Jim Redman, RSR	Honda	(4/6)
1963	Jim Redman, RSR	Honda	(5/7)
1964	Jim Redman, RSR	Honda	(8/8)
1965	Jim Redman, RSR	Honda	(4/9)
1966	Mike Hailwood, GB	Honda	(6/10)
1967	Mike Hailwood, GB	Honda	(6/8)
1968	Giacomo Agostini, I	MV-Agusta	(7/7)
1969	Giacomo Agostini, I	MV-Agusta	(8/10)
1970	Giacomo Agostini, I	MV-Agusta	(9/10)
1971	Giacomo Agostini, I	MV-Agusta	(6/11)
1972	Giacomo Agostini, I	MV-Agusta	(6/12)
1973	Giacomo Agostini, I	MV-Agusta	(4/11)
1974	Giacomo Agostini, I	Yamaha	(5/10)
1975	Johnny Cecotto, YV	Yamaha	(4/10)
1976	Walter Villa, I	Harley-Davidson	(4/10)
1977	Takazumi Katayama, J	Yamaha	(5/11)
1978	Kork Ballington, ZA	Kawasaki	(6/11)
1979	Kork Ballington, ZA	Kawasaki	(5/11)
1980	Jon Ekerold, ZA	Yamaha	(3/6)
1981	Anton Mang, D	Kawasaki	(5/8)
1982	Anton Mang, D	Kawasaki	(1/9)

Past 250 cc World Champions

			(Wins/Races)
1949	Bruno Ruffo, I	Guzzi	(1/4)
1950	Dario Ambrosini, I	Benelli	(3/4)
1951	Bruno Ruffo, I	Guzzi	(2/5)
1952	Enrico Lorenzetti, I	Guzzi	(2/6)
1953	Werner Haas, D	NSU	(2/7)
1954	Werner Haas, D	NSU	(5/7)
1955	Hermann-Peter Müller, D	NSU	(1/5)
1956	Carlo Ubbiali, I	MV-Agusta	(5/6)
1957	Cecil Sandford, GB	Mondial	(2/6)
1958	Tarquinio Provini, I	MV-Agusta	(4/6)
1959	Carlo Ubbiali, I	MV-Agusta	(2/6)
1960	Carlo Ubbiali, I	MV-Agusta	(4/6)
1961	Mike Hailwood, GB	Honda	(4/11)
1962	Jim Redman, RSR	Honda	(6/10)
1963	Jim Redman, RSR	Honda	(4/10)
1964	Phil Read, GB	Yamaha	(5/11)
1965	Phil Read, GB	Yamaha	(7/13)
1966	Mike Hailwood, GB	Honda	(10/12)
1967	Mike Hailwood, GB	Honda	(5/13)
1968	Phil Read, GB	Yamaha	(5/10)
1969	Kel Carruthers, AUS	Benelli	(3/12)
1970	Rod Gould, GB	Yamaha	(6/12)
1971	Phil Read, GB	Yamaha	(3/12)
1972	Jarno Saarinen, SF	Yamaha	(4/13)
1973	Dieter Braun, D	Yamaha	(4/11)
1974	Walter Villa, I	Harley-Davidson	(4/10)
1975	Walter Villa, I	Harley-Davidson	(5/11)
1976	Walter Villa, I	Harley-Davidson	(7/11)
1977	Mario Lega, I	Morbidelli	(1/12)
1978	Kork Ballington, ZA	Kawasaki	(4/12)
1979	Kork Ballington, ZA	Kawasaki	(7/12)
1980	Anton Mang, D	Kawasaki	(4/10)
1981	Anton Mang, D	Kawasaki	(10/12)
1982	Jean-Louis Tournadre, F	Yamaha	(1/12)
1983	Carlos Lavado, YV	Yamaha	(4/11)
1984	Christian Sarron, F	Yamaha	(3/12)
1985	Freddie Spencer, USA	Honda	(7/12)
1986	Carlos Lavado, YV	Yamaha	(6/11)

125 cc World Championship

Position	Rider	Nationality	Machine	Spain	Germany	Italy	Austria	Holland	France	Great Britain	Sweden	Czechoslovakia	San Marino	Portugal	TOTAL
1	Fausto Gresini	I	Garelli	15	15	15	15	15	15	15	15	15	15	–	150
2	Bruno Casanova	I	Garelli	8	10	12	12	12	10	–	12	12	–	–	88
3	Paolo Casoli	I	AGV	10	–	–	10	10	6	–	–	–	10	15	61
4	Domenico Brigaglia	I	AGV	12	6	8	6	–	4	–	10	–	–	12	58
5	August Auinger	A	MBA	4	12	10	8	8	–	–	–	–	12	–	54
6	Ezio Gianola	I	Honda	5	–	–	–	–	12	6	–	8	8	6	45
7	Pier Paolo Bianchi	I	MBA	6	8	6	–	6	–	12	5	–	–	–	43
8	Andrés Marin Sànchez	E	Ducados	–	5	5	5	3	–	–	8	10	4	–	40
9=	Mike Leitner	A	MBA	1	–	–	–	5	8	–	4	–	6	8	32
9=	Lucio Pietroniro	B	MBA	–	1	3	–	–	4	3	6	5	10	32
11	Johnny Wickström	SF	Tunturi	–	–	–	2	–	5	8	6	–	–	–	21
12	Gastone Grassetti	I	MBA	–	–	–	–	–	2	5	2	–	3	5	17
13	Jean-Claude Selini	F	MBA	–	–	–	–	2	–	10	–	–	–	4	16
14	Thierry Feuz	CH	MBA	3	4	–	3	1	–	–	–	1	–	1	13
15	Jussi Hautaniemi	SF	MBA	–	3	4	–	–	–	3	–	–	–	10
16	Adolf Stadler	D	MBA	–	2	–	4	–	–	–	–	–	–	3	9
17	Ivan Troisi	YV	MBA	–	–	–	–	–	1	–	5	–	2	8
18=	Corrado Catalano	I	MBA	–	–	2	–	4	–	–	–	–	–	–	6
18=	Claudio Macciotta	I	MBA	2	–	–	–	–	–	–	4	–	–	6
20=	Esa Kytölä	SF	MBA	–	–	–	–	–	–	1	3	–	–	4
20=	Olivier Liegeois	B	Assmex	–	–	1	–	–	3	–	–	–	–	–	4
22=	Bady Hassaine	DZ	MBA	–	–	–	–	–	–	–	–	2	–	–	2
22=	Robin Milton	GB	MBA	–	–	–	–	–	–	2	–	–	–	2
22=	Håkan Olsson	S	Starol	–	–	–	–	–	–	–	–	2	–	2
25=	Flemming Kistrup	DK	MBA	–	–	–	–	–	1	–	–	–	–	1
25=	Willy Pérez	RA	Zanella	–	–	–	1	–	–	–	–	–	–	1
25=	Norbert Peschke	D	Seel	–	–	–	–	–	–	–	–	1	–	1

Past 125 cc World Champions

			(Wins/Races)
1949	Nello Pagani, I	Mondial	(2/3)
1950	Bruno Ruffo, I	Mondial	(1/3)
1951	Carlo Ubbiali, I	Mondial	(1/4)
1952	Cecil Sandford, GB	MV-Augusta	(3/6)
1953	Werner Haas, D	NSU	(3/6)
1954	Rupert Hollaus, A	NSU	(4/6)
1955	Carlo Ubbiali, I	MV-Augusta	(5/6)
1956	Carlo Ubbiali, I	MV-Agusta	(5/6)
1957	Tarquinio Provini, I	Mondial	(3/6)
1958	Carlo Ubbiali, I	MV-Agusta	(4/7)
1959	Carlo Ubbiali, I	MV-Agusta	(3/7)
1960	Carlo Ubbiali, I	MV-Agusta	(4/5)
1961	Tom Phillis, AUS	Honda	(4/11)
1962	Luigi Taveri, CH	Honda	(6/11)
1963	Hugh Anderson, NZ	Suzuki	(6/12)
1964	Luigi Taveri, CH	Honda	(5/11)
1965	Hugh Anderson, NZ	Suzuki	(7/12)
1966	Luigi Taveri, CH	Honda	(5/10)
1967	Bill Ivy, GB	Yamaha	(8/12)
1968	Phil Read, GB	Yamaha	(6/9)
1969	Dave Simmonds, GB	Kawasaki	(8/11)
1970	Dieter Braun, D	Suzuki	(4/11)
1971	Angel Nieto, E	Derbi	(5/11)
1972	Angel Nieto, E	Derbi	(5/13)
1973	Kent Andersson, S	Yamaha	(5/12)
1974	Kent Andersson, S	Yamaha	(5/10)
1975	Paolo Pileri, I	Morbidelli	(7/10)
1976	Pier Paolo Bianchi, I	Morbidelli	(7/9)
1977	Pier Paolo Bianchi, I	Morbidelli	(7/12)
1978	Eugênio Lazzarini, I	MBA	(4/12)
1979	Angel Nieto, E	Minarelli	(8/13)
1980	Pier Paolo Bianchi, I	MBA	(2/10)
1981	Angel Nieto, E	Minarelli	(8/12)
1982	Angel Nieto, E	Garelli	(6/12)
1983	Angel Nieto, E	Garelli	(6/11)
1984	Angel Nieto, E	Garelli	(6/8)
1985	Fausto Gresini, I	Garelli	(3/10)
1986	Luca Cadalora, I	Garelli	(4/11)

80cc World Championship

Position	Rider	Nationality	Machine	Spain	Germany	Italy	Austria	Yugoslavia	Holland	Great Britain	Czechoslovakia	San Marino	Portugal	TOTAL
1	Jorge Martinez	E	Derbi	15	12	15	15	15	15	15	12	–	15	129
2	Manuel Herreros	E	Derbi	5	6	12	10	6	12	–	8	15	12	86
3	Gerhard Waibel	D	Krauser	8	15	1	12	8	–	10	10	8	10	82
4	Stefan Dörflinger	CH	Krauser	–	10	10	–	12	10	–	15	12	6	75
5	Ian McConnachie	GB	Krauser	4	8	–	6	10	3	12	–	10	–	53
6	Jörg Seel	D	Seel	–	5	6	–	4	–	6	6	6	5	38
7	Hubert Abold	D	Krauser	1	–	8	4	5	4	3	–	–	8	33
8	Luis M. Reyes	E	Autisa	6	–	2	2	–	8	8	5	–	–	31
9	Josef Fischer	A	Krauser	2	–	–	8	–	–	5	4	–	–	19
10	Julian Miralles	E	Derbi	10	–	–	–	–	6	–	–	–	2	18
11=	Alejandro Criville	E	Derbi	12	–	–	–	–	–	–	–	–	–	12
11=	Günther Schirnhofer	D	Krauser	–	3	3	–	–	1	4	1	–	–	12
13	Hans Spaan	NL	Casal	–	–	–	5	3	–	–	–	3	–	11
14=	Juan Ramon Bolart	E	Krauser	–	–	–	1	2	–	3	–	4	10
14=	Károly Juhász	H	Krauser	–	–	5	–	–	5	–	–	–	–	10
16	Paolo Priori	I	Krauser	–	–	4	–	–	–	2	–	–	3	9
17	Alexandre Barros	BR	Arbizu	–	–	–	3	1	–	–	–	4	–	8
18	Giuseppe Ascareggi	I	BBFT	–	–	–	–	–	–	–	–	5	–	5
19	Heinz Paschen	D	Casal	–	4	–	–	–	–	–	–	–	–	4
20=	Richard Bay	D	Ziegler	3	–	–	–	–	–	–	–	–	–	3
20=	Peter Öttl	D	Krauser	–	–	–	–	–	2	–	–	1	–	3
20=	Francisco Torrontegui	I	Cobas	–	–	–	–	–	–	–	–	2	1	3
23=	Michael Gschwander	D	Seel	–	2	–	–	–	–	–	–	–	–	2
23=	Theo Timmer	NL	Casal	–	–	–	–	–	–	–	2	–	–	2
25=	Jacques Bernard	B	Huvo	–	–	–	–	–	1	–	–	–	–	1
25=	Ralf Waldmann	D	Seel	–	1	–	–	–	–	–	–	–	–	1

Sidecar World Championship

Position	Driver & passenger	Nationality	Machine	Spain	Germany	Austria	Holland	France	Great Britain	Sweden	Czechoslovakia	TOTAL
1	Steve Webster/Tony Hewitt	GB / GB	LCR-Yamaha	15	15	8	12	10	15	12	10	97
2	Egbert Streuer/Bernard Schnieders	NL / NL	LCR-Yamaha	–	12	12	15	12	12	–	12	75
3	Rolf Biland/Kurt Waltisperg	CH / CH	LCR-Krauser	–	–	15	8	15	–	15	15	68
4	Alain Michel/Jean-Marc Fresc	F / F	LCR-Krauser	12	10	10	10	8	–	10	8	68
5	Alfred Zurbrügg/Simon Birchall	CH / GB	LCR-Yamaha	10	–	4	5	2	8	6	4	39
6	Steve Abbott/Shaun Smith	GB / GB	Windle-Yamaha	6	6	–	4	3	5	–	2	26
7	Rolf Steinhausen/Bruno Hiller	D / D	Eigenbau	–	–	6	–	10	8	–	–	24
8	Derek Jones/Brian Ayres	GB / GB	LCR-Yamaha	5	–	3	–	6	6	–	3	23
9	Masato Kumano/Markus Fahrni	J / CH	Toshiba	1	4	5	–	–	2	4	5	21
10	Theo van Kempen/Gerardus de Haas	NL / NL	LCR-Yamaha	–	8	1	1	4	–	–	–	14
11	Yoshisada Kumagaya/Brian Barlow/J. Wilson	J / GB / GB	Windle-Yamaha	3	2	–	–	5	3	–	–	13
12	Markus Egloff/Urs Egloff	CH / CH	LCR	4	–	–	–	–	–	2	6	12
13	Pascal Larratte/Jacques Corbier	F / F	LCR-Yamaha	–	3	2	–	–	–	5	1	11
14	Wolfgang Stropek/Hans-Peter Demling	A / A	LCR-Krauser	–	–	6	–	–	–	3	–	9
15=	Derek Bayley/Bryan Nixon	GB / GB	LCR-Yamaha	8	–	–	–	–	–	–	–	8
15=	René Progin/Yves Hunziker	CH / CH	Seymaz	2	5	–	–	–	1	–	8
17	Barry Brindley/Grahame Rose	GB / GB	Windle-Yamaha	–	–	–	2	–	4	–	–	6
18	Bernd Scherer/Wolfgang Gess	D / D	BSR-Yamaha	–	–	–	3	1	–	–	–	4
19=	Ivan Nigrowski/Michel Charpentier/G. Loreille/Frédéric Meunier	F / F / F / F	Seymaz	–	–	–	–	–	1	–	–	1
19=	Fritz Stölzle/Hubert Stölzle	D / D	LCR-Yamaha	–	1	–	–	–	–	–	–	1

Past 50 cc/*80 cc World Champions

			(Wins/ Races)
1962	Ernst Degner, D	Suzuki	(4/10)
1963	Hugh Anderson, NZ	Suzuki	(2/9)
1964	Hugh Anderson, NZ	Suzuki	(4/8)
1965	Ralph Bryans, IRL	Honda	(3/8)
1966	Hans-Georg Anscheidt, D	Suzuki	(2/6)
1967	Hans-Georg Anscheidt, D	Suzuki	(3/7)
1968	Hans-Georg Anscheidt, D	Suzuki	(3/5)
1969	Angel Nieto, E	Derbi	(2/10)
1970	Angel Nieto, E	Derbi	(5/10)
1971	Jan de Vries, NL	Kreidler	(5/9)
1972	Angel Nieto, E	Derbi	(3/8)
1973	Jan de Vries, NL	Kreidler	(5/7)
1974	Henk van Kessel, NL	Kreidler	(6/10)
1975	Angel Nieto, E	Kreidler	(6/8)
1976	Angel Nieto, E	Bultaco	(5/9)
1977	Angel Nieto, E	Bultaco	(3/7)
1978	Ricardo Tormo, E	Bultaco	(5/7)
1979	Eugênio Lazzarini, I	Kreidler	(5/7)
1980	Eugênio Lazzarini, I	Kreidler/Iprem	(2/6)
1981	Ricardo Tormo, E	Bultaco	(6/8)
1982	Stefan Dörflinger, CH	Kreidler	(3/6)
1983	Stefan Dörflinger, CH	Kreidler	(3/7)
1984*	Stefan Dörflinger, CH	Zundapp	(4/8)
1985*	Stefan Dörflinger, CH	Krauser	(2/7)
1986*	Jorge Martinez, E	Derbi	(4/9)

Past Sidecar World Champions

			(Wins/ Races)
1949	Eric Oliver, GB/ Denis Jenkinson, GB	Norton	(2/3)
1950	Eric Oliver, GB/ Lorenzo Dobelli, I	Norton	(3/3)
1951	Eric Oliver, GB/ Lorenzo Dobelli, I	Norton	(3/5)
1952	Cyril Smith, GB/ Bob Clements, GB	Norton	(1/5)
1953	Eric Oliver, GB/ Stanley Dibben, GB	Norton	(4/5)
1954	Wilhelm Noll, D/ Fritz Cron, D	BMW	(3/6)
1955	Wilhelm Faust, D/ Karl Remmert, D	BMW	(3/6)
1956	Wilhelm Noll, D/ Fritz Cron, D	BMW	(3/6)
1957	Fritz Hillebrand, D/ Manfred Grunwald, D	BMW	(3/5)
1958	Walter Schneider, D/ Hans Strauss, D	BMW	(3/4)
1959	Walter Schneider, D/ Hans Strauss, D	BMW	(2/5)
1960	Helmut Fath, D/ Alfred Wohligemuth, D	BMW	(4/5)
1961	Max Deubel, D/ Emil Horner, D	BMW	(3/6)
1962	Max Deubel, D/ Emil Horner, D	BMW	(3/6)
1963	Max Deubel, D/ Emil Horner, D	BMW	(2/5)
1964	Max Deubel, D/ Emil Horner, D	BMW	(2/6)
1965	Fritz Scheidegger, CH/ John Robinson, GB	BMW	(4/7)
1966	Fritz Scheidegger, CH/ John Robinson, GB	BMW	(5/5)
1967	Klaus Enders, D/ Ralf Engelhardt, D	BMW	(5/8)
1968	Helmut Fath, D/ Wolfgang Kallaugh, D	URS	(3/6)
1969	Klaus Enders, D/ Ralf Engelhardt, D	BMW	(4/7)
1970	Klaus Enders, D/ Wolfgang Kallaugh, D	BMW	(5/8)
1971	Horst Owesle, D/ Peter Rutterford, GB	URS-Fath	(3/8)
1972	Klaus Enders, D/ Ralf Engelhardt, D	BMW	(4/8)
1973	Klaus Enders, D/ Ralf Engelhardt, D	BMW	(7/8)
1974	Klaus Enders, D/ Ralf Engelhardt, D	Busch-BMW	(2/8)
1975	Rolf Steinhausen, D/ Josef Huber, D	Busch-König	(3/7)
1976	Rolf Steinhausen, D/ Josef Huber, D	Busch-König	(3/7)
1977	George O'Dell, GB/ Kenny Arthur, GB Cliff Holland, GB	Yamaha	(–/7)
1978	Rolf Biland, CH/ Kenny Williams, GB	Yamaha	(3/8)
1979	*B2A* Rolf Biland, CH/ Kurt Waltisperg, CH	Yamaha	(3/7)
	B2B Bruno Holzer, CH/ Karl Meierhans, CH	Yamaha	(–/6)
1980	Jock Taylor, GB/ Benga Johansson, S	Yamaha	(4/8)
1981	Rolf Biland, CH/ Kurt Waltisperg, CH	Yamaha	(7/10)
1982	Werner Schwärzel, D/ Andreas Huber, D	Yamaha	(–/9)
1983	Rolf Biland, CH/ Kurt Waltisperg, CH	Yamaha	(6/8)
1984	Egbert Streuer, NL/ Bernard Schnieders, NL	Yamaha	(3/7)
1985	Egbert Streuer, NL/ Bernard Schnieders, NL	LCR-Yamaha	(3/6)
1986	Egbert Streuer, NL/ Bernard Schnieders, NL	LCR-Yamaha	(5/8)

Isle of Man Tourist Trophy Races, 30 May-6 June
Isle of Man Tourist Trophy Course, 37.73-mile/60.72-km circuit

TT Formula 1 race

6 laps, 226.38 miles/364.32 km

Place	*No.*	*Rider*	*Nat.*	*Machine*	*Time & speed*
1	3	Joey Dunlop	GB	750 Honda	1h 58m 04.4s 115.03 mph/ 185.12 km/h
2	10	Phil Mellor	GB	750 Suzuki	1h 58m 56.2s
3	2	Geoff Johnson	GB	750 Yamaha	1h 59m 37.4s
4	11	Roger Marshall	GB	750 Suzuki	2h 00m 12.2s
5	5	Trevor Nation	GB	750 Yamaha	2h 00m 18.6s
6	12	Nick Jefferies	GB	750 Honda	2h 00m 45.4s
7	24	Peter Rubatto	D	750 Yamaha	2h 01m 43.2s
8	17	Dave Leach	GB	750 Suzuki	2h 02m 25.8s
9	31	Glenn Williams	NZ	750 Suzuki	2h 03m 26.4s
10	34	Steve Linsdell	GB	750 Yamaha	2h 03m 26.8s
11	22	Anders Andersson	S	750 Suzuki	2h 03m 46.2s
12	29	Eddie Laycock	IRL	750 Yamaha	2h 04m 17.4s
13	18	Ray Swann	GB	750 Suzuki	2h 05m 04.2s
14	33	Tony Moran	GB	750 Yamaha	2h 05m 13.2s
15	25	Steve Ward	GB	750 Suzuki	2h 06m 05.6s
16	68	George Linder	GB	750 Yamaha	2h 06m 06.8s
17	42	Jamie Whitham	GB	750 Suzuki	2h 06m 21.4s
18	57	Bob Jackson	GB	750 Suzuki	2h 07m 04.4s
19	70	Richard Rose	GB	750 Suzuki	2h 07m 08.2s
20	43	Grant Goodings	GB	750 Kawasaki	2h 08m 31.6s

Fastest lap: Dunlop, 19m 15.4s, 117.55 mph/189.18 km/h.

Junior TT

6 laps, 226.38 miles/364.32 km

Place	*No.*	*Rider*	*Nat.*	*Machine*	*Time & speed*
1	7	Eddie Laycock	IRL	250 EMC	2h 05m 09.2s 108.52 mph/ 174.65 km/h
2	1	Brian Reid	IRL	250 EMC	2h 05m 14.8s
3	14	Graeme McGregor	AUS	350 Yamaha	2h 06m 06.4s
4	32	Carl Fogarty	GB	250 Honda	2h 06m 33.0s
5	12	Johnny Rea	GB	350 Yamaha	2h 06m 58.2s
6	10	Bob Heath	GB	350 Yamaha	2h 07m 08.0s
7	25	Derek Chatterton	GB	350 Yamaha	2h 07m 56.8s
8	8	Joey Dunlop	GB	250 Honda	2h 08m 03.4s
9	2	Mark Johns	GB	350 Yamaha	2h 08m 14.8s
10	17	Richard Coates	GB	350 Yamaha	2h 09m 03.4s
11	47	Andrew Nelson	GB	350 Yamaha	2h 09m 35.2s
12	35	Mark Farmer	GB	350 Yamaha	2h 10m 33.4s
13	3	John Weedon	GB	350 Yamaha	2h 10m 59.8s
14	45	Sammy Henry	GB	250 Honda	2h 13m 03.2s
15	20	Kenny Shepherd	GB	250 Spondon	2h 13m 52.6s
16	43	Mick Chatterton	GB	350 Yamaha	2h 14m 21.8s
17	46	Mike Booys	GB	350 Yamaha	2h 14m 21.0s
18	19	Chris Fargher	GB	350 Yamaha	2h 15m 32.8s
19	83	Stephen Johnson	GB	350 Yamaha	2h 15m 36.4s
20	51	Alan Lawton	GB	350 Yamaha	2h 15m 56.8s

Fastest lap: Steve Hislop, GB (350 Yamaha), 20m 18.8s, 111.51 mph/179.46 km/h.

TT Formula 2 race

6 laps, 226.38 miles/364.32 km

Place	*No.*	*Rider*	*Nat.*	*Machine*	*Time & speed*
1	28	Steve Hislop	GB	350 Yamaha	2h 03m 01.4s 110.40 mph/ 177.67 km/h
2	7	Eddie Laycock	IRL	350 Yamaha	2h 03m 18.4s
3	11	Bob Heath	GB	350 Yamaha	2h 04m 18.8s
4	15	Johnny Rea	GB	350 Yamaha	2h 05m 44.0s
5	29	Robert Dunlop	GB	350 Yamaha	2h 06m 28.4s
6	27	Derek Chatterton	GB	350 Yamaha	2h 06m 51.4s
7	10	Michael Seward	GB	600 Honda	2h 07m 38.8s
8	9	Dave Dean	GB	600 Honda	2h 07m 40.6s
9	17	Kevin Hughes	GB	600 Honda	2h 08m 12.4s
10	30	Ian Lougher	GB	350 Yamaha	2h 08m 26.2s
11	25	Peter Bateson	GB	600 Honda	2h 08m 46.8s
12	18	Ray Swann	GB	600 Honda	2h 08m 51.0s
13	66	John Byrne	IRL	350 Yamaha	2h 08m 55.4s
14	57	Bob Jackson	GB	600 Honda	2h 09m 09.8s
15	65	Alan Batson	GB	600 Honda	2h 09m 16.6s
16	32	Steve Boyes	GB	600 Honda	2h 09m 21.8s
17	6	Steve Cull	GB	600 Honda	2h 09m 49.6s
18	33	Malcolm Wheeler	GB	600 Honda	2h 11m 36.4s
19	38	Phil Armes	GB	600 Honda	2h 11m 46.0s
20	37	Colin Beven	GB	600 Honda	2h 11m 47.8s

Fastest lap: Laycock, 20m 08.8s, 112.36 mph/180.83 km/h.

Senior TT

4 laps, 150.92 miles/242.88 km

Place	*No.*	*Rider*	*Nat.*	*Machine*	*Time & speed*
1	3	Joey Dunlop	GB	500 Honda	1h 30m 41.2s 99.85 mph/ 160.69 km/h
2	2	Geoff Johnson	GB	998 Yamaha	1h 31m 39.4s
3	11	Roger Marshall	GB	1100 Suzuki	1h 32m 29.4s
4	4	Andy McGladdery	GB	1100 Suzuki	1h 33m 52.4s
5	12	Nick Jefferies	GB	750 Honda	1h 34m 49.2s
6	5	Trevor Nation	GB	998 Yamaha	1h 34m 50.8s
7	38	David Griffiths	GB	750 Yamaha	1h 35m 29.0s
8	29	Brian Morrison	GB	1100 Suzuki	1h 35m 38.0s
9	14	Graeme McGregor	AUS	750 Yamaha	1h 36m 57.6s
10	26	Eddie Laycock	IRL	750 Yamaha	1h 37m 03.0s
11	30	Glen Williams	NZ	1100 Suzuki	1h 37m 16.8s
12	63	Robert Haynes	GB	1100 Suzuki	1h 37m 38.0s
13	48	Jamie Whitham	GB	750 Suzuki	1h 38m 34.4s
14	39	Gary Radcliffe	GB	750 Yamaha	1h 38m 40.8s
15	23	Steve Ward	GB	750 Suzuki	1h 38m 55.0s
16	24	Des Barry	GB	750 Yamaha	1h 39m 22.6s
17	25	Roger Hurst	GB	750 Yamaha	1h 39m 24.0s
18	1	Klaus Klein	D	750 Yamaha	1h 40m 01.6s
19	88	Anthony Thompson	GB	1100 Suzuki	1h 40m 07.2s
20	44	Howard Selby	GB	1100 Suzuki	1h 40m 09.6s

Fastest lap: Dunlop, 21m 32.6s, 105.08 mph/169.11 km/h.

Production TT

(Class B, 401 cc-500 cc two-strokes/601 cc-750 cc four-strokes)

3 laps, 113.19 miles/182.16 km

Place	*No.*	*Rider*	*Nat.*	*Machine*	*Time & speed*
1	2	Geoff Johnson	GB	750 Yamaha	1h 01m 45.0s 109.98 mph/ 177.00 km/h
2	19	Brian Morrison	GB	750 Suzuki	1h 01m 49.6s
3	5	Trevor Nation	GB	750 Yamaha	1h 01m 53.2s
4	1	Kevin Wilson	CDN	750 Suzuki	1h 01m 58.4s
5	12	Graeme McGregor	AUS	750 Yamaha	1h 02m 08.4s
6	6	Nick Jefferies	GB	750 Honda	1h 02m 12.4s
7	22	Robert Haynes	GB	750 Kawasaki	1h 02m 41.8s
8	21	Glen Williams	NZ	750 Suzuki	1h 03m 00.0s
9	14	Steve Ward	GB	750 Suzuki	1h 03m 00.8s
10	24	Ian Duffus	GB	750 Yamaha	1h 03m 14.0s
11	23	Steve Linsdell	GB	750 Yamaha	1h 03m 23.8s
12	57	Dave Dean	GB	750 Yamaha	1h 03m 23.8s
13	9	Dennis Ireland	NZ	750 Kawasaki	1h 03m 49.0s
14	30	Grant Goodings	GB	750 Kawasaki	1h 03m 50.2s
14	47	Martyn Nelson	GB	750 Suzuki	1h 03m 50.2s

Fastest lap: Nation, 20m 16.6s, 111.64 mph/179.67 km/h.

Production TT

(Class D, 250 cc two-strokes/400 cc four-strokes)

3 laps, 113.19 miles/182.16 km

Place	*No.*	*Rider*	*Nat.*	*Machine*	*Time & speed*
1	86	Barry Woodland	GB	400 Yamaha	1h 05m 56.8s 102.98 mph/ 165.73 km/h
2	88	Malcolm Wheeler	GB	400 Yamaha	1h 06m 52.4s
3	82	Mat Oxley	GB	250 Yamaha	1h 06m 53.4s
4	81	Graham Cannell	GB	250 Yamaha	1h 07m 11.6s
5	96	Steve Hislop	GB	250 Yamaha	1h 07m 15.6s
6	98	Robert Dunlop	GB	250 Honda	1h 07m 17.8s
7	93	Phil Nichols	GB	250 Honda	1h 07m 19.2s
8	85	Chris Fargher	GB	400 Suzuki	1h 07m 24.2s
9	94	Carl Fogarty	GB	250 Yamaha	1h 07m 25.6s
10	84	Peter Bateson	GB	250 Honda	1h 07m 34.4s
11	87	Roger Hurst	GB	250 Yamaha	1h 07m 42.6s
12	123	Gary Thrush	GB	250 Yamaha	1h 08m 29.6s
13	104	Derek Glass	GB	250 Yamaha	1h 08m 45.2s
14	97	Ian Lougher	GB	250 Yamaha	1h 08m 56.4s
15	100	Alan Dugdale	GB	250 Honda	1h 08m 59.4s

Fastest lap: Woodland, 21m 54.8s, 103.36 mph/166.34 km/h.

1000 cc Sidecar TT: Race A

3 laps, 113.19 miles/182.16 km

Place	*No.*	*Driver & Passenger*	*Nat.*	*Machine*	*Time & speed*
1	3	Mick Boddice/ Don Williams	GB GB	700 Ireson-Yamaha	1h 04m 49.6s 104.76 mph/ 168.59 km/h
2	8	Dennis Bingham/ Julia Bingham	GB GB	700 Padgett-Yamaha	1h 05m 16.8s
3	19	Geoff Rushbrook/ Geoff Leitch	GB GB	700 Ireson-Yamaha	1h 05m 29.2s
4	5	Warwick Newman/ Eddie Yarker	GB GB	750 Ireson-Yamaha	1h 05m 36.0s
5	17	Kenny Howles/ Steve Pointer	GB GB	700 Ireson-Yamaha	1h 05m 48.0s
6	12	Martin Murphy/ Alan Langton	GB GB	700 McCavana-Yamaha	1h 06m 48.0s
7	7	Dick Greasley/ Stewart Atkinson	GB GB	700 Yamaha	1h 06m 40.6s
8	22	Eric Cornes/ Graham Wellington	GB GB	750 Ireson-Yamaha	1h 07m 37.4s
9	21	Neil Smith/ Phil Gravel	GB GB	700 NSR-Yamaha	1h 08m 11.2s
10	18	David Molyneux/ Paul Kneale	GB GB	750 Bregazzi-Yamaha	1h 08m 56.2s

Fastest lap: Boddice, 21m 24.6s, 105.73 mph/170.16 km/h.

1000 cc Sidecar TT: Race B

3 laps, 113.19 miles/182.16 km

Place	*No.*	*Driver & passenger*	*Nat*	*Machine*	*Time & speed*
1	2	Lowry Burton/ Pat Cashnahan	GB GB	700 Yamaha	1h 04m 21.0s 105.53 mph/ 169.83 km/h
2	17	Kenny Howles/ Steve Pointer	GB GB	700 Ireson-Yamaha	1h 04m 55.2s
3	6	Warwick Newman/ Eddie Yarker	GB GB	750 Ireson-Yamaha	1h 05m 59.6s
4	11	Lars Schwartz/ Leif Gustavsson	S S	750 Ireson-Yamaha	1h 06m 01.2s
5	4	Nigel Dollason/ Dave Huntington	GB GB	750 Barton-Phoenix	1h 06m 41.4s
6	21	Neil Smith/ Phil Gravel	GB GB	700 NSR-Yamaha	1h 06m 52.4s
7	9	Arthur Oates/ Edward Oates	GB GB	750 CAS-Yamaha	1h 06m 59.2s
8	22	Eric Cornes/ Graham Wellington	GB GB	750 Ireson-Yamaha	1h 07m 19.4s
9	19	Geoff Rushbrook/ Geoff Leitch	GB GB	700 Ireson-Yamaha	1h 07m 24.0s
10	29	Dennis Brown/ William Nelson	GB GB	750 TZ-Yamaha	1h 08m 04.6s

Fastest lap: Burton, 21m 22.2s, 105.93 mph/170.48 km/h.

Shell Oils Transatlantic Challenge

SHELL OILS TRANSATLANTIC CHALLENGE, Race 1. Brands Hatch Indy Circuit, 17 April. 16 laps of the 1.2036-mile/1.9370-km circuit, 19.26 miles/30.99 km.
1 Kevin Schwantz, USA (750 Suzuki), 13m 16.8s, 87.00 mph/140.01 km/h.
2 Wayne Rainey, USA (750 Honda); **3** Michel Mercier, CDN (750 Suzuki); **4** Gary Goodfellow, USA (750 Suzuki); **5** Richard Scott, NZ (750 Honda); **6** Doug Polen, USA (750 Suzuki); **7** Reuben McMurter, CDN (750 Yamaha); **8** Keith Huewen, GB (750 Yamaha); **9** Dan Chivington, USA (750 Honda); **10** John Ashmead, USA (750 Honda).
Fastest lap: Rainey, 49.1s, 88.24 mph/142.01 km/h.
Match points: USA, 129; GB, 78.

SHELL OILS TRANSATLANTIC CHALLENGE, Race 2. Brands Hatch Indy Circuit, 17 April. 16 laps of the 1.2036-mile/1.9370-km circuit, 19.26 miles/30.99 km.
1 Wayne Rainey, USA (750 Honda), 13m 13.3s, 87.39 mph/143.86 km/h.
2 Kevin Schwantz, USA (750 Suzuki); **3** Gary Goodfellow, USA (750 Suzuki); **4** Michel Mercier, CDN (750 Suzuki); **5** Doug Polen, USA (750 Suzuki); **6** Richard Scott, NZ (750 Honda); **7** Keith Huewen, GB (750 Yamaha); **8** Reuben McMurter, CDN (750 Yamaha); **9** Ron Haslam, GB (750 Honda); **10** Mark Phillips, GB (750 Suzuki).
Fastest lap: Rainey, 48.9s, 88.60 mph/142.59 km/h.
Match points: USA, 175; GB, 87. **Total:** USA, 246; GB 165.

SHELL OILS TRANSATLANTIC CHALLENGE, Race 3. Brands Hatch Indy Circuit, 17 April. 16 laps of the 1.2036-mile/1.9370-km circuit, 19.26 miles/30.99 km.
1 Kevin Schwantz, USA (750 Suzuki), 13m 11.5s, 87.58 mph/140.95 km/h.
2 Wayne Rainey, USA (750 Honda); **3** Gary Goodfellow, USA (750 Suzuki); **4** Richard Scott, NZ (750 Honda); **5** Doug Polen, USA (750 Suzuki); **6** Trevor Nation, GB (750 Yamaha); **7** John Ashmead, USA (750 Honda); **8** Keith Huewen, GB (750 Yamaha); **9** Dan Chivington, USA (750 Honda); **10** Mark Phillips, GB (750 Suzuki).
Fastest lap: Rainey, 48.7s, 88.97 mph/143.18 km/h.
Match Points: USA, 109; GB, 95. **Total:** USA, 355; GB, 260.

SHELL OILS TRANSATLANTIC CHALLENGE, Race 4. Donington Park Circuit, 19 April. 8 laps of the 2.500-mile/4.023-km circuit, 20.00 miles/32.18 km.
1 Wayne Rainey, USA (750 Honda), 13m 58.74s, 85.84 mph/138.15 km/h.
2 Kevin Schwantz, USA (750 Suzuki); **3** Gary Goodfellow, USA (750 Suzuki); **4** Richard Scott, NZ (750 Honda); **5** Doug Polen, USA (750 Suzuki); **6** Reuben McMurter, CDN (750 Yamaha); **7** Phil Mellor, GB (750 Suzuki); **8** Mark Phillips, GB (750 Suzuki); **9** Dan Chivington, USA (750 Honda); **10** John Ashmead, USA (750 Honda).
Fastest lap: Rainey, 1m 43.12s, 87.27 mph/140.45 km/h.
Match points: USA, 116; GB, 84. **Total:** USA, 471; GB, 344.

SHELL OILS TRANSATLANTIC CHALLENGE, Race 5. Donington Park Circuit, 19 April. 4 laps of the 2.500-mile/4.023-km circuit, 10.00 miles/16.09 km.
1 Kevin Schwantz, USA (750 Suzuki), 7m 43.87s, 77.60 mph/124.88 km/h.
2 Richard Scott, NZ (750 Honda); **3** Phil Mellor, GB (750 Suzuki); **4** Doug Polen, USA (750 Honda); **5** Michel Mercier, CDN (750 Suzuki); **6** John Ashmead, USA (750 Honda); **7** Dan Chivington, USA (750 Honda); **8** Trevor Nation, GB (750 Yamaha); **9** Roger Hurst, GB (750 Yamaha); **10** Wayne Rainey, USA (750 Honda).
Fastest lap: Goodfellow, 1m 45.17s, 85.57 mph/137.71 km/h.
Match points: USA, 53.5; GB, 48.5. **Total:** USA, 524.5; GB, 392.5.

SHELL OILS TRANSATLANTIC CHALLENGE, Race 6. Donington Park Circuit, 19 April. 8 laps of the 2.500-mile/4.023-km circuit, 20.00 miles/32.18 km.
1 Wayne Rainey, USA (750 Honda), 13m 54.04s, 86.32 mph/138.92 km/h.
2 Kevin Schwantz, USA (750 Suzuki); **3** Gary Goodfellow, USA (750 Suzuki); **4** Michel Mercier, CDN (750 Suzuki); **5** Richard Scott, NZ (750 Honda); **6** Dan Chivington, USA (750 Honda); **7** Phil Mellor, GB (750 Suzuki); **8** Trevor Nation, GB (750 Yamaha); **9** Roger Hurst, GB (750 Yamaha); **10** Jamie Whitham, GB (750 Suzuki).
Fastest lap: Rainey, 1m 42.61s, 87.71 mph/141.16 km/h.
Match points: USA, 103; GB, 93. **Total:** USA, 627.5; GB, 485.5.

SHELL OILS TRANSATLANTIC CHALLENGE, Race 7. Donington Park Circuit, 20 April. 8 laps of the 2.500-mile/4023-km circuit, 20.00 miles/32.18 km.
1 Wayne Rainey, USA (750 Honda), 14m 00.62s, 85.65 mph/137.84 km/h.
2 Kevin Schwantz, USA (750 Suzuki); **3** Gary Goodfellow, USA (750 Suzuki); **4** Richard Scott, NZ (750 Honda); **5** Michel Mercier, CDN (750 Suzuki); **6** Phil Mellor, GB (750 Suzuki); **7** Doug Polen, USA (750 Suzuki); **8** Keith Huewen, GB (750 Yamaha); **9** Trevor Nation, GB (750 Yamaha); **10** Roger Hurst, GB (750 Yamaha).
Fastest lap: Rainey, 1m 43.16s, 87.24 mph/140.40 km/h.
Match points: USA, 102; GB, 87. **Total:** USA, 827.5; GB, 572.5.

SHELL OILS TRANSATLANTIC CHALLENGE, Race 8. Donington Park Circuit, 20 April. 8 laps of the 2.500-mile/4.023-km circuit, 20.00 miles/32.18 km.
1 Kevin Schwantz, USA (750 Suzuki), 13m 56.77s, 86.05 mph/138.48 km/h.
2 Gary Goodfellow, USA (750 Suzuki); **3** Wayne Rainey, USA (750 Honda); **4** Michel Mercier, CDN (750 Suzuki); **5** Richard Scott, NZ (750 Honda); **6** Keith Huewen, GB (750 Yamaha); **7** Phil Mellor, GB (750 Suzuki); **8** Trevor Nation, GB (750 Yamaha); **9** Dan Chivington, USA (750 Honda); **10** Doug Polen, USA (750 Suzuki).
Fastest lap: Schwantz, 1m 43.14s, 87.26 mph/140.43 km/h.
Match points: USA, 104; GB, 85; **Total:** USA, 832.5; GB, 657.5.

SHELL OILS TRANSATLANTIC CHALLENGE, Race 9. Donington Park Circuit, 20 April. 8 laps of the 2.500-mile/4.023-km circuit, 20.00 miles/32.18 km.
1 Wayne Rainey, USA (750 Honda), 13m 57.76s, 85.94 mph/138.31 km/h.
2 Kevin Schwantz, USA (750 Suzuki); **3** Gary Goodfellow, GB (750 Suzuki); **4** Keith Huewen, GB (750 Yamaha); **5** Trevor Nation, GB (750 Yamaha); **6** Michel Mercier, CDN (750 Suzuki); **7** Phil Mellor, GB (750 Suzuki); **8** Doug Polen, USA (750 Suzuki); **9** Geoff Fowler, GB (750 Yamaha); **10** John Lofthouse, GB (750 Suzuki).
Fastest lap: Rainey, 1m 43.32s, 87.10 mph/140.17 km/h.
Match points: USA, 101; GB, 88.

Final match points

1 USA	993.5
2 GB	745.5

Individual riders' points

1 Kevin Schwantz, USA	165
2 Wayne Rainey, USA	161.5
3 Gary Goodfellow, USA	146
4 Richard Scott, NZ	123.5
5 Doug Polen, USA	115.5
6 Michel Mercier, CDN	113

7 Trevor Nation, GB, 104.5; **8** Phil Mellor, GB, 104; **9** Keith Huewen, GB, 85; **10** Dan Chivington, USA, 84; **11** Ray Swann, GB, 61.5; **12** John Ashmead, USA, 52.5; **13** Reuben McMurter, CDN, 51; **14** Geoff Fowler, GB, 45; **15** Roger Hurst, GB, 45; **16** Ottis Lance, USA, 45; **17** Mark Phillips, GB, 40; **18** Jamie Whitham, GB, 39; **19** John Lofthouse, GB, 31.5; **20** Ron Haslam, GB, 29; **21** Gary Lingham, GB, 27; **22** Peter Dalby, GB, 10.5; **23** Simon Buckmaster, GB, 0.

Endurance World Championship

1000 KM DO ESTORIL, Autodromo do Estoril, Portugal, 10 May. Endurance World Championship, round 1. 230 laps of the 2.86-mile/4.35-km circuit, 658 miles/1000.5 km.
1 Hervé Moineau/Bruno le Bihan, F/F (750 Suzuki), 230 laps, 83.52 mph/134.42 km/h.
2 Ulrich Kallen/Robbi Schläfi, CH/CH (750 Honda), 226 laps; **3** Mat Oxley/Geoff Fowler, GB/GB (750 Yamaha), 223; **4** Hans-Peter Bollinger/Hermann Perren, CH/CH (750 Suzuki), 219; **5** Patrick Salles/Olivier Roullet, F/F (750 Suzuki), 219; **6** Dirk Brand/Gerard Flameling, NL/NL (750 Yamaha), 218; **7** Roger Perrotet/Eric Emery, CH/CH (750 Suzuki), 217; **8** Dave Railton/Steve Bonhomme, GB/GB (750 Yamaha), 217; **9** M. Joad/A. Fernandez, E/E (750 Yamaha), 211; **10** Andreas Bartel/H. Meder, A/A (750 Yamaha), 209.
Fastest lap: Moineau, 1m 50.7s, 88.4 mph/142.27 km/h.
Championship points: **1** Moineau and le Bihan, 15; **3** Kallen and Schläfi, 12; **5** Oxley and Fowler, 10; **7** Bollinger and Perren, 8; **9** Salles and Roullet, 6.

DONINGTON PARK 8-HOURS, Great Britain, 24 May. Endurance World Championship, round 2. 259 laps of the 1.96-mile/3.136-km circuit, 507.64 miles/812.224 km.
1 Hervé Moineau/Bruno le Bihan, F/F (750 Suzuki), 7h 58m 19.95s, 81.21 mph/130.70 km/h.
2 Mat Oxley/Geoff Fowler, GB/GB (750 Yamaha), 256 laps; **3** Gérard Jolivet/Michel Simeon, F/F (750 Suzuki), 256; **4** Ulrich Kallen/Robbi Schläfi, CH/CH (750 Honda), 253; **5** Dave Railton/Steve Bonhomme, GB/GB (750 Yamaha), 253; **6** Johan van Vaerenbergh/Eric de Doncker, B/B (750 Kawasaki), 252; **7** Patrice More/Bernard Chateau, F/F (750 Suzuki), 252; **8** M. Teuber/K. Gasser, SF/SF (750 Kawasaki), 250; **9** Hans-Peter Bollinger/ Hermann Perren, CH/CH (750 Suzuki), 248; **10** Patrick Salles/Olivier Roullet, F/F (750 Suzuki), 246.
Fastest lap: not available.
Championship points: **1** Moineau and le Bihan, 30; **3** Oxley and Fowler, 22; **5** Kallen and Schläfi, 20; **7** Bollinger and Perren, Jolivet and Simeon, 10.

6 ORE DI MONZA, Autodromo di Monza, Italy, 21 June. Endurance World Championship, round 3. 176 laps of the 3.604-mile/5.800-km circuit, 634.30 miles/1020.8 km.
1 Virginio Ferrari/Davide Tardozzi, I/I (Bimota), 5h 53m 33.08s, 106.9 mph/172.252 km/h.
2 Hervé Moineau/Bruno le Bihan, F/F (750 Suzuki), 176 laps; **3** Johan van Vaerenbergh/Eric de Doncker, B/B (750 Kawasaki), 170; **4** Klaus Zabka/Peter Häfner, D/D (750 Suzuki), 168; **5** Johann Osendörfer/Wolfhart Kurzhagen, D/D (750 Yamaha), 167; **6** Mat Oxley/Geoff Fowler, GB/GB (750 Yamaha), 167; **7** Dave Railton/Steve Bonhomme, GB/GB (750 Yamaha), 166; **8** Eric Emery/Roger Perrotet, CH/CH (750 Suzuki), 166; **9** Hans-Peter Bollinger/Hermann Perren, CH/CH (750 Suzuki), 165; **10** Patrick Braud/Philippe Carta, F/F (750 Suzuki), 165.
Fastest lap: Ferrari, 1m 57.05s, 110.79 mph/178.385 km/h.
Championship points: **1** Moineau and le Bihan, 42; **3** Oxley and Fowler, 27; **5** Kallen and Schläfi, 20; **7** Ferrari and Tardozzi, van Vaerenbergh and de Doncker, 15.

MOTORRAD MARATHON 6 STUNDEN ÖSTERREICHRING, Zeltweg, Austria, 28 June. Endurance World Championship, round 4. 170 laps of the 3.692-mile/5.942-km circuit, 627.64 miles/1010.14 km.
1 Hervé Moineau/Bruno le Bihan, F/F (750 Suzuki), 6h 00m 45.994s, 104.5 mph/168.013 km/h.
2 Johan van Vaerenbergh/Eric de Doncker, B/B (750 Kawasaki), 166 laps; **3** Walter Oswald/Reinhold Gutzelnig, A/A (750 Honda), 165; **4** Patrick Braud/Philippe Carta, F/F (750 Suzuki), 163; **5** Robbi Schläfi/Ulrich Kallen, CH/CH (750 Honda), 162; **6** Andy Green/Ian Green, GB/GB (750 Suzuki), 161; **7** Andreas Bartel/Dietmar Marehard, A/A (750 Yamaha), 160; **8** Peter Häfner/Roger Perrotet, D/CH (750 Suzuki), 160; **9** Günter Heil/Erhard Sterba, D/D (750 Suzuki), 160; **10** Patrice More/Bernard Chateau, F/F (750 Suzuki), 158.
Fastest lap: Moineau, 2m 03.263s, 107.17 mph/162.588 km/h.
Championship points: **1** Moineau and le Bihan, 57; **3** van Vaerenbergh and de Doncker, Oxley and Fowler, 27; **7** Kallen and Schläfi, 26; **9** Ferrari and Tardozzi, 15.

SUZUKA 8-HOURS, Suzuka International Racing Course, Japan, 26 July. Endurance World Championship, round 5. 200 laps of the 3.675-mile/5.914-km circuit, 735 miles/1182.8 km.
1 Martin Wimmer/Kevin Magee, D/AUS (750 Yamaha), 8h 01m 30.045s, 91.37 mph/147.04 km/h.
2 Garry Goodfellow/Katsuro Takayoshi, CAN/J (750 Suzuki), 200 laps; **3** John Kocinski/Cal Rayborn, USA/USA (750 Yamaha), 198; **4** Hervé Moineau/Bruno le Bihan, F/F (750 Suzuki), 197; **5** Pierre Etienne Samin/Thierry Crine, F/F (750 Kawasaki), 191; **6** Yukiya Ueda/Takao Abe, J/J (600 Honda), 191; **7** Johan van Vaerenbergh/Paul Ramon, B/B (750 Kawasaki), 190; **8** Mitsuo Saito/Ryo Suzuki, J/J (750 Yamaha), 190; **9** Norihiko Fujiwara/Kenmei Matsumoto, J/J (750 Yamaha), 189; **10** Hisahi Yamaha/Toshiaki Hakamada, J/J (750 Suzuki), 189.
Fastest lap: not available.
Championship points: **1** Moineau and le Bihan, 65; **3** van Vaerenbergh, 31; **4** de Doncker, Oxley and Fowler, 27; **7** Kallen and Schläfi, 26; **9** Ferrari and Tardozzi, Wimmer and Magee, 15.

24 HEURES DE LIÈGE, Spa-Francorchamps Grand Prix Circuit, Belgium, 15/16 August. Endurance World Championship, round 6. 513 laps of the 4.335-mile/6.976-km circuit, 2223.855 miles/3578.688 km.
1 Richard Hubin/Michel Simeon/Mark Simul, B/B/B (750 Suzuki), 23h 54m 08.37s, 93.15 mph/149.914 km/h.
2 Johan van Vaerenbergh/Eric de Doncker/Paul Ramon, B/B/B (750 Kawasaki), 505 laps; **3** Hervé Moineau/Bruno le Bihan/Jean-Louis Tournadre, F/F/F (750 Suzuki), 502; **4** Peter Häfner/Roger Perrotet/Rolf Barten, D/CH/D (750 Suzuki), 497; **5** Patrick Braud/Philippe Carta/Gerard Jolivet, F/F/F (750 Suzuki), 492; **6** C. Bouheben/G. Meynet/Jean-Louis Tranois, F/F/F (750 Suzuki), 491; **7** Dominique Savary/Jose Chevalier/Eddy Chevalley, CH/CH/CH (750 Honda), 486; **8** Russell Benney/Steve Bateman/R. Burden, GB/GB/GB (750 Yamaha), 476; **9** P. Delacourt/D. Bonvicini/J. Mergny, B/B/B (750 Yamaha), 471; **10** Eamonn Cleere/Steve Colville/Roger Bennett, GB/GB/GB (750 Suzuki), 468.
Fastest lap: Moineau, 2m 39.01s, 98.8 mph/158.141 km/h.
Championship points: **1** Moineau and le Bihan, 85; **3** van Vaerenbergh, 55; **4** de Doncker, 51; **5** Simeon, 40; **6** Hubin and Simul, 30; **8** Ramon, 28; **9** Oxley, Fowler and Häfner, 27.

JEREZ 1000 KM, Circuito del Jerez, Spain, 6 September. Endurance World Championship, round 7. 234 laps of the 2.621-mile/4.218-km circuit, 613.314 miles/987 km.
1 Hervé Moineau/Bruno le Bihan, F/F (750 Suzuki), 234 laps.
2 Johan van Vaerenbergh/Eric de Doncker, B/B (750 Kawasaki), 231; **3** Dirk Brand/Dirk Bemelman, NL/NL (750 Yamaha), 231; **4** Geoff Fowler/Jean-Pierre Oudin, GB/F (750 Yamaha), 230; **5** Patrice More/Bernard Chateau, F/F (750 Suzuki), 229; **6** Jean-Miguel Pardo/André Garcia, E/E (750 Yamaha), 228; **7** Ulrich Kallen/Robbi Schläfi, CH/CH (750 Honda); **8** Hans-Peter Bollinger/Hermann Perren CH/CH (750 Suzuki), 225; **9** Eric Emery/Olivier Roullet, CH/F (750 Suzuki), 223. **10** Juan Cano/Xavier Cardelus, E/E (750 Yamaha), 222.
Fastest lap: not available.
Championship points: **1** Moineau and le Bihan, 100; **2** van Vaerenbergh, 67; **3** de Doncker, 63; **5** Simeon, 40; **6** Fowler, 35; **7** Huvin and Simul, Kallen and Schläfi, 30.

BOL D'OR, Paul Ricard Circuit, France, 19/20 September. Endurance World Championship, round 8. 651 laps of the 3.610-mile/5.810-km circuit, 2350 miles/3782.31 km.
1 Dominique Sarron/Jean-Louis Battistini/Jean-Michel Mattioli, F/F/F (750 Honda), 23h 40m 28.12s, 100.25 mph/160.396 km/h.
2 Christian Sarron/Patrick Igoa/Jean-Philippe Ruggia, F/F/F (750 Yamaha), 645; **3** Hervé Moineau/Bruno le Bihan/Guy Bertin, F/F/F (750 Suzuki), 639; **4** Johan van Vaerenbergh/Eric de Doncker/Paul Ramon, B/B/B (750 Kawasaki), 625; **5** Dirk Brand/Dirk Bemelman/Henk van der Mark, NL/NL/NL (750 Yamaha), 622; **6** Robbi Schläfi/Ulrich Kallen/Urs Meier, CH/CH/CH (Honda), 620; **7** Roger Perrotet/Peter Häfner/Rolf Barten, CH/D/D (750 Suzuki), 612; **8** D. Heinen/H. Sonnet/Eric Brigard, D/B/B (750 Honda), 611; **9** E. Baldé/Eric Delcamp/H. Jund, F/F/F (750 Suzuki), 696; **10** Peter Sköld/Peter Linden/Per Jansson, S/S/S (750 Honda), 604.
Fastest lap: D. Sarron, 2m 03.90s, 105.32 mph/169.6 km/h.

Final Championship points

1 =	Hervé Moineau, F	120
1 =	Bruno le Bihan, F	120
3	Johan van Vaerenbergh, B	83
4	Eric de Doncker, B	79
5	Paul Ramon, B	44
6 =	Michel Simeon, B	40
6 =	Robbi Schläfi, CH	40
6 =	Ulrich Kallen, CH	40

9 Geoff Fowler, GB, 35; **10** Peter Häfner, D and Roger Perrotet, CH, 34; **12** Dominique Sarron, F, Jean-Louis Battistini, F, Jean-Michel Mattioli, F, Richard Hubin, B and Mark Simul, B, 30; **17** Mat Oxley, GB and Dirk Brand, NL, 27; **19** Christian Sarron, F, Patrick Igoa, F and Jean-Philippe Ruggia, F, 24.

European Championship

CIRCUITO DEL JEREZ, Spain, 15 March. 2.621-mile/4.218-km circuit.
500 cc, round 1 (23 laps, 60.28 miles/97.01 km)
1 Mark Phillips, GB (Suzuki), 45m 44.86s, 79.06 mph/127.23 km/h.
2 Manfred Fischer, D (Honda); **3** Marco Papa, I (Honda); **4** Karl Truchsess, A (Honda); **5** Daniel Amatriain, E (Honda); **6** Andreas Leuthe, LUX (Honda); **7** Alan Jeffery, GB (Suzuki); **8** Peter Schleef, D (Yamaha); **9** Franz Kaserer, A (Suzuki); **10** Daniel Pauget, F (Honda).
Fastest lap: Phillips, 1m 57.97s, 79.98 mph/128.72 km/h.
Championship points: **1** Phillips, 15; **2** Fischer, 12; **3** Papa, 10; **4** Truchsess, 8; **5** Amatriain, 6; **6** Leuthe, 5.

250 cc, round 1 (20 laps, 52.42 miles/87.436 km)
1 Xavier Cardelus, E (Kobas), 39m 14.61s, 80.14 mph/128.97 km/h.
2 Patrick van der Goorbergh, NL (Rotax); **3** Nigel Bosworth, GB (Yamaha); **4** Bernard Hänggeli, CH (Yamaha); **5** Cees Doorakkers, NL (Honda); **6** Rob Orme, GB (Yamaha); **7** Alberto Puig, E (Kobas); **8** Andreas Preining, A (Rotax); **9** Fabrizio Pirovanno, I (Yamaha); **10** Jorge Cavestany, E (Kobas).
Fastest lap: Doorakkers, 1m 56.00s, 81.34 mph/130.90 km/h.
Championship points: **1** Cardelus, 15; **2** van der Goorbergh, 12; **3** Bosworth, 10; **4** Hänggeli, 8; **5** Doorakkers, 6; **6** Orme, 5.

125 cc, round 1 (17 laps, 44.56 miles/71.71 km)
1 Manuel Hernandez, E (Beneti), 34m 59.30s, 76.40 mph/122.96 km/h.
2 Adolf Stadler, D (MBA); **3** Jean-Claude Selini, F (MBA); **4** Fernando Gonzalez, E (Kobas); **5** Chris Galatowicz, GB (Honda); **6** Antonio Oliveros, E (MBA); **7** Massimo Piazza, I (MBA); **8** Michel Escudier, F (MBA); **9** Laurent Chapeau, F (MBA); **10** Pietro Paolucci, I (MBA).
Fastest lap: Hernandez, 2m 01.42s, 77.71 mph/125.06 km/h.
Championship points: **1** Hernandez, 15; **2** Stadler, 12; **3** Selini, 10; **4** Gonzalez, 8; **5** Galatowicz, 6; **6** Oliveros, 5.

80 cc, round 1 (12 laps, 31.45 miles/50.62 km)
1 Julian Miralles, E (Derbi), 26m 16.49s, 71.82 mph/115.58 km/h.
2 Alejandro Criville, E (Derbi); **3** Gunther Schirnhofer, D (Krauser); **4** Károly Juhász, H (Krauser); **5** Ralf Waldmann, D (ERK); **6** Mario Stocco, I (Faccioli); **7** René Dünki, CH (Krauser); **8** Chris Baert, B (Seel); **9** Heinz Paschen, D (Huvo); **10** Jacques Bernard, B (Huvo).
Fastest lap: Criville, 2m 09.36s, 72.94 mph/117.39 km/h.
Championship points: **1** Miralles, 15; **2** Criville, 12; **3** Schirnhofer, 10; **4** Juhász, 8; **5** Waldmann, 6; **6** Stocco, 5.

DONINGTON PARK CIRCUIT, Great Britain, 19/20 April. 2.500-mile/4.023-km circuit.
500 cc, round 2 (25 laps, 62.50 miles/100.58 km)
1 Manfred Fischer, D (Honda), 44m 41.26s, 83.91 mph/135.03 km/h.
2 Steve Manley, GB (Suzuki); **3** Steve Henshaw, GB (Suzuki); **4** Henk van der Mark, NL (Honda); **5** Marco Papa, I (Honda); **6** Maarten Duyzers, NL (Honda); **7** Ari Rämö, SF (Honda); **8** Ian Pratt, GB (Suzuki); **9** Mike Lomas, GB (Suzuki); **10** John Brindley, GB (Yamaha).
Fastest lap: Fischer, 1m 45.07s, 85.65 mph/137.81 km/h.
Championship points: **1** Fischer, 27; **2** Papa, 16; **3** Phillips, 15; **4** Manley, 12; **5** Henshaw, 10; **6** Truchsess and van der Mark, 8.

250 cc, round 2 (20 laps, 50.00 miles/80.46 km)
1 Andreas Preining, A (Rotax), 35m 37.42s, 84.21 mph/135.51 km/h.
2 Rob Orme, GB (Yamaha); **3** Peter van der Goorbergh, NL (Honda); **4** Bernard Hänggeli, CH (Yamaha); **5** Nigel Bosworth, GB (Yamaha); **6** Fabrizio Pirovanno, I (Yamaha); **7** Jochen Schmid, D (Yamaha); **8** Cees Doorakkers, NL (Honda); **9** Alberto Puig, E (Kobas); **10** Engelbert Neumair, A (Rotax).
Fastest lap: Orme, 1m 45.76s, 85.09 mph/136.91 km/h.
Championship points: **1** van der Goorbergh, 22; **2** Preining, 18; **3** Orme, 17; **4** Bosworth and Hänggeli, 16; **6** Cardelus, 15.

125 cc, round 2 (20 laps, 50.00 miles/80.46 km)
1 Corrado Catalano, I (MBA), 37m 46.37s, 79.42 mph/127.80 km/h.
2 Adolf Stadler, D (MBA); **3** Gilles Payraudeau, F (MBA); **4** Flemming Kistrup, DK (MBA); **5** Chris Galatowicz, GB (Honda); **6** Jean-Claude Selini, F (MBA); **7** Peter Sommer, CH (Supeso); **8** Thomas Møller-Pedersen, DK (MBA); **9** Christian le Badezet, F (MBA); **10** Ton Spek, NL (MBA).
Fastest lap: Selini, 1m 51.60s, 80.64 mph/129.78 km/h.
Championship points: **1** Stadler, 24; **2** Hernandez, Selini and Catalano, 15; **5** Galatowicz, 12; **6** Payraudeau, 10.

Sidecars, round 1 (20 laps, 50.00 miles/80.46 km)
1 Ray Gardner/Tony Strevens, GB/GB (Yamaha), 36m 42.83s, 81.71 mph/131.49 km/h.
2 Tony Baker/John Hennigan, GB/GB (Yamaha); **3** Jean-Louis Millet/Claude Debroux, F/F (Yamaha); **4** Gary Knight/Phil Coombes, GB/GB (Yamaha); **5** John Barker/Steve China, GB/GB (Yamaha); **6** Fritz Stölzle/Hubert Stölzle, D/D (Yamaha); **7** Neil Smith/Phil Gravel, GB/GB (Yamaha); **8** Judd Drew/Chris Plant, GB/GB (Yamaha); **9** John Evans/Geoff Wilbraham, GB/GB (Yamaha); **10** Axel von Berg/Werner Riedel, D/D (Busch).

Fastest lap: Gardner, 1m 48.26s, 83.13 mph/133.76 km/h.
Championship points: 1 Gardner, 15; **2** Baker, 12; **3** Millet, 10; **4** Knight, 8; **5** Barker, 6; **6** Stölzle, 5.

SALZBURGRING, Austria, 10 May. 2.636-mile/4.243-km circuit.
250 cc, round 3 (18 laps, 47.44 miles/76.37 km)
1 Stefan Klabacher, A (Schafleitner), 26m 58.75s, 102.81 mph/165.60 km/h.
2 Helmut Bradl, D (Honda); **3** Engelbert Neumair, A (Rotax); **4** Wilhelm Hörhager, A (Honda); **5** Jochen Schmid, D (Yamaha); **6** Urs Jucker, CH (Yamaha); **7** Thomas Bacher, A (Rotax); **8** Josef Hutter, A (Honda); **9** Marcello Iannetta, I (Yamaha); **10** Nigel Bosworth, GB (Yamaha).
Fastest lap: Bacher, 1m 28.10s, 107.75 mph/173.38 km/h.
Championship points: 1 van der Goorbergh, 22; **2** Preining, 18; **3** Bosworth and Orme, 17; **5** Hänggeli, 16; **6** Cardelus and Klabacher, 15.

125 cc, round 3 (17 laps, 44.8 miles/72.13 km)
1 Adolf Stadler, D (MBA), 27m 20.89s, 98.51 mph/158.40 km/h.
2 Corrado Catalano, I (MBA); **3** Norbert Peschke, D (Seel); **4** Gilles Payraudeau, F (MBA); **5** Flemming Kistrup, DK (MBA); **6** Emilio Cuppini, I (MBA); **7** Nicolas Gonzalez, E (Cobas); **8** Alain Kempener, B (MBA); **9** Luciano Garagnani, I (MBA); **10** Thomas Møller-Pedersen, DK (MBA).
Fastest lap: Catalano, 1m 35.70s, 99.20 mph/159.60 km/h.
Championship points: 1 Stadler, 39; **2** Catalano, 27; **3** Payraudeau, 18; **4** Hernandez and Selini, 15; **6** Kistrup, 14.

80 cc, round 2 (12 laps, 31.63 miles/50.91 km)
1 Károly Juhász, H (Krauser), 20m 31.58s, 92.17 mph/148.4 km/h.
2 Julian Miralles, E (Derbi); **3** Peter Öttl, D (Krauser); **4** Alejandro Criville, E (Derbi); **5** René Dünki, CH (Krauser); **6** Raimo Lipponen, SF (Krauser); **7** Mario Stocco, I (Faccioli); **8** Thomas Engl, D (GPE-Esch); **9** Heinz Paschen, D (Casal); **10** Paolo Scappini, I (Unimoto).
Fastest lap: Juhász, 1m 39.30s, 95.58 mph/153.82 km/h.
Championship points: 1 Miralles, 27; **2** Juhász, 23; **3** Criville, 20; **4** Dünki, Öttl and Schirnhofer, 10.

AUTODROM MOST, Czechoslovakia, 14 June. 2.577-mile/4.148-km circuit.
500 cc, round 3 (25 laps, 64.42 miles/103.7 km)
1 Daniel Amatriain, E (Honda), 41m 44.20s, 92.61 mph/149.1 km/h.
2 Karl Truchsess, A (Honda); **3** Manfred Fischer, D (Honda); **4** Henk van der Mark, NL (Honda); **5** Marco Papa, I (Honda); **6** Maarten Duyzers, NL (Honda); **7** Vittorio Gibertini, I (Suzuki); **8** Peter Schleef, D (Honda); **9** Ari Rämö, SF (Honda); **10** Rudolf Zeller, A (Honda).
Fastest lap: Amatriain, 1m 38.76s, 93.96 mph/151.202 km/h.
Championship points: 1 Fischer, 37; **2** Papa, 22; **3** Amatriain, 21; **4** Truchsess, 20; **5** van der Mark, 16; **6** Phillips, 15.

250 cc, round 4 (23 laps, 59.27 miles/95.40 km)
1 Xavier Cardelus, AND (Cobas), 39m 03.32s.
2 Engelbert Neumair, A (Rotax); **3** Alberto Puig, E (Cobas); **4** Nedy Crotta, CH (Armstrong); **5** Andreas Preining, A (Rotax); **6** Cees Doorakkers, NL (Honda); **7** Rob Orme, GB (Yamaha); **8** Urs Jucker, CH (Yamaha); **9** Wilhelm Hörhager, A (Honda); **10** Thomas Bacher, A (Rotax).
Fastest lap: Neumair, 1m 40.15s, 92.60 mph/149.104 km/h.
Championship points: 1 Cardelus, 30; **2** Preining, 24; **3** Neumair, 23; **4** van der Goorbergh, 22; **5** Orme, 21; **6** Bosworth and Doorakkers, 17.

125 cc, round 4 (20 laps, 51.54 miles/82.96 km)
1 Norbert Peschke, D (Seel), 35m 40.79s, 86.67 mph/139.6 km/h.
2 Corrado Catalano, I (MBA); **3** Adolf Stadler, D (MBA); **4** Flemming Kistrup, DK (MBA); **5** Manuel Hernandez, E (Beneti); **6** Peter Sommer, CH (Supeso); **7** Denis Longueville, F (MBA); **8** Fernando Gonzalez, E (Cobas); **9** Robert Zwidl, A (MBA); **10** Bogdan Nikolov, BG (MBA).
Fastest lap: Catalano, 1m 44.35s, 88.92 mph/143.103 km/h.
Championship points: 1 Stadler, 49; **2** Catalano, 39; **3** Peschke, 25; **4** Kistrup, 22; **5** Hernandez, 21; **6** Payraudeau, 18.

80 cc, round 3 (16 laps, 41.23 miles/66.36 km)
1 Károly Juhász, H (Krauser), 29m 54.27s, 82.72 mph/133.2 km/h.
2 Michael Gschwander, D (Seel); **3** Julian Miralles, E (Derbi); **4** Ralf Waldmann, D (Erk); **5** Alejandro Criville, E (Derbi); **6** Günther Schirnhofer, D (Krauser); **7** René Dünki, CH (Krauser); **8** Heinz Paschen, D (Casal); **9** Peter Öttl, D (Krauser); **10** Matthias Ehinger, D (Krauser).
Fastest lap: Juhász, 1m 59.36s, 83.95 mph/135.09 km/h.
Championship points: 1 Juhász, 38; **2** Miralles, 37; **3** Criville, 26; **4** Schirnhofer, 15; **5** Dünki and Waldmann, 14.

Sidecars, round 2 (20 laps, 51.54 miles/82.96 km)
1 Dennis Bingham/Julia Bingham, GB/GB (Yamaha), 34m 32.01s, 89.54 mph/144.2 km/h.
2 Luigi Casagrande/Adolf Hänni, CH/CH (Yamaha); **3** Fritz Stölzle/Hubert Stölzle, D/D (Yamaha); **4** Jean-Louis Millet/Claude Debroux, F/F (Seymaz); **5** Barry Smith/David Smith, GB/GB (Windle); **6** Jacques Heriot/Jean-Luc Sage, F/F (Yamaha); **7** John Barker/Steve China, GB/GB (Yamaha); **8** Paul Atkinson/Graham Simmons, GB/GB (Yamaha); **9** Erwin Weber/Eckart Rösinger, D/D (Yamaha); **10** Neil Smith/Phil Gravel, GB/GB (Yamaha).
Fastest lap: Casagrande, 1m 40.12s, 92.68 mph/149.149 km/h.
Championship points: 1 Millet, 18; **2** Bingham, Gardner and Stölzle, 15; **5** Baker and Casagrande, 12.

CIRCUIT VAN DRENTHE, ASSEN, Holland, 22/27 June. 3.812-mile/6.134-km circuit.
500 cc, round 4 (15 laps, 57.18 miles/92.01 km)
1 Manfred Fischer, D (Honda), 35m 08.59s, 97.55 mph/157.089 km/h.
2 Marco Papa, I (Honda); **3** Henk van der Mark, NL (Honda); **4** Daniel Amatriain, E (Honda); **5** Karl Truchsess, A (Honda); **6** Maarten Duyzers, NL (Honda); **7** Mark Phillips, GB (Suzuki); **8** Rob Punt, NL (Suzuki); **9** Koos van Leyen, NL (Suzuki); **10** Steve Manley, GB (Suzuki).
Fastest lap: Fischer, 2m 18.93s, 98.70 mph/158.946 km/h.
Championship points: 1 Fischer, 52; **2** Papa, 34; **3** Amatriain, 29; **4** Truchsess and van der Mark, 26; **6** Phillips, 19.

250 cc, round 5 (14 laps, 53.36 miles/85.87 km)
1 Jochen Schmid, D (Yamaha), 33m 29.90s, 95.52 mph/153.815 km/h.
2 Xavier Cardelus, AND (Cobas); **3** Engelbert Neumair, A (Rotax); **4** Helmut Bradl, D (Honda); **5** Nigel Bosworth, GB (Yamaha); **6** Patrick van der Goorbergh, NL (Honda); **7** Bernard Hänggeli, CH (Yamaha); **8** Thomas Bacher, A (Rotax); **9** Richard Gauthier, F (Yamaha); **10** Andrew Machin, GB (Yamaha).
Fastest lap: Neumair, 2m 21.31s, 97.04 mph/156.269 km/h.
Championship points: 1 Cardelus, 42; **2** Neumair, 33; **3** van der Goorbergh, 27; **4** Schmid, 25; **5** Preining, 24; **6** Bosworth, 23.

125 cc, round 5 (12 laps, 45.74 miles/73.61 km)
1 Jean-Claude Selini, F (MBA), 30m 38.12s, 89.12 mph/144.163 km/h.
2 Alfred Waibel, D (MBA); **3** Flemming Kistrup, DK (MBA); **4** Adolf Stadler, D (MBA); **5** Norbert Peschke, D (Seel); **6** Manuel Hernandez, E (Beneti); **7** Peter Sommer, CH (Supeso); **8** Anton Straver, NL (Rotax); **9** Corrado Catalano, I (MBA); **10** Jacques Hutteau, F (MBA).
Fastest lap: Payraudeau, F (MBA), 2m 29.33s, 91.83 mph/147.877 km/h.
Championship points: 1 Stadler, 57; **2** Catalano, 41; **3** Kistrup, 32; **4** Peschke, 31; **5** Selini, 30; **6** Hernandez, 26.

80 cc, round 4 (9 laps, 34.30 miles/55.20 km)
1 Alejandro Criville, E (Derbi), 24m 09.01s, 85.17 mph/137.157 km/h.
2 Károly Juhász, H (Krauser); **3** Julian Miralles, E (Derbi); **4** Bert Smit, NL (Minarelli); **5** Jörg Seel, D (Seel); **6** Günther Schirnhofer, D (Krauser); **7** Ralf Waldmann, D (Seel); **8** Peter Öttl, D (Krauser); **9** Stefan Prein, NL (Casal); **10** Reiner Scheidhauer, D (Seel).
Fastest lap: Criville, 2m 37.36s, 87.14 mph/140.33 km/h.
Championship points: 1 Juhász, 50; **2** Miralles, 47; **3** Criville, 41; **4** Schirnhofer, 20; **5** Waldmann, 18; **6** Öttl, 15.

Sidecars, round 3 (12 laps, 45.74 miles/73.61 km)
1 Luigi Casagrande/Adolf Hänni, CH/CH (Yamaha), 29m 42.28s, 92.33 mph/148.68 km/h.
2 Dennis Bingham/Julia Bingham, GB/GB (Yamaha); **3** Fritz Stölzle/Hubert Stölzle, D/D (Yamaha); **4** Tony Baker/John Hennigan, GB/GB (Yamaha); **5** Ray Gardner/Tony Strevens, GB/GB (Yamaha); **6** Jean-Louis Millet/Claude Debroux, F/F (Seymaz); **7** Chris Graf/Kurt Rothenbühler, CH/CH (Yamaha); **8** John Barker/Steve China, GB/GB (Yamaha); **9** Paul Atkinson/Graham Simmons, GB/GB (Yamaha); **10** Herbert Prügl/Christian Parzer, A (Yamaha).
Fastest lap: Bingham, 2m 26.48s, 93.62 mph/150.754 km/h.
Championship points: 1 Bingham and Casagrande, 27; **3** Stölzle, 25; **4** Millet, 23; **5** Gardner, 21; **6** Baker, 20.

MOTODROM HOCKENHEIM, German Federal Republic, 20 September. 4.218-mile/6.789-km circuit.
250 cc, round 6 (12 laps, 50.62 miles/81.46 km)
1 Xavier Cardelus, AND (Cobas), 27m 34.32s, 110.15 mph/177.27 km/h.
2 Helmut Bradl, D (Honda); **3** Jochen Schmid, D (Yamaha); **4** Christian Boudinot, F (Fior); **5** Thomas Bacher, A (Rotax); **6** Bernard Hänggeli, CH (Yamaha); **7** Hermann Holder, D (Yamaha); **8** Patrick van der Goorbergh, NL (Rotax); **9** Andreas Preining, A (Rotax); **10** Martin Füg, D (Honda).
Fastest lap: Bradl, 2m 16.71s, 111.07 mph/178.76 km/h.
Championship points: 1 Cardelus, 57; **2** Schmid, 35; **3** Neumair, 33; **4** Bradl, 32; **5** van der Goorbergh, 30; **6** Preining, 26.

80 cc, round 5 (8 laps, 33.74 miles/54.30 km)
1 Alejandro Criville, E (Derbi), 20m 38.73s, 97.98 mph/157.83 km/h.
2 Károly Juhász, H (Krauser); **3** Julian Miralles, E (Derbi); **4** Jörg Seel, D (Seel); **5** Bogdan Nikolov, BG (Krauser); **6** Stefan Brägger, CH (Casal); **7** Günther Schirnhofer, D (Krauser); **8** Reiner Scheidhauer, D (Seel); **9** Jos van Dongen, NL (Casal); **10** Heinz Paschen, D (Casal).
Fastest lap: Juhász 2m 30.85s, 100.75 mph/162.00 km/h.
Championship points: 1 Juhász, 62; **2** Miralles, 57; **3** Criville, 56; **4** Schirnhofer, 24; **5** Waldmann, 18; **6** Öttl, 15.

Sidecars, round 4 (12 laps, 50.62 miles/81.46 km)
1 Jean-Louis Millet/Claude Debroux, F/F (Seymaz), 28m 47.34s, 105.50 mph/ 169.78 km/h.
2 Toni Wyssen/Kilian Wyssen, CH/CH (Yamaha); **3** Fritz Stölzle/Hubert Stölzle, D (Yamaha); **4** Christian Graf/Kurt Rothenbühler, CH/CH (Yamaha); **5** Hans Hügli/Martin Zurbrügg, CH/CH (Sigwa); **6** Erwin Weber/Eckhart Rösinger, D (Yamaha); **7** Barry Smith/David Smith, GB/GB (Windle-Yamaha); **8** Dennis Bingham/Julia Bingham, GB/GB (Yamaha); **9** Herbert Prügl/Christian Parzer, A (Homa); **10** Jacques Heriot/Jean-Luc Sage, F/F (Yamaha).
Fastest lap: Wyssen, 2m 21.43s, 107.37 mph/172.79 km/h.
Championship points: see final points.

AUTODROMO INTERNATIONALE, MUGELLO, Italy, 4 October. 3.278-mile/5.245-km circuit.
500 cc, round 5 (18 laps, 59.00 miles/94.95 km)
1 Massimo Broccoli, I (Cagiva), 37m 35.42s, 93.64 mph/150.693 km/h.
2 Daniel Amatriain, E (Honda); **3** Fabio Barchitta, RSM (Honda); **4** Marco Papa, I (Honda); **5** Alberto Rota, I (Honda); **6** Peter Schleef, D (Honda); **7** Silvo Habat, YU (Honda); **8** Henny Boerman, NL (Assmex); **9** Romolo Balbi, I (Honda); **10** Henk van der Mark, NL (Honda).
Fastest lap: Broccoli, 2m 03.32s, 94.98 mph/153.114 km/h.

250 cc, round 7 (17 laps, 55.73 miles/89.68 km)
1 Helmut Bradl, D (Honda), 36m 07.91s, 92.03 mph/148.066 km/h.
2 Andrea Brasini, I (Honda); **3** Nedy Crotta, CH (Armstrong); **4** Fabrizio Pirovano, I (Yamaha); **5** Massimo Matteoni, I (Honda); **6** Fabrizio Furlan, I (Yamaha); **7** Bernhard Schick, D (Honda); **8** Roberto Germoni, I (Yamaha); **9** Andrea Borgonovo, I (Honda); **10** Roberto Antonellini, I (Yamaha).
Fastest lap: not available.

125 cc, round 6 (16 laps, 52.45 miles/84.40 km)
1 Corrado Catalano, I (MBA), 35m 30.68s, 87.98 mph/141.791 km/h.
2 Emilio Cuppini, I (MBA); **3** Stefano Pennese, I (MBA); **4** Jean-Claude Selini, F (MBA); **5** Håkan Olsson, S (Starol); **6** Flemming Kistrup, DK (MBA); **7** Peter Sommer, CH (Supeso); **8** Luciano Garagnani, I (MBA); **9** Heinz Litz, D (MBA); **10** Dieter Kindl, CH (Honda).
Fastest lap: Pennese, 2m 10.83s, 89.80 mph/144.325 km/h.

80 cc, round 6 (14 laps, 45.89 miles/73.85 km)
1 Julian Miralles, E (Derbi), 32m 04.33s, 85.35 mph/137.371 km/h.
2 Francisco Torrontegui, I (Derbi); **3** Giuseppe Ascareggi, I (BBFT); **4** Károly Juhász, H (Krauser); **5** Alejandro Criville, E (Derbi); **6** Günther Schirnhofer, D (Krauser); **7** Reiner Koster, CH (Kroko); **8** Heinz Paschen, D (Casal); **9** Janez Pintar, YU (Eberhardt); **10** Alojz Pavlic, YU (Seel).
Fastest lap: Miralles, 2m 14.86s, 87.07 mph/140.012 km/h.

Final Championship points (500 cc)

1	Manfred Fischer, D	52
2	Marco Papa, I	42
3	Daniel Amatriain, E	41
4	Henk van der Mark, NL	27
5	Karl Truchsess, A	26
6	Mark Phillips, GB	19

7 Massimo Broccoli, I and Maarten Duyzers, NL, 15; **9** Steve Manley, GB, 13; **10** Peter Schleef, D, 11; **11** Fabio Barchitta, RSM and Steve Henshaw, GB, 10; **13** Ari Rämö, SF and Alberto Rota, I, 6; **15** Andreas Leuthe, LUX, 5.

Final Championship points (250 cc)

1	Xavier Cardelus, AND	57
2	Helmut Bradl, D	47
3	Jochen Schmid, D	35
4	Engelbert Neumair, A	33
5	Patrick van der Goorbergh	30
6	Andreas Preining, A	26

7 Bernard Hänggeli, CH, 25; **8** Nigel Bosworth, GB, 23; **9** Rob Orme, GB, 21; **10** Nedy Crotta, CH, 18; **11** Cees Doorakkers, NL, 17; **12** Alberto Puig, E, 16; **13** Stefan Klabacher and Fabrizio Pirovano, I, 15; **15** Thomas Bacher, 14.

Final Championship points (125 cc)

1	Adolf Stadler, D	57
2	Corrado Catalano, I	56
3	Jean-Claude Selini, F	38
4	Flemming Kistrup, DK	37
5	Norbert Peschke, D	31
6	Manuel Hernandez, E	26

7 Gilles Payraudeau, F, 18; **8** Emilio Cuppini, I and Peter Sommer, CH, 17; **10** Chris Galatowicz, GB and Alfred Waibel, D, 12; **12** Fernando Gonzalez, E, 11; **13** Stefano Pennese, I, 10; **14** Antonio Oliveros, E, 5.

Final Championship points (80 cc)

1	Julian Miralles, E	72
2	Károly Juhász, H	70
3	Alejandro Criville, E	62
4	Günther Schirnhofer, D	29
5	Ralf Waldmann, D	18
6	Peter Öttl, D	15

7 René Dünki, CH and Jörg Seel, D, 14; **9** Michael Gschwander, D and Francisco Torrontegui, I, 12; **11** Heinz Paschen, D, 11; **12** Giuseppe Ascareggi, I, 10; **13** Mario Stocco, I, 9; **14** Bert Smit, NL, 8; **15** Bogdan Nikolov, BG, 6.

Final Championship points (Sidecars)

1	Jean-Louis Millet, F	38
2	Fritz Stölzle, D	35
3	Dennis Bingham, GB	30
4	Luigi Casagrande, CH	27
5	Ray Gardner, GB	21
6	Tony Baker, GB	20

7 John Barker, GB, 13; **8** Christian Graf, CH and Toni Wyssen, CH, 12; **10** Barry Smith, GB, 10; **11** Gary Knight, GB, 8; **12** Erwin Weber, D, 7; **13** Jacques Heriot, F and Hans Hügli, CH, 6; **15** Paul Atkinson, GB and Neil Smith, GB, 5.

World TT F1 Championship

AUTODROMO SANTAMONICA, MISANO, Italy, 20 April. 2.167-mile/3.488-km circuit.
TT F1, round 1 (75 laps, 162.53 miles/261.60 km)
1 Paul Iddon, GB (Suzuki), 1h 48m 02.2s, 90.27 mph/145.288 km/h.
2 Fred Merkel, USA (Honda); **3** Joey Dunlop, GB (Honda); **4** Peter Rubatto, D (Yamaha); **5** Andy McGladdery, GB (Suzuki); **6** Klaus Caspers, D (Suzuki); **7** Henrik Ottoesen, DK (Yamaha); **8** Glenn Williams, NZ (Suzuki); **9** Jari Suhonen, SF (Yamaha); **10** Steve Williams, GB (Yamaha).
Fastest lap: Roger Marshall, GB (Suzuki), 1m 23.48s, 93.45 mph/150.417 km/h.
Championship points: 1 Iddon, 15; **2** Merkel, 12; **3** Dunlop, 10; **4** Rubatto, 8; **5** McGladdery, 6; **6** Caspers, 5.

HUNGARORING, Hungary, 3 May. 2.494-mile/4.013-km circuit.
TT F1, round 2 (40 laps, 99.76 miles/160.52 km)
1 Virginio Ferrari, I (Bimota), 1h 21m 39.31s, 73.31 mph/117.97 km/h.
2 Davide Tardozzi, I (Bimota); **3** Anders Andersson, S (Suzuki); **4** Peter Rubatto, D (Yamaha); **5** Jari Suhonen, SF (Yamaha); **6** Ernst Gschwender, D (Suzuki); **7** Rene Rasmussen, DK (Suzuki); **8** Joey Dunlop, GB (Honda); **9** Patrick Bettendorf, LUX (Suzuki); **10** Andreas Hoffman, D (Kawasaki).
Fastest lap: Roger Marshall, GB (Suzuki), 1m 59.16s.
Championship points: 1 Rubatto, 16; **2** Ferrari and Iddon, 15; **4** Dunlop, 13; **5** Merkel and Tardozzi, 12.

ISLE OF MAN TT CIRCUIT, Great Britain, 30 May. 37.73-mile/60.72-km circuit.
TT F1, round 3 (6 laps, 226.38 miles/364.32 km)
1 Joey Dunlop, GB (Honda), 1h 58m 04.4s, 115.03 mph/185.135 km/h.
2 Phil Mellor, GB (Suzuki); **3** Geoff Johnson, GB (Yamaha); **4** Roger Marshall, GB (Suzuki); **5** Trevor Nation, GB (Yamaha); **6** Nick Jefferies, GB (Honda); **7** Peter Rubatto, D (Bimota-Yamaha); **8** Dave Leach, GB (Suzuki); **9** Glenn Williams, NZ (Suzuki); **10** Steve Linsdell, GB (Yamaha).
Fastest lap: Joey Dunlop, GB (Honda), 19m 15.4s, 117.55 mph/188.08 km/h.
Championship points: 1 Dunlop, 28; **2** Rubatto, 20; **3** Ferrari and Iddon, 15; **5** Mellor, Merkel and Tardozzi, 12.

CIRCUIT VAN DRENTHE, ASSEN, Holland, 25 June. 3.812-mile/6.134 km-circuit.
TT F1, round 4 (25 laps, 95.30 miles/153.35 km)
1 Virginio Ferrari, I (Bimota), 59m 02.05s, 96.79 mph/155.859 km/h.
2 Davide Tardozzi, I (Bimota); **3** Roger Marshall, GB (Suzuki); **4** Paul Iddon, GB (Suzuki); **5** Peter Rubatto, D (Bimota-Yamaha); **6** Mark Phillips, GB (Suzuki); **7** Anders Andersson, S (Suzuki); **8** Ernst Gschwender, D (Suzuki); **9** Andreas Hoffman, D (Kawasaki); **10** Henk de Vries, NL (Yamaha).
Fastest lap: Davide Tardozzi, I (Bimota), 2m 19.28s, 98.46 mph/158.547 km/h.
Championship points: 1 Ferrari, 30; **2** Dunlop, 28; **3** Rubatto, 26; **4** Tardozzi, 24; **5** Iddon, 23; **6** Marshall, 18.
Note: The scheduled Dundrod round of the World TT F1 Championship was abandoned after the fatal accident to Klaus Klein on 15 August.

SUGO, Japan, 30 August. 2.335-mile/3.737-km circuit.
TT F1, round 5 (50 laps, 116.79 miles/186.875 km)
1 Kevin Magee, AUS (Yamaha), 1h 22m 57.82s, 83.95 mph/135.149 km/h.
2 Yukiya Oshima, J (Suzuki); **3** Michael Doohan, AUS (Yamaha); **4** Katsuro Takayoshi, J (Suzuki); **5** Mitsuo Saito, J (Yamaha); **6** Takahiro Sohwa, J (Kawasaki); **7** Anders Andersson, S (Suzuki); **8** Jun Suzuki, J (Honda); **9** Shohji Hiratsuka, J (Yamaha); **10** Katsunori Shinozaki, J (Suzuki).
Fastest lap: not available.
Championship points: 1 Ferrari, 30; **2** Dunlop, 28; **3** Rubatto, 26; **4** Tardozzi, 24; **5** Iddon, 23; **6** Andersson and Marshall, 18.

MOTODROM HOCKENHEIM, German Federal Republic, 20 September. 4.218-mile/6.789-km circuit.
TT F1, round 6 (23 laps, 97.01 miles/156.15 km)
1 Virginio Ferrari, I (Bimota), 51m 28.26s, 113.09 mph/182.01 km/h.
2 Davide Tardozzi, I (Bimota); **3** Ernst Gschwender, D (Suzuki); **4** Joey Dunlop, GB (Honda); **5** Bodo Schmidt, D (Bimota); **6** Paul Iddon, GB (Suzuki); **7** Fabrizio Pirovano, I (Bimota); **8** Klaus Caspers, D (Suzuki); **9** Jari Suhonen, SF (Yamaha); **10** Edwin Waibel, CH (Honda).
Fastest lap: Virginio Ferrari, I (Bimota), 2m 12.68s, 114.45 mph/184.19 km/h.
Championship points: 1 Ferrari, 45; **2** Dunlop and Tardozzi, 36; **4** Iddon, 28; **5** Rubatto, 26; **6** Andersson, Gschwender and Marshall, 18.

DONINGTON PARK CIRCUIT, Great Britain, 27 September. 2.5-mile/4.02-km circuit.
TT F1, round 7 (40 laps, 100 miles/160.8 km)
1 Paul Iddon, GB (Suzuki), 1h 08m 58.82s, 86.98 mph/139.97 km/h.
2 Roger Marshall, GB (Suzuki); **3** Joey Dunlop, GB (Honda); **4** Fred Merkel, USA (Honda); **5** Anders Andersson, S (Suzuki); **6** Henrik Ottoesen, DK (Yamaha); **7** Virginio Ferrari, I (Bimota); **8** Mark Phillips, GB (Suzuki); **9** Trevor Nation, GB (Yamaha); **10** Edwin Waibel, CH (Honda).
Fastest lap: Roger Marshall, GB (Suzuki), 1m 41.87s, 88.34 mph/142.14 km/h.

Final TT F1 Championship points

1	Virginio Ferrari, I	49
2	Joey Dunlop, GB	46
3	Paul Iddon, GB	43
4	Davide Tardozzi, I	36
5	Roger Marshall, GB	30
6	Peter Rubatto, D	26

7 Anders Andersson, S, 24; **8** Fred Merkel, USA, 20; **9** Ernst Gschwender, D, 18; **10** Kevin Magee, AUS, 15; **11** Phil Mellor, GB and Yukiya Oshima, J, 12; **13** Michael Doohan, AUS, Geoff Johnson, GB and Jari Suhonen, SF, 10.

Major European Meetings

AUTODROMO SANTAMONICA, Misano, Italy, 18/20 April. 2.167-mile/3.488-km circuit.
F1 (24 laps, 52.01 miles/83.71 km)
1 Virginio Ferrari, I (Bimota), 28m 16.80s, 91.98 mph/148.006 km/h.
2 Davide Tardozzi, I (Bimota); **3** Oscar la Ferla, I (Suzuki); **4** Ivo Arnoldi, I (Bimota); **5** Andrea Clerici, I (Yamaha); **6** Luciano Leandrini, I (Yamaha); **7** Walter Villa, I (Yamaha); **8** Ferdinando de Cecco, I (Ducati); **9** Franco Zanardo, I (Bimota); **10** Maurizio Poggi, I (Yamaha).
Fastest lap: Tardozzi, 1m 23.10s, 93.9 mph/151.105 km/h.

500 cc
1 Alessandro Valesi, I (Honda), 32m 00.23s, 93.45 mph/150.402 km/h.
2 Fabio Biliotti, I (Honda); **3** Massimo Broccoli, I

(Honda); **4** Leandro Becheroni, I (Honda); **5** Fabio Barchitta, I (Honda); **6** Romolo Balbi, I (Honda); **7** Massimo Maestri, I (Suzuki); **8** Vittorio Scatola, I (Paton); **9** Michael Jansberg, SF (Suzuki); **10** Bruno Scatola, I (Suzuki).
Fastest lap: Valesi, 1m 22.46s, 94.61 mph/152.77 km/h.

250 cc
1 Loris Reggiani, I (Aprilia), 26m 38.12s, 92.72 mph/149.207 km/h.
2 Luca Cadalora, I (Yamaha); **3** Ezio Gianola, I; **4** Massimo Matteoni, I (Honda); **5** Fausto Ricci, I (Honda); **6** Hans Lindner, A; **7** Alberto Rota, I; **8** Siegfried Minich, A; **9** Roberto Germoni, I (Zamago); **10** Marcellino Lucchi, I (Honda).
Fastest lap: not available.

125 cc
1 Ezio Gianola, I (Honda), 27m 03.13s, 86.52 mph/139.251 km/h.
2 Stefano Bianchi, I (MBA); **3** Marco Cipriani, I (MBA); **4** Roberto Bucci, I (MBA); **5** Mike Leitner, A (EMCO).
Fastest lap: Gianola, 1m 29.29s, 87.37 mph/140.629 km/h.

80 cc
1 Salvatore Milano, I (Krauser), 25m 41.11s, 81.00 mph/130.36 km/h.
2 Giuseppe Ascareggi, I (MBA); **3** Gabriele Gnani, I (Gnani); **4** Vincenzo Saffiotti, I (UFO); **5** Paolo Pozzo, I (Mancini); **6** Claudio Granata, I (Autisa); **7** Luigi Soprano, I (UFO); **8** Sandro Paris, I; **9** Mario Scalinci, I (Huvo); **10** Francesco Fantini, I (RB).
Fastest lap: Milano, 1m 34.80s, 82.30 mph/132.456 km/h.

24 HEURES DU MANS, Bugatti Circuit, Le Mans, France, 18/19 April.
730 laps of the 2.635-mile/4.240-km circuit, 1923.55 miles/3095.2 km.
1 Dominique Sarron/Jean-Louis Battistini/Jean-Michel Mattioli, F/F/F (750 Honda), 23h 55m 25.7s, 80.92 mph/130.201 km/h.
2 Bruno le Bihan/Hervé Moineau/Jean-Louis Tournadre (750 Suzuki), 728 laps; **3** Gérard Coudray/Alex Vieira/Richard Hubin, F/F/F (750 Honda), 726; **4** Pierre-Etienne Samin/Pierre Bolle/Thierry Crine, F/F/F (750 Kawasaki), 715; **5** Jean Monnin/Georges Furling/G. Rolland-Piègue, F/F/F (750 Kawasaki), 698; **6** Robbi Schläfi/Ulrich Kallen/Urs Meier, CH/CH/CH (750 Honda), 693; **7** Patrice More/Bernard Chateau/André Lussiana F/F/F (750 Suzuki), 690; **8** Mat Oxley/P. Jansson/Ken Dobson, GB/S/GB (750 Yamaha), 689; **9** A. Gouin/Maurice Coq/Bouzanne, F/F/F (750 Yamaha), 681; **10** Jean Basselin/A. Bouilloux/Hampe, F/F/F (750 Kawasaki), 666.
Fastest lap: Sarron, 1m 47.5s, 88.75 mph/142.894 km/h.

HUNGARORING, Hungary, 3 May. 2.494-mile/4.013-km circuit.
250 cc (20 laps, 49.88 miles/80.26 km)
1 Wilhelm Hörhager, A (Honda), 41m 42.70s.
2 Andreas Preining, A (Rotax); **3** László Nagy, H (Rotax); **4** Nicolas Schnassmann, CH (Yamaha); **5** Thomas Bacher, A (Rotax); **6** Johann Holtrigter, NL (Honda); **7** Hans Parzer, A (Yamaha); **8** Stefan Stock, D (Honda); **9** Karl Billich, A (Yamaha); **10** Zsolt Iglar, H (Yamaha).
Fastest lap: Hörhager, 2m 02.22s, 73.47 mph/118.23 km/h.

CIRCUIT DE CHIMAY, Belgium, 7 June. 5.903-mile/9.500-km circuit.
Prix La Nouvelle Gazette (10 laps, 59.03 miles/95.00 km)
1 Michel Nicolay, B (Yamaha), 32m 02.97s, 110.1 mph/177.050 km/h.
2 G. Nemeth, N (Honda); **3** Olivier Boers, B (Yamaha); **4** André Pirmez, B (Yamaha); **5** Rudi Balon, B (Yamaha); **6** Jean-François Laval, B (Yamaha); **7** Pascal Lagamme, B (Yamaha); **8** Christian Marcelis, B (Yamaha); **9** Bênoit Warnotte, B (Yamaha); **10** Philippe Noel, B (Yamaha).
Fastest lap: Nicolay, 3m 09.80s, 112.1 mph/180.19 km/h.

Prix Kronenbourg (10 laps, 59.03 miles/95.00 km)
1 Michel Simeon, B (Suzuki), 28m 20.44s, 125.1 mph/201.12 km/h.
2 Michel Simul, B (Suzuki); **3** Johan van Vaerenbergh, B (Kawasaki); **4** Michel Steven, B (Yamaha); **5** Chris Vannieuwenhuyse, B (Suzuki); **6** Eric Bragard, B (Honda); **7** Marc Roobens, B (Yamaha); **8** Johan van Becelaere, B (Suzuki); **9** Joel Mergny, B; **10** Jean-Louis Lesceux, B (Suzuki).
Fastest lap: Simeon, 2m 48.47s, 126.3 mph/203.004 km/h.

Grand Prix Appollinaris, 250 cc (12 laps, 70.84 miles/114.00 km)
1 Andy Machin, GB (Rotax), 35m 08.42s, 120.95 mph/194.64 km/h.
2 Rob Orme, GB (Yamaha); **3** Laurent Naveau, B (Yamaha); **4** Martyn Jupp, GB (Yamaha); **5** Mathias Siebel, D (Rotax); **6** Mario Houssin, B (Yamaha); **7** Henrie van Heist, NL (Honda); **8** Dirk Verwey, NL (Yamaha); **9** Paul Streiker (Honda); **10** Johan Schellings, NL (Honda).
Fastest lap: not available.

Prix Peugeot-Talbot (10 laps, 59.03 miles/95.00 km)
1 Michel Nicolay, B (350 Yamaha), 31m 54.18s, 110.9 mph/178.667 km/h.
2 Rudi Balon, B (Yamaha); **3** Jean-François Laval, B (Yamaha); **4** André Pirmez, B (Yamaha); **5** Pascal Lagamme, B (Yamaha); **6** Bênoit Warnotte, B (Yamaha); **7** Christian Marcelis, B (Yamaha); **8** Philippe Noel, B (Yamaha); **9** Joël Mommen, B (Yamaha); **10** Eric Pohl, B (Yamaha).
Fastest lap: Nicolay, 3m 08.95s, 112.4 mph/118.00 km/h.

Prix Castrol (34 laps, 200.70 miles/323 km)
1 Michel Simeon, B (Suzuki), 1h 35m 31.57s, 126 mph/202.896 km/h.
2 Philippe Polis, B (Suzuki); **3** Gerard Vogt, D (Suzuki); **4** Tony Carey, IRL (Suzuki); **5** M. Roseno; **6** Johan van Vaerenbergh, B (Kawasaki); **7** Jerome van Haeltert, B (Suzuki); **8** Asa Moyce, GB (Kawasaki); **9** Russell Benney, GB (Yamaha); **10** Ronan Sherry, IRL (Suzuki).
Fastest lap: not available.

Grand Prix Martial d'Ardenne, F2 Sidecars (8 laps, 47.22 miles/76 km)
1 Joe Heys/Peter Greetham, GB/GB (Armstrong).
2 Dave Saville/Dave Hall, GB/GB (Sabre); **3** Martin Whittington/Ian Caulton, GB/GB (Yamaha); **4** Dick Hawes/Eddy Kiff, GB/GB (Yamaha); **5** John Coates/Gary Gibson, GB/GB (Yamaha); **6** John Hartell/Tony Newsholme, GB/GB (Armstrong); **7** Jim Norbury/Norman Elcock, GB/GB (Lockyam); **8** Peter Whiteley/John Armitage, GB/GB (Yamaha); **9** David French/Steve Lavender, GB/GB (Windle); **10** Dennis Keen/Robert Parker, GB/GB (Yamaha).
Fastest lap: not available.

ST WENDEL, German Federal Republic, 26-27 September. 1.740-mile/2.800-km circuit.
80 cc (19 laps, 33.06 miles/53.20 km)
1 Peter Öttl, D (Krauser), 27m 42.68s, 71.55 mph/115.187 km/h.
2 Heinz Paschen, D (Kiefer/Casal); **3** Reiner Scheidhauer, D (Seel); **4** Ralf Waldmann, D (Seel); **5** Michael Gschwander, D (Seel); **6** Roland Bosch, D (Casal); **7** Rainer Kunz, D (Ziegler); **8** Bernd Völkel, D (Löffler); **9** Hagen Klein, D (Hess).
Fastest lap: Öttl, 1m 25.21s, 73.49 mph/118.275 km/h.

125 cc (19 laps, 33.06 miles/53.20 km)
1 Alfred Waibel, D (Waibel Spezial), 26m 13.79s, 75.62 mph/121.693 km/h.
2 Norbert Peschke, D (Seel); **3** Adolf Stadler, D (MBA); **4** Jörg Hafeneger, D; **5** Heinz Litz, D (MBA); **6** Karl Dauer, A; **7** Willi Lücke, D (MBA); **8** Reiner Scheidhauer, D (Rotax); **9** Manfred Thurmayer, D (Honda); **10** Klaus Windfuhr, D (MBA).
Fastest lap; Waibel, 1m 20.31s, 77.98 mph/125.513 km/h.

250 cc (19 laps, 33.06 miles/53.20 km)
1 Helmut Bradl, D (Honda), 24m 18.53s, 81.59 mph/131.310 km/h.
2 Jochen Schmid, D (Yamaha); **3** Frank Wagner, D (Honda); **4** Herbert Besendörfer, D (Honda); **5** Bernhard Schick, D (Honda); **6** Harald Eckl, D (Honda); **7** Konrad Hefele, D (Honda); **8** Árpád Harmati, H (Yamaha); **9** Detlef Karthin, D (Honda); **10** Hermann Holder, D (Yamaha).
Fastest lap: Besendörfer, 1m 14.99s, 83.52 mph/134.417 km/h.

350 cc (10 laps, 17.40 miles/28.00 km)
1 Roland Busch, D (WIWA), 13m 09.35s, 79.35 mph/127.70 km/h.
2 Bernhard Schick, D; **3** Jörg Gammerschlag, D (Yamaha); **4** Árpád Harmati, H (Yamaha); **5** Gerhard Häberle, D (Rotax); **6** Rainer Gerwin, D (Rotax); **7** Rainer Braunweiler, D (Juchem); **8** Dieter Gröss, D (Juchem); **9** Rüdi Gächter, CH (Yamaha); **10** Ulli Gläser, D (Yamaha).
Fastest lap: Schülten, D (Honda), 1m 17.10s, 81.23 mph/130.739 km/h.

500 cc (19 laps, 33.06 miles/53.20 km)
1 Gustav Reiner, D (Honda), 24m 03.21s, 82.47 mph/132.704 km/h.
2 Manfred Fischer, D (Honda); **3** Michael Rudroff, D (Honda); **4** Ari Rämö, SF (Honda); **5** Georg Jung, D (Honda); **6** Gerold Fischer, D (GF 500); **7** Pavol Dekánek, CS (Suzuki); **8** Heiner Butz, D (Honda); **9** Hans Klingebiel, D (Suzuki); **10** Josef Doppler, A (Honda).
Fastest lap: Reiner, 1m 13.74s, 84.95 mph/136.696 km/h.

Sidecars (19 laps, 33.06 miles/53.20 km)
1 Rolf Steinhausen/Bruno Hiller, D/D (Krauser), 24m 44.87s, 80.14 mph/128.98 km/h.
2 Bernd Scherer/Wolfgang Gess, D/D (Eigenbau); **3** Masato Kumano/Markus Fahrni, J/CH (Toshiba Tec); **4** Fritz Stölzle/Hubert Stölzle, A/A (Yamaha); **5** Herbert Prügl/Christian Parzer, A/A (Honda-Rotax); **6** Reinhard Link/Walter Link, D/D (LCR); **7** Emil Lauer/Günter Quanz, D/D (Busch); **8** Neil Smith/Wolfgang Bock, GB/D (NSR); **9** Axel von Berg/Norbert Wild, D/D (Busch-Seel); **10** Walter Eggerstorfer/Max Mayer, D/D (LCR).
Fastest lap: Steinhausen/Hiller, 1m 16.31s, 82.05 mph/132.072 km/h.

US ROAD RACING

AMA National Championship Road Race Series (Superbike)

DAYTONA INTERNATIONAL SPEEDWAY, Daytona Beach, Florida, 8 March 1987. 203 miles/326.69 km
1 Wayne Rainey (Honda), 1h 53m 58s, 106.827 mph/171.917 km/h.
2 Satoshi Tsujimoto (Suzuki); **3** Doug Polen (Suzuki); **4** Rueben McMurter (Yamaha); **5** Gary Goodfellow (Suzuki); **6** John Ashmead (Honda); **7** Scott Cantrell (Suzuki); **8** Lance Jones (Yamaha); **9** Larry Shorts (Suzuki); **10** Trevor Nation (Yamaha).

ROAD ATLANTA, Braselton, Georgia, 17 May 1987. 60 miles/96.56 km.
1 Wayne Rainey (Honda), 35m 27s, 102.383 mph/164.765 km/h.
2 Kevin Schwantz (Suzuki); **3** Bubba Shobert (Honda); **4** Dan Chivington (Honda); **5** Mike Harth (Suzuki); **6** Jeff Farmer (Yamaha); **7** Doug Chandler (Honda); **8** Rueben McMurter (Yamaha); **9** Doug Brauneck (Suzuki); **10** Ottis Lance (Suzuki).

BRAINERD INTERNATIONAL RACEWAY, Brainerd, Minnesota, 7 June 1987. 60 miles/96.56 km.
1 Wayne Rainey (Honda), 34m 36s, 104.037 mph/167.427 km/h.
2 Kevin Schwantz (Suzuki); **3** Bubba Shobert (Honda); **4** Dan Chivington (Honda); **5** Doug Polen (Suzuki); **6** Rueben McMurter (Yamaha); **7** Doug Chandler (Honda); **8** Doug Brauneck (Suzuki); **9** Tom Walther (Suzuki); **10** Ottis Lance (Suzuki).

BRYAR MOTORSPORTS PARK, Loudon, New Hampshire, 21 June 1987. 61 miles/98.17 km.
1 Kevin Schwantz (Suzuki), 43m 46s, 83.35 mph/134.135 km/h.
2 Wayne Rainey (Honda); **3** Bubba Shobert (Honda); **4** Doug Polen (Suzuki); **5** Gary Goodfellow (Suzuki); **6** Dan Chivington (Honda); **7** Dave Sadowski (Suzuki); **8** Doug Chandler (Honda); **9** Tom Walther (Suzuki); **10** Stephen Crevier (Suzuki).

ROAD AMERICA RACEWAY, Elkhart Lake, Wisconsin, 28 June 1987. 60 miles/96.56 km.
1 Kevin Schwantz (Suzuki), 35m 36s, 101.123 mph/162.737 km/h.
2 Wayne Rainey (Honda); **3** Doug Polen (Suzuki); **4** Bubba Shobert (Honda); **5** Doug Chandler (Honda); **6** Gary Goodfellow (Suzuki); **7** Dan Chivington (Honda); **8** Larry Shorts (Kawasaki); **9** Stephen Crevier (Suzuki); **10** Rueben McMurter (Yamaha).

LAGUNA SECA RACEWAY, Monterey, California, 12 July 1987. 43.2-mile/69.5-km first segment (red flag), 82.7-mile/100.9-km second segment.

1	Bubba Shobert	3-2	(Honda),
	38m 26s, 97.893 mph/157.539 km/h.		
2	Jim Filice	4-3	(Yamaha);
3	Gary Goodfellow	5-4	(Suzuki);
4	Scott Gray	6-6	(Suzuki);
5	Wayne Rainey	12-1	(Honda);
6	Tom Walther	8-5	(Suzuki);
7	Rich Arnaiz	7-7	(Yamaha);
8	Sam McDonald	11-9	(Yamaha);
9	Larry Shorts	10-10	(Kawasaki);
10	Rueben McMurter	14-11	(Yamaha).

MID-OHIO SPORTS CAR COURSE, Lexington, Ohio, 2 August 1987. 60 miles/96.56 km.
1 Kevin Schwantz (Suzuki), 40m 27s, 89.013 mph/143.249 km/h.
2 Wayne Rainey (Honda); **3** Jim Filice (Yamaha); **4** Bubba Shobert (Honda); **5** Doug Chandler (Honda); **6** Doug Polen (Suzuki); **7** Gary Goodfellow (Suzuki); **8** Dan Chivington (Honda); **9** Larry Shorts (Kawasaki); **10** Jeff Farmer (Yamaha).

MEMPHIS INTERNATIONAL MOTORSPORT PARK, Memphis, Tennessee, 9 August, 1987. 60 miles/96.56 km.
1 Kevin Schwantz (Suzuki), 39m 1s, 92.583 mph/148.994 km/h.
2 Wayne Rainey (Honda); **3** Bubba Shobert (Honda); **4** Doug Polen (Suzuki); **5** Jim Filice (Yamaha); **6** Doug Chandler (Honda); **7** Dan Chivington (Honda); **8** Jeff Farmer (Yamaha); **9** Dale Quarterley (Yamaha); **10** Dave Sadowski (Suzuki).

SEARS POINT INTERNATIONAL RACEWAY, Sonoma, California, 30 August 1987. 61 miles/98.17 km.
1 Kevin Schwantz (Suzuki).
2 Jim Filice (Yamaha); **3** Doug Chandler (Honda); **4** John Ashmead (Honda); **5** Dale Quarterley (Suzuki); **6** Wayne Rainey (Honda); **7** Sam McDonald (Yamaha); **8** Dan Chivington (Honda); **9** Jeff Farmer (Yamaha); **10** Richard Moore (Suzuki).
Note: Race red-flagged; no time or average speed available.

Final points

1	Wayne Rainey	143
2	Kevin Schwantz	134
3	Bubba Shobert	94
4	Doug Polen	71
5	Doug Chandler	65

6 Dan Chivington 61; **7** Jim Filice 55; **8** Gary Goodfellow 50; **9** Rueben McMurter 39; **10** Jeff Farmer 32.

AMA Castrol 250 GP Series

DAYTONA INTERNATIONAL SPEEDWAY, Daytona Beach, Florida, 8 March 1987. 100 miles/160.93 km.
1 Kork Ballington (Honda), 58m 53s, 101.584 mph/163.479 km/h.
2 John Kocinski (Yamaha); **3** Rich Oliver (Honda); **4** Eddie Laycock (EMC); **5** Cal Rayborn III (Yamaha); **6** Franz Lederer (Honda); **7** Luis Lavado (Yamaha); **8** James Stephens (Honda); **9** Andy Leisner (Honda); **10** Doug Brauneck (Yamaha).

ROAD ATLANTA, Braselton, Georgia, 17 May 1987. 50 miles/80.46 km/h.
1 Randy Renfrow (Honda), 30m 53s, 97.895 mph/157.542 km/h.
2 John Kocinski (Yamaha); **3** Don Greene (Honda); **4** Kork Ballington (Honda); **5** Cal Rayborn III (Yamaha); **6** Rich Oliver (Honda); **7** James Stephens (Yamaha); **8** David Curtis (Honda); **9** Garry Griffith (Yamaha); **10** Dave Busby (Honda).

BRAINERD INTERNATIONAL RACEWAY, Brainerd, Minnesota, 7 June 1987. 51 miles/82.07 km.
1 Kork Ballington (Honda), 30m 8s, 101.548 mph/163.421 km/h.
2 Randy Renfrow (Honda); **3** Alan Carter (Honda); **4** John Kocinski (Yamaha); **5** Don Greene (Honda); **6** Cal Rayborn III (Yamaha); **7** Daniel Coe (Rotax); **8** James Stephens (Yamaha); **9** Andy Leisner (Honda); **10** David Curtis (Honda).

BRYAR MOTORSPORTS PARK, Loudon, New Hampshire, 21 June 1987. 51 miles/82.07 km.
1 John Kocinski (Yamaha).
2 Don Greene (Honda); **3** Cal Rayborn III (Yamaha); **4** Rich Oliver (Honda); **5** James Stephens (Yamaha); **6** David Curtis (Honda); **7** Daniel Coe (Rotax); **8** Garry Griffith (Yamaha); **9** Doug Brauneck (Yamaha); **10** Miles Baldwin (Honda).
Note: Race red-flagged; no time or average speed available.

ROAD AMERICA RACEWAY, Elkhart Lake, Wisconsin, 27 June 1987.
1 John Kocinski (Yamaha).
2 Kork Ballington (Honda); **3** Rich Oliver (Honda); **4** Don Greene (Honda); **5** Alan Carter (Honda); **6** Randy Renfrow (Honda); **7** Cal Rayborn III (Yamaha); **8** James Stephens (Yamaha); **9** Daniel Coe (Rotax); **10** David Curtis (Honda).

LAGUNA SECA RACEWAY, Monterey, California, 12 July 1987. 49 miles/78.86 km.
1 John Kocinski (Yamaha), 30m 33s, 97.07 mph/156.215 km/h.
2 Kork Ballington (Honda); **3** Don Greene (Honda); **4** Cal Rayborn III (Yamaha); **5** Alan Carter (Honda); **6** James Stephens (Yamaha); **7** Doug Brauneck (Yamaha); **8** Andy Leisner (Honda); **9** Andrew Price (Yamaha); **10** Mike Sullivan (Honda).

MID-OHIO SPORTS CAR COURSE, Lexington, Ohio, 3 August 1987. 50 miles/80.46 km.
1 John Kocinski (Yamaha), 35m 6s, 86.136 mph/138.619 km/h.
2 Don Greene (Honda); **3** Randy Renfrow (Honda); **4** Cal Rayborn III (Yamaha); **5** Alan Carter (Honda); **6** Rich Oliver (Honda); **7** James Stephens (Yamaha); **8** Garry Griffith (Yamaha); **9** Doug Brauneck (Yamaha); **10** Alan Inglis (Rotax).

MEMPHIS INTERNATIONAL MOTORSPORT PARK, Memphis, Tennessee, 9 August 1987. 51 miles/82.07 km.
1 Randy Renfrow (Honda), 34m 17s, 89.829 mph/144.562 km/h.
2 John Kocinski (Yamaha); **3** Alan Carter (Honda); **4** Kork Ballington (Honda); **5** Don Greene (Honda); **6** Alan Inglis (Honda); **7** Wm. Himmelsbach (Yamaha); **8** James Stephens (Yamaha); **9** David Curtis (Honda); **10** Garry Griffith (Yamaha).

SEARS POINT INTERNATIONAL RACEWAY, Sonoma, California, 30 August 1987. 51 miles/82.07 km.
1 John Kocinski (Yamaha), 36m 8s, 83.026 mph/133.614 km/h.
2 Kork Ballington (Honda); **3** Don Greene (Honda); **4** Randy Renfrow (Honda); **5** James Stephens (Yamaha); **6** Rich Oliver (Honda); **7** Alan Inglis (Rotax); **8** Garry Griffith (Yamaha); **9** Andy Leisner (Honda); **10** Doug Brauneck (Yamaha).

Final Points

1	John Kocinski	159
2	Kork Ballington	110
3	Don Greene	102
4	Randy Renfrow	91
5	James Stephens	73

6 Cal Rayborn III 72; **7** Rich Oliver 66; **8** Alan Carter 56; **9** Doug Brauneck 39; **10** Garry Griffith 37.

ACU Motoprix British Championship

MALLORY PARK CIRCUIT, 6 September. 1.370-mile/2.205-km circuit.
ACU Motoprix British Championship, 1300 cc, round 1 (15 laps, 20.55 miles/33.08 km)
1 Roger Marshall, GB (1100 Suzuki), 15m 18.5s, 80.54 mph/129.60 km/h.
2 Ray Swann, GB (500 Honda); **3** Jamie Whitham, GB (750 Suzuki); **4** Mark Phillips, GB (500 Suzuki); **5** Carl Fogarty, GB (750 Yamaha); **6** Phil Mellor, GB (1100 Suzuki); **7** Steve Williams, GB (750 Yamaha); **8** Mark Phillips, GB (500 Suzuki); **9** Colin Breeze, GB (750 Yamaha); **10** Simon Buckmaster, GB (500 Honda).
Fastest lap: Marshall, 59.1s, 83.45 mph/134.32 km/h.
Championship points: 1 Marshall, 15; **2** Swann, 12; **3** Whitham, 10; **4** Phillips, 8; **5** Fogarty, 6; **6** Mellor, 5.

ACU Motoprix British Championship, 250 cc, round 1 (15 laps, 20.55 miles/33.08 km)
1 Carl Fogarty, GB (Honda), 15m 39s, 78.78 mph/126.9 km/h.
2 Gary Cowan, IRL (Honda); **3** Kevin Mitchell, GB (Yamaha); **4** Phil Borley, GB (Yamaha); **5** Ian Burnett, GB (Honda); **6** Steve Patrickson, GB (Yamaha); **7** Ian Brennan, GB (Yamaha); **8** Dave Redgate, GB (Yamaha); **9** Andrew Nelson, GB (Yamaha); **10** Mark Barker, GB (Honda).
Fastest lap: Fogarty, 1m 01.2s, 80.58 mph/129.68 km/h.
Championship points: 1 Fogarty, 15; **2** Cowan, 12; **3** Mitchell, 10; **4** Borley, 8; **5** Burnett, 6; **6** Patrickson, 5.

ACU Motoprix British Championship, 125 cc, round 1 (12 laps, 16.44 miles/28.46 km)
1 Robin Milton, GB (MBA), 12m 48.4s, 77.02 mph/123.98 km/h.
2 Chris Galatowicz, GB (Honda); **3** Gary Buckle, GB (MBA); **4** Doug Flather, GB (Honda); **5** Patrick Corrigan, GB (Honda); **6** Steve Mason, GB (MBA); **7** Dave Moffitt, GB (MBA); **8** N. Clifton, GB (Yamaha); **9** R. Murphy, GB (Honda); **10** Tony Flinton, GB (Waddon).
Fastest lap: Milton and Galatowicz, 1m 2.1s, 79.52 mph/128.1 km/h.
Championship points: 1 Milton, 15; **2** Galatowicz, 12; **3** Buckle, 10; **4** Flather, 8; **5** Corrigan, 6; **6** Mason, 5.

ACU Motoprix British Championship, Sidecars, round 1 (15 laps, 20.55 miles/33.08 km)
1 Steve Webster/Tony Hewitt, GB/GB (Krauser), 15m 35.1s, 79.11 mph/127.32 km/h.
2 Yoshisada Kumagaya/Brian Barlow, J/GB (Yamaha); **3** Ray Lawrence/Alan Rawlins, GB/GB (Yamaha); **4** Derek Jones/Brian Ayres, GB/GB (Seel); **5** Tony Baker/John Hennigan, GB/GB (Yamaha); **6** Barry Brindley/Grahame Rose, GB/GB (Yamaha); **7** Ray Gardner/Tony Strevens, GB/GB (Yamaha); **8** Gary Thomas/J. Webb, GB/GB (Yamaha); **9** Lindsay Hurst/Gary Hurst, GB/GB (Yamaha); **10** John Evans/Geoff Wilbraham, GB/GB (Yamaha).
Fastest lap: Webster, 59.2s, 83.31 mph/134.08 km/h.

Championship points: 1 Webster, 15; **2** Kumagaya, 12; **3** Lawrence, 10; **4** Jones, 8; **5** Baker, 6; **6** Brindley, 5.

SILVERSTONE CIRCUIT, 19 September. 1.608-mile/2.5878-km circuit.
ACU Motoprix British Championship, 1300 cc, round 2 (15 laps, 24.12 miles/38.82 km)
1 Roger Marshall, GB (1100 Suzuki), 16m 26.20s, 88.05 mph/141.7 km/h.
2 Ray Swann, GB (500 Honda); **3** Keith Huewen, GB (1000 Yamaha); **4** Terry Rymer, GB (1100 Suzuki); **5** Gary Noel, GB (750 Yamaha); **6** Phil Mellor, GB (1100 Suzuki); **7** Jamie Whitham, GB (750 Suzuki); **8** Steve Williams, GB (750 Yamaha); **9** Dave Griffiths, GB (750 Yamaha); **10** Gary Weston, GB (750 Suzuki).
Fastest lap: Noel, 1m 04.30s, 90.03 mph/144.86 km/h.
Championship points: 1 Marshall, 30; **2** Swann, 24; **3** Whitham, 14; **4** Mellor and Huewen, 10; **6** Phillips and Rymer, 8.

ACU Motoprix British Championship, 250 cc, round 2 (15 laps, 24.12 miles/38.82 km)
1 Donnie McLeod, GB (EMC), 15m 45.60s, 91.83 mph/141.79 km/h.
2 Andy Machin, GB (Spondon Rotax); **3** Gary Cowan, GB (Honda); **4** Kevin Mitchell, GB (Yamaha); **5** Peter Hubbard, GB (Yamaha); **6** George Higginson, GB (Honda); **7** Greig Ramsay, GB (Yamaha); **8** Paul Grubb, GB (Yamaha); **9** Phil Borley, GB (Yamaha); **10** Steve Sawford, GB (Yamaha).
Fastest lap: McLeod, 1m 01.40s, 94.28 mph/151.7 km/h.
Championship points: 1 Cowan, 22; **2** Mitchell, 18; **3** McLeod and Fogarty, 15; **5** Machin, 12; **6** Borley, 10.

ACU Motoprix British Championship, Sidecars, round 2.
Race cancelled due to bad weather.

DONINGTON PARK CIRCUIT, 27 September. 2.5-mile/4.02-km circuit.
ACU Motoprix British Championship, 1300 cc, round 3 (15 laps, 37.5 miles/60.3 km)
1 Roger Marshall, GB (1100 Suzuki), 25m 48.88s, 87.15 mph/140.25 km/h.
2 Paul Iddon, GB (750 Suzuki); **3** Jamie Whitham, GB (750 Suzuki); **4** Trevor Nation, GB (750 Yamaha); **5** Simon Buckmaster, GB (500 Honda); **6** Gary Noel, GB (750 Yamaha); **7** Steve Manley, GB (500 Suzuki); **8** Roger Hurst, GB (750 Yamaha); **9** Des Barry, GB (750 Yamaha); **10** Steve Williams, GB (750 Yamaha).
Fastest lap: Marshall, 1m 40.8s, 89.28 mph/143.69 km/h.
Championship points: 1 Marshall, 45; **2** Swann and Whitham, 24; **4** Iddon, 12; **5** Noel, 11; **6** Huewen and Mellor, 10.

ACU Motoprix British Championship, 250 cc, round 3 (15 laps, 37.5 miles/60.3 km)
1 Andy Machin, GB (Spondon/Rotax), 26m 21.2s, 85.37 mph/137.39 km/h.
2 Gary Cowan, IRL (Honda); **3** Steve Patrickson, GB (Yamaha); **4** Ian Newton, GB (Honda); **5** Nigel Bosworth, GB (Yamaha); **6** Peter Hubbard, GB (Yamaha); **7** Rob Orme, GB (Yamaha); **8** Eddie Laycock, GB (EMC); **9** Dave Butler, GB (Yamaha); **10** A. Godber, GB (Yamaha).
Fastest lap: Cowan, 1m 44.15s, 86.41 mph/139.07 km/h.
Championship points: 1 Cowan, 34; **2** Machin, 27; **3** Mitchell, 18; **4** Fogarty, McLeod and Patrickson, 15.

ACU Motoprix British Championship, 125 cc, round 2 (8 laps, 20 miles/32.16 km)
1 Robin Milton, GB (MBA), 15m 14.91s, 78.69 mph/126.64 km/h.
2 Robin Appleyard, GB (MBA); **3** Michael McGarrity, GB (MBA); **4** Ian McConnachie, GB (EMC); **5** Chris Galatowicz, GB (Honda); **6** Gary Buckle, GB (MBA); **7** Steve Mason, GB (MBA); **8** Mark Carkeek, GB (Scitsu); **9** Garry Dickinson, GB (MBA); **10** Patrick Corrigan, GB (Honda).
Fastest lap: McConnachie, 1m 52s, 80.35 mph/129.32 km/h.
Championship points: 1 Milton, 30; **2** Galatowicz, 18; **3** Buckle, 15; **4** Appleyard, 12; **5** McGarrity, 10; **6** Mason, 9.

ACU Motoprix British Championship, Sidecars, round 2 (15 laps, 37.5 miles/60.3 km)
1 Steve Webster/Tony Hewitt, GB/GB (Krauser), 26m 9.2s, 86.03 mph/138.45 km/h.
2 Barry Brindley/Grahame Rose, GB/GB (Yamaha); **3** Yoshisada Kumagaya/J. Wilson, J/GB (Yamaha); **4** Lindsay Hurst/Gary Hurst, GB/GB (Yamaha); **5** Gary Thomas/Syd Naylor, GB/GB (Yamaha); **6** Geoff Rushbrook/Geoff Leitch, GB/GB (Yamaha); **7** Tony Baker/John Hennigan, GB/GB (Yamaha); **8** Brian Gray/Bob Holden, GB/GB (Yamaha); **9** Lowry Burton/Pat Cushanhan, GB/GB (Yamaha); **10** Ray Gardner/Tony Strevens, GB/GB (Yamaha).
Fastest lap: Webster, 1m 42.97s, 87.4 mph/140.66 km/h.
Championship points: 1 Webster, 30; **2** Kumagaya, 22; **3** Brindley, 17; **4** Baker, Lawrence and Hurst, 10.

BRANDS HATCH INDY CIRCUIT, 25 October. 1.2036-mile/1.93-km circuit.
ACU Motoprix British Championship, 1300 cc, round 4 (15 laps, 18.054 miles/28.95 km)
1 Mark Phillips, GB (500 Suzuki), 12m 26.3s, 87.08 mph/140.12 km/h.
2 Roger Marshall, GB (1100 Suzuki); **3** Ray Swann, GB (500 Honda); **4** Paul Iddon, GB (750 Suzuki); **5** Peter Dalby, GB (500 Suzuki); **6** Simon Buckmaster, GB (500 Honda); **7** Mark Farmer, GB (500 Suzuki); **8** Trevor Nation, GB (1000 Yamaha); **9** Jamie Whitham, GB (750 Suzuki); **10** Gary Weston, GB (750 Suzuki).
Fastest lap: Marshall, 48.6s, 89.15 mph/143.47 km/h.

ACU Motoprix British Championship, 250 cc, round 4 (15 laps, 18.054 miles/28.95 km)
1 Donnie McLeod, GB (EMC), 12m 42.7s, 85.21 mph/137.13 km/h.
2 Gary Cowan, IRL (Honda); **3** Andy Machin, GB (Rotax); **4** Peter Hubbard, GB (Yamaha); **5** Steve Patrickson, GB (Yamaha); **6** Eddie Laycock, GB (EMC); **7** Nigel Bosworth, GB (Yamaha); **8** Ian Newton, GB (Honda); **9** Tony Head, GB (Honda); **10** Gary Noel, GB (Exactweld).

Fastest lap: Hubbard and Laycock, 49.5s, 87.53 mph/140.87 km/h.

ACU Motoprix British Championship, Sidecars, round 3 (15 laps, 18.054 miles/28.95 km)
1 Steve Webster/Tony Hewitt, GB/GB (Yamaha), 12m 34.09s, 86.09 mph/138.55 km/h.
2 Barry Brindley/Grahame Rose, GB/GB (Yamaha); **3** Yoshisada Kumagaya/Brian Barlow, J/GB (Yamaha); **4** Lindsay Hurst/Gary Hurst, GB/GB (Yamaha); **5** Ray Gardner/Tony Strevens, GB/GB (LCR); **6** Brian Gray/Robert Holden, GB/GB (Yamaha); **7** Tony Baker/John Hennigan, GB/GB (Yamaha); **8** John Barker/Steve China, GB/GB (Yamaha); **9** Ray Lawrence/Alan Rawlings, GB/GB (Yamaha); **10** Kenny Holmes/Steve Pointer, GB/GB (Yamaha).
Fastest lap: Webster, 48.4s, 89.52 mph/144.08 km/h.

Final Championship points (1300 cc)

1	Roger Marshall	57
2	Ray Swann	34
3	Jamie Whitham	26
4	Mark Phillips	23
5	Paul Iddon	20
6	Simon Buckmaster	12

7 Trevor Nation and Gary Noel, 11; **9** Keith Huewen and Phil Mellor, 10.

Final Championship points (250 cc)

1	Gary Cowan	46
2	Andy Machin	37
3	Donnie McLeod	30
4	Steve Patrickson	21
5	Peter Hubbard	19
6	Kevin Mitchell	18

7 Carl Fogarty, 15; **8** Ian Newton, 11; **9** Nigel Bosworth and Phil Borley, 10.

Final Championship points (Sidecars)

1	Steve Webster/Tony Hewitt	45
2	Yoshisada Kumagaya/Brian Barlow/J. Wilson	32
3	Barry Brindley/Grahame Rose	29
4	Lindsay Hurst/Gary Hurst	18
5	Tony Baker/John Hennigan	14
6	Ray Lawrence/Alan Rawlings	12

7 Ray Gardner/Tony Strevens, 11; **8** Gary Thomas/J. Webb/Syd Naylor, 9; **9** Derek Jones/Brian Ayres and Brian Gray/Bob Holden, 8.

ACU SHELL OILS Superbike Championships

DONINGTON PARK CIRCUIT, 21 June. 1.96-mile/3.136-km circuit.
ACU Shell Oils Superbike Championship, Super One, round 1 (10 laps, 19.6 miles/31.36 km)
1 Roger Marshall, GB (1100 Suzuki), 12m 51.1s, 91.36 mph/147.03 km/h.
2 Phil Mellor, GB (1100 Suzuki); **3** Trevor Nation, GB (1000 Yamaha); **4** Roland Brown, GB (1100 Suzuki); **5** Ray Swann, GB (750 Suzuki); **6** Andy McGladdery, GB (750 Honda); **7** Jamie Whitham, GB (750 Suzuki); **8** Dennis Ireland, GB (1100 Suzuki); **9** Steve Chambers, GB (750 Yamaha); **10** Colin Breeze, GB (750 Yamaha).
Fastest lap: Marshall and Mellor, 1m 15.9s, 92.82 mph/149.38 km/h.
Championship points: 1 Marshall, 15; **2** Mellor, 12; **3** Nation, 10; **4** Brown, 8; **5** Swann, 6; **6** McGladdery, 5.

ACU Shell Oils Superbike Championship, Super Two, round 1
1 Steve Patrickson, GB (250 Yamaha), 10m 31.7s, 89.22 mph/143.6 km/h.
2 Rob Orme, GB (250 Yamaha); **3** Kevin Mitchell, GB (250 Yamaha); **4** Steve Williams, GB (350 Yamaha); **5** Woolsey Coulter, GB (250 Honda); **6** Steve Hislop, GB (350 Yamaha); **7** Dave Butler, GB (250 Yamaha); **8** Peter Hubbard, GB (250 Yamaha); **9** Steve Sawford, GB (250 Yamaha); **10** Chris Lake, GB (350 Yamaha).
Fastest lap: Orme, 1m 16.8s, 91.73 mph/147.62 km/h.
Championship points: 1 Patrickson, 15; **2** Orme, 12; **3** Mitchell, 10; **4** Williams, 8; **5** Coulter, 6; **6** Hislop, 5.

CADWELL PARK CIRCUIT, 28 June. 2.17-mile/3.472-km circuit.
ACU Shell Oils Superbike Championship, Super One, round 2 (8 laps, 17.36 miles/27.77 km)
1 Roger Marshall, GB (1100 Suzuki), 13m 06.3s, 79.62 mph/128.14 km/h.
2 Colin Breeze, GB (750 Yamaha); **3** Roger Hurst, GB (750 Yamaha); **4** John Lofthouse, GB (750 Suzuki); **5** Steve Chambers, GB (750 Yamaha); **6** Steve Henshaw, GB (500 Suzuki); **7** Jamie Whitham, GB (750 Suzuki); **8** Gary Noel, GB (750 Yamaha); **9** Dennis Ireland, GB (750 Yamaha); **10** Paul Iddon, GB (750 Suzuki).
Fastest lap: Mellor and Marshall, 1m 36.7s, 80.93 mph/130.25 km/h.
Championship points: 1 Marshall, 30; **2** Breeze, 13; **3** Mellor, 12; **4** Hurst and Nation, 10; **6** Brown, Chambers and Whitham, 8.

ACU Shell Oils Superbike Championship, Super Two, round 2 (8 laps, 17.36 miles/27.77 km)
1 Steve Patrickson, GB (250 Yamaha), 13m 21.4s, 78.12 mph/125.72 km/h.
2 Andy Machin, GB (250 Rotax); **3** Steve Hislop, GB (350 Yamaha); **4** Carl Fogarty, GB (250 Honda); **5** Ian Burnett, GB (250 Honda); **6** Paul Simmonds, GB (350 Yamaha); **7** Dave Butler, GB (250 Yamaha); **8** Woolsey Coulter, GB (250 Honda); **9** Michael Otter, GB (250 Yamaha); **10** Paul Weston, GB (250 Yamaha).
Fastest lap: Patrickson, 1m 38.1s, 79.77 mph/128.38 km/h.
Championship points: 1 Patrickson, 30; **2** Hislop, 15; **3** Machin and Orme, 12; **5** Mitchell, 10; **6** Coulter, 9.

KNOCKHILL CIRCUIT, 12 July. 1.3-mile/2.08-km circuit.
ACU Shell Oils Superbike Championship, Super One, round 3 (12 laps, 15.6 miles/24.96 km)
1 Roger Marshall, GB (1100 Suzuki), 11m 26.9s, 81.07 mph/130.46 km/h.
2 Phil Mellor, GB (1100 Suzuki); **3** Mark Phillips, GB (500 Suzuki); **4** Paul Iddon, GB (750 Suzuki); **5** Keith Huewen, GB (750 Yamaha); **6** Roger Hurst, GB (750 Yamaha); **7** Steve Spray, GB (750 Yamaha); **8** Gary Noel, GB (750 Yamaha); **9** Ray Swann, GB (500 Honda); **10** Steve Chambers, GB (750 Yamaha).
Fastest lap: Marshall, 56.5s, 82.13 mph/132.2 km/h.
Championship points: 1 Marshall, 45; **2** Mellor, 24; **3** Hurst, 15; **4** Breeze, 13; **5** Nation and Phillips, 10.

ACU Shell Oils Superbike Championship, Super Two, round 3 (6 laps, 7.8 miles/12.48 km)
1 Andy Machin, GB (250 Rotax), 5m 51s, 79.32 mph/127.68 km/h.
2 Carl Fogarty, GB (250 Honda); **3** Steve Hislop, GB (350 Yamaha); **4** Greig Ramsay, GB (250 Yamaha); **5** Steve Patrickson, GB (250 Rotax); **6** Ian Burnett, GB (250 Honda); **7** Derek Young, GB (350 Yamaha); **8** Ian Lougher, GB (350 Yamaha); **9** Micky Bridges, GB (350 Yamaha); **10** Phil Borley, GB (250 Yamaha).
Fastest lap: Ramsay, 57.3s, 80.98 mph/130.32 km/h.
Championship points: 1 Patrickson, 36; **2** Machin, 27; **3** Hislop, 25; **4** Fogarty, 20; **5** Orme, 12; **6** Burnett, 11.

SNETTERTON CIRCUIT, 19 July. 1.917-mile/3.085-km circuit.
ACU Shell Oils Superbike Championship, Super One, round 4 (12 laps, 23 miles/37.02 km)
1 Phil Mellor, GB (1100 Suzuki), 14m 3.5s, 98.17 mph/157.8 km/h.
2 Roger Marshall, GB (1100 Suzuki); **3** Ray Swann, GB (500 Honda); **4** Paul Iddon, GB (750 Suzuki); **5** Ricky McMillan, GB (1100 Suzuki); **6** Colin Breeze, GB (750 Yamaha) and Steve Chambers, GB (750 Yamaha); **8** Mark Farmer, GB (500 Suzuki); **9** Des Barry, GB (750 Yamaha); **10** Andy McGladdery, GB (750 Honda).
Fastest lap: Mellor and Marshall, 1m 8.5s, 100.74 mph/161.9 km/h.
Championship points: 1 Marshall, 57; **2** Mellor, 39; **3** Swann, 18; **4** Breeze, 17.5; **5** Iddon, 17; **6** Chambers, 13.5.

ACU Shell Oils Superbike Championship, Super Two, round 4 (12 laps, 23 miles/37.02 km)
1 Andy Machin, GB (250 Rotax), 14m 36.5s, 94.48 mph/151.9 km/h.
2 Steve Patrickson, GB (250 Yamaha); **3** Kevin Mitchell, GB (250 Yamaha); **4** Steve Hislop, GB (350 Yamaha); **5** Carl Fogarty, GB (250 Honda); **6** Dave Butler, GB (250 Yamaha); **7** Steve Williams, GB (250 Yamaha); **8** R. Johnson, GB (250 Exactweld); **9** Woolsey Coulter, GB (250 Honda); **10** Glen English, GB (350 Yamaha).
Fastest lap: Williams, 1m 11.9s, 95.98 mph/153.9 km/h.
Championship points: 1 Patrickson, 48; **2** Machin, 42; **3** Hislop, 33; **4** Fogarty, 26; **5** Mitchell, 20; **6** Butler, 13.

MALLORY PARK CIRCUIT, 26 July. 1.370-mile/2.205-km circuit.
ACU Shell Oils Superbike Championship, Super One, round 5 (12 laps, 16.44 miles/26.46 km)
1 Mark Phillips, GB (500 Suzuki), 10m 36.4s, 92.99 mph/149.66 km/h.
2 Ray Swann, GB (500 Honda); **3** Phil Mellor, GB (1100 Suzuki); **4** Paul Iddon, GB (750 Suzuki); **5** Roger Marshall, GB (1100 Suzuki); **6** Mark Farmer, GB (500 Suzuki); **7** Roger Hurst, GB (750 Yamaha); **8** Simon Buckmaster, GB (500 Honda); **9** Jamie Whitham, GB (750 Suzuki); **10** Steve Williams, GB (750 Yamaha).
Fastest lap; Marshall and Phillips, 52.1s, 94.66 mph/152.38 km/h.
Championship points: 1 Marshall, 63; **2** Mellor, 49; **3** Swann, 30; **4** Iddon and Phillips, 25; **6** Hurst, 19.

ACU Shell Oils Superbike Championship, Super Two, round 5 (10 laps, 13.7 miles/22.05 km)
1 Carl Fogarty, GB (250 Honda), 10m 12.2s, 80.56 mph/129.64 km/h.
2 Andy Machin, GB (250 Rotax); **3** Kevin Mitchell, GB (250 Yamaha); **4** Steve Patrickson, GB (250 Yamaha); **5** Phil Borley, GB (250 Yamaha); **6** Peter Hubbard, GB (250 Yamaha); **7** D. Heal, GB (350 Yamaha); **8** Steve Bevington, GB (350 Yamaha); **9** Steve Sawford, GB (250 Yamaha) and T. Sanders, GB (350 Yamaha).
Fastest lap: Fogarty, 58.9s, 83.73 mph/134.75 km/h.
Championship points: 1 Patrickson, 56; **2** Machin, 54; **3** Fogarty, 41; **4** Hislop, 33; **5** Mitchell, 30; **6** Butler, 13.

THRUXTON CIRCUIT, 23 August. 2.356-mile/3.792-km circuit.
ACU Shell Oils Superbike Championship, Super One, round 6 (12 laps, 28.27 miles/45.50 km)
1 Roger Marshall, GB (1100 Suzuki), 16m 54.2s, 100.35 mph/161.5 km/h.
2 Mark Phillips, GB (500 Suzuki); **3** Phil Mellor, GB (1100 Suzuki); **4** Steve Henshaw, GB (500 Suzuki); **5** Trevor Nation, GB (1000 Yamaha); **6** Roger Hurst, GB (750 Yamaha); **7** Gary Noel, GB (750 Yamaha); **8** Gary Lingham, GB (750 Kawasaki); **9** Steve Chambers, GB (750 Yamaha); **10** Steve Williams, GB (750 Yamaha).
Fastest lap: Marshall, 1m 22.4s, 102.93 mph/165.65 km/h.
Championship points: 1 Marshall, 78; **2** Mellor, 59; **3** Phillips, 37; **4** Swann, 30; **5** Iddon, 25; **6** Hurst, 24.

ACU Shell Oils Superbike Championship, Super Two, round 6 (10 laps, 23.56 miles/37.92 km)
1 Carl Fogarty, GB (250 Honda), 14m 56.4s, 94.62 mph/152.28 km/h.
2 Rob Orme, GB (250 Yamaha); **3** Steve Patrickson, GB (250 Yamaha); **4** Andy Machin, GB (250 Rotax); **5** Woolsey Coulter, GB (250 Honda); **6** Peter Hubbard, GB (250 Yamaha); **7** Steve Williams, GB (350 Yamaha); **8** Steve Johnson, GB (350 Yamaha); **9** Phil Borley, GB (250 Yamaha); **10** Dave Redgate, GB (250 Yamaha).
Fastest lap: Patrickson, 1m 25.6s, 99.08 mph/159.6 km/h.
Championship points: 1 Patrickson, 66; **2** Machin, 62; **3** Fogarty, 56; **4** Hislop, 33; **5** Mitchell, 30; **6** Orme, 24.

OLIVER'S MOUNT CIRCUIT, 12/13 September. 2.4136-mile/3.8842-km circuit.
ACU Shell Oils Superbike Championship, Super One, round 7 (12 laps, 28.96 miles/46.61 km)
1 Roger Marshall, GB (1100 Suzuki), 21m 30.6s, 80.79 mph/130.04 km/h.
2 Phil Mellor, GB (1100 Suzuki); **3** Mark Phillips, GB (500 Suzuki); **4** Jamie Whitham, GB (750 Suzuki); **5** Roger Hurst, GB (750 Yamaha); **6** Colin Breeze, GB (750 Yamaha); **7** John Lofthouse, GB (750 Suzuki); **8** Mark Westmorland, GB (750 Yamaha); **9** Steve Ward, GB (750 Suzuki); **10** Ian Wilson, GB (750 Suzuki).
Fastest lap: Marshall, 1m 46.2s, 81.89 mph/131.79 km/h.
Championship points: 1 Marshall, 93; **2** Mellor, 71; **3** Phillips, 47; **4** Hurst and Swann, 30; **6** Iddon, 25.

ACU Shell Oils Superbike Championship, Super Two, round 7 (10 laps, 24.1 miles/38.84 km)
1 Carl Fogarty, GB (250 Honda), 18m 35.3s, 77.91 mph/125.38 km/h.
2 Steve Hislop, GB (350 Yamaha); **3** Steve Patrickson, GB (250 Yamaha); **4** Steve Johnson, GB (350 Yamaha); **5** Mark Barker, GB (250 Honda); **6** T. Sanders, GB (350 Yamaha); **7** Tony Head, GB (350 Yamaha); **8** Mark Ward, GB (600 Ducati); **9** Mike Seward, GB (600 Honda); **10** Dave Woolams, GB (600 Kawasaki).
Fastest lap: Hislop, 1m 49.5s, 79.35 mph/127.70 km/h.
Championship points: 1 Patrickson, 76; **2** Fogarty, 71; **3** Machin, 62; **4** Hislop, 45; **5** Mitchell, 30; **6** Orme, 24.

SILVERSTONE CIRCUIT, 20 September. 1.608-mile/2.588-km circuit. ACU Shell Oils Superbike Championship, Super One and Super Two, round 8.
Races cancelled due to bad weather.

BRANDS HATCH INDY CIRCUIT, 24 October. 1.2035-mile/1.9370-km circuit.
ACU Shell Oils Superbike Championship, Super One, round 8 (10 laps, 12.03 miles/19.37 km)
1 Mark Phillips, GB (500 Suzuki), 8m 22.1s, 86.29 mph/138.88 km/h.
2 Roger Marshall, GB (1100 Suzuki); **3** Mark Farmer, GB (500 Suzuki); **4** Roger Hurst, GB (750 Yamaha); **5** Simon Buckmaster, GB (500 Honda); **6** Des Barry, GB (750 Yamaha); **7** Steve Henshaw, GB (500 Suzuki); **8** Alan Irwin, GB (500 Honda); **9** Peter Dalby, GB (500 Suzuki); **10** Jamie Whitham, GB (750 Suzuki).
Fastest lap: Irwin, Marshall and Phillips, 49s, 88.42 mph/143.9 km/h.

ACU Shell Oils Superbike Championship, Super Two, round 8 (10 laps, 12.03 miles/19.37 km)
1 Steve Williams, GB (350 Yamaha), 8m 30.5s, 84.87 mph/136.58 km/h.
2 Rob Orme, GB (250 Yamaha); **3** Steve Patrickson, GB (250 Yamaha); **4** Steve Hislop, GB (350 Yamaha); **5** Ian Newton, GB (250 Yamaha); **6** Gary Cowan, IRL (250 Honda); **7** Woolsey Coulter, GB (250 Honda); **8** Eddie Laycock, GB (250 EMC); **9** Donnie McLeod, GB (250 EMC); **10** Steve Johnson, GB (250 Yamaha).
Fastest lap: Hislop, 49.6s, 87.35 mph/140.58 km/h.

Final Championship points (Super One)

1	Roger Marshall, GB	105
2	Phil Mellor, GB	71
3	Mark Phillips, GB	62
4	Roger Hurst, GB	38
5	Ray Swann, GB	30
6	Paul Iddon, GB	25

7 Steve Chambers, GB, 22.5; **8** Jamie Whitham, GB, 19; **9** Mark Farmer, GB, 18; **10** Steve Henshaw, GB, 17; **11** Trevor Nation, GB, 16; **12** Steve Chambers, GB, 15.5; **13** John Lofthouse, GB, 12; **14** Gary Noel, GB, 10; **15** Simon Buckmaster, GB, 9.

Final Championship points (Super Two)

1	Steve Patrickson, GB	86
2	Carl Fogarty, GB	71
3	Andy Machin, GB	62
4	Steve Hislop, GB	53
5	Rob Orme, GB	36
6	Steve Williams, GB	31

7 Kevin Mitchell, GB, 30; **8** Woolsey Coulter, 21; **9** Dave Butler, GB and Peter Hubbard, GB, 13; **11** Steve Johnson, GB, 12; **12** Ian Burnett, GB, 11; **13** Phil Borley, GB, 9; **14** Greig Ramsay, GB, 8; **15** T. Sanders, GB, 6.5.

750 cc Metzeler Production Championship

DONINGTON PARK CIRCUIT, 21 June. 1.96-mile/3.136-km circuit.
750 cc Metzeler Production Championship, round 1 (8 laps, 15.68 miles/25.088 miles)
1 Phil Mellor, GB (Suzuki), 10m 48.4s, 86.92 mph/139.89 km/h.
2 Dean Ashton, GB (Suzuki); **3** John Lofthouse, GB (Suzuki); **4** Colin Gable, GB (Suzuki); **5** Ray Stringer, GB (Suzuki); **6** Adrian Jupp, GB (Suzuki); **7** Graham Read, GB (Suzuki); **8** Tom Blackwell, GB (Suzuki); **9** Geoff Johnson, GB (Kawasaki); **10** Mark Linscott, GB (Suzuki).
Fastest lap: Mellor, 1m 20s, 88.06 mph/141.72 km/h.
Championship points: 1 Mellor, 15; **2** Ashton, 12; **3** Lofthouse, 10; **4** Gable, 8; **5** Stringer, 6; **6** Jupp, 5.

CADWELL PARK CIRCUIT, 28 June. 2.17-mile/3.472-km circuit.
750 cc Metzeler Production Championship, round 2 (8 laps, 17.36 miles/27.77 km)
1 Phil Mellor, GB (Suzuki), 13m 35.1s, 76.81 mph/123.62 km/h.
2 Ray Stringer, GB (Suzuki); **3** John Lofthouse, GB (Suzuki); **4** Eric McFarlane, GB (Suzuki); **5** Dean Ashton, GB (Suzuki); **6** Colin Gable, GB (Suzuki); **7** Rob Talton, GB (Honda); **8** Gary Thrush, GB (Yamaha); **9** Brian Morrison, GB (Suzuki); **10** Antony Cummins, GB (Suzuki).
Fastest lap: Mellor, 1m 40.8s, 77.64 mph/124.95 km/h.

Championship points: 1 Mellor, 30; **2** Lofthouse, 20; **3** Ashton and Stringer, 18; **5** Gable; 13; **6** McFarlane, 8.

KNOCKHILL CIRCUIT, 12 July. 1.3-mile/2.08-km circuit.
750 cc Metzeler Production Championship, round 3 (12 laps, 15.6 miles/24.96 km)
1 Ray Stringer, GB (Suzuki), 11m 58s, 77.56 mph/124.83 km/h.
2 Brian Morrison, GB (Suzuki); **3** Phil Mellor, GB (Suzuki); **4** John Lofthouse, GB (Suzuki); **5** Eric McFarlane, GB (Suzuki); **6** Geoff Johnson, GB (Kawasaki); **7** Antony Cummins, GB (Suzuki); **8** Tom Blackwell, GB (Suzuki); **9** Tom Webb, GB (Suzuki); **10** G. Lawson, GB (Suzuki).
Fastest lap: Mellor, Morrison and Stringer, 58.6s, 79.19 mph/127.45 km/h.
Championship points: 1 Mellor, 40; **2** Stringer, 33; **3** Lofthouse, 28; **4** Ashton, 18; **5** McFarlane and Morrison, 14.

SNETTERTON CIRCUIT, 19 July. 1.917-mile/3.085-km circuit.
750 cc Metzeler Production Championship, round 4 (12 laps, 23 miles/37.02 km)
1 Phil Mellor, GB (Suzuki), 14m 49.5s, 93.1 mph/149.85 km/h.
2 Ray Stringer, GB (Suzuki); **3** Brian Morrison, GB (Suzuki); **4** Geoff Johnson, GB (Suzuki); **5** Graham Read, GB (Kawasaki); **6** John Lofthouse, GB (Suzuki); **7** Adrian Jupp, GB (Suzuki); **8** Antony Cummins, GB (Suzuki); **9** Mark Linscott, GB (Kawasaki); **10** Grant Goodings, GB (Kawasaki).
Fastest lap: McFarlane, GB (Suzuki), 1m 13s, 94.53 mph/152.14 km/h.
Championship points: 1 Mellor, 55; **2** Stringer, 45; **3** Lofthouse, 33; **4** Morrison, 24; **5** Ashton, 18; **6** Johnson, 15.

MALLORY PARK CIRCUIT, 26 July. 1.370-mile/2.205-km circuit.
750 cc Metzeler Production Championship, round 5 (12 laps, 16.44 miles/26.46 km)
1 John Lofthouse, GB (Suzuki), 13m 3.1s, 75.57 mph/121.63 km/h.
2 Phil Mellor, GB (Suzuki); **3** Ray Stringer, GB (Suzuki); **4** Brian Morrison, GB (Suzuki); **5** Graham Read, GB (Suzuki); **6** Tony Thompson, GB (Suzuki); **7** Colin Gable, GB (Suzuki); **8** Alan Batson, GB (Honda); **9** Antony Cummins, GB (Suzuki); **10** Adrian Jupp, GB (Suzuki).
Fastest lap: Lofthouse and Morrison, 1m 3.1s, 78.16 mph/125.78 km/h.
Championship points: 1 Mellor, 67; **2** Stringer, 55; **3** Lofthouse, 48; **4** Morrison, 32; **5** Ashton, 18; **6** Gable, 17.

THRUXTON CIRCUIT, 23 August. 2.356-mile/3.792-km circuit.
750 cc Metzeler Production Championship, round 6 (8 laps, 18.85 miles/30.33 km)
1 Eric McFarlane, GB (Suzuki), 12m 2.7s, 93.89 mph/151.14 km/h.
2 Phil Mellor, GB (Suzuki); **3** John Lofthouse, GB (Suzuki); **4** Ray Stringer, GB (Suzuki); **5** Rob Haynes, GB (Kawasaki); **6** Colin Gable, GB (Suzuki); **7** Adrian Jupp, GB (Suzuki); **8** Brian Morrison, GB (Suzuki); **9** Geoff Johnson, GB (Suzuki); **10** Gary Thrush, GB (Suzuki).
Fastest lap: Haynes, 1m 28.4s, 95.95 mph/154.2 km/h.
Championship points: 1 Mellor, 79; **2** Stringer, 63; **3** Lofthouse, 58; **4** Morrison, 35; **5** McFarlane, 29; **6** Gable, 23.

OLIVER'S MOUNT CIRCUIT, 13 September. 2.4136-mile/3.8842-km circuit.
750 cc Metzeler Production Championship, round 7 (10 laps, 24.13 miles/38.84 km)
1 Phil Mellor, GB (Suzuki), 18m 45.3s, 77.21 mph/124.28 km/h.
2 Brian Morrison, GB (Suzuki); **3** John Lofthouse, GB (Suzuki); **4** Ray Hutchison, GB (Suzuki); **5** Geoff Johnson, GB (Suzuki); **6** Ray Stringer, GB (Suzuki); **7** Gary Thrush, GB (Suzuki); **8** Colin Gable, GB (Suzuki); **9** M. Parvin, GB (Honda); **10** Tony Thompson, GB (Suzuki).
Fastest lap: Mellor, 1m 51.2s, 78.14 mph/125.76 km/h.
Championship points: 1 Mellor, 94; **2** Lofthouse and Stringer, 68; **4** Morrison, 47; **5** McFarlane, 29; **6** Gable, 26.

SILVERSTONE CIRCUIT, 20 September. 1.608-mile/2.588-km circuit.
750 cc Metzeler Production Championship, round 8 (10 laps, 16.08 miles/25.88 km)
1 Antony Cummins, GB (Suzuki), 11m 09.70s, 86.44 mph/139.12 km/h.
2 Brian Morrison, GB (Suzuki); **3** Ray Stringer, GB (Suzuki); **4** Phil Mellor, GB (Suzuki); **5** Mark Linscott, GB (Kawasaki); **6** Geoff Johnson, GB (Suzuki); **7** John Lofthouse, GB (Suzuki); **8** Mike Hodges, GB (Suzuki); **9** Mark Plato, GB (Kawasaki); **10** Graham Read, GB (Suzuki).
Fastest lap; Cummins, 1m 05.60s, 88.24 mph/142.05 km/h.
Championship points: 1 Mellor, 102; **2** Stringer, 78; **3** Lofthouse, 72; **4** Morrison, 59; **5** McFarlane, 29; **6** Johnson, 28.

BRANDS HATCH INDY CIRCUIT, 24 October. 1.2036-mile/1.9370-km circuit.
750 cc Metzeler Production Championship, round 9 (10 laps, 12.03 miles/19.37 km)
1 Brian Morrison, GB (Suzuki), 8m 45.5s, 82.45 mph/132.69 km/h.
2 Phil Mellor, GB (Suzuki); **3** Ray Stringer, GB (Suzuki); **4** Graham Read, GB (Suzuki); **5** Mark Linscott, GB (Kawasaki); **6** Ian Cobby, GB (Suzuki); **7** Eric McFarlane, GB (Suzuki); **8** Antony Cummins, GB (Suzuki); **9** Geoff Johnson, GB (Honda); **10** John Gainey, GB (Honda).
Fastest lap: Morrison, 51.6s, 83.97 mph/135.14 km/h.

Final Championship points

1	Phil Mellor, GB	114
2	Ray Stringer, GB	88
3	Brian Morrison, GB	74
4	John Lofthouse, GB	72
5	Eric McFarlane, GB	33
6	Geoff Johnson, GB	30

7 Antony Cummins, GB, 28; **8** Colin Gable, GB and Graham Read, GB, 26; **10** Dean Ashton, GB, 18; **11** Adrian Jupp, GB and Mark Linscott, GB, 15; **13** Ray Hutchison, GB and Gary Thrush, GB, 8; **15** Tom Blackwell, GB and Tony Thompson, GB, 6.

1300 cc Metzeler Production Championship

DONINGTON PARK CIRCUIT, 21 June. 1.96-mile/3.136-km circuit.
1300 cc Metzeler Production Championship, round 1 (8 laps, 15.68 miles/25.088 km)
1 Geoff Johnson, GB (1000 Yamaha), 10m 40s, 87.99 mph/141.61 km/h.
2 Phil Mellor, GB (1100 Suzuki); **3** Ian Wilson, GB (1100 Suzuki); **4** Trevor Nation, GB (1000 Yamaha); **5** Iain Duffus, GB (1000 Yamaha); **6** Tony Thompson, GB (1100 Suzuki); **7** Eric McFarlane, GB (1000 Yamaha); **8** Rob Haynes, GB (1100 Suzuki); **9** Dennis Ireland, GB (1100 Suzuki); **10** Ricky McMillan, GB (1100 Suzuki).
Fastest lap: Wilson and A. Batson (1100 Suzuki), 1m 18.3s, 89.97 mph/144.73 km/h.
Championship points: 1 Johnson, 15; **2** Mellor, 12; **3** Wilson, 10; **4** Nation, 8; **5** Duffus, 6; **6** Thompson, 5.

CADWELL PARK CIRCUIT, 28 June. 2.17-mile/3.472-km circuit.
1300 cc Metzeler Production Championship, round 2 (8 laps, 17.36 miles/27.77 km)
1 Ian Wilson, GB (1100 Suzuki), 13m 41.4s, 76.22 mph/122.66 km/h.
2 Geoff Johnson, GB (1000 Yamaha); **3** Trevor Nation, GB (1000 Yamaha); **4** Phil Mellor, GB (1100 Suzuki); **5** Tony Thompson, GB (1100 Suzuki); **6** Brian Morrison, GB (1100 Suzuki); **7** Eric McFarlane, GB (1100 Suzuki); **8** John Lofthouse, GB (1100 Suzuki); **9** Paul Ruckledge, GB (1100 Suzuki); **10** Martin Wells, GB (1000 Yamaha).
Fastest lap: Johnson, 1m 40.9s, 77.56 mph/124.84 km/h.
Championship points: 1 Johnson, 27; **2** Wilson, 25; **3** Mellor, 20; **4** Nation 18; **5** Thompson, 11; **6** McFarlane, 8.

KNOCKHILL CIRCUIT, 12 July. 1.3-mile/2.08-km circuit.
1300 cc Metzeler Production Championship, round 3 (12 laps, 15.6 miles/24.96 km)
1 Brian Morrison, GB (1100 Suzuki), 11m 50.2s, 78.41 mph/126.19 km/h.
2 Iain Duffus, GB (1000 Yamaha); **3** Eric McFarlane, GB (1100 Suzuki); **4** Phil Mellor, GB (1100 Suzuki); **5** Ian Wilson, GB (1100 Suzuki); **6** Geoff Johnson, GB (1000 Yamaha); **7** John Lofthouse, GB (1100 Suzuki); **8** Tony Thompson, GB (1100 Suzuki); **9** Rory Thompson, GB (1100 Suzuki); **10** David Goodley, GB (1100 Suzuki).
Fastest lap: Morrison, 57.7s, 80.46 mph/129.52 km/h.
Championship points: 1 Johnson, 32; **2** Wilson, 31; **3** Mellor, 28; **4** Morrison, 20; **5** Duffus, McFarlane and Nation, 18.

SNETTERTON CIRCUIT, 19 July. 1.917-mile/3.085-km circuit.
1300 cc Metzeler Production Championship, round 4 (12 laps, 23 miles/37.02 km)
1 Brian Morrison, GB (1100 Suzuki), 14m 34.5s, 94.69 mph/152.5 km/h.
2 Geoff Johnson, GB (1000 Yamaha); **3** Phil Mellor, GB (1100 Suzuki); **4** Ian Wilson, GB (1100 Suzuki); **5** Tony Thompson, GB (1100 Suzuki); **6** Iain Duffus, GB (1000 Yamaha); **7** Eric McFarlane, GB (1100 Suzuki); **8** Steve Bonhomme, GB (1100 Suzuki); **9** Mark Bowen, GB (1000 Yamaha); **10** Ricky McMillan, GB (1100 Suzuki).
Fastest lap: Johnson and Morrison, 1m 11.8s, 96.11 mph/154.677 km/h.
Championship points: 1 Johnson, 44; **2** Wilson, 39; **3** Mellor, 38; **4** Morrison, 35; **5** Duffus, 23; **6** McFarlane, 22.

MALLORY PARK CIRCUIT, 26 July. 1.370-mile/2.205-km circuit.
1300 cc Metzeler Production Championship, round 5 (12 laps, 16.44 miles/26.46 km)
1 Brian Morrison, GB (1100 Suzuki), 10m 53.8s, 90.52 mph/145.69 km/h.
2 Phil Mellor, GB (1100 Suzuki); **3** Eric McFarlane, GB (1100 Suzuki); **4** Iain Duffus, GB (1000 Yamaha); **5** Geoff Johnson, GB (1000 Yamaha); **6** John Lofthouse, GB (1100 Suzuki); **7** Ian Wilson, GB (1100 Suzuki); **8** Rob Haynes, GB (1100 Suzuki); **9** Howard Selby, GB (1100 Suzuki); **10** Simon Sloan, GB (1100 Suzuki).
Fastest lap: Morrison, 53.6s, 92.01 mph/148.07 km/h.
Championship points: 1 Johnson, Mellor and Morrison, 50; **4** Wilson, 43; **5** McFarlane, 32; **6** Duffus, 31.

THRUXTON CIRCUIT, 23 August. 2.356-mile/3.792-km circuit.
1300 cc Metzeler Production Championship, round 6 (8 laps, 18.85 miles/30.33 km)
1 Phil Mellor, GB (1100 Suzuki), 11m 35.7s, 97.53 mph/157.25 km/h.
2 Ian Wilson, GB (1100 Suzuki); **3** Brian Morrison, GB (1100 Suzuki); **4** Tony Thompson, GB (1100 Suzuki); **5** Rob Haynes, GB (1100 Suzuki); **6** Eric McFarlane, GB (1100 Suzuki); **7** Trevor Nation, GB (1000 Yamaha); **8** Rory Thompson, GB (1100 Suzuki); **9** David Pickworth, GB (1000 Yamaha); **10** T. Smith, GB (1100 Suzuki).
Fastest lap: Wilson, 1m 25.5s, 99.2 mph/159.73 km/h.
Championship points: 1 Mellor, 65; **2** Morrison, 60; **3** Wilson, 55; **4** Johnson, 50; **5** McFarlane, 37; **6** Duffus, 31.

OLIVER'S MOUNT CIRCUIT, 13 September. 2.4136-mile/3.8842-km circuit.
1300 cc Metzeler Production Championship, round 7 (10 laps, 24.13 miles/38.84 km)
1 Brian Morrison, GB (1100 Suzuki), 18m 37.4s, 77.76 mph/125.13 km/h.
2 Phil Mellor, GB (1100 Suzuki); **3** Geoff Johnson, GB (1000 Yamaha); **4** Ian Wilson, GB (1100 Suzuki); **5** Iain Duffus, GB (1000 Yamaha); **6** S. Dowey, GB (1000 Yamaha); **7** Tony Thompson, GB (1100 Suzuki); **8** Rob Haynes, GB (1100 Suzuki); **9** M. Searle, GB (1000 Yamaha); **10** David O'Leary, GB (1100 Suzuki).
Fastest lap: Morrison, 1m 50.6s, 78.56 mph/126.42 km/h.
Championship points: 1 Mellor, 77; **2** Morrison, 75; **3** Wilson, 63; **4** Johnson, 60; **5** Duffus and McFarlane, 37.

SILVERSTONE CIRCUIT, 20 September. 1.608-mile/2.588-km circuit.
1300 cc Metzeler Production Championship round 8.
Race cancelled due to bad weather.

BRANDS HATCH INDY CIRCUIT, 24 October. 1.2036-mile/1.9370-km circuit.
1300 cc Metzeler Production Championship, round 9 (10 laps, 12.03 miles/19.37 km)
1 Brian Morrison, GB (1100 Suzuki), 8m 39.9s, 83.34 mph/134.14 km/h.
2 Tony Thompson, GB (1100 Suzuki); **3** Geoff Johnson, GB (1000 Yamaha); **4** Rob Haynes, GB (1100 Suzuki); **5** Howard Selby, GB (1100 Suzuki); **6** Eric McFarlane, GB (1100 Suzuki); **7** Steve Bonhomme, GB (1100 Yamaha); **8** Mark Bowen, GB (1100 Yamaha); **9** David Pickworth, GB (1000 Yamaha); **10** Iain Duffus, GB (1000 Yamaha).
Fastest lap: Johnson and Thompson, 51.1s, 84.79 mph/136.45 km/h.

Final Championship points

1	Brian Morrison, GB	90
2	Phil Mellor, GB	77
3	Geoff Johnson, GB	70
4	Ian Wilson, GB	63
5	Tony Thompson, GB	44
6	Eric McFarlane, GB	42

7 Iain Duffus, GB, 38; **8** Rob Haynes, GB, 23; **9** Trevor Nation, GB, 22; **10** John Lofthouse, GB, 12; **11** Howard Selby, GB, 8; **12** Steve Bonhomme, GB, 7; **13** Mark Bowen, GB, S. Dowey, GB and Rory Thompson, GB, 5.

Motor Cycle News/ EBC Brakes Superstock Series

BRANDS HATCH INDY CIRCUIT, 4 May. 1.2036-mile/1.9370-km circuit.
MCN/EBC Superstock Series, round 1 (15 laps, 18.05 miles/29.06 km)
1 Terry Rymer, GB (750 Yamaha), 12m 49.0s, 84.51 mph/136.01 km/h.
2 Keith Huewen, GB (750 Yamaha); **3** Trevor Nation, GB (750 Yamaha); **4** Ian Muir, GB (750 Suzuki); **5** Phil Mellor, GB (750 Suzuki); **6** Steve Chambers, GB (750 Yamaha); **7** Andy McGladdery, GB (750 Honda); **8** Darren Dixon, GB (750 Kawasaki); **9** Steve Spray, GB (750 Yamaha); **10** Mark Plato, GB (750 Suzuki).
Fastest lap: Rymer, 50.5s, 85.80 mph/138.08 km/h.
Championship points: 1 Rymer, 15; **2** Huewen, 12; **3** Nation, 10; **4** Muir, 8; **5** Mellor, 6; **6** Chambers, 5.

MALLORY PARK CIRCUIT, 14 June. 1.370-mile/2.205-km circuit.
MCN/EBC Brakes Superstock Series, round 2 (15 laps, 20.55 miles/ 33.08 km)
1 Terry Rymer, GB (Yamaha), 13m 41.7s, 90.03 mph/144.88 km/h.
2 Roger Hurst, GB (Yamaha); **3** Keith Huewen, GB (Yamaha); **4** Colin Breeze, GB (Yamaha); **5** Phil Mellor, GB (Suzuki); **6** Ray Swann, GB (Suzuki); **7** Steve Spray, GB (Yamaha); **8** Trevor Nation, GB (Yamaha); **9** Andy McGladdery, GB (Honda); **10** Steve Chambers, GB (Yamaha).
Fastest lap: Rymer, 53.1s, 92.88 mph/149.49 km/h.
Championship points: 1 Rymer, 34; **2** Huewen, 22; **3** Nation, 13; **4** Hurst and Mellor, 12; **6** Breeze and Muir, 8.

DONINGTON PARK CIRCUIT, 21 June. 1.96-mile/3.136-km circuit.
MCN/EBC Brakes Superstock Series, round 3 (10 laps, 19.6 miles/31.36 km)
1 Trevor Nation, GB (Yamaha) and Phil Mellor, GB (Suzuki), 12m 56.6s, 90.71 mph/145.98 km/h.
3 Keith Huewen, GB (Yamaha); **4** Terry Rymer, GB (Yamaha); **5** Andy McGladdery, GB (Honda); **6** Steve Chambers, GB (Yamaha); **7** Jamie Whitham, GB (Suzuki); **8** Ray Swann, GB (Suzuki); **9** Ray Stringer, GB (Suzuki); **10** Colin Breeze, GB (Yamaha).
Fastest lap: Nation, 1m 16.7s, 91.85 mph/147.82 km/h.
Championship points: 1 Rymer, 42; **2** Huewen, 32; **3** Nation, 28.5; **4** Mellor, 25.5; **5** Hurst and McGladdery, 12.

KNOCKHILL CIRCUIT, 12 July. 1.3-mile/2.08-km circuit.
MCN/EBC Brakes Superstock Series, round 4 (15 laps, 19.5 miles/31.2 km)
1 Andy McGladdery, GB (Honda), 14m 30.7s, 79.94 mph/128.65 km/h.
2 Phil Mellor, GB (Suzuki); **3** Steve Chambers, GB (Yamaha); **4** Keith Huewen, GB (Yamaha); **5** Ray Swann, GB (Suzuki); **6** Gary Noel, GB (Yamaha); **7** Colin Breeze, GB (Yamaha); **8** Geoff Fowler, GB (Yamaha); **9** John Lofthouse, GB (Suzuki); **10** Gary Lingham, GB (Kawasaki).
Fastest lap: McGladdery, 56.5s, 82.13 mph/132.18 km/h.
Championship points: 1 Rymer, 42; **2** Huewen, 40; **3** Mellor, 37.5; **4** McGladdery, 29; **5** Nation, 28.5; **6** Chambers, 21.

SNETTERTON CIRCUIT, 19 July. 1.917-mile/3.085-km circuit.
MCN/EBC Brakes Superstock Series, round 5 (12 laps, 23 miles/37.02 km)
1 Roger Hurst, GB (Yamaha), 14m 24s, 95.76 mph/153.85 km/h.
2 Andy McGladdery, GB (Honda); **3** Keith Huewen, GB (Yamaha); **4** Gary Noel, GB (Yamaha); **5** Steve Chambers, GB (Yamaha); **6** Colin Breeze, GB (Yamaha); **7** Trevor Nation, GB (Yamaha); **8** Terry Rymer, GB (Yamaha); **9** Keith Nicholls, GB (Yamaha); **10** Geoff Fowler, GB (Yamaha).
Fastest lap: Noel and Spray (Yamaha), 1m 10.5s, 97.88 mph/157.5 km/h.
Championship points: 1 Huewen, 50; **2** Rymer, 45; **3** McGladdery, 41; **4** Mellor, 37.5; **5** Nation, 32.5; **6** Chambers and Hurst, 27.

CADWELL PARK WOODLAND CIRCUIT, 9 August. 0.849-mile/1.358-km circuit.
MCN/EBC Brakes Superstock Series, round 6 (20 laps, 16.98 miles/27.16 km)
1 Keith Huewen, GB (Yamaha), 16m 43.80s, 60.90 mph/98.01 km/h.
2 Jamie Whitham, GB (Suzuki); **3** Andy McGladdery, GB (Honda); **4** Roger Hurst, GB (Yamaha); **5** Trevor Nation, GB (Yamaha); **6** Terry Rymer, GB (Yamaha); **7** Colin Breeze, GB (Yamaha); **8** Phil Mellor, GB (Suzuki); **9** Des Barry, GB (Yamaha); **10** Chris White, GB (Suzuki).
Fastest lap: Huewen and McGladdery, 49.0s, 62.38 mph/100.39 km/h.
Championship points: 1 Huewen, 66; **2** McGladdery, 52; **3** Rymer, 50; **4** Mellor, 40.5; **5** Nation, 38.5; **6** Hurst, 35.

THRUXTON CIRCUIT, 23 August. 2.356-mile/3.792-km circuit.
MCN/EBC Brakes Superstock Series, round 7 (10 laps, 23.56 miles/37.92 km)
1 Phil Mellor, GB (Suzuki), 14m 9.9s, 99.8 mph/160.55 km/h.
2 Gary Noel, GB (Yamaha); **3** Terry Rymer, GB (Yamaha); **4** Trevor Nation, GB (Yamaha); **5** Keith Nicholls, GB (Yamaha); **6** Roger Hurst, GB (Yamaha); **7** Mark Phillips, GB (Honda); **8** Steve Spray, GB (Yamaha); **9** Steve Henshaw, GB (Suzuki); **10** Steve Chambers, GB (Yamaha).
Fastest lap: Mellor and Noel, 1m 23.7s, 101.33 mph/163.12 km/h.
Championship points: 1 Huewen, 66; **2** Rymer, 60; **3** Mellor, 56.5; **4** McGladdery, 52; **5** Nation, 46.5; **6** Hurst, 40.

MALLORY PARK CIRCUIT, 6 September. 1.370-mile/2.205-km circuit.
MCN/EBC Brakes Superstock Series, round 8 (15 laps, 20.55 miles/ 33.08 km)
1 Jamie Whitham, GB (Suzuki), 14m 57s, 82.47 mph/132.72 km/h.
2 Keith Huewen, GB (Yamaha); **3** Brian Morrison, GB (Honda); **4** Darren Dixon, GB (Kawasaki); **5** Roger Hurst, GB (Yamaha); **6** Gary Lingham, GB (Kawasaki); **7** Colin Breeze, GB (Yamaha); **8** Ray Swann, GB (Suzuki); **9** David Griffith, GB (Suzuki); **10** Trevor Nation, GB (Yamaha).
Fastest lap; Whitham, 57.9s, 85.19 mph/137.10 km/h.
Championship points: 1 Huewen, 78; **2** Rymer, 60; **3** Mellor, 56.5; **4** McGladdery, 52; **5** Nation, 47.5; **6** Hurst, 46.

CADWELL PARK CIRCUIT, 4 October. 2.17-mile/3.472-km circuit.
MCN/EBC Brakes Superstock Series, round 9 (8 laps, 17.36 miles/27.77 km)
1 Keith Huewen, GB (Yamaha), 13m 15.4s, 78.57 mph/126.43 km/h.
2 Roger Hurst, GB (Yamaha); **3** Geoff Fowler, GB (Yamaha); **4** Ray Stringer, GB (Suzuki); **5** Colin Breeze, GB (Yamaha); **6** Phil Mellor, GB (Suzuki); **7** John Lofthouse, GB (Suzuki); **8** Steve Chambers, GB (Yamaha); **9** Darren Dixon, GB (Kawasaki); **10** Brian Morrison, GB (Honda).
Fastest lap: Huewen, 1m 37.9s, 79.94 mph/128.66 km/h.
Championship points: 1 Huewen, 95; **2** Mellor, 61.5; **3** Rymer, 60; **4** Hurst, 58; **5** McGladdery, 52; **6** Nation, 47.5.

BRANDS HATCH INDY CIRCUIT, 24 October. 1.2036-mile/1.9370-km circuit.
MCN/EBC Brakes Superstock Series, round 10 (15 laps, 18.05 miles/29.06 km)
1 Jamie Whitham, GB (Suzuki), 12m 42.8s, 85.2 mph/137.13 km/h.
2 Des Barry, GB (Yamaha); **3** Trevor Nation, GB (Yamaha); **4** Roger Hurst, GB (Yamaha); **5** Keith Huewen, GB (Yamaha); **6** Steve Chambers, GB (Yamaha); **7** G. Weston, GB (Suzuki); **8** Ray Stringer, GB (Suzuki); **9** Mick Preston, GB (Suzuki); **10** Gerry Mahaffy, GB (Suzuki).
Fastest lap: Chambers, 49s, 88.42 mph/143.9 km/h.

Final Championship points

1	Keith Huewen, GB	101
2	Roger Hurst, GB	66
3	Phil Mellor, GB	61.5
4	Terry Rymer, GB	60
5	Trevor Nation, GB	57.5
6	Andy McGladdery, GB	52

7 Jamie Whitham, GB, 48; **8** Steve Chambers, GB, 38; **9** Colin Breeze, GB, 32; **10** Gary Noel, GB, 27; **11** Ray Swann, GB, 17; **12** Des Barry, GB, and Geoff Fowler, GB, 14; **14** Darren Dixon, GB, and Ray Stringer, GB, 13.

MCA/ACU Star UK Championship

THRUXTON CIRCUIT, 5 April. 2.356-mile/3.792-km circuit.
MCA/ACU Star 125 cc Championship, round 1 (5 laps, 11.78 miles/18.96 km)
1 Doug Flather, GB (Honda), 8m 29.20s, 83.28 mph/134.01 km/h.
2 Chris Galatowicz, GB (Honda); **3** Robin Appleyard, GB (MBA); **4** Gary Buckle, GB (MBA); **5** Garry Dickinson, GB (Morbidelli); **6** Mark Carkeek, GB (Scitsu); **7** Michael Hose, GB (Honda); **8** Dave Brown, GB (MBA); **9** Patrick Corrigan, GB (Honda); **10** Dave Moffitt, GB (MBA).
Fastest lap: Galatowicz, 1m 38.1s, 86.45 mph/139 km/h.
Championship points: 1 Flather, 15; **2** Galatowicz, 12; **3** Appleyard, 10; **4** Buckle, 8; **5** Dickinson, 6; **6** Carkeek, 5.

MCA/ACU Star 250 cc Championship, round 1 (6 laps, 14.14 miles/22.75 km)

1 Gary Cowan, IRL (Honda), 9m 13.80s, 91.89 mph/147.86 km/h.
2 Nigel Bosworth, GB (Yamaha); **3** Ian Newton, GB (Honda); **4** Steve Patrickson, GB (Yamaha); **5** Ian Burnett, GB (Honda); **6** Rob Orme, GB (Yamaha); **7** Dave Redgate, GB (Yamaha); **8** Greig Ramsay, GB (Yamaha); **9** Paul Grubb, GB (Yamaha); **10** Robin Appleyard, GB (Honda).
Fastest lap: Cowan, 1m 30.2s, 94.03 mph/151.34 km/h.
Championship points: 1 Cowan, 15; **2** Bosworth, 12; **3** Newton, 10; **4** Patrickson, 8; **5** Burnett, 6; **6** Orme, 5.

MCA/ACU Star 350 cc Championship, round 1 (6 laps, 14.14 miles/22.75 km)
1 Gary Cowan, IRL (Yamaha), 9m 34.20s, 88.62 mph/142.60 km/h.
2 Steve Williams, GB (Yamaha); **3** Andy Muggleton, GB (Yamaha); **4** David Heal, GB (Yamaha); **5** Darrell Higgins, GB (Yamaha); **6** Richard Alldis, GB (Yamaha); **7** Neil Tomlinson, GB (Yamaha); **8** Ian Burnett, GB (Yamaha); **9** Brad Wilcox, GB (Yamaha); **10** Steve Hislop, GB (Yamaha).
Fastest lap: Cowan, 1m 31.6s, 92.59 mph/148.85 km/h.
Championship points: 1 Cowan, 15; **2** Williams, 12; **3** Muggleton, 10; **4** Heal, 8; **5** Higgins, 6; **6** Alldis, 5.

MCA/ACU Star 375–1300 cc Championship, round 1 (6 laps, 14.14 miles/22.75 km)
1 Steve Williams, GB (750 Yamaha), 9m 27.50s, 89.67 mph/144.29 km/h.
2 Roger Hurst, GB (750 Yamaha); **3** Mark Plato, GB (750 Suzuki); **4** Terry Rymer, GB (750 Yamaha); **5** Ray Stringer, GB (750 Suzuki); **6** Mark Farmer, GB (500 Suzuki); **7** Mark Harrison, GB (750 Suzuki); **8** Les Burgan, GB (750 Suzuki); **9** Dave Burford, GB (1100 Suzuki); **10** Steve Spray, GB (750 Yamaha).
Fastest lap: Williams, 1m 31.10s, 93.10 mph/149.92 km/h.
Championship points: 1 Williams, 15; **2** Hurst, 12; **3** Plato, 10; **4** Rymer, 8; **5** Stringer, 6; **6** Farmer, 5.

MCA/ACU Star TT Formula 2 Championship, round 1 (6 laps, 14.14 miles/22.75 km)
1 Steve Williams, GB (350 Yamaha), 9m 24.70s, 90.11 mph/145.00 km/h.
2 Ian Burnett, GB (350 Yamaha); **3** Andy Muggleton, GB (350 Yamaha); **4** Brad Wilcox, GB (350 Yamaha); **5** Steve Hislop, GB (350 Yamaha); **6** Chris Lake, GB (350 Yamaha); **7** Brian Nicholson, GB (600 Honda); **8** Mike Booys, GB (350 Yamaha); **9** Mike Hose, GB (350 Yamaha); **10** Dave Seidel, GB (350 Yamaha).
Fastest lap: Williams, 1m 31.60s, 92.59 mph/149.01 km/h.
Championship points: 1 Williams, 15; **2** Burnett, 12; **3** Muggleton, 10; **4** Wilcox, 8; **5** Hislop, 6; **6** Lake, 5.

MCA/ACU Star 375–1300 cc Sidecar Championship, round 1 (6 laps, 14.14 miles/22.75 km)
1 Barry Brindley/Grahame Rose, GB/GB (Yamaha), 9m 23.50s, 90.30 mph/145.31 km/h.
2 Warwick Newman/Eddie Yarker, GB/GB (Yamaha); **3** Ray Lawrence/R. Chandler, GB/GB (Yamaha); **4** Geoff Rushbrook/Geoff Leitch, GB/GB (Yamaha); **5** Gary Knight/Phil Coombes, GB/GB (Redline); **6** Mike Boddice/Donny Williams, GB/GB (Yamaha); **7** Steve Pullan/Steve Parker, GB/GB (Yamaha); **8** Mick Smith/Kev Webster, GB/GB (Yamaha); **9** Kenny Howles/Steve Pointer, GB/GB (Yamaha); **10** Derek Jones/Brian Ayres, GB/GB (Seel).
Fastest lap: Brindley, 1m 31.00s, 93.20 mph/149.00 km/h.
Championship points: 1 Brindley, 15; **2** Newman, 12; **3** Lawrence, 10; **4** Rushbrook, 8; **5** Knight, 6; **6** Boddice, 5.

MCA/ACU Star Formula 2 Sidecar Championship, round 1 (6 laps, 14.14 miles/22.75 km)
1 Joe Heys/Peter Greetham, GB/GB (Armstrong), 10m 08.50s, 83.63 mph/134.56 km/h.
2 Dennis Keen/Robert Parker, GB/GB (Yamaha); **3** Mike Hamblin/Rob Smith, GB/GB (Yamaha); **4** Eddy Wright/Ian Marchant, GB/GB (Yamaha); **5** Keith Galtress/Neil Shelton, GB/GB (Yamaha); **6** Alan Delmont/Wallace Brammer, GB/GB (Windle); **7** Roy Hanks/Tom Hanks, GB/GB (Yamaha); **8** Adrian Dawson/Nigel Steel, GB/GB (Yamaha); **9** John Hartell/Chris Broughton, GB/GB (Armstrong); **10** Dick Hawes/Eddy Kiff, GB/GB (Ireson).
Fastest lap: Wright, 1m 37.8s, 86.72 mph/139.53 km/h.
Championship points: 1 Heys, 15; **2** Keen, 12; **3** Hamblin, 10; **4** Wright, 8; **5** Galtress, 6; **6** Delmont, 5.

SNETTERTON CIRCUIT, 3 May. 1.917-mile/3.085-km circuit.
MCA/ACU Star 125 cc Championship, round 2 (7 laps, 13.41 miles/21.59 km)
1 Chris Galatowicz, GB (Honda), 9m 44.7s, 82.62 mph/133.00 km/h.
2 Gary Buckle, GB (MBA); **3** Doug Flather, GB (Honda); **4** Garry Dickinson, GB (Morbidelli); **5** Patrick Corrigan, GB (Honda); **6** Andy Mundy, GB (Twirly); **7** Carl Dickinson, GB (Honda); **8** Andrew Cooper, GB (MBA); **9** Dave Moffitt, GB (MBA); **10** Chris Palmer, GB (MBA).
Fastest lap: Galatowicz, 1m 21.3s, 84.88 mph/136.63 km/h.
Championship points: 1 Galatowicz, 27; **2** Flather, 25; **3** Buckle, 20; **4** G. Dickinson, 14; **5** Appleyard, 10; **6** Corrigan, 8.

MCA/ACU Star 250 cc Championship, round 2 (7 laps, 13.41 miles/21.59 km)
1 Greig Ramsay, GB (Yamaha), 9m 09.9s, 87.84 mph/141.30 km/h.
2 Steve Patrickson, GB (Yamaha); **3** Dave Butler, GB (Yamaha); **4** Ian Newton, GB (Honda); **5** Rob Orme, GB (Yamaha); **6** Phil Borley, GB (Yamaha); **7** Gary Cowan, IRL (Honda); **8** Mark Barker, GB (Honda); **9** Nicholas Bradbury, GB (Yamaha); **10** Mark Heath, GB (Honda).
Fastest lap: Ramsay, 1m 14.6s, 92.50 mph/148.85 km/h.
Championship points: 1 Patrickson, 20; **2** Cowan, 19; **3** Newton and Ramsay, 18; **5** Bosworth, 12; **6** Orme, 11.

MCA/ACU Star 350 cc Championship, round 2 (7 laps, 13.41 miles/21.59 km)
1 David Heal, GB (Yamaha), 9m 04.6s, 88.70 mph/142.82 km/h.
2 Andy Collingwood, GB (Saxon); **3** Ian Burnett, GB (Yamaha); **4** Steve Bevington, GB (Yamaha); **5** Christopher Lake, GB (Yamaha); **6** Neil Tomlinson, GB (Yamaha); **7** Gary Cowan, GB (Yamaha); **8** Barrie Middleton, GB (Yamaha); **9** Richard Alldis, GB (Yamaha); **10** David Griffiths, GB (Yamaha).
Fastest lap: Collingwood, 1m 14.6s, 92.50 mph/148.85 km/h.
Championship points: 1 Heal, 23; **2** Cowan, 19; **3** Burnett, 13; **4** Collingwood and Williams, 12; **6** Muggleton, 10.

MCA/ACU Star 375–1300 cc Championship, round 2 (7 laps, 13.41 miles/21.59 km)
1 Mark Stone, GB (500 Suzuki), 9m 42.3s, 81.96 mph/131.91 km/h.
2 Ray Stringer, GB (750 Suzuki); **3** John Brindley, GB (500 Yamaha); **4** Gary Thrush, GB (750 Yamaha); **5** Ricky McMillan, GB (1080 Suzuki); **6** Marc Harrison, GB (750 Suzuki); **7** Mark Edge, GB (750 Suzuki); **8** Steve Chambers, GB (750 Yamaha); **9** Steve Ward, GB (750 Suzuki); **10** Steve Tabrett, GB (500 Suzuki).
Fastest lap: Stone and Stringer, 1m 21.2s, 84.99 mph/136.77 km/h.
Championship points: 1 Stringer, 18; **2** Stone and Williams, 15; **4** Hurst, 12; **5** Brindley and Plato, 10.

MCA/ACU Star TT Formula 2 Championship, round 2 (7 laps, 13.41 miles/21.59 km)
1 Christopher Lake, GB (350 Yamaha), 10m 27.3s, 77.01 mph/124 km/h.
2 Mark Linscott, GB (600 Honda); **3** Peter Warden, GB (350 Yamaha); **4** Ian Burnett, GB (350 Yamaha); **5** Brad Wilcox, GB (350 Yamaha); **6** Steve Richardson, GB (350 Yamaha); **7** Derek Hopkins, GB (592 Kawasaki).
Fastest lap: Linscott, 1m 22.2s, 83.95 mph/135.11 km/h.
Championship points: 1 Burnett and Lake, 20; **3** Williams, 15; **4** Wilcox, 14; **5** Linscott, 12; **6** Muggleton and Warden, 10.

MCA/ACU Star 375–1300 cc Sidecar Championship, round 2 (7 laps, 13.41 miles/21.59 km)
1 Kenny Howles/Steve Pointer, GB/GB (Yamaha), 8m 45.4s, 91.94 mph/147.94 km/h.
2 Lindsay Hurst/Gary Hurst, GB/GB (Yamaha); **3** Mick Smith/Kev Webster, GB/GB (Yamaha); **4** Andy Westhead/John Skews, GB/GB (Yamaha); **5** Mark Reddington/Phil Gravel, GB/GB (Yamaha); **6** Mark Searle/Bernard Thear, GB/GB (RCL); **7** Neville Fisk/Philip Hampton, GB/GB (Yamaha); **8** Brian Roberts/Dave Roberts, GB/GB (Yamaha); **9** Ward Scarth/Lin Scarth, GB/GB (Yamaha); **10** David Lee/Richard Lee, GB/GB (Windle).
Fastest lap: Howles, 1m 12.5s, 95.18 mph/153.12 km/h.
Championship points: 1 Howles, 17; **2** Brindley, 15; **3** Smith, 13; **4** Hurst and Newman, 12; **6** Lawrence, 10.

MCA/ACU Star Formula 2 Sidecar Championship, round 2 (7 laps, 13.41 miles/21.59 km)
1 Joe Heys/Peter Greetham, GB/GB (Armstrong), 9m 38.1s, 83.56 mph/134.48 km/h.
2 Eddy Wright/Ian Marchant, GB/GB (Windle-Yamaha); **3** Mike Hamblin/Robert Smith, GB/GB (Windle-Yamaha); **4** David Saville/Dave Hall, GB/GB (Sabre); **5** Roy Hanks/Tom Hanks, GB/GB (Yamaha); **6** Keith Galtress/Neil Shelton, GB/GB (Yamaha); **7** Alan Delmont/Wallace Brammer, GB/GB (Windle); **8** Gary Golder/David Fordham, GB/GB (Yamaha); **9** Dennis Keen/Robert Parker, GB/GB (Yamaha); **10** Andre Witherington/John Jackson, GB/GB (Yamaha).
Fastest lap: Wright.
Championship points: 1 Heys, 30; **2** Hamblin and Wright, 20; **4** Keen, 14; **5** Galtress, 11; **6** Hanks, 10.

MALLORY PARK CIRCUIT, 17 May. 1.370-mile/2.205-km circuit.
MCA/ACU Star 80 cc Championship, round 1 (10 laps, 13.7 miles/22.05 km)
1 Dennis Batchelor, GB (Krauser), 11m 12.8s, 73.3 mph/118 km/h.
2 David O'Leary, GB (Suzuki); **3** John Cresswell, GB (Lusuardi); **4** Mark Harrison, GB (Honda); **5** Steven Lawton, GB (Eberhardt); **6** D. Green, GB (Honda); **7** Michael Ford, GB (Honda); **8** Ian Rearney, GB (Honda); **9** Douglas Wightman, GB (Honda); **10** R. Simpkin, GB.
Fastest lap: Batchelor, 1m 4.8s, 76.11 mph/122.51 km/h.
Championship points: 1 Batchelor, 15; **2** O'Leary, 12; **3** Cresswell, 10; **4** Harrison, 8; **5** Lawton, 6.

MCA/ACU Star 125 cc Championship, round 3 (10 laps, 13.7 miles/22.05 km)
1 Chris Galatowicz, GB (Honda), 10m 17.6s, 79.85 mph/128.51 km/h.
2 Doug Flather, GB (Honda); **3** Gary Buckle, GB (MBA); **4** Mark Carkeek, GB (Scitsu); **5** Dave Moffitt, GB (MBA); **6** Reg Lennon, GB (MBA); **7** Andrew Cooper, GB (MBA); **8** M. Ollerenshaw, GB (Honda); **9** P. Baldock, GB (Honda); **10** Dean Hodgson, GB (Honda).
Fastest lap: Galatowicz, 59.8s, 82.47 mph/132.73 km/h.
Championship points: 1 Galatowicz, 42; **2** Flather, 37; **3** Buckle, 30; **4** G. Dickinson, 14; **5** Carkeek, 13; **6** Appleyard, 10.

MCA/ACU Star 250 cc Championship, round 3 (10 laps, 13.7 miles/22.05 km)
1 Steve Patrickson, GB (Yamaha), 10m 10.2s, 80.82 mph/130.10 km/h.
2 Andy Machin, GB (Rotax); **3** Andy Godber, GB (Yamaha); **4** Dave Butler, GB (Yamaha); **5** Peter Hubbard, GB (Yamaha); **6** Greig Ramsay, GB (Yamaha); **7** Ian Burnett, GB (Yamaha); **8** Mark Heath, GB (Honda); **9** M. Nelson, GB (Yamaha); **10** Steve Sawford, GB (Yamaha).
Fastest lap: Patrickson and Godber, 59.2s, 83.31 mph/134.10 km/h.
Championship points: 1 Patrickson, 35; **2** Ramsay, 23; **3** Cowan, 19; **4** Butler and Newton, 18; **6** Bosworth and Machin, 12.

MCA/ACU Star 350 cc Championship, round 3 (10 laps, 13.7 miles/22.05 km)
1 Steve Williams, GB (Yamaha), 10m 7.7s, 81.17 mph/130.61 km/h.
2 Andy Muggleton, GB (Yamaha); **3** Steve Bevington, GB (Yamaha); **4** Ian Burnett, GB (Yamaha); **5** David Heal, GB (Yamaha); **6** Christopher Lake, GB (Yamaha); **7** Mark Farmer, GB (Yamaha); **8** Barry Stanley, GB (Yamaha); **9** P. Warden, GB (Yamaha); **10** J. Davis, GB (Yamaha).
Fastest lap: Williams, 58.4s, 84.45 mph/135.90 km/h.
Championship points: 1 Heal, 29; **2** Williams, 27; **3** Muggleton, 22; **4** Burnett, 21; **5** Cowan, 19; **6** Bevington, 18.

MCA/ACU Star 375–1300 cc Championship, round 3 (12 laps, 16.44 miles/26.46 km)
1 Colin Breeze, GB (750 Yamaha), 12m 2.6s, 81.9 mph/131.79 km/h.
2 Ray Stringer, GB (750 Suzuki); **3** Mark Plato, GB (750 Suzuki); **4** Steve Williams, GB (750 Yamaha); **5** Mark Edge, GB (750 Suzuki); **6** T. Thompson, GB (1100 Suzuki); **7** Steve Spray, GB (750 Yamaha); **8** Mark Stone, GB (500 Yamaha); **9** Mark Farmer, GB (500 Suzuki); **10** W. Taylor, GB (750 Suzuki).
Fastest lap: Breeze, 58.1s, 86.88 mph/139.80 km/h.
Championship points: 1 Stringer, 30; **2** Williams, 23; **3** Plato, 20; **4** Stone, 18; **5** Breeze, 15; **6** Hurst, 12.

MCA/ACU Star TT Formula 2 Championship, round 3 (10 laps, 13.7 miles/22.05 km)
1 Ian Burnett, GB (350 Yamaha), 9m 51.7s, 83.35 mph/134.13 km/h.
2 Steve Williams, GB (350 Yamaha); **3** Andy Muggleton, GB (350 Yamaha); **4** Mike Hose, GB (350 Yamaha); **5** Barry Stanley, GB (350 Yamaha); **6** Ian Lawton, GB (350 Yamaha); **7** Brad Wilcox, GB (350 Yamaha); **8** Dave Seidel, GB (350 Yamaha); **9** B. Evans, GB (350 Yamaha); **10** Phil Armes, GB (350 Yamaha).
Fastest lap: Williams, 57.8s, 81.32 mph/130.90 km/h.
Championship points: 1 Burnett, 35; **2** Williams, 27; **3** Lake and Muggleton, 20; **5** Wilcox, 18; **6** Linscott, 12.

MCA/ACU Star 375-1300 cc Sidecar Championship, round 3 (10 laps, 13.7 miles/22.05 km)
1 Lindsay Hurst/Gary Hurst, GB/GB (Yamaha), 10m 9.5s, 80.91 mph/130.20 km/h.
2 Mick Smith/Kev Webster, GB/GB (Yamaha); **3** D. Molyneux/P. Kneale, GB/GB (Yamaha); **4** Neville Fisk/Philip Hampton, GB/GB (Yamaha); **5** Geoff Rushbrook/Geoff Leitch, GB/GB (Yamaha); **6** Andy Westhead/John Skews, GB/GB (Yamaha); **7** P. Davis/T. Darby, GB/GB (Yamaha); **8** Mark Reddington/Phil Gravel, GB/GB (Yamaha); **9** C. Betts/G. Scott, GB/GB (Yamaha); **10** P. Whiteside/P. Chappel, GB/GB (Yamaha).
Fastest lap: Rushbrook, 58.7s, 84.02 mph/135.21 km/h.
Championship points: 1 Hurst, 27; **2** Smith, 25; **3** Howles, 17; **4** Brindley, 15; **5** Rushbrook, 14; **6** Westhead, 13.

MCA/ACU Star Formula 2 Sidecar Championship, round 3 (10 laps, 13.7 miles/22.05 km)
1 Eddy Wright/Ian Marchant, GB/GB (Yamaha), 10m 6.5s, 81.31 mph/130.84 km/h.
2 David Saville/Dave Hall, GB/GB (Sabre); **3** Joe Heys/Peter Greetham, GB/GB (Armstrong); **4** Keith Galtress/Neil Shelton, GB/GB (Yamaha); **5** Martin Whittington/Iain Caulton, GB/GB (Armstrong); **6** Andre Witherington/John Jackson, GB/GB (Yamaha); **7** Roy Hanks/Tom Hanks, GB/GB (Yamaha); **8** Mike Hamblin/Robert Smith, GB/GB (Windle-Yamaha); **9** Alan Delmont/Wallace Brammer, GB/GB (Windle); **10** Adrian Dawson/Nigel Steel, GB/GB (Yamaha).
Fastest lap: not available.
Championship points: 1 Heys, 40; **2** Wright, 35; **3** Hamblin, 23; **4** Saville, 20; **5** Galtress, 19; **6** Hanks and Keen, 14.

OLIVER'S MOUNT CIRCUIT, 5 July. 2.4136-mile/3.8842-km circuit.
MCA/ACU Star 80 cc Championship, round 2 (6 laps, 14.46 miles/23.30 km)
1 Dennis Batchelor, GB (Krauser), 13m 22.4s, 64.79 mph/104.27 km/h.
2 David Shields, GB (Yamaha); **3** David O'Leary, GB (Suzuki); **4** Steven Lawton, GB (Eberhardt); **5** Terry Wales, GB (Yamaha); **6** Peter Banks, GB (Yamaha).
Fastest lap: Batchelor, 2m 11.5s, 66.08 mph/106.34 km/h.
Championship points: 1 Batchelor, 30; **2** O'Leary, 22; **3** Lawton, 14; **4** Shields, 12; **5** Cresswell, 10; **6** Harrison, 8.

MCA/ACU Star 125 cc Championship, round 4 (8 laps, 19.28 miles/31.07 km)
1 Chris Galatowicz, GB (Yamaha), 16m 21.9s, 70.79 mph/113.90 km/h.
2 Doug Flather, GB (Honda); **3** Peter Banks, GB (MBA); **4** Andrew Cooper, GB (MBA); **5** Reg Lennon, GB (Morbidelli); **6** Carl Dickinson, GB (Honda); **7** Bill Robertson, GB (MBA); **8** Andy Mundy, GB (Honda); **9** Martin Pollard, GB (Honda); **10** John Cresswell, GB (Honda).
Fastest lap: Galatowicz, 2m 00.2s, 72.29 mph/116.33 km/h.
Championship points: 1 Galatowicz, 57; **2** Flather, 49; **3** Buckle, 30; **4** Cooper, 15; **5** G. Dickinson, 14; **6** Carkeek, 13.

MCA/ACU Star 250 cc Championship, round 4 (8 laps, 19.28 miles/31.07 km)
1 Andy Machin, GB (Spondon), 14m 46.6s, 78.40 mph/126.16 km/h.
2 Carl Fogarty, GB (Honda); **3** Ian Burnett, GB (Honda); **4** Phil Borley, GB (Yamaha); **5** Stephen Smith, GB (Yamaha); **6** David Hirst, GB (Yamaha); **7** Andrew Sproston, GB (Yamaha).
Fastest lap: Machin, 1m 48.2s, 80.30 mph/129.25 km/h.
Championship points: 1 Patrickson, 35; **2** Machin, 27; **3** Ramsay, 23; **4** Burnett, 20; **5** Cowan, 19; **6** Butler and Newton, 18.

MCA/ACU Star 350 cc Championship, round 4 (8 laps, 19.28 miles/31.07 km)
1 Ian Burnett, GB (Yamaha), 15m 17.7s, 75.75 mph/121.91 km/h.
2 Tony Hutchinson, GB (Yamaha); **3** Stephen Johnson, GB (Yamaha); **4** Terry Sanders, GB (Yamaha); **5** Barry Stanley, GB (Yamaha); **6** Stephen Smith, GB (Yamaha); **7** David Heal, GB (Yamaha); **8** Steve Mason, GB (Yamaha); **9** Ralph Sutcliffe, GB (Yamaha); **10** Neil Kent, GB (Maxton).
Fastest lap: Hislop (Yamaha), 1m 51.4s, 78 mph/125.60 km/h.

Championship points: 1 Burnett, 36; **2** Heal, 33; **3** Williams, 27; **4** Muggleton, 22; **5** Cowan, 19; **6** Bevington, 18.

MCA/ACU Star 375-1300 cc Championship, round 4 (8 laps, 19.28 miles/31.07 km)
1 Steve Henshaw, GB (500 Suzuki), 14m 34.9s, 79.45 mph/127.83 km/h.
2 Gary Thrush, GB (750 Yamaha); **3** Ian Bell, GB (750 Yamaha); **4** Steve Ward, GB (750 Suzuki); **5** Carl Fogarty, GB (750 Yamaha); **6** Richard Crossley, GB (750 Suzuki); **7** Colin Breeze, GB (750 Yamaha); **8** Andrew Ross, GB (750 Suzuki); **9** Michael Seward, GB (750 Yamaha); **10** Robert Gourlay, GB (500 Suzuki).
Fastest lap: Henshaw, 1m 47.7s, 80.68 mph/129.85 km/h.
Championship points: 1 Stringer, 30; **2** Williams, 23; **3** Plato and Thrush, 20; **5** Breeze, 19; **6** Stone, 18.

MCA/ACU Star TT Formula 2 Championship, round 4 (8 laps, 19.28 miles/31.07 km)
1 Ian Burnett, GB (350 Yamaha), 15m 31.9s, 74.59 mph/120.05 km/h.
2 Barry Stanley, GB (350 Yamaha); **3** Dave Woolams, GB (600 Kawasaki); **4** Michael Parvin, GB (600 Honda); **5** Martin Birkinshaw, GB (600 Honda); **6** Gary Dickinson, GB (350 Yamaha); **7** Martin James, GB (750 Suzuki); **8** Michael Williams, GB (350 Yamaha); **9** Adrian Starles, GB (350 Yamaha); **10** Geoffrey Sawyer, GB (350 Yamaha).
Fastest lap: Burnett, 1m 54.5s, 75.89 mph/122.12 km/h.
Championship points: 1 Burnett, 50; **2** S. Williams, 27; **3** Lake and Muggleton, 20; **5** Stanley and Wilcox, 18.

MCA/ACU Star Formula 2 Sidecar Championship, round 4 (8 laps, 19.28 miles/31.07 km)
1 Eddy Wright/Ian Marchant, GB/GB (Yamaha), 16m 22.3s, 70.76 mph/113.85 km/h.
2 David Saville/Dave Hall, GB/GB (Sabre); **3** Mike Hamblin/Robert Smith, GB/GB (Sabre); **4** Martin Whittington/Iain Caulton, GB/GB (Armstrong); **5** Boyd Hutchinson/Steve Birkett, GB/GB (Yamaha); **6** Bill Crook/John Hornby, GB/GB (Yamaha); **7** Alan Delmont/Wallace Brammer, GB/GB (Yamaha); **8** Adrian Dawson/Nigel Steel, GB/GB (Yamaha).
Fastest lap: Wright, 2m 01.3s, 71.63 mph/115.30 km/h.
Championship points: 1 Wright, 50; **2** Heys, 40; **3** Hamblin, 33; **4** Saville, 32; **5** Galtress, 19; **6** Delmont, 15.

CARNABY RACEWAY, 16 August. 1.21-mile/1.95-km circuit.
MCA/ACU Star 80 cc Championship, round 3 (8 laps, 9.68 miles/15.6 km)
1 Steve Lawton, GB (Eberhardt), 8m 49.5s, 65.81 mph.
2 John Cresswell, GB (Lusuardi); **3** David O'Leary, GB (Suzuki); **4** Ian Rearney, GB (Wigler); **5** Mark Harrison, GB (Yamaha); **6** Douglas Wightman, GB (Honda).
Fastest lap: Lawton, 1m 0.47s, 67.33 mph.
Championship points: 1 O'Leary, 32; **2** Batchelor, 30; **3** Lawton, 29; **4** Cresswell, 22; **5** Harrison, 14; **6** Shields, 12.

MCA/ACU Star 125 cc Championship, round 5 (10 laps, 12.1 miles/19.5 km)
1 Gary Buckle, GB (MBA), 10m 17.9s, 70.50 mph/113.48 km/h.
2 David Lemon, GB (Yamaha); **3** Steve Mason, GB (MBA); **4** Garry Dickinson, GB (MBA); **5** Mark Carkeek, GB (Yamaha); **6** Andrew Cooper, GB (MBA); **7** Patrick Corrigan, GB (Honda); **8** Dave Moffitt, GB (MBA); **9** Doug Flather, GB (Honda); **10** Dean Hodgson, GB (Honda).
Fastest lap: Buckle, 1m 00.4s, 72.11 mph/116.05 km/h.
Championship points: 1 Galatowicz, 57; **2** Flather, 51; **3** Buckle, 45; **4** G. Dickinson, 22; **5** Cooper, 20; **6** Carkeek, 19.

MCA/ACU Star 250 cc Championship, round 5 (15 laps, 18.15 miles/29.25 km)
1 Andy Machin, GB (Rotax), and Steve Patrickson, GB (Yamaha), 14m 17.3s, 76.2 mph/122.64 km/h.
3 Peter Hubbard, GB (Yamaha); **4** Greig Ramsay, GB (Yamaha); **5** David Wisdom, GB (Yamaha); **6** Phil Borley, GB (Yamaha); **7** Ian Burnett, GB (Honda); **8** Tom Hutton, GB (Yamaha); **9** Steve Sawford, GB (Yamaha).
Fastest lap: Patrickson, 55.7s, 78.2 mph/125.84 km/h.
Championship points: 1 Patrickson, 48.5; **2** Machin, 40.5; **3** Ramsay, 31; **4** Burnett, 24; **5** Cowan, 19; **6** Borley, Butler and Newton, 18.

MCA/ACU Star 350 cc Championship, round 5 (15 laps, 18.15 miles/29.25 km)
1 Steve Williams, GB (Yamaha), 14m 23.0s, 75.71 mph/121.85 km/h.
2 Andy Machin, GB (Rotax); **3** Ian Burnett, GB (Yamaha); **4** Stephen Johnson, GB (Yamaha); **5** Andy Muggleton, GB (Yamaha); **6** Terry Sanders, GB (Yamaha); **7** Barry Stanley, GB (Yamaha); **8** Andy Atkinson, GB (Spondon); **9** Stephen Bevington, GB (Yamaha); **10** Braddon Evans, GB (Yamaha).
Fastest lap: Williams, 56.0s, 77.79 mph/125.20 km/h.
Championship points: 1 Burnett, 46; **2** Williams, 42; **3** Heal, 33; **4** Muggleton, 28; **5** Bevington, 20; **6** Cowan, 19.

MCA/ACU Star 375-1300 cc Championship, round 5 (15 laps, 18.15 miles/29.25 km)
1 Mark Westmorland, GB (750 Yamaha), 14m 12.1s, 76.68 mph/123.40 km/h.
2 Ray Stringer, GB (750 Yamaha); **3** John Brindley, GB (700 Yamaha); **4** Colin Breeze, GB (750 Yamaha); **5** Steve Williams, GB (750 Yamaha); **6** Lloyd Glew, GB (500 Suzuki); **7** Dennis Winterbottom, GB (750 Yamaha); **8** David O'Leary, GB (500 Suzuki); **9** Steve Spray, GB (750 Yamaha); **10** Simon Bastow, GB (1100 Suzuki).
Fastest lap: Westmorland, 55.8s, 78.06 mph/125.62 km/h.
Championship points: 1 Stringer, 42; **2** Williams, 29; **3** Breeze, 27; **4** Brindley, Plato and Thrush, 20.

MCA/ACU Star TT Formula 2 Championship, round 5 (12 laps, 14.52 miles/23.4 km)

1 Steve Williams, GB (350 Yamaha), 11m 39.2s, 74.76 mph/119.82 km/h.
2 Ian Burnett, GB (350 Yamaha); **3** Mark Ward, GB (998 Ducati); **4** Barry Stanley, GB (350 Yamaha); **5** Andy Muggleton, GB (350 Yamaha); **6** Allan MacDonald, GB (600 Honda); **7** Michael Seward, GB (600 Honda); **8** Stephen Johnson, GB (600 Honda); **9** Garry Dickinson, GB (350 Yamaha); **10** Martin James, GB (600 Honda).
Fastest lap: Williams, 56.6s, 79.96 mph/123.85 km/h.
Championship points: 1 Burnett, 62; **2** Williams, 42; **3** Muggleton and Stanley, 26; **5** Lake, 20; **6** Wilcox, 18.

MCA/ACU Star 375-1300 cc Sidecar Championship, round 4 (7 laps, 8.47 miles/13.65 km)
1 Lindsay Hurst/Gary Hurst, GB/GB (Yamaha), 8m 35.8s, 76.00 mph/122.31 km/h.
2 Kenny Howles/Steve Pointer, GB/GB (Yamaha); **3** Rob Bellas/Geoff Knight, GB/GB (Suzuki); **4** Gordon Shand/Johnny Sheddon, GB/GB (Shand); **5** Mick Hudson/Norm Oxley, GB/GB (Yamaha); **6** Mark Reddington/Phil Gravel, GB/GB (Yamaha); **7** Stuart Leaning/Simon Christie, GB/GB (Suzuki); **8** Ward Scarth/Lin Scarth, GB/GB (Yamaha); **9** Barry Laidlow/Carl Laidlow, GB/GB (Suzuki); **10** Eric Cornes/Graham Wellington, GB/GB (Yamaha).
Fastest lap: Hurst and Howles, 55.9s, 77.92 mph/125.40 km/h.
Championship points: 1 Hurst, 42; **2** Howles, 29; **3** Smith, 25; **4** Brindley, 15; **5** Reddington and Rushbrook, 14.

MCA/ACU Star 375-1300 cc Sidecar Championship, round 5 (12 laps, 14.52 miles/23.4 km)
1 Kenny Howles/Steve Pointer, GB/GB (Yamaha), 11m 33.9s, 75.33 mph/121.22 km/h.
2 Dennis Bingham/Julia Bingham, GB/GB (Padgetts); **3** Mick Smith/Kev Webster, GB/GB (Yamaha); **4** Rob Bellas/Geoff Knight, GB/GB (Suzuki); **5** Gordon Shand/Johnny Sheddon, GB/GB (Shand); **6** Mick Hudson/Norm Oxley, GB/GB (Yamaha); **7** Mark Reddington/Phil Gravel, GB/GB (Yamaha); **8** Barry Laidlow/Carl Laidlow, GB/GB (Yamaha); **9** Stuart Leaning/Simon Christie, GB/GB (Suzuki); **10** Stuart Applegate/Andrew Gibson, GB/GB (Mitchell).
Fastest lap: Howles and Smith, 56.0s, 77.79 mph/125.16 km/h.
Championship points: 1 Howles, 44; **2** Hurst, 42; **3** Smith, 35; **4** Bellas and Reddington, 18; **6** Brindley, 15.

MCA/ACU Star Formula 2 Sidecar Championship, round 5 (12 laps, 14.52 miles/23.4 km)
1 Joe Heys/Peter Greetham, GB/GB (Armstrong), 12m 14.9s, 71.13 mph/114.48 km/h.
2 Andre Witherington/John Jackson, GB/GB (Yamaha); **3** Eddy Wright/Ian Marchant, GB/GB (Yamaha); **4** Martin Whittington/Iain Caulton, GB/GB (Yamaha); **5** Mike Hamblin/Robert Smith, GB/GB (Yamaha); **6** Alan Delmont/Wallace Brammer, GB/GB (Yamaha); **7** John Coates/Gary Gibson, GB/GB (Powershuttle); **8** Roy Hanks/Tom Hanks, GB/GB (Yamaha); **9** Keith Galtress/Neil Shelton, GB/GB (Yamaha); **10** Gordon Hogg/William Hogg, GB/GB (BMW).
Fastest lap: Heys and Wright, 59.5s, 73.21 mph/117.82 km/h.
Championship points: 1 Wright, 60; **2** Heys, 55; **3** Hamblin, 39; **4** Saville, 32; **5** Galtress, 21; **6** Delmont, 20.

CADWELL PARK CIRCUIT, 31 August. 2.250-mile/3.621-km circuit.
MCA/ACU Star 80 cc Championship, round 4 (6 laps, 13.04 miles/21.72 km)
1 Doug Flather, GB (Wicks), 11m 32.7s, 67.79 mph.
2 John Cresswell, GB (Lusuardi); **3** A. Patterson, GB (Huvo); **4** D. Hodgson, GB (Huvo); **5** Ian Rearney, GB (Wigler); **6** A. Stanway, GB (Huvo); **7** David O'Leary, GB (Suzuki); **8** Mark Harrison, GB (Yamaha); **9** Terry Wales, GB (Yamaha); **10** B. Skelton, GB (Famos).
Fastest lap: Flather, 1m 52.3s, 69.69 mph/112.15 km/h.
Championship points: 1 O'Leary, 36; **2** Cresswell, 34; **3** Batchelor, 30; **4** Lawton, 29; **5** Harrison and Rearney, 17.

MCA/ACU Star 125 cc Championship, round 6 (8 laps, 17.39 miles/28.96 km)
1 Gary Buckle, GB (MBA), 14m 14.2s, 73.29 mph/117.96 km/h.
2 Patrick Corrigan, GB (Honda); **3** Garry Dickinson, GB (MBA); **4** Doug Flather, GB (Honda); **5** Mark Carkeek, GB (Scitsu); **6** Dean Hodgson, GB (Honda); **7** Dave Moffitt, GB (MBA); **8** A. Patterson, GB (Honda); **9** M. Noble, GB (Honda); **10** D. Parman, GB (MBA).
Fastest lap: Galatowicz (Honda), 1m 45.1s, 74.46 mph/119.82 km/h.
Championship points: 1 Buckle, 60; **2** Flather, 59; **3** Galatowicz, 57; **4** G. Dickinson, 32; **5** Carkeek, 25; **6** Corrigan, 24.

MCA/ACU Star 250 cc Championship, round 6 (8 laps, 17.39 miles/28.96 km)
1 Nigel Bosworth, GB (Yamaha), 13m 13.0s, 78.95 mph/127.08 km/h.
2 Andy Machin, GB (Rotax); **3** Steve Patrickson, GB (Yamaha); **4** Peter Hubbard, GB (Yamaha); **5** Dave Butler, GB (Yamaha); **6** Ian Burnett, GB (Honda); **7** Ian Newton, GB (Honda); **8** Phil Borley, GB (Yamaha); **9** T. Rogers, GB (Yamaha); **10** David Wisdom, GB (Yamaha).
Fastest lap: Hubbard, 1m 37.0s, 80.68 mph/129.85 km/h.
Championship points: 1 Patrickson, 58.5; **2** Machin, 52.5; **3** Ramsay, 31; **4** Burnett, 29; **5** Bosworth, 27; **6** Butler and Hubbard, 24.

MCA/ACU Star 350 cc Championship, round 6 (8 laps, 17.39 miles/28.96 km)
1 Steve Hislop, GB (Yamaha), 13m 28.8s, 77.41 mph/124.58 km/h.
2 Steve Williams, GB (Yamaha); **3** Ian Burnett, GB (Yamaha); **4** Andy Machin (Rotax); **5** Terry Sanders, GB (Yamaha); **6** Stephen Johnson, GB (Yamaha); **7** David Heal, GB (Yamaha); **8** M. Nelson, GB (Yamaha); **9** Barry Stanley, GB (Yamaha); **10** Andy Muggleton, GB (Yamaha).
Fastest lap: Hislop, 1m 38.7s, 79.29 mph/127.61 km/h.
Championship points: 1 Burnett, 56; **2** Williams, 54; **3** Heal, 37; **4** Muggleton, 29; **5** Johnson, 23; **6** Bevington and Machin, 20.

MCA/ACU Star 375-1300 cc Championship, round 6 (6 laps, 13.04 miles/21.72 km)
1 Steve Henshaw, GB (Suzuki), 9m 50.4s, 79.53 mph/128.02 km/h.
2 Keith Huewen, GB (Yamaha); **3** Geoff Fowler, GB (Yamaha); **4** Mark Farmer, GB (Suzuki); **5** J. Lofthouse, GB (Suzuki); **6** Ray Stringer, GB (Suzuki); **7** Trevor Nation, GB (Yamaha); **8** Jamie Whitham, GB (Suzuki); **9** Colin Breeze, GB (Yamaha); **10** Steve Spray, GB (Yamaha).
Fastest lap: Henshaw, 1m 36.6s, 81.01 mph/130.39 km/h.
Championship points: 1 Stringer, 47; **2** Henshaw, 30; **3** Breeze and Williams, 29; **5** Brindley, Plato and Thrush, 20.

MCA/ACU Star TT Formula 2 Championship, round 6 (8 laps, 17.39 miles/28.96 km)
1 Steve Williams, GB (Yamaha), 13m 22.0s, 78.06 mph/125.63 km/h.
2 Steve Hislop, GB (Yamaha); **3** Ian Burnett, GB (Yamaha); **4** Barry Stanley, GB (Yamaha); **5** Mark Ward, GB (Ducati); **6** R. Bradley, GB (Yamaha); **7** Brad Wilcox, GB (Yamaha); **8** Ian Lougher, GB (Yamaha); **9** Garry Dickinson, GB (Yamaha).
Fastest lap: Williams, 1m 36.9s, 80.76 mph/129.98 km/h.
Championship points: 1 Burnett, 72; **2** Williams, 57; **3** Stanley, 34; **4** Muggleton, 26; **5** Wilcox, 22; **6** Lake, 20.

MCA/ACU Star 375-1300 cc Sidecar Championships, round 6 (8 laps, 17.39 miles/28.96 km)
1 Tony Baker/John Hennigan, GB/GB (Yamaha); **2** Lindsay Hurst/Gary Hurst, GB/GB (Yamaha); **3** Paul Atkinson/Graham Simmons, GB/GB (Yamaha); **4** Neil Smith/G. Ape, GB/GB (Yamaha); **5** John Evans/Geoff Wilbraham, GB/GB (Yamaha); **6** Steve Sinott/D. Wells, GB/GB (Yamaha); **7** M. Staiano/A. Fisher, GB/GB (Yamaha); **8** Philip Croft/Nigel Harding, GB/GB (Yamaha); **9** Ken Williams/Mick Williams, GB/GB (Suzuki).
Fastest lap: Barker, 1m 38.7s, 79.29 mph/127.61 km/h.
Championship points: 1 Hurst, 54; **2** Howles, 44; **3** Smith, 35; **4** Bellas and Reddington, 18; **6** Barker and Brindley, 15.

MCA/ACU Star Formula 2 Sidecar Championship, round 6 (8 laps, 17.39 miles/28.96 km)
1 Eddy Wright/Ian Marchant, GB/GB (Yamaha), 14m 12.0s, 73.48 mph/118.25 km/h.
2 Andre Witherington/John Jackson, GB/GB (Yamaha); **3** Martin Whittington/Iain Caulton, GB/GB (Yamaha); **4** Keith Galtress/Neil Shelton, GB/GB (Yamaha); **5** John Coates/Gary Gibson, GB/GB (Powershuttle); **6** Gordon Hogg/William Hogg, GB/GB (BMW); **7** S. Noble/M. Parker, GB/GB (Yamaha); **8** Alan Delmont/Wallace Brammer, GB/GB (Yamaha); **9** Jim Norbury/Norman Elcock, GB/GB (Yamaha); **10** Mike Hamblin/Rob Smith, GB/GB (Yamaha).
Fastest lap: Witherington, 1m 44.3s, 75.03 mph/120.75 km/h.
Championship points: 1 Wright, 75; **2** Heys, 55; **3** Hamblin, 40; **4** Saville, 32; **5** Witherington, 30; **6** Galtress, 29.

DONINGTON PARK CIRCUIT, 26/27 September, 2.5-mile/4.02-km circuit.
MCA/ACU Star 80 cc Championship, round 5 (8 laps, 20 miles/32.16 km)
1 Doug Flather, GB (Wicks), 16m 34.41s, 72.4 mph/116.52 km/h.
2 Dennis Batchelor, GB (Krauser); **3** John Cresswell, GB (Lusuardi); **4** Dean Hodgson, GB (Huvo); **5** David O'Leary, GB (Suzuki); **6** Alistair Stanway, GB (Huvo); **7** Mark Harrison, GB (Yamaha); **8** J. Dodd, GB (Honda); **9** M. Marman, GB (Honda).
Fastest lap: Flather, 2m 2.11s, 73.7 mph/118.61 km/h.
Championship points: *see final points.*

MCA/ACU Star 125 cc Championship, round 7 (8 laps, 20 miles/32.16 km)
1 Robin Milton, GB (MBA), 15m 25.95s, 77.75 mph/125.12 km/h.
2 Ian McConnachie, GB (EMC); **3** Robin Appleyard, GB (MBA); **4** M. McGarrity, GB (MBA); **5** Gary Buckle, GB (MBA); **6** Chris Galatowicz, GB (Honda); **7** Mark Carkeek, GB (Scitsu); **8** Andrew Cooper, GB (MBA); **9** Rob Blow, GB (Waddon); **10** C. Morgan, GB (Rotax).
Fastest lap: McConnachie, 1m 53.03s, 79.62 mph/128.14 km/h.
Championship points: *see final points*

MCA/ACU Star 250 cc Championship, round 7 (8 laps, 20 miles/32.16 km)
1 Donnie McLeod, GB (EMC), 14m 16.86s, 84.02 mph/135.22 km/h.
2 Steve Patrickson, GB (Yamaha); **3** Andy Machin, GB (Rotax); **4** Gary Cowan, IRL (Honda); **5** Ian Newton, GB (Honda); **6** Kevin Mitchell, GB (Yamaha); **7** Nigel Bosworth, GB (Yamaha); **8** Peter Hubbard, GB (Yamaha); **9** Woolsey Coulter, GB (Honda); **10** Rob Orme, GB (Yamaha).
Fastest lap: McLeod, 1m 45.18s, 85.56 mph/137.70 km/h.
Championship points: *see final points*

MCA/ACU Star 350 cc Championship, round 7 (8 laps, 20 miles/ 32.16 km)
1 Gary Cowan, IRL (Yamaha), 14m 27.27s, 83.01 mph/133.59 km/h.
2 Steve Williams, GB (Yamaha); **3** Andy Machin, GB (Rotax); **4** Steve Hislop, GB (Yamaha); **5** David Heal, GB (Yamaha); **6** Terry Sanders, GB (Yamaha); **7** Barry Stanley, GB (Yamaha); **8** T. Clow, GB (Armstrong); **9** Ian Lougher, GB (Yamaha); **10** M. Nelson, GB (Yamaha).
Fastest lap: Cowan and Machin, 1m 46.13s, 84.8 mph/136.5 km/h.
Championship points: *see final points.*

MCA/ACU Star 375-1300 cc Championship, round 7 (8 laps, 20 miles/32.16 km)
1 Mark Phillips, GB (500 Suzuki), 14m 3.62s, 85.34 mph/137.35 km/h.
2 Jamie Whitham, GB (750 Suzuki); **3** Ray Stringer, GB (750 Suzuki); **4** Steve Henshaw, GB (500 Suzuki); **5** Terry Rymer, GB (750 Yamaha); **6** Roger Hurst, GB (750 Yamaha); **7** Steve Williams, GB (750 Yamaha); **8** Gary Noel, GB (750 Yamaha); **9** Steve Manley, GB (500 Suzuki); **10** Alan Carter, GB (750 Suzuki).
Fastest lap: Phillips, 1m 43.14s, 87.26 mph/140.45 km/h.
Championship points: *see final points.*

MCA/ACU Star TT Formula 2 Championship, round 7 (8 laps, 20 miles/32.16 km)
1 Steve Williams, 14m 28.13s, 82.93 mph/133.48 km/h.
2 Steve Hislop, GB (Yamaha); **3** Eddie Laycock, GB (Yamaha); **4** Ian Burnett, GB (Yamaha); **5** Barry Stanley, GB (Yamaha); **6** Andy Muggleton, GB (Yamaha); **7** Ian Lougher, GB (Yamaha); **8** D. Woolams, GB (Kawasaki); **9** J. Mossey, GB (Yamaha); **10** B. Evans, GB (Yamaha).
Fastest lap: Williams, 1m 46.89s, 84.19 mph/135.49 km/h.
Championship points: *see final points.*

MCA/ACU Star 375-1300 cc Sidecar Championship, round 7 (8 laps, 20 miles/32.16 km)
1 Barry Brindley/Grahame Rose, GB/GB (Yamaha), 14m 19.92s, 83.72 mph/134.73 km/h.
2 Geoff Rushbrook/Geoff Leitch, GB/GB (Yamaha); **3** Kenny Howles/Steve Pointer, GB/GB (Yamaha); **4** Lindsay Hurst/Gary Hurst, GB/GB (Yamaha); **5** Lowry Burton/Grahame Wellington, GB/GB (Yamaha); **6** Gary Knight/Phil Coombes, GB/GB (Yamaha); **7** Dennis Bingham/Julia Bingham, GB/GB (Yamaha); **8** Ray Lawrence/Dave Rawlings, GB/GB (Yamaha); **9** Mark Reddington/Phil Gravel, GB/GB (Yamaha); **10** Andy Westhead/C. Parkinson, GB/GB (Yamaha).
Fastest lap: Brindley, 1m 45.13s, 85.6 mph/137.74 km/h.
Championship points: *see final points.*

MCA/ACU Star Formula 2 Sidecar Championship, round 7 (8 laps, 20 miles/32.16 km)
1 Andre Witherington/John Jackson, GB/GB (Yamaha), 15m 39.49s.
2 Eddy Wright/Ian Marchant, GB/GB (Yamaha); **3** Martin Whittington/Iain Caulton, GB/GB (Yamaha); **4** David Saville/Dave Hall, GB/GB (Yamaha); **5** Alan Delmont/Wallace Brammer, GB/GB (Yamaha); **6** Roy Hanks/Tom Hanks, GB/GB (Yamaha); **7** Mike Hamblin/Rob Smith, GB/GB (Yamaha); **8** Keith Galtress/Neil Shelton, GB/GB (Yamaha); **9** John Coates/Gary Gibson, GB/GB (Yamaha); **10** Dennis Keen/Robert Parker, GB/GB (Yamaha).
Fastest lap: Witherington, 1m 55.01s, 78.25 mph/125.93 km/h.
Championship points: *see final points.*

Final Championship points (80 cc)

1	John Cresswell	44
2 =	Dennis Batchelor	42
2 =	David O'Leary	42
4	Doug Flather	40
5	Steven Lawton	29
6	Mark Harrison	21

7 Ian Rearney, 17; **8** Dean Hodgson, 16; **9** David Shields, 12; **10** = A. Patterson and B. Skelton, 10.

Final Championship points (125 cc)

1	Gary Buckle	66
2	Chris Galatowicz	62
3	Doug Flather	59
4	Garry Dickinson	32
5	Mark Carkeek	29
6	Patrick Corrigan	24

7 Andrew Cooper, 23; **8** Robin Appleyard, 20; **9** Dave Moffitt, 16; **10** Robin Milton, 15.

Final Championship points (250 cc)

1	Steve Patrickson	70.5
2	Andy Machin	62.5
3 =	Nigel Bosworth	31
3 =	Greig Ramsay	31
5	Ian Burnett	29
6	Ian Newton	28

7 Gary Cowan and Peter Hubbard, 27; **9** Dave Butler, 24; **10** Phil Borley, 21.

Final Championship points (350 cc)

1	Steve Williams	66
2	Ian Burnett	56
3	David Heal	43
4	Gary Cowan	34
5	Andy Machin	30
6	Andy Muggleton	29

7 Steve Hislop and Terry Sanders, 24; **9** Stephen Johnson, 23; **10** Steve Bevington, 20.

Final Championship points (375–1300 cc)

1	Ray Stringer	57
2	Steve Henshaw	38
3	Steve Williams	33
4	Colin Breeze	29
5 =	John Brindley	20
5 =	Mark Plato	20
5 =	Gary Thrush	20

8 Mark Stone, 18; **9** Roger Hurst, 17; **10** Mark Farmer and Mark Westmorland, 15.

Final Championship points (TT Formula 2)

1	Ian Burnett	80
2	Steve Williams	72
3	Barry Stanley	40
4	Andy Muggleton	31
5	Steve Hislop	30
6	Brad Wilcox	22

7 Chris Lake, 20; **8** Mark Ward, 16; **9** Mark Linscott, 12.

Final Championship points (375–1300 cc Sidecars)

1	Lindsay Hurst/Gary Hurst	62
2	Kenny Howles/Steve Pointer	54
3	Mick Smith/Kev Webster	35
4	Barry Brindley/Grahame Rose	30
5	Geoff Rushbrook/Geoff Leitch	26
6	Mark Reddington/Phil Gravel	21

7 Rob Bellas/Geoff Knight, 18; **8** Dennis Bingham/Julia Bingham, 17; **9** Tony Baker/John Hennigan, 15.

Final Championship points (Formula 2 Sidecars)

1	Eddy Wright/Ian Marchant	87
2	Joe Heys/Peter Greetham	55
3	Andre Witherington/John Jackson	45
4	Mike Hamblin/Rob Smith	44
5	David Saville/Dave Hall	40
6	Keith Galtress/Neil Shelton	32

7 Alan Delmont/Wallace Brammer, 29; **8** Martin Whittington/Iain Caulton, 28; **9** Roy Hanks/Tom Hanks, 22; **10** Dennis Keen/Robert Parker, 15.

Manx Grand Prix

MANX GRAND PRIX, Isle of Man, 29 August/3 September. 37.73-mile/69.72-km circuit.
Senior Race 1000 cc (6 laps, 226.38 miles/364.32 km)
1 Brian Raynor, GB (1000 Yamaha), 2h 06m 42.0s, 107.20 mph/172.52 km/h (record)
2 Steve Dowey, GB (1000 Yamaha); **3** Pete Beale, GB (1000 Yamaha); **4** Kenny Harmer, GB (1000 Honda); **5** Dave Sharratt, GB (750 Suzuki); **6** Kevin Jackson, GB (750 Suzuki); **7** Stephen Hazlett, GB (350 Yamaha); **8** Stuart Marshall, GB (600 Honda); **9** Geoff Martin, GB (750 Suzuki); **10** John McBride, IOM (750 Suzuki).
Fastest lap: Raynor, 20m 38.2s, 109.69 mph/176.52 km/h.

Junior Race 350 cc (6 laps, 226.38 miles/364.32 km)
1 Craig Ryding, GB (Kimoco), 2h 09m 53.4s, 104.57 mph/168.29 km/h.
2 Stephen Hazlett GB (Yamaha); **3** Mark Linton, GB (Yamaha); **4** Mick Robinson, GB (Yamaha); **5** Decca Kelly, IOM (Yamaha); **6** Tony Martin, GB (Yamaha); **7** Dave Montgomery, GB (Yamaha); **8** Stewart Rae, GB (Yamaha); **9** Ian Jones, GB (Yamaha); **10** Serek Allan, GB (Yamaha).
Fastest lap: Ryding, 21m 20.4s, 106.08 mph/170.72 km.h.

Lightweight Race 250 cc (4 laps, 150.92 miles/242.88 km)
1 Craig Ryding, GB (Kimoco), 1h 28m 22.8s, 102.45 mph/164.87 km/h.
2 Mick Robinson, GB (Yamaha); **3** Billy Craine, IOM (Yamaha); **4** John Davies, GB (Honda); **5** Derek Glass, GB (Yamaha); **6** Martin Birkinshaw, GB (Armstrong); **7** Ian Dugdale, GB (Honda); **8** Derek Young, GB (Rotax); **9** Andy Bassett, GB (Yamaha); **10** Vaughan Smith, GB (Yamaha).
Fastest lap: Ryding, 21m 47.2s, 103.98 mph/167.34 km/h.

Newcomers Race 1000 cc four-stroke/750 cc two-stroke (4 laps, 150.92 miles/242.88 km)
1 Colin Gable, GB (750 Suzuki), 1h 26m 03.0s, 105.23 mph/169.35 km/h (record).
2 Phil Hogg, IOM (750 Suzuki); **3** Al Dalton, GB (1000 Yamaha); **4** Dave Lawson, GB (750 Suzuki); **5** Steve Bushell, GB (1000 Yamaha); **6** Graham Read, GB (750 Suzuki); **7** Neil Munro, GB (750 Suzuki); **8** Steve Allen, GB (750 Suzuki); **9** Dave Birtles, GB (750 Suzuki); **10** Karl Ellison, IOM (750 Yamaha).
Fastest lap: Gable, 21m 05.4s, 107.33 mph/172.73 km/h (record).

Newcomers Race 350 cc (4 laps, 150.92 miles/242.88 km)
1 Billy Craine, IOM (Yamaha) 1h 29m 51.4s, 100.77 mph/162.17 km/h.
2 Derek Young, GB (Yamaha); **3** Lee Finney, GB (Yamaha); **4** Geoff Swann, GB (Yamaha); **5** Steven Clements, GB (Yamaha); **6** Paul Ward, GB (Yamaha); **7** Mike Blake, GB (Yamaha); **8** Chris Angold, GB (Yamaha); **9** Geoff Sawyer, GB (Yamaha); **10** Kevin Griffiths, GB (Yamaha).
Fastest lap: Craine, 22m 01.4s, 102,79 mph/165.42 km/h.

Newcomers Race 250 cc (4 laps, 150.92 miles/242.88 km)
1 Ian Morris, GB (Yamaha), 1h 33m 31.8s, 96.81 mph/155.80 km/h.
2 Ian Simpson, GB (Yamaha); **3** Kenneth Virgo, GB (Yamaha); **4** Nigel Jennings, GB (Yamaha); **5** Steve Cook, GB (Yamaha); **6** Royston Edwards, GB (Yamaha); **7** Ewan Hamilton, GB (Yamaha); **8** Kevin Liddle, GB (Yamaha); **9** Gareth Ridgway, GB (Yamaha); **10** Dean Blackwell, GB (Yamaha).
Fastest lap: Morris, 23m 06.6s, 97.95 mph/157.63 km/h.

Classic Race 500 cc (3 laps 113.19 miles/209.16 km)
1 Dave Pither, GB (Matchless), 1h 07m 45.8s, 100.22 mph/161.28 km/h (record).
2 Chris Turner, GB (Matchless); **3** Selwyn Griffiths, GB (Matchless); **4** John Goodall, GB (Matchless); **5** Richard Cutts, GB (Matchless); **6** Dave Storrey, GB (Matchless); **7** David Dearden, GB (Seeley); **8** John Knowles, GB (Seeley); **9** Brian Richards, GB (Seeley); **10** Roger Sutcliffe, IOM (Matchless).
Fastest lap: Pither, 22m 20.6s, 101.31 mph/163.04 km/h (record).

Classic Race 350 cc (3 laps 113.19 miles/209.16 km)
1 Richard Swallow, GB (Aermacchi), 1h 10m 01.4s, 96.98 mph/156.07 km/h (record).
2 John Kidson, GB (Aermacchi); **3** Cliff Gobell, GB (Aermacchi); **4** Chris Bladon, GB (Aermacchi); **5** Anthony Ainslie, GB (Ducati); **6** Les Trotter, GB (Suzuki); **7** Peter Byrne, GB (Ducati); **8** Trevor Beharrell, GB (AJS); **9** Eddie Crooks, IOM (Suzuki); **10** Michael Cain, IOM (Suzuki).
Fastest lap: Swallow, 23m 14.2s, 97.42 mph/156.78 km/h (record).

ULSTER GRAND PRIX, Dundrod Circuit, Northern Ireland, 15 August, 7.401-mile/11.911-km circuit. 250-350 cc (10 laps, 74.01 miles/119.11 km)
1 Brian Reid, GB (EMC), 41m 00.60s, 108.28 mph/174.26 km/h.
2 Gary Cowan, IRL (Honda); **3** Woolsey Coulter, GB (Honda); **4** Steve Hislop, GB (Yamaha); **5** Mark Farmer, GB (Yamaha); **6** Robert Dunlop, GB (Yamaha); **7** Donny Robinson, GB; **8** George Higginson, GB (Honda); **9** Ian Lougher, GB (Yamaha); **10** Derek Chatterton, GB (Yamaha).
Fastest lap: Reid, 4m 2.4s, 109.87 mph/176.81 km/h.
Note: The remaining races scheduled for this meeting were abandoned after the fatal accident to Klaus Klein.